法律英语高级教程

A Course-book of
the English Language of Law

宋 雷　郑达轩 主编

北京大学出版社
PEKING UNIVERSITY PRESS

图书在版编目(CIP)数据

法律英语高级教程/宋雷,郑达轩主编. —北京:北京大学出版社,2012.9
(21世纪法学规划教材)
ISBN 978-7-301-21260-8

Ⅰ.①法… Ⅱ.①宋… ②郑… Ⅲ.①法律-英语-高等学校-教材 Ⅳ.①H31

中国版本图书馆CIP数据核字(2012)第218508号

书　　　名：法律英语高级教程
著作责任者：宋　雷　郑达轩　主编
责 任 编 辑：郭薇薇
标 准 书 号：ISBN 978-7-301-21260-8/D·3181
出 版 发 行：北京大学出版社
地　　　址：北京市海淀区成府路205号　100871
网　　　址：http://www.pup.cn
电　　　话：邮购部 62752015　发行部 62750672　编辑部 62752027　出版部 62754962
电 子 信 箱：law@pup.pku.edu.cn
印 刷 者：北京富生印刷厂
经 销 者：新华书店
　　　　　　787毫米×1092毫米　16开本　35.75印张　870千字
　　　　　　2012年9月第1版　2019年5月第3次印刷
定　　　价：56.00元

未经许可,不得以任何方式复制或抄袭本书之部分或全部内容。
版权所有,侵权必究
举报电话:010-62752024　电子信箱:fd@pup.pku.edu.cn

丛书出版前言

秉承"学术的尊严,精神的魅力"的理念,北京大学出版社多年来在文史、社科、法律、经管等领域出版了不同层次、不同品种的大学教材,获得了广大读者好评。

但一些院校和读者面对多种教材时出现选择上的困惑,因此北京大学出版社对全社教材进行了整合优化。集全社之力,推出一套统一的精品教材。

"21世纪法学规划教材"即是本套精品教材的法律部分。本系列教材在全社法律教材中选取了精品之作,均由我国法学领域颇具影响力和潜力的专家学者编写而成,力求结合教学实践,推动我国法律教育的发展。

"21世纪法学规划教材"面向各高等院校法学专业学生,内容不仅包括了16门核心课教材,还包括多门传统专业课教材,以及新兴课程教材;在注重系统性和全面性的同时,强调与司法实践、研究生教育接轨,培养学生的法律思维和法学素质,帮助学生打下扎实的专业基础和掌握最新的学科前沿知识。

本系列教材在保持相对一致的风格和体例的基础上,以精品课程建设的标准严格要求各教材的编写;汲取同类教材特别是国外优秀教材的经验和精华,同时具有中国当下的问题意识;增加支持先进教学手段和多元化教学方法的内容,努力配备丰富、多元的教辅材料,如电子课件、配套案例等。

为了使本系列教材具有持续的生命力,我们将积极与作者沟通,结合立法和司法实践,对教材不断进行修订。

无论您是教师还是学生,在适用本系列教材的过程中,如果发现任何问题或有任何意见、建议,欢迎及时与我们联系(发送邮件至 bjdxcbs1979@163.com)。我们会将您的意见或建议及时反馈给作者,供作者在修订再版时进行参考,从而进一步完善教材内容。

最后,感谢所有参与编写和为我们出谋划策提供帮助的专家学者,以及广大使用本系列教材的师生,希望本系列教材能够为我国高等院校法学专业教育和我国的法治建设贡献绵薄之力。

北京大学出版社
2012年3月

前　言

随着法律语言学(Legal Language 或 the Language of Law)在中国的兴起和蓬勃发展,以英语作为介质的法律英语(Legal English 或 the English Language of Law)在我国的发展蔚为壮观。同时,世界政治、法律、经济、贸易、金融、文化等交流活动的发展也为法律英语的学习带来便利,法律文件的翻译活动也日渐普及,为此,法律英语相关教材不断问世,但如何更好教会学生拓展其专业水平的教科书在国内相对鲜见。基于此,我们在编写了多种法律英语教材的基础上重新设计和编写了本教程,旨在让读者认识为"法律人"(Lawyer)所适用的法律语言,帮助他们提高法律英语水平,期待他们最终能掌握和比较熟练地应用法律英语实际开展各种相关工作或研究。

法律英语的涉及面极广,一般可以将有关材料分为两大类,即 Black Letter Law(严谨的法律原则,包括法律、法规、条例、命令、合同等等)和 Legal Literature(法学著述),而属于 Legal Literature 的范围很广泛,它包括法律评论文章(law review articles)、法学论文(treaties)、专著(monograph)、法官判决词(judge's opinion)等。这类著述相对晦涩深奥,常有不为非法律人理解的行话(legalese)在内,作者一般从交叉学科的视角对法学等进行诠释、剖析、解构和建构。

本书所选课文的语篇、语义及语用结构等均属中等以上难度,编者对不少课文都作有比较详尽的注释。此外,每课课文之后还附有大量的涉及法律英语的词汇、阅读理解、交互作用、案例赏析等练习。本书更具特色的是每课练习均设有一定的法律语言特征分析与法律翻译技能培养的简单介绍,并配有相关的翻译练习,以期帮助读者提高以英语作为介质的法律翻译能力。

本教程编写人员主要有:宋雷、郑达轩、倪清泉、谢金荣、谯莉、耿茜茜、薛婷婷等人。其中,倪清泉负责第16课的编写,谢金荣负责第8、15课的编写,谯莉负责第13课的编写,耿茜茜负责第6课的编写,薛婷婷负责第10课的编写,尹延安参加了第1、12、18课的部分编写,刘雅晴、王涛、王玉华、邓莎等参加了第7、9、11、14、17课的部分编写,张瑜参加了第1、4、18课的部分编写,郝立蓉参加了第3、12课的编写。

本书主编除材料收集和整理外,还参加了第2、3、4、5、7、9、11、14、17等课的编写,第1、12、18课的部分编写工作,并负责全书统编、刊校工作。

教材编写是件极科学和极艰巨的任务,尽管本书的编写得到西南政法大学研究生教研室各位同仁的指导和帮助,但鉴于编者的经验、水平等关系,错误在所难免,恳请不吝赐教。

宋　雷　郑达轩
2012 年于西南政法大学

目 录

1　Lesson One　Separation of Parties, Not Powers

- *1* Text
- *13* Legal Terminology
- *13* Exercises

27　Lesson Two　Sample Sales Agency Contract

- *27* Text
- *36* Legal Terminology
- *38* Exercises

58　Lesson Three　About Contracts

- *58* Text
- *70* Legal Terminology
- *72* Exercises

95　Lesson Four　Code of Judicial Conduct

- *95* Text
- *106* Legal Terminology
- *108* Exercises

129　Lesson Five　Terms and Conditions of Commercial Letter of Credit and Security Agreement

- *129* Text
- *136* Legal Terminology
- *137* Exercises

155　Lesson Six　The Skepticism in Law and Morals

- 155　Text
- 161　Legal Terminology
- 163　Exercises

188　Lesson Seven　Rules of Legal Interpretation

- 188　Text
- 195　Legal Terminology
- 199　Exercises

218　Lesson Eight　U.S. Legal History on Capital Punishment
——Crime of Homicide in Chicago from 1870 to 1930

- 218　Text
- 226　Legal Terminology
- 228　Exercises

260　Lesson Nine　Judicial Discipline and Judicial Independence

- 260　Text
- 268　Legal Terminology
- 269　Exercises

285　Lesson Ten　Investor Protection and Corporate Governance

- 285　Text
- 291　Legal Terminology
- 294　Exercises

313　Lesson Eleven　Using Theory to Study Law: A Company Law Perspective

- 313　Text
- 323　Legal Terminology
- 327　Exercises

344　Lesson Twelve　Ethical Implications of Energy for Sustainable Development

344	Text
353	Legal Terminology
354	Exercises

377　Lesson Thirteen　Virtual Civil Litigation: A Visit to John Bunyan's Celestial City

377	Text
390	Legal Terminology
392	Exercises

407　Lesson Fourteen　Successive Confessions and the Poisonous Tree

407	Text
416	Legal Terminology
418	Exercises

435　Lesson Fifteen　Due Process and Targeted Killing of Terrorists

435	Text
445	Legal Terminology
446	Exercises

469　Lesson Sixteen　Sexual Predator Laws: A Two-Decade Retrospective

469	Text
479	Legal Terminology
480	Exercises

502　Lesson Seventeen　Introduction to International Law

502	Text
509	Legal Terminology
511	Exercises

538 | Lesson Eighteen　Recent Developments in International Intellectual Property Litigation

- *538* | Text
- *545* | Legal Terminology
- *547* | Exercises

Lesson One

Separation of Parties, Not Powers

> **Learning objectives**
>
> After learning the text and having done the exercises in this lesson, you will:
>
> —familiarize with knowledge of the legal characteristics and the nature of separation of parties rather than separation of powers;
>
> —acquire an appreciation of the vocabulary and grammar or syntax relevant to separation of powers and separation of parties in the constitutional setting;
>
> —become aware of the information required in order to understand the separation of parties in the US constitutionality;
>
> —cultivate the practical abilities to put to use the language in the specific context;
>
> —be able to do some translation from Chinese to English and from English to Chinese.

 Text

Separation of Parties, Not Powers

- **Introduction**

American political institutions were founded upon the Madisonian① assumption of vigorous, self-sustaining political competition between the legislative and executive branches. Congress and the President would check and balance② each other; officeholders would defend the distinct interests of their distinct institutions, and ambition would counteract ambition.

---

① James Madison, Jr.：詹姆斯·麦迪逊(1751—1836)，美国著名政治家和政治理论家，第四任美国总统(1809—1817)，因起草美利坚合众国联邦宪法被人尊称为"宪法之父"，并极力主张和草拟美国"权利法案"。起草宪法后，极力推动各州批准该宪法的工作，他和亚历山大·汉密尔顿以及约翰·杰伊的合作成果造就了备受后人瞩目的《联邦党人文集》(1788年)的诞生。他担任总统期间曾领导进行第二次美英战争，保卫了美国的共和制度，为美国赢得彻底独立建立了功绩。他在1776年参加弗吉尼亚宪法的制定，并且是弗吉尼亚会议的一位领导人。他还是出席大陆会议的代表，是制宪会议的主要人物、众议院议员、民主共和党的组织者。

② check and balance：制衡,制约与平衡。check and balance principle(分权制衡原则)是美国政治制度中一个非常重要的概念。

To this day, the idea of building self-sustaining political competition into the structure of government is frequently portrayed as the unique genius of the U.S. Constitution and largely credited for① the success of American democracy. Yet the truth is closer to the opposite. The success of American democracy overwhelmed the branch-based design of separation of powers② almost from the outset, preempting the political dynamics that were supposed to provide each branch with a will of its own. What the Framers③ did not count on was the emergence of robust democratic competition, in government and in the electorate. Political competition and cooperation along relatively stable lines of policy and ideological disagreement quickly came to be channeled not through the branches of government but rather through an institution the Framers could imagine only dimly but nevertheless despised④: political parties. Parties came to serve as the primary organizational vehicle for mobilizing, motivating, and defining the terms of democratic political competition, creating alliances among constituents and officeholders that cut across the boundaries between the branches and undermined Madisonian assumptions of branch-based competition. Few aspects of the Founding generation's political theory are now more clearly anachronistic⑤ than their vision of legislative-executive separation of powers.

Nevertheless, few of the Framers' ideas continue to be taken as literally or sanctified as deeply by courts and constitutional scholars as the passages about interbranch relations⑥ in Madison's *Federalist 51*⑦. This Article re-envisions the law and theory of separation of powers by viewing it through the lens of party competition. In particular, it points out that during periods—like the present—of cohesive and polarized⑧ political parties, the degree and kind of competition between the legislative and executive branches will vary significantly and may all but disappear, depending on whether party control of the House, Senate, and presidency is divided or unified. The practical distinction between party-divided and party-unified government thus rivals, and often dominates, the constitutional distinction between the branches in predicting and explaining interbranch political dynamics. Recognizing that these dynamics will shift from competitive when government is divided to cooperative when it is unified calls into question basic assumptions of separation of powers, law and theory. More constructively, refocusing the separation of powers on parties casts nu-

---

① be credited for:归功于某人,如:He is credited with the invention(这个发明是他的功劳)。To credit (sb.) with (an amount /a quality),把(某数)记入(某人)账户的贷方,记入为(某人)存款;相信(某人)具有(某性质)。To credit success to (sb.),把成功归于某人。

② branch-based design of separation of powers:基于国家权力的不同部门而设定权力的分立。

③ Framers:在文中指美国的制宪者、开国元勋们,开国一代(Founding Fathers of the United States)。

④ an institution the Framers could imagine only dimly but nevertheless despised:制宪者们可以隐隐约约想象得到却不屑为之的一种制度。

⑤ anachronistic:年代出错的,时代错误的,不合时代潮流。源自 anachronism:时代错误,弄错年代;与时代不合的事物,如:Contemporary monarchy is an anachronism(现代的君主政体是不合时宜的事物)。

⑥ interbranch relations:国家各部门之间权力的关系。

⑦ Federalist 51:指《联邦党人文集》第51篇。《联邦党人文集》或称《联邦论》、《联邦主义论文集》(Federalist Papers),是18世纪80年代数位美国政治家在制定美国宪法的过程中所写作的有关美国宪法和联邦制度的评论文章的合集,共收有85篇文章。这些文章最早连载于纽约地区的报纸,之后在1788年,首次出版了合集,书名为《联邦党人》(The Federalist)。此书主要对美国宪法和美国政府的运作原理进行了剖析和阐述,是研究美国宪法的最重要的历史文献之一。

⑧ polarized:极化的,两极分化的;偏振的,如:The public opinion has polarized on this issue(在这个问题上公众的意见已两极分化)。

merous aspects of constitutional structure, doctrine, and institutional design in a new and more realistic light.

• Madison and the Mechanisms of Political Competition

According to the political theory of the Framers, "the great problem to be solved" was to design governance institutions① that would afford "practical security" against the excessive concentration of political power. Constitutional provisions specifying limited domains of legitimate authority were of minimal utility, for, as Madison explained, "a mere demarcation on parchment of the constitutional limits of the several departments is not a sufficient guard against those encroachments which lead to a tyrannical concentration of all the powers of government in the same hands." The solution to this great problem was, instead, to link the power-seeking motives of public officials to the interests of their branches. By giving "those who administer each department the necessary constitutional means and personal motives to resist encroachments of the others," the Framers hoped to create a system in which competition for power among the branches would constrain each safely within its bounds. With multiple government departments pitted against each other② in a competition for power, an invisible-hand dynamic might prevail in which "ambition would be made to counteract ambition."

Madison's vision of competitive branches balancing and checking one another has dominated constitutional thought about the separation of powers through the present. Yet it has never been clear exactly how the Madisonian machine was supposed to operate. Particularly puzzling is Madison's personification of political institutions, his hope that each branch might come to possess "a will of its own." If branches of government pursued their own interests, and if these interests were similar to the power-mongering interests③ that the Framers attributed to individual political actors, then branches might indeed compete with one another for power. But of course, government institutions do not have wills or interests of their own; their behavior is a product of the wills or interests that motivate the individual officials who compose them. Madison saw the need for a linkage between "the interest of the man" and "the constitutional rights of the place," but he never provided a mechanism by which the interests of actual public officials would be channeled into maintaining the proper role for their respective branches.

---

① governance institutions:治理制度,治理机制。governance:治理,管治,统治,管理,支配;统治方式,管理方法,如 global governance(全球治理);ownership structure and corporate governance performance(股权结构与公司治理绩效);the community governance(社区治理);collaboration game and governance of relation of governments(合作博弈与府际治理)。

② pit against:使竞争,使相互角斗,如:The government leadership and rural social forces pitted against each other(政府主导与乡村社会力量相互对垒);For many women, profession and family are pitted against one another on a high—stakes collision course (对许多女性来说,职业和家庭在一个高风险的冲突过程上是互相抵触的)。

③ power-mongering interests:角逐权利者的利益,争权夺利者的利益,power-monger:角逐权力者,争权者。

From the modern perspective of consolidated democracy①, it is hard to see how such a mechanism would arise. Even assuming, with the founding generation, that officeholders are driven by a "lust for self-aggrandizement," the structure of democratic politics effectively channels those ambitions into a different set of activities that has nothing to do with aggrandizing their departments or defending them against encroachments. Individual politicians gain and exercise power by winning competitive elections and effectuating political or ideological goals. Neither of these objectives correlates in any obvious way with the interests or power of branches of government as such. Madison's will-based theory of separation of powers would seem to require government officials who care more about the intrinsic interests of their departments than their personal interests or the interests of the citizens they represent. Democratic politics is unlikely to generate such officials.

The founding generation's assumptions about the workings of representative democracy② may help account for Madison's optimism. First, elections were not then conceived as the competitive contests they soon became. Instead, they were understood and practiced largely as matters of acclamation, focusing on personal qualities more than issues and interests and primarily serving to ratify existing social and political hierarchies. George Washington's③ assumption of the presidency is a paradigmatic example. Second, to the extent political issues were discussed, it was in the civic republican vocabulary of disinterested concern for the common good④, shunning explicit appeals to interest. With large election districts for the House⑤ and indirect election of the Senate and President providing further insulation from the self-interested demands of constituents, it was possible to envision officeholders who would "refine and enlarge the public views" and whose "wisdom might best discern the true interest of their country." In this kind of political, or apolitical, world, it was possible to imagine that, once elected, officeholders would not be tempted by constituent pressures and competing ideological or policy goals to sacrifice the constitutionally assigned duties and powers of their branches—simply because constituent pressures and divergent interests were kept to a minimum.

Less optimistically, the founding generation also had good reason to doubt whether representative democracy would work at all and, consequently, good reason to fear that government officials

---

① Consolidated democracy：统一(整合)民主制，如：一国绝大多数的人民把民主体制当作是合法制度予以接受，民众接受有关民主的基本准则并参与到各个层面的市民社会生活。(A democracy is considered "consolidated" when it is the only game in town. What this means is that a large majority of the countries' population accepts the democratic institutions as legitimate and thus they exist relatively unchallenged. However, this also means that there must be a strong democratic culture in place as well. This means that, in general, the population believes in the basic tenets of democracy and participates in various aspects of civil society.)

② representative democracy：代议制民主，公民选举代表掌握国家决策权力的民主形式。代议制民主下，公民的民主权利主要体现在选举代表的权利上。与直接民主制(direct democracy)相对。

③ George Washington：美国首任总统(1789—1797)，由于他扮演了美国独立战争和建国中最重要的角色，故被尊称为美国国父。

④ common good：公益/共同利益；在苏格兰指公共财产，如：law is an ordinance of reason for the common good(法律是维护公众利益的理性条令)。

⑤ House：此处指 House of Representatives，〔美〕众议院，美国立法机构两院的下院，上院为参议院(Senate)。

would pursue interests entirely disconnected not just from those of their nominal constituents①, but from the public good as well. Madison's scheme for pitting competing branches against one another may have been meant only as a fail-safe②, in case Antifederalist③ fears of radical democratic failure came to pass. If one branch fell under the control of a would-be monarch or tyrannical cabal, the other branches might provide a check by using their constitutional powers to block oppressive measures or, as the founding generation vividly recalled from the English Civil War④, by leading an opposing army to fight for control of the state. In the worst-case scenario, better to be ruled by several warring tyrants than a single omnipotent one. For the Federalist Framers, however, this kind of figurative and literal interbranch warfare was meant only as an "auxiliary precaution." The "primary control on the government" would be its "dependence on the people," which would link the political self-interest of legislators to the interests of the voters who determined their professional fates. If representative democracy worked as the Framers hoped, in other words, competition for power among the branches would be replaced by competition for power among politicians and groups of constituents.

In fact, this is just what happened: Madison's design was eclipsed almost from the outset by the emergence of robust democratic political competition. Rather than tying their ambitions to the constitutional duties or power base of their departments, officials responded to the material incentives of democratic politics in ways that now seem natural and inevitable: by forming incipient organizations that took sides on contested policy and ideological issues and by competing to marshal support for their agendas. These efforts led inexorably, though haltingly, to the organization of enduring parties that would facilitate alliances among groups of like-minded elected officials and politically mobilized citizens on a national scale.

The idea of political parties, representing institutionalized divisions of interest, was famously anathema to the Framers, as it had long been in Western political thought. Equating parties with nefarious "factions," the Framers had attempted to design a "Constitution Against Parties." But the futility of this effort quickly became apparent. By the end of the first Congress⑤, it had become clear that political competition organized around issues and programs had the potential to divide coalitions of officeholders and cut through the constitutional boundaries between the branches.

---

① Constituents: adj. 组成的,形成的(部分);有权制宪、修宪的(会议)如"立宪会议"(constituent council); n. 委任人(指委任并授权他人为自己的代理人);选民(在自己所在的选区选出代表该选区并在公共事务中关注他们利益的议员的人)。此处指选民。
② fail-safe: n. 自动防故障装置; adj. 自动防故障装置的,故障自动保险的;能组织军事攻击的;万无一失的。
③ Antifederalist:反联邦主义者,反联邦党员,是1642年至1651年在英国议会派与保皇派之间发生的一系列武装冲突及政治斗争;英国辉格党称之为清教徒革命(Puritan Revolution)。此事件对英国和整个欧洲都产生了巨大的影响,并由此将革命开始的1640年作为世界近代史的开端。
④ English Civil War:英国内战(1642—1651),也被称作 The Civil War in Great Britain。
⑤ 此处应指第一次大陆会议(First Continental Congress)。第一次大陆会议在1774年召开,组建了军队并任命乔治·华盛顿为大陆军总司令,讨论殖民地反抗英国统治的问题。1775年4月19日,英国士兵与殖民地反叛者在马萨诸塞州列克星敦发生遭遇战,战争爆发了。1776年7月4日,大陆会议通过了《独立宣言》。

The earliest efforts toward alliance formation were initiated by Treasury Secretary Alexander Hamilton①, who in 1790 began to recruit members of Congress to forge a coalition in favor of his economic development program. His leading congressional opponent, James Madison, joined with Thomas Jefferson② to organize opposition. As the political battle in Congress intensified, both sides recognized the need to cultivate public support. By the 1796 elections, Federalists and Republicans③ had coalesced into competing groupings, with party leaders controlling nominations and, at least in some states, rudimentary party machinery organizing campaigns focused more on issues and platforms than on the local stature of the candidates. When Congress convened in 1797, its members were clearly identified as Federalist or Republican and regularly voted along those lines. The precursors of the modern political parties had taken root, planted by the very Framers who had authored a Constitution against them.

To be sure, the early organizations, caucuses, and proto-parties were organized with regret and regarded as temporary expediencies that would fade when the urgent need to defeat a treasonous enemy had passed—as they did, to some extent, after the collapse of the Federalist Party inaugurated the "Era of Good Feelings."④ The Jacksonian period, however, brought lasting recognition and acceptance of a "party system" of democratic politics: an ongoing competition, as Professor Richard Hofstadter⑤ later defined it, between stable, organized parties, alternating power and control within shared acceptance of a constitutional framework. Acceptance of this idea has rightly been called a "revolution in political structure that lies at the foundation of modernity."

At the very least, the rise of partisan politics worked a revolution in the American system of separation of powers, radically realigning the incentives of politicians and officeholders. As an initial example, consider the role of parties in transforming the presidency into a genuinely independent counterweight to Congress. During the country's first forty years or so, a chasm emerged between the predicted and actual effects of the constitutional design on the President's capacity to

---

① Treasury Secretary,是指美国财政部长,而在英国,财政部长为 Treasury Chief。
Alexander Hamilton:亚历山大·汉密尔顿(1757—1804),是美国的开国元勋之一,宪法的起草人之一,财经专家,是美国的第一任财政部长,美国政党制度的创建者,在美国金融、财政和工业发展史上,占有重要地位。因政党相争而决斗丧生。2006 年,汉密尔顿被美国的权威期刊《大西洋月刊》评为影响美国的 100 位人物第 5 名。

② Thomas Jefferson:托马斯·杰斐逊(1743—1826),美国政治家、思想家、哲学家、科学家、教育家,第三任美国总统。他是美国独立战争期间的主要领导人之一,1776 年,作为一个包括约翰·亚当斯和本杰明·富兰克林在内的起草委员会的成员,起草了美国《独立宣言》。此后,他先后担任了美国第一任国务卿、第二任副总统和第三任总统。他在任期间保护农业,发展民族资本主义工业。从法国手中购买路易斯安那州,使美国国土近乎增加了一倍。他被普遍视为美国历史上最杰出的总统之一,同华盛顿、林肯和罗斯福齐名。

③ Federalists:联邦党(Federalist Party 或 Federal Party)是在 1792 年到 1816 年期间存在的一个美国政党。由美国首任财政部长亚历山大·汉密尔顿(Alexander Hamilton)成立。联邦党是美国在 1801 年之前的执政党。主张增强联邦政府的权力。主要的支持者来自新英格兰和一些南方较富有的农民。其竞争对手为民主共和党。联邦党是后来辉格党和共和党的前身。
Republican:共和党(Republican Party),又常被简称为 GOP(Grand Old Party,大佬党),是美国当代的两大主要政党之一,另一个是民主党。1856 年创党以来,共和党在 39 届总统选战中赢得了 23 届,包括了最近 10 届中的 6 届;自从那时开始 29 位美国总统有 18 位都是共和党人。共和党创立于 1854 年,结合了当时反对奴隶制度扩张的政治势力。在现代政治中,共和党则被视为是社会保守主义和经济古典自由主义的政党。

④ Era of Good Feelings:"和睦时代",是美国历史上一个独特的时代,这个时期主要包括詹姆斯·门罗任职总统的 8 年(1817—1825)。

⑤ Richard Hofstadter:理查德·霍夫施塔特(1916—1970),20 世纪 50 年代的美国公共知识分子、历史学家。

stand apart from Congress. The Framers had specifically rejected congressional appointment of the President on the ground that making the President reliant on congressional support would deny him the requisite independence. Yet after Washington's presidency, party caucuses in Congress quickly became the mechanism for identifying and selecting credible presidential candidates. The rise of legislative parties as gatekeepers for the presidency, together with the expectation that elections would often be decided in the House of Representatives (as they were in two of the four open-seat presidential elections from 1800 to 1824), meant that Congress played a major role in selecting the President. As a result, the American government effectively operated for much of its first forty years with a congressionally dominated fusion of legislative and executive powers. So much for Madison's prediction that separated powers would create checks and balances by joining "the interest of the man" with "the constitutional rights of the place." The political interests of the man who held the presidency, it turned out, had little to do with furthering some abstract conception of the presidency's proper role, but were instead rooted in the necessity of winning and keeping office. Presidents maximized their political prospects not by creating an independent "will" for the executive branch or competing with Congress for power, but instead by acquiescing in congressionally dominated government.

Not until the presidency of Andrew Jackson① did American government begin to resemble in practice the Madisonian system of separation of powers that existed on paper. Jackson was the first President to circumvent Congress by appealing directly to the people, claiming that his office embodied the American people as a whole. His revolutionary use of the veto backed up this claim.② As a leading historian of the presidency puts it, for the first time the presidency "was thrust forward as one of three equal departments of government, and to each and every of its powers was imparted new scope, new vitality."

The inauguration of the independent presidency under Jackson was made possible by two institutional changes, both emerging from the invention of political parties. First, Martin Van Buren's③ creation of the mass-scale political party generated pressure for popular control over presidential nominations, leading to the replacement of the congressional caucus system by national

---

① Andrew Jackson:安德鲁·杰克逊,是美国第七任总统(1829—1837)。首任佛罗里达州州长、新奥尔良之役战争英雄、民主党创建者之一,杰克逊式民主因他而得名。在美国政治史上,19世纪二三十年代第二党体系(Second Party System)以他为极端的象征。杰克逊始终被美国的专家学者评为美国最杰出的10位总统之一。

② His revolutionary use of the veto backed up this claim:他革命性地使用总体否决权以支持这种主张。Jackson 所行使的总统否决权比历史上所有总统使用否决权之和还要多,其中包括最著名的美利坚合众国第二银行案的否决,其早期行使否决权主要还是基于宪法,而后期则更多是基于他和国会的不和,这些较为典型地反映出美国总统的独立性。(Jackson vetoed more bills than all previous Presidents combined, Presidential Vetoes, including his famous veto of the Second Bank of the United States, which was accompanied by the strongest statement of the presidency's independent role that had thus far been issued in American history. Even the course of his vetoes reflected the increasing functional separation of the Presidency from Congress: Jackson's early vetoes were based on constitutional objections, traditionally a more widely accepted basis for exercise of the veto, while his later ones rested on mere policy disagreement with Congress.)

③ Martin Van Buren:马丁·范布伦,美国第八任副总统(1833—1837)及美国第八任总统(1837—1841)。他是美国《独立宣言》正式签署后出生的第一位总统。为人圆滑,诡计多端,是一个出色的政党组织者,有"魔术师"和"红狐狸"之称。是前总统安德鲁·杰克逊最得力的助手。1837年继位上台后,和加拿大爆发了边界争端,他灵活处理。但后来美国又爆发了第一次经济危机。虽然这不是他的错,但人民对范布伦失去信心。1840年他竞选连任时,败于威廉·亨利·哈里森。后来又两度参加竞选,都遭到失败,从此退出政坛,回到故乡。

nominating conventions as of 1832. Second, the Democratic Party's novel practice of running presidential electors pledged in advance to vote for particular candidates undermined the electoral college[①] by turning it into a mere tabulating device, one likely to yield a majority winner; this all but eliminated the role of the House of Representatives in resolving presidential elections. Taken together, these two institutional changes wrested control of the presidency away from Congress by forging an independent, popular electoral base for the President.

Thus, it took the mass-scale Democratic Party of Van Buren and Jackson to create the possibility of Madisonian competition between Congress and the President that the original constitutional design had promised but failed to deliver. For all of the Framers' aversion to parties, credit for the belated birth of genuinely separated powers must go to the mass political party—the embodiment of the factionalized politics the Framers most loathed. One failure of constitutional design was corrected, ironically, by another.

The correction, however, was neither permanent nor complete. Just as parties can create the conditions necessary for interbranch competition to emerge, they can also submerge competition by effectively reuniting the branches. As we elaborate below, if government officials are motivated primarily by policy and partisan goals, then single-party control of multiple branches of government will tend to create cross-branch cooperation among like-minded officeholders. Once again, parties can—and often do—change the relationship between Congress and the President from competitive to cooperative.

For present purposes, however, it is enough to see that from the outset of government under the Constitution, practical politics undermined the Madisonian vision of rivalrous branches pitted against one another in a competition for power. The emergence of a robust system of democratic politics tied the power and political fortunes of government officials to issues and elections. This, in turn, created a set of incentives that rendered these officials largely indifferent to the powers and interests of the branches per se. In Madison's terms, "the interests of the man" have become quite disconnected from the interests of "the place."

Instead, the electoral and policy interests of politicians have become intimately connected to political parties. Since the early conflicts between Federalists and Republicans, politicians have affiliated themselves with the party whose platform comes closest to their own policy preferences, and parties, in turn, have exerted influence over members' policy goals and their ability to achieve them in office. The result has been a strong correlation between party affiliation and political behavior. Even the most casual observer of Washington politics understands that congressional opposition to a President's initiatives and nominees will come predominantly, if not entirely, from members of the opposite party.

To observe that the political interests of elected officials generally correlate more strongly with party than with branch is not to assert that political interests perfectly track party affiliation. They

---

① electoral college: 美国由各州所选出的总统选举团制度。美国国父们在宪法中确定"选举团"制度是为了在国会选票与大众选票之间搞妥协,但宪法文本中并没有 Electoral College 这个术语,《宪法》第 2 条与第十二修正条款所使用的均为"elector"。

obviously do not. For well-understood structural reasons, American parties have never achieved the near-perfect unity of political parties in European parliamentary systems. In the American system, policy agreement and disagreement on some issues has been, and continues to be, structured along lines that cut across party affiliations. On certain aspects of trade and environmental policy, for example, the relevant cleavages may correspond more closely to geography and interest-group support than to party. And sometimes the lines of policy disagreement actually do correspond to the branches, reflecting the divergent preferences of the different temporal and geographical majorities that the House, Senate, and President represent (as opposed to the institutional interests of the branches as such). Conventional wisdom has it, for example, that the President tends to focus more on national-scale problems and is generally inclined to resist the persistent efforts of Congress to dole out local pork①. This creates the possibility, and occassionally the reality, of political battles between the branches—not because anyone has any intrinsic interest in the power of the branches qua② branches, but simply because, on some issues, branch affiliation will correlate with policy preferences (and party affiliation will not). When it comes to highway bills, party labels may fall by the wayside.

Nevertheless, the bottom line remains that in the broad run of cases—which is, after all, the relevant perspective for constitutional law—party is likely to be the single best predictor of political agreement and disagreement. It is impossible to grasp how the American system of government works in practice without taking account of how partisan③ political competition has reshaped the constitutional structure of government in ways the Framers would find unrecognizable.

Yet the constitutional law and theory of separation of powers has proceeded, for the most part, as if parties did not exist and the branches behaved in just the way Madison imagined.

• Presidential, Parliamentary, and Party Government

In contrast to courts and constitutional scholars, political scientists have long appreciated political parties' leading role in enforcing the separation of powers, though from the opposite normative perspective. Their focus on parties emerges from a traditional line of political thought juxtaposing the American "presidential" system of separation of powers with the classic British system of parliamentary government. In contrast to the Madisonian model, in which democratic legitimacy and lawmaking authority are formally divided between the independently elected President and Congress, the Westminster executive is formed by the legislative majority and essentially wields plenary control over governance. Power in the Westminster system④ is unified, not separated.

For admirers of the British system, the Madisonian design was critically flawed in its inception. The parliamentarian critique of the American separation of powers dates back at least to the

---

① dole out local pork: dole out 指分配; pork 指猪肉,政治恩惠(政府用以笼络人心的工程或款项),合起来即分配获得利益。
② qua:拉丁语,作为,以……的资格/或身份的。
③ partisan:党徒;信徒,指与整体的公共利益相对立的某一党派或某一事业的拥护者。
④ Westminster system:威斯敏斯特体制,英国的代议制政体。

early Woodrow Wilson①, who, writing in the late nineteenth century, saw the Framers' decision to divide powers between Congress and the Executive as a "grievous mistake." Wilson argued that Madisonian government was dramatically ineffective and vulnerable to paralysis and stalemate because significant policymaking could not be accomplished without somehow inducing cooperation between the inherently competitive political branches. He also argued that, because voters had no single government institution on which to focus political credit or blame, the constitutional separation of powers sacrificed democratic accountability. Wilson judged the parliamentary system's unification of authority and responsibility in the prime minister② and his cabinet to be clearly superior along both of these dimensions.

Wilson's parliamentarian critique of presidential government became the conventional wisdom of the field he founded and has been reiterated and elaborated by political scientists through the present. But political scientists have also appreciated the ironic possibility that political parties could redeem American government from its inherently flawed constitutional structure. As the standard argument goes, "the institutions that the framers had so deliberately separated had to be brought together in some degree of unity for the government to function—and the instrument for that purpose was the political party." The hope is that, by uniting the interests of government officials across branch lines, parties might defeat the Framers' design and, in practice, fuse the formally separated legislature and Executive into a second-best approximation of Westminster. This view, which has both descriptive and normative③ components, has been known as the doctrine of "(responsible) party government."④

The party government view is premised on⑤ the widespread belief among political scientists that party lines predict political behavior better than branch ones. If instead the political interests of members of Congress and the President corresponded predominantly to branch membership, then regardless of party we would expect to see competition rather than cooperation between the branches—just as Madison envisioned, Wilson once feared, and courts and constitutional theorists continue to take for granted. This would make parties at best peripheral features of the political system—which, again, is exactly how they have generally been regarded by constitutional scholars.⑥ If parties are to link "the executive and legislative branches in a bond of common interest," then party identification must dominate branch identification. Generations of political scientists have proceeded from this well-grounded assumption, putting them precisely at odds with genera-

---

① Thomas Woodrow Wilson:托马斯·伍德罗·威尔逊,美国第 28 任总统,是进步主义时代的一个领袖级知识分子,1912 年总统大选中,以民主党人身份当选总统。迄今为止,他是唯一一名拥有哲学博士头衔的美国总统(法学博士衔除外),也是唯一一名任总统以前曾在新泽西州担任公职的美国总统,被认为是美国历史上学术成就最高的一位总统。

② prime minister:(1) 首相;(内阁)总理,常用大写,指议会制政府(parliamentary government)的行政首脑,内阁的负责人。(2) 此处指英国首相,首相是政府的行政首脑,英国首相同时也是首席财政大臣(First Lord of the Treasury)和文官事务大臣(Minister for Civil Service)。

③ descriptive and normative:描述性和规范性。

④ party government:政党政治,通常指一个国家通过政党行使国家政权的形式。

⑤ is premised on:以……为前提。

⑥ 就钻研民主制度和选举法的法律学者而言,政党政治中法律学术中总是居于核心的位置。(Among public law scholars who specialize in the law of democracy and election law, of course, political parties have long occupied a central place in legal scholarship.)

tions of constitutional lawyers.

But another necessary condition for successful party government, of course, is that the same party control both the legislative and executive branches. When control is divided between parties, we should expect party competition to be channeled through the branches, resulting in interbranch political competition resembling the Madisonian dynamic of rivalrous branches (perhaps even fueling more extreme competition than the Framers envisioned). True, the underlying mechanism would be entirely different: branches would continue to lack wills of their own, and politicians would continue to lack any interest in the power of branches qua branches. The branches would simply serve a politically contingent role as vehicles for party competition.

Writing in the midst of a quarter century of mostly divided government, the early Wilson had witnessed exactly that. His mistake was to overgeneralize features of the political system he was observing at that moment, assuming them to be inevitable features of the Madisonian design. Later generations of political scientists, writing against the background norm of unified government that had prevailed for the first half of the twentieth century, replicated Wilson's mistake in the opposite direction. By the 1950s, Wilsonian criticism of the Madisonian design had been displaced by calls for stronger and more programmatic political parties of the European variety. This made perfect sense on the assumption that government would usually be unified: strengthening parties might then be all that stood between Washington and a system of responsible party government that would closely approximate the Westminster ideal. Under conditions of divided party control, however, strong parties would only exacerbate the inefficiency and unaccountability of separated powers by making interbranch cooperation all the more difficult.

As fate would have it, the responsible party government movement coincided with the beginning of a prolonged period of divided government. Once again, political scientists rallied around the Wilsonian lamentation that the Madisonian system was living down to its defective design. The peak of despair was marked by the 1987 report of the Committee on the Constitutional System. Representing the consensus view among political scientists and Washington insiders①, the Committee bemoaned the deleterious consequences of divided party control—precisely the same problems of gridlock and diminished accountability that Wilson had (mis)identified as essential features of the Madisonian design. Short of rewriting the structural constitution from scratch, the country's best hope, according to the Committee and its fellow travelers, lay in a set of constitutional and statutory reforms designed to reunify government (some similar to reforms suggested by Wilson a century earlier). These included requiring or encouraging straight-ticket voting②, allowing sitting members③ of Congress to serve in the President's cabinet, and altering the electoral timing and term lengths for the President and members of Congress. Not surprisingly, none of these measures has proven politically feasible.

Most constitutional lawyers would bid them good riddance. The pseudo-parliamentarian, re-

---

① insiders: 内幕人士, 知情人士。
② straight-ticket voting: 清一色选票(美国选举中支持某一政党全部候选人的选票)。
③ sitting members: 任期内的成员。

sponsible party government project of fusing the branches under the control of a single, strong party takes Wilson's critique of Madisonian separation of powers as its normative touchstone. Yet each of the features of Madisonian separationism that parliamentarians criticize is, in fact, celebrated in American constitutional discourse. Thus, the inefficiency of requiring the agreement of multiple, mutually antagonistic institutions to make laws becomes, in the view of constitutional lawyers, the great virtue of preserving "liberty" and preventing "tyranny." And while separated powers may blur the lines of political accountability, constitutional lawyers emphasize that creating multiple channels of democratic responsiveness helps keep government accountable to the popular will by encouraging interbranch deliberation, defeating demagoguery, and impeding capture by narrow interests.

From the Madisonian perspective that undergirds much of constitutional law and theory, therefore, the primary threat posed by political parties to the separation of powers comes not from party division of government but from party unification. Far from dreading divided government, Madisonians in a modern democracy must count on party division to recreate a competitive dynamic between the branches. And far from encouraging unified party control of the House, Senate, and presidency, Madisonians will view the prospect of unchecked and unbalanced governance by a cohesive majority party as cause for constitutional alarm.

- **Conclusion: Separation of Parties**

Whether it is party unification or party division of government that is cause for the most concern, any understanding of the American system of separation of powers should start from the recognition that it encompasses both. Contrary to the foundational assumption of constitutional law and theory since Madison, the United States has not one system of separation of powers but (at least) two. When government is divided, party lines track branch lines, and we should expect to see party competition channeled through the branches. The resulting interbranch political competition will look, for better or worse, something like the Madisonian dynamic of rivalrous branches. On the other hand, when government is unified and the engine of party competition is removed from the internal structure of government, we should expect interbranch competition to dissipate. Intraparty① cooperation (as a strategy of interparty competition) smoothes over branch boundaries and suppresses the central dynamic assumed in the Madisonian model.

The functional differences between these two systems of separation of powers—party separated and party unseparated—are described in more detail in the next Part, but the challenge to the constitutional law and theory of separation of powers should already be clear. The Madisonian model of inherently competitive branches checking and balancing one another, around which the constitutional law of separation of powers has been designed, has existed only in a few passages of *Federalist 51* and the imagination of courts and constitutional theorists ever since. To the extent constitutional law is concerned with the real as opposed to the parchment government, it would do well to shift focus from the static existence of separate branches to the dynamic interactions of the political parties that animate those branches.

---

① intraparty:党内的,一党内部的,而后文出现的 interparty 则是"党派之间、党与党之间"的意思。

Lesson One   Separation of Parties, Not Powers   13

 ## Legal Terminology

1. separation of powers 与 division of powers

前者指"三权分立"或"三权分立原则",指为了相互制约而使立法、司法和行政权力的相互分立。而后者指"权力分配",指在如美国这样的联邦制国家里,联邦政府和州政府之间权力的分配。

2. decentralization 与 devolution

两者均有中央政府将权力下放地方政府的含义,区别在于前者下放的权力要少于后者。在实行 devolution 的国家,地方当局几乎等于自治区政府,而在实行 decentralization 的国家则不然。故而在翻译"联邦政府将警察权下放各州"时应用 devolution。

3. legislative fact 与 adjudicative fact

两者之间的差别在于前者(法定事实)泛指与案件具体当事人的个人问题无关,即不属于个案性质而属于法律规定的具有一般属性的社会、经济、科技等的事实问题。而后者(裁定事实)指诉讼,尤其是行政诉讼中与当事人具体相关的事实,如个人动机、故意等,其为个案属性。

4. legislator 与 law-maker

二者均有"立法者"的含义。区别在于前者与 legislature 相关,故其多指属于立法机关成员者。而后者的范围较广,除包括 legislator 外,通过判例制定法律的法官,甚至缔结合同的双方当事人在某种意义上都可以称为 law maker。

5. primary legislation 与 delegated legislation

二者指不同分类的两种立法。前者指"本位立法"或"最高立法",多指议会直接制定的法律,在英国还包括根据皇家特权经枢密院令形式所颁布的法律。后者则为"受权立法"(与授权法相区别),也可称为"次位立法"(secondary legislation),指经议会法令,即母法(parent law)授权的人或机构在限定的范围内制定的法律。

 ## Exercises

I   Verbal Abilities

Part One

Directions: *For each of these completing questions, read each item carefully to get the sense of it. Then, in the proper space, complete each statement by supplying the missing word or phrase.*

1. The rules of blood _____ were closely regulated by law and custom: in the type of vengeance that might be taken, in the amount of compensation that might be exacted, in the place at which the compensation should be paid, and in the circumstances under which compensation need not be paid.

   A. aversions   B. enmity   C. grudge   D. animosity   E. feuds

2. These three chief procedural designs have the common principle of law equality and _____, which is expounded in this essay form two aspects: the structure of procedure and the op-

erating of procedure.

　　A. neurasthenia　　B. injustice　　C. bovine　　D. equalization　　E. adulation

3. They gave no clear-cut mandate to any leaders, vesting large parliamentary powers in small parties whose priorities sometimes _____ and sometimes contradict one another.

　　A. break away　　B. alienate　　C. dovetail　　D. retaliate　　E. harmonize

4. Having been officially banned, the political party was obliged to meet and operate _____.

　　A. tremendously　　B. ungainly　　C. clandestinely　　D. overtly　　E. in succession

5. The government is looking for new ways to prevent _____ and misleading advertising.

　　A. repulsive　　B. fraudulent　　C. integrated　　D. anticipated　　E. sufficient

6. The fireman wore masks that were _____ to the acid smok.

　　A. impervious　　B. wavering　　C. widespread　　D. menacing　　E. feeble

7. All countries _____ themselves to pursue internal and external economic policies designed to accelerate economic growth throughout the world.

　　A. pleaded　　B. premeditate　　C. plotted　　D. maneuvered　　E. pledged

8. As a general rule, the directors of a corporation may _____ a corporation only when they act as a legal meeting of the board.

　　A. obligate　　B. bind　　C. strap　　D. encumber　　E. constrain

9. When he realized the enormity of his criminal behavior, he became _____.

　　A. perforate　　B. penitent　　C. flamboyant　　D. pompous　　E. cerebrate

10. Whereas a per se analysis _____ a bright line prohibition to avoid the difficulties that would be presented by looking to the particular circumstances of the individual case, a prophylactic rule arguably moves a step beyond that analysis by requiring the state to take certain affirmative steps to ensure against the possible violation of an individual rights.

　　A. cast roach upon　　　　B. cast a slur on　　　　C. carves out

　　D. carve into　　　　　　E. carve up

Part Two

Directions: *Choose the one word or phase that best keep the meaning of the original sentence if it were substituted for the underlined part.*

1. The concept of retributive justice is reflected in many parts of the legal documents and procedures of modern times.

　　A. autocephalous　　B. retaliatory　　C. retrospective　　D. punishable　　E. automorphic

2. The most elementary means of settling international disputes is resort to negotiation between the contending parties.

　　A. elevated　　　　　　　B. egomaniacal　　　　　　C. swell-headed

　　D. rudimentary　　　　　E. individualistic

3. Such scholarship might take the form of an article addressing a knotty doctrinal problem.

　　A. problematical　　B. considerable　　C. profound　　D. challenging　　E. political

4. The trend <u>manifests</u> itself in a number of ways.
   A. monopolizes   B. brings to the open   C. lays barely
   D. summarizes   E. holds up to view

5. Furthermore, the DOC <u>objected to</u> Ukraine's regulations of the matter in which workers are paid.
   A. disagreed with   B. opposed   C. traced   D. obligated to   E. objurated to

6. An individual company may <u>rebut</u> this presumption by proving the absence of both de facto and de jure government control.
   A. reprimand   B. controvert   C. confute   D. reclaim   E. recapitulate

7. She lived lonely and had little <u>commerce</u> with her neighbors.
   A. trade   B. bargain   C. contact   D. transaction   E. communication

8. Great efforts were made to <u>curb</u> the air pollution
   A. wipe out   B. eliminate   C. hinder   D. slow down   E. decrease

9. Equally unresolved, and, indeed, ignored by most scholars, is the problem presented by most scholars, is the problem presented by a change in the configuration of contacts after the <u>accrual</u> of the cause of action.
   A. deduction   B. alteration   C. change   D. addition   E. reduce

10. Another of the salient features of the antitrust laws is the unique <u>panoply</u> of remedies available for their enforcement.
    A. award   B. character   C. datum   D. provision   E. protection

II Blank-filling

Directions: *Fill in the blanks in the following sentences with the words or phrases taken from the text.*

Constitutional provisions _____ limited domains of legitimate authority were of minimal utility, for, as Madison explained, "a mere demarcation on parchment of the constitutional limits of the several departments is not a sufficient guard against those encroachments which lead to a tyrannical _____ of all the powers of government in the same hands." The _____ to this great problem was, instead, to link the power-seeking motives of public officials to the interests of their branches.

Individual politicians gain and _____ power by winning competitive elections and effectuating political or ideological goals. Neither of these objectives correlates in any obvious way with the interests or power of branches of government as such. Madison's will-based theory of _____ of powers would seem to require government officials who care more about the _____ interests of their departments than their personal interests or the interests of the citizens they represent.

Instead, they were understood and practiced largely as matters of acclamation, _____ on personal qualities more than issues and interests and primarily serving to _____ existing social and political hierarchies. George Washington's assumption of the presidency is a _____ example.

The Framers had specifically rejected congressional _____ of the President on the ground that making the President reliant on congressional support would deny him the requisite _____. Yet after Washington's presidency, party caucuses in Congress quickly became the _____ for identifying and selecting credible presidential candidates.

It is _____ to grasp how the American system of government works in practice without taking _____ of how partisan political competition has reshaped the constitutional structure of government in ways the Framers would find _____.

Even as political scientists _____ to explain the tectonic shift to divided government in the 1950s and to come to grips with its _____, the political world, once again, seems to be changing underneath them. The turn of this century _____ a return of unified government.

Party organizations not only survived, but over the past couple decades also have managed to _____ an increasingly important role for themselves by providing campaign consulting and capital to their preferred candidates. Few _____ can now afford to turn down the fundraising, advertising, and polling assistance of parties, though accepting assistance means _____ some political independence.

Thus, the electoral _____ of the Westminster system might be contrasted with a Madisonian, intragovernmental form of accountability that operates during the _____ between elections and allows government officials not just to report each other's bad behavior to the electorate, but also to _____ it through the exercise of constitutional powers.

Nevertheless, especially as the parties have become more _____ and polarized, divisive electoral and policy competition should translate into greater congressional _____ and institutionalized resistance to executive actions during periods of divided government. This prediction will _____ with observers of relatively recent Washington history.

Similarly, the War Powers Resolution, Congress's most significant post-World War II attempt to stand up for itself in the foreign affairs _____, was passed by a Democratic Congress over President Nixon's _____. The three Supreme Court nominees who have been voted down by the Senate since World War II were _____ by Republican Presidents and defeated by Democratic Senates.

III Reading Comprehension

Part One

Directions: *In this section passages bellow is followed by questions or unfinished statements, each with four suggested answers. Choose the one you think is the best answer.*

What should a law firm do if it faces a media storm?

Sensational newspaper stories about one's law firm are every senior partner's nightmare. Stray e-mails are a particularly common source of law firm embarrassment. A recent case involved London firm Head and Lister: senior associate Terry Galpin gained worldwide notoriety after an e-mail row with a secretary. Mr Galpin e-mailed Cora Tomkins, asking her to pay for the cleaning of a jacket of his that she had spilled coffee on. Her outraged reply was seized upon by national newspapers. Head and Lister declined to contribute to this article, but made it clear when Mr Galpin resigned from his post that he did so before the media frenzy in order to pursue long-term study plans.

According to solicitor Natalie Egan, 'Most of the recent reputational disasters in major firms have resulted from lawyers forwarding e-mails outside the firm, or gossiping to legal journalists.' She says it is good to involve staff closely in the success of a firm, and help them understand how actions that can lead to the reputation of the firm being damaged can impact adversely on staff and on their own careers. She adds that although every story should be separately assessed and an appropriate strategy devised for each one, staying silent is sometimes best. 'I advise people upset by a story that unless it is actually untrue or defamatory, they should make no comment and console themselves that it will be history in a day or two.'

Ms Egan continues, 'However, if you're actually trying to campaign for a miscarriage of justice to be corrected, you need to build support with the widest audiences, from the public through to the law officers, and to brief the media. You should never dissemble, but prepare thoroughly, brief journalists comprehensively and be prepared for the fact that changing attitudes takes time.

David Abecia, a public relations expert, comments, 'There are times, especially with law firms, where confidentiality clauses require them to make no comment. However, if at all possible, I'd advise firms to put over their side of the story instead of saying "no comment", which always looks worse than if you've said your piece.'

Mr Abecia claims he can bring a detached viewpoint to a situation that may not be as big an issue as the client thinks it is. However, he says it is imperative that he is called in early on during a story so a news management plan can be devised. 'It's all a question of packaging. A story about a law firm sacking 60 people can be disastrous, but if you put it across as a restructuring exercise, done in consultation with staff due to tough market conditions, it doesn't look quite so bad.' He says that in the last seven years, how law firms handle media enquiries has changed 'out of all recognition'. There is now much better appreciation of the power of the media, he says.

Tony Mawson, a London-based partner, has also received adverse publicity after clashes with the media. However, it doesn't concern him unduly. 'If you're in the public eye, you just have to live with it. If you don't like it, you should go and do something easier like residential conveyancing.' He says that using the UK's privacy laws or criminal libel laws in other jurisdictions can be dangerous. 'That way you could make enemies. Most of my clients have low media profiles because we don't seek conflict with editors or journalists. An editor may get a small fine for criminal libel and although you might hope it will have a deterrent effect, in reality you're just encouraging them to put their best investigative journalist onto you.' But he says the threat of a libel suit can be a good way of killing a story. Even if the writ isn't served, the story usually isn't taken up by other newspapers.

1. What was Head and Lister's reaction to the 'coffee stain' incident?

A. They became annoyed when they were misquoted in the press.

B. They were quick to disassociate themselves from Mr Galpin.

C. They were anxious to prevent Ms Tomkins from making further comments.

D. They insisted that Mr Galpin's departure had nothing to do with the press coverage.

2. What does Natalie Egan say about media storms?

A. Strong action should be taken against staff who leak information.

B. It is best to adopt a uniform approach when dealing with them.

C. Bad publicity will quickly be forgotten if it is ignored.

D. They tend to affect senior lawyers more adversely.

3. What does David Abecia suggest about confidentiality clauses?

A. They are often difficult to implement.

B. They may turn out to be counter-productive.

C. They are useful in keeping a situation under control.

D. They must be carefully drafted to be effective.

4. According to David Abecia, when important stories are announced to the press,

A. staff briefings need to have taken place first.

B. appropriate timing is essential in order to minimize the impact.

C. the information needs to be framed in as positive a way as possible.

D. law firms should not attempt to deal with the media directly.

5. What does Tony Mawson say about the media criticism that has been aimed at him?

A. He accepts it is the price he has to pay.

B. It has become unnecessarily unpleasant.

C. He tries hard not to get too unsettled by it.

D. It has made him consider doing something less demanding.

6. Tony Mawson says that bringing a libel action against a newspaper

A. ought to discourage it from printing damaging stories in future.

B. is only advisable for those who are not in the public eye.

C. could deter other newspapers from investigating similar stories.

D. may well do more harm than good.

Part Two   Short-answer questions

Direction: *In this part of the exercise, there is a passage with several questions. Read the passage carefully and answer the following questions.*

The expression "sources of law" can mean at least two different things. It can refer to the historical origins from which the law has come, such as common law and equity. Second, it can refer to the body of rules which a judge will draw upon in deciding a case, and where these rules are to be found. In this second sense the sources of English law today are: Community law, legislation, delegated legislation, case law, legal textbooks, and custom.

Community Law

Since the United Kingdom joined the European Economic Community, now the European Community, it has progressively, but effectively, passed the power to create laws which are operative in this country to the wider European institutions. The United Kingdom is now subject to Community law, not just as a direct consequence of the various treaties of accession passed by the United Kingdom Parliament, but increasingly it is subject to the secondary legislation generated by the various institutions of the European Community.

European law takes three distinct forms: regulations, directives and decisions. Regulations are immediately effective without the need for the United Kingdom Parliament to produce its own legislation. Directives, on the other hand, require specific legislation to implement their proposals but the United Kingdom Parliament is under an obligation to enact such legislation as will give effect to the implementation of the directives. Decisions of the European Court of Justice are binding throughout the community and take precedence over any domestic law.

Legislation

Parliament makes law in the form of legislation, i. e. Acts of Parliament. There are various types of legislation. Whereas public Acts affect the public generally; private Acts only affect a limited sector of the populace, either particular people or people within a particular locality. Within the category of public Acts a further distinction can be made between government Bills and private members Bills. The former are usually introduced by the government whilst the latter axe the product of individual initiative on the part of particular members of Parliament.

Before enactment the future Act is referred to as a bill. Without going into the details of the procedure, bills have to be considered by both Houses of Parliament and have to receive Royal Assent before they are actually enacted.

Delegated Legislation

Delegated legislation has to be considered as a source of law in addition, but subordinate, to general Acts of Parliament. Generally speaking, delegated legislation is law made by some person or body to whom Parliament has delegated its general law making power. The output of delegated legislation in any year greatly exceeds the output of Acts of Parliament and, according to Professor Zander's computation, each year there are over 2000 sets of rules and regulations made in the form of delegated legislation as opposed to less than 100 public Acts of Parliament.

Case Law

The next source of law that has to be considered is case law, the effective creation and refinement of law in the course of judicial decisions. It should be remembered that the United Kingdom's law is still a common law system and even if legislation is of ever increasing importance, the significance and effectiveness of judicial creativity should not be discounted. Judicial decisions are a source of law through the operation of the doctrine of judicial precedent. This process depends on the established hierarchy of the courts, and operates in such a way that generally a court is bound by the *ratio decidendi* or rule of law implicit in the decision of a court above it in the hierarchy and usually by a court of equal standing in that hierarchy. Where statute law does not cover a particular area or where the law is silent generally it will be necessary for a court deciding cases relating to such an area to determine what the law is and, in so doing, that court will inescapably and unarguably be creating law. The scope for judicial creativity should not be underestimated and it should be remembered that the task of interpreting the actual meaning of legislation in particular cases also falls to the judiciary and provides it with a further important area of discretionary creativity. As the highest court in the land, the House of Lords has particular scope for creating or extending the common law, and a relatively contemporary example of its adopting such an active stance can be seen in the way in which it overruled the longstanding presumption that a man could not be guilty of the crime of rape against his wife. It should of course always be remembered that Parliament remains sovereign as regards the creation of law and any aspect of the judicially created common law is subject to direct alteration by statute.

Legal Textbook

An extension of the doctrine of judicial precedent leads to a consideration of a further possible source of law, for when the court is unable to locate a precise or analogous precedent it may refer to legal textbooks for guidance and assistance. Such books are subdivided, depending on when they were written. In strict terms only certain venerable works of antiquity are actually treated as authoritative sources of law. Amongst the most important of these works are those by Bracton from the thirteenth century, Coke from the seventeenth century and Blackstone from the eighteenth century. Legal works produced after Blackstone's Commentaries of 1765 are considered to be of recent origin, but although they cannot be treated as authoritative sources the courts on occasion will look at the most eminent works by accepted experts in particular fields in order to help determine what the law is or should be.

Custom

The final source of law that remains to be considered is custom. The romantic view of the common law is that it represented a crystallization of common customs distilled by the judiciary in the course of its travels round the land. Although some of the common law may have had its basis in general custom, as Professor Zander points out, a large proportion of these so called customs were invented by the judges themselves and represented what they wanted the law to be, rather than what people generally thought it was.

There is however a second possible customary source of law and that is with regard to specific local customs. Here there is the possibility that the local custom might differ from the common law and thus limit its operation. Even in this respect, however, reliance, on customary law as opposed to common law, although not impossible, is made unlikely by the stringent test that any appeal to it has to satisfy. Amongst these requirements are that the custom must have existed from "time immemorial", i. e. 1189, and must have been exercised continuously within that period, and without opposition. The custom must also have been felt as obligatory, have been consistent with other customs and in the final analysis must be reasonable. Given this list of requirements it can be seen why local custom does not loom large as an important source of law.

1. Is there any difference between legislation and case law? Why?
2. How many legal sources are there as you know? What?
3. What are the main differences legislation and custom?
4. What is the position of the legal textbook in the sources of English Law?
5. What are the main differences between legislation and delegated legislation?

6. Summarize the differences between custom and case law?
7. Please give some comments on the sources of Anglo-American law?

IV Translation Abilities

法律语言特征分析与法律翻译技能培养之一：

英汉思维方式及对语言的影响（一）

长期以来，东西方民族在思维方式上存在着巨大的差异。东方民族的思维方式常常被描述为"整体的"、"辨证的"、"具象的"、"主观的"和"模糊的"；而西方民族的思维方式被描述为"具体的"、"分析的"、"抽象的"、"客观的"和"精确的"。其对两种语言的影响则各具不同的特点，具体表现在如下几个方面：

1. 具象思维和抽象思维

从总体上加以分析，我们就可以发现，中国文化思维方式具有较强的具象性，而西方文化思维方式中具有较多的抽象性。不同的思维方式直接反映在句子词汇的使用层面上。除科技文体、哲学和政论性文体等外，汉语较少使用表示抽象概念的名词，而较多使用具有实指意义的具体名词；但英语中抽象名词的使用频率明显高出汉语。如：Wisdom prepares for the worst; but the folly leaves the worst for the day it comes (R. Cecil).（聪明人防患未然，愚蠢者临渴掘井。）句中 wisdom 和 folly 表示具有系统概念的一类人，对于习惯抽象思维的英美人而言，词义明确、措辞简练，但对习惯于具象思维的中国人而言，则须将抽象名词所要表达的抽象概念具体化，才符合汉语读者的思维习惯和汉语遣词造句的行文习惯。

2. 综合性思维与分析性思维

分析性思维和综合性思维乃人类思维的两种基本思维方式。所谓"分析"，就是将事物的整体分解成为各个组成部分，其优点在于可以深入地观察事物的本质，但其缺点在于：只见树木，不见森林；而所谓"综合"，即把事物的各个组成部分联系起来，使之成为一个统一的整体，其特点在于该思维方式强调事物的普遍联系，既见树木，又见森林。但任何民族的思维方式均不可能只有分析性思维或只有综合性思维。为此，这两者乃中西文化的共有特点，但由于传统文化的不同，于是形成了"东方重综合，西方重分析"的思维习惯。两种不同的思维方式，对英汉语的结构形态则产生了不同的影响：分析性的思维方式使英语具有明显的词形变化，形式多样的语法形式和组词造句中较为灵活的语序结构；而综合性的思维方式则使得汉语没有词型的变化，语法形式的表达则主要靠词汇手段，组词造句中完全依靠语义逻辑和动作发生时间的先后来决定词语和分句的排列顺序。

3. 本体型思维和客体型思维

中国文化以人本为主体，西方文化以物本为主体。本体型和客体型思维方式的不同在语言形态上的表现就是，在描述事物和阐述事理的过程中，特别是涉及行为主体时，汉语习惯上用表示人或生物的词作为主语（或潜在主语），而英语则常用非生物名词来作主语。如：Memoranda were prepared in advance of private meetings on matters to be discussed.（举行个别交谈之前，所要讨论的问题预先就拟好了备忘录。）

4. 顺向思维和逆向思维

英汉民族在观察事物和现象时，所取的角度和思维的方向有时是不相同的，表现在语言上,各个民族可能采取截然不同的甚至相反的语言形式来描述某一事物、行为或现象。如汉语中我们常用"您(先)请"等表示出于礼貌请对方先走、先吃或先做某事,但在英语中,却常用"After you!"等来表示。此外,在观察事物时所取的视角倾向有时也是不同的。如在汉语中"寒衣"在英语中却只能用"warm clothes"表示,其他,如"太平门"(emergency exit)、"听电话"(answer the telephone)、"红眼"(green-eyed)、"乘客止步"(crew only)、"Theft Act"(防止/反盗窃法)、"law of unfair competition"(反不当竞争法)、"Riot Act"(防止暴乱法)等等。

Translation Exercises:

Part One *Put the Following into Chinese*

Less optimistically, the founding generation also had good reason to doubt whether representative democracy would work at all and, consequently, good reason to fear that government officials would pursue interests entirely disconnected not just from those of their nominal constituents, but from the public good as well. Madison's scheme for pitting competing branches against one another may have been meant only as a fail-safe, in case Antifederalist fears of radical democratic failure came to pass.

The correction, however, was neither permanent nor complete. Just as parties can create the conditions necessary for interbranch competition to emerge, they can also submerge competition by effectively reuniting the branches. As we elaborate below, if government officials are motivated primarily by policy and partisan goals, then single-party control of multiple branches of government will tend to create cross-branch cooperation among like-minded officeholders.

Far from dreading divided government, Madisonians in a modern democracy must count on party division to recreate a competitive dynamic between the branches. And far from encouraging unified party control of the House, Senate, and presidency, Madisonians will view the prospect of unchecked and unbalanced governance by a cohesive majority party as cause for constitutional alarm.

Part Two *Put the Following into English*

国会掌握立法权,制定法律。国会由选民直接选举产生,只对选民负责,不受行政机关的干预。为了保障国会能够独立的行使权力,不受总统的干预,宪法还设定了保障机制:总统无权解散国会,不能决定议员的工资待遇。在国会内部又进一步对权力进行了分配,国会由参议院和众议院组成。国会的权力体现在:制定法律权、修改宪法权、对总统、副总统的复选权及弹劾权等。行政权由总统行使。总统由选民选举产生,只对选民负责,不对国会负责。国会不得增减总统的报酬,非经审判定罪不得罢免总统。总统的主要权力体现在:统领陆海军,对外缔结条约,宣布缓刑和特赦,任命大使、公使、领事、最高法院的法官等官员,签署或拒绝签署国会通过的法案。最后一项权力是司法权。司法权由联邦最高法院以及国会随时下令设立的低级法院来行使,最高法院有终审权。联邦法院的法官均由总统征得参议院同意后进行任命,法官只要忠于职守,可以终身任职,非经国会弹劾不能被免职。宪法对司法权适用的范围进行了界定:应包括在本宪法、合众国法律和合众国已订的及将订的条约之下发生的一切涉及普通法及衡平法的案件;一切有关大使、公使及领事的案件;一切有关海上裁判权及海事裁判的案件……。另外,作为联邦最高法院还拥有一项重要权力——司法监督权。虽然在美国宪法中没有明确规定,但已经发挥了重要作用。为了保障三种权力行使的独立性,美国宪法还规定,这三个机关的官员在任职上应保持彼此的独立:任何一个机关的官员不得在任职期间担任另一机关的职务。

V Interaction

Discuss with your tutor(s) or the People's judges in your locality about the relationship between law and politics. Then based on the discussion, you are supposed to write a composition about how the judges overcome the political difficulties in their handling the cases. Remember that you are required to express your ideas clearly.

VI Appreciation of Judge's Opinions

(1) Case Name(案件名): *United States v. Kirby Lumber Co.*

U.S. Supreme Court

U S v. KIRBY, 74 U.S. 482 (1868)

74 U.S. 482 (Wall.)

UNITED STATES

v.

KIRBY.

December Term, 1868

United States v. Kirby Lumber Co.

Supreme Court of the United States

Argued October 21, 1931
Decided November 2, 1931

Full case name	United States v. Kirby Lumber Company
Citations	284 U.S. 1 (more)
	52 S. Ct. 4; 76 L. Ed. 131; 1931 U.S. LEXIS 457; 2 U.S. Tax Cas. (CCH) P814; 10 A.F.T.R. (P-H) 458
Prior history	Cert. to the Court of Claims, 283 U.S. 814, to review a judgment allowing a claim for refund of money collected as income tax. 71 Ct. Cls. 290; 44 F.2d 885

Holding

If a corporation purchases and retires bonds at a price less than their face value or issuing price, the excess amount of the purchase price over the issuing price is a taxable gain.

Court membership

Chief Justice
Charles E. Hughes
Associate Justices
Oliver W. Holmes, Jr. · Willis Van Devanter
James C. McReynolds · Louis Brandeis
George Sutherland · Pierce Butler
Harlan F. Stone · Owen J. Roberts

Case opinions

Majority   Holmes, joined by unanimous court

Laws applied

§213 of the Revenue Act of 1921

(2) Case Summary(案情简介)

United States v. Kirby Lumber Co., 284 U. S. 1 (1931), was a case in which the United States Supreme Court held that when a corporation settles its debts for less than the face amount, a taxable gain has occurred.

Facts & procedural history

In 1923, the Kirby Lumber Company issued bonds (证券,公债,债券;借据;证券纸;付款保证书;保证人;海关扣存) which had a par value(票面价值) of $12,126,800. Later that same year, the company repurchased the same bonds in the open market for a sum less than par value. The difference between the issue price of the bonds and the price at which the company repurchased them was $137,521.30. The regulations promulgated by the United States Department of the Treasury(美国财政部) stated that such a cost savings to a corporation was to be considered taxable income. The Court of Claims(小额索赔法院), however, found in favor of the taxpayer, analogizing the situation in this case to the one in *Bowers v. Kerbaugh-Empire Co.*, 271 U. S. 170 (1925), a case in which a loan repaid in devalued German marks (德国马克) was not considered to be a taxable gain for the taxpaying company.

Decision

In a brief, concise, unanimous opinion, Justice Holmes upheld the validity of the Treasury regulations. He distinguished Bowers v. Kerbaugh-Empire Co. on the grounds that the enterprise in that case had been on the whole a failure, and had lost money. In this case, the taxpayer had made a clear and obvious gain. By paying off its debts for less than the issue price, it had freed up assets to spend on other things. Interestingly, Justice Holmes said nothing in his opinion about the Treasury's definition of income. Later cases before the Court did however address directly the Treasury's definition in connection with related cases.

(3) Excerpts of the Judgment(法官判决词)

THE defendants were indicted for knowingly and willfully obstructing and retarding(有意和故意阻碍和妨碍) the passage of the mail and of a mail carrier, in the District Court for the District of Kentucky. The case was certified to the Circuit Court for that district.

The indictment was founded upon the ninth section of the act of Congress, of March 3, 1825, 'to reduce into one the several acts establishing and regulating the post office department,' which provides 'that, if any person shall knowingly or willfully obstruct or retard the passage of the mail, or of any driver or carrier, or of any horse or carriage carrying the same, he shall, upon conviction, for every such offence, pay a fine not exceeding one hundred dollars; and if any ferryman shall, by willful negligence, or refusal to transport the mail across the ferry(渡轮), delay the same, be shall forfeit(因被罚而丧失所有权,因犯罪等而失去职位、生命等;因过劳等而失掉健康等,罚金,没收物,权利、名誉、生命等的丧失) and pay, for every ten minutes that the same shall be so delayed, a sum not exceeding ten dollars.'

The indictment contained four counts(罪名), and charged the defendants with knowingly and wilfully obstructing the passage of the mail of the United States, in the district of Kentucky, on the first of February, 1867, contrary to the act of Congress; and with knowingly and wilfully obstructing and retarding at the same time in that district, the passage of one Farris, a carrier of the mail(邮递员), while engaged in the performance of this duty; and with knowingly and wilfully retarding [74 U. S. 482, 484] at the same time in that district, the passage of the steamboat(蒸汽船) General Buell, which was then carrying the mail of the United States from the city of Louisville, in Kentucky, to the city of Cincinnati, in Ohio.

To this indictment the defendants, among other things, pleaded specially to the effect, that at the September Term, 1866, of the Circuit Court of Gallation County, in the State of Kentucky, which was a court of competent jurisdiction(具有适当管辖权的法院), two indictments were found by the grand jury(大陪审团) of the county against the said Farris for murder; that by order of the court bench warrants(法院拘票,逮捕令:由法官或法庭发出的命令逮捕罪犯的逮捕状) were issued upon these indictments, and placed in the hands of Kirby, one of the defendants, who was then sheriff of the county, commanding him to arrest the said Farris and bring him before the court to answer the indictments; that in obedience to these warrants he arrested Farris, and was accompanied by the other defendants as a posse(武装队;警察等的一队;乌合之众,暴徒) who were lawfully summoned to assist him in effecting the arrest; that they entered the steamboat Buell to make the arrest, and only used such force as was necessary to accomplish this end; and that they acted without any intent or purpose to obstruct or retard the mail, or the passage of the steamer. To this plea the district attorney of the United States demurred(表示异议,反对;抗辩) and upon the argument of the demurrer two questions arose:

First. Whether the arrest of the mail-carrier(邮递员) upon the bench warrants from the Circuit Court of Kentucky was, under the circumstances, an obstruction of the mail within the meaning of the act of Congress.

Second. Whether the arrest was obstructing or retarding the passage of a carrier of the mail within the meaning of that act.

Upon these questions the judges were opposed in opinion, and the questions were sent to this court upon a certificate of division.

Mr. Ashton, Assistant Attorney-General, for the United States:

There are authorities which perhaps favor the position of the government, that the arrest of the carrier of the mail [74 U. S. 482, 485] under the warrant, was an obstruction of the mail and of the carrier thereof, within the intent and meaning of the act of Congress. United States v. Barney, decided by Winchester, J., in Maryland district, in 1810, is in that direction. The Indictment was under an act in the same words as the act of 1825. The detention was by an innkeeper, under a lien(留置权) for the keeping of the horses employed in carrying the mail; and the court held that the defendant was not justified. The court says:

'The statute is a general prohibitory act. It has introduced no exceptions. The law does not allow any justification of a willful and voluntary act of obstruction to the passage of the mail,' etc.

So in United States v. Harvey, where the indictment (which was under the act of 1825) was against a constable(警察,警官,王室总管,城堡的主管) for arresting the mail-carrier under a warrant in an action of trespass, Taney, C. J., held that the mere serving of the warrant would not render the party liable; yet 'if by serving the warrant he detained the carrier, he would then be liable.'

Contrary, however, to these decisions, is the ruling of Mr. Justice Washington in *United States v. Hart*. In that case it was held that the act of Congress was not to be construed so as to prevent the arrest of the driver of a carriage in which the mail is carried, when he is driving through a crowded city at an improper rate.

No opposing counsel.

Mr. Justice FIELD, after stating the case, delivered the opinion of the court, as follows:

There can be but one answer, in our judgment, to the questions certified to us. The statute of Congress by its terms applies only to persons who 'knowing and willfully' obstruct or retard the passage of the mail, or of its carrier; that is, to those who know that the acts performed will have that effect, and perform them with the intention that such shall be their operation. When the acts which create the obstruction are in themselves unlawful, the intention to obstruct will be imputed to(把……归咎于;把……归因于,把……推给;把……转嫁于) their author, although the attainment of other ends may have been his primary object. The statute has no reference to acts lawful in themselves, from the execution of which a temporary delay to the mails unavoidably follows. All persons in the public service are exempt, as a matter of public policy, from arrest upon civil process while thus engaged. Process of that kind can, therefore, furnish no justification for the arrest of a carrier of the mail. This is all that is decided by the case of the *United States v. Harvey*, to which we are referred by the counsel of the government. The rule is different when the process is issued upon a charge of felony(重罪). No officer or employee of the United States is placed by his position, or the services he is called to perform, above responsibility to the legal tribunals of the country, and to the ordinary processes for his arrest and detention, when accused of felony, in the forms prescribed by the Constitution and laws. The public inconvenience which may occasionally follow from the temporary delay in the transmission of the mail caused by the arrest of its carriers upon such charges, is far less than that which would arise from extending to them the immunity for which the counsel of the government contends. Indeed, it may be doubted whether it is competent for Congress to exempt the employees of the United States from arrest on criminal process from the State courts, when the crimes charged against them are not merely *mala prohibita*(法律所禁止的行为), but are *mala in se*(本身错误的,自身不法的,指的是违反自然的、道德的、善风良俗的行为,如杀人、防火、投毒等). But whether legislation of that character be constitutional or not, no intention to extend such exemption should be attributed to Congress unless clearly manifested by its language. All laws should receive a sensible construction(合理解释). General terms(一般用语) should be so limited in their application as not to lead to injustice, oppression, or an absurd consequence. It will always, therefore, be presumed that the legislature intended exceptions to its language, which would avoid results of this character. The reason of the law in such cases should prevail over its letter.

The common sense of man approves the judgment mentioned by Puffendorf(普芬道夫), that the Bolognian(意大利城市博洛尼亚的形容词形式) law which enacted, 'that whoever drew blood in the streets should be punished with the utmost severity,' did not extend to the surgeon who opened the vein of a person that fell down in the street in a fit. The same common sense accepts the ruling, cited by Plowden, that the statute of 1st Edward II, which enacts that a prisoner who breaks prison shall be guilty of felony, does not extend to a prisoner who breaks out when the prison is on fire 'for he is not to be hanged because he would not stay to be burnt.' And we think that a like common sense will sanction(许可,允许) the ruling we make, that the act of Congress which punishes the obstruction or retarding of the passage of the mail, or of its carrier, does not apply to a case of temporary detention of the mail caused by the arrest of the carrier upon an indictment for murder.

The questions certified to us must be answered IN THE NEGATIVE; and it is SO ORDERED.

Mr. Justice MILLER, having been absent at the hearing, took no part in this order.

Lesson Two

Sample Sales Agency Contract

> **Learning objectives**
>
> After learning the text and having done the exercises in this lesson, you will:
>
> —familiarize with knowledge of the legal characteristics and the nature of sales agency;
>
> —acquire an appreciation of the vocabulary and grammar or syntax relevant to sales agency;
>
> —become aware of the information required in order to understand sales agency;
>
> —cultivate the practical abilities to put to use the language in the specific context;
>
> —be able to do some translation from Chinese to English and from English to Chinese.

 Text

SAMPLE SALES AGENCY AGREEMENT

(The "Agreement")

between

(name)

of (address)

(hereinafter known as "_____ Company");

And

(name)

of (address)

(hereinafter known as "Representative");

(together referred to as "the Parties")

Date:_____

1. DEFINITIONS

1.1 "Products" initially shall mean those products listed in Exhibit① A attached hereto and any such additional products that Company may manufacture or sell. Products may be changed, discontinued, or added by mutual agreement of the Parties. Representative shall have the right of first refusal to represent any additional product, including Product upgrades② and modifications, represented, sold, or marketed by Company.

1.2 "Territory③" means the geographic areas listed on Exhibit B hereto.

2. APPOINTMENT AND AUTHORITY OF REPRESENTATIVE

Exclusive Sales Representative. Subject to the terms and conditions herein, Company appoints Representative as Company's exclusive sales representative for the Products in the Territory, and Representative shall

(i) give either party the power to direct and control the day-to-day activities of the other, or

(ii) constitute the parties as partners, joint venturers④, co-owners or otherwise as participants in a joint undertaking, or

(iii) be allowed to create or assume any obligation on behalf of Company for any purpose whatsoever.

All financial and other obligations associated with Representative's business are the sole responsibility of Representative, Representative shall be responsible for, and shall indemnify⑤ and hold Company free and harmless from, any and all claims, damages or lawsuits (including Company's attorneys' fees) arising solely out of the acts or omissions of Representative, its employees or its agents.

3. COMMISSION⑥

3.1 Sole Compensation. Representative's sole compensation under the terms of this Agree-

---

① exhibit: vt. 表明,显示,显出;陈列,展览;法律上提出证据等;医学上的用药;n. 展出,展览会;陈列品,展览品;法律上的证据,证物。此处的 exhibit 等同于"Annex",表示"附件"的意思。

② Product upgrades:升级换代产品。

③ territory:领土,版图,领地;科学知识、行动等的领域,范围;商业上的势力范围;(野鸟的)生活范围。如:a leased territory:租借地;in the territory/sphere/field/domain of physics:在物理学的领域内;take in too much territory 走极端;说得过分;牵涉过多。

④ joint venturers:合资企业者。注意:joint venture 表示"合资企业,合资经营;合资,由于共同承担风险而形成的伙伴关系或联合大企业"等的意思,有时已可表示"共同风险"的意思,为此,可以用 joint investment venture 来表示"合资企业",其他如:equity joint venture:股份制合营企业。

⑤ indemnify: v. 赔偿;补偿;保护;保障;责任免除。如: to indemnify sb. from harm:保证某人不受伤害;to indemnify sb. for the loss incurred: 赔偿某人所受的损失;Everyone should learn to indemnify oneself against harm:每个人都应学会保护自己不受伤害。Indemnify 的名词形式是 indemnification,表示"赔偿,补偿;赔偿物(赔偿金);免罚,赦免;保证金,赔偿物;提供保障的事物;对损失的补偿;责任免除"的意思,如:export indemnification:出口补偿。

⑥ Commission:课文中表示"佣金"的意思。该词作为名词时,可以表示佣金(a fee for services rendered based on a percentage of an amount received or collected or agreed to be paid (as distinguished from a salary));委员会(a special group delegated to consider some matter));委托;委任(the act of granting authority to undertake certain functions);犯罪(the act of committing a crime)等意思,也可以作为动词使用,表示"授予;使服役;委托"等意思。

ment shall be a commission ("Commission") as provided in Exhibit C hereof on the net sales of all Products ordered, delivered or sold in the Territory.

3.2 Basis of Commission. The Commission shall apply to all orders to the Territory, whether or not such orders were solicited by Representative. Commissions shall be computed on the net sales amount invoiced by Company to the customer, provided no commission shall be paid with respect to charges for handling, freight, taxes, C. O. D. charges[①], insurance, tariffs and duties[②], cash and trade discounts[③], rebates, amounts allowed or credited for returns, uncollected or uncollectible amounts, services, and the like.

3.3 Payment. Commissions shall be paid in United States dollars and shall be subject to all applicable governmental laws, regulations and rulings, including the withholding of taxes[④].

3.4 Time of Payment. The Commission for a given order shall be earned by Representative when that order is placed. The Commission on a given order shall be due and payable thirty (30) days after the end of the calendar month in which Company invoices and ships that order.

3.5 Commission Charge-Back[⑤]. Company shall have the right, while this Agreement is in effect, to write off as bad debts such overdue customer accounts as it deems advisable after notifying Representative and providing Representative the opportunity to attempt to induce payment. In each such case, Company may charge back to Representative's account only any amounts previously paid to Representative. If such accounts are paid at any time, Representative shall be entitled to the applicable commissions.

3.6 Monthly Statements. Company shall submit to Representative monthly statements of the commissions due and payable to Representative under the terms of this Agreement, with reference to the specific orders on invoices on which the commissions are being paid.

3.7 Inspection of Records. Representative shall have the right, at its own expense and not more than once in any twelve (12) month period, to authorize Representative's independent auditors[⑥] to inspect, at reasonable times during Company's ordinary business hours, Company's relevant accounting records to verify the accuracy of Commissions paid by Company hereunder.

---

① C. O. D. charges:货到付款,C. O. D. = cash on delivery:货到付款。

② tariffs and duties:各种关税,其中 duty 作为名词使用时的意思有"义务(the social force that binds you to the courses of action demanded by that force);职责,责任(work that you are obliged to perform for moral or legal reasons);税,关税(a government tax on imports or exports)等。如:active duty 现役;customs duty 关税;death duty (英)遗产税;specific duty 从量税;stamp duty(英)印花税;transit duty 通行税。与 duty 有关的短语表达方式有:do duty for 起……的作用;go beyond one's duty 超越职权范围;off duty 下班;on duty 值班。duty-free 指不用交税的,免税的;如:duty -free goods 指免税商品;duty-free stores 表示免税商店;offshore duty-free policy 即指离岛免税政策,是指对乘飞机离岛(不包括隔境)旅客实行限次、限值、限量和限品种免进口税购物,在岛免税店内付款,在机场隔离区提货离岛的税收优惠政策。

③ cash and trade discounts:现金和商业折扣。trade discount:商业折扣;同行折扣;批发折扣。

④ withholding of taxes:预扣税;预扣所得税,多数时候使用 withholding tax 或 retention tax,是世界很多国家或地区的税项之一。由于纳税人长期居于外国其他地方等原因,税务局难以接触此类纳税当事人,所以税法规定支付如下费用的代理人有义务,预先"代扣代缴"此类税额予税务局,仅支付余额予纳税当事人。预扣所得税的主要目的,在于减少逃税,及避免届时无力缴税的可能。

⑤ charge-back:退款,信用卡退单,退单,拒付。主要指在产品经销过程中,当供应商以高于其最终用户的价格把产品给予经销商时,则经销商可以向产品供应商提出返还该部分价款的差价以弥补其损失。

⑥ independent auditor:独立审计师,独立审计员,独立核数师。

4. SALE OF THE PRODUCTS

4.1　Prices and Terms of Sale. Company shall provide Representative with copies of its current price lists, its delivery schedules①, and its standard terms and conditions of sale, as established from time to time. Representative shall quote to customers only those authorized prices, delivery schedules, and terms and conditions, and shall have no authority to quote or offer any discount to such prices or change any such terms and conditions, without the consent of Company. Company may change the prices, delivery schedules, and terms and conditions, provided that it gives Representative at least thirty (30) days prior written notice of any changes; however, such changes shall not affect any existing contacts or pricing agreements. Each order for a Product shall be governed by the prices, delivery schedules, and terms and conditions in effect at the time the order is accepted, and all quotations by Representative shall contain a statement to that effect②.

4.2　Quotations. The parties shall furnish to each other copies of all quotations submitted to customers.

4.3　Orders. All orders for the Products shall be in writing, and the original shall be submitted to Company. Company shall promptly furnish to Representative informational copies of all commissionable orders sent by customers in the Territory.

4.4　Acceptance. All orders obtained by Representative shall be subject to acceptance by Company at its principal office currently located at the address listed for Company at the beginning of this Agreement, and all quotations by Representative shall contain a statement to that effect. Representative shall have no authority to make any acceptance or delivery commitments to customers. Company specifically reserves the right to reject any order or any part thereof for any reasonable reason. Company shall send copies to Representative of any written acceptances on commissionable orders.

4.5　Credit Approval. Company shall have the sole right of credit approval or credit refusal for its customers in all cases.

4.6　Collection. It is expressly understood by Representative that full responsibility for all collection rests with Company, provided, at Company's request, Representative will provide reasonable assistance in collection of any accounts receivable③. In the event that Representative, with the approval of Company, purchases Products from Company and resells said Products to its own customers, Representative shall have the sole right of credit approval or credit refusal for its own customers and full responsibility for all collection for such customers rests with Representative.

4.7　Inquiries from Outside the Territory. Representative shall promptly submit to Company, for Company's attention and handling, the originals of all inquiries received by Representative from customers outside the Territory.

---

①　delivery schedule：交付进度，交货计划表；交货日程表；交货时间表。
②　to that effect：大意如此；是那个意思的。
③　accounts receivable：应收账款。

4.8 Product Availability. Company shall not be responsible to Representative or any other party for its failure to fill accepted orders, or for its delay in filling accepted orders, when such failure or delay is due to a cause beyond Company's reasonable control.

5. ADDITIONAL OBLIGATIONS OF REPRESENTATIVE

5.1 Annual Quota Commitment. Within 30 days of the Effective Date and within thirty days before the start of each subsequent calendar year, Company may assign to Representative an annual quota. Any annual quota must be fair and reasonable, taking into account factors including but not limited to sales in prior years, the competitive and economic situation in the Territory and marketplace, and Company's market share nationally and in the Territory.

5.2 Promotion of the Products. Representative shall, at its own expense, promote the sale of the Products in the Territory. Representative may hire or contract with sales representatives or service personnel to promote the Products and perform the duties hereunder.

5.3 Facilities. Representative shall provide itself with, and be solely responsible for,

(i) such facilities, employees, and business organization, and

(ii) such permits, licenses, and other forms of clearance from governmental or regulatory agencies, if any, as it deems necessary for the conduct of its business operations in accordance with this Agreement.

5.4 Customer and Sales Reporting. Representative shall, at its own expense, and in a manner consistent with the sales policies of Company:

(a) attend a reasonable number of trade shows as Company requests;

(b) provide adequate contact with existing and potential customers within the Territory on a regular basis; and

(c) assist Company in assessing customer requirements for the Products.

5.5 Customer Service. Representative shall diligently assist its customers' personnel in using the Products and shall perform such additional customer services as good salesmanship requires and as Company may reasonably request.

5.6 Product Complaints. Representative shall promptly investigate and monitor all customer and/or regulatory complaints and/or correspondence concerning the use of the Product in the Territory. Representative shall immediately notify Company of all such complaints and/or correspondence in accordance with the following:

(a) Representative shall advise Company of all complaints relating to incidents of serious and unexpected reactions to the Product as promptly as possible but not more than two (2) calendar days following the date Representative receives such complaint

(b) All complaints other than those related to incidents of serious and unexpected reactions to the Product shall be reported to Company within five (5) calendar days following the date Representative receives such complaint

(c) For purposes of this Section 5.6, a reaction shall be deemed to be "unexpected" if it is one that is not listed in the current package insert for the Product approved by Company and a reaction shall be deemed to be "serious" if it is fatal or life threatening, requires inpatient hospitalization, prolongs hospitalization, is permanently disabling, or requires intervention to prevent impairment or damage.

5.7 Expense of Doing Business. Representative shall bear the entire cost and expense of conducting its business in accordance with the terms of this Agreement.

5.8 Representations. Representative shall not make any false or misleading representations to customers or others regarding Company or the Products. Representative shall not make any representations, warranties or guarantees with respect to the specifications, features or capabilities of the Products that are not consistent with Company's documentation accompanying the Products or Company's literature describing the Products.

6. ADDITIONAL OBLIGATIONS OF COMPANY

6.1 Training by Company. Company shall provide sales training to Representative's personnel at periodic intervals, with the frequency and content of the training to be determined by Company. When possible, such training shall be given at Representative's facilities, but it may be necessary to provide training at a geographically central location near but not in the Territory.

6.2 Regulatory Approvals. Company shall be responsible for obtaining FDA[①] and any other approvals necessary to distribute the Products in the United States.

6.3 Materials. Company shall provide Representative with marketing and technical information concerning the Products as well as reasonable quantities of brochures, instructional material, advertising literature, demonstration product samples, and other Product data at no charge.

6.4 Telephone Marketing and Technical and Sales Support. Company shall provide a reasonable level of telephone marketing and technical support to Representative and its representatives. Company shall use its best efforts to support Representative's sales and marketing activities.

6.5 Delivery Time. Company shall use its best efforts to fulfill delivery obligations as committed in acceptances.

6.6 New Developments. Company shall promptly inform Representative of new product developments relating to the Products.

7. TRADEMARKS

During the term of this Agreement, Representative shall have the right to indicate to the public that it is an authorized representative of the Products and to advertise (within the Territory) such Products under the trademarks, marks, and trade names that Company may adopt from time to time ("Trademarks"). Representative shall not alter or remove any Trademark applied to the Products. Except as set forth in this Article 7, nothing contained in this Agreement shall grant to Representative any right, title or interest in the Trademarks.

---

① FDA：美国食品和药物管理局(Food and Drug Administration)的简称，成立于1906年，是一个专门从事食品与药品管理的最高执法机关，由医生、律师、微生物学家、药理学家、化学家和统计学家等专业人士组成，是一个致力于保护、促进和提高国民健康的政府卫生管制的监控机构。

Lesson Two Sample Sales Agency Contract

8. CONFIDENTIAL INFORMATION

Representative acknowledges that by reason of its relationship to Company hereunder it will have access to certain information and materials concerning Company's technology, and products that are confidential and of substantial value to Company, which value would be impaired if such information were disclosed to third parties. Representative agrees that it will not use in any way for its own account or the account of any third party, nor disclose to any third party, any such confidential information revealed to it in written or other tangible form or orally, identified as confidential, by Company without the prior written consent of Company.

Representative shall take every reasonable precaution to protect the confidentiality of such information. Upon request by Representative, Company shall advise whether or not it considers any particular information or materials to be confidential. In the event of termination of this Agreement, there shall be no use or disclosure by Representative of any confidential information of Company, and Representative shall not manufacture or have manufactured any devices, components or assemblies utilizing any of Company's confidential information. This section shall not apply to any confidential information which is or becomes generally known and available in the public domain① through no fault of Representative.

9. INDEMNIFICATION

The Company shall be solely responsible for the design, development, supply, production and performance of its products and the protection of its trade names and patents. The Company agrees to indemnify, hold the Representative harmless against and pay all losses, costs, damages or expenses, whatsoever, including counsel fees, which the Representative may sustain or incur on account of infringement or alleged infringements of patents, trademarks or trade names resulting from the sale of the Company's products, or arising on account of warranty② claims, negligence claims, product liability claims or similar claims by third parties.

The Representative shall promptly deliver to the Company any notices or papers served upon it in any proceeding covered by this Indemnification Agreement, and the Company shall defend such litigation at its expense. The Representative shall, however, have the right to participate in the defense at its own expense unless there is a conflict of interest, in which case, the Representative shall indemnify the Company for the expenses of such defense including counsel fees.

The Company shall provide the Representative with a certificate of insurance evidencing the Representative as an additional insured on the Company's product liability insurance policy. This provision shall survive and remain in full force and effect after the termination or nonrenewal of this Agreement.

---

① public domain:公知领域,公共领域;美国的官产,公地;公有财产;不受版权/专利权限制的状态。
② warranty:保证书;根据,理由;授权(证);(商品等的)保单。

10. TERM AND TERMINATION

10.1 Term. This Agreement shall continue in full force and effect for a period of three years from the date above, unless terminated earlier under the provisions of this Agreement. Thereafter, this Agreement shall be renewed automatically for successive additional three year terms under the same terms and conditions unless either party chooses not to continue the relationship and provides written notice 180 days prior to the natural expiration of the existing three-year term.

10.2 Termination. This Agreement may be terminated by as follows:

- 10.2.1 By Company if Representative fails to achieve its annual quota requirement.
- 10.2.2 By either party if the other party becomes insolvent or bankrupt, or files a voluntary petition in bankruptcy, or has had filed for an involuntary petition in bankruptcy (unless such involuntary petition① is withdrawn or dismissed within ten days after filing) in which event termination may be immediate upon notice; or
- 10.2.3 By either party if the other party fails to cure any breach of a material covenant, commitment or obligation under this Agreement, within 45 days after receipt of written notice specifically setting forth the breach from the other party; or
- 10.2.4 By either party if the other party is convicted or pleads to a crime or an act of fraud that materially impacts on its performance or its fiduciary duties② hereunder, in which event termination may be immediate upon notice.

10.3 Return of Materials. All Confidential Information and other property belonging to Company shall remain the property of Company and will be immediately returned by Representative upon termination. Representative shall not make or retain any copies of any Confidential Information that may have been entrusted to it.

10.4 Return of the Products. Upon the termination of this Agreement, Company shall repurchase any inventory③ and instrumentation of the Representative at Representative's cost.

11. MISCELLANEOUS

11.1 Notices. Any notice required or permitted by this Agreement shall be in writing and shall be sent by prepaid registered or certified mail, return receipt requested, addressed to the other party at the address shown above or at such other address for which such party gives notice hereunder. Such notice shall be deemed to have been given three (3) days after deposit in the mail.

11.2 Assignment. The parties may not assign or transfer this Agreement or any of its rights and obligations under this Agreement without the prior written consent of the other party, which

---

① files a voluntary petition in bankruptcy, or has had filed for an involuntary petition in bankruptcy (unless such involuntary petition……:提出自动破产申请,或已经被强制破产清算。其中 involuntary bankruptcy 表示"恶性倒闭;强制性破产清理"的意思,而 voluntary bankruptcy 指的是"自动破产申请;自愿破产"的意思。

② fiduciary duties:诚信义务;诚信责任;受信责任;受托责任;受信义务;受信责任;信托义务;信义义务;忠实义务。

③ inventory:盘存,存货,也可指财产等的清单,报表,商品的目录。如 physical inventory:实地盘存;inventory liquidating:减少存货;to make/take/draw up/an inventory of:编制……的目录,开列……的清单。

shall not be unreasonably withheld. This Agreement shall be binding upon and inure to the benefit of the parties hereto and their successors and assigns including purchasers of their assets constituting a bulk sale pursuant to the provisions of the "Uniform Commercial Code."

11.3　Compliance with Law. Company and Representative agree that they will comply with all US Government laws, regulations and requirements applicable to the duties conducted hereunder.

11.4　Property Rights. Representative agrees that Company owns all right, title, and interest in the product lines that include the Products and in all of Company's patents, trademarks, trade names, inventions, copyrights, know-how, and trade secrets relating to the design, manufacture, operation or service of the Products. The use by Representative of any of these property rights is authorized only for the purposes herein set forth, and upon termination of this Agreement for any reason such authorization shall cease.

11.5　Severability[①]. If any provision(s) of this Agreement shall be held invalid, illegal or unenforceable by a court of competent jurisdiction[②], the remainder of the Agreement shall be valid and enforceable and the parties shall negotiate in good faith a substitute, valid and enforceable provision which most nearly effects the parties' intent in entering into this Agreement.

11.6　Modification; Waiver. This Agreement may not be altered, amended or modified in any way except by a writing signed by both parties. The failure of a party to enforce any provision of the Agreement shall not be construed to be a waiver of the right of such party to thereafter enforce that provision or any other provision or right.

11.7　Entire Agreement. This Agreement and the Exhibits hereto represent and constitute the entire agreement between the parties, and supersedes and merges all prior negotiations, agreements and understandings, oral or written, with respect to any and all matters between the Representative and Company.

This Agreement was agreed to on the date written above.

SIGNED by
(Name)_____
Signature _____
For and on behalf of the Company
In the presence of:
(Name)_____
Signature _____
SIGNED by
(Name)_____
Signature _____

---

① Severability: 可分开性;权益或职责范围可分开;条款独立性;亦称为 salvatorius,源自拉丁语,指合同的条款规定中,若某一部分合同内容被认为是无效或不予以履行时,其他合同内容仍然有效。

② court of competent jurisdiction:具有管辖权的法院。

For and on behalf of the Representative
In the presence of:
(Name)_____
Signature_____
EXHIBIT A—PRODUCTS
EXHIBIT B—TERRITORY
EXHIBIT C—COMMISSION SCHEDULE

 ## Legal Terminology

1. agency in estoppel 与 agency in fact

Agency in estoppel 表示"表见代理,表意代理,不可否认的代理",等同于"apparent agency, ostensible agency 或者 agency by operation of law",而 agency in fact 表示"事实代理关系"。两者区别在于,Agency in estoppel 并不存在真实的代理关系,即委托人与代理人之间并不存在代理协议,只是因为委托人的行为让第三人合理地确认他与代理人之间存在着代理关系,且第三人因此种确认行为而受到伤害,此时应由法院根据推定认定代理关系成立而委托人不得否认。而 agency in fact 所表示的代理关系则是委托人和代理人之间经协议事实确立的,与 Agency in estoppel 相反。

2. exhibit

Exhibit 一词是 15 世纪中期进入英语,源自古典拉丁语的 exhibit,最初源自古典拉丁语的 exhibitum。

(作名词使用时) exhibition, exhibit, show, exposition, fair, display 的辨析
这些名词都可表示"展览"的意思,但区别在于:
exhibition:一般指较正规的展览会。
exhibit:多指个人或团体陈列的展览品,规模可大可小。
show:指艺术品、农产品、工业品或商品等的任何形式的公开展览。
exposition:多指大型博览会或国际博览会。
fair:侧重指为促销商品而举办的展览会或商品交易会。
display:指展销会,商店橱窗或柜台上的陈列品。

(作动词使用时) show, exhibit, display, manifest 与 demonstrate 的辨析
show:泛指任何有意或无意地把东西给别人看的行为。
exhibit:指公开或正式地展示,以便引人注目或让人检查。
display:多指将某物陈列在显眼之处以便让发现其优点,侧重有意识地显示。
manifest:书面正式用词,指明确地表明。
demonstrate:指明显地表露感情。也指用实例、实验推理等手段表演证明,或论证某一问题。

3. committee 与 commission

commission:1344 年进入英语,直接源自古典拉丁语的 commissionem,意为商务代表团。而 committeee 则于 1621 年进入英语,直接源自盎格鲁法语的 commite(commettre 的过去分

词),意为犯,做;最初源自古典拉丁语的 committere。其既用作普通名词,也用作集体名词,指通过选举或其他方式而成立的一般委员会。

commission:指为了某项任务专门成立的委员会。commission 表示"委员会"的意思时,比 committee 的范围要宽。

与 committee 有关的习惯用语:

to be on a committee(任委员会委员); to sit on a committee(任委员会委员); to go into committee(在英国议会中)交委员会详细审查。

4. duty 与 obligation, responsibility, function

duty 一词大约于 1300 年左右进入英语,直接源自盎格鲁法语的 duete;最初源自古典拉丁语的 debitus(debere 的过去分词),意为欠,负债。其指按道德和法律的标准,一个人永远要尽的义务,强调自觉性。

Duty 与 obligation, responsibility, function 等词的区别

obligation:指道义上或法律上对他人的义务,强调强制性。也指因作出承诺而被迫履行的某种义务。

responsibility:指任何义务、职责、责任或职务上所应尽的本分,强调对他人的责任。

function:指因职务或职业关系去履行某种职责。

duty-free 指不用交税的,免税的;如:duty-free goods 指免税商品;duty-free stores 表示免税商店;offshore duty-free policy 即指离岛免税政策,是指对乘飞机离岛(不包括离境)旅客实行限次、限值、限量和限品种免进口税购物,在离岛免税店内付款,在机场隔离区提货离岛的税收优惠政策。

5. representations 与 warranties

warranty:表示"财产转让保证书,合同中的保证(尤其指卖方保证其商品的质量等),商品等的保单,保修证书"的意思。为此,与 guaranty, suretyship 等词都有"担保或保证"的意思。但是区别在于:

指合同时,guaranty 所作的担保属于附属性质的担保,对担保人不构成主要责任,有时也可以表示对某些瑕疵或事故的一种有条件担保,等同于"一般担保或赔偿责任保证";而 suretyship 虽然也可以指对他人的行为或债务的一种担保,但多属于独立和单独性质的一种担保,有些类似"连带担保","连带责任保证"的意思;而 warranty 则属于对自己的行为或产品的担保,其对担保人构成主要责任,属于一种严格法律责任意义上的担保,可以翻译为"单方承诺保证",在商事交易过程中,warranty 经常指对产品瑕疵、质量、数量的绝对担保,如我国的"三包卡"所提供的保证,对于合同而言,warranty 则是一种严格的责任担保,即除非担保人严格按照字面意义执行合同,否则合同便视为无效。

If a party commits any material breach of this contract or its representation and warranties hereunder, the other party shall have the right to terminate this contract and claim damages. 如果一方实质上违反本合同或其在本合同项下的陈述和保证,另一方有权终止本合同,并要求赔偿损失。

在英文合同法律中,通常可以发现如下类似表达:

(1) If any of the above representations and warranties of distributor are not accurate in all material respects on the date hereof (or the effective date), then distributor shall be in material breach of this contract. (如果在本合同签订日或生效日经销商的上述陈述及担保的任何一项

与实际情况有实质性不符,则构成经销商重大违约。)

(2) Representations and warranties: We express no opinion as to the accuracy of any representation or warranty made in the documents save insofar as any matters represented or warranted are the subject of a specific opinion in this letter and are matters of law and not fact. (声明和保证:我们对文件中所做的任何声明和保证的准确性不表达任何意见,但作为本意见书中某一特定意见的,以及作为法律而非事实的任何被声明和保证的事项除外。)

warranty 作为动词使用时,应注意与如下词汇的区别:

ensure, insure, assure, guarantee, pledge, promise

这些动词都有"保证"之意。但是:

ensure:侧重使人相信某个行为或力量产生的结果。

insure:常与 ensure 换用,但前者多指经济方面的保证、保险。

assure:侧重指消除某人思想上的怀疑或担心,从而有达到目的的保证感,但不如 ensure 普通。

guarantee:指对事物的品质或人的行为及履行义务、义务等承担责任的保证。

pledge:正式用词,指通过郑重许诺、协议或立誓等保证承担某一义务或遵守某一原则。

promise:侧重表自己的主观意向,设法用语言使人感到稳当可靠。

 ## Exercises

I Verbal Abilities

Part One

Directions: *For each of these completing questions, read each item carefully to get the sense of it. Then, in the proper space, complete each statement by supplying the missing word or phrase.*

1. An agency is a legal relationship where one person, the agent, is legally authorized to act _____ another person, the principal.

　　A. against　　　　B. on behalf of　　　　C. in place of　　　　D. in harmony with

2. Agency relationships are important to understand because if you _____ an agent to act on your behalf, then you become the principal, and a principal can be legally liable for the acts of the agent.

　　A. accredit　　　　B. legitimize　　　　C. sanction　　　　D. authorize

3. An agent is required to always act in the best interest of the principal, so if you take a business opportunity that rightfully could have been taken by your principal, then you might _____ your principal.

　　A. be victorious over　B. be in arrears with　　C. be liable to　　　　D. be parallel to

4. In the U.S., agency relationships are generally governed by common law, which means there may not be a state statute _____ agency relationships.

　　A. defining　　　　B. delineating　　　　C. enumerating　　　　D. formalizing

5. The only requirement for creating an agency relationship is that the principal _____ mani-

Lesson Two Sample Sales Agency Contract

fest some intention for the agent to act on the principal's behalf.

A. ostensibly B. perspicuously C. overtly D. definitely

6. Sales outsourcing represents a quick way by which service providers or manufactures can _____ distribution, and is becoming more and more popular

A. gain entry to B. access
C. gain the upper hand of D. gain liberty against

7. Full sales outsourcing is different from telemarketing in that it requires direct _____ of sales personnel with specific backgrounds for each sales campaign.

A. muster B. augmentation C. conscription D. recruitment

8. Always have an attorney write, or at least review, every contract you sign so that you can be sure you, your employees and your company are as protected as you can be in a legal, _____ contract.

A. compulsory B. mandatory C. binding D. requisite

9. Sales outsourcing is expected to be cheaper than the fully loaded cost of employing salespeople, but calculating the cost comparison over time is far from _____.

A. uncontrived B. straightforward. C. undeviating D. unwavering

10. The aims of an outsourcer can be closely aligned with the aims and _____ of the contracting company.

A. objectives B. aspiration C. expectation D. set pursuit

Part Two

Directions: *Choose the one word or phase that best keep the meaning of the original sentence if it were substituted for the underlined part.*

1. Works in the public domain are those whose intellectual property rights have expired, been <u>forfeited</u>, or are inapplicable.

A. disgorged B. capitulated C. foregone D. relinquished

2. The public domain did not <u>come to fruition</u> as a term until the mid-17th century, although as a concept "it can be traced back to the ancient Roman Law, as a preset system included in the property right system".

A. go into realization B. gain momentum
C. go into satisfaction D. come to growth

3. When looking at the public domain from a historical perspective, one could say the construction of the idea of "public domain" <u>sprouted</u> from the concepts of *res commune* (things that could be commonly enjoyed by mankind, such as air, sunlight and ocean), *res publicae* (things that were shared by all citizens), and *res universitatis* (things that were owned by the municipalities of Rome) in early Roman Law.

A. germinated B. flourished C. originated D. thrived

4. The public domain is under pressure from the "commoditization of information" as items of information that previously had little or no economic value have <u>acquired</u> independent economic value in the information age.

  A. assimilated   B. appropriated   C. assumed   D. procured

  5. Bankruptcy is a legal status of an <u>insolvent</u> person or an organization, that is, one who cannot repay the debts they owe to creditors.

  A. destitute   B. impoverished   C. insolent   D. flippant

  6. The principal focus of modern insolvency legislation and business debt restructuring practices no longer rests on the elimination of insolvent entities but on the remodeling of the financial and organizational structure of debtors experiencing financial distress so as to permit the <u>rehabilitation</u> and continuation of their business.

  A. regeneration   B. redemption   C. reorganization   D. reparation

  7. An agent who acts within the scope of authority <u>conferred</u> by his or her principal binds the principal in the obligations he or she creates against third parties.

  A. bestowed   B. transmitted   C. negotiated   D. adjudged

  8. <u>Apparent</u> authority exists where the principal's words or conduct would lead a reasonable person in the third party's position to believe that the agent was authorized to act, even if the principal and the purported agent had never discussed such a relationship.

  A. conjectural   B. tangible   C. ostensible   D. discernible

  9. Where the principal is not bound because the agent has no actual or apparent authority, the purported agent is liable to the third party for breach of the <u>implied</u> warranty of authority.

  A. implicit   B. suggestive   C. unpronounced   D. inherent

  10. If the agent has acted within the scope of the actual authority given, the principal must <u>indemnify</u> the agent for payments made during the course of the relationship whether the expenditure was expressly authorized or merely necessary in promoting the principal's business.

  A. make restitution   B. make good   C. save harmless   D. reimburse

II Cloze

  Directions: *For each blank in the following passage, there are five answers marked A, B, C, D, and E, you are to choose the best answer from the choices given to complete the sentence.*

  The purpose of agency relationships is   (1) , and sometimes necessity. Because an agent is authorized to act on behalf of a principal, a principal can essentially be two places at once. The principal can   (2)   business in one setting, while the agent handles the principal's business in another setting, all at the same time. Another practical benefit of an agency relationship is that it gives   (3)   to professional services. For example, you might consider hiring an attorney to represent you in a legal dispute, and the attorney is your agent authorized to represent your legal interests. This is beneficial to you, the client, because you get the advantage of the attorney's professional   (4) . Another benefit of the agency relationship is that an agent can take care of a principal who is not able to take care of himself or herself. Imagine a handicapped, elderly individual who has difficulty   (5)   daily functions, including managing personal finances. That person can   (6)   an agency relationship with a trusted individual, his or her agent, so that the agent can handle personal finances, manage wealth and provide for daily sustenance.

Lesson Two   Sample Sales Agency Contract   41

One of the risks of the agency relationship is that a principal is exposed to ___(7)___ liability for the acts of the agent. Because an agent is legally authorized to represent the principal, the principal is responsible for whatever the agent does under that ___(8)___. The principal could, for example, ___(9)___ a contract signed by the agent on behalf of the principal, even if the principal never read that contract. Or, if an agent is involved in a car crash while acting on the principal's business, the principal might be responsible for paying for the ___(10)___ sustained in the crash. For this reason, agency relationships should generally be in writing, and the written agreement should clearly limit the actions the agent is authorized or not authorized to take.

An agency relationship is a powerful tool that is easy to use. An agency relationship can be based on a written agreement, or sometimes even a ___(11)___ agreement. When you create an agency relationship, you are authorizing someone to make decisions ___(12)___, so you should always be sure you trust your agent. Or, if you are going to ___(13)___ an agent, you should always make sure you act in the best interest of your principal, or your principal could sue you for ___(14)___ the agency relationship. The agency relationship can be helpful, but also hurtful, so it should be used ___(15)___.

(1) A. convenience   B. benefit   C. suitability
    D. conduciveness   E. eligibility

(2) A. carry forth   B. handle   C. carry onto
    D. carry out   E. trade off

(3) A. effect   B. force   C. access
    D. way   E. availability

(4) A. expertise   B. competence   C. efficiency
    D. efficacy   E. mastermind

(5) A. pursuing   B. perpetrating   C. executing
    D. performing   E. commissioning

(6) A. encroach   B. ensue   C. enter for
    D. enter upon   E. enter into

(7) A. effectual   B. potential   C. permissible
    D. performable   E. workable

(8) A. authority   B. dominance   C. percept
    D. precept   E. precedent

(9) A. be a drag on   B. be an agent for   C. be bound to
    D. be attentive to   E. be bent on

(10) A. depreciation   B. remuneration   C. reimbursement
     D. reparation   E. damages

(11) A. parole   B. verbal   C. recited
     D. veracious   E. veridical

(12) A. on all counts   B. on the docket   C. on the market
     D. on your behalf   E. on the way

(13) A. act on   B. act as   C. act a part

                    D. act the part of   E. act together
(14) A. trespassing   B. vindicating   C. violating
                    D. vitiating   E. vouching
(15) A. with care   B. with deference   C. with fidelity
                    D. with simplicity   E. with ease

III Reading Comprehension

Passage one

Directions: *Choose the best answer from the given choices for each question.*

China's dollar dilemma

The flotation of Blackstone in June 2007 has already gone down as one of the symbolic events in America's financial bubble—the end-of-an-era deal when some of Wall Street's savviest insiders decided to cash out.

Yet the listing of the private equity group could also be the turning point in another chapter of financial history; one that will shape the world that emerges from the current crisis: the moment when China really began to question its deep financial entanglement with the US.

China Investment Corporation, the country's sovereign wealth fund, had not even begun formally operating when it spent $3bn on a 9.9 per cent stake in the private equity group. With Blackstone's shares down 84 per cent since flotation, CIC's new executives have become the target of furious attacks by bloggers who think China was conned. "They are worse than wartime traitors," says one recent chat-room posting. "Blind worship of the US by so-called 'experts'," complains another.

China's near $2,000bn (£1,380bn, €1,560bn) in reserves, the world's largest, are often viewed outside the country as a great strength—an insurance policy against economic turbulence. But within China, they are increasingly seen by the public and even some policymakers as something of an albatross—a huge pool of resources not being used at home that will plunge in value if the US dollar collapses. Why, people ask, should such a relatively poor country bankroll such a rich one?

Even at the elite level, the sense of frustration occasionally bubbles over. "We hate you guys," Luo Ping, a director-general at the China Banking Regulatory Commission (CBRC), complained last week on a visit to New York. "Once you start issuing $1— $2 trillion ... we know the dollar is going to depreciate, so we hate you guys, but there is nothing much we can do."

As China's economy slows sharply, the debate on how to manage its reserves is intensifying. Some propose spending the money at home; others want more diversification of investments. But the consensus behind recycling foreign currency into US government securities is coming under attack.

The discussion is hugely important for the Obama administration. At the very least, the Chinese government is likely to become much more forceful in trying to influence US economic policy. "There should be more give and take; some sort of guarantee that our interests will be defended," says Yu Yongding, a leading economist at the Chinese Academy of Social Sciences. Given the vital role that China has played in financing US deficits, Washington "should at least be a little nicer", he says.

The explosion in China's foreign exchange reserves has been one of the more remarkable episodes in recent financial history. The official total is $1,950bn, but Brad Setser, of the Council on Foreign Relations, a New York-based think-tank, who tracks China's foreign assets, puts the real figure at nearer $2,300bn—equivalent to more than $1,600 for every Chinese citizen.

From that total, Mr Setser calculates that about $1,700bn is invested in dollar assets, making the Chinese government by far the largest creditor of the US. Last year, when its economy was under extreme stress, China lent the US more than $400bn—equivalent to more than 10 per cent of Chinese gross domestic product. "Day after day, China is the single biggest buyer of Treasury bonds in the market," he wrote in a recent report. "Never before has the US relied so heavily on another country's government for financing."

But like most senior leaders, he rarely talks publicly about the Chinese currency. Analysts say any significant shift in policy either on the exchange rate or on foreign reserves would have to be approved by the nine-member standing committee of the Communist party political bureau.

Within China, a popular backlash against the scale of these investments in the US has been building for some time. Founded in 2007, CIC controls assets equivalent to only about 10 per cent of the total reserves, yet it has become a lightning rod for criticism. Not only has its Blackstone investment gone sour, but CIC also invested $5bn in Morgan Stanley before the bank's shares slumped. CIC also had money in Reserve Primary Fund, the US money market fund which froze redemptions after the collapse of Lehman Brothers.

A European banker who has been advising CIC on its overseas strategy says: "This is a completely unique situation for Chinese bureaucrats to face—having their every decision debated, analysed and often attacked in the media and on the internet. I get the feeling that they are all shell-shocked."

Almost every week, a new proposal is launched to find a better way of investing the money. State media reported this week that a fund might be set up using reserves to back overseas investments by oil companies. Such ideas follow a flurry of recent natural-resources deals involving Chinese companies—most notably Chinalco's planned investment in Rio Tinto—although none of these deals has directly involved foreign exchange reserves.

Another much-touted plan is for China's finance ministry to "borrow" dollar reserves from the central bank, which would be swapped into local currency and spent on social projects.

Even the body that manages the bulk of the reserves, the State Administration of Foreign Exchange (Safe), admitted last week that it was debating new approaches. "We will actively expand channels and ways to use the foreign exchange reserves. In particular, we will explore how the reserves can better serve domestic economic development," said Deng Xianhong, deputy director of Safe.

Yet officials recognise that there are still powerful reasons for China to keep buying Treasury bonds. If the authorities want to maintain most of their vast holdings in liquid assets, there are few options that match the depth of the US government bond market. And if China did not want to accumulate so many reserves, it would have to let its currency strengthen—exactly what the government does not want at a time when exports are crumbling.

China's leaders have made it clear that, in the short-term at least, they will keep supporting US markets. They want to be thought of as responsible global citizens during the crisis. They also know that a strong signal that China was backing away from dollar investments would damage the value of the enormous holdings it already has.

"We believe that to maintain a stable international financial market is in the interests of shoring up market confidence ... and facilitating early recovery of the international markets," said Wen Jiabao, the Chinese premier, in a recent interview with the Financial Times, although he hinted at a shift in strategy when the crisis was over. As Arthur Kroeber, managing editor of the China Economic Quarterly, puts it: "China's default policy is to pursue stability at all costs. They do not want to rock the boat when things are unstable."

Yet if China has few options but to keep buying US Treasuries, it can still try to turn its investments into some sort of leverage. Think-tanks close to the government have been given the task of devising concessions that China can seek in recognition of its bigger role in international economic affairs. Zha Xiaogang, of the Shanghai Institute for International Studies, has published an "economic wish-list", which includes a relaxation of US restrictions on exports of sophisticated technology to China.

China economy

Chinese policymakers are also becoming increasingly critical of US financial policies. Last week's barbed comments from Mr Luo of CBRC were the most colourful indication of Chinese fears of a dollar crisis. But there have been other hints from senior leaders. "We hope the US side will ... guarantee the safety of China's assets and investments in the US," Wang Qishan, a vice-premier, told Hank Paulson when the former US Treasury secretary visited Beijing in December. Given public skepticisms over the reserves, a tougher approach from Beijing would be well-received at home.

One of the ideas being discussed in Beijing is pushing for the International Monetary Fund to have greater authority to issue critical judgments about the health of the US economy and its financial system. Officials also hope to use purchases of US debt as a diplomatic weapon against protectionist measures in the US.

Arguably, China has already shown it can influence US decisions. One of the reasons the Bush administration was forced to recapitalize Fannie Mae and Freddie Mac last year, economists say, was because China had started to sell its bond holdings in the US agencies in favour of Treasuries. "China is beginning to behave like a normal creditor," says Mr. Setser.

Ultimately, China's influence on US policy faces two big constraints. The dollar's status as the world's reserve currency gives the US huge flexibility that other countries with large deficits do not enjoy, much to the frustration of many Chinese officials. China's unwillingness to let its currency appreciate more also limits its leverage.

But the political debate is likely to be very different. The Sino-US relationship used to involve lectures from Washington about China's undervalued currency and its closed financial markets. Now they will include Chinese warnings on the risks of inflation in the US and dollar weakness. Fiscal conservatives in the US, worried about the country's impending borrowing binge, have an unlikely new ally: Beijing.

(By Geoff Dyer)

1. Why did the author mention Blackstone?
   A. To humiliate CIC officials for their bad judgement.
   B. To lead to his central subject of this article.
   C. To show how Wall Street's insiders cashed out.
   D. To explain that China is no match to U.S. in terms of financial savvyness.
2. Which of the following is most likely to happen, according to the article?
   A. China tries harder to influence US economic policy.
   B. China tries harder to influence US economic policy.
   C. China let RMB appreciate aggressively.
   D. China stop buying U.S. treasury
3. Who ultimately decide how to use China's huge reserves?
   A. The financial markets
   B. CIC
   C. SAFE
   D. Chinese top leaders
4. Why does China have to continue buying U.S. treasury?
   A. There are few other options.
   B. The perception that China was backing away from dollar investments would damage the value of the enormous holdings it already has.
   C. So that RMB doesn't have to appreciate.
   D. China wants to be thought of as responsible global citizens during the crisis.
   E. All of the above

Passage Two

Directions: *Choose the best answer from the given choices for each question.*

Choices made in 2009 will shape the globe's destiny

Welcome to 2009. This is a year in which the fate of the world economy will be determined, maybe for generations. Some entertain hopes that we can restore the globally unbalanced economic growth of the middle years of this decade. They are wrong. Our choice is only over what will replace it. It is between a better balanced world economy and disintegration. That choice cannot be postponed. It must be made this year.

We are in the grip of the most significant global financial crisis for seven decades. As a result, the world has run out of creditworthy, large-scale, willing private borrowers. The alternative of relying on vast US fiscal deficits and expansion of central bank credit is a temporary—albeit necessary—expedient. But it will not deliver a durable return to growth. Fundamental changes are needed.

Already it must be clear even to the most obtuse and complacent that this crisis matches the most serious to have affected advanced countries in the postwar era. In a recent update of a seminal paper, released a year ago, Carmen Reinhart of Maryland University and Kenneth Rogoff of Harvard spell out what this means. They note the similarities among big financial crises in advanced and emerging countries and, by combining a number of severe cases, reach disturbing conclusions.

Banking crises are protracted, they note, with output declining, on average, for two years. Asset market collapses are deep, with real house prices falling, again on average, by 35 per cent over six years and equity prices declining by 55 per cent over 3 and a half years. The rate of unemployment rises, on average, by 7 percentage points over four years, while output falls by 9 per cent.

Not least, the real value of government debt jumps, on average, by 86 per cent. This is only in small part because of the cost of recapitalizing banks. It is far more because of collapses in tax revenues.

How far will the present crisis match the worst of the past? The continuing willingness of the world to finance at least the US—though not necessarily the smaller and more peripheral deficit countries, such as the UK—is a reason for optimism. It does allow the US government to mount a vast fiscal and monetary rescue programme.

Cumulative increase in real public debt in the three years following a bank crisis.

Yet, as Profs Reinhart and Rogoff note in another paper, this is a global crisis, not a regional one (see chart). It has reminded us that the US is still, for good or ill, the core of the world economy. In the big crises of recent decades, US demand has rescued the world. This was true during the 1990s, after the Asian crisis, and again after the stock market crash of 2000. But who, apart from its government, will rescue the US? And on what scale must it act?

This issue is addressed in another seminal paper, the latest in the series co-written by Wynne Godley and two others for the Levy Economics Institute of Bard College. The underlying argument is one with which readers of this column should, by now, be all too familiar.

What makes rescue so difficult is the force that drove the crisis: the interplay between persistent external and internal imbalances in the US and the rest of the world. The US and a number of other chronic deficit countries have, at present, structurally deficient capacity to produce tradable goods and services. The rest of the world or, more precisely, a limited number of big surplus countries—particularly China—have the opposite. So demand consistently leaks from the deficit countries to surplus ones.

In times of buoyant demand, this is no problem. In times of collapsing private spending, as now, it is a huge one. It means that US rescue efforts need to be big enough not only to raise demand for US output but also to raise demand for the surplus output of much of the rest of the world. This was a burden that crisis-hit Japan did not have to bear.

What has happened to US private spending follows from the collapse in borrowing: between the third quarter of 2007 and the third quarter of 2008 net lending to the US private sector fell by about 13 per cent of gross domestic product—by far the steepest fall in the history of the series (see chart). With borrowing out of the picture, private net saving—the difference between income and expenditure—is likely to remain positive for years, as households pay down debt, willingly or not.

Given the persistent structural current account deficit, how large does the fiscal deficit need to be to balance the economy at something close to full employment? Assuming, for the moment, that the private sector runs a financial surplus of 6 per cent of GDP and the structural current account deficit is 4 per cent of GDP, the fiscal deficit must be 10 per cent of GDP, indefinitely.

And to get to this point the fiscal boost must be huge. A discretionary boost of $760bn or 5.3 per cent of GDP is not enough. The authors argue that "even with the application of almost unbelievably large fiscal stimuli, output will not increase enough to prevent unemployment from continuing to rise through the next two years".

Now think what will happen if, after two or more years of monstrous fiscal deficits, the US is still mired in unemployment and slow growth. People will ask why the country is exporting so much of its demand to sustain jobs abroad. They will want their demand back. The last time this sort of thing happened—in the 1930s—the outcome was a devastating round of beggar-my-neighbour devaluations, plus protectionism. Can we be confident we can avoid such dangers? On the contrary, the danger is extreme. Once the integration of the world economy starts to reverse and unemployment soars, the demons of our past—above all, nationalism—will return. Achievements of decades may collapse almost overnight.

Yet we have a golden opportunity to turn away from such a course. We know better now. The US has, in Barack Obama, a president with vast political capital. His administration is determined to do whatever it can. But the US is not strong enough to rescue the world economy on its own. It needs helpers, particularly in the surplus countries. The US and a few other advanced countries can no longer absorb the world's surpluses of savings and goods. This crisis is the proof. The world has changed and so must policy. It must do so now. (By Martin Wolf)

1. Which of the following is the real root behind the financial crisis, according to the author?
A. Bad risk management by US banks
B. Flawed regulation by governments
C. Unbalanced globally economic growth
D. Economic cycle

2. The author implied that 86 more government debt are issued mainly to raise money for:
A. Buying stakes in troubled banks
B. Buying bad assets
C. Compensate for lower tax revenue
D. Lower the government bond prices

3. What's the author's solution to the financial crisis?
A. The US work with the surplus countries to solve the problem of global imbalance
B. Stricter financial and banking regulation
C. Stimulate demand in the US

D. Big fiscal stimulus from the western countries

4. If the author continues to write, he would most likely talk about:

A. How the financial crisis of 1930 is solved by the New Deal
B. How the global financial system was shaped after World War II
C. How Surplus countries will be affected by the crisis
D. How Obama convince surplus countries to help solve the imbalance problem

IV Translation Abilities

法律语言特征分析与法律翻译技能培养之二：
英汉思维差异及对语言的影响（二）

翻译活动的基础乃人类思维规律的共同性，翻译的本质乃不同思维形式的转换。思维的单位是概念、判断和推理，而语言的单位是词、句、语段和语篇。思维和语言之间的对应关系也就决定了语言的表达形式。为此，在翻译的过程中，我们必须按照目的语民族思维的习惯，调整语句结构，以符合其表达习惯。英汉翻译中主要的调整手段有：

1. 调整句子长度

西方民族中惯有的分析型思维方式使得西方人注重分析方法，采用"由一及多"的思维方式，句子结构以主语和谓语为核心，统摄各种短语和从句，由主到次，递相跌加，结构复杂，但形散而意合，于是形成一种"树杈型"的句式结构；而东方民族中的综合性思维方式使得中国人注重整体与和谐，强调"从多归一"的思维方式，句子结构上以动词为核心，以时间顺序为逻辑语序，横向铺叙，层层推进，归纳总结，于是形成"流水型"的句式结构。故有人说英语句子结构犹如"参天大树，枝繁叶茂"，汉语句子结构犹如"大江流水，后浪推前浪"。汉语里特多流水句，一个小句接一个小句，很多地方可断可连。汉语中的这种流水式用节节短句逐点交代，层层展开问题的表达方式，使得表达内容相同的汉语句子在数量上要比英语多。为此在翻译过程中，英语的一个长句往往需要转译为汉语的几个短句，而汉语的一个意群中的数个短句常常可以译为英语的一个句子，正因为如此，英汉翻译中的分译和合译，是调整句子长度的常用方法。

2. 调整句子结构

东西方不同的思维模式所形成的"树杈型"和"流水型"的句子结构，不仅表现在句子的外部长度上，还体现在句子内部组词造句的规律上。英语句子依靠关联词语和各种短语，对中心词语"随举随释"，因此一个中心词可以有多个短语或从句进行修饰说明；汉语是以分析性为主的语言，组词造句主要靠词序和虚词，而词序手段大大限制了中心词语的负载量，为此汉语中习惯于采用"双提分述"的叙述方法，以体现层次分明、条理清晰的老哟机语义结构。为此，在英汉翻译过程中，英语的"随举随释"和"双提分述"的句法结构要求我们挑战句子语序，以符合英汉语不同的表达习惯，否则会出现汉译"欧化"句式或英译"汉化"的句子。

除此以外，汉语"流水型"的句子结构还取决于句中动词的安排，动词的高频率使用乃汉语词组的重要特色，动词的频繁使用不仅表达了汉语强有力的表达功能，而且还取决于动作发生的时间顺序，为此决定了句子的语序结构。也就是说，汉语句子以动词为关键词，以时间顺序为语序链，而英语则以动词为谓语，以分词、介词、不定式、动名词或介词短语等表示相应动词的语义和动作的先后顺序,为此,在英汉翻译过程中,就必须调整句子结构。

3. 调整句子中心

英汉语句子的语义中心基本相同,在含有表示条件、假设、原因、让步或分析推理的复合句中,语义的重心均落在结果、结论或事实上,但英汉语句子语义中心的位置是极不相同的。英语句子一般采用前中心位置,而汉语句子一般采用后中心位置。也就是说,西方民族"由一及多"的思维方式往往将句子的语义重心置于句子后面,而东方民族"从众归一"的思维方式则常常将句子的次要部分放在句首,而将句子的重心放在句子的末尾。为此,英语主从复合句中,表示条件、让步、假设等内容的从句的位置比较灵活,可以置前,也可以位后,但相应的现代汉语偏正复句中,一般是偏句在前,正句在后。为此,英语到汉语的翻译过程中,常常将英语"主前从后"的语序调整为"偏前正后"的语序。同样,汉语到英语的翻译过程中,为了符合西方思维方式和英语的表达习惯,我们也拟前移句子的重心。

4. 变化句子视点

习惯于本体思维方式的中国人在描述或记录动作或事件发生与演变的过程中,观察或叙述的视点落在动作的发出者,并常常将动作的发出者作为句子的主语,为此汉语中主动语态的使用较为频繁,而习惯于客体思维方式的西方人常常将观察或叙述的视点放在行为、动作的结果或承受者身上,并以此作为句子的主语,为此英语中被动语态的使用较为广泛。翻译过程中,我们则必须根据语义逻辑改换或增添句子的主语,相应调整句子的语态。

5. 转换修辞方式

不同的思维方式决定了不同的语言表达形式,不同的语言形式又有着不同的修辞形式和特点,英汉翻译过程中,有时就必须根据目的语的表达习惯和读者的审美情趣,对原文的修辞形式作相应的调整,以使译文文通字顺,语意畅达。主要的手段有:

(1) 正反转换

正反转换指肯定于否定的思维方向的互换,亦称正说反译或反说正译,也就是说,在保持原文意思的情况下,变换表达角度,把词义或句子形式从正面表达该为反面表达,或从反面表达该为正面表达,目的在于使译文符合目的语的表达习惯,增强表达效果。

(2) 虚实转换

虚实转换指词汇抽象概念与具体意义的相互转换。抽象思维方式中多用抽象概念的词语描述事物,阐述事理,而具象思维方式中常常用表示具体概念的词语描述事物、述情达理。为此英汉翻译过程中就需要进行词语虚实意义的相互转换,英语中抽象名词的使用频率明显高于汉语,故翻译时,往往需要将英语中表示抽象概念的名词转换成汉语中的表示具体概念的名词以符合汉语的表达习惯。虚实转换包括虚转实和实转虚。前者指对原文中城乡、含蓄或朦胧的词义,通过释义、补偿等手段,使词义具体、明确或清晰,以利于读者的理解或译文语句的顺畅,或达到文化移植的目的。而后者指词义从具体到抽象、由个别到一般、特殊到概括,是译文为了适应表情达意或行文通顺而答对原文进行的词义的延伸或扩展。

(3) 词量增减

翻译中词量的增减可以使译文语句通顺,语义流畅,可以有效提高译文的可读性,有利于读者增强对原文的理解。正如刘勰所说::"善删者字去而意留,善敷者辞殊而义显"。但增词也好,减词也好,读者均得依托具体语境,做大增词有理,减词有据。所谓增词译法指的是出于遣词造句的需要,或依据语境补充语义。减词译法指同样由于修辞的需要,减少赘词冗语,使译文简洁流畅,更符合目的语的表达习惯。如,在汉语中,为了句子结构平衡、增强气势、强化音韵,常常使用排比、对仗、重复等修辞手段,为此,汉语句子中词或词组的重复使用或结构相似、含义相同的多个词组的连续应用现象较为多见,故在汉语翻译成英语的过程中,我们可以只将主要意思译出,而不必字比句对,拘泥于原文的表达形式。

Part One *Put the following into Chinese*

America must remember it is not just any other country

In this young century, the 9/11 attacks, the global financial crisis and the unrest in the Arab world have struck at the heart of vital US interests. If Americans want the tectonic plates of the international system to settle in a way that makes the world safer, freer and more prosperous, the US must overcome its reluctance to lead. We will have to stand up for and promote the power and promise of free markets and free peoples, and affirm that American pre-eminence safeguards rather than impedes global progress.

The list of US foreign policy challenges is long and there will be a temptation to respond tactically to each one. But today's headlines and posterity's judgment often differ. The task at hand is to strengthen the pillars of our influence and act with the long arc of history in mind.

In the Middle East we must patiently use our aid, expertise and influence to support the creation of inclusive democratic institutions. The fundamental problem in the region is the absence of institutions that can bridge the Sunni-Shia divide, and protect the rights of women and minorities. Even as we make necessary immediate choices—including arming the Syrian rebels—we must insist upon inclusive politics. The US cannot afford to stand aside; regional powers will bring their own agendas that could exacerbate confessional divisions.

As we work with reformers across the region, we should not forget that Iraq has the kind of institutions that are meant to overcome these divisions. Given its geostrategic importance, the chaos engulfing its neighbors and Iran's destructive influence, our re-engagement with Baghdad is sorely needed.

The US needs to turn again to the development of responsible and democratic sovereigns beyond the Middle East. The George W. Bush administration doubled aid spending worldwide and quadrupled it to Africa. It channeled assistance to countries that were investing in their people's health and education, governing wisely and democratically, building open economies and fighting corruption. Ultimately, these states will make the transition from aid to private investment, becoming net contributors to the international economy and global security. US tax dollars will have been well spent.

We must also not lose sight of how democracy is solidifying in the western hemisphere. US assistance and trade policy can help democracies in Latin America to provide an answer to populist dictators. At the same time, we must speak out for dissidents—from Cuba to Venezuela to Nicaragua. Mexico needs attention across a broad agenda that includes the devastating security challenge that threatens both it and the US.

The US "pivot" to Asia (a region that had hardly been abandoned) has focused heavily on security issues. America should remain the pre-eminent military power in the Pacific. But consider this: China has signed free-trade agreements with 15 nations over the past eight years and has explored FTAs with some 20 others; since 2009 the US has ratified three FTAs negotiated during the Bush administration and it has continued—but not concluded—talks on the Trans-Pacific Partnership, which began in 2008. One of the US's best assets in managing China's rise is its regional economic engagement.

A robust free trade policy will strengthen our economy and influence abroad, as will developing our domestic resources, such as the North American energy platform. High oil prices empower Venezuela, Russia and Iran. We are developing alternative sources of energy but they will not replace hydrocarbons for a long time. It is a gift that much of our demand—possibly all of it—can be met domestically and in co-operation with US allies, Mexico and Canada.

Part Two *Put the following into English*

最重要的是,我们需要让我们在全球的朋友放心。仓促树敌的做法,给我们与可信赖的盟友的关系蒙上了阴影。我们与欧洲的合作一直是零星的,有时还带有不屑的意味。近些年来,我们与印度、巴西和土耳其的战略关系既没有得到加强,也没有深化。委内瑞拉总统乌戈·查韦斯(Hugo Chávez)以及伊朗人没有接受我们伸出的橄榄枝。巴勒斯坦国并不存在,因为这只有通过与一个安全无忧、对自身与美国关系有信心的以色列进行谈判才能实现。放弃在波兰和捷克部署导弹防御体系(以"重置"美国与俄罗斯关系)的决定,被弗拉基米尔·普京(Vladimir Putin)所窃取,他迅速恢复了反美立场。朋友必须能够相信我们对他们做出的承诺的一致性。

最后,我们不能忘记源于国内的优势。我们是否具备全球领导能力,取决于我们是否拥有建立在财政纪律和私营部门稳健增长基础之上的强大经济。归根结底,我们的成功取决于我们调动人们潜能的能力,在历史上,美国在这方面的表现胜过其他任何一个国家。美国从来都充满了可能性,我们不是怀着怨恨、依靠福利取得成功的。雄心勃勃的人们从世界各地赶来,寻找美国提供的机遇。缺乏人道、可持续的国家移民政策将危及这一伟大资产。

从历史上来说,我们的人才来自于美国社会的各个方面,与阶级和经济状况无关。但当一个儿童的所在地决定她是否会获得良好的教育时,我们的几代人将输给贫穷和失望。美国教育危机是影响我们国家实力和团结的最大威胁。

美国人民必须振奋起来,再次发挥带头作用。他们需要记住,美国不是其他任何一个国家。我们之所以特殊,是因为我们的信念是明确的:自由市场和自由人民是未来的关键,而且我们愿意根据这些信念采取行动。做不到这点将会留下一个真空,而那些不支持"势力均衡"(有利于自由程度的提高)的国家将会取而代之。对于美国的利益和价值观以及那些拥有相同利益和价值观的同道者而言,这将是一场悲剧。

V Interaction

Discuss with your tutor(s) or the People's judges in your locality about the relationship between law and politics. Then based on the discussion, you are supposed to write a composition about how the judges overcome the political difficulties in their handling the cases. Remember that you are required to express your ideas clearly.

VI Appreciation of Judge's Opinions

(1) **Case Name**(案件名) *Water Waste Land Inc Westec v. Lanham*

WATER WASTE LAND INC WESTEC v. LANHAM

WATER, WASTE & LAND, INC., d/b/a WESTEC, Petitioner, v. Donald LANHAM;
Larry Clark; and Preferred Income Investors, L. L. C., Respondents.

97SC199. No.

—March 09, 1998

(2) **Case Summary**(案情简介)

Brief Fact Summary

Plaintiff company, Water, Waste & Land, Inc., brought this action to collect from Defendant individuals, Donald Lanham and Larry Clark, for work performed by Plaintiff. Defendants claimed that they could not be held personally liable as agents of a limited Liability Corporation (LLC).(不能代表有限责任公司承担责任)

Synopsis of Rule of Law(所适用法律规则概要). State statutes providing constructive notice(推定通知) to third parties when an LLC has been incorporated do not extend to agency law.

Facts. Clark contacted Plaintiff to have Plaintiff perform some engineering work. Although a written agreement never emerged, both sides made an oral agreement regarding the work eventually performed by Plaintiff. During the negotiations, Defendants never notified Plaintiff that they were acting as agents on behalf of their LLC, Preferred Income Investors (P.I.I.). The only reference to P.I.I. available to Plaintiff was the initials "P.I.I." on Defendants' business cards(名片). When Plaintiff tried to collect for the work performed, Defendants could not pay. Clark and Lanham asserted that they were not liable because Colorado's statutes regarding LLC's provided constructive notice to third parties by the act of incorporation. Defendants further argued that the Plaintiff should have inquired into the LLC status, and the business card sufficed to give some warning as to the possible existence of an LLC. Although the county court found for Plaintiff(做出有利于原告的判决), the district court overturned(推翻), agreeing with Defendant's reasoning.

Issue. The issue is whether state statutes providing constructive notice of LLC's to third parties were intended to cover agency law claims wherein the agents never fully disclosed the principle to the outside party.

Held. The court reversed the district court and reinstated the findings for Plaintiff. The LLC statutes never intended on being read so broadly as to absolve agents from deceptively withholding the existence or name of the principle. Common law agency principles(普通法代理原则) still apply regardless of the statute. Colorado's agency law holds agents responsible when they do not fully disclose the principle, and the notation of "P.I.I." on Defendants' business cards does not fully disclose the principle.

Discussion. The court's decision upholds public policy(维护公序良俗/公共政策).

(3) **Excerpts of the Judgment**(法官判决词)

Justice SCOTT delivered the Opinion of the Court.

This case requires us to decide whether the members or managers of a limited liability company (LLC)(有限责任公司成员或管理人员) are excused from personal liability on a contract where the other party to the contract did not have notice that the members or managers were negotiating on behalf of a limited liability company at the time the contract was made. Because the county court(郡法院) found that the party dealing with the members or managers was unaware that they were acting as agents of a limited liability company when they negotiated the contract(合同协商), and the evidence in the record supports the county court's findings, we see no legal basis to excuse the agents of the LLC from liability and therefore we reverse the judgment of the district court(推翻地区法院的判决).

Lesson Two Sample Sales Agency Contract

I.

The Company is a limited liability company organized under the Colorado Limited Liability Company Act(《科罗拉多州有限责任公司法》). At the time of the events in this case, Donald Lanham and Larry Clark were managers and also members of Preferred Income Investors, L. L. C. (Company or P. I. I.). Land, Inc., the petitioner, is a land development and engineering company(土地开发和工程公司) doing business under the name "Westec."

However, there was no indication as to what the acronym(首字母缩略词) meant or that P. I. I. was a limited liability company. While the Company's name was not on the business card, the letters "P. I. I." appeared above the address on the card. The business card included Lanham's address, which was also the address listed as the Company's principal office and place of business in its articles of organization(公司组织大纲) filed with the secretary of state. In the course of preliminary discussions, Clark gave his business card to representatives of Westec. In March 1995, Clark contacted Westec about the possibility of hiring Westec to perform engineering work in connection with a development project which involved the construction of a fast-food restaurant known as Taco Cabaña.

On August 2, 1995, Westec sent Lanham a form of contract, which Lanham was to execute(签署合同) and return to Westec. Clark instructed Westec to send a written proposal of its work to Lanham and the proposal was sent in April 1995. After further negotiations, an oral agreement was reached concerning Westec's involvement with the Company's restaurant project. No payments were made on the bill. Westec completed the engineering work and sent a bill for $9,183.40 to Lanham. Although Westec never received a signed contract, in mid-August it did receive verbal authorization from Clark to begin work.

Lanham appealed, seeking review in the Larimer County District Court. Accordingly, the county court dismissed Clark from the suit, concluding he could not be held personally liable, and entered judgment in the amount of $9,183 against Lanham and the Company. Based on its findings, the county court ruled that: (1) Clark was an agent of both Lanham and the Company with "authority to obligate Lanham and the Company"; (2) a valid and binding contract existed for the work; (3) Westec "did not have knowledge of any business entity" and only dealt with Clark and Lanham "on a personal basis"; and (4) Westec understood Clark to be Lanham's agent and therefore "Clark is not personally liable." The county court found that: (1) Clark had contacted Westec to do engineering work for Lanham; (2) it was "unknown" to Westec that Lanham had organized the Company as a limited liability company; and (3) the letters "P. I. I." on Clark's business card were insufficient to place Westec on notice that the Company was a limited liability company. The county court entered judgment in favor of Westec. At trial, the Company admitted liability for the amount claimed by Westec. Westec filed a claim in county court against Clark and Lanham individually as well as against the Company.

In the district court's view, the notice provision, as well as Westec's failure to investigate or request a personal guarantee, relieved Lanham of personal liability for claims against the Company. In addressing that issue, the district court found that Westec was placed on notice that it was dealing with a limited liability company based on two factors: (1) the business card containing the letters "P. I. I."; and (2) the notice provision of section 7-80-208, of the LLC Act. Principally in reliance upon the LLC Act's notice provision, section 7-80-208, which provides that the filing of the articles of organization serve as constructive notice of a company's status as a limited liability company, the district court held that "the County Court erred in finding that Westec had no notice that it was dealing with an L. L. C." Contrary to the trial court's findings, the district court held that "evidence presented at trial was uncontradicted that Westec knew it was dealing with a business entity (P. I. I.). The district court reversed, concluding that "the issue which the court must address is whether the County Court erred in holding Lanham, a member and primary manager of the company, personally liable for a debt of the company."

II.

However, before doing so, it may prove helpful to first discuss the history and development of limited liability companies and their use in business enterprise. Resolution of the controversy between Westec and Lanham requires us to analyze the relationship between the common law of agency and the reach of our statutes governing managers and members of a limited liability company.

Wyoming adopted the first LLC statute in 1977, but the majority of states did not adopt LLC legislation until the 1990s, largely because the tax treatment of such companies was in doubt. The limited liability company is a relatively recent innovation in the law governing business entities. The ability to avoid two levels of income taxation is an especially attractive feature of organization as a limited liability company. These doubts have been largely resolved, and the LLC has become a popular form of business organization because it offers members the limited liability protection of a corporation, together with the single-tier tax treatment of a partnership along with considerable flexibility in management and financing.

In 1990, our General Assembly(州议会) adopted the LLC Act, a statute currently codified as amended at sections 7-80-101 through 7-80-1101, 2 C.R.S. (1997), making Colorado the third state, behind Wyoming and Florida, to do so. In any case, the LLC Act includes the same basic features of limited liability, single-tier tax treatment, and planning flexibility shared by the Uniform Limited Liability Company Act and LLC legislation adopted by other states. Unlike a number of other states, where LLC statutes were based on a model act drafted by the National Conference of Commissioners on Uniform State Laws(美国统一各州法律全国代表大会), Colorado's LLC Act combined features of the state's existing limited partnership and corporation statutes.

Thus, it is clear that the "primary force of LLC statutes" has been to create a business entity that will meet the federal requirements for pass-through tax treatment. Colorado passed the LLC Act into law for several reasons, but the importance of the tax benefits derived from the use of the LLC should not be overlooked.

III.

A.

In essence, this course of analysis assumed that the LLC Act displaced(换置,移置;顶替,取代) certain common law agency doctrines, at least insofar as these doctrines otherwise would be applicable to suits by third parties seeking to hold the agents of a limited liability company liable for their personal actions as agents. We hold, however, that the statutory notice provision applies only where a third party seeks to impose liability on an LLC's members or managers simply due to their status as members or managers of the LLC. When a third party sues a manager or member of an LLC under an agency theory, the principles of agency law apply notwithstanding the LLC Act's statutory notice rules.

B.

As a leading treatise explains: In other words, an agent who negotiates a contract with a third party can be sued for any breach of the contract unless the agent discloses both the fact that he or she is acting on behalf of a principal (本人;委托人) and the identity of the principal. Under the common law of agency, an agent is liable on a contract entered on behalf of a principal if the principal is not fully disclosed.

But where the principal is partially disclosed (i.e. the existence of a principal is known but his identity is not), it is usually inferred that the agent is a party to the contract. If both the existence and identity of the agent's principal are fully disclosed to the other party, the agent does not become a party to any contract which he negotiates.

Other scholars agree that under the common law of agency, the duty to disclose the identity(披露身份的义务) as well as the existence of the principal lies with the agent:

The duty of disclosure clearly lies with the agent alone; □the third party with whom the agent deals(与代理人进行交易的第三方) has no duty to discover the existence of an agency or the identity of the principal. It is not sufficient that the third party has knowledge of facts and circumstances which would, if reasonably followed by inquiry, disclose the identity of the principal.

C.

Having so decided, it was bound to accept the facts as found by the county court and its review was limited to the sufficiency of the evidence. Instead, the district court exercised its authority to decide the case based on the record developed below. On appeal from the county court, the district court had the power to find the facts independently by ordering a trial de novo(重审;重新审讯). Whether a principal is partially or completely disclosed is a question of fact.

The trial record was sufficient to support the county court's finding that Clark was an agent for Lanham and this conclusion should not have been disturbed by the district court. For the same reason, the district court erred in concluding that Clark was not acting as Lanham's agent. We are, therefore, bound to accept the county court's finding that Westec did not know Clark was acting as an agent for the Company or that the letters "P. I. I." stood for "Preferred Income Investors," a limited liability company registered under Colorado law. Indeed, neither the business card nor the unsigned contract documents, both of which are of obvious significance in evaluating whether Westec knew the identity of the entity represented by Clark and Lanham, are in the record before us. However, we see the evidence as sufficient to support the county court's finding to the contrary. If the district court had held a trial de novo, its conclusion that the letters "P. I. I." on Clark's business card sufficiently alerted Westec's representatives to the fact of Clark's agency relationship with the Company and to the Company's identity would be entitled to deference if supported by evidence in the record. These precepts(训导,告诫;格言,箴言;戒律;技术上的格式;规程;方案;命令书,令状), then, lead us to conclude that the district court erred in substituting its own factual determinations for the findings of the county court.

D.

We conclude, however, that the LLC Act's notice provision was not intended to alter the partially disclosed principal doctrine. Still, if the General Assembly has altered the common law rules applicable to this case by adopting the LLC Act, then these rules must yield in favor of the statute. In light of the partially disclosed principal doctrine, the county court's determination that Clark and Lanham failed to disclose the existence as well as the identity of the limited liability company they represented is dispositive(事件、行为等具有决定性的) under the common law of agency.

Section 7-80-208, C. R. S. (1997) states:

The fact that the articles of organization are on file in the office of the secretary of state is notice that the limited liability company is a limited liability company and is notice of all other facts set forth therein which are required to be set forth in the articles of organization.

We are not persuaded that the statute can bear such an interpretation. In order to relieve Lanham of liability, this provision would have to be read to establish a conclusive presumption(推定) that a third party who deals with the agent of a limited liability company always has constructive notice(推定通知,推定知悉) of the existence of the agent's principal.

However, an equally plausible interpretation of the words used in the statute is that once the limited liability company's name is known to the third party, constructive notice of the company's limited liability status has been given, as well as the fact that managers and members will not be liable simply due to their status as managers or members. Section 7-80-208 could be read to state that third parties who deal with a limited liability company are always on constructive notice of the company's limited liability status, without regard to whether any part of the company's name or even the fact of its existence has been disclosed. Such a construction exaggerates the plain meaning of the language in the statute.

For this reason alone, a broad reading of the notice provision would be suspect. We may presume that in adopting section 7-80-208, the General Assembly did not intend to create a safe harbor(安全港) for deceit. While Westec has not alleged that Clark or Lanham deliberately tried to conceal the Company's identity or status as a limited liability company, Lanham's construction(法律的解释) would open the door to sharp practices and outright fraud. Moreover, the broad interpretation urged by Lanham would be an invitation to fraud, because it would leave the agent of a limited liability company free to mislead third parties into the belief that the agent would bear personal financial responsibility under any contract, when in fact, recovery would be limited to the assets of a limited liability company not known to the third party at the time the contract was made.

If the legislature had intended a departure of such magnitude, its desires would have been expressed more clearly. For the reasons outlined above, the interpretation urged by Lanham would be a radical departure from the settled rules of agency under the common law. In addition, statutes in derogation(毁损;减损) of the common law are to be strictly construed.

By way of further support for our conclusion, section 7-80-107 provides two bases of individual liability for members: □(1) for "alleged improper actions," and (2) "the failure of a limited liability company to observe the formalities or requirements relating to the management of its business and affairs when coupled with some other wrongful conduct." For example, section 7-80-201(1)(1997), requires limited liability companies to use the words "Limited Liability Company" or the initials "LLC" as part of their names, implying that the legislature intended to compel any entity seeking to claim the benefits of the LLC Act to identify itself clearly as a limited liability company. Other LLC Act provisions reinforce the conclusion that the legislature did not intend the notice language of section 7-80-208 to relieve the agent of a limited liability company of the duty to disclose its identity in order to avoid personal liability.

As one commentator opined:

That means that participants in closely held enterprises will continue to be liable for their acts taken in the entity's name that are wrongful or violate regulatory provisions either under agency law or by a court piercing the entity's veil. It would be an unwarranted stretch to say that these laws intend to extend the insulation of limited liability beyond that traditionally provided by the corporate form.

Hence, even if we were sympathetic to Lanham's plight, he had within his control the means to clearly state to Westec and the world. He did not do so. At that point, he could have clarified his relationship to the Company. Lanham received from Westec a form of contract demonstrating Westec's assumption that Lanham was the principal. Moreover, we must avoid straying from long established legal precepts and inserting uncertainty into accepted rules that govern business relationships that he was acting only for the limited liability company.

Section 7-80-208 is of little force, however, in determining whether a limited liability company's agent is personally liable on the theory that the agent has failed to disclose the identity of the company. In sum, then, section 7-80-208 places third parties on constructive notice that a fully identified company—that is, identified by a name such as "Preferred Income Investors, LLC," or the like—is a limited liability company provided that its articles of organization have been filed with the secretary of state.

IV.

The notice provision protects the members from suit based on their status as members, as opposed to their acts as agents of the corporate entity. Under our interpretation, section 7-80-208 still offers significant protection to the members of a limited liability company. The distinction between the use of an agency theory and the doctrine of piercing the corporate(揭开公司面纱) or limited liability company. If a third party such as Westec had tried to pierce the corporate veil to hold Clark and Lanham personally responsible for the Company's contractual debt based on the fact that they were members of the LLC, section 7-80-208 would protect them from liability. As one treatise explains: veil is significant.

The undisclosed principal theory is a rule of law and applies regardless of a defendant's intent to engage in wrongful conduct; however, the doctrine of piercing the corporate veil is based in equity so that a failure to disclose must coexist with wrongful conduct or improper purpose or intent for the latter theory to apply and render personal liability.

V.

Where the third party does not know the identity of the principal entity, however, the situation is fundamentally different because the third party is without notice and the law does not contemplate that he has any way of finding the relevant records. When a third party deals with an agent acting on behalf of a limited liability company, the existence and identity of which has been disclosed, the third party is conclusively presumed to know that the entity is a limited liability company and not a partnership or some other type of business organization. For these reasons, we conclude that where an agent fails to disclose either the fact that he is acting on behalf of a principal or the identity of the principal, the notice provision of our LLC Act, section 7-80-208, cannot relieve the agent of liability to a third party.

The "missing link" between the limited disclosure made by Clark and the protection of the notice statute was the failure to state that "P. I. I. ," the Company, stood for "Preferred Income Investors, LLC."The county court, however, found that Lanham and Clark did not identify Preferred Income Investors, LLC, as the principal in the transaction. If Clark or Lanham had told Westec's representatives that they were acting on behalf of an entity known as "Preferred Income Investors, LLC", the failure to disclose the fact that the entity was a limited liability company would be irrelevant by virtue of the statute, which provides that the articles of organization operate as constructive notice of the company's limited liability form.

Accordingly, the judgment of the district court is reversed and this case is remanded to that court with instructions that it reinstate(恢复,此处可以理解为"维持") the judgment of the county court.

Lesson Three

About Contracts

> **Learning objectives**
>
> After learning the text and having done the exercises in this lesson, you will:
>
> —familiarize with knowledge of the legal characteristics and the nature of the formation of contract;
>
> —acquire an appreciation of the vocabulary and grammar or syntax relevant to contract law;
>
> —become aware of the information required in order to understand the contract;
>
> —cultivate the practical abilities to put to use the language in the specific context;
>
> —be able to do some translation from Chinese to English and from English to Chinese.

 Text

About Contracts

Chapter 1 Meaning of Terms

§1 Contract Defined

A contract is a promise or a set of promises① for the breach of which the law gives a remedy②, or the performance③ of which the law in some way recognizes as a duty.

§2 Promise; Promisor; Promisee; Beneficiary④

(1) A promise is a manifestation of intention⑤ to act or refrain from acting in a specified

---

① a promise or a set of promises:一个允诺或一组允诺。
② remedy:救济,救济措施;补救行为(remedial action)。
③ performance:履行。
④ Promise; Promisor; Promisee; Beneficiary:允诺;允诺人;受允诺人;受益人。Beneficiary:作为形容词时,表示"封建制度下受封的、采邑的、臣服的"的意思。作为名词使用时,表示"封臣、受俸牧师"的意思,但后经不断演变,表示"遗嘱、保险等的受益人;退休金等的领受人;美国大学的公费生;国际汇兑的收款人"等意思,此处表示合同法上的受益人。
⑤ manifestation of intention:意思表示。

way, so made as to justify a promisee in understanding that a commitment has been made.

(2) The person manifesting the intention is the promisor.

(3) The person to whom the manifestation is addressed is the promisee.

(4) Where performance will benefit a person other than the promisee, that person is a beneficiary.

§4　How a Promise May Be Made

A promise may be stated in words, either oral or written, or may be inferred wholly or partly from conduct.

Chapter 2　Formation of Contracts—Parties and Capacity①

§12　Capacity to Contract

(1) No one can be bound by contract who has not legal capacity to incur at least voidable② contractual duties. Capacity to contract may be partial and its existence in respect of a particular transaction may depend upon the nature of the transaction or upon other circumstances.

(2) A natural person③ who manifests assent to a transaction has full legal capacity to incur contractual duties thereby unless he is

(a) under guardianship④, or

(b) an infant, or

(c) mentally ill or defective, or

(d) intoxicated.

§13　Persons Affected by Guardianship

A person has no capacity to incur contractual duties if his property is under guardianship by reason of an adjudication⑤ of mental illness or defect.

§14　Infants

Unless a statute provides otherwise, a natural person has the capacity to incur only voidable contractual duties until the beginning of the day before the person's eighteenth birthday.

§15　Mental Illness or Defect

(1) A person incurs only voidable contractual duties by entering into a transaction if by reason of mental illness or defect (a) he is unable to understand in a reasonable manner the nature and consequences of the transaction, or (b) he is unable to act in a reasonable manner in relation to the transaction and the other party has reason to know of his condition.

(2) Where the contract is made on fair terms and the other party is without knowledge of the mental illness or defect, the power of avoidance⑥ under Subsection (1) terminates to the extent

---

① Formation of Contracts—Parties and Capacity:合同的订立——当事人及其缔约能力。

② voidable:可撤销的;voidable contract:可撤销合同;void contract:无效合同。

③ natural people:自然人。其对应的 legal person 为法人。

④ guardianship:监护,监护职责,监护关系,监护权。

⑤ adjudication:判决,裁定。by reason of adjudication of mental illness or defec:因为其被裁定为具有精神病或精神障碍/缺陷。

⑥ avoidance: 避免,回避;罪名不成立的抗辩;撤销,无效的主张,职位的空缺。avoidance of contract:合同的撤销;avoidance of contractual liabilities:逃脱合同责任;avoidance of tax:避税(用合法手段规避纳税)。

that the contract has been so performed in whole or in part or the circumstances have so changed that avoidance would be unjust. In such a case a court may grant relief as justice requires.

§16　Intoxicated Persons

A person incurs only voidable contractual duties by entering into a transaction if the other party has reason to know that by reason of intoxication

(a) he is unable to understand in a reasonable manner the nature and consequences of the transaction, or

(b) he is unable to act in a reasonable manner in relation to the transaction.

Chapter 3　Formation of Contracts—Mutual Assent①

§17　Requirement of a Bargain

(1) Except as stated in Subsection (2), the formation of a contract requires a bargain in which there is a manifestation of mutual assent to the exchange and a consideration②.

(2) Whether or not there is a bargain a contract may be formed under special rules applicable to formal contracts or under the rules stated in §§82—94.

§18　Manifestation of Mutual Assent

Manifestation of mutual assent to an exchange requires that each party either make a promise or begin or render a performance.

The predecessor of §18 is §20 of the First Restatement③. It read as follows: *§20　Requirement of Manifestation of Mutual Assent:A manifestation of mutual assent by the parties to an informal contract is essential to its formation and the acts by which such assent is manifested must be done with the intent to do those acts; but, except as qualified by §§55, 71 and 72, neither mental assent to the promises in the contract nor real or apparent intent that the promises shall be legally binding is essential.*

§20　Effect of Misunderstanding

(1) There is no manifestation of mutual assent to an exchange if the parties attach materially different meanings to their manifestations and (a) neither party knows or has reason to know the meaning attached by the other; or (b) each party knows or each party has reason to know the meaning attached by the other.

(2) The manifestations of the parties are operative in accordance with the meaning attached to them by one of the parties if (a) that party does not know of any different meaning attached by the other, and the other knows the meaning attached by the first party; or

(b) that party has no reason to know of any different meaning attached by the other, and the other has reason to know the meaning attached by the first party.

---

① mutual assent:合意,合意是指双方当事人订立合同的意思表示相一致。
② consideration:约因或对价,是普通法系合同法中的重要概念,其内涵是一方为换取另一方做某事的承诺而向另一方支付的金钱代价或得到该种承诺的允诺。
③ First Restatement:合同法重述(第一次)。

§22 Mode of Assent: Offer and Acceptance①

(1) The manifestation of mutual assent to an exchange ordinarily takes the form of an offer or proposal by one party followed by an acceptance by the other party or parties.

(2) A manifestation of mutual assent may be made even though neither offer nor acceptance can be identified and even though the moment of formation cannot be determined.

§24 Offer Defined

An offer is the manifestation of willingness to enter into a bargain, so made as to justify another person in understanding that his assent to that bargain is invited and will conclude it.

§25 Option Contracts②

An option contract is a promise which meets the requirements for the formation of a contract and limits the promisor's power to revoke an offer.

§26 Preliminary Negotiations

A manifestation of willingness to enter into a bargain is not an offer if the person to whom it is addressed knows or has reason to know that the person making it does not intend to conclude a bargain until he has made a further manifestation of assent.

§27 Existence of Contract Where Written Memorial③ is Contemplated④

Manifestations of assent that are in themselves sufficient to conclude a contract will not be prevented from so operating by the fact that the parties also manifest an intention to prepare and adopt a written memorial thereof, but the circumstances may show that the agreements are preliminary negotiations.

§30 Form of Acceptance Invited

(1) An offer may invite or require acceptance to be made by an affirmative answer in words, or by performing or refraining from performing a specified act, or may empower the offeree⑤ to make a selection of terms in his acceptance.

(2) Unless otherwise indicated by the language or the circumstances, an offer invites acceptance in any manner and by any medium reasonable in the circumstances.

§32 Invitation of Promise or Performance

In case of doubt an offer is interpreted as inviting the offeree to accept either by promising to perform what the offer requests or by rendering the performance, as the offeree chooses.

§33 Certainty

(1) Even though a manifestation of intention is intended to be understood as an offer, it cannot be accepted so as to form a contract unless the terms of the contract are reasonably certain.

(2) The terms of a contract are reasonably certain if they provide a basis for determining the

---

① mode of assent: offer and acceptance:表示合意的方式:要约与承诺。
② option contracts:选择权合同,任择性合同。选择权/任择性合同属于一种保护受允诺人免受要约人取消合同的合同类型。
③ memorial:纪念物,纪念品;纪念日;纪念馆;纪念碑;纪念仪式;(常 pl.)记录,备忘录;年代记,编年史;提交议会等的建议书;外交上的备忘录;请愿书;抗议书。句中表示"备忘录"的意思。written memorial 表示书面记录,书面备忘录的意思。
④ Existence of Contract Where Written Memorial is Contemplated:在书面备忘录存在情况下合同的存在。
⑤ offeree:受约人。

existence of a breach and for giving an appropriate remedy.

(3) The fact that one or more terms of a proposed bargain are left open or uncertain may show that a manifestation of intention is not intended to be understood as an offer or as an acceptance.

§34 Certainty and Choice of Terms; Effect of Performance or Reliance

(1) The terms of a contract may be reasonably certain even though it empowers one or both parties to make a selection of terms in the course of performance.

(2) Part performance under an agreement may remove uncertainty and establish that a contract enforceable as a bargain has been formed.

(3) Action in reliance on an agreement may make a contractual remedy appropriate even though uncertainty is not removed.

§35 The Offeree's Power of Acceptance

(1) An offer gives to the offeree a continuing power to complete the manifestation of mutual assent by acceptance of the offer.

(2) A contract cannot be created by acceptance of an offer after the power of acceptance has been terminated in one of the ways listed in §36.

§36 Methods of Termination of the Power of Acceptance

(1) An offeree's power of acceptance may be terminated by

(a) rejection or counter-offer① by the offeree, or

(b) lapse of time②, or

(c) revocation by the offeror, or

(d) death or incapacity of the offeror or offeree.

(2) In addition, an offeree's power of acceptance is terminated by the nonoccurrence of any condition of acceptance under the terms of the offer.

§38 Rejection

(1) An offeree's power of acceptance is terminated by his rejection of the offer, unless the offeror has manifested a contrary intention.

(2) A manifestation of intention not to accept an offer is a rejection unless the offeree manifests an intention to take it under further advisement.

§39 Counter-offers

(1) A counter-offer is an offer made by an offeree to his offeror relating to the same matter as the original offer and proposing a substituted bargain differing from that proposed by the original offer.

(2) An offeree's power of acceptance is terminated by his making of a counteroffer, unless the offeror has manifested a contrary intention or unless the counteroffer manifests a contrary intention of the offeree.

---

① counter-offer：反要约。
② lapse of time：期间届满,时效终止。

§40 Time When Rejection or Counter-offer Terminates the Power of Acceptance

Rejection or counter-offer by mail or telegram does not terminate the power of acceptance until received by the offeror, but limits the power so that a letter or telegram of acceptance started after the sending of an otherwise effective rejection or counter-offer is only a counter-offer unless the acceptance is received by the offeror before he receives the rejection or counter-offer.

§41 Lapse of Time

(1) An offeree's power of acceptance is terminated at the time specified in the offer, or, if no time is specified, at the end of a reasonable time.

(2) What is a reasonable time is a question of fact, depending on all the circumstances existing when the offer and attempted acceptance are made.

(3) Unless otherwise indicated by the language or the circumstances, and subject to[①] the rule stated in §49, an offer sent by mail is seasonably accepted if an acceptance is mailed at any time before midnight on the day on which the offer is received.

§42 Revocation by Communication from Offeror Received by Offeree

An offeree's power of acceptance is terminated when the offeree receives from the offeror a manifestation of an intention not to enter into the proposed contract.

§43 Indirect Communication of Revocation

An offeree's power of acceptance is terminated when the offeror takes definite action inconsistent with an intention to enter into the proposed contract and the offeree acquires reliable information to that effect.

§45 Option Contract Created by Part Performance or Tender

(1) Where an offer invites an offeree to accept by rendering a performance and does not invite a promissory acceptance[②], an option contract is created when the offeree tenders or begins the invited performance or tenders a beginning of it.

(2) The offeror's duty of performance under any option contract so created is conditional on completion or tender of the invited performance in accordance with the terms of the offer.

§46 Revocation of General Offer

Where an offer is made by advertisement in a newspaper or other general notification to the public or to a number of persons whose identity is unknown to the offeror, the offeree's power of acceptance is terminated when a notice of termination is given publicity by advertisement or other general notification equal to that given to the offer and no better means of notification is reasonably available.

§48 Death or Incapacity[③] of Offeror or Offeree

An offeree's power of acceptance is terminated when the offeree or offeror dies or is deprived of legal capacity to enter into the proposed contract.

---

① subject to: 依据, 根据。
② Promissory acceptance: 允诺性的承诺。
③ incapacity: 丧失行为能力。

§50 Acceptance of Offer Defined; Acceptance by Performance; Acceptance by Promise①

(1) Acceptance of an offer is a manifestation of assent to the terms thereof made by the offeree in a manner invited or required by the offer.

(2) Acceptance by performance requires that at least part of what the offer requests be performed or tendered and includes acceptance by a performance which operates as a return promise.

(3) Acceptance by a promise requires that the offeree complete every act essential to the making of the promise.

§51 Effect of Part Performance without Knowledge of Offer

Unless the offeror manifests a contrary intention, an offeree who learns of an offer after he has rendered part of the performance requested by the offer may accept by completing the requested performance.

§52 Who May Accept an Offer②

An offer can be accepted only by a person whom it invites to furnish the consideration.

§53 Acceptance by Performance; Manifestation of Intention Not to Accept

(1) An offer can be accepted by the rendering of a performance only if the offer invites such an acceptance.

(2) Except as stated in §69, the rendering of a performance does not constitute an acceptance if within a reasonable time the offeree exercises reasonable diligence to notify the offeror of non-acceptance.

(3) Where an offer of a promise invites acceptance by performance and does not invite a promissory acceptance, the rendering of the invited performance does not constitute an acceptance if before the offeror performs his promise the offeree manifests an intention not to accept.

§54 Acceptance by Performance; Necessity of Notification to Offeror

(1) Where an offer invites an offeree to accept by rendering a performance, no notification is necessary to make such an acceptance effective unless the offer requests such a notification.

(2) If an offeree who accepts by rendering a performance has reason to know that the offeror has no adequate means of learning of the performance with reasonable promptness and certainty, the contractual duty of the offeror is discharged unless

(a) the offeree exercises reasonable diligence to notify the offeror of acceptance, or

(b) the offeror learns of the performance within a reasonable time, or

(c) the offer indicates that notification of acceptance is not required.

§55 Acceptance of Non-Promissory Offers③

Acceptance by promise may create a contract in which the offeror's performance is completed when the offeree's promise is made.

---

① Acceptance of Offer Defined; Acceptance by Performance; Acceptance by Promise:承诺的定义;通过履行义务而为承诺;通过允诺作出承诺。

② Who May Accept an Offer:有权作出承诺的人。

③ Non-Promissory Offers:非允诺要约。

§56 Acceptance by Promise; Necessity of Notification to Offeror

Except as stated in §69 or where the offer manifests a contrary intention, it is essential to an acceptance by promise either that the offeree exercise reasonable diligence to notify the offeror of acceptance or that the offeror receive the acceptance seasonably.

§58 Necessity of Acceptance Complying with Terms of Offer

An acceptance must comply with the requirements of the offer as to the promise to be made or the performance to be rendered.

§59 Purported Acceptance Which Adds Qualifications①

A reply to an offer which purports to accept it but is conditional on the offeror's assent to terms additional to or different from those offered is not an acceptance but is a counter-offer.

§60 Acceptance of Offer Which States Place, Time or Manner of Acceptance

If an offer prescribes the place, time or manner of acceptance its terms in this respect must be complied with in order to create a contract. If an offer merely suggests a permitted place, time or manner of acceptance, another method of acceptance is not precluded.

§61 Acceptance Which Requests Change of Terms

An acceptance which requests a change or addition to the terms of the offer is not thereby invalidated unless the acceptance is made to depend on an assent to the changed or added terms.

§62 Effect of Performance by Offeree Where Offer Invites Either Performance or Promise

(1) Where an offer invites an offeree to choose between acceptance by promise and acceptance by performance, the tender or beginning of the invited performance or a tender of a beginning of it is an acceptance by performance.

(2) Such an acceptance operates as a promise to render complete performance.

§63 Time When Acceptance Takes Effect

Unless the offer provides otherwise,

(a) an acceptance made in a manner and by a medium invited by an offer is operative and completes the manifestation of mutual assent as soon as put out of the offeree's possession, without regard to whether it ever reaches the offeror; but

(b) an acceptance under an option contract is not operative until received by the offeror.

§66 Acceptance Must be Properly Dispatched②

An acceptance sent by mail or otherwise from a distance is not operative when dispatched, unless it is properly addressed and such other precautions③ taken as are ordinarily observed to insure safe transmission of similar messages.

---

① Purported Acceptance Which Adds Qualifications:附带有限制条件所称的承诺。

② dispatch:作为动词使用时,表示"火速发出信件,电讯等,急速送出公文等,快速派出军队等"意思。作为名词使用时,表示"迅速发送,火速派遣;急报,快信,急件,新闻电讯;特电,特别公报;就地处决犯人"等意思。如:the date of the dispatch of the parcel(包裹发出的日期);a dispatch carrier(急件递送员);quick dispatch of business(快速处理事务);send (sth.) by dispatch (用快件寄发);with dispatch(火速,从速)。

③ precaution:预防措施。

§69 Acceptance by Silence or Exercise of Dominion[①]

(1) Where an offeree fails to reply to an offer, his silence and inaction operate as an acceptance in the following cases only:

(a) Where an offeree takes the benefit of offered services with reasonable opportunity to reject them and reason to know that they were offered with the expectation of compensation.

(b) Where the offeror has stated or given the offeree reason to understand that assent may be manifested by silence or inaction, and the offeree in remaining silent and inactive intends to accept the offer.

(c) Where because of previous dealings or otherwise, it is reasonable that the offeree should notify the offeror if he does not intend to accept.

(2) An offeree who does any act inconsistent with the offeror's ownership of offered property is bound in accordance with the offered terms unless they are manifestly unreasonable. But if the act is wrongful as against the offeror it is an acceptance only if ratified by him.

Chapter 4 Formation of Contracts—Consideration

§71 Requirement of Exchange; Types of Exchange

(1) To constitute consideration, a performance or a return promise must be bargained for.

(2) A performance or return promise is bargained for if it is sought by the promisor in exchange for his promise and is given by the promisee in exchange for that promise.

(3) The performance may consist of

(a) an act other than a promise, or

(b) a forbearance[②], or

(c) the creation, modification, or destruction of a legal relation.

(4) The performance or return promise may be given to the promisor or to some other person. It may be given by the promisee or by some other person.

§73 Performance of Legal Duty

Performance of a legal duty owed to a promisor which is neither doubtful nor the subject of honest dispute is not consideration; but a similar performance is consideration if it differs from what was required by the duty in a way which reflects more than a pretense of bargain.

§74 Settlement of Claims[③]

(1) Forbearance to assert or the surrender of a claim or defense which proves to be invalid is not consideration unless

(a) the claim or defense is in fact doubtful because of uncertainty as to the facts or the law, or

---

① Acceptance by Silence or Exercise of Dominion:通过沉默或实施控制权/支配权作出承诺。Dominion:表示"统治权,主权,支配;管辖(over);所有权。pl. 疆土,领土,版图;领地。英帝国的自治领:加拿大"等的意思,如 to have/hold/exercise/dominion over(具有对……的支配权,对……使行使统治权);the overseas dominions(海外领地);Dominion Day(加拿大自治纪念日——七月一日)。Dominion of Canada(加拿大自治领,俗称为 the Dominion);Dominion Parliament(加拿大议会);the Old Dominion(美国 Virginia 州的通称)。

② forbearance:权力之不行使或行为之容忍,不作为。

③ Settlement of Claims:请求权争议的解决。

(b) the forbearing or surrendering party believes that the claim or defense may be fairly determined to be valid.

(2) The execution of a written instrument surrendering a claim or defense by one who is under no duty to execute it is consideration if the execution of the written instrument is bargained for even though he is not asserting the claim or defense and believes that no valid claim or defense exists.

§77 Illusory and Alternative Promises①

A promise or apparent promise is not consideration if by its terms the promisor or purported promisor reserves a choice of alternative performances unless

(a) each of the alternative performances would have been consideration if it alone had been bargained for; or

(b) one of the alternative performances would have been consideration and there is or appears to the parties to be a substantial possibility that before the promisor exercises his choice events may eliminate the alternatives which would not have been consideration.

§79 Adequacy of Consideration; Mutuality of Obligation②

If the requirement of consideration is met, there is no additional requirement of

(a) a gain, advantage, or benefit to the promisor or a loss, disadvantage, or detriment to the promisee; or

(b) equivalence in the values exchanged; or

(c) "mutuality of obligation."

§81 Consideration as Motive or Inducing Cause③

(1) The fact that what is bargained for does not of itself induce the making of a promise does not prevent it from being consideration for the promise.

(2) The fact that a promise does not of itself induce a performance or return promise does not prevent the performance or return promise from being consideration for the promise.

§82 Promise to Pay Indebtedness; Effect on the Statute of Limitations④

(1) A promise to pay all or part of an antecedent contractual or quasi-contractual⑤ indebtedness owed by the promisor is binding if the indebtedness is still enforceable or would be except for the effect of a statute of limitations.

(2) The following facts operate as such a promise unless other facts indicate a different intention:

(a) A voluntary acknowledgment to the obligee, admitting the present existence of the antecedent indebtedness; or

(b) A voluntary transfer of money, a negotiable instrument, or other thing by the obligor to

---

① Illusory and Alternative Promises: 空泛和选择性允诺。
② Adequacy of Consideration; Mutuality of Obligation: 约因/对价的适当性/适切性; 义务的相互性。
③ Consideration as Motive or Inducing Cause: 作为诱因的约因/对价。
④ Promise to Pay Indebtedness; Effect on the Statute of Limitations: 给付债务之允诺; 时效法的效力。
⑤ Quasi-contract: 准合同。

the obligee①, made as interest on or part payment of or collateral security for the antecedent indebtedness; or

(c) A statement to the obligee that the statute of limitations will not be pleaded as a defense.

§83   Promise to Pay Indebtedness Discharged in Bankruptcy

An express promise to pay all or part of an indebtedness of the promisor, discharged or dischargeable in bankruptcy proceedings begun before the promise is made, is binding.

§84   Promise to Perform a Duty in Spite of Non-occurrence of a Condition②

(1) Except as stated in Subsection (2), a promise to perform all or part of a conditional duty under an antecedent contract in spite of the non-occurrence of the condition is binding, whether the promise is made before or after the time for the condition to occur, unless

(a) occurrence of the condition was a material part of the agreed exchange for the performance of the duty and the promisee was under no duty that it occur; or

(b) uncertainty of the occurrence of the condition was an element of the risk assumed by the promisor.

(2) If such a promise is made before the time for the occurrence of the condition has expired and the condition is within the control of the promisee or a beneficiary, the promisor can make his duty again subject to the condition by notifying the promisee or beneficiary of his intention to do so if

(a) the notification is received while there is still a reasonable time to cause the condition to occur under the antecedent terms or an extension given by the promisor; and

(b) reinstatement of the requirement of the condition is not unjust because of a material change of position by the promisee or beneficiary; and

(c) the promise is not binding apart from the rule stated in Subsection (1).

§86   Promise for Benefit Received

(1) A promise made in recognition of a benefit previously received by the promisor from the promisee is binding to the extent necessary to prevent injustice.

(2) A promise is not binding under Subsection (1)

(a) if the promisee conferred the benefit as a gift or for other reasons the promisor has not been unjustly enriched; or

(b) to the extent that its value is disproportionate to the benefit.

§87   Option Contract

(1) An offer is binding as an option contract if it

(a) is in writing and signed by the offeror, recites a purported consideration for the making of the offer, and proposes an exchange on fair terms within a reasonable time; or

(b) is made irrevocable by statute.

(2) An offer which the offeror should reasonably expect to induce action or forbearance of a

---

① Obligor and obligee：债务人和债权人。
② Promise to Perform a Duty in Spite of Non-occurrence of a Condition：条件不成就时而履行义务之允诺。

substantial character on the part of the offeree before acceptance and which does induce such action or forbearance is binding as an option contract to the extent necessary to avoid injustice.

§89 Modification of Executory Contract①

A promise modifying a duty under a contract not fully performed on either side is binding

(a) if the modification is fair and equitable in view of② circumstances not anticipated by the parties when the contract was made; or

(b) to the extent provided by statute; or

(c) to the extent that justice requires enforcement in view of material change of position in reliance on the promise.

§90 Promise Reasonably Inducing Action or Forbearance

(1) A promise which the promisor should reasonably expect to induce action or forbearance on the part of the promisee or a third person and which does induce such action or forbearance is binding if injustice can be avoided only by enforcement of the promise. The remedy granted for breach may be limited as justice requires.

(2) A charitable subscription or a marriage settlement is binding under Subsection (1) without proof that the promise induced action or forbearance.

§95 Requirements for Sealed Contract or Written Contract or Instrument③

[The Introduction to this topic notes that the effect of a seal is governed by statute in most states.]

(1) In the absence of statute a promise is binding without consideration if

(a) it is in writing and sealed; and

(b) the document containing the promise is delivered; and

(c) the promisor and promisee are named in the document or so described as to be capable of identification when it is delivered.

(2) When a statute provides in effect that a written contract or instrument is binding without consideration or that lack of consideration is an affirmative defense to an action on a written contract or instrument, in order to be subject to the statute a promise must either

(a) be expressed in a document signed or otherwise assented to by the promisor and delivered; or

(b) be expressed in a writing or writings to which both promisor and promisee manifest assent.

---

① Executory Contract:待履行合同。
② in view of:鉴于,考虑到。
③ Requirements for Sealed Contract or Written Contract or Instrument:盖印合同或书面合同之要求。

Legal Terminology

1. agreement 与 contract

均表达两个或以上的当事人合意的文件,在英美法中,agreement 常常用作 contract 的同义词,但其内涵远比 contract 宽广,也可以用来指不具备合同要素或要件的某些协议。一份协议要成为合同,则需符合合同的要件构成规定。有时还需要当事人在整个交易过程中通过语言或经过交易过程或商业习惯等的默示予以补充条件。

2. remedy, redress 与 relief

三个词语均可以表示"司法救济"的意思,但区别在于:relief 主要指衡平法上的救济,如以 injunction(强制令)或 specific performance(合同或协议的强制履行)等方式而非以损害赔偿金进行的救济;remedy 这既可以指衡平法上的救济,也可指普通法上的救济。如 the most common remedies are judgments that plaintiffs are entitled to collect sums of money from defendants(普通法上的救济) and orders to defendants to refrain from their wrongful conduct or to undo consequences(衡平法上的救济)。Redress 也可以指衡平法和普通法上的救济,其通常用以替代 remedy 和 relief。在 Black's Law Dictionary 中,redress 等于 remedy 或 relief。如:Money damages as opposed to equitable relief, is the only redress available.(金钱赔偿,相对于衡平法上的救济,才是唯一可获得的救济手段),该句中的 redress 这属于普通法上的救济。

作为动词使用时,rmedy 还以表示"治疗,补救,矫正,改善,修补,修缮"等意思。此时,应该注意其与下列词语之间的辨析:

Correct, rectify, remedy, revise, amend

这些动词均含"纠正,改正"之意。但:

correct 指纠正或改正不正确、不真实或有缺点的东西。

rectify 正式用词,意义较抽象,侧重指彻底改正偏离子正确标准或规则的东西。

remdedy 正式用词,通常指在局部范围内进行纠正,尤指对困难或棘手问题的解决。

rervise 指通过仔细阅读、反复思考后而进行改正、订正或修订,使趋于完善。

amend 书面语用词。指进行更正或改变,使之更好,符合更高的要求。

有关 remedy 的童谣或谚语:

For Every Evil Under the Sun

For every evil under the sun
There is a *remedy* or there is none.
If there be one, seek till you find it;
If there be none, never mind it.

Notes:

A slightly different version from *The Little Mother Goose* (1912), illustrated by Jessie Willcox Smith and illustrated by Blanche Fisher Wright. The illustration can be found in *The Sleeping Beauty Picture Book*, illustrated by Walter Crane.

中文翻译：世间的一切弊病，有的可以救药，有的不可救药；有救药的，努力去找；无救药的，就别太烦恼。

3. ability, capacity, capability, genius, talent, competence, faculty, gift 与 aptitude

上述各词均可以表示"能力"的意思，但各自在语言应用中具有如下区别：

ability：普通用词，指人先天的或后天学来的各种能够做好某事的能力，在法律中尤指实施法律行为的能力(power to carry out a legal act);

capacity：侧重指人的潜在能力，通常不指体力，多指才智，尤指接受与领悟能力，表示在法律上或其他意义上的一种资格；capacity 比 ability 更加正式，表示具有做某事所必需的特质：如：the capacity for hard work（能吃苦耐劳）；

capability：多用于人，指胜任某项具体工作的能力，也指本身具有、尚未发挥的潜在能力，常与 of 或 for 连用，表示能完成的工作量及工作质量：a job beyond the capability of one man（个人力所不及的工作）；

genius：语气最强，指高度的天赋、才能与智力；

talent：着重指人某方面具有可发展和培养的突出天赋才能，但语意比 genius 弱；

competence：正式用词，侧重指令人满意的业务能力与水平，达到胜任某项工作等的要求；法律上，表示"权能、权限"的意思；

faculty：主要指具有某种特殊行为的天赋能力；

gift：着重个人的天赋的才能或在某方面的显著本领，常暗含不能用一般规律作解释的意味；

aptitude：多指先天或后天习得的运用自如的能力，常暗示接受能力强，能迅速掌握一种学术训练或艺术技巧。

4. discharge of contract

discharge of contract 指"解除合同"，使得各方当事人不再有合同间的义务关系。在法律中，discharge 具有"排放废水；解除；清偿；撤职，辞退，开除；卸货；撤销；清偿债务；履行职责，完成任务；释放"等意思，拟根据语境判断其意义。如 The discharge of a contract means in general that the parties are freed from mutual obligations. (合同的解除/解约一般指的是双方当事人免去相互承担的义务。)

Discharge generally refers to the act or an instance of removing an obligation, burden, or responsibility. It may mean the fulfillment of the terms of something, such as a debt or promise or a performance, as of an office or duty(In relation to employees and persons in appointed and other positions, it refers to dismissal or release from employment, service, care, or confinement. It is also an official document certifying such release, especially from military service. Discharge, in labor law, refers to the dismissal of an employee, usually for breaking the rules or policies of management, incompetence, or some other reason. Collective bargaining agreements usually protect employees from arbitrary or discriminatory discharge. Legal strikers are protected from discharge, although they may be replaced during a strike and regain employment rights only if vacancies open within a certain period of time. Discharge is used in other legal contexts, such as the discharge of a lien or debt, as in the discharge of a debtor in bankruptcy.

中文翻译：Discharg 一般指清除债务、负担或责任的行为或情况；也可以指履行了某些条件，如债务、允诺的履行或者从事某职位或岗位的事务的完成。就雇员或指定某职位工作者而言，特指解雇，解聘；其还可以证明一个人不再服兵役等之类的官方文件。Discharge 亦指劳动法上因为某一员工违反规则、政策或不称职或其他原因被解雇（因为集体磋商协议常常可以保护他们免受武断或不具有任何理由的解雇，如合法罢工者也不得解除其工作，即使罢工期间被人替代。Discharge 还可以用于其他法律语境，如留置权或债务的清偿）。

此外，discharge 表示"解雇，解聘"的意思时应注意其与 dismiss 和 fire 的区别：

三个词均可表示解聘或解雇的意思，但 discharge 语气较重，指有理由的解雇，含几乎不再复用的意味；discharge：正式用词，是这组词中语气最轻的一个词，一般只有从上文才能看解雇的原因或理由；而 fire：口语用词，多指被断然地突然解雇，其行动犹如开枪一样干净利落。

5. promise, acceptance 与 offer

三个词均为合同法中的常用词，promise 指要约人向被要约人所作的邀约，是一种主动的"允诺"或"许诺"，一种说了就必然去做或给予的陈述（A promise is a statement which you make to a person in which you say that you will definitely do something or give them something）；acceptance 则为"承诺"，是被要约人对邀约的一种认可；而 offer 则与 promise 相同，主动对他人的一种"邀约"。

Exercises

I Verbal Abilities

Part One

Directions: *For each of these completing questions, read each item carefully to get the sense of it. Then, in the proper space, complete each statement by supplying the missing word or phrase.*

1. A contract is an agreement entered into _____ by two parties or more with the intention of creating a legal obligation.
  A. optional B. voluntarily C. compulsory D. voluntary E. required
2. The remedy for _____ of contract can be "damages" or compensation of money.
  A. accept B. breach C. implementation D. complete E. break
3. In equity, the remedy can be _____ performance of the contract or an injunction.
  A. concrete B. specific C. special D. exact E. extremely

4. Both of these remedies award the party at loss the "benefit of the bargain" or expectation damages, which are greater than mere reliance damages, as in _____ estoppel.

  A. promissory   B. proposed   C. promise   D. valid   E. promis

5. The parties may be natural persons or _____ persons.

  A. corporate   B. natural   C. juristic   D. artificial   E. conventional

6. A contract is a legally _____ promise or undertaking that something will or will not occur.

  A. voluntary   B. coercible   C. enforceable   D. compellable   E. unbidden

7. The word promise can be used as a legal synonym for contract. , although care is required as a promise may not have the full standing of a contract, as when it is an agreement without _____.

  A. consideration   B. concern   C. quid pro-puo   D. conclusion   E. acceptance

8. Contract law varies largely from one jurisdiction to another, including differences in common law compared to _____ law, the impact of received law, particularly from England in common law countries, and of law codified in regional legislation.

  A. criminal   B. civil   C. case   D. martial   E. canon

9. Contract theory is the body of legal theory that _____ normative and conceptual questions in contract law.

  A. addresses   B. mentioned   C. prepares   D. occur   E. aforesaid

10. One of the most important questions asked in contract theory is why contracts are _____.

  A. accpeted   B. implementation   C. enforced   D. impregnated   E. imputed

Part Two

Directions: *Choose the one word or phase that best keep the meaning of the original sentence if it were substituted for the underlined part.*

1. Law is the system of rules of conduct established by the sovereign government of a society to correct wrongs, maintain the <u>stability</u> of political and social authority, and deliver justice.

  A. constancy   B. weak   C. fragile   D. delicate   E. vulnerable

2. Working as a lawyer involves the practical application of abstract legal theories and knowledge to solve specific individualized problems, or to advance the interests of those who retain lawyers to <u>perform</u> legal services.

  A. deliver   B. accomplish   C. neglect   D. slight   E. pass over

3. The role of the lawyer varies <u>significantly</u> across legal jurisdictions, and so it can be treated here in only the most general terms.

  A. overwhelming   B. largely   C. tiny
  D. in general   E. far

4. A <u>treaty</u> is an express agreement under international law entered into in international law, namely sovereign states and international organizations.

  A. agreement   B. derangement   C. arrangement   D. negotiate   E. record

5. Treaties can be loosely compared to contracts: both are means of willing parties assuming obligations among themselves, and a party to either that fails to live up to their obligations can be held liable under international law.
  A. intention B. willing C. method D. meager E. deed

6. Since the late 19th century, most treaties have followed a fairly consistent format.
  A. senseless B. inconsistent C. illogical D. uniform E. invalid

7. A treaty is an official, express written agreement that states use to legally bind themselves.
  A. criminal B. illegal C. lawfully D. valid E. unlawful

8. A treaty typically begins with a preamble describing the contracting parties and their joint objectives in executing the treaty, as well as summarizing any underlying events.
  A. as same as B. in addition C. otherwise D. moreover E. as to

9. A treaty is that official document which expresses that agreement in words; and it is also the objective outcome of a ceremonial occasion which acknowledges the parties and their defined relationships.
  A. conclusion B. beginning C. outset D. commence E. outcast

10. The contracting parties' full names or sovereign titles are often included in the preamble, along with the full names and titles of their representatives, and a boilerplate clause about how their representatives have communicated (or exchanged) their full powers and found them in good or proper form.
  A. exclude B. keep out C. contain D. reject E. prohibit

II Cloze

Directions: *For each blank in the following passage, there are several answers marked A, B, C, D, and E. You are to choose the best answer from the choices given to complete the sentence.*

Chapter 5 The Stattute of Frauds

§131 General Requisites of a Memorandum

Unless additional requirements are prescribed by the particular statute, a contract within the Statute of Frauds is enforceable if it is evidenced by any writing, signed by or ___(1)___ the party to be charged, which

(a) reasonably identifies the subject matter of the contract,

(b) is sufficient to indicate that a contract with respect thereto has been made between the parties or offered by the signer to the other party, and

(c) states with reasonable certainty the essential terms of the unperformed promises in the contract.

§132 Several Writings

The memorandum may consist of several writings if one of the writings is signed and the writings in the circumstances clearly indicate that they relate to the same transaction.

§139 Enforcement ___(2)___ Action in Reliance

(1) A promise which the ___(3)___ should reasonably expect to induce action or forbearance

on the part of the promisee or a third person and which does induce the action or forbearance is enforceable notwithstanding the Statute of Frauds if injustice can be avoided only by enforcement of the promise. The __(4)__ granted for breach is to be limited as justice requires.

(2) In determining whether injustice can be avoided only by enforcement of the promise, the following circumstances are significant:

(a) the availability and adequacy of other remedies, particularly cancellation and restitution;

(b) the definite and substantial character of the action or forbearance in relation to the remedy sought;

(c) The extent to which the action of forbearance __(5)__ evidence of the making and terms of the promise, or the making and terms are otherwise established by clear and convincing evidence;

(d) the reasonableness of the action or forbearance;

(e) the extent to which the action of forbearance was foreseeable by the promisor.

CHAPTER 6 MISTAKE

§151 Mistake Defined

A mistake is a belief that is not __(6)__ the facts.

§152 When Mistake of Both Parties Makes a Contract Voidable

(1) Where a mistake of both parties at the time a contract was made as to a basic assumption on which the contract was made has a material effect on the agreed exchange of performances, the contract is voidable by the adversely affected party unless he bears the risk of the mistake under the rule stated in §154.

(2) In determining whether the mistake has a __(7)__ effect on the agreed exchange of performances, account is taken of any relief by way of reformation, restitution, or otherwise.

§153 When Mistake of One Party Makes a Contract Voidable

Where a mistake of one party at the time a contract was made as to a basic assumption on which he made the contract has a material effect on the agreed exchange of performances that is adverse to him, the contract is voidable by him if he does not bear the risk of the mistake under the rule stated in §154, and

(a) the effect of the mistake is such that enforcement of the contract would be __(8)__, or

(b) the other party had reason to know of the mistake or his fault caused the mistake.

§154 When a Party Bears the Risk of a Mistake

A party bears the risk of a mistake when

(a) the risk is __(9)__ him by agreement of the parties, or

(b) he is aware, at the time the contract is made, that he has only limited knowledge __(10)__ the facts to which the mistake relates but treats his limited knowledge as sufficient, or

(c) the risk is allocated to him by the court __(11)__ that it is reasonable in the circumstances to do so.

§155 When Mistake of Both Parties as to Written Expression justifies __(12)__

Where a writing that evidences or embodies an agreement in whole or in part fails to express the agreement because of a mistake of both parties as to the contents or effect of the writing, the court may at the request of a party reform the writing to express the agreement, except to the extent that rights of third parties such as ___(13)___ purchasers for value will be unfairly affected.

§157 Effect of Fault of Party Seeking Relief

A mistaken party's fault in failing to know or discover the facts before making the contract does not ___(14)___ him from avoidance or reformation under the rules stated in this Chapter, unless his fault amounts to a failure to act in good faith and in accordance with reasonable standards of fair dealing.

§158 Relief Including Restitution

(1) In any case governed by the rules stated in this Chapter, either party may have a claim for relief including restitution under the rules stated in §§240 and 376.

(2) In any case governed by the rules stated in this Chapter, if those rules together with the rules stated in Chapter 16 will not avoid injustice, the court may grant relief on such terms as justice requires including protection of the parties' ___(15)___ interests.

(1) A. represent   B. on behalf of   C. toward
    D. voluntary   E. required
(2) A. accident   B. by chance   C. by virtue of
    D. as far as   E. as to
(3) A. party   B. signer   C. promisee
    D. promisor   E. offeree
(4) A. remind   B. remedy   C. damage
    D. codify   E. correct
(5) A. corroborates B. invalid   C. validation
    D. make sure   E. sustain
(6) A. inconformity B. in line   C. in accord with
    D. disaccord   E. consistency
(7) A. damage   B. material   C. practice
    D. enforceable   E. unbidden
(8) A. unconscionable B. reasonable   C. greatly
    D. badly   E. conscionable
(9) A. turn back   B. allocated to   C. assign to
    D. delivered to E. passed over
(10) A. concern with B. withheld   C. with a view to
     D. withdraw   E. with respect to
(11) A. on the ground B. On the side   C. On top of
     D. Moreover   E. Attached
(12) A. information B. reformation   C. reform
     D. convert   E. revise
(13) A. good faith   B. bad faith   C. good belief
     D. religion   E. under no case

(14) A. solid B. curb C. bar
     D. block E. hinder
(15) A. reliance B. valid C. reliant
     D. relic E. reliable

III Reading Comprehension

Directions: *In this part, there are some questions or unfinished statements, each with four suggested answers. Choose the one you think is the best answer.*

Passage One

The future of human beings is what matters

For me, capitalism has never been an abstract concept. It is a real, concrete part of everyday life. When I was a boy, my family left the rural misery of Brazil's north-east and set off for São Paulo. My mother, an extraordinary woman of great courage, uprooted herself and her children and moved to the industrial centre of Brazil in search of a better life. My childhood was no different from that of many boys from poor families: informal jobs; very little formal education. My only diploma was as a machine lathe operator, from a course at the National Service for Industry.

I began to experience the reality of factory life, which awoke in me my vocation as a union leader. I became a member of the Metalworkers' Union of São Bernardo, in the outskirts of São Paulo. I became the union's president and, as such, led the strikes of 1978—1980 that changed the face of the Brazilian labour movement and played a big role in returning democracy to the country, then under military dictatorship.

The impact of the union movement on Brazilian society led us to create the Workers' party, which brought together urban and rural workers, intellectuals and militants from civil society. Brazilian capitalism, at that time, was not only a matter of low salaries, insalubrious working conditions and repression of the union movement. It was also expressed in economic policy and in the whole set of the government's public policies, as well as in the restrictions it placed on civil liberties. Together with millions of other workers, I discovered it was not enough merely to demand better salaries and working conditions. It was fundamental that we should fight for citizenship and for a profound reorganisation of economic and social life.

I fought and lost four elections before being elected president of the republic in 2002. In opposition, I came to know my country intimately. In discussions with intellectuals I thrashed out the alternatives for our society, living out on the periphery of the world a drama of stagnation and profound social inequality. But my greatest understanding of Brazil came from direct contact with its people through the "caravans of citizenship" that took me across tens of thousands of kilometres.

When I arrived in the presidency, I found myself faced not only by serious structural problems but, above all, by an inheritance of ingrained inequalities. Most of our governors, even those that enacted reforms in the past, had governed for the few. They concerned themselves with a Brazil in which only a third of the population mattered.

The situation I inherited was one not only of material difficulties but also of deep-rooted prejudices that threatened to paralyse our government and lead us into stagnation. We could not grow, it was said, without threatening economic stability—much less grow and distribute wealth. We would have to choose between the internal market and the external. Either we accepted the unforgiving imperatives of the globalised economy or we would be condemned to fatal isolation.

Over the past six years, we have destroyed those myths. We have grown and enjoyed economic stability. Our growth has been accompanied by the inclusion of tens of millions of Brazilian people in the consumer market. We have distributed wealth to more than 40m who lived below the poverty line. We have ensured that the national minimum wage has risen always above the rate of inflation. We have democratised access to credit. We have created more than 10m jobs. We have pushed forward with land reform. The expansion of our domestic market has not happened at the expense of exports—they have tripled in six years. We have attracted enormous volumes of foreign investment with no loss of sovereignty.

All this has enabled us to accumulate $207bn (164bn, £150bn) in foreign reserves and thereby protect ourselves from the worst effects of a financial crisis that, born at the centre of capitalism, threatens the entire structure of the global economy.

Nobody dares to predict today what will be the future of capitalism.

As the governor of a great economy described as "emerging", what I can say is what sort of society I hope will emerge from this crisis. It will reward production and not speculation. The function of the financial sector will be to stimulate productive activity—and it will be the object of rigorous controls, both national and international, by means of serious and representative organisations. International trade will be free of the protectionism that shows dangerous signs of intensifying. The reformed multilateral organisations will operate programmes to support poor and emerging economies with the aim of reducing the imbalances that scar the world today. There will be a new and democratic system of global governance. New energy policies, reform of systems of production and of patterns of consumption will ensure the survival of a planet threatened today by global warming.

But, above all, I hope for a world free of the economic dogmas that invaded the thinking of many and were presented as absolute truths. Anti-cyclical policies must not be adopted only when a crisis is under way. Applied in advance—as they have been in Brazil—they can be the guarantors of a more just and democratic society.

As I said at the outset, I do not give much importance to abstract concepts.

I am not worried about the name to be given to the economic and social order that will come after the crisis, so long as its central concern is with human beings. (By Luiz Inácio Lula da Silva, President of Brazil)

1. The article is a comment on a topic initiated by the Financial Times. Which of the following is the most likely topic?

　　A. The future of human beings

　　B. The future of finance

　　C. The future of capitalism

　　D. The future of Brazil

2. Why did the author talk about his life?

A. To illustrate his train of thoughts

B. To get closer to the audience by being personal

C. To strengthen his arguments

D. All of the above

3. Which of the following would the author DISAGREE?

A. Financial sectors should be regulated strictly.

B. Protectionism is a bad thing.

C. The current energy policy needs to be changed.

D. Free trade caused the current crisis.

4. The author's view can be generalized by which of the following famous statement?

A. It doesn't matter you are black or white. As long as you catches mice, you are a good cat.

B. Under capitalism, man exploits man. Under communism, it's just the opposite.

C. Capitalism is the astounding belief that the most wickedest of men will do the most wickedest of things for the greatest good of everyone.

D. Capitalism has destroyed our belief in any effective power but that of self interest backed by force.

Passage Two

Who will mourn local newspapers?

They say that journalists prefer bad news to good news. There is plenty of that close to home.

This is becoming a terrible week for the US newspaper industry. On Monday, the Tribune Company, which owns the Chicago Tribune and the Los Angeles Times, filed for bankruptcy. The New York Times Company followed by saying it might mortgage its Renzo Piano-designed headquarters building by Times Square to reduce debt.

The recession has turned the long, slow decline of newspapers into a brisk fall. On Tuesday, I dropped into a UBS investor conference in New York to catch Gary Pruitt, chief executive of the McClatchy newspaper chain, calling its results "lousy". At this rate, US newspapers will be lucky to make it to the weekend.

Many American journalists, facing job losses and the death of an industry they loved, regard it as a tragedy not just for them but for society. They fear that television, radio and blogs can never replace what newspapers provided for readers.

Bill Keller, executive editor of The New York Times, put the point succinctly to National Public Radio earlier this month: "Good journalism does not come cheap. And, therefore, you're not going to find a lot of blogs or non-profit websites that are going to build a Baghdad bureau."

Up to a point, Lord Keller. The failure of papers will deprive US readers—and those in countries where similar forces are at work—of plenty of useful information. But, let us face it, the industry also plays host to an immense amount of duplication and self-indulgence.

The internet brought trouble for regional and city papers not only because it gave an outlet to bloggers, and broke the monopoly they had on classified and display advertising, but because it let

Philadelphians, for example, peruse publications other than the Inquirer.

There are things you can only learn about Philadelphia from the Inquirer, or Chicago from the Tribune, or Miami from the Herald. If they went away, they would also take with them a check on local abuses of political power, as the phone-tapped desire of Rod Blagojevich, the governor of Illinois, to get his critics on the Tribune fired shows.

Nor is it obvious that such coverage could be produced by internet sites instead. In theory, information about local events can be just as efficiently distributed online as in print—in some ways, better. In practice, papers' dominance of local print advertising brought them a revenue base that is unlikely to be replicated.

This week, I had a chat with Joel Kramer, the founder of MinnPost, a news and analysis internet site devoted to politics and civic affairs in Minneapolis and St Paul. He was formerly publisher of the Minneapolis Star Tribune, which has cut jobs as it gets financially squeezed.

MinnPost is among a new breed of non-profit sites, including Voice of San Diego and ProPublica, which are trying to fill the gap left by the decline of city papers. He raised $1.5m (including $250,000 from himself) to start the site, which employs six editors and pays freelances to write.

It does some valuable work. But Mr Kramer admits that it functions more as a "complement" to the Star Tribune and its rival, the Pioneer Press, than as a substitute. He says that it tries to add depth and analysis to stories that are already in the news more than dig up news itself.

As Mr Keller says, reporting is expensive. It requires someone to get on the phone, gather information, balance conflicting views of what has just occurred, and present the result. Papers have done this basic work for cities and states for so long that we take it for granted.

Other aspects of US journalism will not, however, be missed. Some things, such as sports scores and weather forecasts, can be collated in a more timely and user-friendly way online. In addition, there is a swath of national and foreign coverage that is no longer needed.

There used to be a logic to the Chicago Tribune or the Miami Herald having large Washington bureaux and even foreign correspondents. People who lived in those places could not access The New York Times or The Washington Post online and relied instead on the local paper.

These days, they can do so free, which eliminates the need for a lot of coverage to be duplicated. Aggregation sites such as Google News have shone a harsh spotlight on the overlap and repetition in national coverage in hundreds of newspapers.

I am sure US citizens would lose something if fewer papers or wire services covered national affairs. But would it really be insufficient for society if five or six organisations (including Reuters and Bloomberg) competed to cover, for example, the Federal Reserve? I doubt it.

The question for national and international reporting is not whether city papers survive but whether news organisations such as The New York Times do. Clearly, if they did not, and blogs were left alone to provide coverage of Washington and Iraq, there would be a problem.

The honest answer is: we do not know. The New York Times, with its thriving online readership and global clout, seems in better shape than The New York Times Company, which has been indifferently managed by the Sulzberger family. A change of ownership might fix that.

My working assumption, in more ways than one, is that consolidation—or, more accurately, eradication—of local newspapers will strengthen the editorial position of the remaining elite: The New York Times, The Wall Street Journal, Bloomberg, the Financial Times etc.

I also assume that this elite will find some way to cover its costs. Here's hoping, anyway. (By John Gapper)

1. Which of the following best describes the author's attitude toward US newspaper?

A. Indifferent

B. Optimistic

C. Sarcastic

D. Pesimistic yet hopeful

2. Which of the following would the author agree?

A. Blogs can replace newspapers.

B. There's plenty of replacements for newspapers.

C. New York Times serves only local people.

D. Good papers like Financial Times should and probably will survive.

3. The author used Google News to show that:

A. More and more people go to the web for news.

B. News can come cheap.

C. Too many papers are wrting about the same things.

D. New types of media is going to fill the void left by newspapers.

4. According to the author, which of the following is most likely to happen?

A. Local newspapers in US disappear, but good ones like New York Times survive.

B. The entire newspaper industry is wiped out.

C. Google News became the only news source.

D. After the crisis, most newspapers survive.

IV Translation Abilities

法律语言特征分析与法律翻译技能培养之三:

法律和语言的关系

法律是通过语言建构的规范,其字面背后的逻辑规则和学理内容可以通过对法律语言的剖析而明了,其如美国语言学家 David Mellinkoff 所说,"法律是一种词语的职业"(Law is a profession of words)(Sarat,1996:1),由此导致国内外许多人达成一个共识,即"法律问题就是语言问题"(A legal problem is a linguistic problem.)。也有人认为"法律是仅为法律人讲用的专门语言"(Law is a specialized language that only lawyers can speak)(Morrison,1999:271)。由于法律事实就是一种"语言行为",因而 Sarat(1996)将严格意义上的法律界定为:"从最一般和该术语最容易理解和接受的字面意义上说,法律一词可以说是一个具有权力的理智的人对另外理智的人设定的一种向导"(吕世伦,2000)。Conley(1998:3)甚至说,If the law is failing to live up to its ideals, the failure must lie in the details of everyday legal practice—details that consist almost entirely of language(如果法律没有实现其理想,失败肯定应当归咎于日常实践之细节,即完全与语言相关的细节)(John M. Conley. 1998)。事实上,法律是一个展示言辞技巧、语言能力和辩护水平的舞台,其间,语言所起的作用是人类其他任何主要经验都无法相比的。

就语言对法律的关系和作用而言,人们归纳出以下四点:

(1) 语言是法律的载体:语言是法律的记录工具,所有的法典、法条、法律阐述都是通过语言(主要是狭义的有声语言符号和书面文字)记录而巩固保存的结果。

(2) 语言是法律思维的工具:语言和法律具有形至影随的关系,语言整理、规范人们对于法律纷繁复杂的感知经验,使人的法律意识、思想、感情、观念得以成为现实的存在体。

(3) 法律语言是法律人的生产资料和生产工具:法律人掌握法律语言的话语权,借助语言替当事人提供法律服务、解释法律以及依据法律判决案件。法律语言是法律人从事其生产和生活所必需的物质条件,是其劳动资料和劳动对象的总和。

(4) 语言是法律文化载体和发展工具:尽管法律语言包含在法律文化之中,但法律文化的精髓,包括法律体制、立法规范、法律价值、人们对法律的信仰和态度、对争议解决模式的选择倾向等却都是借助法律语言方才得以张扬和发展。

然而语言对于法律的最大功能却在于语言是人们阅读、理解和阐释法律的工具。作为一种语言构筑之规范,法律自身需要通过语言予以阐释,否则法律的效力便无法得到最大化的实施。正是通过语言,人们才得以将不同的事物规定和矛盾的主体需求——事实世界转换成符号文本,从而为人类通过法律创生秩序提供公共认知基础(谢晖,2003:325)。然而法律的理解和诠释,则有赖于语言的作用。正如加达默尔所说,语言是阐释得以进行的媒介,因而他把自己的诠释学归结于是以语言为主线的学问。人们通过语言阐释法律的确定性和不确定性,解决法律存在的模糊和疑问,从而最终确立法律在实践中的效力。离开语言的阐释,法律的作用必将大打折扣。

与此同时,法律也对语言的发展产生深刻影响。法律的产生与法律语言的问世犹如鸡生蛋与蛋生鸡一样难以确认,然而我们能肯定的一点就是它们之间的互动关系。首先是语言的强制作用:语言对法律具有某种程度的制约性,法律领域的所有活动必须遵从一定的语言法则,否则便会导致歧义和误解。此外,法律还必须屈从于语言的模糊性(vagueness)与不确定性(uncertainty),尽管由此会导致法律的含混与不确定。另一方面则是法律对于语言的强制作用。从其诞生之时起,法律就对其所使用的语言提出特殊要求,无论从技术层面或交流层面上讲,法律语言的出现都是为了适应法律客观需要的结果。一旦进入法律领域,语言即成为专门用途语言,导致以下一些情况出现:被迫丧失了一般语言原有的诸多特质,如失去语言的感情色彩,不带任何褒贬意想而呈现出一副"中性"面孔;丧失某些原有含义,而被赋予特定的法律涵义,如句子 Is it an assault or conversation?(究竟其是强奸或是通奸?)中的单词 assault(强奸)与 conversation(通奸)均被赋予了特定语境中的特殊含义;词义或者被扩大(extending)或缩小(narrowing),如在香港的 Commodities Trading Ordinance(《商品交易条例》)中,单词 constitution 被其"释义条款"界定为:"constitution," in relation to a company, means the memorandum and articles of association of the company or other instrument providing the constitution of the company("章程",在涉及一个公司时,指该公司的组织大纲和内部管理章程,或其他有关该公司章程规定的文件)。

Lesson Three About Contracts

Translation Exercises:

Part One *Put the Following into Chinese*

US inequality is at its highest point for nearly a century. Those at the top—no matter how you slice it—are enjoying a larger share of the national pie; the number below the poverty level is growing. The gap between those with the median income and those at the top is growing, too. The US used to think of itself as a middle-class country—but this is no longer true.

Economists have justified such disparities by citing "marginal productivity theory", which explains higher incomes through greater societal contributions. But those who have really transformed our society, by providing the knowledge that underpins the advances in technology, earn a relative pittance. Just think of the inventors of the laser, the Turing machine or the discoverers of DNA. The innovation of those on Wall Street, while well compensated, brought the global economy to the brink of ruin; and these financial entrepreneurs walked off with mega-incomes.

One might feel better about inequality if there were a grain of truth in trickle-down economics. But the median income of Americans today is lower than it was a decade and a half ago; and the median income of a full-time male worker is lower than it was more than four decades ago. Meanwhile, those at the top have never had it so good.

Some argue that increased inequality is an inevitable byproduct of the market. False: several countries are reducing inequality while maintaining economic growth.

Markets are shaped by the rules of the game. Our political system has written rules that benefit the rich at the expense of others. Financial regulations allow predatory lending and abusive credit-card practices that transfer money from the bottom to the top. So do bankruptcy laws that provide priority for derivatives. The rules of globalisation—where capital is freely mobile but workers are not-enhance an already large asymmetry of bargaining: businesses threaten to leave the country unless workers make strong concessions.

Textbooks teach us that we can have a more egalitarian society only if we give up growth or efficiency. However, closer analysis shows that we are paying a high price for inequality: it contributes to social, economic and political instability, and to lower growth. Western countries with the healthiest economies (for example those in Scandinavia) are also the countries with the highest degree of equality.

The US grew far faster in the decades after the second world war, when inequality was lower, than it did after 1980, since when the gains have gone disproportionately to the top. There is growing evidence looking across countries over time that suggests a link between equality, growth and stability.

There is good news in this: by reducing rent-seeking—finding ways of getting a larger share of the pie, rather than making the pie larger—and the distortions that give rise to so much of America's inequality we can achieve a fairer society and a better-performing economy. Laws that tax speculators at less than half the rate of those who work for a living or make the innovations that are transforming our society, say something about our values; but they also distort our economy, encouraging young people to move into gambling rather than into more productive areas. Since so much of the income at the top is derived from rent seeking, higher taxes at the top would discourage rent-seeking.

Part Two *Put the Following into English*

过去,人们觉得美国遍地是机会。可在如今的美国,一个孩子在人生机遇方面依赖父母收入的程度,超过欧洲或有数据记录的其他任何发达工业国家。昔日的美国努力创造机会均等的"美国梦"。但如今,"美国梦"只是个神话。

美国能够再次变成一个遍地是机会的地方,但这种变化不会自动发生。只要我们还在实行这样的政策——削减公共教育和有助于增加中下层发展机会的其他项目、同时削减收入最高人群适用的税率——这种变化就不会发生。美国总统巴拉克·奥巴马(Barack Obama)支持公共教育等投资,并支持"巴菲特规则"(要求针对收入最高人群的所得税税率至少达到普通人的水平),这些举措的方向都是正确的。共和党总统候选人米特·罗姆尼(Mitt Romney)提出要裁减公务员,同时在另一个问题上(投机产生的资本利得适用税率是否应低于辛勤工作所得)保持沉默,这些都令人担忧。

美国将不得不面临一个抉择:如果继续走近几十年的老路,机会的匮乏将意味着社会分化更加严重,经济增长率降低,社会、政治和经济更加不稳定。抑或,美国可以意识到:经济已失衡。黄金时代之后迎来进步时代,咆哮的二十年代(Roaring Twenties)的过分行为引发大萧条(Depression),而大萧条又引出罗斯福新政(New Deal)。每次发现自己正走向极端之后,这个国家都把自己拉回了正常轨道。问题是,这一次还会这样吗?

V Interaction

Discuss with your tutor(s) or the People's judges in your locality about the formation of contract. Then based on the discussion, you are supposed to write a composition about the technicalities in the formation of Chinese contract. Remember that you are required to express your ideas clearly.

VI Appreciation of Judge's Opinions

(1) Case Name(案件名): *Disan Williams v Roffey Bros & Nicholls (Contractors) Ltd*

Court	Court of Appeal
Full case name	*Williams v. Roffey Bros & Nicholls (Contractors) Ltd*
Citation(s)	[1989] EWCA Civ 5, [1991] 1 QB 1, [1990] 2 WLR 1153
Transcript(s)	Full text of judgment
Judge(s) sitting	Glidewell, Russell and Purchas, L. JJ.

BAILII Citation Number: [1989] EWCA Civ 5

Case No.

IN THE SUPREME COURT OF JUDICATURE
COURT OF APPEAL (CIVIL DIVISION)
ON APPEAL FROM THE KINGSTON-UPON-THAMES COUNTY COURT
MR. ASSISTANT RECORDER RUPERT JACKSON Q.C.

Royal Courts of Justice
23rd November 1989

Before:
LORD JUSTICE PURCHAS
LORD JUSTICE GLIDEWBLL
and
LORD JUSTICE RUSSELL

LESTER WILLIAMS	Respondent (Plaintiff)
and	
ROFFEY BROTHERS & NICHOLLS (CONTRACTORS) LIMITED	Appellants (Defendants)

(Transcript of the Shorthand Notes of The Association of Official Shorthandwriters Ltd., Room 329, Royal Courts of Justice, and 2, New Square, Lincoln's Inn, London WC2A 3RU)

MR. FRANKLIN EVANS (instructed by Messrs John Pearson & Co) appeared on behalf of the Appellants (Defendants).
MR. MR. CHRISTOPHER MAKEY (instructed by Messrs Terrence W. Lynch & Co.) appeared on behalf of the Respondent (Plaintiff).

HTML VERSION OF JUDGMENT

Crown Copyright
(Revised)

(2) Case Brief(案情简介)

Williams v Roffey Bros & Nicholls (Contractors) Ltd [1989] is a leading English contract law case, which decided that in varying a contract(变更合同), the court will be quick to find consideration(对价,约因) if "factual benefits", are given from one to another party.

Facts

Roffey Bros was contracted by Shepherds Bush Housing Association Ltd to refurbish 27(再刷新;整修;翻新) flats at Twynholm Mansions, Lillie Road, London SW6. They subcontracted carpentry(木工活) to Mr Lester Williams for £20,000 payable in installments(分期支付). Some work was done and £16,200 was paid. Then Williams ran into financial difficulty because the price was too low. Roffey Bros was going to be liable under a penalty clause for late completion, so they had a meeting on 9 April 1986 and promised an extra £575 per flat for on time completion(及时完工). Williams did eight flats and stopped because he had only got £1,500. New carpenters were brought in. Williams claimed.

Mr Rupert Jackson QC held Williams should get the eight times £575 with a few deductions for defects and some of the £2,200 owing from the original sum. He said that they had agreed that the original price was too low, and that raising it to a reasonable level was in both sides' interests.

Judgment

Glidewell LJ(Lord Justice 的缩写形式,在英国对法官的尊称)held Williams had provided good consideration even though he was merely performing a pre-existing duty. Williams got £3,500 (not full expectation damages). He said that the idea of promissory estoppel(不得自食其言;允诺后不得否认的原则;允诺禁反言;禁反悔) was not properly argued and 'not yet been fully developed'. The concept of economic duress(胁迫) provided an answer to Stilk's old problem. The test for understanding whether a contract could legitimately be varied was set out as follows:

a) if A has a contract with B for work

b) before it is done, A has reason to believe B may not be able to complete

c) A promises B more to finish on time

d) A 'obtains in practice a benefit, or obviates a disbenefit' from giving the promise

e) there is no economic duress or fraud...

f) The practical benefit of timely completion, even though a pre-existing duty is performed, constitutes good consideration.

On *Stik v. Myrick*, Glidewell LJ said,

"It is not in my view surprising that a principle enunciated in relation to the rigours of seafaring life during the Napoleonic wars should be subjected during the succeeding 180 years to a process of refinement and limitation in its application to the present day."

Russell LJ said 'the courts nowadays should be more ready to find consideration's existence so as to reflect the intention of the parties to the contract where the bargaining powers are not unequal'. He noted that Roffey Bros' employee, Mr Cottrell had felt the original price to be less than reasonable, and there was a further need to replace the 'haphazard method of payment by a more formalised scheme' of money per flat. "True it was that the plaintiff did not undertake to do any work additional to that which he had originally undertaken to do but the terms upon which he was to carry out the work were varied and, in my judgment, that variation was supported by consideration which a pragmatic approach to the true relationship between the parties readily demonstrates."

Purchas LJ concurred with Glidewell LJ.

(3) **Excerpts of the Judgment**(法官判决词)

LORD JUSTICE GLIDEWELL:

This is an appeal(上诉) against the decision of Mr. Rupert Jackson Q.C., an assistant recorder, given on 31st January 1989 at Kingston-upon-Thames County Court, entering judgment for the plaintiff(作为有利于原告的判决) for £3,500 damages with £1,400 interest and costs and dismissing the defendants' counterclaim(驳回被告的反诉).

The facts

The plaintiff is a carpenter. The defendants are building contractors(建筑承包商) who in September 1985 had entered into a contract with Shepherds Bush Housing Association Ltd. to refurbish a block of flats(整修公寓大楼) called Twynholm Mansions, Lillie Road, London S.W.6. The defendants were the main contractors for the works(主要工程承包商). There are 28 flats in Twynholm Mansions, but the work of refurbishment was to be carried out in 27 of the flats.

The defendants engaged the plaintiff to carry out the carpentry work in the refurbishment of the 27 flats, including work to the structure of the roof. Originally the plaintiff was engaged on three separate sub-contracts, but these were all superseded by a sub-contract in writing made on 21st January 1986 by which the plaintiff undertook to provide the labour for the carpentry work to the roof of the block and for the first and second fix carpentry work required in each of the 27 flats for a total price of £20,000.

The judge found that, though there was no express term providing for payment to be made in stages, the contract of 21st January 1986 was subject to an implied term(默示条款) that the defendants would make interim payments to the plaintiff, related to the amount of work done, at reasonable intervals.

The plaintiff and his men began work on 10th October 1985. The judge found that by 9th April 1986 the plaintiff had completed the work to the roof, had carried out the first fix to all 27 flats, and had substantially completed the second fix to 9 flats. By this date the defendants had made interim payments totalling £16,200.

It is common ground that by the end of March 1986 the plaintiff was in financial difficulty. The judge found that there were two reasons for this, namely:

(i) That the agreed price of £20,000 was too low to enable the plaintiff to operate satisfactorily and at a profit. Mr. Cottrell, a Surveyor(测量员,勘测员,测地员;检查员;调查员;英国度量衡等的检查官;美国入口货的检验官;鉴定人) employed by the defendants said in evidence that a reasonable price for the works would have been £23,783.

(ii) That the plaintiff failed to supervise his workmen adequately(未适当地监督工人).

The defendants, as they made clear, were concerned lest the plaintiff did not complete the carpentry work on time. The main contract contained a penalty clause(惩罚条款). The judge found that on 9th April 1986 the defendants promised to pay the plaintiff the further sum of £10,300, in addition to the 620,000, to be paid at the rate of £575 for each flat in which the carpentry work was completed.

The plaintiff and his men continued work on the flats until the end of May 1986. By that date the defendants, after their promise on 9th April 1986, had made only one further payment of El,500. At the end of May the plaintiff ceased work on the flats. I will describe later the work which, according to the judge's findings, then remained to be done. Suffice it to say that the defendants engaged other carpenters to complete the work, but in the result incurred one week's time penalty in their contract with the building owners.

The plaintiff commenced this action by specially endorsed writ on 10th May 1987. He originally claimed the sum of £32,708.70. In a re-amended statement of claim served on 3rd March 1986 his claim was reduced to £10,847.07. It was, I think, at about this time that the matter was transferred to the county court.

It is not necessary to refer to the statement of claim. On every important issue on which the plaintiff's case differed from that of the defendants, the judge found that the plaintiff was mistaken, and preferred the evidence for the defendants. In particular, the plaintiff denied the defendants' promise of 9th April 1986 to pay him an additional £10,300, instead alleging an earlier and different agreement which the judge found had not been made.

In the amended defence the defendants' promise to pay an additional £10,300 was pleaded as part of paragraph 5 in the following terms:

"... In or about the month of May 1986 at a meeting at the offices of the defendants between Mr. Hooper and the plaintiff on the one hand and Mr. Cottrell and Mr. Roffey on the other it was agreed that the defendants would pay the plaintiff an extra £10,300 over and above the contract sum of £20,000. 9 flats had been first and second fixed completely at the date of this meeting and there were 18 flats left that had been first fixed but on which the second fixing had not been completed. The sum of £10,300 was to be paid at a rate of £575 per flat to be paid on the completion of each flat".

The defence then alleged that neither the balance of the original contract sum nor the £10,300 addition was payable until the work was completed, that the plaintiff did not complete the work before he left the site, and thus that no further sum was due to him. By their amended counterclaim the defendants claimed that the plaintiff was in breach of contract in ceasing work at the end of May 1986, as a result of which they had suffered damage to the extent of £18,121.46.

The judge's conclusions

The judge found that the defendants' promise to pay an additional £10,300, at the rate of £575 per completed flat, was part of an oral agreement made between the plaintiff and the defendants on 9th April 1986, by way of variation to the original contract(对原合同的变更).

The judge also found that before the plaintiff ceased work at the end of May 1986 the carpentry in 17 flats had been substantially (but not totally) completed(大部分完工). This means that between the making of the agreement on 9th April 1986 and the date when the plaintiff ceased work, eight further flats were substantially completed.

The judge calculated that this entitled the plaintiff to receive £4,600 (8 × £575) "less some small deduction for defective and incomplete items". He held that the plaintiff was also entitled to a reasonable proportion of the £2,200 which was outstanding from the original contract sum. Adding these two amounts, he decided that the plaintiff was entitled to further payments totalling £5,000 against which he had only received £1,500, and that the defendants were therefore in breach of contract, entitling the plaintiff to cease work.

The issues

Before us Mr. Evans for the defendants(代理被告的 Evans 先生) advances two arguments. His principal submission is that the defendants' admitted promise to pay an additional £10,300, at the rate of £575 per completed flat, is unenforceable since there was no consideration for it(因为不存在对价). This issue was not raised in the defence, but we are told that the argument was advanced at the trial(一审,原审) without objection, and that there was equally no objection to it being argued before us.

Mr. Evans' secondary argument is that the additional payment was only payable as each flat was completed. On the judge's findings, 8 further flats had been "substantially" completed. Substantial completion was something less than completion. Thus none of the 8 flats had been completed, and no further payment was yet due from the defendants. I will deal with this subsidiary argument first.

Does substantial completion entitle the plaintiff to payment?

The agreement which the judge found was made between the parties on 9th April 1986 provided for payment as follows:

"The sum of £10,300 was to be paid at the rate of £575 per flat to be paid on the completion of each flat".

Mr. Evans argues that the agreement provided for payment on completion, not on substantial completion(大部分完工), of each flat. Since the judge did not find that the work in any additional flat was completed after 9th April 1986, the defendants were under no obligation to pay any part of the £10,300 before the plaintiff ceased work at the end of May. In his judgment the judge does not explain why in his view substantial completion entitled the plaintiff to payment. In support of the judgment on this issue, however, Mr. Makey for the plaintiff(代理原告的 Makey 先生), refers us to the decision of this court in *Hoenig v. Isaac*. In that case the plaintiff was engaged to decorate and furnish the defendant's flat for £750, to be paid "net cash, as the work proceeds, and balance on completion". The defendant paid £400, moved into the flat and used the new furniture, but refused to pay the balance(拒绝支付余额) on the ground that some of the work was defective. The official referee found that there were some defects, but that the contract had been substantially performed. The Court of Appeal held that accordingly the plaintiff was entitled to be paid the balance due, less only a deduction for the cost of making good(修复,成功;兑现诺言;实现;补偿;消除不良影响;成功;实现;纠正) the defects or omissions.

Somervell L. J. said at page 179G:

"The learned official referee regarded *H. Dakin & Co. Ltd. v. Lee* [1916] as laying down that the price must be paid subject to the set-off or counterclaim if there was a substantial compliance with the contract. I think on the facts of this case where the work was finished in the ordinary sense, though in part defective, this is right. It expresses in a convenient epithet what is put from another angle in the Sale of Goods Act, 1893. The buyer cannot reject if he proves only the breach of a term collateral to the main purpose. I have, therefore, come to the conclusion that the first point of counsel for the defendant fails".

Denning L. J. said at page 180H-181D:

"In determining this issue the first question is whether, on the true construction of the contract(对于合同的真实解释), entire performance was a condition precedent to payment(先于支付的一个先决条件). It was a lump sum(一次结清的总额) contract, but that does not mean that entire performance was a condition precedent to payment. When a contract provides for a specific sum to be paid on completion of specified work, the courts lean against a construction of the contract which would deprive the contractor of any payment at all simply because there are some defects or omissions. The promise to complete the work is, therefore, construed as a term of the contract, but not as a condition(合同的一个条款,而非一种条件). It is not every breach of that term which absolves the employer from his promise to pay the price, but only a breach which goes to the root of the contract, such as an abandonment of the work when it is only half done. Unless the breach does go to the root of the matter, the employer cannot resist payment of the price. He must pay it and bring a cross-claim for the defects and omissions, or, alternatively, set them up in diminution (减少,缩小)of the price. The measure is the amount which the work is worth less by reason of the defects and omissions, and is usually calculated by the cost of making them good. It is, of course, always open to the parties by express words(明示的用语) to make entire performance a condition precedent. A similar instance is when the contract provides for progress payments(按进度分期付款,到货后支付;分阶段付款;工程进度款;计件付款;验工计价). The contractor is entitled to payment pro rata(按比例地) as the work proceeds, less a deduction for retention money(保留金;保留款项;保留款额;工程累积保证金;扣留款项,保留款项;留存款项). But he is not entitled to the retention money until the work is entirely finished, without defects or omissions. In the present case the contract provided for 'net cash, as the work proceeds; the balance on completion'. If the balance could be regarded as retention money, then it might well be that the contractor ought to have done all the work correctly, without defects or omissions, in order to be entitled to the balance. But I do not think the balance should be regarded as retention money. Retention money is usually only ten per cent., or fifteen per cent., whereas this balance was more than fifty per cent. I think this contract should be regarded as an ordinary lump sum contract. It was substantially performed. The contractor is entitled, therefore, to the contract price, less a deduction for the defects".

Romer L. J. said:

"The defendant's only attack on the plaintiff's performance of his obligations was in relation to certain articles of furniture which the plaintiff supplied and which the defendant says were faulty and defective in various important respects. The finding of the learned official referee on this was 'that the furniture supplied constituted a substantial compliance with the contract so far as the supply of furniture was concerned'.

That is a finding of fact, and whether or not another mind might have taken a different view it appears to me impossible to say that there was no sufficient evidence on which the finding could be based. This, then, being a lump sum contract for the supply of furniture (and the carrying out of certain minor work) which was substantially complied with by the plaintiff, the question is whether the official referee was wrong in law in applying the principle of *H. Dakin & Co. Ltd. v. Lee* and rejecting the defendant's submissions that the plaintiff had failed to perform a condition on the fulfillment of which his right to sue(诉权,起诉的权利) depended. In my judgment, he was quite right in applying the *H. Dakin & Co. Ltd. v. Lee* principle to the facts of the present case. I can see no reason why that principle should be approached with wariness and applied with caution. In certain cases it is right that the rigid rule for which the defendant contends should be applied, for example, if a man tells a contractor to build a ten foot wall for him in his garden and agrees to pay Ex for it, it would not be right that he should be held liable for any part of the contract price if the contractor builds the wall to two feet and then renounce (抛弃,放弃,背弃) further performance of the contract, or builds the wall of a totally different material from that which was ordered, or builds it at the wrong end of the garden. The work contracted for has not been done and the corresponding obligation to pay consequently never arises. But when a man fully performs his contract in the sense that he supplies all that he agreed to supply but what he supplies is subject to defects of so minor a character that he can be said to have substantially performed his promise, it is, in my judgment, far more equitable to apply the *H. Dakin & Co. Ltd v. Lee* principle than to deprive him wholly of his contractual rights and relegate (委托,移交事件;指示某人向某人打听;命令撤离,驱逐/出境;充军;降职,贬黜;丢弃,束之高阁) him to such remedy (if any) as he may have on a quantum meruit(无合同规定时按合理价格支付,合理给付), nor, in my judgment, are we compelled to a contrary view (having regard to the nature and terms of the agreement and the official referee's finding) by any of the cases in the books".

In my view this authority(权威判例) entirely supports the judge's decision on this issue.

Was there consideration for the defendants' promise made on 9th April 1986 to pay an additional price at the rate of £575 per completed flat?

The judge made the following findings of fact which are relevant on this issue.

(i) The sub-contract price agreed was too low to enable the plaintiff to operate satisfactorily and at a profit. Mr. Cottrell, the defendants' surveyor, agreed that this was so.

(ii) Mr. Roffey (managing director of the defendants) was persuaded by Mr. Cottrell that the defendants should pay a bonus to the plaintiff. The figure agreed at the meeting on 9th April 1986 was 610,300.

The judge quoted and accepted the evidence of Mr. Cottrell to the effect(大意是)that a main contractor who agrees too low a price with a sub-contractor is acting contrary to his own interests. He will never get the job finished without paying more money.

The judge therefore concluded:

"In my view where the original sub-contract price is too low, and the parties subsequently agree that the additional monies shall be paid to the subcontractor, this agreement is in the interests of both parties. This is what happened in the present case, and in my opinion the agreement of 9th April 1986 does not fail for lack of consideration".

In his address to us, Mr. Evans outlined the benefits to his clients the defendants which arose from their agreement to pay the additional £10,300 as:

(i) seeking to ensure that the plaintiff continued work and did not stop in breach of the subcontract;

(ii) avoiding the penalty for delay;

(iii) avoiding the trouble and expense of engaging other people to complete the carpentry work. However, Mr. Evans submits that, though his clients may have derived, or hoped to derive, practical benefits from their agreement to pay the "bonus", they derived no benefit in law, since the plaintiff was promising to do no more than he was already bound to do by his subcontract i.e. continue with the carpentry work and complete it on time. Thus there was no consideration for the agreement.

Mr. Evans relies on the principle of law which, traditionally, is based on the decision in *Stilk v. Myrick* (1809). That was a decision at first instance of Lord Ellenborough C. J. On a voyage to the Baltic, two seamen deserted(逃跑,当逃兵). The captain agreed with the rest of the crew that if they worked the ship back to London without the two seamen being replaced, he would divide between them the pay which would have been due to the two deserters. On arrival at London this extra pay was refused, and the plaintiff's action to recover his extra pay was dismissed. Counsel for the defendant argued that such an agreement was contrary to public policy(公共政策,公序良俗), but the Chief Justice's judgment was based on lack of consideration. It reads:

"I think *Harris v. Watson* was rightly decided; but I doubt whether the ground of public policy, upon which Lord Kenyon is stated to have proceeded, be the true principle on which the decision is to be supported. Here, I say the agreement is void for want of consideration(由于缺乏对价). There was no consideration for the ulterior pay promised to the mariners who remained with the ship. Before they sailed from London they had undertaken to do all they could under the emergencies of the voyage. They had sold all their services till the voyage should be completed. If they had been at liberty to quit the vessel at Cronstadt, the case would have been quite different; or if the captain had capriciously discharged the two men who were wanting, the others might not have been compellable to take the whole duty upon themselves, and their agreeing to do so might have been a sufficient consideration for the promise of an advance of wages. But the desertion of a part of the crew is to be considered an emergency of the voyage as much as their death, and those who remain are bound by the terms of their original contract to exert themselves to the utmost to bring the ship in safety to her destination port(目的港). Therefore, without looking to the policy of this agreement, I think it is void for want of consideration, and that the plaintiff can only recover at the rate of £5 a month".

In *North Ocean Shipping Co. Ltd. v. Hyundai Construction Co. Ltd.* [1979], Mocatta J. regarded the general principle of the decision in *Stilk v. Myrick* as still being good law. He referred to two earlier decisions of this court, dealing with wholly different subjects, in which Denning L. J., as he then was, sought to escape from the confines of the rule, but was not accompanied in his attempt by the other members of the court.

In *Ward v. Byham* [1956] the plaintiff and the defendant lived together unmarried for five years, during which time the plaintiff bore their child. After the parties ended their relationship, the defendant promised to pay the plaintiff El per week to maintain the child, provided that she was well looked after and happy. The defendant paid this sum for some months, but ceased to pay when the plaintiff married another man. On her suing for the amount due at El per week, he pleaded that there was no consideration for his agreement to pay for the plaintiff to maintain her child, since she was obliged by law to do so. The county court judge upheld the plaintiff mother's claim, and this court dismissed the defendant's appeal.

Denning L. J. said at page 498:

"I approach the case, therefore, on the footing that the mother, in looking after the child, is only doing what she is legally bound to do. Even so, I think that there was sufficient consideration to support the promise. I have always thought that a promise to perform an existing duty, or the performance of it, should be regarded as good consideration, because it is a benefit to the person to whom it is given. Take this very case. It is as much a benefit for the father to have the child looked after by the mother as by a neighbour. If he gets the benefit for which he stipulated, he ought to honour his promise(兑现其承诺); and he ought not to avoid it by saying that the mother was herself under a duty to maintain the child.

I regard the father's promise in this case as what is sometimes called a unilateral contract(单诺合同), a promise in return for an act(以行为换取允诺), a promise by the father to pay El a week in return for the mother's looking after the child. Once the mother embarked on the task of looking after the child, there was a binding contract. So long as she looked after the child, she would be entitled to El a week. The case seems to me to be within the decision of *Hicks v. Gregory*, on which the judge relied. I would dismiss the appeal".

However, Morris L. J. put it rather differently. He said:

"... Mr. Lane submits that there was a duty on the mother to support the child; that no affiliation proceedings were in prospect or were contemplated; and that the effect of the arrangement that followed the letter was that the father was merely agreeing to pay a bounty (赐物,赠物;赐金,赠金;慷慨,仁爱,博爱,宽大;恩惠;赏金;奖金) to the mother.

It seems to me that the terms of the letter negative(作为动词使用是,表示"否认;否定;驳斥;否决;拒绝;反证;反对;使无效,使中和"的意思) those submissions, for the husband says 'providing you can prove that she'—that is Carol—'will be well looked after and happy and also that she is allowed to decide for herself whether or not she wishes to come and live with you'. The father goes on to say that Carol is then well and happy and looking much stronger than ever before. 'If you decide what to do let me know as soon as possible'. It seems to me, therefore, that the father was saying, in effect: Irrespective of what may be the strict legal position, what I am asking is that you shall prove that Carol will be well looked after and happy, and also that you must agree that Carol is to be allowed to decide for herself whether or not she wishes to come and live with you. If those conditions were fulfilled the father was agreeable to pay. Upon those terms, which in effect became operative, the father agreed to pay El a week. In my judgment, there was ample consideration there to be found for his promise, which I think was binding."

Parker L. J. agreed. As I read the judgment of Morris L. J., he and Parker L. J. held that, though in maintaining the child the plaintiff was doing no more than she was obliged to do by law, nevertheless her promise that the child would be well looked after and happy was a practical benefit to the father which amounted to consideration for his promise.

In *Williams v. Williams* [1957], a wife left her husband, and he promised to make her a weekly payment for her maintenance. On his failing to honour his promise, the wife claimed the arrears (欠款,尾款,欠工,尾活) of payment, but her husband pleaded that, since the wife was guilty of desertion she was bound to maintain herself, and thus there was no consideration for his promise. Denning L. J. reiterated his view that "a promise to perform an existing duty is, I think, sufficient consideration to support a promise, so long as there is nothing in the transaction which is contrary to the public interest".

However, the other members of the court (Hodson and Morris L. JJ.) declined to agree with this expression of view, though agreeing with Denning L. J. in finding that there was consideration because the wife's desertion might not have been permanent, and thus there was a benefit to the husband.

It was suggested to us in argument that, since the development of the doctrine of promissory estoppel, it may well be possible for a person to whom a promise has been made, on which he has relied, to make an additional payment for services which he is in any event bound to render under an existing contract or by operation of law, to show that the promisor is estopped from claiming that there was no consideration for his promise. However, the application of the doctrine of promissory estoppel to facts such as those of the present case has not yet been fully developed. Moreover, this point was not argued in the court below, nor was it more than adumbrated(暗示,预示;画……的轮廓) before us. Interesting though it is, no reliance can in my view be placed on this concept in the present case.

There is, however, another legal concept of relatively recent development which is relevant, namely, that of economic duress(经济胁迫). Clearly if a sub-contractor has agreed to undertake work at a fixed price, and before he has completed the work declines to continue with it unless the contractor agrees to pay an increased price, the subcontractor may be held guilty of securing the contractor's promise by taking unfair advantage of the difficulties he will cause if he does not complete the work. In such a case an agreement to pay an increased price may well be voidable because it was entered into under duress. Thus this concept may provide another answer in law to the question of policy which has troubled the courts since before *Stilk v. Myrick*, and no doubt led at the date of that decision to a rigid adherence to the doctrine of consideration.

This possible application of the concept of economic duress was referred to by Lord Scarman, delivering the judgment of the Judicial Committee of the Privy Council(枢密院司法委员会) in *Pao On v. Lau Yiu Long* [1989]. He said:

"Their Lordships do not doubt that a promise to perform, or the performance of, a pre-existing contractual obligation to a third party can be valid consideration. In *New Zealand Shipping Co. Ltd. V. A. M. Satterthwaite & Co. Ltd* (*The Eurymedon*), the rule and the reason for the rule were stated:

'An agreement to do an act which the promisor is under an existing obligation to a third party to do, may quite well amount to valid consideration ... the promisee obtains the benefit of a direct obligation ... This proposition is illustrated and supported by *Scotson v. Pegg*(1861) which their Lordships consider to be good law'.

Unless, therefore, the guarantee was void as having been made for an illegal consideration or voidable on the ground of economic duress, the extrinsic evidence establishes that it was supported by valid consideration.

Mr. Leggatt for the defendants submits that the consideration is illegal as being against public policy. He submits that to secure a party's promise by a threat of repudiation of a pre-existing contractual obligation owed to another can be and in the circumstances of this case was, an abuse of a dominant bargaining position and so contrary to public policy. This submission found favour with the majority in the Court of Appeal. Their Lordships, however, considered it misconceived".

Lord Scarman then referred to *Stilk v. Myrick* and its predecessor *Harris v. Watson* (1791), and to *Williams v. Williams*, before turning to the development of this branch of the law in the United States of America. He then said:

"Their Lordships' knowledge of this developing branch of American law is necessarily limited. In their judgment it would be carrying audacity to the point of foolhardiness(蛮勇；有勇无谋；愚勇) for them to attempt to extract from the American case law a principle to provide an answer to the question now under consideration. That question, their Lordships repeat, is whether, in a case where duress is not established, public policy may nevertheless invalidate the consideration if there has been a threat to repudiate a pre-existing contractual obligation or an unfair use of a dominating bargaining position. Their Lordships' conclusion is that where businessmen are negotiating at arms' length it is unnecessary for the achievement of justice, and unhelpful in the development of the law, to invoke such a rule of public policy. It would also create unacceptable anomaly. It is unnecessary because justice requires that men, who have negotiated at arm's length, be held to their bargains unless it can be shown that their consent was vitiated(损害,使失效,使道德败坏) by fraud, mistake or duress. If a promise is induced by coercion (强制)of a man's will, the doctrine of duress suffices to do justice. The party coerced, if he chooses and acts in time, can avoid the contract. If there is no coercion, there can be no reason for avoiding the contract where there is shown to be a real consideration which is otherwise legal.

Such a rule of public policy as is now being considered would be unhelpful because it would render the law uncertain. It would become a question of fact and degree to determine in each case whether there had been, short of duress, an unfair use of a strong bargaining position. It would create anomaly because, if public policy invalidates the consideration, the effect is to make the contract void. But unless the facts are such as to support a plea of 'non est factum'(拉丁语,否认订立契约的答辩；否认立约), which is not suggested in this case, duress does no more than confer upon the victim the opportunity if taken in time, to avoid the contract. It would be strange if conduct less than duress could render a contract void, whereas duress does no more than render a contract voidable. Indeed, it is the defendants' case in this appeal that such an anomaly is the correct result. Their case is that the plaintiffs, having lost by cancellation the safeguard of the subsidiary agreement, are without the safeguard of the guarantee because its consideration is contrary to public policy, and that they are debarred from restoration to their position under the subsidiary agreement because the guarantee is void, not voidable. The logical consequence of Mr. Leggatt's submission is that the safeguard which all were at all times agreed the plaintiffs should have—the safeguard against fall in value of the shares—has been lost by the application of a rule of public policy. The law is not, in their Lordships' judgment, reduced to countenancing(默许,纵容)such stark injustice; nor is it necessary, when one bears in mind the protection offered otherwise by the law to one who contracts in ignorance of what he is doing or under duress. Accordingly, the submission that the additional consideration established by the extrinsic evidence is invalid on the ground of public policy is rejected".

It is true that *Pao On* is a case of a tripartite relationship i.e. a promise by A to perform a pre-existing contractual obligation owed to B, in return for a promise of payment by C. But Lord Scarman's words at page 634/5 seem to me to be of general application, equally applicable to a promise made by one of the original two parties to a contract.

Accordingly, following the view of the majority in *Ward v. Byham* and of the whole court in *Williams v. Williams* and that of the *Privy Council in Pao On* the present state of the law on this subject can be expressed in the following proposition:

(i) if A has entered into a contract with B to do work for, or to supply goods or services to, B in return for payment by B; and

(ii) at some stage before A has completely performed his obligations under the contract B has reason to doubt whether A will, or will be able to, complete his side of the bargain; and

(iii) B thereupon promises A an additional payment in return for A's promise to perform his contractual obligations on time; and

(iv) as a result of giving his promise, B obtains in practice a benefit, or obviates a disbenefit; and

(v) B's promise is not given as a result of economic duress or fraud on the part of A; then

(vi) the benefit to B is capable of being consideration for B's promise, so that the promise will be legally binding.

As I have said, Mr. Evans accepts that in the present case by promising to pay the extra £10,300 his client secured benefits. There is no finding, and no suggestion, that in this case the promise was given as a result of fraud or duress.

If it be objected that the propositions above contravene the principle in *Stilk v. Myrick*, I answer that in my view they do not; they refine, and limit the application of that principle, but they leave the principle unscathed e.g. where B. secures no benefit by his promise. It is not in my view surprising that a principle enunciated(宣布，阐明) in relation to the rigours of seafaring life during the Napoleonic wars should be subjected during the succeeding 180 years to a process of refinement and limitation in its application in the present day.

It is therefore my opinion that on his findings of fact in the present case, the judge was entitled to hold, as he did, that the defendants' promise to pay the extra £10,300 was supported by valuable consideration, and thus constituted an enforceable agreement.

As a subsidiary argument, Mr. Evans submits that on the facts of the present case the consideration, even if otherwise good, did not "move from the promisee". This submission is based on the principle illustrated in the decision in *Tweddle v. Atkinson* (1861). My understanding of the meaning of the requirement that "consideration must move from the promisee" is that such consideration must be provided by the promisee, or arise out of his contractual relationship with the promisor. It is consideration provided by somebody else, not a party to the contract, which does not 'move from the promisee'. This was the situation in *Tweddle v. Atkinson*, but it is, of course, not the situation in the present case. Here the benefits to the defendants arose out of their agreement of 9th April 1986 with the plaintiff, the promisee. In this respect I would adopt the following passage from *Chitty on Contracts*(25th edition, paragraph 173), and refer to the authorities there cited:

"The requirement that consideration must move from the promisee is most generally satisfied where some detriment is suffered by him e.g. where he parts with money or goods, or renders services, in exchange for the promise. But the requirement may be equally well satisfied where the promisee confers a benefit on the promisor without in fact suffering any detriment".

That is the situation in this case.

I repeat, therefore, my opinion that the judge was, as a matter of law, entitled to hold that there was valid consideration to support the agreement under which the defendants promised to pay an additional £10,300 at the rate of £575 per flat.

For these reasons I would dismiss this appeal.

...

Opinion by Lord Justice Russell(omitted)

Opinion By Lord Justice Purchas(omitted)

Lesson Four

Code of Judicial Conduct

Learning objectives

After learning the text and having done the exercises in this lesson, you will:

—familiarize with knowledge of the legal characteristics and the nature of judicial conduct;

—acquire an appreciation of the vocabulary and grammar or syntax relevant to judicial conduct;

—become aware of the information required in order to understand the judicial conduct;

—cultivate the practical abilities to put to use the language in the specific context;

—be able to do some translation from Chinese to English and from English to Chinese.

Text

Code of Judicial Conduct[①]

- **Preamble**

An independent, fair and impartial judiciary[②] is indispensable to our system of justice. The United States legal system is based upon the principle that an independent, impartial, and competent judiciary, composed of men and women of integrity[③], will interpret and apply the law that governs our society. Thus, the judiciary plays a central role in preserving the principles of justice

---

① Code of Judicial Conduct:调整法官职业行为的一系列规则。本文选自美国律师协会(ABA)1972 年制定的《法官行为示范法典》(Model Code of Judicial Conduct),有的翻译为《司法行为示范法典》。该法典本身并没有法律效力,但是却得到联邦政府和各州政府的广泛采用,作为对法官行为的规范以及惩戒的根据。

② judiciary:司法部门,司法机关;法院系统,法院体系;法官的总称。作为形容词使用时表示"法院的,司法的,涉及司法机关的"的意思。

③ integrity:完整;完善;正直;诚实,指人的品格纯真,正直诚实(moral soundness),man of integrity(刚直不阿的人,正直的人)。

and the rule of law. Inherent in all the Rules contained in this Code are the precepts[①] that judges, individually and collectively, must respect and honor the judicial office[②] as a public trust[③] and strive to maintain and enhance confidence in the legal system.

Judges should maintain the dignity of judicial office at all times, and avoid both impropriety and the appearance of impropriety in their professional and personal lives. They should aspire at all times to conduct that ensures the greatest possible public confidence in their independence, impartiality, integrity, and competence.

The Model Code of Judicial Conduct establishes standards for the ethical conduct of judges and judicial candidates. It is not intended as an exhaustive guide for the conduct of judges and judicial candidates, who are governed in their judicial and personal conduct by general ethical standards as well as by the Code. The Code is intended, however, to provide guidance and assist judges in maintaining the highest standards of judicial and personal conduct, and to provide a basis for regulating their conduct through disciplinary agencies.

- **Terminology**

"**Aggregate**" in relation to contributions for a candidate, means not only contributions in cash or in kind[④] made directly to a candidate's campaign committee, but also all contributions made indirectly with the understanding that they will be used to support the election of a candidate or to oppose the election of the candidate's opponent.

"**Appropriate authority**" means the authority having responsibility for initiation of disciplinary process in connection with the violation to be reported.

"**Contribution**"[⑤] means both financial and in-kind contributions, such as goods, professional or volunteer services, advertising, and other types of assistance, which, if obtained by the recipient otherwise, would require a financial expenditure.

"**De minimis**" in the context of interests pertaining to disqualification of a judge, means an insignificant interest that could not raise a reasonable question regarding the judge's impartiality.

---

① precept：命令,训令,指令,指示；法院命令,令状；规诫,戒律；行为准则；格言,箴言；法国古法中的国王命令,即要求法官作出或容忍违法之事；英格兰古法中的唆使犯罪,犯罪教唆。
② judicial office：作为法官这样的职位,法官职务,与司法权的行使相关的职位。
③ public trust：群众/公众的信任；公益信托(为慈善事业或公共目的设立的信托)。
④ in kind：以实物,以货物或劳务,而不以货币；以同类方式,以相同方法,课文中与 in cash 相对应,指第一层意思。
⑤ contribution：捐献,捐赠；分摊额；分担额,指负有责任的几人中任一人应当承担的份额,它通常发生于以下几种情形：(1) 共同侵权人(joint tortfeasors)之间,每一行为人均应分担因侵权行为而给他人造成的损害。在美国,一部分州已采纳了《统一侵权人责任分担法》(Uniform Contribution Among Tortfeasors Act)。(2) 在共同保险(co-insurance)中,每一保险人根据共同保险条款而与其他保险人对同一损失承担赔偿责任,如其承担全部赔偿责任或超过其应分担的赔偿份额的,则有权向其他保险人求偿。(3) 在海商法上,如果发生共同海损(general average),而损失已由一个当事人承担,则所有有关利益的当事人应当根据其在获救财产中的比例分摊该项损失。(4) 财产分配,指破产案件中的债权人之间按照其各自的债权比例而对债务人的财产进行分割,亦指继承人之间对遗产及债务根据其应承担的比例分割。(5) 社会保险基金中应强制缴纳的保险金。(6) 捐献；出资额。(7) 占领军税,指占领军向被占领地居民征收的一种税金,亦作 war contribution。

Lesson Four Code of Judicial Conduct

"**Domestic partner**"① means a person with whom another person maintains a household and an intimate relationship, other than a person to whom he or she is legally married.

"**Economic interest**" means ownership of more than a de minimis legal or equitable② interest. Except for situations in which the judge participates in the management of such a legal or equitable interest, or the interest could be substantially affected by the outcome of a proceeding before a judge, it does not include:

(1) an interest in the individual holdings within a mutual or common investment fund③;

(2) an interest in securities held by an educational, religious, charitable, fraternal, or civic organization in which the judge or the judge's spouse, domestic partner, parent, or child serves as a director, an officer, an advisor, or other participant;

(3) a deposit in a financial institution or deposits or proprietary interests④ the judge may maintain as a member of a mutual savings association or credit union⑤, or similar proprietary interests; or

(4) an interest in the issuer⑥ of government securities held by the judge.

"**Fiduciary**" includes relationships such as executor⑦, administrator⑧, trustee⑨, or guardian⑩.

"**Impartial**" "**impartiality**" and "**impartially**" mean absence of bias or prejudice in favor of, or against, particular parties or classes of parties, as well as maintenance of an open mind in considering issues that may come before a judge.

"**Impending matter**" is a matter that is imminent or expected to occur in the near future.

"**Impropriety**" includes conduct that violates the law, court rules, or provisions of this

---

① domestic partner:非婚同居者(与之因性关系而同居的伙伴:a person with whom one cohabits in a sexual relationship);非婚同居伴侣,但是拥有许多合法婚姻伴侣的权利(比如许多公司购买健康保险时是为全家购买,还有些公司买保险时就会同意包括职员的非婚同居伴侣)。同性恋者由于不能结婚,就会注册成为 domestic partner,享受这些福利。

② legal or equitable:此处是一对相对的概念,legal 意义缩小为"普通法的,或普法上的",而 equitable 指的是有关衡平法的。

③ mutual or common investment fund:共同投资基金,一种集体投资机制,在英国,其属于慈善委员会根据《1993 年慈善法》的规定而建立的同样具有慈善性质的多方位投资机制。

④ proprietary interests:所有人权益,包括财产所有人的所有权及各项从属权利,例如股东按股份的表决权及对公司事务的参与管理权。

⑤ Credit union:信用合作社;信贷互助会;利用社员储蓄,以优惠利息贷给本社成员,为本社成员提供信用,以促进共同发展。

⑥ issuer:证券发行人,发行和销售证券的公司、政府机构及其他实体;信用证开证人,指开立信用证的银行或其他人;权利凭证签发人,签发权利凭证的货物保管人,但在交货指示尚未被接受时,指向货物占有人发出交货指示的人。

⑦ executor:遗嘱执行人,指由立遗嘱人在遗嘱中指定在其死后依遗嘱处理其遗产的人;大陆法中判决的执行官;执行者;实施者。课文中表示"遗嘱执行人"之意。

⑧ administrator:遗产管理人;行政人员;机构。

⑨ trustee:受托人,依照信托委任或法律规定拥有信托财产、执行信托业务,并将所得利益交与受益人的人,其对信托财产和受益人都承担责任;破产法中的破产财产管理人,指由债权人选任或由法官指定充当破产财产管理人的法院官员,其负有多项职责,如清理破产财产、处理债务人相关业务、参加债权人会议、向利害关系人提供相关信息等,又称为"bankruptcy trustee"、"trustee in bankruptcy";担任受托人,指定受托人;将人或财产交托给受托人。课文中表示破产财产管理者的意思。

⑩ guardian:监护人,对于年龄不足、缺乏理解和自控能力而不能处理自己事务的人,依法有权并有责任照顾和保护其人身、财产及其他合法权益的人;监护人依法有责任保护和照顾被监护人的人身权益,或管理其财产,或兼负这两种职责。

Code, and conduct that undermines a judge's independence, integrity, or impartiality.

"**Independence**" means a judge's freedom from influence or controls other than those established by law.

"**Integrity**" means probity, fairness, honesty, uprightness, and soundness of character.

"**Judicial candidate**" means any person, including a sitting judge, who is seeking selection for or retention in judicial office by election or appointment. A person becomes a candidate for judicial office as soon as he or she makes a public announcement of candidacy, declares or files as a candidate with the election or appointment authority, authorizes or, where permitted, engages in solicitation or acceptance of contributions or support, or is nominated for election or appointment to office.

"**Knowingly**" "**knowledge**" "**known**" and "**knows**" mean actual knowledge[①] of the fact in question. A person's knowledge may be inferred from circumstances.

"**Law**" encompasses court rules as well as statutes, constitutional provisions, and decisional law.

"**Member of the candidate's family**" means a spouse, domestic partner, child, grandchild, parent, grandparent, or other relative or person with whom the candidate maintains a close familial relationship.

"**Member of the judge's family**" means a spouse, domestic partner, child, grandchild, parent, grandparent, or other relative or person with whom the judge maintains a close familial relationship.

"**Member of a judge's family residing in the judge's household**" means any relative of a judge by blood or marriage, or a person treated by a judge as a member of the judge's family, who resides in the judge's household.

"**Nonpublic information**" means information that is not available to the public. Nonpublic information may include, but is not limited to[②], information that is sealed by statute or court order[③] or impounded[④] or communicated in camera[⑤], and information offered in grand jury[⑥] pro-

---

① actual knowledge：实际知悉，指直接且清楚地知悉某种事实或状况，与"推定知悉"（constructive knowledge）相对；指知晓某种信息或情况，而该信息或情况会使得一个有理性的人（reasonable person）对事实作进一步的探究或查询，这种情形也称为默示实际知悉（implied actual knowledge），这种知悉可替代及时、充分的实际通知（actual notice）。

② include but is not limited to：法律英语中非常常见的固定句式，可译作：包括但不限于。

③ court order：法庭秩序，法院命令（A direction or command of the court which, if not complied with, may result in contempt of court. The directions given to the parties to the litigation which follow from the decision of the court constitute court orders）。

④ impound：扣押，指警察或法院在有关的程序或诉讼中扣押某物，如车辆、资金或其他动产等，但应在该程序或诉讼终结时将被扣押物完整地返还；为指控犯罪而扣押某物以便在诉讼中作为证据使用，如为实施犯罪使用的车辆、伪造的文件或其他物品等。

⑤ in camera：拉丁语，在法官办公室；在非公开法庭上，在无旁听者的法庭上；某一司法措施在法院休庭期内采取的；在用于指法官的判决意见时，该词等同于 in chambers。

⑥ grand jury：大陪审团。在刑事法庭审案期间由行政司法官选定并召集。其职责为受理刑事指控，听取控方提出的证据，决定是否将犯罪嫌疑人交付审判，而不是认定其是否有罪。称为大陪审团，因其成员的人数较通常的陪审团即小陪审团为多；普通法上由 12—23 人组成。大陪审团起源于 1166 年的《克拉伦敦法》（Assize of Clarendon）。开始时对案件既负责起诉，又负责审理。逐渐演变为只决定是否对犯罪嫌疑人起诉，对案件的审理则由小陪审团承担。在英国，除个别情况外，大陪审团已于 1933 年取消；至 1948 年则被彻底废除。美国宪法第五修正案规定，对可能判处死刑的犯罪和不名誉罪的指控，原则上必须经由大陪审团起诉。联邦法院的大陪审团由 16—23 人组成。各州法院大陪审团的人数，则各有不同。

ceedings, presentencing reports, dependency cases, or psychiatric reports.

"Pending matter" is a matter that has commenced. A matter continues to be pending through any appellate process until final disposition.①

"Personally solicit" means a direct request made by a judge or a judicial candidate for financial support or in-kind services, whether made by letter, telephone, or any other means of communication.

"Political organization" means a political party or other group sponsored by or affiliated with a political party or candidate, the principal purpose of which is to further the election or appointment of candidates for political office. For purposes of this Code, the term does not include a judicial candidate's campaign committee created as authorized by Rule 4.4.

"Public election" includes primary and general elections②, partisan elections, nonpartisan elections, and retention elections.③

"Third degree of relationship" includes the following persons: great-grandparent, grandparent, parent, uncle, aunt, brother, sister, child, grandchild, great-grandchild, nephew, and niece.

Canon 1

A judge shall uphold and promote the independence, integrity, and impartiality of the judiciary, and shall avoid impropriety and the appearance of impropriety.

RULE 1.1 Compliance with④ the Law

A judge shall comply with the law, including the Code of Judicial Conduct.

RULE 1.2 Promoting Confidence in the Judiciary

A judge shall act at all times in a manner that promotes public confidence in the independence, integrity, and impartiality of the judiciary, and shall avoid impropriety and the appearance of impropriety.

RULE 1.3 Avoiding Abuse of the Prestige of Judicial Office

A judge shall not abuse the prestige of judicial office to advance the personal or economic interests of the judge or others, or allow others to do so.

Canon 2

A judge shall perform the duties of judicial office impartially, competently, and diligently.

RULE 2.1 Giving Precedence to the Duties of Judicial Office

The duties of judicial office, as prescribed by law, shall take precedence over all of a judge's personal and extrajudicial⑤ activities.

RULE 2.2 Impartiality and Fairness

A judge shall uphold and apply the law, and shall perform all duties of judicial office fairly

---

① final disposition：（对标的物）最终处分、终局处分，指在法院判决、裁定或决定作出后，不再对当事人的权利和义务进一步确定，并且不再有引起诉讼的进一步的争议，从而达到对标的物的终局性决定。
② primary and general election：初选和大选（普选）。
③ retention election：法官留任待选。
④ compliance with：固定短语，译作"遵守"。
⑤ extrajudicial：法庭外的；诉讼外的；正常司法程序之外的；超出法庭职权的；法庭管辖之外的。

and impartially.

RULE 2.3 Bias, Prejudice, and Harassment①

(A) A judge shall perform the duties of judicial office, including administrative duties, without bias or prejudice.

(B) A judge shall not, in the performance of judicial duties, by words or conduct manifest bias or prejudice, or engage in harassment, including but not limited to bias, prejudice, or harassment based upon race, sex, gender, religion, national origin, ethnicity, disability, age, sexual orientation, marital status, socioeconomic status, or political affiliation, and shall not permit court staff, court officials, or others subject to the judge's direction and control to do so.

(C) A judge shall require lawyers in proceedings② before the court to refrain from manifesting bias or prejudice, or engaging in harassment, based upon attributes including but not limited to race, sex, gender, religion, national origin, ethnicity, disability, age, sexual orientation, marital status, socioeconomic status, or political affiliation, against parties, witnesses, lawyers, or others.

(D) The restrictions of paragraphs (B) and (C) do not preclude judges or lawyers from making legitimate reference to the listed factors, or similar factors, when they are relevant to an issue in a proceeding.

RULE 2.4 External Influences on Judicial Conduct

(A) A judge shall not be swayed by public clamor or fear of criticism.

(B) A judge shall not permit family, social, political, financial, or other interests or relationships to influence the judge's judicial conduct or judgment.

(C) A judge shall not convey or permit others to convey the impression that any person or organization is in a position to influence the judge.

RULE 2.5 Competence, Diligence, and Cooperation

(A) A judge shall perform judicial and administrative duties, competently and diligently.

(B) A judge shall cooperate with other judges and court officials in the administration of court business.

RULE 2.6 Ensuring the Right to be Heard③

(A) A judge shall accord to④ every person who has a legal interest in a proceeding, or that person's lawyer, the right to be heard according to law.

(B) A judge may encourage parties to a proceeding and their lawyers to settle⑤ matters in

---

① harassment:骚扰;烦扰,指非出于合法目的,用语言、身势或行为搅扰、威吓或辱骂他人,造成其巨大情感压抑和精神痛苦。如缠诉行为,在不适当时间或用冒犯性粗俗语言与他人通讯等。在美国,禁止以骚扰方式收债;雇主对雇员的性骚扰可依 1964 年《民权法》(Civil Rights Act) 提起诉讼。

② proceeding:(1) 程序;诉讼程序,可指完整的正规的诉讼程序,包括从诉讼开始到作出判决其间所进行的全部行为和步骤;也可指在一个大的诉讼过程中的某一程序阶段或步骤,或指向法庭或其他机构寻求救济的程序手段;(2) 听审;听证,指法院或其他官方机构所处理的事务;(3) 破产法中在诉讼进行期间产生的特定争议或事项,区别于作为整体的案件本身。

③ Right to be Heard:听讯权;发表意见的权利;听证权;陈情权。

④ accord to:给予、赋予。

⑤ settle:和后面的名词形式 settlement 在此处表示"和解"的含义。

dispute but shall not act in a manner that coerces any party into settlement.

RULE 2.7   Responsibility to Decide

A judge shall hear and decide matters assigned to the judge, except when disqualification is required by Rule 2.11 or other law.

RULE 2.8   Decorum, Demeanor, and Communication with Jurors

(A) A judge shall require order and decorum in proceedings before the court.

(B) A judge shall be patient, dignified, and courteous to litigants, jurors, witnesses, lawyers, court staff, court officials, and others with whom the judge deals in an official capacity, and shall require similar conduct of lawyers, court staff, court officials, and others subject to the judge's direction and control.

(C) A judge shall not commend or criticize jurors for their verdict[①] other than in a court order or opinion in a proceeding.

RULE 2.9   Ex Parte[②] Communications

(A) A judge shall not initiate, permit, or consider ex parte communications, or consider other communications made to the judge outside the presence of the parties or their lawyers, concerning a pending or impending matter, except as follows:

(1) When circumstances require it, ex parte communication for scheduling, administrative, or emergency purposes, which does not address substantive matters, is permitted, provided:

(a) The judge reasonably believes that no party will gain a procedural, substantive, or tactical advantage as a result of the ex parte communication; and

(b) The judge makes provision promptly to notify all other parties of the substance of the ex parte communication, and gives the parties an opportunity to respond.

(2) A judge may obtain the written advice of a disinterested expert on the law applicable to a proceeding before the judge, if the judge gives advance notice to the parties of the person to be consulted and the subject matter of the advice to be solicited, and affords the parties a reasonable opportunity to object and respond to the notice and to the advice received.

(3) A judge may consult with court staff and court officials whose functions are to aid the judge in carrying out the judge's adjudicative responsibilities, or with other judges, provided the judge makes reasonable efforts to avoid receiving factual information that is not part of the record, and does not abrogate the responsibility personally to decide the matter.

(4) A judge may, with the consent of the parties, confer separately with the parties and their

---

① verdict:陪审团的裁断,裁决,陪审团就提交其审理的事项所作的正式裁决。通常可分为概括裁断(general verdict),即确定原告胜诉还是被告胜诉(民事案件中)或被告人有罪还是无罪(刑事案件中)的裁断;和特别裁断(special verdict),即陪审团仅对案件中的特定事项作出裁决,而将对该事实适用法律的问题留给法官解决,通常只有在很特殊的案件中才作出特别裁断/裁决。在英国,根据1974年《陪审团法》(Juries Act),民事案件中的陪审团裁断必须是一致裁断/裁决(unanimous verdict),除非当事人双方同意接受多数裁断(majority verdict);刑事案件中在某些情况下,法庭可以接受多数裁断。在苏格兰,民事诉讼中的裁断可以是一般裁断或特别裁断,且接受多数裁断;刑事诉讼中的裁断则包括有罪裁断(guilty)、罪证不足的裁断(not proven)和无罪裁断(not guilty),其中后两者都具有宣告无罪的效力。在美国,传统上要求陪审团裁断须是一致裁断,但现在已有改变。在刑事案件中,若所涉罪行轻微,有些州允许陪审团作出多数裁断;在民事案件中,许多州已放弃了对一致性的要求,允许作出12人陪审团中有10人同意的裁断,联邦法院则允许当事人约定将一定多数陪审员同意的裁断作为陪审团的裁断。

② ex parte:拉丁语,单方面的;为一方利益的;依单方申请的。

lawyers in an effort to settle matters pending before the judge.

(5) A judge may initiate, permit, or consider any ex parte communication when expressly authorized by law to do so.

(B) If a judge inadvertently receives an unauthorized ex parte communication bearing upon the substance of a matter, the judge shall make provision① promptly to notify the parties of the substance of the communication and provide the parties with an opportunity to respond.

(C) A judge shall not investigate facts in a matter independently, and shall consider only the evidence presented and any facts that may properly be judicially noticed.

(D) A judge shall make reasonable efforts, including providing appropriate supervision, to ensure that this Rule is not violated by court staff, court officials, and others subject to the judge's direction and control.

RULE 2.10 Judicial Statements on Pending and Impending Cases②

(A) A judge shall not make any public statement that might reasonably be expected to affect the outcome or impair the fairness of a matter pending or impending in any court, or make any nonpublic statement that might substantially interfere with a fair trial or hearing.

(B) A judge shall not, in connection with cases, controversies, or issues that are likely to come before the court, make pledges, promises, or commitments that are inconsistent with the impartial performance of the adjudicative duties of judicial office.

(C) A judge shall require court staff, court officials, and others subject to the judge's direction and control to refrain from making statements that the judge would be prohibited from making by paragraphs (A) and (B).

(D) Notwithstanding③ the restrictions in paragraph (A), a judge may make public statements in the course of official duties, may explain court procedures, and may comment on any proceeding in which the judge is a litigant④ in a personal capacity.

(E) Subject to the requirements of paragraph (A), a judge may respond directly or through a third party to allegations in the media or elsewhere concerning the judge's conduct in a matter.

RULE 2.11 Disqualification

(A) A judge shall disqualify himself or herself in any proceeding in which the judge's impartiality might reasonably be questioned, including but not limited to the following circumstances:

(1) The judge has a personal bias or prejudice concerning a party or a party's lawyer, or personal knowledge of facts that are in dispute in the proceeding.

(2) The judge knows that the judge, the judge's spouse or domestic partner, or a person within the third degree of relationship to either of them, or the spouse or domestic partner of such a person is:

---

① make provision to do：为……采取措施。

② a pending case：待决案件，已受理但未最终决定的案件；an impending case：期待中但未开始的案件。

③ notwithstanding：拉丁语（non obstante）不抵抗或处于某事的地位；意思是"不管、不顾、虽然、不过、无论如何、即使、但是、仍然；在法律草拟中，用以发出最重要情况的讯号"等的意思，既可以连接句子，也可以和短语使用。

④ litigant：诉讼当事人，如原告和被告。一般指实际参加诉讼者，而非名义上的当事人（nominal parties）。

Lesson Four Code of Judicial Conduct

(a) a party to the proceeding, or an officer, director, general partner①, managing member, or trustee of a party;

(b) acting as a lawyer in the proceeding;

(c) a person who has more than a de minimis interest that could be substantially affected by the proceeding; or

(d) likely to be a material witness② in the proceeding.

(3) The judge knows that he or she, individually or as a fiduciary, or the judge's spouse, domestic partner, parent, or child, or any other member of the judge's family residing in the judge's household, has an economic interest in the subject matter in controversy or is a party to the proceeding.

(4) The judge knows or learns by means of a timely motion③ that a party, a party's lawyer, or the law firm of a party's lawyer has within the previous(insert number)year/s made aggregate contributions to the judge's campaign in an amount that [is greater than $[insert amount] for an individual or $[insert amount for an entity] [is reasonable and appropriate for an individual or an entity].

(5) The judge, while a judge or a judicial candidate, has made a public statement, other than in a court proceeding, judicial decision, or opinion, that commits④ or appears to commit the judge to reach a particular result or rule in a particular way in the proceeding or controversy.

(6) The judge:

(a) served as a lawyer in the matter in controversy, or was associated with a lawyer who participated substantially as a lawyer in the matter during such association;

(b) served in governmental employment, and in such capacity participated personally and substantially as a lawyer or public official concerning the proceeding, or has publicly expressed in such capacity an opinion concerning the merits⑤ of the particular matter in controversy;

(c) was a material witness concerning the matter; or

(d) previously presided as a judge over the matter in another court.

(B) A judge shall keep informed about the judge's personal and fiduciary economic interests, and make a reasonable effort to keep informed about the personal economic interests of the judge's

---

① general partner:普通合伙人;无限(责任)合伙人,指在普通合伙(general partnership)中的合伙人;也指在有限合伙(limited partnership)中完全参与合伙组织的经营管理,分享利益,分担亏损,并以个人财产对合伙组织的全部债务承担责任的合伙人,故与有限合伙人(limited partner)相对,后者仅以其出资为限对合伙债务承担责任。

② material witness:重要证人,能够就与重要事实有某种逻辑联系的事项提供证言的证人,尤其是在几乎没有他人知道这些事项的情况下。

③ motion:(1) 提议;动议。议会中由议员提出建议或解决方法以供议会考虑及采取措施所用的一种正式方式。(2) 申请;请求;动议。向法庭或法官提出的、请求作出对申请人有利的裁决、命令或指示的行为。此种申请通常是在诉讼过程中提出的,且一般要在通知对方当事人后方可提出,但在某些案件中,也可以不经通知对方而直接提出申请,称为单方面申请(ex parte motion)。申请提出的形式可以是书面的,也可以是口头的。申请提出的时间在法院开庭审理前(如申请驳回起诉)、开庭审理过程中(如申请指示陪审团作出裁断)、开庭审理后(如申请重审)均可。有时法庭也可以依自己的申请或动议作出裁定、命令或指示,如法庭有权依自己的动议而召开审前会议。

④ commit:犯罪,作恶;委托,把……托付给;使作出保证;押交或提交,依法将某人送交监狱或精神病院、教养院、感化院等地方看管。此处应指第三个含义。

⑤ merits:当事人的法定权利;诉求或答辩的实质依据;案件的是非曲直。

spouse or domestic partner and minor children① residing in the judge's household.

(C) A judge subject to disqualification under this Rule, other than for bias or prejudice under paragraph (A)(1), may disclose on the record the basis of the judge's disqualification and may ask the parties and their lawyers to consider, outside the presence of the judge and court personnel, whether to waive② disqualification. If, following the disclosure, the parties and lawyers agree, without participation by the judge or court personnel, that the judge should not be disqualified, the judge may participate in the proceeding. The agreement shall be incorporated into the record of the proceeding.

RULE 2.12 Supervisory Duties

(A) A judge shall require court staff, court officials, and others subject to the judge's direction and control to act in a manner consistent with the judge's obligations under this Code.

(B) A judge with supervisory authority for the performance of other judges shall take reasonable measures to ensure that those judges properly discharge③ their judicial responsibilities, including the prompt disposition of matters before them.

RULE 2.13 Administrative Appointments

(A) In making administrative appointments, a judge:

(1) shall exercise the power of appointment impartially and on the basis of merit; and

(2) shall avoid nepotism④, favoritism⑤, and unnecessary appointments.

(B) A judge shall not appoint a lawyer to a position if the judge either knows that the lawyer, or the lawyer's spouse or domestic partner, has contributed more than $[insert amount] within the prior [insert number] year[s] to the judge's election campaign, or learns of such a contribution by means of a timely motion by a party or other person properly interested in the matter, unless:

(1) the position is substantially uncompensated;

(2) the lawyer has been selected in rotation from a list of qualified and available lawyers compiled without regard to their having made political contributions; or

(3) the judge or another presiding or administrative judge⑥ affirmatively finds that no other lawyer is willing, competent, and able to accept the position.

---

① minor children:未成年子女。

② waive:(英格兰古法)被剥夺法律保护的妇女,与被剥夺法律保护的男子(outlaw)相对。作为动词使用时,表示"放弃,放弃权利,弃权"的意思,句中的意思为该词的此义。

③ discharge:v. & n. (1) 清偿(债务);(2) 履行(义务);(3) 免除(债务、义务的履行,包括在破产程序终止后免除破产人的剩余债务);(4) 释放;出狱;允许离开;(5) 解雇;解聘;使退役;解除(军职);(6) 驳回(诉讼);(7) 撤销(法院命令);(8) 起(卸)货;(9) 排放;排泄。句中的意思是"履行职责"。

④ nepotism:裙带关系;任人唯亲。

⑤ favoritism:主要考虑友情或其他因素而非其才德的任人唯亲;偏袒,偏爱。

⑥ presiding or administrative judge:分别指主审法官、行政法官。

(C) A judge shall not approve compensation[①] of appointees beyond the fair value of services rendered.

RULE 2.14 Disability[②] and Impairment[③]

A judge having a reasonable belief that the performance of a lawyer or another judge is impaired by drugs or alcohol, or by a mental, emotional, or physical condition, shall take appropriate action, which may include a confidential referral to a lawyer or judicial assistance program.

RULE 2.15 Responding to Judicial and Lawyer Misconduct

(A) A judge having knowledge that another judge has committed a violation of this Code that raises a substantial question regarding the judge's honesty, trustworthiness, or fitness as a judge in other respects shall inform the appropriate authority.

(B) A judge having knowledge that a lawyer has committed a violation of the Rules of Professional Conduct that raises a substantial question regarding the lawyer's honesty, trustworthiness, or fitness as a lawyer in other respects shall inform the appropriate authority.

(C) A judge who receives information indicating a substantial likelihood that another judge has committed a violation of this Code shall take appropriate action.

(D) A judge who receives information indicating a substantial likelihood that a lawyer has committed a violation of the Rules of Professional Conduct shall take appropriate action.

---

① compensation：(1) 补偿；赔偿，指对他人的损失给予价值相当的货币，或其他等价物，以使受损一方当事人回复其原有状况。(2) 土地补偿金，因公共目的而致土地被征用或受到破坏性影响，从而给予土地所有人或占有人的价值相当的货币。如，英国1961年《土地补偿法》(Land Compensation Law) 规定土地补偿的一般原则是按土地的市场价值进行赔偿，即将土地在公开市场上自愿出售的卖主所期望实现的土地价值。1973年《土地补偿法》则规定，因使用公用设施所引起的喧嚣、振动、废气、烟气、热气或排放液体、固体物质从而造成土地价值贬损的，应予补偿。(3) 劳灾补偿，工人抚恤金，根据《劳工赔偿法》(workmen's compensation act)，由雇主向受伤雇员发放的款项。该术语在劳工赔偿法中是指根据该法所指定的人员和确定的额度提供的金钱补助，而不是指针对不法行为或违反合同依法起诉所获得的补偿性赔偿金。(4) 工作、劳务报酬，因提供工作或劳务而获得的回报，可以采用固定工资、费用、佣金或事先规定的其他方式。(5) 因捕获罪犯而获得的赏金。(6) 苏格兰法或大陆法中或美国路易斯安那州法中的抵消，双方当事人互为金钱或种类物的债权人和债务人，由于法律规定或双方的约定而使各自的债务归于消灭。

② disability：(1) 无能力；无资格，指在法律上缺乏实施行为或享有某些利益的能力，诸如无能力提起诉讼、缔结婚姻或转让财产。导致当事人无能力的原因可能是不足法定年龄、精神缺陷或被追究刑事责任等。与其相对应的概念是豁免(immunity)，它可以分为一般无能力(general disability)与特殊无能力(special disability)，前者指缺乏从事所有行为的能力，精神病人或未成年人即为殊例，其不能缔约或转让财产。在古代，罪犯不能就其自己的权利提起诉讼。后者是指缺乏从事特定行为的能力或暂时无能力，例如某人无权签订某一种类的合同。它也可以分为本人无能力(personal disability)与绝对无能力(absolute disability)，后一种情况除使当事人本人无能力外，尚及于其后代或继承人，例如，在以前，某人若构成叛国罪或其他重罪，则其继承人不得主张继承非限嗣继承地产。(2) 残疾，伤残，在有关劳工赔偿法上，伤残是由以下两个条件综合构成的：① 实际上无法从事雇佣工作并由此而失去工资；② 身体受到损害。基于社会保障利益之目的，该词在制定法上的定义则须符合三个条件：(a) 发生医学上可确定的肉体或精神损害，该损害将导致死亡或在很长时期或不确定期间内持续存在；(b) 缺乏从事任何可获得实质性收入的雇佣工作的能力；(c) 该无能力系由前述损害所致。

③ impairment：(1) 人体上的损伤、丧失身体上的或智力上的功能；(2) 愈变愈差，价值消损，或由以往没有受损或较少损伤的状况恶化。受损/损伤亦包括损害某人的思想过程、对现实的理解、情绪或判断的状况，或引致行为紊乱的状况；或引致需要依赖补救工具(例如导盲犬或轮椅等)的损害。

Legal Terminology

1. judiciary 与 judicial

Judiciary：表示所有法官，审判人员，法院系统，司法机关等意思，注意使用该词时，司法的概念非我国所理解的司法概念，为此，与 judicial 搭配使用的词在翻译中常常不分青红皂白就翻译成"司法……"的意思，如：judicial independence（司法独立），但使用时，英美主要指的是法官或法院。Judicial interpretation：法律解释，但该词常常被认为是司法解释，其与该词本意相距甚远。Judicial opinion：法官在其判决书中的判决词，而非通常所谓的法官意见。

2. integrity, honesty 与 justice

三个词都可以表示"正直"等意思，但：

integrity：指品格纯正，有高度是非感，正直诚实，受人敬佩。此外，integrity 还强调"完整，完善"等意思。如：data integrity（数据完整性）；business integrity（商业信誉）；territorial integrity（领土完整）。

honesty：普通用词，侧重为人忠厚，老实，正直，不欺骗，不说谎。

justice：侧重办事或处事公正，公道不偏心，此外，justice 更强调"公平；公正；正义；司法"的意思，此外还具有"法官；法律制裁"等意思。如：chief justice（首席大法官，首席法官）；failure of justice（审判不公，审判失当）；jungle justice（私刑）；miscarriage of justice（审判不公）；summary justice（即决裁判）；to bring sb. to justice（把某人送交法院审判；把……交付审判……）；to temper justice with mercy（宽严并济，恩威兼施）。

3. impartiality, integrity 与 fairness

三者都有"公正、正义"的意义，但着重点不同。

impartiality：n．公正，不偏不倚，不偏袒，居中审判案件，通常认为是法官和执法者所应具备的素质，要求平等地对待争议的各方当事人，对所有人平等地、公正地适用法律，没有偏见和偏袒。例如：impartiality of taxation（税收的公平原则）；impartiality of the judge（法官的居中审判，不偏不倚；法官公正性）；impartiality of tria（审判的公正性）。

integrity：n. 正直；诚实，用以指官员、受托人等的品性，与"probity"、"honesty"、"uprightness"同义。除此之外，integrity 还有另一层意义：完整（性），完善，尊严等意义。如：integrity right（著作的完整权，属于 moral rights 的一部分）；integrity of the individual（个人的尊严）。

fairness："公平/公允性，合理性，公平适当（指财务报告），公正，适当"等意思。如 fairness doctrine（公正使用原则，指对广播机构提供社会重大问题的影响范围所规定的责任，该范围应是广泛的且能反映不同观点，对于有关政治和社会争点问题的双方辩论人均应得到公正和等同的机会来广播他们的观点）。

4. rule of law

（1）法律原则，经有权机关批准认可，通常以基本原理（maxim）或者逻辑命题（logic proposition）的形式表达的、具有普适性的法律原则。之所以称为"原则"，是因为其在有疑问的案件中作出判决时所起到的指导或规范作用。因对法律原则的具体适用过程中不允许有自由裁量权，因此该项原则有时又被称为"法律至上"（supremacy of law）。

（2）法治，与人治相对，与"以法而治"（rule by law）相区别，与前者的区别在于法治是以法律而非个人的意志作为决策的依据;与后者的区别在于在法治中法律已被视作一种价值取向而不仅仅是一种治理的工具。"法治"是一个极为重要的概念,其历史与西方文明差不多同样悠久。但其具体含义依语境的变化而有所不同。最常见的含义是指与恣意的人治相对,根据现存既定规则(法律)进行的治理。第二个含义是指"法律之下的治理"(rule under law),即无任何人或政府机构凌驾法律之上或者超越于法律许可之外。第三个含义是指治理应符合更高的法律(rule according to a higher law),即,任何成文法律如果不符合某些非成文的、普遍存在的公正、道德性和正义等原则,则政府不得强制执行。这些含义意味着法律作为规则尽管具有某些功能性作用,但并不表明它是作为一种纯粹的工具而存在的。它实际上暗含了对于公民个体的至上价值和尊严的尊重。

5. canon 与 rule

两词均可以表示"规则,原则"的意思,但各自的内涵不同。

canon 的含义有:(1) 法律;法规;规则;准则;(2) 纪律;戒;(3) 判断标准;(4) 成套的准则、规则、规范或标准等;(5) 教会法;教规,特别是由教皇或宗教会议制定的,包含在教会法令的官方汇编中的行为规则;(6) 英格兰国教教规,由该国教会神职人员代表大会颁布的教会法令,无论其是否有法律效力;(7) 英国法政牧师,主教座堂的教会官员,指导举行宗教仪式,由国王或主教任命。教会法规定每个主教座堂至少必须有两个驻堂法政牧师专门从事教堂礼拜仪式。

rule:

作为动词使用时,主要含义有:(1)(依法院规则)命令;要求;(2) 法官解决案件;裁决庭审中出现的法律问题。

作为名词使用时,主要含义有:(1) 规则;细则;准则,由有权机关制定的,可导致确定的法律后果的行为规则或指导性准则,通常适用于较具体的事项;(2) 法庭的裁决;裁定;命令。

6. bias 与 prejudice

两个词意义相近,都有"偏见、成见"的意思。

bias:偏见;成见;倾向;预断;先入为主的观点,指对争议的一方存在赞成或反对的个人的且通常是不合理的判断的主观状态。在诉讼中它会使法官在案件审理中不能公正地履行职责。因此,避免存在实际的或明显的偏见是司法权行使过程中的一个重要方面。如果法官与案件有任何金钱上的利害关系,就不应参与案件的审理,不管这种利害关系有多小或多么间接,并且法官的任何表明其具有偏见的表述都将可能使判决无效。但作为使法官回避的理由的偏见,通常指法官对诉讼的一方当事人存在某种主观上的倾向或预断,而非法官对诉讼标的可能存在的任何观点。

prejudice:偏见;成见,指未了解事实或不顾事实真相而形成的观点或判断。除这个含义外,还有"损害;侵害"的意义,包括对权利及物质利益的侵害。法律英语中常见的短语有 without prejudice to...(不损害……的情况下)。

Exercises

I Verbal Abilities

Part One

Directions: *For each of these completing questions, read each item carefully to get the sense of it. Then, in the proper space, complete each statement by supplying the missing word or phrase.*

1. To _____ all the deficiencies of the international order in the resolution of conflict, a new system—international supervision—has gradually been introduced for the purpose of scrutinizing the behaviour of States which are parties to a specific treaty.

    A. rule out   B. deter   C. obviate   D. interpose   E. intervene

2. The clearing house guarantees that all of the futures trades in the futures market will _____ their obligations.

    A. honour   B. sublime   C. magnify   D. uprear   E. aggrandize

3. By _____ the compensatory interest to an overriding principle of damage calculation, the proposed Code opens up virtually all remedies to a defendant's claim.

    A. elevating   B. imposing   C. impacting   D. embedding   E. invoking

4. This section _____ remedial policies that control the applications of the mare specific remedial rules.

    A. sets forth   B. sets in   C. sets out   D. impresses on   E. extracts from

5. Pleas in favor of theoretical legal scholarship have in fact _____ a positive response in the United Kingdom.

    A. bought through   B. provided for   C. acquiesced in

    D. rendered important   E. yielded

6. While many lawyers in the United States may indeed feel _____ from their profession, law school teaching is unlikely to be the primary cause.

    A. alienated   B. remote   C. far   D. detached   E. separated

7. It should be emphasized that a corporation possesses the statutory attributes not because it is an artificial entity but because the statute so _____.

    A. accommodates   B. provides   C. prostrates   D. sustains   E. neglects

8. The publicly held corporations unquestionably _____ immense economic power when they make decisions.

    A. apply   B. brandish   C. utilize   D. swing   E. wield

9. While giving his ruling, an independent judge should be unmindful of personal, political, or financial _____.

    A. effects   B. backgrounds   C. capacities

    D. repercussions   E. millenaries

10. Misuse of office, undignified behavior, bias or _____, harmful or offensive conduct should be considered misconduct of judges.

A. burglar   B. prejudgment   C. threatening
D. slurs   E. precondition

Part Two

Directions: *Choose the one word or phase that best keep the meaning of the original sentence if it were substituted for the underlined part.*

1. As used in the law, a fee (derived from the Latin 'feodum', meaning a feof, or feudal estate) is an <u>eternal</u> interest in property.
   A. terminable   B. 9supertemporal   C. debateable
   D. remitting   E. undying

2. In spite of the <u>momentous</u> importance, the general duty to settle legal or political disputes peacefully is marred by the absence of any provision establishing by what modalities conflict and disagreement should be solved.
   A. momentary   B. impulsive   C. epochal   D. considerate   E. substantive

3. This existence of this cost may help explain why businessman <u>attach so much importance to</u> the reputations of their transactional partners.
   A. grant more attention to   B. think highly of
   C. are of primary importance to   D. devote to   E. pay no heed to

4. As a consequence, the aggrieved party may not <u>file suit</u> and may therefore receive no compensation.
   A. lodge an appeal   B. deliver a file   C. suit well
   D. appease a complaint   E. document its claims

5. Instead, they must be mindful of how the law in action can <u>diverge from</u> the law in books.
   A. react to   B. reason for   C. increase by   D. impress on   E. differ from

6. This is of importance because the legal system is not <u>marked off</u> neatly from other systems in society.
   A. divided into   B. produced   C. characterized   D. fortified   E. hedged

7. Private enterprises are required to create a similar system that <u>parallels</u> the government system.
   A. compares   B. correlates   C. corresponds   D. parcels out   E. parts with

8. Although commentators have described achieving market as a "reward", the benefits of the market economy designation may not be so great <u>in light of</u> the burdens attached.
   A. in terms of   B. by means of   C. in virtue of
   D. in nature with   E. free from

9. The Commission shall establish for appropriate cases an <u>expedited procedure</u> for consideration and determination of the question of a stay.
   A. special proceeding   B. extra procedure
   C. ad hoc formality   D. accelerated procedure   E. delayed process

10. When the Supreme Court <u>affirms</u> a lower court it is approving the decision made and leaving it unchanged.

A. supports   B. holds   C. upholds   D. backs   E. retains

II Cloze

Directions: *For each blank in the following passage, there are five answers marked A, B, C, and D. You are to choose the best answer from the choices given to complete the sentence.*

Judges have the ___(1)___ responsibility for decisions regarding freedoms, rights and duties of natural and legal persons within their jurisdiction. The independence of each individual judge ___(2)___ every person's right to have their case decided solely on the basis of the law, the evidence and facts, without any improper influence. A well-functioning, efficient and independent judiciary is an essential requirement for a fair, consistent and ___(3)___ administration of justice. Consequently, judicial independence is an indispensable element of the right to due process, the rule of law and democracy.

The separation of powers is a fundamental guarantee of the independence of the judiciary. In the decision-making process, judges should have freedom to decide cases impartially, in accordance with their ___(4)___ of the law and the facts. They should be able to act without any restriction or improper influence. Direct or indirect pressure, threats or interferences, should not come from any quarter or for any reason.

The principle of independence of the judiciary has been ___(5)___ in various human rights instruments, including the *Universal Declaration of Human Rights* and the *International Covenant on Civil and Political Rights*. There are also a number of UN standards, in particular the *Basic Principles on the Independence of the Judiciary* endorsed by the United Nations General Assembly in 1985 and the *Bangalore Principles of Judicial Conduct of 2002*.

Within the European framework, the right to an independent and ___(6)___ tribunal is guaranteed by Article 6 of the European Convention on Human Rights (ECHR). Apart from the ECHR, there exist a number of more detailed texts, among them the Council of Europe Recommendation on Judges: Independence, Efficiency and Responsibilities adopted by the Committee of Ministers in 2010.

The basic principles ensuring the independence of the judiciary should be ___(7)___ in the constitution. Judges are subject only to the law and their decisions should not be revised outside the ___(8)___ procedure. All decisions regarding the appointment and the professional career of judges should be based on ___(9)___, by means of the application of objective criteria. The evaluation of judges should never be based on the content of their decisions and, in particular, acquittals should in no way be considered as a sign of failure.

One of the most important standards underpinning the ___(10)___ of the judiciary is irremovability. That is, for ordinary judges to be appointed permanently until retirement. The irremovability of judges, including protection from involuntary transfers, as well as adequate remuneration ___(11)___ the dignity of the office are other factors that constitute the backbone of genuine independence.

Furthermore, it is important to ___(12)___ the appropriate balance between judges' accountability and their independence in adjudication. Disciplinary responsibility of judges shall not extend to the content of their verdicts or to judicial mistakes. Also, the body that initiates cases of judicial discipline should not be the one that adjudicates them. Judges facing these bodies should enjoy ___(13)___ safeguards and disciplinary hearings must be fully transparent.

It is axiomatic that a judge deciding a case should not act on any order or instruction of any third party, inside or outside the judiciary. A hierarchical organization of the judiciary which would amount to ___(14)___ of the judges to the court chairpersons or to higher instances in their judicial decision-making activities would be a clear infringement of this principle. In order for freedom from external influence to be ensured, the law should provide ___(15)___ against outside actors seeking to influence judges in any manner.

(1) A. fundamental   B ultimate   C. conclusive   D. eventual
(2) A safeguards   B. shelters   C. protects   D. harbors
(3) A. uninterested   B. disinterested   C. neutral   D. dispassionate
(4) A. explication   B. clarification   C. explanation   D. interpretation
(5) A. lay by   B. laid down   C. specified   D. lay about
(6) A. impartial   B. evenhanded   C. indifferent   D. impersonal
(7) A. set about   B. set forth   C. set out   D. set aside
(8) A. petitions   B. entreats   C. appeals   D. pleads
(9) A. merit   B. distinction   C. credit   D. accomplishment
(10) A. self-direction   B. autonomy   C. self-sufficiency   D. sovereignty
(11) A. in conformity with B. in light of   C. with pursuance to
     D. in accordance with
(12) A. assault   B. strike   C. overtake   D. thrash
(13) A. bureaucratic   B. ceremonial   C. procedural   D. routine
(14) A. subservience   B. subordination   C. dependency   D. relegation
(15) A. authorizations   B. endorsements   C. affirmation   D. sanctions

III Reading Comprehension

Part One   Short-answer Questions

Directions: *In this section, there are questions or unfinished statements, read the section carefully and answer the questions.*

Canon 3

A judge shall conduct the judge's personal and extrajudicial activities to minimize the risk of conflict with the obligations of judicial office.

RULE 3.1 Extrajudicial Activities in General

A judge may engage in extrajudicial activities, except as prohibited by law or this Code. However, when engaging in extrajudicial activities, a judge shall not:

(A) participate in activities that will interfere with the proper performance of the judge's judicial duties;

(B) participate in activities that will lead to frequent disqualification of the judge;

(C) participate in activities that would appear to a reasonable person to undermine the judge's independence, integrity, or impartiality;

(D) engage in conduct that would appear to a reasonable person to be coercive; or

(E) make use of court premises, staff, stationery, equipment, or other resources, except for incidental use for activities that concern the law, the legal system, or the administration of justice, or unless such additional use is permitted by law.

RULE 3.2 Appearances before Governmental Bodies and Consultation with Government Officials

A judge shall not appear voluntarily at a public hearing before, or otherwise consult with, an executive or a legislative body or official, except:

(A) in connection with matters concerning the law, the legal system, or the administration of justice;

(B) in connection with matters about which the judge acquired knowledge or expertise in the course of the judge's judicial duties; or

(C) when the judge is acting pro se in a matter involving the judge's legal or economic interests, or when the judge is acting in a fiduciary capacity.

RULE 3.3 Testifying as a Character Witness

A judge shall not testify as a character witness in a judicial, administrative, or other adjudicatory proceeding or otherwise vouch for the character of a person in a legal proceeding, except when duly summoned.

RULE 3.4 Appointments to Governmental Positions

A judge shall not accept appointment to a governmental committee, board, commission, or other governmental position, unless it is one that concerns the law, the legal system, or the administration of justice.

RULE 3.5 Use of Nonpublic Information

A judge shall not intentionally disclose or use nonpublic information acquired in a judicial capacity for any purpose unrelated to the judge's judicial duties.

RULE 3.6 Affiliations with Discriminatory Organizations

(A) A judge shall not hold membership in any organization that practices invidious discrimination on the basis of race, sex, gender, religion, national origin, ethnicity, or sexual orientation.

(B) A judge shall not use the benefits or facilities of an organization if the judge knows or should know that the organization practices invidious discrimination on one or more of the bases identified in paragraph (A). A judge's attendance at an event in a facility of an organization that the judge is not permitted to join is not a violation of this Rule when the judge's attendance is an isolated event that could not reasonably be perceived as an endorsement of the organization's practices.

RULE 3.7 Participation in Educational, Religious, Charitable, Fraternal, or Civic Organizations and Activities

(A) Subject to the requirements of Rule 3.1, a judge may participate in activities sponsored by organizations or governmental entities concerned with the law, the legal system, or the administration of justice, and those sponsored by or on behalf of educational, religious, charitable, fraternal, or civic organizations not conducted for profit, including but not limited to the following activities:

(1) assisting such an organization or entity in planning related to fund-raising, and participating in the management and investment of the organization's or entity's funds;

(2) soliciting contributions for such an organization or entity, but only from members of the judge's family, or from judges over whom the judge does not exercise supervisory or appellate authority;

(3) soliciting membership for such an organization or entity, even though the membership dues or fees generated may be used to support the objectives of the organization or entity, but only if the organization or entity is concerned with the law, the legal system, or the administration of justice;

(4) appearing or speaking at, receiving an award or other recognition at, being featured on the program of, and permitting his or her title to be used in connection with an event of such an organization or entity, but if the event serves a fund-raising purpose, the judge may participate only if the event concerns the law, the legal system, or the administration of justice;

(5) making recommendations to such a public or private fund-granting organization or entity in connection with its programs and activities, but only if the organization or entity is concerned with the law, the legal system, or the administration of justice; and

(6) serving as an officer, director, trustee, or nonlegal advisor of such an organization or entity, unless it is likely that the organization or entity:

(a) will be engaged in proceedings that would ordinarily come before the judge; or

(b) will frequently be engaged in adversary proceedings in the court of which the judge is a member, or in any court subject to the appellate jurisdiction of the court of which the judge is a member.

(B) A judge may encourage lawyers to provide pro bono publico legal services.

RULE 3.8 Appointments to Fiduciary Positions

(A) A judge shall not accept appointment to serve in a fiduciary position, such as executor, administrator, trustee, guardian, attorney in fact, or other personal representative, except for the estate, trust, or person of a member of the judge's family, and then only if such service will not interfere with the proper performance of judicial duties.

(B) A judge shall not serve in a fiduciary position if the judge as fiduciary will likely be engaged in proceedings that would ordinarily come before the judge, or if the estate, trust, or ward becomes involved in adversary proceedings in the court on which the judge serves, or one under its appellate jurisdiction.

(C) A judge acting in a fiduciary capacity shall be subject to the same restrictions on engaging in financial activities that apply to a judge personally.

(D) If a person who is serving in a fiduciary position becomes a judge, he or she must comply with this Rule as soon as reasonably practicable, but in no event later than [one year] after becoming a judge.

RULE 3.9 Service as Arbitrator or Mediator

A judge shall not act as an arbitrator or a mediator or perform other judicial functions apart from the judge's official duties unless expressly authorized by law.

RULE 3.10 Practice of Law

A judge shall not practice law. A judge may act pro se and may, without compensation, give legal advice to and draft or review documents for a member of the judge's family, but is prohibited from serving as the family member's lawyer in any forum.

RULE 3.11 Financial, Business, or Remunerative Activities

(A) A judge may hold and manage investments of the judge and members of the judge's family.

(B) A judge shall not serve as an officer, director, manager, general partner, advisor, or employee of any business entity except that a judge may manage or participate in:

(1) a business closely held by the judge or members of the judge's family; or

(2) a business entity primarily engaged in investment of the financial resources of the judge or members of the judge's family.

(C) A judge shall not engage in financial activities permitted under paragraphs (A) and (B) if they will:

(1) interfere with the proper performance of judicial duties;

(2) lead to frequent disqualification of the judge;

(3) involve the judge in frequent transactions or continuing business relationships with lawyers or other persons likely to come before the court on which the judge serves; or

(4) result in violation of other provisions of this Code.

RULE 3.12 Compensation for Extrajudicial Activities

A judge may accept reasonable compensation for extrajudicial activities permitted by this Code or other law unless such acceptance would appear to a reasonable person to undermine the judge's independence, integrity, or impartiality.

RULE 3.13 Acceptance and Reporting of Gifts, Loans, Bequests, Benefits, or Other Things of Value

(A) A judge shall not accept any gifts, loans, bequests, benefits, or other things of value, if acceptance is prohibited by law or would appear to a reasonable person to undermine the judge's independence, integrity, or impartiality.

(B) Unless otherwise prohibited by law, or by paragraph (A), a judge may accept the following without publicly reporting such acceptance:

(1) items with little intrinsic value, such as plaques, certificates, trophies, and greeting cards;

(2) gifts, loans, bequests, benefits, or other things of value from friends, relatives, or other persons, including lawyers, whose appearance or interest in a proceeding pending or impending before the judge would in any event require disqualification of the judge under Rule 2.11;

(3) ordinary social hospitality;

(4) commercial or financial opportunities and benefits, including special pricing and discounts, and loans from lending institutions in their regular course of business, if the same opportunities and benefits or loans are made available on the same terms to similarly situated persons who are not judges;

(5) rewards and prizes given to competitors or participants in random drawings, contests, or other events that are open to persons who are not judges;

(6) scholarships, fellowships, and similar benefits or awards, if they are available to similarly situated persons who are not judges, based upon the same terms and criteria;

(7) books, magazines, journals, audiovisual materials, and other resource materials supplied by publishers on a complimentary basis for official use; or

(8) gifts, awards, or benefits associated with the business, profession, or other separate activity of a spouse, a domestic partner, or other family member of a judge residing in the judge's household, but that incidentally benefit the judge.

(C) Unless otherwise prohibited by law or by paragraph (A), a judge may accept the following items, and must report such acceptance to the extent required by Rule 3.15:

(1) gifts incident to a public testimonial;

(2) invitations to the judge and the judge's spouse, domestic partner, or guest to attend without charge:

(a) an event associated with a bar-related function or other activity relating to the law, the legal system, or the administration of justice; or

(b) an event associated with any of the judge's educational, religious, charitable, fraternal or civic activities permitted by this Code, if the same invitation is offered to nonjudges who are engaged in similar ways in the activity as is the judge; and

(3) gifts, loans, bequests, benefits, or other things of value, if the source is a party or other person, including a lawyer, who has come or is likely to come before the judge, or whose interests have come or are likely to come before the judge.

RULE 3.14 Reimbursement of Expenses and Waivers of Fees or Charges

(A) Unless otherwise prohibited by Rules 3.1 and 3.13(A) or other law, a judge may accept reimbursement of necessary and reasonable expenses for travel, food, lodging, or other incidental expenses, or a waiver or partial waiver of fees or charges for registration, tuition, and similar items, from sources other than the judge's employing entity, if the expenses or charges are associated with the judge's participation in extrajudicial activities permitted by this Code.

(B) Reimbursement of expenses for necessary travel, food, lodging, or other incidental expenses shall be limited to the actual costs reasonably incurred by the judge and, when appropriate to the occasion, by the judge's spouse, domestic partner, or guest.

(C) A judge who accepts reimbursement of expenses or waivers or partial waivers of fees or charges on behalf of the judge or the judge's spouse, domestic partner, or guest shall publicly report such acceptance as required by Rule 3.15.

RULE 3.15 Reporting Requirements

(A) A judge shall publicly report the amount or value of:

(1) compensation received for extrajudicial activities as permitted by Rule 3.12;

(2) gifts and other things of value as permitted by Rule 3.13(C), unless the value of such items, alone or in the aggregate with other items received from the same source in the same calendar year, does not exceed $[insert amount]; and

(3) reimbursement of expenses and waiver of fees or charges permitted by Rule 3.14(A), unless the amount of reimbursement or waiver, alone or in the aggregate with other reimbursements or waivers received from the same source in the same calendar year, does not exceed $[insert amount].

(B) When public reporting is required by paragraph (A), a judge shall report the date, place, and nature of the activity for which the judge received any compensation; the description of any gift, loan, bequest, benefit, or other thing of value accepted; and the source of reimbursement of expenses or waiver or partial waiver of fees or charges.

(C) The public report required by paragraph (A) shall be made at least annually, except that for reimbursement of expenses and waiver or partial waiver of fees or charges, the report shall be made within thirty days following the conclusion of the event or program.

(D) Reports made in compliance with this Rule shall be filed as public documents in the office of the clerk of the court on which the judge serves or other office designated by law, and, when technically feasible, posted by the court or office personnel on the court's website.

1. What does Canon 3 mainly contain?

2. Give a definition of Character Witness according to your understanding after reading the **RULE 3.3**.

3. What are the compensation for extrajudicial activities?

4. List some rules designed to eliminate bias and prejudice.

5. Please give some comments on the Canon 3.

6. Summarize the judge's duties in general.

Part Two True or False Questions

Canon 4

A judge or candidate for judicial office shall not engage in political or campaign activity that is inconsistent with the independence, integrity, or impartiality of the judiciary.

RULE 4.1 Political and Campaign Activities of Judges and Judicial Candidates in General

(A) Except as permitted by law, or by Rules 4.2, 4.3, and 4.4, a judge or a judicial candidate shall not:

(1) act as a leader in, or hold an office in, a political organization;

(2) make speeches on behalf of a political organization;

(3) publicly endorse or oppose a candidate for any public office;

(4) solicit funds for, pay an assessment to, or make a contribution to a political organization or a candidate for public office;

(5) attend or purchase tickets for dinners or other events sponsored by a political organization

or a candidate for public office;

(6) publicly identify himself or herself as a candidate of a political organization;

(7) seek, accept, or use endorsements from a political organization;

(8) personally solicit or accept campaign contributions other than through a campaign committee authorized by Rule 4.4;

(9) use or permit the use of campaign contributions for the private benefit of the judge, the candidate, or others;

(10) use court staff, facilities, or other court resources in a campaign for judicial office;

(11) knowingly, or with reckless disregard for the truth, make any false or misleading statement;

(12) make any statement that would reasonably be expected to affect the outcome or impair the fairness of a matter pending or impending in any court; or

(13) in connection with cases, controversies, or issues that are likely to come before the court, make pledges, promises, or commitments that are inconsistent with the impartial performance of the adjudicative duties of judicial office.

(B) A judge or judicial candidate shall take reasonable measures to ensure that other persons do not undertake, on behalf of the judge or judicial candidate, any activities prohibited under paragraph (A).

RULE 4.2 Political and Campaign Activities of Judicial Candidates in Public Elections

(A) A judicial candidate in a partisan, nonpartisan, or retention public election shall:

(1) act at all times in a manner consistent with the independence, integrity, and impartiality of the judiciary;

(2) comply with all applicable election, election campaign, and election campaign fund-raising laws and regulations of this jurisdiction;

(3) review and approve the content of all campaign statements and materials produced by the candidate or his or her campaign committee, as authorized by Rule 4.4, before their dissemination; and

(4) take reasonable measures to ensure that other persons do not undertake on behalf of the candidate activities, other than those described in Rule 4.4, that the candidate is prohibited from doing by Rule 4.1.

(B) A candidate for elective judicial office may, unless prohibited by law, and not earlier than [insert amount of time] before the first applicable primary election, caucus, or general or retention election:

(1) establish a campaign committee pursuant to the provisions of Rule 4.4;

(2) speak on behalf of his or her candidacy through any medium, including but not limited to advertisements, websites, or other campaign literature;

(3) publicly endorse or oppose candidates for the same judicial office for which he or she is running;

(4) attend or purchase tickets for dinners or other events sponsored by a political organization or a candidate for public office;

(5) seek, accept, or use endorsements from any person or organization other than a partisan political organization; and

(6) contribute to a political organization or candidate for public office, but not more than $[insert amount] to any one organization or candidate.

(C) A judicial candidate in a partisan public election may, unless prohibited by law, and not earlier than [insert amount of time] before the first applicable primary election, caucus, or general election:

(1) identify himself or herself as a candidate of a political organization; and

(2) seek, accept, and use endorsements of a political organization.

RULE 4.3 Activities of Candidates for Appointive Judicial Office

A candidate for appointment to judicial office may:

(A) communicate with the appointing or confirming authority, including any selection, screening, or nominating commission or similar agency; and

(B) seek endorsements for the appointment from any person or organization other than a partisan political organization.

RULE 4.4 Campaign Committees

(A) A judicial candidate subject to public election may establish a campaign committee to manage and conduct a campaign for the candidate, subject to the provisions of this Code. The candidate is responsible for ensuring that his or her campaign committee complies with applicable provisions of this Code and other applicable law.

(B) A judicial candidate subject to public election shall direct his or her campaign committee:

(1) to solicit and accept only such campaign contributions as are reasonable, in any event not to exceed, in the aggregate, $[insert amount] from any individual or $[insert amount] from any entity or organization;

(2) not to solicit or accept contributions for a candidate's current campaign more than [insert amount of time] before the applicable primary election, caucus, or general or retention election, nor more than [insert number] days after the last election in which the candidate participated; and

(3) to comply with all applicable statutory requirements for disclosure and divestiture of campaign contributions, and to file with [name of appropriate regulatory authority] a report stating the name, address, occupation, and employer of each person who has made campaign contributions to the committee in an aggregate value exceeding $[insert amount]. The report must be filed within [insert number] days following an election, or within such other period as is provided by law.

RULE 4.5 Activities of Judges Who Become Candidates for Nonjudicial Office

(A) Upon becoming a candidate for a nonjudicial elective office, a judge shall resign from judicial office, unless permitted by law to continue to hold judicial office.

(B) Upon becoming a candidate for a nonjudicial appointive office, a judge is not required to resign from judicial office, provided that the judge complies with the other provisions of this Code.

1. A judge or candidate for judicial office shall not engage in political or campaign activity. ( )

2. A judge or a judicial candidate is allowed to solicit funds for, pay an assessment to, or make a contribution to a political organization or a candidate for public office. ( )

3. A judge or judicial candidate should engage in political or campaign activity prescribed by Code and do not need to pay attention to what others do. ( )

4. A judicial candidate can not disseminate their campaign statements and materials directly. ( )

5. A candidate for elective judicial office may, unless prohibited by law, seek endorsements for the appointment from any person or organization other than a partisan political organization before the first applicable primary election, caucus, or general or retention election. ( )

6. A judge may not, for example, act as a leader or hold an office in a political organization, publicly endorse a political candidate, or make speeches on behalf of a political organization. ( )

IV Translation Abilities

法律语言特征分析与法律翻译技能培养之四：

法律语言学

20 世纪以来,随着文学、历史、哲学等人文社会学科纷纷受到"语言帝国主义"的侵袭,法学中也出现了以哈特(H. L. A. Hart)为代表的语义分析法学,佩雷尔曼(Perelman)的新修辞法学及法律解释学,故有"法学的语言学转向"之称。同时,随着语言学、心理语言学和社会语言学的发展及言语行为理论、会话分析和交际能力研究的加强,以及在过去几十年中,律师、司法人员、执法人员在实践中碰到诸多与语言和话语相关的问题,他们经常向语言学家请教,两大学科的渗透与交叉性日渐突出,一门新的学科——法律语言学的形成时机日益成熟。1993 年 7 月在德国波恩召开的首届国际法律语言学家协会(The International Association of Forensic Linguists, IAFL)大会为其成立标志。

我们可以说,法律语言学的研究对象是以立法语言和司法语言为基础,以语言变异为对象,以语言学基本理论为指导,结合相关法律原理去解决法务中各种语言问题的语言行为。进而,法律语言学的研究领域是广泛的。英国伯明翰大学将其归纳为语段分析、法庭语言、法律可读性、作者鉴定、语言变体、口语笔录、口语翻译、专家举证、法律统计学、笔迹学、语料库建议、历史回顾、语言权利与政策及书评等二十个方面。国内有学者将其研究领域概括为理论研究与实用研究两方面,前者包括法律语言与哲学、法律语用学、法律语言与文化、法律语言修辞学、法律语义学等,后者包括法庭语言研究、法庭翻译、法律双语及多语研究、法律语言技能分析与训练、法律语料库建设等。

法庭语言研究是目前国外法律语言学研究的中心。这与国际法律语言学家协会的狭义研究范围相吻合,即侧重语言在法律语境中的具体应用,并与具体案例相联系。他们在这方面的研究成果颇丰,如:Maley, O'Barr, Conley & O'Barr, Fuler, Berk-Selig 和 Edwards, Storywhyte, Hale & Gibbons 等分别在法庭语篇的结构、法庭权力的体现、法庭翻译等方面影响较大。而早期对法律语言学理论进行研究的有亚里士多德(Aristotle)的《修辞学》,西塞罗

(Cicero),大卫·梅林可夫(David Mellinkoff)的《法律语言》,克里斯多(Crystal)与戴维(Davy)的《英语语体研究》及古德里奇(Goodrich)等。

我国法律语言学研究立足于本国实际,侧重于语言本身的研究,如法律语言的句法特点,法律语体的表现风格,法庭辩论的语言艺术与修辞以及法律语言学基本理论探讨,如法律语言学学科定位及构建、任务、研究对象等。另外,由于英国的地位与作用,许多人从事于法律英语方面的研究及成果也集中于语言本身(法律英语的语言特征)。即主要侧重于用"文体学"和"句法学"理论来分析法律英语的文体特点,如法律书面语言的语体,以及其句法特征等等;"词汇学"理论用来研究法律术语特征、分类、词源、语义特征等;用"术语学"理论来研究法律术语的概念构成、定义以及术语标准化等;用"语义学"理论来研究法律术语静态的字面意义;用"语用学"理论来研究法律英语动态的应用中的意义。还有部分研究者运用"社会语言学"理论来研究法律语言与社会的关系;"语言与文化"理论了解法律语言与不同文化背景的关系和相互作用;"模糊语言学"理论从不同侧面了解法律语言的精确性是相对的,以及法律语言模糊的成因和如何正确理解和应用法律语言的模糊性。

就目前研究看,我国法律语言学研究领域比较有影响的有:刘愫贞的《法律语言:立法与司法的艺术》(1990),姜剑云的《法律语言与言语研究》(1995),王洁的《法律语言学教程》(1997年),孙懿华、周广然的《法律语言学》(1997),潘庆云的《跨世纪的中国法律语言》(1997),李振宇的《法律语言学初探》(1998),陈炯的《法律语言学概论》(1998),彭京宜的《法律语言的文化解析》(2001),吴伟平的《语言与法律——司法领域的语言学研究》(2002),刘红婴的《法律语言学》(2003),刘蔚铭的《法律语言学研究》(2003),杜金榜的《法律语言学》(2003),廖美珍的《法庭问答及其互动研究》(2004),宋雷的《法律同义近义词辨析翻译指南》(2005),宋雷、张绍全的《英汉对比法律语言学》(2010)等。

Translation Exercises:

Part One *Put the Following into Chinese*

As the director of President Reagan's strike force against unfair trade, I targeted Airbus subsidies and a variety of Japanese trade barriers. Although we achieved positive results in specific cases, in a broader sense we got nowhere. Airbus still found ways to get subsidies and Japan remained largely impervious to imports.

My experience taught me that in today's globalised world two different games are being played. One is suggested by the formal rules of the World Trade Organization. The other is a silent mercantilism played by countries that use subsidies and domestic regulations to exploit ambiguities in the formal WTO rules—or that simply ignore them.

I have therefore been bemused by the recent filing of WTO complaints from Washington, Brussels, and Tokyo against China's export restrictions on rare earths(稀土). Not that I think the filings unjustified. Indeed, I believe they are a step in the right direction. But they are a sideshow.

Consider that just this past weekend, in the wake of these filings, Brazilian finance minister Guido Mantega vowed to manipulate the Brazilian real and to provide whatever subsidies are necessary to keep Brazilian manufacturers competitive against imports.

The WTO may well find against China. But so what? Will that actually result in a surge of unrestricted rare earth exports? I sympathize with the sentiments of complainants in this and other cases. But will they produce desired results? Will Mr Mantega repent actions that most call protectionist but he calls "defensive measures"? I submit that the answer to these questions is no.

President Barack Obama keeps insisting that "everyone has to play by the same rules". But the problem is not a matter of a few discrete instances of rule-breaking. It is a much broader free-trade charade. It has long been the unspoken premise of globalization that all the members of the WTO and other international organizations are playing the private enterprise, free market, free-trade game—and that no systemic differences exist between the rules in different countries. Let's call the game "trade rugby", an international game played between everyone in the same way. In this view of the game, any difficulties are understood as discrete problems that can be resolved through application of the rules. And it is assumed that similar problems will not arise again. But as I know from experience and as we see in the cases of China and Brazil, the same problems keep returning. That means only one thing—not everyone is playing the same game.

Consider that China's rare-earth export restraints are not the action of some private monopoly. They are a policy decision that favors production of certain products in China. The recent General Electric deal to do avionics(航空电子学;航空控制系统) with China's Avic was not the result of the invisible hand. Rather, GE understood from reading China's five-year plan that if it wanted to sell avionics in China it had better produce them there.

This is a different game to trade rugby. It's a game adapted to suit particular countries, a bit like American football. Taking advantage of the rules' ambiguity, it can be played in the shadows of the global institutions but it cannot be disciplined by them because it is a game with its own very different rules and scoring system.

Part Two *Put the Following into English*

WTO必须意识到全球化所面临的两套游戏规则并存的现状,并建立起一套清晰的标准,以区分哪些经济体遵守的是哪一套规则,以及WTO规则在何种情况下适用。举例来说,WTO可以阐明,一个国家将某些重点行业列为优先发展对象的五年计划,是属于美式还是英式橄榄球的范畴。众所周知,这类计划涉及对相关行业的扶持,这会导致产能过剩,从而成为出口的动力并出现倾销,因此,或许应该有这样一套规则,当出现类似巴西的情况时,它能够为"防御性"反击措施赋予合法性。通过这种方式,所有的参与者都可以在不损害他人利益的情况下,发展各自想要发展的行业,而现行这种具有破坏作用且拘泥于法律条文的说教式争议解决程序将变得多余。

对奥巴马来说,他应该做的不是徒劳无益地坚持所有人都应遵守"同样的游戏规则",而是呼吁"同一种全球化,两套游戏规则"。

V Interaction

Discuss with your tutor(s) or the People's judges in your locality about the judicial conduct and judicial discipline. Then based on the discussion, you are supposed to write a composition about how the judicial conduct and judicial discipline in Chinese People's Courts. Remember that you are required to express your ideas clearly.

VI Appreciation of Judge's Opinions

(1) **Case Name**(案件名): *Inquiry Concerning A Judge, No. 09-01 Re: N. James Turner*

Inquiry Concerning A Judge, No. 09-01 Re: N. James Turner
Supreme Court of Florida

No. SC09-1182

INQUIRY CONCERNING A JUDGE, NO. 09-01 RE: N. JAMES TURNER.
[November 18, 2011]

(2) **Case Summary**(案情简介)

The court reviewed the recommendation of the Florida Judicial Qualifications Commission (JQC) that N. James Turner, Circuit Judge, be removed from office for a series of violations of the Code of Judicial Conduct. After considering all the evidence presented and conducting a final hearing, the Investigative Panel of the JQC found Judge Turner guilty of six specific charges as well as a separate charge asserting that certain specific charges constituted a pattern of misconduct. The court accepted the Panel's findings of guilt with respect to five of the specific charges, as well as the charge of a pattern of misconduct. The court removed Judge Turner from office based on these violations. The court did not reach the other specific charge—a charge regarding the solicitation of campaign contributions, which Judge Turner challenged on constitutional grounds.

(3) **Excerpts of the Judgment**(法官判决词)

PER CURIAM(法院/法庭共同决议,无需标记出各法官意见的法院判决).

We have for review the recommendation of the Florida Judicial Qualifications Commission (JQC)(佛罗里达州法官行为委员会,根据美国巡回法院而设立的各州就法官行为或司法行为而设立的惩戒或起诉法官的委员会) that N. James Turner, Circuit Judge(巡回法院) for Florida's Ninth Judicial Circuit, be removed from office(撤销法官职务) for a series of violations of the Code of Judicial Conduct. We have jurisdiction. For the reasons we explain, we approve the JQC's recommendation of removal.

On July 8, 2009, the Investigative Panel(调查小组) of the JQC filed a notice of formal charges against Judge Turner, pursuant to article V, section 12(b) of the Florida Constitution. After several amendments, the matter proceeded to the JQC Hearing Panel (the Panel)(听审小组) on an amended notice charging thirteen counts of judicial misconduct(以十三项罪名指控其不端司法行为). Some of these counts stemmed from Judge Turner's actions during his ultimately successful 2008 campaign for circuit judge(成功竞选为巡回法院法官), and some stemmed from his conduct after he assumed office(就职). After considering all of the evidence presented and conducting a final hearing, the Panel found Judge Turner guilty of six specific charges as well as a separate charge asserting that certain of the specific charges constituted a pattern of misconduct. Based on Judge Turner's commission of multiple canon violations(违背法官行为示范法典的基本准则), the Panel recommended his removal from office. As explained in detail below, we accept the Panel's findings of guilt with respect to five of the specific charges, as well as the charge of a pattern of misconduct. We remove Judge Turner from office based on these violations. We need not reach the other specific charge—a charge regarding the solicitation of campaign contributions(政治献金), which Judge Turner challenges on constitutional grounds. In judicial disciplinary proceedings(司法惩戒程序), this Court must independently review the JQC's findings to determine whether they are established by clear and convincing evidence(明确且令人信服的证据). This is so because the JQC is in a position to evaluate the testimony and evidence first hand.

We now examine the specific charges on which the Panel found Judge Turner guilty.

Lesson Four Code of Judicial Conduct

Count 5

Count 5 alleges a campaign contribution solicitation in violation of Canon 7C(1), which proscribes the personal solicitation of campaign funds by judicial candidates. Judge Turner challenges the constitutionality of Canon 7C(1), contending that the canon violates the First Amendment of the United States Constitution. In finding Judge Turner guilty on count 5, the Panel discussed Judge Turner's constitutional argument but ultimately declined to make a finding or conclusion regarding the matter, recognizing that any such determination should come from this Court. Because we conclude that Judge Turner's misconduct apart from the charges contained in count 5 requires his removal, we too decline to decide the constitutional issue at this juncture(在此时,值此之际;在这个当口,在这个节骨眼上).

Count 7

The allegations in count 7 focus on Judge Turner's inappropriate campaign finance conduct(不适当的竞选筹资行为), which occurred before he took the bench(就任法官):

7. During the campaign for the office you now hold, you knowingly accepted and received a very substantial campaign contribution made for the purpose of influencing the results of the election, whether characterized as a gift or loan, far in excess of the $500 limit established by Ch. 106, Florida Statutes, from your mother (Mignon Gordon) which you used to pay for your campaign, in violation of Chapter 106, Florida Statutes, and Canons 1, 2A and 7C(1) of the Code of Judicial Conduct.

The Panel determined that Judge Turner was guilty of violating chapter 106 and Canon 7C(1), but determined that Canons 1 and 2A were not applicable to Judge Turner's misconduct. The gravity of the misconduct(其不端行为的严重性) charged in count 7 lies in Judge Turner's violation of Florida's campaign finance laws, set forth in chapter 106, Florida Statutes. In light of our decision not to address the constitutionality of Canon 7C(1), we do not address the Panel's finding that Judge Turner's conduct described in count 7 violates that canon. Contrary to the Panel's determination that Canons 1 and 2A were not applicable, we conclude that Judge Turner's violations of chapter 106 also constituted violations of the requirement of Canon 1 that judges maintain "high standards of conduct" and the requirement of Canon 2A that judges "respect and comply with the law and ... act at all times in a manner that promotes public confidence in the integrity ... of the judiciary." Florida law provides that

"except for political parties, no person, political committee, or committee of continuous existence may, in any election, make contributions in excess of $500 to any candidate for election to or retention in office(留任) or to any political committee supporting or opposing one or more candidates."

A "loan" is included in the definition of "contribution". Moreover, any contribution received by the candidate for election—on the day of that election or less than 5 days prior to the day of that election must be returned by him or her to the person or committee contributing it and may not be used or expended by or on behalf of the candidate. The Panel found that near the end of his 2008 campaign, Judge Turner solicited funds from his mother, Mignon Gordon, to help pay off outstanding (unsettled) campaign debt. At Judge Turner's request, Ms. Gordon refinanced her condominium(多层公寓中有独立所有权的一套公寓房间,一个住宅单元,实质上有点类似我国现在的连排住房) and on November 5, 2008—one day after Judge Turner was elected to office—wired $42,288.75 into Judge Turner's personal account. On that same day, Judge Turner transferred $15,000 from his personal account to his campaign account and two days later transferred another $15,000. During the JQC investigation, Judge Turner admitted that the money he loaned to his campaign came from the funds that his mother loaned him.

The Panel concluded that the $30,000 that Judge Turner's campaign received from his mother was in excess of the $500 limit on individual campaign contributions(个人政治献金额度不得超过500美元) established in section 106.08(1)(a), Florida Statutes, and that the loan was received after the cut-off date established in section 106.08(3)(a), Florida Statutes. Judge Turner does not dispute the fact that he received a loan from his mother in violation of the contribution limitations established by Florida law. We accept these findings and the Panel's determination of guilt.

Counts 8 and 9

The charges contained in counts 8 and 9 stem from actions taken by Judge Turner—after he became a sitting judge(在任法官)—regarding a foreclosure(丧失赎取权/赎回权) action against his mother. The counts allege:

8. As a sitting circuit court judge, on or about November 20, 2009, you knowingly filed a notice of appearance in pending litigation in Dade County, Florida (CitiMortgage, Inc. v. Gordon, Case No. 2009-74992-CA-01) where you purported to appear to represent your mother in foreclosure proceedings brought against her therein, in violation of Canons 1, 2A and 5G of the Code of Judicial Conduct.

9. As a sitting circuit court judge, you knowingly represented and acted as litigation counsel for your mother in the foreclosure proceeding in Dade County, Florida, described above by, inter alia, communicating with counsel for the mortgagee(接受抵押者,受押人,抵押权人) on her behalf, in Osceola County, Florida, in violation of Canons 1, 2A and 5G of the Code of Judicial Conduct.

Regarding both counts, the Panel determined that Judge Turner was guilty of violating Canons 1, 2A, and 5G. Canon 1 of Florida's Code of Judicial Conduct states:

"An independent and honorable judiciary is indispensable to justice in our society. A judge should participate in establishing, maintaining, and enforcing high standards of conduct, and shall personally observe those standards so that the integrity and independence of the judiciary may be preserved. The provisions of this Code should be construed and applied to further that objective."

Canon 2A provides that:

"A judge shall respect and comply with the law and shall act at all times in a manner that promotes public confidence in the integrity and impartiality of the judiciary."

In furtherance of maintaining the integrity, independence, and impartiality of Florida's judiciary, Canon 5G prohibits judges from practicing law except in certain narrow circumstances:

Practice of Law. A judge shall not practice law. Notwithstanding this prohibition, a judge may act pro se(拉丁语,代表自己) and may, without compensation, give legal advice to and draft or review documents for a member of the judge's family.

The commentary to Canon 5G states that the Code allows a judge to give legal advice to and draft legal documents for members of the judge's family, so long as the judge receives no compensation. A judge must not, however, act as an advocate or negotiator for a member of the judge's family in a legal matter.

The Panel found that Judge Turner violated Canons 1, 2A, and 5G after his mother had become unable to repay the loan she incurred when refinancing her condominium and was facing foreclosure. In September 2009, Judge Turner began negotiating with his mother's mortgage company and wrote a letter on September 22, 2009, to her mortgage broker:

Dear Mr. Steiner:

I am a lawyer from Orlando and my mother is facing foreclosure on a CitiMortgage mortgage. My mother is trying to do a reverse mortgage and has been approved for a Federally-Insured Reverse Mortgage. However, the appraisal came in low and we are seeking to have a short payoff of $150,000.00. I have tried calling your office to discuss this matter with you personally but was not able to get through. If you and your client are in agreement, we can close this before November 30, 2009. For your information, my mother had a flawless payment record but was completely wiped out by Bernard Madoff.

Thank you very much.

N. James Turner

When attorneys for the mortgage company requested a signed authorization from Ms. Gordon to discuss her situation with Judge Turner, Judge Turner requested and secured such authorization. On November 20, 2009, Judge

Turner filed a notice of appearance in his mother's case, and on December 1, 2009, Judge Turner wrote to opposing counsel:

I am an attorney licensed to practice in Florida but I do not practice. My mother is Mignon Gordon and I filed a Notice of Appearance in the above matter on her behalf solely to avoid a default. I understood we were negotiating with your client toward a short payoff so that my mother could obtain a reverse mortgage.

When notified on December 7, 2009, that a short sale would not be permitted, Judge Turner instructed lender's counsel to "proceed with the foreclosure action. We will defend accordingly."

The Panel was not persuaded by Judge Turner's explanation that he was in a panic and mistakenly believed that the canons permitted his actions. The Panel determined that Judge Turner had intentionally and carefully crafted the language of his correspondence to hide the fact that he was a sitting judge in order to circumvent the prohibition on judges practicing law. The Panel was not convinced by Judge Turner's argument that he failed to disclose his position so as not to appear to be wielding undue influence. The record contains clear and convincing evidence that Judge Turner knowingly engaged in the practice of law, in violation of judicial canons, by negotiating with counsel for his mother's mortgagee and by filing a notice of appearance on her behalf. Accordingly, we accept the Panel's findings and determination of guilt.

Count 10

The Panel next found Judge Turner guilty—in part—of violating count 10, which set forth the following accusation:

10. While performing the duties of the office you now hold, you made inappropriate comments and had improper, unwanted and uninvited physical contact with subordinate female personnel, including hugging, kissing and massaging them, attempting to force yourself into the personal and private lives of subordinate female employees, including loaning them money, inviting yourself to their homes and family activities and/or appearing without invitation at their homes and family activities and injecting yourself into their families' lives without being invited or asked to do so, insisting on communicating with and seeing certain subordinate female court employees for reasons unrelated to the performance of your or their official duties, and intemperately(无节制的,放纵的;过度的,激烈的) and vexatiously(令人烦恼/着急的,气人的;令人苦恼的) screaming and yelling at, berating, belittling and humiliating certain subordinate female employees, including your judicial assistants and court clerks in open court and otherwise, thus creating a hostile work environment in violation of Fla. Stat. §760.10 and Canons 1 and 2A of the Code of Judicial Conduct.

The Panel determined that Judge Turner was guilty of injecting himself into the personal life of one subordinate female employee—Heather Shelby—in violation of Canons 1 and 2A, but not guilty of the remainder of the charge. The Panel found that Ms. Shelby, an employee of the Osceola County Clerk of Court, had begun working with Judge Turner in February 2009, when Judge Turner began handling the domestic violence docket(家庭暴力案件). In April or May of 2009, Judge Turner summoned Ms. Shelby to his chambers on the sixth floor of the courthouse, where he was in a T-shirt and gym shorts. Judge Turner closed the door to his office and began to have a personal discussion with Ms. Shelby for nearly half an hour. When Ms. Shelby informed Judge Turner that she needed to return to her desk on the second floor of the courthouse, he thanked her for coming and kissed her on the cheek. The Panel found that although Ms. Shelby felt that this meeting crossed professional boundaries, she decided not to report it after conferring with a coworker, who agreed that it might be an isolated occurrence.

The Panel found, however, that Judge Turner's actions toward Ms. Shelby only became increasingly inappropriate. Judge Turner soon began calling Ms. Shelby at her desk and, one morning in October 2009, was sitting at Ms. Shelby's desk when she arrived at work. Judge Turner asked Ms. Shelby to lunch, to which she initially agreed despite feeling uncomfortable. When Ms. Shelby tried to cancel the lunch, she was not able to do so because Judge Turner had cleared his afternoon docket in order to be available at Ms. Shelby's convenience. When Ms.

Shelby inquired into the purpose of the lunch, Judge Turner told her it was for various personal reasons. The Panel found that Ms. Shelby would not have gone to lunch with Judge Turner had he not been a judge. The situation further progressed to the point where Judge Turner would call Ms. Shelby constantly—including from the bench—and would show up at her desk several times a day, starting in the morning. If he did not see her at the beginning of a work day, Judge Turner would send Ms. Shelby emails. Judge Turner would invent reasons to see Ms. Shelby, to the point that Ms. Shelby described it as "an everyday thing; ... he was down at my desk continuously all day long ... I would turn around and he would be there." Another clerk's office employee, who sat next to Judge Turner during domestic violence hearings and who knew Ms. Shelby, observed that Judge Turner's efforts to locate Ms. Shelby in the courthouse "got worse" over time.

The Panel found that a central theme of Judge Turner's fixation on Ms. Shelby's personal life was Ms. Shelby's then twelve-year-old son, a cancer patient. Judge Turner—himself a cancer survivor—would inquire about treatment and medical bills and repeatedly sought to visit Ms. Shelby's son in the hospital during his treatment. Ms. Shelby considered her son's treatment a private family matter and consistently rebuffed(拒绝,驳斥;击退) Judge Turner's efforts, but to no effect. Judge Turner continued to ask if he could visit Ms. Shelby's son at their home or drive him to treatment. When Judge Turner found out that Ms. Shelby and her son would be attending a local performance of a Broadway musical, he suggested that he come to the theater at intermission (interval) to take photos. Ms. Shelby politely declined, but Judge Turner persisted, even finding out the scheduled intermission time in order to coordinate his arrival. Despite Ms. Shelby's rebuffs, Judge Turner showed up at the theater at intermission, met Ms. Shelby and her son, and took photos of them. He later told Ms. Shelby that he could not wait to spend more time with her son, which she again refused. The Panel further found that in February 2010, Ms. Shelby was forced to physically hide in order to avoid Judge Turner. Judge Turner, undeterred, began to search for the hiding Ms. Shelby, asking loudly, "Where's Heather"? The Chief Judge of the circuit had to call Judge Turner on his cell phone and order him to stop searching for Ms. Shelby, and the clerk's office had to change Ms. Shelby's phone number and move her desk to another area.

The Panel found that Judge Turner's interest in Ms. Shelby was not romantic or sexual, but instead stemmed from Judge Turner's loneliness and need to be needed. Dr. Barbara Mara, a psychologist to whom Judge Turner submitted himself for a psychological evaluation at the recommendation of the Chief Judge, reported that Judge Turner suffered from "no major mental illness or gross pathology." Instead, Dr. Mara determined that Judge Turner's inappropriate behavior was a result of a "somewhat self-centered opinion of himself and others" and a "lack of psychological insight and minimization trends." Dr. Mara concluded: In my clinical opinion, Judge Turner's evaluation results suggest an individual who prefers to be in control, with a need to please others, and might push boundaries and rules to meet some of his needs. His lack of psychological insight, or simply put, sometimes he does not get it, might lead to poor judgment behavior whose intent is to receive attention, social approval and to fulfill the need to help others. His social behavior might be seen as audacious (daring, bold) and uninhibited. All of these clinical characteristics relate to personality traits and not any major mental health concerns.

The Panel concluded its findings regarding Judge Turner's conduct toward Ms. Shelby by noting that although Judge Turner was an expert employment attorney before he joined the bench, he was oblivious to the fact(无视这样的事实) that his superior position would exploit Ms. Shelby's need for a job and reluctance to anger or upset him. The Panel found that although there was no sexual component to Judge Turner's actions, they were nonetheless unwarranted and unwelcome and thus constituted an inappropriate intrusion into Ms. Shelby's personal and family life.

The record contains clear and convincing evidence to support the Panel's findings. Judge Turner does not dispute the substance of Ms. Shelby's allegations but only challenges the frequency with which he intruded into Ms. Shelby's life and the attitude with which Ms. Shelby met his advances. The differences between Judge Turner's account of events and Ms. Shelby's account are explained by Dr. Mara's testimony that Judge Turner lacked insight into the true dynamics of his relationship with Ms. Shelby. Moreover, Ms. Shelby's testimony was corroborated—at least in part—by the testimony of another court employee. The Panel's decision to find Ms. Shelby's testimony more credible than Judge Turner's is therefore supported by an abundance of evidence. We accept the Panel's findings and determination of guilt.

Count 12

The final specific charge of which the Panel found Judge Turner guilty alleged:

12. While acting as a sitting circuit court judge in open court in State v. John Doe, a Child, on or about March 12, 2010, you unlawfully ordered the seizure of jewelry from a child, arbitrarily determined its value and proposed to offset the court costs owed by the child against your summary determination of the value of the jewelry, in violation of Canons 1, 2A and 3[B](3)1 of the Code of Judicial Conduct.

The Panel determined that Judge Turner was guilty of an error in judgment and a technical violation of the canons but recommended that no punishment be imposed based on the violation.

Canon 3B(3) provides that "a judge shall require order and decorum in proceedings before the judge." The Panel found that Judge Turner violated this canon—as well as Canons 1 and 2A—when, while questioning a juvenile appearing before him about the juvenile's nonpayment of costs, Judge Turner noticed that the juvenile was wearing a "nice diamond earring." When asked about the worth of the jewelry, the juvenile informed Judge Turner that it was fake and had cost seven dollars. Judge Turner offered to give the juvenile a credit of ten dollars toward his court costs in exchange for the earring. When the juvenile agreed, Judge Turner instructed the deputy to take the earring from the juvenile and place it in an evidence bag and stated that he would credit ten dollars toward the juvenile's outstanding court costs. The Panel found, however, that Judge Turner did not know his conduct was prohibited and that—when the Chief Judge called shortly thereafter and informed Judge Turner that his conduct was inappropriate—Judge Turner immediately directed the clerk to prepare the necessary paperwork and return the earring.

The transcript from the hearing in which the alleged conduct occurred contains clear and convincing evidence to support the Panel's findings. Accordingly, we accept the Panel's findings of fact regarding count 12. We do not, however, accept the Panel's recommendation that Judge Turner be spared punishment for this conduct. Instead, we consider this violation as a part of the pattern of misconduct engaged in by Judge Turner.

Count 13

Finally, the Panel found Judge Turner guilty—in part—of count 13, which alleged that the charged violations, "taken collectively, constituted a pattern of misconduct which raises serious questions regarding his fitness to perform the duties of the office he now holds." The Panel determined that Judge Turner was guilty of the pattern of misconduct alleged in count 13 to the extent that he was found guilty of counts 5, 7, 8, 9, and, in part, 10. Based on our acceptance of the Panel's findings of fact described above, we modify the Panel's findings regarding count 13 to reflect a pattern of misconduct based on the conduct described in counts 7, 8, 9, 10, in part, and 12. We accept the Panel's conclusion that the pattern of misconduct established by Judge Turner's many ethical violations raises serious questions regarding Judge Turner's fitness to perform the duties of his office.

DISCIPLINE

"Although this Court gives the findings and recommendations of the JQC great weight, the ultimate power and responsibility in making a determination to discipline a judge rests with this Court."

Here, Judge Turner engaged in a broad variety of serious misconduct both before and upon being elevated to the bench. Because Judge Turner gained his office partially through illegal means and committed serious violations of the judicial canons upon assuming his role as a judge, we determine that he has engaged in conduct unbecoming (不适当的,不相称的,不相配的) a member of Florida's judiciary and is unfit to perform the duties of his office. Accordingly, we conclude that removing Judge Turner from the bench is the appropriate discipline for the serious violations established here, and we accept the Panel's recommendation.

...

CONCLUSION

We hold that Judge Turner is unfit to hold judicial office and that removal is the only appropriate sanction. For the reasons stated above, N. James Turner is hereby removed as a judge of Florida's Ninth Judicial Circuit, effective upon this opinion becoming final.

It is so ordered.

Lesson Five

Terms and Conditions of Commercial Letter of Credit and Security Agreement

> **Learning objectives**
>
> After learning the text and having done the exercises in this lesson, you will:
>
> —familiarize with knowledge of the legal characteristics and the nature of commercial letter of credit and security agreement;
>
> —acquire an appreciation of the vocabulary and grammar or syntax relevant to commercial letter of credit and security agreement;
>
> —become aware of the information required in order to understand commercial letter of credit and security agreement; ;
>
> —cultivate the practical abilities to put to use the language in the specific context;
>
> —be able to do some translation from Chinese to English and from English to Chinese.

 Text

Terms and Conditions of
Commercial Letter of Credit① and Security Agreement

In consideration of your issuing the Credit, substantially according to the Application appearing on the reverse side hereof or as attached thereto and initialed② by us, we, the undersigned, hereby jointly and severally agree as follows:

1. As to drafts③ or acceptances under or purporting to be under the Credit, which are payable

---

① Commercial letter of credit: 商业信用证,常用缩写: L/C,国际结算中一种主要的方式。因其为银行风险而非商业风险,较为安全可靠,故广泛被采用为交易方法,但相对地,信用证的相关费用较高,导致交易成本的增加。

② initial: 作为动词使用时,表示"在……上记上姓名的词首字母,用词首字母在……上署名";草签,临时签署条约等;作为名词释使用时,表示词首字母,词首大写字母;(pl.)姓名中的大写字母,如 John Smith 中的"J. S"。

③ draft: 汇票,又称 bill of exchange。

in United States Dollars, we agree: (a) in the case of each sight draft①, to reimburse you at your office, on demand, in legal tender② of United States of America, the amount paid on such drafts, or, if so demanded by you, to pay you at your office in advance in legal tender³ of the United States of America, the amount required to pay such draft; and (b) in the case of each acceptance, to pay to you at your office, in legal tender of the United States of America the amount thereof, on demand but in any event not later than the date of maturity.

2. As to drafts or acceptances under or purporting to be under the Credit which are payable in currency other than United States Dallas, we agree:

(a) in the case of each sight draft, to reimburse you at your office, on demand, the equivalent of the amount paid, in legal tender of the United States of America at the rate of exchange then current in Los Angeles for cable transfers to the place of payment in the currency in which such draft is drawn, with interest from the date of payment of the instrument, or if so demanded by you, to pay you, at your office in advance, in United States currency, the equivalent of the amount required to pay the same; and

(b) in the case of each acceptance, to pay you at your office, on demand, the equivalent of the acceptance in the legal tender of the United States of America at the current rate of exchange for demand drafts③ on the place of payment, if payment is made by us in time to reach the place of payment in the course of the mails not later than the date of maturity, or at the current rate in Los Angeles for cable transfers at time of transmission to the place of payment in the currency in which the acceptance is payable, if such payment is made at your office an the maturity date. If, for any cause whatsoever, there exists at the time in question no rate of exchange generally current in Los Angeles for effective cable transfers of the sort above provided for, we agree to pay you on demand an amount in United States Dallas equivalent to the actual cost of settlement of your obligation to the payor of the draft or acceptance or any holder thereof, as the case may be, and however and whenever such settlement may be made by you, including interest on the amount of dollars payable by us from the date of payment of such draft or acceptance to the date of our payment to you at the rate customarily charged by you in like circumstances.

3. In the event④ that any United States Dollar drafts are drawn by us on you in order to refinance any obligation set forth in the preceding two sections, and such drafts, at your option, are accepted by you, we agree to pay you on demand, but in any event not later than the maturity date the amount of each such acceptance. Each amount which may become due and payable to you under this Agreement may, in your discretion and if not otherwise paid, be charged by you to any available funds then held by you for our account.

4. We agree to pay you on demand⑤, with respect to the Credit, a commission at such rate as you may determine to be proper, and any and all charges and expenses which may be paid or

---

① sight draft:见票即付的即期汇票。
② legal tender:法定货币。
③ demand drafts:即期汇票。
④ in the event that:如果……,等于 if 或 provided 等引导的从句,表示条件。
⑤ pay sb. on demand:按某人的要求支付。

Lesson Five Terms and Conditions of Commercial Letter of Credit and Security Agreement

incurred by you in connection with the Credit, together with interest where chargeable. Interest payable hereunder shall be at the rate customarily charged by you at the time in like circumstances.

5. As security for all of our obligations and liabilities to you, we hereby recognize and admit your security interest in all property shipped under or pursuant to or in connection with the Credit or in any way relative thereto or to the drafts drawn thereunder, whether or not released to us or to our agents on security agreements, and also in and to all shipping documents, warehouse receipts, policies or certificates of insurance and other documents accompanying or relative to drafts drawn under or in connection with the Credit, and in and to the proceeds of each and all of the foregoing, until such time as all the obligations and liabilities of us or any of us to you at any time existing under or with reference to the Credit or this Agreement, or any other obligation or liability to you have been fully paid and discharged; and that all or any of such property and documents, and the proceeds of any thereof, coming into your possession or that of any of your correspondents, may be held and disposed of as hereinafter provided. You shall have all of the rights of a secured party under the Uniform Commercial Code① in the aforesaid property and, in addition, shall have all of the rights specified herein. We agree to execute such financing statements and other writings as shall be necessary to perfect and maintain your security interest in all said property and to pay all costs of filing financing, continuation and termination statements with respect to your security interest hereunder. The receipt by you or any of your correspondents at time of other security of whatsoever nature, including cash, shall not be deemed a waiver of any of your rights or powers herein recognized.

6. In the absence of written instructions expressly to the contrary, we agree that you or any of your correspondents may receive and accept as "bills of lading"② under the Credit, any document issued or purporting to be issued by or on behalf of any carrier, which acknowledges receipt of property for transportation, whatever the other specific provisions of such document(s), and that the date of each such document shall be regarded as the date of shipment of the property mentioned therein; however, on an ocean bill of lading③ the date of an onboard notation④ is to be considered the shipment date. Any such bill of lading issued by or on behalf of an ocean carrier may be accepted by you as an "ocean bill of lading" whether or not the entire transportation is by water. Unless otherwise specifically agreed in writing, partial shipments may be made and you may honor the relative drafts, our liability to reimburse you for payments made or obligations incurred on such drafts being limited to the amount of the Credit. If the Credit specified shipments in installments within given periods, and any installment is not shipped within the period allowed for that installment, the Credit ceases to be available for that or any subsequent installment, unless otherwise expressly provided in the Credit. You and any of your correspondents may receive and accept as doc-

---

① Uniform Commercial Code:美国《统一商法典》。
② bill of lading:提单,是一种有法律效力的单据。它是一种货物所有权的凭证,也是托运人和承运人之间所订的运输契约的证明。
③ ocean bill of lading:海运提单。
④ an onboard notation:已装船通知。

uments of insurance under the Credit either insurance policies or insurance certificates[①]which need not be for an amount of insurance greater than the amount paid by you under or relative to the Credit. You and any of your correspondents may receive, accept, at pay as complying with the terms of the Credit, any drafts or other documents, otherwise in order, which may be signed by, or issued to, the administrator or executor of, or the trustee in bankruptcy[②]or the receiver for any of the property[③]of, the party in whose name it is provided in the Credit that any drafts or other documents should be drawn or issued.

7. (a) If at our special request the Credit is issued in transferable form, it is understood and agreed that you are under no duty to determine the proper identity of any one appearing in the draft or documents as transferee, nor shall you be charged with responsibility of any nature or character for the validity or correctness of any transfer or successive transfers, and payment by you to any purported transferee or transferees as determined by you is hereby authorized and approved, and we further agree to hold you harmless and indemnified against[④]any liability or claim in connection with or arising out of the foregoing.

(b) If it is a condition of this Credit that payment may be made upon receipt by you of a cable advising negotiation[⑤], we hereby agree to reimburse you on demand for the amount indicated in the said cable advice, and further agree to hold you harmless if the documents fail to arrive, or when, as and if documents arrive it should develop that the terms of the credit have not been complied with, and that the documents are not in order.

8. We agree that in the event of any extension of the maturity or time for presentation of drafts, acceptances, or documents, or any other modification of the terms of the Credit, at the request of any of us, with or without notification to the others, or in the event of any increase in the amount of the Credit at our request, this Agreement shall be binding upon us with regard to the Credit so increased or otherwise modified, to drafts, documents, and property covered thereby, and to any action taken by you or any of your correspondents in accordance with such extension, increase, or other modification.

9. The users of the Credit shall be deemed our agents and neither you nor your correspondents shall be responsible for: (a) the use which may be made of the Credit or for any acts or omissions of the users of the Credit; (b) the existence of the property purporting to be represented by documents; (c) any difference in character, quality, quantity, condition, or value of the property and that purporting to be represented by documents; (d) the validity, sufficiency or genuineness of documents, even if such documents should in fact prove to be in any or all respects invalid, fraudulent, or forged; (e) particular conditions stipulated in the documents or superimposed thereon; (f) the time, place, manner or order in which shipment is made; (g) partial or incomplete shipment, or failure or omission to ship any and all of the property referred to in the Credit;

---

① insurance policies or insurance certificates:保险单或保险凭证。
② the trustee in bankruptcy:破产财产和受托人。
③ the receiver for any of the property:破产案产业管理人,(争执财产等的)委托管理人。
④ hold sb. harmless and indemnified against:使不受到损害等。
⑤ advising negotiation:通知议付。

Lesson Five Terms and Conditions of Commercial Letter of Credit and Security Agreement

(h) the character, adequacy, validity, or genuineness of any insurance, the solvency or responsibility of any insurance, or any other risk connected with insurance; (i) any deviation from instructions, delay, default, or fraud by the shipper or any one else in connection with the property or the shipping thereof; (j) the solvency, responsibility, or relationship to the property of any party issuing any documents in connection with the property; (k) delay in arrival or failure to arrive of either the properly or any of the documents relating thereto; (l) delay in giving or failure to give notice of arrival or any other notice; (m) any breach of contract between the shippers or vendors and ourselves or any of us; (n) failure of any instrument to bear any reference or adequate reference to the Credit, or failure of documents to accompany any draft at negotiation, or failure of any person to note the amount of any draft on the reverse of the Credit or to surrender or take up the Credit or to send forward documents apart from drafts as required by the terms of the Credit, each of which provisions, if contained in the Credit itself, it is agreed may be waived by you; (o) errors, omissions, interruptions, or delays in transmission, or delivery of any messages by mail, cable, telegraph, wireless or otherwise, whether or not they may be in cipher. You shall not be responsible for any act, error, neglect, or default, omission[15], insolvency or failure in the business of any of your correspondents or for any refused by you or any of your correspondents to pay or honor drafts drawn under the Credit because of any applicable law, decree or edict, legal or illegal, of any governmental agency now or hereafter in farce or for any matter beyond your control. The happening of any one or more of the contingencies referred to in the preceding clauses of this paragraph shall not affect, impair, or prevent the vesting of any of your rights or powers hereunder, or our obligation to make reimbursement. In furtherance and extension and not in limitation of the specific provisions hereinabove set forth, we agree that any action taken by you or by any correspondent of yours under or in connection with the Credit or the relative drafts, documents, or property, if taken in good faith, shall be binding on us and shall not put you or any of your correspondents under any resulting liability to us and we make like agreement as to any inaction or omission unless in breach of good faith.①

10. If it is a condition of this Credit that the accreditees are authorized to draw clean drafts, you are authorized to accept and pay drafts without requiring, and without responsibility for, the delivery of shipping documents, either at the time of acceptance or of payment or thereafter.

11. We agree to procure promptly any necessary import and export or other licenses for the import, export, or shipping of the property and to comply with all foreign and domestic governmental regulations in regard to the shipment of the property or the financing thereof, and to furnish such certificates in that respect as you may at any time require, and to keep the property adequately covered by insurance acceptable to you, and to assign the policies or certificates of insurance to you, or to make the loss or adjustment, if any, payable to you, at your option, and to furnish you, if demanded, with evidence of acceptance by the insurers of such assignment.

12. In the event you deliver to us, or to any of us, or to a Custom House Broker at our request any of the documents of title pledged hereunder prior to having received payment in full of all

---

① good faith:诚实信用,诚信。

of our liabilities to you, we agree to obtain possession of any goods represented by documents within twenty-one days from the date of such delivery of said documents and if we should fail to do so, we agree to return said documents or to have them returned by the Custom House Broker to you prior to the expiration of the said twenty-one day period. We agree to execute and deliver to you receipts for such documents and the goods represented thereby identifying and describing such documents and goods, which said receipts shall constitute a part of this Agreement.

13. Each of us agrees at any time and from time to time, on demand, to deliver, convey, transfer, or assign to you, as security for any and all of his and/or our obligations and liabilities, contingent or absolute, due or to become due, which are now or may at any time hereafter be owing by him or us to you, additional security of a character and value satisfactory to you, or to make such payment as you may require. Each of us agrees that all property belonging to him, or us, in which he or we may have an interest, of every name and nature whatsoever, now or at any time hereafter delivered, conveyed, transferred, assigned, or paid to you, or coming into your possession in any manner whatsoever, whether expressly as security for any of the obligations or liabilities of him or us to you, or for safekeeping or otherwise, including any items received for collection or transmission and the proceeds thereof, whether or not such property is in whole or part released to us on security agreement, are hereby made security for each and all such obligations and liabilities.

14. Each of us agrees that upon his or our failure at any time to keep a margin of security with you satisfactory to you, or upon the making by him or us of any assignment for the benefit of creditors, or upon the filing of any voluntary or involuntary petition in bankruptcy by or against him or us, or upon the application for the appointment of a receiver of any of his or our property, or upon any act of insolvency of him or us, all of such obligations and liabilities shall become and be immediately due and payable without demand or notice, notwithstanding any credit or time allowed to him or us, or any instrument evidencing any such obligations or liabilities or otherwise. Each of us, as to property in which he may have any interest, and all of us, as to property in which we may have any interest, expressly authorize you in any such event or upon his failure to pay any of such obligations or liabilities when it or they shall become or be made due, to sell immediately, without demand for payment, without advertisement and without notice to us or any of us, all of which are hereby expressly waived, any and all such property, arrived or to arrive, at private sale or at public auction or at broker's board or otherwise, at your option, in such parcel or parcels and at such time or times and at such place or places and for such price or prices and upon such terms and conditions as you may deem proper, and to apply the net proceeds of such sale or sales, together with any balance of deposits and any sums credited by or due from you to him or us in general account or otherwise, to the payment of any and all of such obligations or liabilities to you however arising. If any such sale be at broker's board or at public auction, you may yourself be a purchaser at such sale, free from any right of redemption which we hereby expressly waive and release.

Lesson Five Terms and Conditions of Commercial Letter of Credit and Security Agreement

15. The rights and liens①which you possess hereunder shall continue unimpaired, and we and each of us shall remain obligated in accordance with the terms and provisions hereof, notwithstanding the release or substitution of any property which may be held as security hereunder at any time, or of any right or interest therein. No delay, extension of time, renewal, compromise, or other indulgence which may occur, shall impair your rights or powers hereunder. You shall not be deemed to have waived any of your rights hereunder unless you or your authorized agent shall have signed such waiver in writing. No such waiver, unless expressly as stated therein, shall be effective as to any transaction which occurs subsequent to the date of such waiver, nor as to any continuance of a breach after such waiver.

16. Except as otherwise expressly provided in this Application and Agreement or as you and we may otherwise expressly agree with regard to, and prior to your issuance of the Credit, the "Uniform Customs and Practice for Documentary Credits (1982 Revision), International Chamber of Commerce Brochure No. 222"②shall be binding on the Credit and shall serve, in the absence of proof expressly to the contrary, as evidence of general banking usage.

17. The word "property" as used herein includes goods and merchandise, as well as any and all documents relative thereto, also, securities, funds, choses in action③, and any and all other forms of property, whether real, personal or mixed and any right or interest therein.

18. This Agreement shall be binding upon us, our heirs, executors, administrators, successors, and assigns④and shall inure to⑤the benefit of, and be enforceable by you, your successors, transferees, and assigns. If this Agreement should be terminated or revoked as to us by operation of law, we will indemnify and save you harmless from any loss which may be incurred by you in acting hereunder prior to the receipt by you or your successors, transferees, or assigns of notice in writing of such termination or revocation. If this Agreement is signed by one individual, the terms "we," "our," "us," shall be read throughout as "I", "my," "me," as the case may be. If this Agreement is signed by two or more parties, it shall be the joint and several agreement of such parties; and in any such case, this Agreement shall not be revoked or impaired as to any one or more of such parties by the death of any of the others or by the revocation or release of any obligations hereunder of any one or more of such parties.

19. This Agreement and all rights, obligations, and liabilities arising thereunder shall be construed in accordance with the laws of the State of California.

---

① lien：留置权，留置权（德语：Zurückbehaltungsrecht, 法语：Droit de rétention），乃债权人占有他人之动产, 而其债权之发生与该动产有牵连关系, 于债权已届清偿期未受清偿时, 得留置该动产之权, 用以偿付一般在法律效力之下产生的债务或税务。若债权人因侵权行为或其他不法之原因而占有动产者, 不适用前项之规定。其占有之始明知或因重大过失而不知该动产非为债务人所有者。

② Uniform Customs and Practice for Documentary Credits (1982 Revision), International Chamber of Commerce Brochure No. 222：《跟单信用证统一惯例》, 国际商会第 222 号。

③ chose in action：无体财产。

④ assign：受让人, 如：heirs and assigns（继承人和受让人）。作为动词使用时, 表示"把财产、权利等转让, 让与, 过户给……"的意思。

⑤ inure to：法律等的生效, 适用；有助于, 如 to inure to the prosperity and welfare of the nation（有利于全国国民的繁荣与福利）。

Legal Terminology

1. letter of credit 与 bill of lading

Letter of Credit,or L/C(信用证),是国际结算的一种主要方式。因其为银行风险而非商业风险,较为安全可靠,故广泛被采用为交易方法,但相对地,信用证的相关费用较高,导致交易成本的增加。

信用证的开具必须由付款人向银行申请。开证行在付款人缴纳开证费用和保证金之后,开证行会开具信用证,保证在符合一定条件的情况下向受益人付款。根据开具方式的不同,可以分为信开信用证和电开信用证两种。信开信用证是指开证行开具纸质信用证,并且上面盖章和加编密押,通过邮寄的形式送达通知行。电开信用证是指开证行在信用证上面加编密押之后通过电传的形式送达通知行。

虽然开具信用证的时候是以购销合同为依据,但是信用证开具以后不会受到购销合同的约束,如果合同发生变更,只要受益人符合信用证上面记载的条件,银行仍然会向受益人付款。

根据分类依据的不同,信用证可分为跟单信用证和光票信用证、保兑信用证和非保兑信用证、即期信用证和远期信用证、可撤销信用证和不可撤销信用证等。

Bill of Lading,or B/L(提单),是一种有法律效力的单据,它是一种货物所有权的凭证,也是托运人与承运人之间所订的运输契约的证明。

根据内容繁简可以把提单分为全式提单(Long Form B/L)和简式提单(Short Form B/L)两种,根据是否转船,可以把提单分为"直运提单"(Direct B/L)、"转运提单"(Transhipment B/L)、"联运提单"(Through B/L)以及"多式联运提单"(Combined Transport B/L,简称 C.T.B.)等种类。提单是最重要的信用证交单文件之一。

提单一般有如下内容:托运人(Shipper 或 Consignor);收货人(Consignee);被通知人(Notified Party);货物描述(Description of goods);毛重(Gross weight);尺码(体积)(Measurement);装运港(Port of Loading);卸货港(Port of Discharge);运费条款(填写 Freight Prepaid:运费预付或 Freight Collect:运费到付);签发时间和地点(Place and date of issue);正本的总数量(Numbers of original B(s)/L)等。

2. act or omission 与 act or forbearance

这两个术语的意思通常表示"作为与不作为"的意思,其中 omission 表示非故意地不实施某项行为,为此,在合同法中,就常常采用"act or forbearance"来表示"作为与不作为",该处的 forbearance 指的是允诺人要求对方"故意地不实施某项行为",比如,为了让某人不抽烟,一方允诺给对方一定的报酬。

3. insolvent,bankrupt 与 broke

bankrupt,insolvent and broke 三词均有"破产"的意思。insolvent 常用于指公司的破产,用于个人时,则指债务人(个人与法人均可)资不抵债,无法向债权人清偿债务,故处于破产状态;而 bankrupt 则多指个人的破产。经过司法程序宣布某债务人 insolvent 后,该债务人就可以称为 bankrupt。broke 则是非正式用语。

4. executor 与 administrator

两个词均可以表示对遗产进行清理、管理、变卖以及分配财产的职责,但区别在于 executor 指遗嘱上载明的由立遗嘱人指定的"遗嘱执行人"。而 administrator 则指因遗嘱上没有指定或无遗嘱继承中需要由法院指定的法定继承中的遗产管理人。

5. transfer，assignment，conveyance 与 negotiation

几个词均可以表示"转让"的意思，但 transfer 为一般术语，可以泛指各种形式的转让；assignment 多为民事法律或合同法上的债权的转让，常常指转让无形财产的权利；conveyance 常常指的不动产的转让，如土地物权的转让，也包括土地其他权利的转让或租赁（lease）、按揭（mortgage）、抵押（encumbrance）；negotiation 则属于票据法上的权利转让等。

Exercises

I Verbal Abilities

Part One

Directions: *For each of these completing questions, read each item carefully and complete each statement by supplying the missing word or phrase.*

1. A negotiable instrument is a document _____ the payment of a specific amount of money, either on demand, or at a set time.

   A. assuring   B. ensuring   C. warranting   D. guaranteeing

2. As a negotiable instrument is a promise of a payment of money, the instrument itself can be used by the _____ as a store of value.

   A. holder in good faith   B. holder in due course
   C. holder for value   D. holder of a lien

3. A _____ is essentially an order made by one person to another to pay money to a third person.

   A. cheque   B. promissory note
   C. bill of exchange   D. negotiable instrument

4. The person who draws the bill is called the _____, who gives the order to pay money to the third party.

   A. drawer   B. payer   C. payee   D. drawee

5. The party upon whom the bill is drawn is called the drawee, who is the person to whom the bill is _____ and who is ordered to pay.

   A. sought address   B. pleaded   C. called upon   D. addressed

6. The drawee becomes an acceptor when he indicates his _____ to pay the bill.

   A. voluntariness   B. willingness   C. disposition   D. bestowal

7. The party in whose favor the bill is drawn or is payable is called the _____.

   A. addressee   B. addressor   C. payor   D. payee

8. A bill of exchange may be _____ by the payee in favour of a third party, who may in turn do it to a fourth, and so on indefinitely.

   A. endorsed   B. endowed   C. bequeathed   D. subsidized

9. The "holder in due course" may claim the amount of the bill against the drawee and all previous endorsers, regardless of any _____ that may have disabled the previous payee or endorser from doing so.

  A. counteractions   B. counterclaims   C. countermands   D. counterfoils

10. A writing which does not contain the words "to the order of" within the four corners of the instrument or in endorsement on the note or indicate that it is payable to the individual holding the contract document (analogous to the holder in due course) is not a _____.

  A. negotiable instrument   B. marketable instrument
  C. conveyable instrument   D. vendible instrument

Part Two

Directions: *Choose the one word or phase that best keep the meaning of the original sentence if it were substituted for the underlined part.*

1. One of the primary <u>peculiarities</u> of the documentary credit is that the payment obligation is abstract and independent from the underlying contract of sale or any other contract in the transaction.

  A. differentiations   B. distinguishableness
  C. anomaly   D. distinguished

2. If the responsibility for the validity of documents was thrown onto banks, they would <u>be burdened with</u> investigating the underlying facts of each transaction, and would thus be less inclined to issue documentary credits as the transaction would involve great risk and inconvenience.

  A. assigned   B. inflicted   C. mandated   D. hindered

3. The fact that the basic function of the credit is to provide a seller with the certainty of payment for documentary duties suggests that banks should <u>honor</u> their obligation notwithstanding allegations of misfeasance by the buyer.

  A. applaud   B. pay tribute to   C. memorialize   D. ennoble

4. The courts have emphasize that buyers always have a remedy for an action upon the contract of sale, and that it would be a <u>calamity</u> for the business world if, for every breach of contract between the seller and buyer, a bank were required to investigate said breach.

  A. hardship   B. stroke   C. adverse fortune   D. disaster

5. The "principle of strict compliance" also aims to make the bank's duty of <u>effecting</u> payment against documents easy, efficient and quick.

  A. developing   B. resulting   C. achieving   D. realizing

6. If the documents tendered under the documentary credit <u>deviate</u> from the language of the credit the bank is entitled to withhold payment even if the deviation is purely terminological.

  A. effectuate   B. set apart   C. diverge   D. converge

7. All the charges for issuance of Letter of Credit, negotiation of documents, <u>reimbursements</u> and other charges like courier are to the account of applicant or as per the terms and conditions of the Letter of credit.

  A. refund   B. rebate   C. recoupment   D. remuneration

8. A promissory note is an unconditional promise in writing made by one person to another, signed by the maker, <u>engaging</u> to pay on demand to the payee, or at fixed or determinable future time, certain in money, to order or to bearer.

    A. enlisting   B. reserving   C. undertaking   D. retaining

9. The consideration constituted by a negotiable instrument is <u>cognizable</u> as the value given up to acquire it (benefit) and the consequent loss of value (detriment) to the prior holder.

    A. ascertainable   B. recognizable   C. decipherable   D. perceptible

10. Negotiation often enables the transferee to become the party to the contract through a contract <u>assignment</u> (provided for explicitly or by operation of law) and to enforce the contract in the transferee-assignee's own name.

    A. transfer   B. delegation   C. conveyance   D. consignment

II   Cloze Test

Directions: *Read the following passage concerning the letter of credit and fill in the blanks with the contextual information.*

A letter of credit is a document that a _____ or similar party issues to a seller of goods or services which provides that the _____ will pay the seller for goods or services the seller _____ to a third-party buyer. The issuer then _____ reimbursement from the buyer or from the buyer's bank. The document serves essentially as a _____ to the seller that it will be paid by the issuer of the letter of credit regardless of whether the buyer ultimately fails to pay. In this way, the risk that the buyer will fail to pay is _____ from the seller to the letter of credit's issuer.

Letters of credit are used primarily in international trade for large transactions between a supplier in one country and a customer in another. In such cases, the International Chamber of Commerce Uniform Customs and Practice for Documentary Credits _____ (UCP 600 being the latest version). They are also used in the land development process to ensure that approved public facilities (streets, sidewalks, storm water ponds, etc.) will be built. The parties to a letter of credit are the supplier, usually called the _____, the issuing bank, of whom the buyer is a client, and sometimes an advising bank, of whom the beneficiary is a client. Almost all letters of credit are _____, i.e., cannot be amended or canceled without the consent of the beneficiary, issuing bank, and confirming bank, if any. In _____ a transaction, letters of credit incorporate functions common to giros and traveler's check.

III   Reading Comprehension

Directions: *In this section there are passages followed by questions or unfinished statements, you are to choose the one you think is the best answer.*

Passage one   America's lessons in killing off toxic banks

A couple of years ago, I spent some time brainstorming with officials from America's mighty Federal Deposit Insurance Corporation. It felt rather like meeting doctors from ER, or an emergency medical ward. For FDIC officials have handled so many sick American banks in recent years, they have developed a slick drill: if a bank is deemed bust, FDIC "shock troops" will arrive, typically on Friday night, seize control, reassure staff and depositors—before either closing the banks or selling it on.

Performing this operation demands tricks of the trade; FDIC officials have learnt from bitter experience that electricity bills need to be prepaid to avoid panic if the lights go off. But the drill is usually slick enough to avoid alarm. So much so, in fact, that many people do not even know that 445 ailing banks have been closed in America since 2008 (or an average of two a week). And while many are tiddlers, the deceased banks include big(ish) groups such as Washington Mutual.

There is an important lesson for Europe here. Two weeks ago, Eurozone leaders announced plans to create a banking union, in their latest effort to quell panic. The news duly sparked a brief market rally, amid hopes that European politicians are finally trying to grasp their banking nettle.

Last week, however, I met European financial officials in Dublin, and was clear that many elements of this "union" remain uncertain; it is unknown, for example, whether a union will "just" involve joint bank recapitalization, or include joint deposit insurance and supervision too. So, as European regulators and policy makers thrash out their ideas about how to rebuild confidence, they might do well to take a look at how "union" has worked in America, and how this has helped quell the 2008 US banking shock.

Part of this story revolves around the so-called Troubled Asset Relief Program (Tarp) that the US government implemented in 2008; this provided badly needed recapitalization and transparency for the banks. However, the other, less-discussed element is the FDIC, and the Friday night "death drill". For this has also stabilized the system, and as such offers lessons for Eurozone politicians and regulators.

One is that it pays to have a predictable and consistent routine for spotting and killing troubled banks. More specifically, the FDIC system works well because there are clear rules of the game (most notably, that when the FDIC judges a bank insolvent, it can seize its operations, wipe out shareholders, then sell or liquidate it.) This does not always prevent controversy; in 2008, for example, there was a row about how the FDIC handled WaMu's bonds. But the FDIC has the benefit of having existed for eight decades, and so has a well-worn, credible routine.

Second, a regulator needs to have a powerful "brand" in the eyes of the public—in the sense of embodying simple, easy-to-understand principles. Consumers in America do not usually know the details of how the FDIC operates; but they know that accounts with the FDIC stamp are guaranteed against losses, up to $250,000. The message is crystal clear, and thus readily understood. This is crucial for quelling panic and contagion. Witness the contrast with the money market fund sector, whose status is more ambiguous.

Third, the FDIC benefits by having federal, not regional, status. This ensures that the supervisors who take the decision to kill a troubled bank are not from the same, local community, and so cannot be co-opted or influenced. It also means that the FDIC draws its funding from a wide base (in this case the financial industry). That puts it on a stronger financial footing, which is important, given that it has cost the FDIC about $88bn to protect depositors since 2008, as those

Lesson Five Terms and Conditions of Commercial Letter of Credit and Security Agreement

445 banks have died—and the agency expects to spend $12bn more in the next four years.

Fourth, the FDIC's experience shows that regulation need not be a zero-sum game; on the contrary, the agency has a long history of collaborating with other regulators in America to supervise banks. Banks sometimes complain this creates unnecessary, wasteful duplication; it also occasionally causes issues to fall between the cracks. But mostly, it is beneficial, since collaboration creates checks and balances.

Now it will not be easy to transplant all these lessons to Europe. The FDIC, after all, has mostly "only" dealt with domestic banks, not cross-border banking behemoths, and the legal code in Europe is radically different. Most crucially, Germans politicians appear unconvinced that a mutual insurance scheme is a good idea at all.

However, leaving aside these legal and political niceties, the most important lesson is that having a simple message and purpose is crucial for building trust. The FDIC "works" because it does what it says: kills ailing banks, while protecting depositors. If the Eurozone could build similar clarity, with whatever regulatory structure it chooses, it might start building a better financial world. Or, put another way, if the Eurozone could kill 450-odd Spanish, Greek or French banks without a consumer or market panic, the euro might have a more viable future. Politicians take note.

1. Which of the following is correct according to the passage?

A. In fact, people know that 445 ailing banks have been closed in US since 2008.

B. Many deceased banks in America didn't include the big banks.

C. Eurozone leaders announced plans to create a financial union.

D. The European regulators should think about how to rebuild confidence.

2. What should the Eurozone learn from America in author's opinion?

A. To bailout the toxic banks.

B. To kill off the ailing banks.

C. o kill off the toxic banks without consumers or market panic.

D. All of above is correct.

3. Which is not the lesson from US to eurozone politicians and regulators?

A. The FDIC's experience shows that regulation need be a zero-sum game.

B. The FDIC's experience shows that regulation need be a zero-sum game.

C. It pays to have a predictable and consistent routine for spotting and killing troubled banks.

D. A regulator needs to have a powerful "brand" in the eyes of the public-in the sense of embodying simple, easy-to-understand principles.

4. What is the most important lesson from the FDIC works?

A. To pay more attention in legal and political niceties.

B. Try to protect the banks until last moment.

C. To have a simple message and purpose for building trust.

D. none is correct.

Passage Two   Breaking up banks will win investor approval

The debate on bank reform has reached a curious moment. In one half of the conversation, regulators are discussing how to make banks safer for society. In the other half, equity investors are discussing how to make banks safer for their portfolios. If you put the two halves of the debate together, you soon realise that the regulatory conversation is topsy turvy—at least in one crucial respect.

The regulatory discussion generally presumes that "reasonable" reform must leave banks intact. Breaking up too-big-to-fail lenders would do violence to the private sector; by contrast, demanding that banks raise extra capital is a market-friendly way to avoid taxpayer bailouts. But the actual conversation in the markets inverts this presumption. Among equity investors, breaking up banking behemoths is increasingly regarded as desirable; by contrast, boosting banks' capital is anathema. If a "reasonable" reform is one that goes with the grain of preferences in the market, busting up the banks may actually be more reasonable than forcing them to hold capital they absolutely do not want.

It is easy to see why investors are eager to dismember the big banks. The promises of synergies trotted out by empire-building bosses in the 1990s have proved largely empty; clients don't necessarily want to buy underwriting or wealth management services from the same supermarket that provides their ordinary loans. Meanwhile, the risks in empire building are evident. If even the respected JPMorgan Chase can lose billions on a sloppy trade in one wayward outpost, then imperial overstretch is everywhere. "Banks are increasingly regarded as unanalysable and uninvestable," says Mike Mayo, an analyst for CLSA on Wall Street.

Investors' skepticism shows up in share prices. The stock market capitalizations of Citigroup and Bank of America languish at half and three fifths of tangible book value, respectively—liquidating Citi could hand shareholders a gain of 100 per cent. Indeed, because banks' assets include infrastructure that could be sold for much more than book value, the bonanza might be even bigger. JPMorgan's market capitalisation is roughly equal to its book value, but analysts reckon that the bank might be worth about a third more dismembered than intact.

If the attraction of bank break-ups is obvious, so is the hostility to regulatory efforts to require banks to raise more capital. Traditionally, banks have preferred to issue debt rather than equity because the government has perversely subsidised leverage. The double taxation of corporate profits has rendered debt tax-efficient; deposit guarantees have subsidised borrowing from retail customers; central bank liquidity has made short-term wholesale borrowing artificially cheap. However, these long-standing incentives for leverage have now been fortified by two new ones.

The first comes from the realisation of banks' too-big-to-fail status. Since 2008, it has been clear that banks' unsecured bondholders stand a good chance of being bailed out in a crisis. This has created a subsidy for bond issuance, distinct from the old subsidies for collecting deposits and issuing short-term paper. Whereas in the past it was only quasi-government lenders such as Fannie Mae that issued bonds cheaply, thanks to an implicit government backstop, now all the big banks enjoy this privilege.

While bond issuance has acquired a subsidy, equity issuance has grown more expensive. To

Lesson Five Terms and Conditions of Commercial Letter of Credit and Security Agreement

limit moral hazard, crisis bailouts were crafted so as to make shareholders suffer; thus AIG's shareholders were taken to the cleaners even as the banks that had incautiously bought its derivatives got off scot-free. As a result, equity investors today do not expect the government to rescue them. In contrast to bondholders, shareholders see banking behemoths as scarily complex, not comfortingly protected.

This too-big-to-fail effect shows up clearly in the prices of equity and debt. A non-financial corporation choosing between equity issuance and bond issuance could reasonably go either way. For example, Coca-Cola's shares sell for 17 times next year's expected earnings, meaning that equity investors demand a return of 5.8 per cent in order to buy the shares. Since Coke can issue long-term bonds at just over 4 per cent, equity is only 1.6 percentage points more costly. By contrast, Bank of America, JPMorgan, and Citigroup face a far larger wedge: 7.5 percentage points, 10.4 percentage points and 11.8 percentage points, respectively. Banks frequently moan that equity is expensive. Thanks to regulators' selective concern with moral hazard, they have a point.

Finally, as Stanford's Anat Admati has noted, bank shareholders do not want to cut leverage because of a classic debt overhang effect. Normally, the owners of a healthy company may accept the expense of issuing equity rather than debt. They do so to reduce the risk of bankruptcy, since equity investors, unlike bond investors, agree in advance to forgo payouts in hard times. But when a company is already unhealthily indebted, creditors resemble owners; the odds of bankruptcy are rising, so bondholders also face the danger that their cash receipts may stop. In this circumstance of debt overhang, the effect of deleveraging is to cut the risk borne by bondholders—or by the government that backstops them. Equity holders get stuck with higher financing costs and no compensating fall in risk.

None of this means that bank regulators should stop insisting on more capital. On the contrary, bank investors' losses from deleveraging will be society's gain. But the capital adequacy police should be aware that they are pushing against powerful incentives to evade their edicts. If regulators want a "reasonable" policy that will be accepted by the equity market, they should break up the giant banks.

1. According to the passage, what about the presumption the regulatory discussed actually?
    A. It was been proved it's right.
    B. It was inverted.
    C. It was been overthrown by clients.
    D. None of them is correct.
2. Traditionally, why did not the bank prefer to issue equity?
    A. Because the government has perversely subsidised leverage.
    B. Because the government has no energy to balance it.
    C. Because the bank can't afford so many debts.
    D. Because the bank has no ability to contend with government
3. Which of the following intensified the incentives for leverage according to the passage?
    A. The banks'too-big-to-fail status has been realised.
    B. Bank shareholders do not want to cut.

C. The realisation of banks' stable status and the bank shareholders's expectation that they don't want to cut.

D. Equity investors today do not expect the government to rescue them.

4. What is the result of the deleveraging in author's opinion ?

A. Bank investors' losses will be society's gain.

B. The bank regulators will insist on more capital.

C. The bank regulators will stop insist on more capital.

D. none is correct.

Passage Three   Vickers is not enough to stop another Libor scandal

In response to the latest banking scandal—Barclays' rigging of Libor rates—David Cameron is calling for better banking culture. Good luck with that. What the prime minister should do is rethink the feckless reforms of the Independent Commission on Banking. This is a throwback to the Glass-Steagall Act, which prompts much nostalgia, but will not and cannot keep banking safe, as the eurozone crisis shows.

The commission was charged with keeping the still-reeling UK economy safe from its banking system. It has done nothing of the kind. Instead the commission plays lip service to real reform with its call to ringfence banks' retail operations. The government is blithely adopting the commission's recommendations. Instead it should replace them with what I call Limited Purpose Banking, where banks stick to their core roles: mediating the payments system and connecting lenders to borrowers.

The history of bank failures is a sorry record of promises that cannot be kept for legitimate reasons as well as fraud. But, unlike standard bankruptcies, bank failures have far greater economic fallout. Banks not only market financial products, they also make financial markets. Markets, be they for apples or loans, constitute critical public goods whose provision should not be jeopardised. The financial market is particularly fragile, and yet the Vickers commission, as it is known after its chairman, perpetuates faith-based casino banking and vast leverage.

The Vickers report discusses neither the public goods aspect of banking nor why banking requires special regulation. It also fails to identify the root causes of the financial crisis—opacity and leverage. Markets do not operate well in the dark. When people cannot tell what they are buying, the slightest evidence of misrepresentation or fraud can trigger a run.

In 1982 several bottles of Tylenol in Chicago pharmacies were laced with cyanide and sold to unsuspecting customers, who promptly died. News of the deaths quickly rendered worthless 31m Tylenol bottles across the world. To prevent further losses, Johnson & Johnson repackaged new Tylenol in safety-sealed containers. This was an act of disclosure, since customers were now assured the bottles contained only Tylenol shipped from the company.

No such disclosure occurs in banking. And so fraud, suspicions of fraud, or suspicions of suspicions of fraud can spark bank runs. Those who run first are short-term creditors induced to lend with the promise of quick escape if they smell something rotten. Other creditors escape as soon as possible. The greater the borrowing, the faster the run, since to the swift go the spoils. Thus opacity and leverage are not only the sine qua non for bank failure, they are the catalyst.

Lesson Five Terms and Conditions of Commercial Letter of Credit and Security Agreement

Instead of restricting leverage and enforcing disclosure, the Vickers report rearranges the proverbial deck chairs by ringfencing "good" banks. Under the commission's plan, good banks hold good assets (eg "safe" mortgages and sovereign bonds), have only good customers (eg retail depositors, and small and medium-sized enterprises), and do only good things (ie no proprietary trading or transacting in derivatives). Good banks are also closely monitored and bailed out as needed.

"Bad" banks are the investment banks and other "shadow/shady" financial corporations. Bad banks have bad customers—large corporations, foreigners and other bad banks. They hold bad assets such as derivatives, engage in bad practices and should not expect government rescue. Both good and bad banks retain more capital against "risky" assets, submit to stress tests and make their longer-term debt loss-absorbing to speed up financial funerals. Unfortunately, good assets go bad. Spanish and other eurozone periphery junk bonds used to be top rated. So did Lehman and AIG bonds, and top tranches of bundled subprime mortgages.

Today, gilts are ultra "safe" assets. But, given the UK's long-term fiscal position, gilts are very risky. Yet the commission would allow good, ringfenced banks to borrow £25 for every pound of equity and invest it all in gilts. In this case, the commission's ringfenced banks would fail if gilt prices dropped by just 4 per cent.

The commission's higher capital requirements would not help, since they pertain to "risky" assets. Furthermore, its capital requirements are lower than Lehman's reported capital level three days before it failed—a report its regulator apparently approved.

When trust takes a holiday, creditors find no comfort in capital ratios. The banks' opacity makes it impossible to verify if their capital ratios are as high as advertised. Finally, in suggesting that bad banks will be left to sink or swim, the commission raises the risk of financial collapse in times of crisis. If the bad banks' bad customers actually believe the commission's intimations that their credits will not be honoured, they will exit at the first sign of trouble. As a result, the instability of the bad banks and the entire financial system will increase.

For all the good intentions and hard work of its members, the commission protects neither good nor bad banks. Nor does it protect the public from the failure of opaque, leveraged banking. What the commission protects are the bankers, who, apparently, are too big to cross.

1. What did the author think about the opacity and leverage?
A. They are the primary factors for the bank failure.
B. They are the catalyst.
C. Not only are they the major causes, but they also accelerate the bad status.
D. None is correct.
2. Which of the following is correct on the Vickers report?
A. The report discusses the public goods aspect of banking.
B. The report couldn't identify the root causes of the financial crisis.
C. The report discusses why banking requires special regulation.
D. The report involves the root causes of the financial crisis

3. In author's eyes, what is the characteristic of the "bad" banks?

   A. They have bad customers

   B. They are the investment banks.

   C. They have some invisible financial corporations.

   D. Above all is right.

4. What is the result of the stupid customers of bad banks believing that their credit won't be accepted?

   The bad banks' instability and the entire financial system will enhance.

   A. he bad banks' instability and the entire financial system will enhance.

   B. The instability of bad banks and the entire financial system will enhance.

   C. The bank will increase their bad credit.

   D. The financial system will be broken.

IV Translation Abilities

法律语言特征分析与法律翻译技能培养之五：

法律语言学的研究内容

法律语言学是研究法律语言的学科。法律语言是法律语言学的研究对象的总称，二者之间不是相等的。法律语言学的主要职责是，分析和总结在法制定、法研究和法执行过程中的特点和规律，从而为法的制定、法学研究和法律的执行中语言运用应遵循的原则和规范提供理论依据。其研究对象由此可大致归纳为：一是法律行为中的语词、语义、语序特点和规律；二是法律行为中语言机体能力，即法律语言内在的创造力、表意的能量、一定时空范围内的活力体现；三是法律行为中语言的文化属性；四是法律行为中语言的实用效力。

根据吴伟平、庞继贤的介绍，国外的法律语言学所探讨的主要内容有以下几个方面：一是法律程序中的口语问题。包括法庭上的语言交流问题，如法官、律师和证人的语言，以及在法庭语境中对语言交流产生的限制和影响等。二是法律文件的书面语问题。包括所有文件的可读性；法律文件区别于一般文件或读物的特征；法律文件在语法、语义上的歧义.语段的衔接；代词的所指；上下文对意义的影响等。三是语言学分析在法律中的应用问题。包括语言本身的分析，如语音、词素和语法分析、语义和语用方面的分析、话题分析、对比分析、反应分析、会话分析、社会语言学分析、心理语言学分析等。四是法庭中的多语和双语问题。包括语言证据的翻译、翻译的程序、方言的处理、如何以书面语表现口语、法庭上的口译以及对法庭所用语言的不熟悉所带来的一切问题等。五是语言学家出庭作证所涉及的问题。包括出庭的语言学家的资格、语言学家在审案中的作用、如何保持中立的证人态度、己方律师和对方律师提问的方式和目的、如何对没有受过语言学训练的人谈语言学等。在上述这些方面国内的研究基本上没有较为深入的探讨。

而国内目前的研究方向主要有三个方面：一是对法律语言本体的研究。如法律语言在词汇、语法、修辞等方面的特点、法律术语体系的构建等。二是对法律语体的研究.如法律文本的语言特点。如法律语体中立法、司法、庭讯、庭辩、侦查、诉讼等语体的语言特点。三是对法律实践中的语言研究。如话语分析、语用学、语言变体理论、民族学、跨文化交际学以及聋哑人和外国人的语言翻译等在法律实践中的应用。

我们认为,语言学研究语言的一般规律,法律语言学则研究语言一般规律在法律各类活动中的体现及其变体。因此,法律语言学除了有关语言的一般性的研究、从法律的角度抽象语言的一般规律以外,更为重要的是进行法律语言的特殊性研究。这种特殊性研究相对于法律语言研究内部的各方面来看,又可以是法律语言学自身的一般性研究,如图1:

图1　语言学、法律语言学及法律语言学分支三者的关系

因而,法律语言学的研究对象既不同于法学的基本研究对象,也不同于语言学的基本研究对象。语言学是研究语言的一般规律,而法律语言学是研究语言一般规律在法律各类活动中的体现及其变体。它所研究的对象包括:描写法律语言现象,研究法律和语言的关系,探讨法律语言的特点、规律及其运用。还应该包括法律语言的语言层次,表述层次和总体文本语言结构三个方面的研究。这样既对法律语言的语言层面进行了描写与探求,同时也对法律事务中涉及的各种活动的言语进行了探究。法律语言讲究严谨性、准确性、逻辑性。受其影响,学者们的研究已经不再限定在笔迹辨认、语音识别、词义解释、法律文献翻译、法庭辩论及法庭翻译等方面,而是从哲学、文化、逻辑学、心理学、社会学、语用学、方言学等角度对法律语言进行全方位的研究,并且也取得了丰硕的成果。此类研究既包括了理论性的探讨,也注重了实用性的研究,使得法律语言学的研究呈现出一种相互斗艳、大放异彩的局面。理论性的探讨是指围绕语言与法律的关系,运用各种不同的理论从多个侧面进行探究,包括:法律语言的特点、功能、所涉及的语言行为,所表现的社会关系(如上下关系、强弱关系、平等或不平等关系、权利层次等),对法律实施过程和结果的影响、法律对语言的要求和制约、法律实施过程中语言使用的特点等。而实用性的研究运用的方法包括:比较、分析、统计,利用语料库的研究等方法。

Translation exercises

Part One　*Put the following into Chinese*

True conservatives despise America's crony capitalism

Elections are a means to an end, not an end in and of themselves. In the face of our present national crisis, merely electing a Republican president and Congress is not ambitious enough. Any Republican victory must be fuelled by a reform agenda that addresses the fiscal, economic, and trust deficits in the US.

The founding fathers' vision of limited government, one that empowers free markets and creates a level playing field for all citizens, is being replaced by a form of crony capitalism where powerful economic interests blur the distinction between regulators and regulated. Campaign finance super-political action committees are but the latest manifestation of this phenomenon.

This cancer has spread across both parties and reduces the prospects of finding solutions to the deepening public policy problems facing the US. Meanwhile, precious time slips away that should be used to bolster the prospects of the next generation. Republicans are better than this!

We must campaign on structural reforms focused on reigniting the marketplace for jobs and innovation. This is the challenge facing conservatives: how to roll back the political power of incumbent business and political interests in order to protect the dynamism that has always been the cornerstone of America's success.

The Republicans should begin by eliminating the tax code's labyrinth of subsidies, loopholes and corporate welfare in favor of lower, flatter individual rates. For the party of Ronald Reagan, national debt should be seen as an enemy and framed as a national security issue.

Developing our human capital is critical to our economy but it is also a moral imperative: we owe our children the same opportunities our parents gave us. Education reform starts with recognizing the need for an expanded marketplace. This, along with tighter federal-local co-ordination of vocational skills training, will be necessary to win back our manufacturing base.

Protecting our natural resources is our joint responsibility but "environmental protection" has become a façade for special interests at the expense of competing energy sources. We must open markets and distribution channels to allow cleaner fuels such as natural gas to compete with gasoline and diesel.

We need financial reform so that innovators and entrepreneurs have access to capital without turning our banking system into a public utility. This means creating a world where we are no longer held hostage to banks that are too big to fail.

Republicans should recognize that full repeal of "Obamacare" is unlikely and drop the pointless sound bites, and instead roll up our sleeves and start slogging towards alternative healthcare solutions. In the run-up to 2014, state governors should aggressively seek more diverse and affordable private health insurance options regulated at the local level. Private health insurance and Medicare should increasingly be based on a defined contribution model. This realistic approach should be coupled with attacking the real cost-drivers such as frivolous litigation and fee-for-service care.

Part Two *Put the following into English*

美国外交政策和国防预算应该着眼于长期的威胁和自身的弱点，而不应受制于20年前发展起来的没有意义的采购模式，当今为数众多的游说者、政治顾问、竞选活动者使这种模式进一步得到强化。当前最大的威胁在国内，解决好内部的问题才是一切外交政策目标的重中之重，特别是在应对中国重新崛起的问题上。本国经济得不到贸易伙伴尊重的国家是无法获得成功的。当前美国势头荏弱，华盛顿的"轴心说"被斥为空洞的无稽之谈。

我认为，大部分共和党人对这些目标并没有很大的分歧，那么为什么完成这些目标如此之难呢？我们政治体制内部的结构性问题催生了裙带资本主义：最有人脉的人试图将政治优势永久化，不管是过时的武器系统还是为大银行提供纾困资助，从中都可以看出这一点。

问题的核心是，监管者和被监管者之间有一道"旋转门"，可供他们彼此互换角色。华尔街和政府之间也变得人员几乎可以互相流动。武器制造者和五角大楼"臭味相投"。国会税收委员会也开始与华盛顿K街的"古琦峡谷"(Gucci Gulch)志同道合。

最终，为了解决民众和政府之间的信任赤字，我们必须改变华盛顿的激励体制。国会任期的限制、合理的竞选募资改革、堵住可供国会和白宫人员通行的"旋转门"是改革的核心。

共和党人是泰迪·罗斯福(Teddy Roosevelt)的同仁,我们应当怀着发起切实改革、推动真正变化的愿景,并且宣之于口,否则,生命、自由和追求幸福这些就没有希望可言。

V Interaction

Discuss with your tutor(s) or the People's judges in your locality about how the courts have handled the cases concerning the legal problems in the letter of credits. Then based on the discussion, you are supposed to write a composition about how the judges overcome the technical difficulties in their handling the cases. Remember that you are required to express your ideas clearly.

VI Appreciation of Judge's Opinions

(1) Case Name(案件名):　　　United States v. Sheneman
In the
United States Court of Appeals
For the Seventh Circuit
No. 11-3161

UNITED STATES OF AMERICA,

Plaintiff-Appellee,

v.

MICHAEL SHENEMAN,

Defendant-Appellant.

Appeal from the United States District Court
for the Northern District of Indiana, South Bend Division.
No. 3:10-CR-126—**Jon E. DeGuilio**, *Judge*.
ARGUED APRIL 13, 2012—DECIDED JUNE 1, 2012

(2) Case Summary(案情简介)

Sheneman and his son purchased distressed properties(被扣押的财产), then flipped the properties by operating an elaborate mortgage fraud scheme(按揭欺诈计划) that convinced unwitting buyers to purchase properties they could neither afford nor rent out after purchasing. Mortgage lenders(按揭贷款者) were duped into(受骗) financing the purchases through misrepresentations(虚假陈述) about the buyers and their financial stability. Four buyers with few assets and no experience in the real estate market(不动产市场,房地产市场) purchased 60 homes. Most of the homes were eventually foreclosed upon(因超过限期等取消赎取权,取消抵押人的赎取权). The buyers and lenders each suffered significant losses. Sheneman was convicted of four counts of wire fraud(电信诈骗,通讯诈欺,透过电子通信方式所为的诈骗行为,如使用电话或是调制解调器), and sentenced to 97 months' imprisonment. The Seventh Circuit affirmed, rejecting challenges to the sufficiency of the evidence(证据的充足性) and to application of sentencing enhancements for use of sophisticated means and for losses of more than one million dollars.

From 2003 to 2005, Sheneman and Jeremie worked in tandem to defraud both real estate buyers and mortgage lenders through a series of calculated misrepresentations. Generally speaking, their plan involved acquiring control over a large number of rental properties, inducing buyers to purchase the properties through a host of false promises, and ensuring that lenders would finance the purchases by falsifying loan documents and misrepresenting the buyers' financial standing.

Sheneman and Jeremie began by acquiring control over a large number of rental properties being sold by landlords in the South Bend and Mishawaka areas of Indiana. Many of these sellers had difficulty renting out their properties—some were in very poor condition—and were, by and large, simply looking to cut their losses and walk away from the homes with their mortgages and taxes paid. They agreed to sell their properties to either Sheneman or Jeremie, both of whom had a reputation for "flipping" homes and selling them at a profit. Although most sellers believed they had sold their properties directly to either Sheneman or Jeremie, the sellers had in fact merely granted one of the two power of attorney over their properties. By exercising powers of attorney, Sheneman and Jeremie took control over the properties without ever appearing on any chain of title. The sellers, for their part, did not notice much of a practical difference. Each seller received the amount of money agreed upon as the selling price—albeit not from a title company, as would normally be the case, but directly from either Sheneman or Jeremie. After they "flipped" the houses and sold them to new buyers for more than the seller's asking price, Sheneman and Jeremie then endorsed and deposited the checks issued by the title company directly into their own accounts, yielding them hefty profits.

Once granted control, Sheneman and Jeremie then set about searching for buyers to purchase the dilapidated properties(破败的资产). Eventually, they found their marks, selling sixty properties to four buyers with no relevant real estate experience: Gladys Zoleko, a Cameroonian citizen in the United States on a student visa, bought fifteen homes; Paul Davies, a Liberian citizen also on a student visa, bought fourteen homes; David Dootlittle, an electrician, bought twenty-one homes; and Gary Denaway, a maintenance worker, bought ten homes. For each buyer, a very similar pattern of conduct transpired.

Sheneman and Jeremie made a wide range of promises to the buyers—false promises, as it turns out—in order to induce the sales. The buyers were all looking for an additional source of income, and Sheneman promised them just that. Significant profits could be made by purchasing homes and then renting them out—the more homes purchased, the bigger the profit. The homes were all in excellent condition, buyers were assured, and either Sheneman or Jeremie would make any necessary repairs. There was also little risk because most of the homes already had paying tenants living in them, and Sheneman and Jeremie would help find new tenants for vacant homes. And if the buyers ever wanted to get out of the real estate business, Sheneman and Jeremie promised to buy back properties that they no longer wanted. Perhaps most enticing of all, Sheneman and Jeremie also promised to cover all down payments(分期付款的首期付款,头期款;订金;首付,首付款,第一期付款;分期付款的第一次清算部分或定金) and closing costs(结算价格,地产成交价). The buyers, despite their relatively modest incomes, could therefore purchase a large number of homes and begin earning an immediate profit—without having to spend a dime out-of-pocket.

They jumped at the chance.

The buyers, for their part, ignored some clear red flags(危险信号,惹人生气的事物). Most obviously, they were only permitted to see one or two of the properties they were purchasing prior to closing. The other homes, buyers were told, had tenants already living in them and a visit to those homes might disturb the tenants. But the buyers were assured that the other homes were all in similar condition and located in comparable neighborhoods. Buyers filled out only minimal paperwork throughout the process. Sheneman brought each potential buyer to Superior Mortgage, a mortgage broker(按揭经纪人) where Jeremie worked as a loan officer. There, each buyer completed a few documents with some very basic information. Shortly thereafter, Jeremie informed the buyer that he or she was approved to buy a large number of properties. In order to ensure that mortgage lenders approved the loan applications, however, Jeremie falsified(篡改,伪造文件等;歪曲) key parts of the documents. Among other misrepresentations, numerous loan applications falsely stated the buyers' citizenship, employment status, and finances, and the buyers' signature on many documents was often forged(伪造).

Beyond falsifying documents, Sheneman and Jeremie took other steps to secure financing from lenders and ensure the closings took place. First, they artificially inflated(抬高) buyers' bank accounts, depositing tens of thousands of dollars in order to make it appear as though the buyers had sufficient assets to take on the loans.

After the transactions were completed, the money was returned to Sheneman and Jeremie. Second, they masked the buyers' financial infirmities(虚弱,衰弱;病症;优柔寡断,懦弱;弱点,缺点) from lenders by utilizing certified checks to cover down payments and closing costs. Lenders therefore had no way of knowing that the buyers were not the true source behind these payments, as the loan documents contemplated. After closing, each of the buyers quickly discovered that the deals they were promised were too good to be true.

A number of the newly purchased homes were hardly habitable. Some had faulty plumbing(管道问题), others had significant mold(发霉) and termite(白蚁) damage, and yet others had structural damage and leaky roofs (屋顶漏水). Moreover, paying tenants were difficult to come by. Many of the homes did not have tenants living in them—despite previous assurances to the contrary—while others had tenants who never paid rent. Often, the few homes that the buyers had actually viewed prior to closing were not even included among the properties they had purchased. Many of the properties were also located in worse neighborhoods than the ones they had visited. When the buyers contacted Sheneman and Jeremie to repair the homes or assist them in finding tenants, as they had promised to do, they were suddenly difficult to reach. The buyers' calls would often be ignored, or Sheneman and Jeremie would hang up when the buyers began complaining. In the end, Sheneman and Jeremie made very few repairs to the properties and reneged(否认,拒绝) on their promise to buy any of them back. Unsurprisingly, each of the buyers was soon unable to make timely mortgage payments. Of the sixty properties: thirty-six were foreclosed upon, eleven were deeded back to the lender in lieu of foreclosure, six were demolished by the city, and four were sold in tax sales.

Sheneman and Jeremie were indicted(起诉) on October 13, 2010, and charged with four counts of wire fraud in violation of 18 U.S.C. §1343. After a four-day jury trial(陪审审判), they were convicted on all four counts (四项罪名). At sentencing, the district court calculated Sheneman's advisory sentencing guidelines range to be 87 to 108 months' imprisonment. In doing so, the court applied several sentencing enhancements, including enhancements for a loss amount of more than $1 million, using sophisticated means, having ten or more victims, and gaining more than $1 million in gross receipts from a financial institution. The district court then sentenced Sheneman to 97 months' imprisonment.

(3) Excerpts of the Judgment(法官判决词)

Before BAUER, KANNE, and TINDER, *Circuit Judges*.

KANNE, Circuit Judge.

I Background *see* (2) case brief

II Analysis

On appeal, Sheneman challenges the sufficiency of the evidence underlying his conviction for wire fraud. He also challenges two of the district court's findings at 8 No. 11-3161 sentencing that resulted in sentencing enhancements, arguing: (1) that the loss amount was not in excess of $1 million, and (2) that the offense did not involve the use of sophisticated means. We take each of these arguments in turn.

A. Sufficiency of the Evidence

Sheneman first challenges his conviction, arguing there was insufficient evidence to establish wire fraud.

Typically, we will reverse a conviction only where the evidence, viewed in the light most favorable to the government, is "devoid of evidence from which a reasonable jury could find guilt beyond a reasonable doubt." Although we have characterized this standard as "highly deferential" and "nearly insurmountable," the even more stringent plain error standard applies here because Sheneman did not move for a judgment of acquittal in the district court. Under the plain error standard, Sheneman must show that "a manifest miscarriage of justice will occur if his conviction is not reversed."

To establish wire fraud under 18 U.S.C. §1343, the government must prove (1) Sheneman's participation in a scheme to defraud, (2) his intent to defraud, and (3) his use of interstate wires in furtherance of the fraud.

Sheneman challenges the sufficiency of the evidence with respect to all three of these elements.

Sheneman begins by contending that the evidence is insufficient to establish there was any scheme to defraud. "A scheme to defraud requires 'the making of a false statement or material misrepresentation, or the concealment of a material fact.'" Sheneman's argument is a non-starter(不可能成功的构想,无成功的机会); there was an abundance of evidence presented at trial detailing the numerous false statements and material misrepresentations made by both he and Jeremie throughout the course of their fraudulent enterprise. The jury heard evidence that Jeremie falsified key portions of loan documents, that Sheneman made a series of misrepresentations to buyers about the homes, and that both Jeremie and Sheneman concealed the true nature of the buyers' finances by inflating bank accounts and using certified checks at closings. Plainly, there was sufficient evidence of a scheme to defraud.

But even if there was a scheme to defraud, Sheneman maintains, he was an unwitting participant. "Intent to defraud requires a willful act by the defendant with the specific intent to deceive or cheat, usually for the purpose of getting financial gain for one's self or causing financial loss to another." Sheneman lacked the specific intent to deceive because he was a hapless(unlucky) pawn(爪牙,走卒) in his son's fraudulent scheme, or so the argument goes. It was Jeremie, after all, who forged documents and completed loan applications riddled with material misstatements. Sheneman was merely selling homes to interested buyers; how was he to know the extent of Jeremie's wrongdoing?

We are not convinced; there was ample circumstantial evidence of Sheneman's intent to defraud. A specific intent to defraud may be established both from circumstantial evidence (旁证) and inferences drawn by examining the scheme itself. As we have already stated, Sheneman took an active part in misleading the banks and causing them to believe that the buyers were financially capable of taking on the loans. More fundamentally, Sheneman played a crucial role in nearly every aspect of the fraudulent scheme from beginning to end. He induced buyers to purchase the homes through various misrepresentations, then immediately referred them to Jeremie so that loan documents could be falsified. He also attended closings and was present at many of Jeremie's meetings with buyers, and therefore was involved in every step of the process. This is all to say that the evidence is more than adequate to support the jury's determination that Sheneman was no unwitting pawn in Jeremie's fraudulent scheme, but rather an active participant with the requisite level of intent. The last element of wire fraud requires that interstate wire communications were used in furtherance of the fraud. Wire fraud statutes, like mail fraud statutes, are not intended to reach all frauds but only those "limited instances in which the use of the [wires] is a part of the execution of the fraud." The use of the wires need not be an essential element of the scheme; it is enough if the use is "incident to an essential part of the scheme" or "a step in the plot." Moreover, it is not necessary for the use of the wires to contain any false or fraudulent material, and even a routine or innocent use of the wires may satisfy this element so long as that use is part of the execution of the scheme.

The wire uses at issue are four bank-to-bank wire transfers, one for each count charged in the indictment. In each case, the lending bank wired funds interstate to the title company on or about the closing date. Sheneman primarily advances two arguments as to why evidence of these wire transfers is insufficient to sustain his conviction. First, he contends that he did not "cause" the transfers, and was unaware that they occurred. Second, Sheneman argues that the wire transfers did not play any role in the execution of the scheme. Instead, Sheneman posits, he would have received the sales proceeds from the title company regardless of whether or not the lending bank ever wired funds to the title company, and thus the scheme's success in no way depended on the wire transfers taking place. We disagree.

Although Sheneman did not "cause" the transfers to occur, there is no requirement that a defendant personally cause the use of the wire. Rather, it will suffice if the use of the wire "will follow in the ordinary course of business, or where such use can be reasonably foreseen, even though not actually intended." Here, it was well within

Lesson Five Terms and Conditions of Commercial Letter of Credit and Security Agreement   153

reason for the jury to conclude that Sheneman, given his involvement in the real estate market, could reasonably foresee that lending banks would use wire transfers to transmit loan proceeds in the course of real estate transactions. Sheneman's second argument, that the wire transfers played no role in the scheme, fares no better. In each case, Sheneman received disbursements(支付,支出)from the title company only after the mortgage lender approved the loan and wire transferred the funds interstate to the title company. As such, there was evidence that Sheneman would not have received any disbursements from the title company absent the wire transfers, and the fraudulent scheme thus would have been foiled. There was simply no manifest miscarriage of justice in the jury's verdict.

B. Sentencing

Next, Sheneman challenges two of the district court's determinations at sentencing. First, he argues that the district court erred in finding that the loss amount was in excess of $1 million, which resulted in a sixteen-level enhancement to Sheneman's offense level. Second, Sheneman contends that the district court erred in finding that sophisticated means were used in the mortgage fraud scheme, which resulted in a two-level enhancement.

We review the district court's application of the sentencing guidelines de novo and its findings of fact for clear error. Under the clear error standard, we will affirm a district court unless "we are left with the definite and firm conviction that a mistake has been committed."

1. Loss Amount

The district court found that mortgage lenders suffered losses totaling $1,084,671.54 for the sixty properties sold as part of the mortgage fraud scheme. Sheneman does not challenge the district court's method of calculating these losses. Instead, he argues that the court erred in considering the lenders' losses at all. Echoing his earlier argument, Sheneman points out that he did not falsify loan documents—again, that was Jeremie. Because Jeremie was responsible, Sheneman contends that the scope of the fraud he agreed to did not extend to the loan application process, and that Jeremie's acts were not reasonably foreseeable. Thus, Sheneman maintains that Jeremie's misconduct alone caused the lenders' losses, and should not have been considered. But, for similar reasons that we have already discussed in addressing Sheneman's earlier challenges, we disagree.

Section 1B1.3(a)(1)(B) of the sentencing guidelines allows a defendant to be held accountable for the conduct of others, but only if that conduct was "in furtherance of a jointly undertaken criminal activity and reasonably foreseeable in connection with that criminal activity." The scope of jointly undertaken criminal activity, however, is not necessarily the same as the scope of the entire scheme. In determining the scope of the criminal activity that a particular defendant agreed to jointly undertake, "the district court 'may consider any explicit agreement or implicit agreement fairly inferred from the conduct of the defendant and others.'" Several factors are relevant in this determination, including: (1) the existence of a single scheme; (2) similarities in modus operandi(做法;办事方式;操作法;手术法;运作方法;作案方法); (3) coordination of activities among schemers; (4) pooling of resources or profits; (5) knowledge of the scope of the scheme; and (6) length and degree of the defendant's participation of the scheme."

The district court properly found the scope of the criminal activity that Sheneman and Jeremie agreed to jointly undertake involved the fraudulent sale of real estate, and this included fraudulently securing the buyers' financing. The scheme as a whole hinged on unqualified buyers securing financing, and necessitated a high level of coordination between Sheneman and his son. In each case, Sheneman quickly referred potential buyers to Jeremie for financing, and profits were pooled throughout the duration of the scheme, which lasted over two years. Moreover, Sheneman could have reasonably foreseen that fraudulent funding was being secured for the unqualified buyers. Not only was he aware that the buyers were on shaky financial grounds, he helped conceal this fact from lenders. And yet, each time he brought a buyer to Jeremie, the buyer was able to secure enough financing to buy as many as twenty one homes. The district court did not err in considering the lenders' losses at sentencing.

2. Sophisticated Means

Finally, Sheneman argues that the district court erred in applying a two-level enhancement because the mortgage fraud scheme did not involve the use of sophisticated means. Sophisticated means are defined as "especially complex or especially intricate offense conduct pertaining to the execution or concealment of an offense." The sophisticated means enhancement is proper when "the conduct shows a greater level of planning or concealment than a typical fraud of its kind." In other words, "the offense conduct, viewed as a whole, was notably more intricate than that of the garden-variety offense." Sheneman primarily argues that the scheme at issue was nothing more than a "garden variety home 'flipping' scam", and therefore was no more complex than a typical fraud of its kind. But we think it clear that the district court's application of the sophisticated means enhancement was proper. Sheneman and Jeremie carefully orchestrated an intricate scheme that fooled buyers, sellers, and mortgage lenders, resulting in four unsophisticated buyers of limited means purchasing sixty properties. In doing so, they relied on their extensive knowledge of the real estate market and lending industry to perpetrate the scheme and avoid detection for several years. This was no simple scam: Sheneman and Jeremie utilized powers of attorney to conceal their activity; convinced buyers that the run-down properties would make sound investments; and fooled mortgage lenders into financing the purchases by falsifying loan documents, misrepresenting the source of down payments and closing costs, and artificially inflating buyers' bank accounts. Moreover, we have previously upheld the application of a sophisticated means enhancement in cases involving similar mortgage fraud schemes.

III Conclusion

For the foregoing reasons, we AFFIRM Sheneman's conviction and sentence.

Lesson Six

The Skepticism in Law and Morals

> **Learning objectives**
> After leaning the text and having done the exercises in this lesson, you will:
> —familiarize yourself with knowledge of the legal characteristics and the nature of law and morals;
> —acquire an appreciation of the vocabulary and grammar or syntax relevant to legal philosophy;
> —become aware of the information required in order to understand legal philosophy;
> —cultivate the practical abilities to put to use the language in the specific context;
> —be able to do some translation from Chinese to English and from English to Chinese.

 Text

The Skepticism in Law and Morals

"Suppose that Socrates was wrong, that we have not once seen the Truth, and so will not, intuitively, recognize it when we see it again. This means that when the secret police① come, when the torturers violate the innocent, there is nothing to be said to them of the form, There is something within you which you are betraying. Though you embody the practices of a totalitarian society which will endure forever, there is something beyond those practices which condemns you."

——Richard Rorty②

---

① The secret police:御用警力,在很多语境当中都有一定的贬义,用于指称那些维护专制政权的暴力工具。
② Richard Rorty:里查德·罗蒂,当代美国最有影响力的哲学家、思想家,也是美国新实用主义哲学的主要代表之一。他的影响力主要来自两个方面:第一,他利用英美分析哲学所擅长的严格方法和精密论说,详细分析了当代诸多分析哲学和历史主义思潮,结合欧陆哲学的解构思想,发展出一套独特的新实用主义的思路和话语。第二,他擅长以宏观的历史视野,向人们显示,新实用主义的信仰对于我们的行为有什么影响。

"Saying that the Aztecs① were wrong to practice human sacrifice simply means we do not want to change in the ways required to make their practices understandable."

——Joan Williams

Stanley Fish tells us that moral issues are intelligible only "within the precincts of the... paradigms② or communities that give them their local and changeable shape". This is one formulation of antifoundationalism③, which rejects the idea of a transcultural moral reality that binds all people. Antifoundationalists see value judgments as contingent cultural products that cannot be objectively true.

But can we do anything with this thesis in practice? Postmodern pragmatists④ like Richard Rorty and Joan Williams believe that we can; they say we would benefit by understanding our moral principles as no more than cultural preferences. The author of this Article takes issue with that approach and provides a series of pragmatic counterarguments in favor of objectivist moral and legal discourse⑤. By investigating the relationship between the anti-foundationalist claim and the universal human rights claim, the author has demonstrated that (a) the thesis that our moral commitments are produced through a contingent historical process can never tell us what commitments we should have; (b) to formulate such commitments, we require an objectivist language of evaluation, one which is not confined to diagnosing the play of cultural and psychological forces but which stands apart from them; and (c) in law and morals this objectivist discourse expresses the distinctions we experience as morally sensitive beings, including the difference between the fair and illegitimate uses of power. A truly pragmatic view would recognize that objective moral claims are not a way we stake out a metaphysical position⑥, but the way we inhabit and describe a nuanced normative world. These are pragmatic arguments which show that anti-foundationalist theory

---

① Azte:阿兹特克人,北美洲南部墨西哥人数最多的一支印第安人。其中心在墨西哥的特诺奇,故又称墨西哥人或特诺奇人。约130万人(1977年),主要分布在中部的韦拉克鲁斯、莫雷洛斯、格雷罗等州。属蒙古人种美洲支。使用纳华特语,属印第安语系犹他—阿兹特克语族。原有象形文字。多信天主教和众神,如"太阳神"、"月亮神"、"春神"等,特别是守护神"威济洛波特利"(战神)。阿兹特克文化的一大特色是喜欢用祭品。有这么一个传说:必须用人的鲜血供奉太阳,他才有力量每天从东边升起。用活人当祭品的数量更是可观,一天之内用掉数千人是常有的事。这些人牲通常被斩首或剥皮,或是活活被挖出心脏。他们被带到金字塔的顶端(最接近太阳的地方),让血沿着石阶流下。由于阿兹特克的经济主要依靠玉米的生产,而他们相信农作要有好收成得依靠祭祀鲜血才行。

② within the precincts of the... paradigms:在范式的范围内。precinct:建筑物等的围地,附近范围;英国教会的会内,寺院的院内;境域内;(复数)境界;美国县以下的管区;美国选举区,分界,分区;(复数)(城镇的周围,附近,郊区)。如:city precincts (市区);an election precinct (选区);a police precinct (警察管区);a shopping precinct (商业区)。

③ antifoundationalism:反基础主义,一种理论倾向,与反理性主义、解构主义、反本质主义、新实用主义等思想倾向紧密联系,相互为用。反基础主义反对基本理性标准的存在,不认为理性主义所谓"放之四海而皆准"的原则或信条有存在的可能。代表人物有 John Dewey, Stanley Fish, Michel Foucault, G. W. F. Hegel, William James, Friedrich Nietzsche, Charles Sanders Peirce, Richard Rorty, Wilfrid Sellars, Ludwig Wittgenstein 等。

④ pragmatists:实用主义者。Pragmatism:实用主义。冯友兰先生在《三松堂自序》中有言:"实用主义的特点在于它的真理论。它的真理论实际是一种不可知论。它认为,认识来源于经验,人们所能认识的,只限于经验。至于经验的背后还有什么东西,那是不可知的,也不必问这个问题。这个问题是没有意义的。因为无论怎么说,人们总是不能走出经验范围之外而有什么认识。要解决这个问题,还得靠经验。所谓真理,无非就是对于经验的一种解释,对于复杂的经验解释得通。如果解释得通,它就是真理,是对于我们有用。有用就是真理。所谓客观的真理是没有的。"此处,该词与 postmodern 搭配,表示的是"新实用主义哲学"(或后现代实用主义哲学),其对传统哲学予以批判,否定真理的绝对性和永恒性。

⑤ objectivist moral and legal discourse:客观主义道德与法律话语。objectivism:客观主义;客观性,如:blending of criminal objectivism and subjectivism in criminal law(刑法客观主义和主观主义的融合)。

⑥ a metaphysical position:形而上学的立场。metaphysics:形而上学,玄学。

Lesson Six The Skepticism in Law and Morals

is so divorced from the human experience of agency and choice that we cannot utilize it in practice. The author also offers some affirmative reasons to believe that the universal human rights claim states a transcultural moral truth.

In an early, influential essay, Duncan Kennedy argued that "there is never a 'correct legal solution' that is other than the correct ethical and political solution to that legal problem". This was an attractive claim, at least to those lawyers who rejected the Langdellian[①] faith that legal concepts are tied to nature and logic in a way that can produce uncontroversial right answers to legal questions. It reflected the efforts of many critical legal scholars[②], and of the legal realists[③] before them, to dismantle the formalist dichotomy[④] separating decisions based on legal reasoning (pictured as an autonomous, determinate form of conceptual thinking) from outcome-driven decisions (pictured as decisions based on individual prejudice or sentiment). Where formalists saw the rule of law, these scholars saw a rule's fetish—a sort of institutionalized Milgram experiment[⑤] directing judges to ignore the consequences of their rulings.

There are various ways to pursue this antiformalist program. For legal academics, the most direct is to do what Kennedy suggested—expose the real political and ethical stakes underlying legal controversies. An example is the abundant critical scholarship on particular legal doctrines[⑥], which is less concerned with the doctrine's theoretical soundness than with how it operates in practice, or whose interests it serves, or whose vision it reflects. Such efforts can reveal suffering and injustice that go unnoticed because of their formal legitimacy.

There are also less fruitful paths. This author attempts to elucidate the drawbacks of one of them: the production of postmodern legal theory, a cottage industry that has consumed the best efforts of a number of progressive legal scholars. Postmodern theory seems a useful antidote to formalist ideology because it denies the possibility of neutral and objective answers in any domain, and thus necessarily in the legal one. But because of its generality, this approach inherently es-

---

① 此处的 Langdellian 是 Langdell 的形容词形式,Langdell,即 Christopher Columbus Langdell,美国著名法学家,其主要成就体现在将案例教学法引入到法学教育当中。

② critical legal scholars:批判法学家们,其中,critical legal studies:批判法学,利用诸如法兰克福学派的批判理论或法律解构理论等方法分析和研究法律的一个学派。

③ legal realist:法律现实主义者,坚持现实主义,也叫规则怀疑论,兴盛于20世纪初期的一个法哲学流派。法律现实主义坚持认为,传统法学理论是虚构的,因为它们把法律规范视为抽象的实体,认为法律概念具有形而上学的本质。与法律形式主义相对立,法律现实主义对法律规则的概念持怀疑态度。规则就其实质而言并不能控制法院的判决,法律的功能是解决实际的纠纷。对法律的理解必须参考实际存在的法律体系这一现实。法律现实主义有两个传统。以 O.W.小霍尔姆斯和 K.卢埃林为代表的美国的法律现实主义受到"实用主义"的影响,认为法律是由法规如何制定和法院实际作出的判决构成的。以 A.哈格施特勒姆、K.奥里维克鲁纳和 A.罗斯为代表的斯堪的纳维亚的法律现实主义受到孔德的实证主义的影响,认为对法律规范的解释必须根据法官的、或公民的、或两者的心理反应。法律现实主义试图按照实际的法律以及它们是如何起作用的去理解法律。它的长处在于,它深深植根于律师的实际活动、洞察力和实践艺术中,其不足之处是既不能说明判决的法律推理,也不能解释法律改革的必要性。

④ Formalist dichotomy:形式主义者的二分法,其所坚持的形式主义是法学中的一个流派,着重审讯过程中的公平更甚于最后的实质结果。课文中的二分法指的是基于法律推理而作出的判决(decisions based on legal reasoning)和由于结果的驱动而作出的判决(outcome-driven decisions)。

⑤ institutionalized Milgram experiment:制度化的米尔格兰姆实验。斯坦利·米尔格兰姆(Stanley Milgram,1933—1984)美国著名的社会心理学家,在社会心理学领域从事了大量研究,由于对从众行为的研究而著名。

⑥ legal doctrines:英美法中,该词主要指的是"通过法官判决而抽象出的基本原则或原理",为此,法学界通常将其看作是"法律",或曰"法之通货手段"。而在大陆法系中,该词多指"法律教义学"之类的内容。

chews specific ethical and political claims and operates on a much more abstract level. Consequently, it risks producing a scholarship as conceptual, arid, and removed from experience as the formalism which is its target. And so it has.

What do these theorists assert? There are many, sometimes conflicting claims, but as a first approximation we can say they present a contemporary version of what Nietzsche①called perspectivism②(to adopt his term from among many). On this view, all judgments are contingent cultural products that cannot be "objectively true." We each necessarily see through particular lenses shaped by our cultural and personal histories, so that our beliefs are always situated and partial and no one can properly claim to have privileged, unmediated access to the "real" description of the world or to "natural" standards of rationality. The claim that one has achieved this impartial view from nowhere is really an exercise of power. Gary Peller③writes: according to the new critical approaches, there is no objective reference point, separate from culture and politics, available to distinguish truth from ideology, fact from opinion, or representation from interpretation... These new critical approaches deny the central Enlightenment④notion... that there is a difference between rational, objective representation and interested, biased interpretation... The most successful form of social power is one that presents itself not as power, but as reason, truth, and objectivity. But there is no place that is outside politics and independent of social struggle...."

Perspectivist theory challenges the separation of law and politics in this way, but it also leaves the third term in Kennedy's formulation—"the correct ethical solution"—in a jurisprudential limbo. For although ethics differs from formalist legal reasoning in that it does not aspire to value-neutrality, it does presuppose that objectively correct answers exist and that there is an impartial position from which to distinguish legitimate from illegitimate uses of power. If we describe *Bowers v. Hardwick*, the so-called anti-sodomy case, not merely as an inevitably partial decision reflecting the homophobic perspective of particular judges, but as *unjust*, we do so from the conviction that there are correct ethical answers across persons. But the perspectivist critique deconstructs the ethical claim no less than the Langdellian one, and reduces ethics to a heavily mystified form of politics.

Applied to ethics, perspectivism challenges the idea that ideals like justice and equality refer to anything at all, except as particular cultures come to define them. The problem is not just that people have divergent ideals (such as individualism and communitarianism⑤), but that they con-

---

① Nietzsche:全称是 Friedrich Wilhelm Nietzsche(1844—1900),弗里德里希·威廉·尼采,德国著名哲学家。西方现代哲学的开创者,同时也是卓越的诗人和散文家。他最早开始批判西方现代社会,然而他的学说在他的时代却没有引起人们重视,直到 20 世纪,才激起深远的调门各异的回声。后来的生命哲学,存在主义,弗洛伊德主义,后现代主义,都以各自的形式回应尼采的哲学思想。

② perspectivism:尼采的透视主义(视点论),认为解释存在多种可能性,解释的标准是透视的权力意志本身,权力意志是理解透视主义的关键。透视主义动摇了真理有绝对的、客观的标准的信仰。

③ Gary Peller:美国左翼批判法学学者,他在《美国法的形而上学》一文中提出,法律既反映它试图调整的更大的文化的价值、规范、实践和风尚,又建构于它们,因此法律是一种社会建构。

④ Enlightenment:启蒙运动,发生于 18 世纪初至 1789 年法国大革命期间的一个新思维不断涌现的时代,其核心理念就是理性主义。法语中,"启蒙"的本意是"光明"。当时先进的思想家认为,迄今为止,人们处于黑暗之中,应该用理性之光驱散黑暗,把人们引向光明。他们著书立说,积极地批判专制主义和宗教愚昧,宣传自由、平等和民主。

⑤ communitarianism:社群主义,1993 年兴起的一种政治理论,主张个人和社团/社群之间的密切关联。

struct different descriptions of the world (is the fetus a person?): One can only make moral judgments with a picture of the world in mind, and what looks like discrimination in one picture will look natural and just in a different one. A slaveholder's picture might combine the conviction that all human beings have inalienable rights with the belief that slaves are not human beings. To put this another way, the perspectivist can argue that the most rudimentary requirement of justice—to "treat like cases alike"—is formal and empty, because there are no natural essences to cases but only theory-laden, culture-bound interpretations attached to them. "The world does not split itself up, on its own initiative, into sentence-shaped chunks called 'facts'"; worlds are made, not found, and in some of them "treating like cases alike" means assigning roles according to caste, or treating abortion as murder, or limiting the vote to the propertied class.

The problem with yoking this postmodern view to the antiformalist cause is that it blinds us to the difference in kind between transcendental legal nonsense like "the nature of a corporation," which can be usefully deconstructed, and meaningful transcendental ethical ideals like equality and universal human rights, which cannot. And as the quotations that preface this article show, committed perspectivists are indeed willing to hold these moral claims equally hostage to perspectivist theory. Richard Rorty, a pragmatist philosopher who has greatly influenced legal theory, believes that his theoretical commitment to antifoundationalism means he cannot claim that a totalitarian society betrays any moral principle that transcends its practices. Joan Williams, a legal pragmatist, suggests that we can "benefit... from redefining our moral certainties as cultural rather than as reflective of eternal truth". She views her opposition to human sacrifice as a cultural epiphenomenon with no transcultural validity. According to these theorists and many others who advocate a postmodern legal and ethical practice, we should stop thinking we can be impartial and own up to the fact that the moral standards we apply are simply our standards: There can be no objective standards of justice because each culture constructs its own.

This perspectivist thesis now permeates academia, and is "as dominant in legal theory as any paradigm was in the past" according to one observer. But there is much wrong with it, not least a non-sequitur① that conflates morality and history. We do all see from somewhere, encumbered by our particular histories and interests; but that does not mean that we should give up seeking a wider, more impartial view, or that the effort is futile. What is futile, I believe, is a theory that leaves no room for this basic moral aspiration.

This present endeavor explains as precisely as possible why perspectivism is such a black hole for legal theory and legal scholars. It offers a map of the circular trails and blind alleys that plague the theoreticians who enter this maze, hoping to find some kind of liberation or political promise within. What they actually find, I argue, is the unnuanced formalism they thought they left behind. The ethical stakes in legal cases remain obscure, this time because the perspectivist approach supplants moral considerations with (anti-)metaphysical ones.

In what follows, I explore the relationships among perspectivism, law and morals primarily

---

① non sequitur:拉丁语,不根据前提的推论/结论,不根据前提的推论或推理,不合逻辑的推论/推理,不合逻辑的陈述或结论;前后不连贯的陈述;与所说无关的评论。

through the example of universal human rights. The human rights claim reveals the conflicting arguments at their strongest, because it combines the most deeply-held moral convictions with the most metaphysical, least plausible assertion of objectivity, cross-cultural objectivity. On the one hand, it does appear self-evident that human beings have certain inalienable rights, such as rights against enslavement and torture. On the other hand, it is difficult to understand how objective moral standards could exist wholly independent of a culture's particular traditions, against which cultural practices such as caste and clitoridectomy① might be judged. It is equally difficult to envision how such a transcultural, ahistorical moral reality might be accessible to people whose beliefs and motivations seem formed by their diverse cultural and personal circumstances. Community consensus is insufficient, and locating transcultural truth in Platonic Forms, human nature, or human or divine reason may seem unacceptably metaphysical.

The author will argue against perspectivists who have said that the transcultural human rights claim is either false or not useful in practice. What, I ask, can the perspectivist possibly mean when she says a universal moral claim is false? And why would she think that depriving ourselves of the language of transcultural human rights could be useful? By charting these logical and practical limits of perspectivism, I hope to demonstrate that this kind of postmodern skepticism can be no objection to the claim that all human beings have certain objective and fundamental moral rights. Apart from this, this article will examine two perspectivist alternatives—neopragmatism② and cultural relativism③—and show how each misconceives ethics in the impossible attempt to translate anti-metaphysical theory into practice. Neopragmatists and cultural relativists often disagree about particular human rights policies. Unlike cultural relativists, many neopragmatists favor human rights laws, but purport to do so on ethnocentric④ rather than moral, grounds. But their theories reject the idea that some actions violate an ahistorical, transcultural moral stricture, and I argue that neither theory provides a convincing alternative. Both of my counter-arguments are internal critiques, for they demonstrate that these programs fail by their own standards.

Cultural relativism's theory of "local" truth cannot be applied without making the kind of objective, transcultural claims that the theory rejects. Thus, there is really no intelligible difference between "cultural relativism" and "cultural absolutism": as practiced, cultural relativism looks just like an objectivist ethical judgment that every culture should be the final arbiter of its practices. The neopragmatist program also fails on its own terms, at least to the degree that it holds out

---

① clitoridectomy:阴蒂切开术;阴蒂切除术。

② Neopragmatism:新实用主义,又称为 linguistic pragmatism,1960 年来,由 Richard Rorty 所发展的实用主义的后现代版本,传统实用主义注重的是经验,而 Rorty 十分强调语言,语言依赖于使用,其意义产生就在于在类似方式下使用词语。

③ cultural relativism:文化相对主义,该理论的核心人物是梅尔赫斯科维茨,他认为"文化相对主义的核心是尊重差别并要求相互尊重的一种社会训练,它强调多种生活方式的价值,这种强调以寻求理解与和谐共处为目的,而不去批判甚至摧毁那些与自己原有文化不相吻合的东西"。简单点说就是承认并尊重不同的文化,并在平等的基础上交流。

④ ethnocentric:以民族为中心的。民族中心主义(ethnocentrism),是一种认为自己文化优于他文化的信条。广义上说就是轻视其他群体的成员。美国社会学家孙墨楠(William Graham Sumner)给它下的定义是:"以其个人所属群体为一切事物的中心为出发点来看待事物,对其他所有群体则按照自己的标准把它们分成等级……每个群体都认为只有自己的社会习俗是恰当的,看到别的群体有不同的社会习俗,就会嘲笑。"总之,它是一种主观主义的态度,偏爱本群体的生活方式,以自己的生活方式为标准,用否定的态度,否定或贬低其他民族群体的生活方式和文化成就。所有文化及其成员都有一定程度上的民族中心主义,人类学被认为是一门民族中心主义最少的社会科学。

perspectivism as useful in practice. In Part III (B), I suggest that proposals by Rorty, Williams and others to redefine truth instrumentally as "what it is better to believe," or ethnocentrically as "cultural preferences," cannot serve as an adequate basis for practice. In this discussion, I argue that a pragmatist should favor a more nuanced approach that is capable of expressing the difference between a matter of taste, a breach of etiquette and an extreme injustice; and that objectivist discourse is necessary for that purpose.

We should address the difficult ethical problems presented by diversity directly, rather than bury them in formalistic, antimetaphysical myths. Part IV suggests that we can do this only by crediting our intuitive moral sense that there is a meaningful difference in kind between fairness and self-assertion that can guide us even in cases of cultural conflict. On this view, locating oneself in history and understanding one's positioned perspective are very important, but they are importantly ethically only because they are crucial parts of the project of seeking a more just and inclusive view.

Legal Terminology

1. lawyer, attorney, attorney-at-law, barrister, solicitor, counsel, counselor, conveyancer, law agent 与 advocate

以上词汇均有律师的含义。lawyer 为最通用词,可泛指取得法律专业资格有权从事法律工作者,在英国,其可包括法官、开业律师、法学教师等。在美国,其可指参与法庭诉辩或提供法律咨询的任何人,该单词有时也用于专指开业律师。现有人将其译为"法律人"。attorney 在英国是指与当事人指定,以委托人名义行使职责,代写诉讼文书、财产转让书等的法律代理人,在英国现该词已鲜用。在美国,该词广泛用来指行使英格兰的巴律师、沙律师和代理人等全部职能的律师。attorney-at-law 为美国用语,通常在名片上使用。barrister 和 solicitor 多用于英国或一些曾属于英联邦的国家或地区,如香港,这与美国和加拿大等国的律师不分类别的情况不同。这两个单词的译法很多,前者有出庭律师、高级律师、专门律师、大律师等,后者有诉状律师、初级律师等,这些译法均不太准确,易误导读者。事实上,这两种律师的职能各有差异,根本不能用高级和低级区分。此外,solicitor 也常常可在高等法院之外的其他法庭上出庭辩护,故也不能用出庭律师或不出庭律师加以区别。有鉴于此,笔者推崇上海陈忠诚教授的音译法,即将前者译为巴律师,后者译为沙律师。counsel 为顾问律师,在英国多指为沙律师提供意见或建议的巴律师,有时也指成为王室法律顾问的巴律师,即 Queen's(或 King's) Counsel;在美国,其多指为公司或政府担当法律顾问的律师,如 in-house counsel。counselor 在英国已经被废弃,其在爱尔兰和美国等地有时仍在使用,主要是指提供法律咨询、处理各种法律事务,出庭进行诉辩等的法律代理人,其含义等同于 attorney。conveyancer 主要指从事财产转让事务的律师,包括巴律师和沙律师。advocate 为出庭律师,此外,苏格兰的巴律师也被称为 advocate,而沙律师则被称为 law agent。

2. legal doctrine, legal principle 与 legal rule

三个词都是指法律规范(legal norm)的种类,但各表述的范围以及普遍性程度具有差异。legal doctrine(法律原理)的概括性最强,常表示实质性的法律规范,包括带共同主题的、系统的一套处理特殊情况、典型事例和法律秩序的原则、规则和准则,它们在逻辑上相互关联,结合为有机的统一体,可从其基础和逻辑前提进行法律推理,如英美法系中的合同对价原理以及公共政策原理等。legal principle(法律原则)多指对较具体的简单陈述、法律适用进行论证、统一和解释,并作为更进一步的法律推理的权威前提的普遍性规范。legal rule(法律规则)则多指比较专门和具体的规范,用以规定某种法律事实的特定法律后果,如必须有两人或两人以上者证明遗嘱方能生效规则等。

3. neopragmatism

新实用主义,代表人物:R.罗蒂。他一方面否认皮尔士对实用主义的贡献将其开除出实用主义传统,认为他走上了科学主义的错误道路,并否认皮尔士的真理界定即"真理是理想共同体进行探究时所达到的最终的意见一致";另一方面,罗蒂放弃了詹姆斯彻底的经验主义路线而只保留詹姆斯在真理理论上的实用主义,这样一来,就走上了康德式的抛弃"经验作为连接我们与世界的桥梁"的狭窄路线,从而有陷入相对主义和语言唯心论泥潭的嫌疑;再次,罗蒂对杜威的自然主义的理解也是狭窄的、扭曲的,是背离其精神内核的。虽然他利用了杜威那里的对真理的达尔文主义—工具主义的诠释,但他同时走向了塞拉斯—戴维森式的"融贯论+整体论",从而放弃了"指称"、"映现"等可能存在于我们的(作为第二自然的)经验、实践活动中的维度,因此强行地割裂了世界与语言或心灵的天然联系,而滑向了后现代主义。由于新实用主义是一个非常模糊的、并没有如维也纳学派或新儒家那样有着集体宣言的理论运动,对其成员的认定、对其核心理论的理解莫衷一是。一般来说,这项运动的中心立场涵盖维特根斯坦的"意义即使用"的用法论、塞拉斯对心灵的语言学解释以及其在意义推理论(inferential theory of meaning)上的原创贡献、蒯因的意义整体论、戴维森的三角定位理论、麦克道威尔的最低限度经验论、罗蒂与普特南的新实用主义以及布兰顿的分析实用主义。

4. ruling

多指在诉讼中就动议所作出的裁决,以及为解释法律、法令、法规、条例等而作出裁定;此外,award、decision、judgment、sentence、verdict、decree 和 disposition 均有裁定、判决的含义。decision 为通用词汇,如 arbitral decision(仲裁裁决)或 judicial decision(司法判决)等;award 专指仲裁裁决;judgment 用于诉讼案件,其可指民事判决,也可用于指刑事判决,尤其是指结果为赦免、撤销原判、驳回上诉等不科处刑罚之判决;而 sentence 的中心含义为科刑"inflicting punishment on the convicted",故其只限于指刑事判决,且为处以刑罚之判决,如无罪开释则应用其他词,如 decision 或 judgment 等来表示;verdict 是指陪审团作出的有关事实的裁决;decree 是指法院根据衡平法上的权利所作的裁定,故多用于指衡平法院、海事法院以及继承和离婚法院所作的判决或裁定;disposition 在民事上多指法官就某事项或动议的裁定,等于 judge's ruling,其更多用于刑事案件方面,指科刑,如 probation is often a desirable disposition,此外,其还常用作未成年罪犯的判决,指科刑或给予其他规定的处遇。

5. affirmation

声称,断言,其与 allegation 构成关系。其中,allegation 主要指诉辩状或证词中关于事实的陈述,在教会法中,其还可指在作为原告人控诉之后的任何抗辩,包括应答抗辩、反对抗辩或例外抗辩等;而 affirmation 则多指正式严肃的声明,表示声明人将提供真实情况,对某事进行确认。除此之外,affirmation 的形容词 affirmative 与不同的法律词汇搭配后,会被赋予多种法律含义,如 affirmative charge(法官给陪审团所作的)不得按起诉罪名定罪的指示、affirmative defense 积极抗辩(指对刑事指控超出仅仅是否认的一种回应,被告承认指控事实但却以其他理由,如精神失常、混合过失、时效等为由进行抗辩,此种抗辩是为了从陪审团处获得无罪裁决而采用的一种策略)。

Exercises

I Verbal Abilities

Part One

Directions: *For each of these completing questions, read each item carefully to get the sense of it. Then, in the proper space, complete each statement by supplying the missing word or phrase.*

1. When a public officer is a party to an appeal in an official capacity and during its pendency dies, the action does not _____.

　　A. curtail　　　　B. diminish　　　　C. lower　　　　D. abate

1. If the contract was void for traditional reasons such as fraud or _____, the parties to this contract will make the registration accordingly.

　　A. currency　　　B. downplaying　　C. overreaching　　D. budgeting

2. A party aggrieved by a _____ may bring an action for relief.

　　A. repudiation　　B. party　　　　　C. contract　　　　D. experience

3. A purchaser who buys in good faith at a _____ takes the goods free of any rights of the original buyer.

　　A. selling　　　　B. check　　　　　C. resale　　　　　D. bill

4. The justices _____ d the question because it was not an issue in the case.

　　A. satisfy　　　　B. reserve　　　　C. hold　　　　　D. batch

5. A person can have more than one _____ but only one domicile.

　　A. friend　　　　B. box　　　　　　C. residence　　　　D. batch

6. An _____ is the partial or complete prohibition of commerce and trade with a particular country, in order to isolate it.

　　A. embargo　　　B. injunction　　　C. reputation　　　D. beholding

7. In accordance with one party's report, it was the _____ that caused by budgetary deficit.

　　A. price　　　　　B. inflation　　　　C. exchange　　　　D. transaction

8. The parol evidence rule is a substantive _____ law rule in contract cases.

　　A. civil　　　　　B. criminal　　　　C. administrative　　D. common

9. In civil law countries, if lawsuits are presented after that time, an institution called _____ applies.

　　A. time　　　　　B. period　　　　　C. prescription　　　D. rule

Part Two

Directions: *Choose the one word or phrase that best keep the meaning of the original sentence if it were substituted for the underlined part.*

1. People may bring forth the <u>wrongful termination action</u> in case of unfairness.
   A. unfair competition   B. torts action
   C. wrongful discharge action   D. unjust manipulation

2. Armed with these studies, defense attorneys sought to use <u>the XYY defense</u> to protect for the client.
   A. XYY chromosome defense   B. dissatisfaction defense
   C. aggrieved defense   D. affirmative defense

3. The adjudicator said to Helen that he would give <u>the 2000 warranty</u> to the party.
   A. civilized promise   B. guarantee   C. surety   D. Y2K warranty

4. The judge held that the violating act had been going on for a <u>year and day</u>.
   A. 360 days   B. year and a day   C. 366 days   D. 12 months and a day

5. The dying man told his lawyer to make a <u>testament</u> for him.
   A. declaration   B. guarantee   C. word   D. will

6. Something voluntarily <u>abandoned</u> by its owner with the intention of not retaking it is a derelict.
   A. give up   B. rescinded   C. throw   D. neglect

7. A <u>waiver</u> is the voluntary relinquishment or surrender of some known right or privilege.
   A. give in   B. consent   C. admit   D. abandonment

8. To aid and <u>abet</u> is to knowingly order, encourage, assist or attempted to assist another person in the commission of a crime.
   A. incite   B. bet   C. gamble   D. play

9. A <u>charge</u> is a formal allegation by the state against a person who is suspected of committing a crime.
   A. report   B. announcement   C. accusation   D. claim

10. That <u>law</u> was enacted by the Parliament in 1980.
    A. rule   B. ordinance   C. act   D. by-law

II Cloze

Directions: *For each blank in the following passage, choose the best answer from the choices given.*

Secret police (sometimes political police) are a police agency which operates ___(1)___ to protect the power and authority of a political regime or state. Secret police ___(2)___ are associated with authoritarian regimes, as they are, ___(3)___, used to support the political power of an individual government or regime rather than ___(4)___ the common rule of law. Instead of ___(5)___ enforcing the rule of law and being ___(6)___ to public scrutiny as ordinary police agencies do, secret police organizations are specifically intended to operate beyond and above the law in order to

Lesson Six The Skepticism in Law and Morals

　　__(7)__ political dissent through clandestine acts of terror and intimidation (such as kidnapping, coercive interrogation, torture, internal exile, forced disappearance, and __(8)__) targeted against political enemies of the ruling authority. Secret police forces are accountable only __(9)__ the executive branch of the government, sometimes only to a dictator. They operate entirely or partially in secrecy, that is, most or all of their operations are obscure and hidden from the general public and government except for the topmost executive officials. This semi-official capacity allows the secret police to __(10)__ the government's control over their citizens while also allowing the government to deny prior knowledge of any violations of civil liberties. Secret police agencies have often been used as an instrument of political __(11)__ . States where the secret police wield significant power are sometimes referred to as police states or __(12)__ states. Secret police differ from the domestic __(13)__ agencies in modern liberal democracies, because domestic security agencies are generally subject to government regulation, reporting requirements, and other accountability measures. Despite such overview, there still exists the possibility of domestic-security agencies acting __(14)__ and taking on some characteristics of secret police. In some cases, certain police agencies are accused of being secret police and deny being such. For example, radical groups in the United States have at various times accused the Federal Bureau of Investigation of being secret police. Which government agencies may be classed or characterized, in whole or part, as "secret police" is __(15)__ by political scientists.

  (1) A. in secrecy   B. in pubic   C. in proceeding   D. in time
  (2) A. arms   B. navies   C. forces   D. institutions
  (3) A. for example   B. as aforesaid   C. for instance   D. by definition
  (4) A. fighting   B. battling   C. upholding   D. applauding
  (5) A. transparently   B. secretly   C. profoundly   D. greatly
  (6) A. likely   B. subject   C. willing   D. speculating
  (7) A. advocate   B. suppress   C. hope   D. get
  (8) A. assassination   B. dissertation   C. propaganda   D. publication
  (9) A. for   B. of   C. to   D. in
  (10) A. let   B. go   C. bolster   D. do
  (11) A. repression   B. subordination   C. acceleration   D. enrichment
  (12) A. digital   B. high-tech   C. counterintelligence
     D. poorly-managed
  (13) A. security   B. public   C. private   D. administrative
  (14) A. actively   B. unlawfully   C. excitedly   D. suddenly
  (15) A. fought   B. disputed   C. discussed   D. focused

III Reading Comprehension

Part One

Directions: *In this section there are passages followed by questions or unfinished statements, each with four suggested answers. Choose the one you think is the best answer.*

Passage One

Justice Holmes laid the foundation of healthy and constructive skepticism in the law. Hughes writes: "Though another half century was to elapse before the appearance of Ogden and Richard's *The Meaning of Meaning*, exploration of meaning of meaning of law was Holmes's pioneer enterprise." Hughes further writes: "To me, Mr. Justice Holmes is a prophet of the Law."

In 1881, Holmes published The Common Law, representing a new departure in legal philosophy. By his writings, he changed attitude to law. An excerpt from the opening passage captures the pragmatic theme of that work and of Holmes's philosophy of law: 'The life of the law has not been logic; it has been experience.' In a dissenting opinion in *Lochner v. New York* (1905), Holmes declared that the law should develop along with society and that the 14th Amendment did not deny states a right to experiment with social legislation. He also argued for judicial restraint, asserting that the Court should not interpret the Constitution according to its own social philosophy. Francis Biddle writes: "He was convinced that one who administers constitutional law should multiply his skepticisms to avoid heading into vague words like 'liberty', and reading into law his private convictions or the prejudices of his class." Biddle also tells us that Holmes "refused to let his preferences (other men were apt to call them convictions) interfere with his judicial decisions... The steadily held determination to keep his own views isolated from his professional work is aptly shown by his famous remark in the Lochner case—the Fourteenth Amendment does not enact Mr. Herbert Spencer's *Social Statistics*... A constitution is not intended to embody a particular economic theory."

According to Holmes, 'men make their own laws;... these laws do not flow from some mysterious omnipresence in the sky, and... judges are not independent mouthpieces of the infinite'. The common law is not a brooding omnipresence in the sky. Holmes compared the Law to a bad man "who cares only for the material consequences of things." Holmes defined the law in accordance with his pragmatic judicial philosophy. Rather than a set of abstract, rational, mathematical, or in any way unwordly set of principals, Holmes said that 'he prophecies of what the courts will do in fact, and nothing more pretentious, are what I mean by the law'. Accordingly, Holmes thought that only a judge or lawyer who is acquainted with the historical, social, and economic aspects of the law will be in a position to fulfill his functions properly.

As a justice of US Supreme Court, Holmes introduced a new method of constitutional interpretation. He challenged the traditional concept of constitution. Holmes also protested against the method of abstract logical deduction from general rules in the judicial process. According to Holmes, lawyers and judges are not logicians and mathematicians. The books of the laws are not books of logic and mathematics. He writes: "The life of the law has not been logic; it has been experience. The felt necessities of the time, the prevalent moral and political theories, intuitions of public policy, avowed or unconscious, and even the prejudices which judges share with their fellow-men, have had a good deal more to do than syllogism in determining the rules by which men should be governed. The law embodies the story of a nation's development through many centuries, and it cannot be dealt with as if it contained only the axioms and corollaries of a book of mathematics.

1. To say "Holmes is a prophet of the Law" means _____.
   A. Holmes is a pioneer in the legal thought circles.
   B. Holms can foresee the future of the law.
   C. Holms will give orders to other judges in the United States.
   D. Holms is regarded as the forefather of the law in America.

2. *The Common Law* published by Holms represents _____.
   A. Legal scholars began to pay attention to the importance of common law in legal system.
   B. Legal scholars began to change their attitude toward justice.
   C. A new departure in legal philosophy at that time began to arise.
   D. Great concurrency occurred concerning the problem of legislature.

3. Concerning the problem of judicial restraint, which of the following ideas belong to Holms _____?
   A. The court should interpret the law in accordance with the legal texts.
   B. The court should interpret any statutes on its own initiative.
   C. The court should interpret the special vocabulary in the legal texts with reference to legal dictionaries.
   D. The Court should not interpret the Constitution according to its own social philosophy.

4. Why does Holms think the law is like a bad man "who cares only for the material consequences of things"?
   A. The common law is not a brooding omnipresence in the sky
   B. The law can only operate in accordance with its own functions.
   C. The civil law could also be effective under the guidance of the wise leaders.
   D. Law is not an eleemosynary institution.

5. Which of the following does not belong to Holms according to this passage?
   A. The law should develop along with society.
   B. The Court should not interpret the Constitution according to its own social philosophy.
   C. The life of the law has not been experience; it has been logic.
   D. The 14th Amendment did not deny states a right to experiment with social legislation.

Passage Two

Postmodern philosophy is a philosophical direction which is critical of the foundational assumptions and structures of philosophy. Beginning as a critique of Continental philosophy, it was heavily influenced by phenomenology, structuralism and existentialism, including writings of Georg Wilhelm Friedrich Hegel, Søren Kierkegaard, Friedrich Nietzsche, and Martin Heidegger. Postmodern philosophy is skeptical or nihilistic toward many of the values and assumptions of philosophy that derive from modernity, such as humanity having an essence which distinguishes humans from animals, or the assumption that one form of government is demonstrably better than another. Postmodern philosophy is often particularly skeptical about simple binary oppositions characteristic of structuralism, emphasizing the problem of the philosopher cleanly distinguishing knowledge from ignorance, social progress from reversion, dominance from submission, and presence from absence. Postmodern philosophy has strong relations with the substantial literature of critical theory. The most influential early postmodern philosophers were Jean Baudrillard, Jean-François Lyotard, and Jacques Derrida. Michel Foucault is also often cited as an early postmodernist although he personally rejected that label. Following Nietzsche, Foucault argued that knowledge is produced through the operations of *power*, and changes fundamentally in different historical periods. The writings of Lyotard were largely concerned with the role of narrative in human culture, and particularly how that role has changed as we have left modernity and entered a "postindustrial" or postmodern condition. He argued that modern philosophies legitimized their truth-claims not (as they themselves claimed) on logical or empirical grounds, but rather on the grounds of accepted stories (or "metanarratives") about knowledge and the world—comparing these with Wittgenstein's concept of language-games. He further argued that in our postmodern condition, these meta-narratives no longer work to legitimize truth-claims. He suggested that in the wake of the collapse of modern meta-narratives, people are developing a new "language game"—one that does not make claims to absolute truth but rather celebrates a world of ever-changing relationships (among people and between people and the world). Derrida, the father of deconstruction, practiced philosophy as a form of textual criticism. He criticized Western philosophy as privileging the concept of presence and *logos*, as opposed to absence and markings or writings. In America, the most famous pragmatist and self-proclaimed postmodernist was Richard Rorty. An analytic philosopher, Rorty believed that combining Willard Van Orman Quine's criticism of the analytic-synthetic distinction with Wilfrid Sellars's critique of the "Myth of the Given" allowed for an abandonment of the view of the thought or language as a mirror of a reality or external world. Further, drawing upon Donald Davidson's criticism of the dualism between conceptual scheme and empirical content, he challenges the sense of questioning whether our particular concepts are related to the world in an appropriate way, whether we can justify our ways of describing the world as compared with other ways. He argued that truth was not about getting it right or representing reality, but was part of a social practice and language was what served our purposes in a particular time; ancient languages are sometimes untranslatable into modern ones because they possess a different vocabulary and are unuseful today. Donald Davidson is not usually considered a postmodernist, although he and Rorty have both acknowledged that there are few differences between their philosophies.

For the most part, postmodern philosophy has spawned substantial literature of critical theory. Recently, it is noticeable that some of the ideas found in postmodernism, as the lack of belief in absolute truth or the idea of a reality *constructed*, are promoted in a new paradigm within constructivist epistemology. Some writers and theorists fear Kalle Lasn's description of our contemporary society: Post-modernism is arguably the most depressing philosophy ever to spring from the western mind. It is difficult to talk about post-modernism because nobody really understands it. It's allusive to the point of being impossible to articulate. But what this philosophy basically says is that we've reached an endpoint in human history. That the modernist tradition of progress and ceaseless extension of the frontiers of innovation are now dead. Originality is dead. The avant-garde artistic tradition is dead. All religions and utopian visions are dead and resistance to the status quo is impossible because revolution too is now dead. Like it or not, we humans are stuck in a permanent crisis of meaning, a dark room from which we can never escape.

1. What does structuralism emphasize in accordance with this passage?

A. The essence of the truth lies with the God.

B. Any parts of one integrity can be dissolved and assembled together in another way.

C. Binary oppositions distinguishing knowledge from ignorance.

D. All creatures in the world are equal and entitled with the right to live.

2. Which of the following ideas belongs to Foucault in this passage?

A. Knowledge is produced through the operations of *power*.

B. Knowledge can cultivate a person to be good.

C. Knowledge is power.

D. Knowledge will not change in different historical periods

3. Which of the following statements concerning those of Lyotard is false?

A. Rarely wrote something concerned with the role of narrative in human culture.

B. The writings of Lyotard were particularly concerned with how the role of narrative in human culture has changed.

C. Modern philosophies legitimized their truth-claims not on logical or empirical grounds, but rather on the grounds of accepted stories.

D. In the wake of the collapse of modern metanarratives, people are developing a new "language game"

4. Which of the following is true according to this passage?

A. Richard Rorty, the father of deconstruction, practiced philosophy as a form of textual criticism.

B. Derrida criticized Western philosophy as privileging the concept of presence and *logos*, as opposed to absence and markings or writings.

C. Donald Davidson shared the same opinions with Rorty in their philosophies.

D. Rorty believed that combining Willard Van Orman Quine's criticism of the analytic-synthetic distinction with Wilfrid Sellars's critique of the "Myth of the Given" allowed for an resurrection of the view of the thought or language as a mirror of a reality or external world.

5. In according with this passage, the defects lying in the postmodern theories may be _____.

A. Post-modernism is arguably the most active philosophy ever to spring from the western mind.

B. What this philosophy basically says is that we've reached an endpoint in human history

C. It's absolutely possible to articulate.

D. It is easy to talk about post-modernism because every body can understands it.

Part Two   True or False Questions

Directions: *In this part of the exercise, there is a passage with ten true or false questions. Read the passage carefully and mark T if it is true and F if it is false.*

I have explored two perspectivist approaches, each of which challenges the human rights discourse of non-contingent moral obligations and rights. I have endeavored to show that neither cultural relativism nor Rorty's version of neopragmatism offers any convincing reason to abandon our ethical conviction that every human being has certain fundamental moral rights. If we take these theories seriously, we find that each one fails on its own terms, and neither can address our inescapable ethical concerns.

The cultural relativist challenges human rights policies on theoretical grounds, urging us instead to defer to whatever traditions have arisen in diverse cultures. Although the relativist argument for doing so is that there are no transcultural moral truths, I have claimed that cultural relativism is itself based on certain dubious, nonrelative ethical choices, especially including the selection of a value-creating group. The particular weakness of relativism is that it rejects the possibility of nuanced ethical judgments and makes these choices by default, privileging one or another framework which then becomes the source of all value. The kind of relativism asserted against human rights claims, status quo cultural relativism, is a procedural theory which inherently obscures the political divisions and ethical issues within a society. In this way, the relativist flight from "metaphysical" discourse results in a kind of formalism that relieves us of the need to think through the hard problems presented by diversity.

Neopragmatists such as Rorty and Williams present a different perspectivist position. They object not to human rights policies, but to the objectivist moral discourse invoked to develop and justify such policies. I have addressed this position by applying a pragmatic test to the alternative practice they suggest, and have argued that objectivist moral discourse serves our needs in ways that these perspectivist proposals cannot. When we seek to implement these suggestions, intractable problems arise. We have problems at the outset even understanding whether there is a relationship between Rorty's perspectivist claims and the universalist language we use in legal and ethical discourse. Does perspectivism teach us that people who rely on the ethical and legal language of universal human rights are speaking the "wrong" way? Or are they pursuing their own "local truth", engaging in their own cultural practice which they have no reason to abandon?

However this choice gets resolved, neither path is a particularly compelling one. A perspectivism that has nothing to say about the normative language we use leaves human rights discourse untouched, but should be uninteresting to a pragmatist because it makes no difference to practice. The alternative revisionist path does make a difference by excising entire discourses as improperly foundationalist or essentialist, including the moral discourse of human rights, but we might wonder whether this version of perspectivism is any more pragmatic than the first. I have described the practical difficulties involved in attempting to live according to a theory that denies or obscures the distinctions between justice and convention, reasons and causes, truth and coherence, and impartiality and bias. On pragmatic grounds alone, we should question whether such a post-metaphysical language could provide us with the tools we need to live in and describe a normative world or communicate in meaningful ways with each other. On pragmatic grounds, why would we want to deprive ourselves of the ability to describe torture as a non-contingent moral atrocity and a violation of a human right, however well accepted it might be in a culture?

Both of these arguments constitute internal critiques which demarcate the limits of moral skepticism. I have endeavored to show that transcultural moral judgments are part of our humanity, and that therefore we should not object to the human rights claim on the ground that it is such a judgment.

Rather than evaluating human rights claims according to the exorbitant demands of a mythical postmetaphysical practice, we should consider them on their moral merits. There is no way to recognize a human right against slavery without accepting that it is what it claims to be: an inalienable and absolute moral right in any culture. We mistake morality for something else if we think that the existence of countless centuries of slave societies, with their paradigms that made slavery look natural, demonstrate that the moral right is in any way illusory or contingent.

1. Our ethical conviction that every human being has certain fundamental moral rights conforms to the neopragmatist thinking. (　　)

2. The cultural relativist challenges lies in the fact that there are no transcultural moral truths. (　　)

3. Neopragmatists such as Rorty and Williams have placed greater emphasis on the "local truth". (　　)

4. The foundationalists or essentialists should question whether a post-metaphysical language could provide the people with the tools they need to live in and describe a normative world or communicate in meaningful ways with each other. (　　)

5. That the existence of countless centuries of slave societies, with their paradigms that made slavery look natural has demonstrated that the moral right is in any way illusory or contingent was believed to be what the author's proposal that there in no objective truth. (　　)

IV Translation Abilities

法律语言特征分析与法律翻译技能培养之六:

国外法律语言学的研究内容

Forensic linguistics: an umbrella science for many fields of study.

——*John Olsson. Forensic Linguistics*, *London*, *Continuum*, 2004, 5

在西方,属于法律语言学(forensic linguistics)研究范畴的内容和形式繁多,但他们的研究主要注重法庭语言适用,与法庭语言证据科学密切相关。Olsson认为,其主要研究的形式和类别一般可分为:

- 作者身份识别(authorship identification):识别法律文本作者身份。
- 文本模式认证(mode identification):认证法律文本源于书面或口语或部分书面部分口语。
- 法律口译和笔译(legal interpretation and translation):在法庭上进行口译和笔译,或在

警方和被告/证人之间进行翻译；翻译口供或其他法律文件。涉及翻译的准确性和公正性问题，以及译者的地位和作用，译者的资格，以及对译者的"管控"。

• 将口供记录译为笔录（transcribing verbal statements）：在某些法律体制中，口供被磁带记录，法庭上要求将其录为笔录。涉及记录的完整性和避免偏见等问题。

• 法庭语言和话语研究（the language and discourse of courtrooms）：司法程序参与人之间的关系及他们使用之语言。涉及诸如权力、偏见、文化冲突等问题。

• 话语权研究（language rights）：生活在由其他语言或其他方言主宰的文化区域之少数民族的话语权研究；无自己语言的少数民族的话语权；官方语言的压迫性。

• 证言证词之分析（statement analysis）：分析证人言辞的真实性（veracity）。

• 法庭语音学（forensic phonetics）：分析音像材料，用语鉴定语者身份或其他目的；做声音识别以锁定嫌疑犯。

• 篇章状况分析（textual status）：分析文本和声响资料话语状况以鉴别真伪，如鉴别报警电话、自杀、赎金勒索条等的真伪；从篇章话语中估计危险大小。

而 AILA Science Commission on Forensic Linguistics（AILA 法律语言学委员会）也认为 forensic linguistic 所研究的主要内容应当包括：

• The study of the language of the law, including the language of legal documents and the language of the courts, the police and prisons（研究法律语言，包括法律文件以及法庭、警察和监狱用语）；

• The study, the provision and the improvement of professional legal interpreting and translation services（研究、提供和改进法律解释和翻译服务）；

• The alleviation of disadvantage produced by language in legal processes（减少司法程序中因语言而产生的不利因素）；

• The provision of forensic linguistic evidence that is based on the best available linguistic expertise（提供基于最佳语言学专家鉴定的法庭语言证据）；

• The provision of linguistic expertise in issues of legal drafting and interpretation, including plain language drafting（就法律起草和法律阐释、包括普通语言起草问题提供语言学专业技术知识）。

Translation Exercises

Part One *Put the following into Chinese*

Perspectivists tell us that moral issues are only intelligible "within the precincts of the... paradigms or communities that give them their local and changeable shape." In the preceding sections, I have questioned whether this thesis teaches us anything about the universal human rights claim. As a theoretical matter, it is simply a nonsequitur to conclude that the thesis requires us to abandon the idea that every person has certain moral rights. As a practical matter, the thesis that our commitments are produced through an historical process can never tell us what commitments we should have. Most importantly, recognizing the fact that cultures produce diverse value systems does not obviate the question of how to deal with conflicts between them. For people who see this as an ethical question, it is important to reach a resolution that is morally justified and not simply a form of domination or cultural imperialism. I have argued that perspectivist theory cannot help elucidate this question because it makes these ethical stakes unintelligible. Someone who rejects the idea of an impartial standpoint as transcendental nonsense can describe the difference between a Jim Crow law and a civil rights law only in terms of whose ox is gored, not in terms of legitimate and illegitimate power, or justice and injustice, because these claims purport to be non-perspectival. For someone who seeks to discover a just resolution across diverse viewpoints, perspectivism can be of no help.

Part Two *Put the following into English*

显而易见,反对透视主义理论的这种说法不能证明,任何人权组织是对的还是错的,或许,通过集中于个人行为者的公正评价,我完完全全地回避了透视主义的主张。因为根据透视主义的描述,这种体验是虚幻的。如斯坦利·费仕所言,每个人所体验的"内心确认是千真万确的,真实的,而非地方的……即使自身清晰的个人批判性自我意识无法取得,其所取得的方法与内心确认的体验一模一样"。因此就该观点而言,若我确信有关歧视黑人法律的残酷性没有什么主观性或透视主义观点的话,不过是因为我还没能充分理解我自身观点的偏颇性而已。

V Interaction

Discuss with your tutor(s) or the People's judges in your locality about the relationship between law and morality. Then based on the discussion, you are supposed to write a composition about what morality can do in the absence of law. Remember that you are required to express your ideas clearly.

VI Appreciation of the Judge's Opinions

(1) Case Name(案件名): *Holder v. Humanitarian Law Project*

Holder v. Humanitarian Law Project

Supreme Court of the United States

Argued February 23, 2010
Decided June 24, 2010

Full case name   Holder et al. v. Humanitarian Law Project et al.
Docket nos.   08-1498
Citations   561 U.S. ____ (2010)

Holding

The federal government may prohibit providing non-violent material support for terrorist organizations, including legal services and advice, without violating the free speech clause of the First Amendment. Ninth Circuit Court of Appeals reversed and remanded.

Court membership	
Chief Justice	
John G. Roberts	
Associate Justices	
John P. Stevens · Antonin Scalia	
Anthony Kennedy · Clarence Thomas	
Ruth Bader Ginsburg · Stephen Breyer	
Samuel Alito · Sonia Sotomayor	
Case opinions	
Majority	Roberts, joined by Stevens, Scalia, Kennedy, Thomas and Alito
Dissent	Breyer, joined by Ginsburg and Sotomayor
Laws applied	

U.S. Const. amend. I; 18 U.S.C. §2339B

(2) **Case Summary**(案件简介)

Holder v. Humanitarian Law Project, 561 U. S. _____ (2010), was a case decided in June 2010 by the United States Supreme Court regarding the USA PATRIOT Act(《美国爱国者法》) which prohibits material support (物质支持) to groups designated as terrorists(指定为恐怖分子的集团). The court held that a prohibition of these types of support—"training"(培训), "expert advice or assistance"(专家意见或援助), "service", and "personnel"—were constitutional as applied to the forms of support that plaintiffs in the case, represented by the Humanitarian Law Project, sought to provide to foreign terrorist organizations. The court noted that the proposed actions of the Humanitarian Law Project were general and "entirely hypothetical", implying that a post-enforcement challenge to the application of the "material support" provisions is not foreclosed(取消抵押人的赎取权;逐出;排除妨碍;结束,停止讨论等). The plaintiffs sought to help the Kurdistan Workers' Party(库尔德工人党) in Turkey and the Liberation Tigers of Tamil Eelam(猛虎组织,全称泰米尔·伊拉姆猛虎解放组织,斯里兰卡泰米尔族的反政府武装组织,擅长游击战术) learn means of peacefully resolving conflicts(学习和平解决纠纷的方式).

This case represents the only time in U.S. First Amendment jurisprudence that a restriction on political speech has passed the strict scrutiny test.

Facts of the Case

Among the plaintiffs in this case are supporters of the Kurdistan Workers Party ("KWP", 库尔德工人党) and the Liberation Tigers of Tamil Eelam ("LTTE", 猛虎组织). The KWP and LTTE engage in a variety of both lawful and unlawful activities. They sought an injunction(禁止令) to prevent the government from enforcing sections of the Antiterrorism and Effective Death Penalty Act ("AEDPA")(《反恐怖与有效死刑法》). Section 302 authorizes the Secretary of State(美国国务卿) to designate a group as a "foreign terrorist organization". (外国恐怖主义组织) Section 303 makes it a crime for anyone to provide "material support or resources"(物质支持或资源提供) to even the nonviolent activities of a designated organization. In previous cases, the courts have held that Section 303 was unconstitutionally vague. Congress then passed the Intelligence Reform and Terrorism Prevention Act ("IRTPA")(《情报与反恐预防法》) which amended the AEDPA. It added a state of mind requirement that individuals "knowingly"(有意地或故意地) provide "material support or resources" in order to violate the Act. Congress also added terms to the Act that further clarified what constituted "material support or resources." The government moved for summary judgment arguing that challenged provisions of the AEDPA were not unconstitutionally vague. The district court granted a partial motion for summary judgment, but held that some parts of the Act were unconstitutionally vague(模糊).

On appeal(上诉后), the U. S. Court of Appeals for the Ninth Circuit(美国联邦第九巡回法院) affirmed, holding that the terms "service", "training" or "other specialized knowledge" within the AEDPA, as applied to the plaintiffs, were unconstitutionally vague.

Question: Are provisions of the AEDPA which prohibit providing "any... service,... training, or other specialized knowledge" to designated foreign terrorist organizations unconstitutionally vague?

Conclusion

Decision: 6 votes for both parties, 3 vote(s) against

Legal provision: AEDPA(the Antiterrorism and Effective Death Penalty Act) ("AEDPA")

Not as applied to the plaintiffs. The Supreme Court held that the material support provision of the AEDPA is constitutional as applied to the particular forms of support that the plaintiffs seek to provide to terrorist organizations. With Chief Justice John G. Roberts writing for the majority(代表多数决撰写判决书), the Court reasoned that, as applied, the provision in question is not vague. Here, the statutory terms at issue—"training", "expert advice or assistance", "service" and "personnel"—are not similar to terms like "annoying" and "indecent" that the Court has struck down as being too vague. The Court recognized that the statute may not be clear in every respect, but it is clear enough with respect to the plaintiffs in this case.

Justice Stephen G. Breyer, joined by Justices Ruth Bader Ginsburg and Sonia Sotomayor, dissented(持异议). He agreed that the statute was not unconstitutionally vague. However, Justice Breyer disagreed that the Constitution permits the government to prosecute the plaintiffs criminally for engaging in coordinated teaching and advocacy furthering the designated organizations' lawful political objectives. He reasoned that the government had not met its burden to show that the speech prohibited by the statute served a compelling governmental interest(国家利益).

(3) Excerpts of the Judgment(法官判决词)

Chief Justice Roberts delivered the opinion of the Court.

Congress has prohibited the provision of "material support or resources" to certain foreign organizations that engage in terrorist activity. That prohibition is based on a finding that the specified organizations "are so tainted(玷污,使感染,毒化思想、感情等,使腐败,使坠落) by their criminal conduct that any contribution to such an organization facilitates that conduct". The plaintiffs in this litigation seek to provide support to two such organizations. Plaintiffs claim that they seek to facilitate only the lawful, nonviolent purposes of those groups, and that applying the material-support law to prevent them from doing so violates the Constitution. In particular, they claim that the statute is too vague(法律存在模糊性), in violation of the Fifth Amendment, and that it infringes their rights to freedom of speech and association(言论自由与结社自由), in violation of the First Amendment. We conclude that the material-support statute is constitutional as applied to the particular activities plaintiffs have told us they wish to pursue. We do not, however, address the resolution of more difficult cases that may arise under the statute in the future.

I

This litigation concerns 18 U. S. C. §2339B, which makes it a federal crime to "knowingly provide material support or resources to a foreign terrorist organization". Congress has amended the definition of "material support or resources" periodically, but at present it is defined as follows:

"The term 'material support or resources' means any property, tangible or intangible(有形或无形的), or service, including currency or monetary instruments(货币工具) or financial securities, financial services, lodging, training, expert advice or assistance, safehouses(藏身之所,藏身地), false documentation or identification, communications equipment(通讯设备), facilities, weapons, lethal substances(有毒物质), explosives, personnel (1 or more individuals who may be or include oneself), and transportation, except medicine or religious materials."

The authority to designate an entity a "foreign terrorist organization" rests with the Secretary of State(将某一实体当做"外国恐怖主义组织"的权利属于美国国务卿). She may, in consultation with the Secretary of the Treasury(财政部长) and the Attorney General(总检察长), so designate an organization upon finding that it is foreign, engages in "terrorist activity" or "terrorism", and thereby "threatens the security of United States nationals(国民) or the national security(国家安全) of the United States." "'National security' means the national defense(国防), foreign relations(对外关系), or economic interests of the United States." An entity designated a foreign terrorist organization may seek review of that designation before the D. C. Circuit within 30 days of that designation.

In 1997, the Secretary of State designated 30 groups as foreign terrorist organizations. Two of those groups are the Kurdistan Workers' Party (also known as the Partiya Karkeran Kurdistan, or PKK) and the Liberation Tigers of Tamil Eelam (LTTE). The PKK is an organization founded in 1974 with the aim of establishing an independent Kurdish state in southeastern Turkey. The LTTE is an organization founded in 1976 for the purpose of creating an independent Tamil state in Sri Lanka. The District Court in this action found that the PKK and the LTTE engage in political and humanitarian activities. The Government has presented evidence that both groups have also committed numerous terrorist attacks, some of which have harmed American citizens. The LTTE sought judicial review(司法审查) of its designation as a foreign terrorist organization; the D. C. Circuit upheld that designation. The PKK did not challenge its designation.

Plaintiffs in this litigation are two U. S. citizens and six domestic organizations: the Humanitarian Law Project (HLP) (a human rights organization with consultative status to the United Nations); Ralph Fertig (the HLP's president, and a retired administrative law judge); Nagalingam Jeyalingam (a Tamil physician, born in Sri Lanka and a naturalized U. S. citizen); and five nonprofit groups dedicated to the interests of persons of Tamil descent. In 1998, plaintiffs filed suit in federal court challenging the constitutionality of the material-support statute. Plaintiffs claimed that they wished to provide support for the humanitarian and political activities of the PKK and the LTTE in the form of monetary contributions, other tangible aid, legal training, and political advocacy, but that they could not do so for fear of prosecution under §2339B.

As relevant here, plaintiffs claimed that the material-support statute was unconstitutional on two grounds: First, it violated their freedom of speech and freedom of association under the First Amendment, because it criminalized their provision of material support to the PKK and the LTTE, without requiring the Government to prove that plaintiffs had a specific intent to further the unlawful ends of those organizations. Second, plaintiffs argued that the statute was unconstitutionally vague.

Plaintiffs moved for a preliminary injunction, which the District Court granted in part. The District Court held that plaintiffs had not established a probability of success on their First Amendment speech and association claims. But the court held that plaintiffs had established a probability of success on their claim that, as applied to them, the statutory terms "personnel" and "training" in the definition of "material support" were impermissibly(不允许的,不许可的) vague.

The Court of Appeals affirmed. The court rejected plaintiffs' speech and association claims, including their claim that §2339B violated the First Amendment in barring them from contributing money to the PKK and the LTTE. But the Court of Appeals agreed with the District Court that the terms "personnel" and "training" were vague because it was "easy to imagine protected expression that falls within the bounds" of those terms.

With the preliminary injunction issue decided, the action returned to the District Court, and the parties moved for summary judgment on the merits. The District Court entered a permanent injunction against applying to plaintiffs the bans on "personnel" and "training" support. The Court of Appeals affirmed.

Lesson Six　The Skepticism in Law and Morals

Meanwhile, in 2001, Congress amended the definition of "material support or resources" to add the term "expert advice or assistance". In 2003, plaintiffs filed a second action challenging the constitutionality of that term as applied to them.

In that action, the Government argued that plaintiffs lacked standing and that their pre-enforcement claims were not ripe. The District Court held that plaintiffs' claims were justiciable(可由法庭裁判的,可在法庭裁判/决的,可予审理的) because plaintiffs had sufficiently demonstrated a "genuine threat of imminent prosecution," and because §2339B had the potential to chill plaintiffs' protected expression. On the merits, the District Court held that the term "expert advice or assistance" was impermissibly vague. The District Court rejected, however, plaintiffs' First Amendment claims that the new term was substantially overbroad and criminalized associational speech.

The parties cross-appealed(反诉). While the cross-appeals were pending, the Ninth Circuit granted en banc (全体法官列席的,全席的) rehearing of the panel's 2003 decision in plaintiffs' first action (involving the terms "personnel" and "training"). The en banc court heard reargument on December 14, 2004. Three days later, Congress again amended §2339B and the definition of "material support or resources."

In IRTPA(《情报与反恐预防法》), Congress clarified the mental state necessary to violate §2339B, requiring knowledge of the foreign group's designation as a terrorist organization or the group's commission of terrorist acts. Congress also added the term "service" to the definition of "material support or resources," and defined "training" to mean "instruction or teaching designed to impart a specific skill, as opposed to general knowledge". It also defined "expert advice or assistance" to mean "advice or assistance derived from scientific, technical or other specialized knowledge." Finally, IRTPA clarified the scope of the term "personnel" by providing:

"No person may be prosecuted under §2339B in connection with the term 'personnel' unless that person has knowingly provided, attempted to provide, or conspired(合谋) to provide a foreign terrorist organization with 1 or more individuals (who may be or include himself) to work under that terrorist organization's direction or control or to organize, manage, supervise, or otherwise direct the operation of that organization. Individuals who act entirely independently of the foreign terrorist organization to advance its goals or objectives shall not be considered to be working under the foreign terrorist organization's direction and control."

Shortly after Congress enacted IRTPA, the en banc Court of Appeals issued an order in plaintiffs' first action. The en banc court affirmed the rejection of plaintiffs' First Amendment claims for the reasons set out in the Ninth Circuit's panel decision in 2000. In light of IRTPA, however, the en banc court vacated the panel's 2003 judgment with respect to vagueness, and remanded to the District Court for further proceedings. The Ninth Circuit panel assigned to the cross-appeals in plaintiffs' second action (relating to "expert advice or assistance") also remanded in light of IRTPA.

The District Court consolidated the two actions on remand. The court also allowed plaintiffs to challenge the new term "service." The parties moved for summary judgment, and the District Court granted partial relief to plaintiffs on vagueness grounds.

The Court of Appeals affirmed once more. The court first rejected plaintiffs' claim that the material-support statute would violate due process unless it were read to require a specific intent to further the illegal ends of a foreign terrorist organization. The Ninth Circuit also held that the statute was not overbroad in violation of the First Amendment. As for vagueness, the Court of Appeals noted that plaintiffs had not raised a "facial vagueness challenge." The court held that, as applied to plaintiffs, the terms "training," "expert advice or assistance" (when derived from "other specialized knowledge"), and "service" were vague because they "continued to cover constitutionally protected advocacy", but the term "personnel" was not vague because it "no longer criminalized pure speech protected by the First Amendment".

The Government petitioned for certiorari, and plaintiffs filed a conditional cross-petition. We granted both petitions.

II

Given the complicated 12-year history of this litigation, we pause to clarify the questions before us. Plaintiffs challenge §2339B's prohibition on four types of material support—"training", "expert advice or assistance", "service" and "personnel". They raise three constitutional claims. First, plaintiffs claim that §2339B violates the Due Process Clause of the Fifth Amendment because these four statutory terms are impermissibly vague. Second, plaintiffs claim that §2339B violates their freedom of speech under the First Amendment. Third, plaintiffs claim that §2339B violates their First Amendment freedom of association.

Plaintiffs do not challenge the above statutory terms in all their applications. Rather, plaintiffs claim that §2339B is invalid to the extent it prohibits them from engaging in certain specified activities. With respect to the HLP and Judge Fertig, those activities are: (1) "training members of the PKK on how to use humanitarian and international law to peacefully resolve disputes"; (2) "engaging in political advocacy on behalf of Kurds who live in Turkey"; and (3) "teaching PKK members how to petition various representative bodies such as the United Nations for relief". With respect to the other plaintiffs, those activities are: (1) "training members of the LTTE to present claims for tsunami-related aid(海啸有关的援助) to mediators and international bodies"; (2) "offering their legal expertise in negotiating peace agreements between the LTTE and the Sri Lankan government"; and (3) "engaging in political advocacy on behalf of Tamils who live in Sri Lanka".

Plaintiffs also state that "the LTTE was recently defeated militarily in Sri Lanka", so "much of the support the Tamil organizations and Dr. Jeyalingam sought to provide is now moot." Plaintiffs thus seek only to support the LTTE "as a political organization outside Sri Lanka advocating for the rights of Tamils". Counsel for plaintiffs specifically stated at oral argument that plaintiffs no longer seek to teach the LTTE how to present claims for tsunami-related aid, because the LTTE now "has no role in Sri Lanka." For that reason, helping the LTTE negotiate a peace agreement with Sri Lanka appears to be moot as well. Thus, we do not consider the application of §2339B to those activities here.

One last point. Plaintiffs seek pre-enforcement review of a criminal statute. Before addressing the merits, we must be sure that this is a justiciable case or controversy under Article III. We conclude that it is: Plaintiffs face "a credible threat of prosecution" and "should not be required to await and undergo a criminal prosecution as the sole means of seeking relief."

Plaintiffs claim that they provided support to the PKK and the LTTE before the enactment of §2339B and that they would provide similar support again if the statute's allegedly unconstitutional bar were lifted. The Government tells us that it has charged about 150 persons with violating §2339B, and that several of those prosecutions involved the enforcement of the statutory terms at issue here. The Government has not argued to this Court that plaintiffs will not be prosecuted if they do what they say they wish to do.

III

Plaintiffs claim, as a threshold matter, that we should affirm the Court of Appeals without reaching any issues of constitutional law. They contend that we should interpret the material-support statute, when applied to speech, to require proof that a defendant intended to further a foreign terrorist organization's illegal activities. That interpretation, they say, would end the litigation because plaintiffs' proposed activities consist of speech, but plaintiffs do not intend to further unlawful conduct by the PKK or the LTTE.

We reject plaintiffs' interpretation of §2339B because it is inconsistent with the text of the statute. Section 2339B(a)(1) prohibits "knowingly" providing material support. It then specifically describes the type of knowledge that is required: "To violate this paragraph, a person must have knowledge that the organization is a designated terrorist organization..., that the organization has engaged or engages in terrorist activity..., or that the organization has engaged or engages in terrorism...." Congress plainly spoke to the necessary mental state for a violation of §2339B, and it chose knowledge about the organization's connection to terrorism, not specific intent to further the organization's terrorist activities.

Plaintiffs' interpretation is also untenable(站不住脚) in light of the sections immediately surrounding §2339B, both of which do refer to intent to further terrorist activity. Congress enacted §2339A in 1994 and §2339C in 2002. Yet Congress did not import the intent language of those provisions into §2339B, either when it enacted §2339B in 1996, or when it clarified §2339B's knowledge requirement in 2004.

Finally, plaintiffs give the game away when they argue that a specific intent requirement should apply only when the material-support statute applies to speech. There is no basis whatever in the text of §2339B to read the same provisions in that statute as requiring intent in some circumstances but not others. It is therefore clear that plaintiffs are asking us not to interpret §2339B, but to revise it. "Although this Court will often strain to construe legislation so as to save it against constitutional attack, it must not and will not carry this to the point of perverting the purpose of a statute."

Scales (Scales v. United States (1961)) is the case on which plaintiffs most heavily rely, but it is readily distinguishable. That case involved the Smith Act, which prohibited membership in a group advocating the violent overthrow of the government(暴力推翻政府). The Court held that a person could not be convicted under the statute unless he had knowledge of the group's illegal advocacy and a specific intent to bring about violent overthrow. This action is different: Section 2339B does not criminalize mere membership in a designated foreign terrorist organization. It instead prohibits providing "material support" to such a group. Nothing about Scales suggests the need for a specific intent requirement in such a case. The Court in Scales, moreover, relied on both statutory text and precedent that had interpreted closely related provisions of the Smith Act to require specific intent. Plaintiffs point to nothing similar here.

We cannot avoid the constitutional issues in this litigation through plaintiffs' proposed interpretation of §2339B.

IV

We turn to the question whether the material-support statute, as applied to plaintiffs, is impermissibly vague under the Due Process Clause of the Fifth Amendment. "A conviction fails to comport with due process if the statute under which it is obtained fails to provide a person of ordinary intelligence fair notice of what is prohibited, or is so standardless that it authorizes or encourages seriously discriminatory enforcement." We consider whether a statute is vague as applied to the particular facts at issue, for "a plaintiff who engages in some conduct that is clearly proscribed(禁止,排斥,使失去法律保护) cannot complain of the vagueness of the law as applied to the conduct of others." We have said that when a statute "interferes with the right of free speech or of association, a more stringent vagueness test should apply." "But 'perfect clarity and precise guidance have never been required even of regulations that restrict expressive activity'."

The Court of Appeals did not adhere to these principles. Instead, the lower court merged plaintiffs' vagueness challenge with their First Amendment claims, holding that portions of the material-support statute were unconstitutionally vague because they applied to protected speech—regardless of whether those applications were clear. The court stated that, even if persons of ordinary intelligence understood the scope of the term "training", that term would "remain impermissibly vague" because it could "be read to encompass speech and advocacy protected by the First Amendment". It also found "service" and a portion of "expert advice or assistance" to be vague because those terms covered protected speech.

Further, in spite of its own statement that it was not addressing a "facial vagueness challenge", the Court of Appeals considered the statute's application to facts not before it. Specifically, the Ninth Circuit relied on the Government's statement that §2339B would bar filing an amicus brief in support of a foreign terrorist organization—which plaintiffs have not told us they wish to do, and which the Ninth Circuit did not say plaintiffs wished to do—to conclude that the statute barred protected advocacy and was therefore vague. By deciding how the statute applied in hypothetical circumstances, the Court of Appeals' discussion of vagueness seemed to incorporate elements of First Amendment overbreadth doctrine.

In both of these respects, the Court of Appeals contravened(违反) the rule that "a plaintiff who engages in some conduct that is clearly proscribed cannot complain of the vagueness of the law as applied to the conduct of others". That rule makes no exception for conduct in the form of speech. Thus, even to the extent a heightened vagueness standard applies, a plaintiff whose speech is clearly proscribed cannot raise a successful vagueness claim under the Due Process Clause of the Fifth Amendment for lack of notice. And he certainly cannot do so based on the speech of others. Such a plaintiff may have a valid overbreadth claim under the First Amendment, but our precedents make clear that a Fifth Amendment vagueness challenge does not turn on whether a law applies to a substantial amount of protected expression. Otherwise the doctrines would be substantially redundant.

Under a proper analysis, plaintiffs' claims of vagueness lack merit. Plaintiffs do not argue that the material-support statute grants too much enforcement discretion to the Government. We therefore address only whether the statute "provide[s] a person of ordinary intelligence fair notice of what is prohibited."

As a general matter, the statutory terms at issue here are quite different from the sorts of terms that we have previously declared to be vague. We have in the past "struck down statutes that tied criminal culpability(刑事可责性) to whether the defendant's conduct was 'annoying' or 'indecent'—wholly subjective judgments without statutory definitions, narrowing context, or settled legal meanings." Applying the statutory terms in this action—"training", "expert advice or assistance", "service" and "personnel"—does not require similarly untethered, subjective judgments.

Congress also took care to add narrowing definitions to the material-support statute over time. These definitions increased the clarity of the statute's terms. And the knowledge requirement of the statute further reduces any potential for vagueness, as we have held with respect to other statutes containing a similar requirement.

Of course, the scope of the material-support statute may not be clear in every application. But the dispositive point here is that the statutory terms are clear in their application to plaintiffs' proposed conduct, which means that plaintiffs' vagueness challenge must fail. Even assuming that a heightened standard applies because the material-support statute potentially implicates speech, the statutory terms are not vague as applied to plaintiffs.

Most of the activities in which plaintiffs seek to engage readily fall within the scope of the terms "training" and "expert advice or assistance". Plaintiffs want to "train members of the PKK on how to use humanitarian and international law to peacefully resolve disputes" and "teach PKK members how to petition various representative bodies such as the United Nations for relief". A person of ordinary intelligence would understand that instruction on resolving disputes through international law falls within the statute's definition of "training" because it imparts a "specific skill," not "general knowledge". Plaintiffs' activities also fall comfortably within the scope of "expert advice or assistance": A reasonable person would recognize that teaching the PKK how to petition for humanitarian relief before the United Nations involves advice derived from, as the statute puts it, "specialized knowledge". In fact, plaintiffs themselves have repeatedly used the terms "training" and "expert advice" throughout this litigation to describe their own proposed activities, demonstrating that these common terms readily and naturally cover plaintiffs' conduct.

Plaintiffs respond by pointing to hypothetical situations designed to test the limits of "training" and "expert advice or assistance". They argue that the statutory definitions of these terms use words of degree—like "specific", "general" and "specialized"—and that it is difficult to apply those definitions in particular cases.

Whatever force these arguments might have in the abstract, they are beside the point(不切题) here. Plaintiffs do not propose to teach a course on geography, and cannot seek refuge in imaginary cases that straddle the boundary between "specific skills" and "general knowledge". We emphasized this point in Scales, holding that even if there might be theoretical doubts regarding the distinction between "active" and "nominal" membership in an organization—also terms of degree—the defendant's vagueness challenge failed because his "case presented no such problem."

Gentile was different. There the asserted vagueness in a state bar rule was directly implicated by the facts before the Court: Counsel had reason to suppose that his particular statements to the press would not violate the rule, yet he was disciplined nonetheless. We did not suggest that counsel could escape discipline on vagueness grounds if his own speech were plainly prohibited.

Plaintiffs also contend that they want to engage in "political advocacy" on behalf of Kurds living in Turkey and Tamils living in Sri Lanka. They are concerned that such advocacy might be regarded as "material support" in the form of providing "personnel" or "service/s," and assert that the statute is unconstitutionally vague because they cannot tell.

As for "personnel", Congress enacted a limiting definition in IRTPA that answers plaintiffs' vagueness concerns. Providing material support that constitutes "personnel" is defined as knowingly providing a person "to work under that terrorist organization's direction or control or to organize, manage, supervise, or otherwise direct the operation of that organization." The statute makes clear that "personnel" does not cover independent advocacy: "Individuals who act entirely independently of the foreign terrorist organization to advance its goals or objectives shall not be considered to be working under the foreign terrorist organization's direction and control."

"Service" similarly refers to concerted activity, not independent advocacy. See *Webster's Third New International Dictionary 2075* (1993) (defining "service" to mean "the performance of work commanded or paid for by another: a servant's duty: attendance on a superior"; or "an act done for the benefit or at the command of another"). Context confirms that ordinary meaning here. The statute prohibits providing a service "to a foreign terrorist organization". The use of the word "to" indicates a connection between the service and the foreign group. We think a person of ordinary intelligence would understand that independently advocating for a cause is different from providing a service to a group that is advocating for that cause.

Moreover, if independent activity in support of a terrorist group could be characterized as a "service", the statute's specific exclusion of independent activity in the definition of "personnel" would not make sense. Congress would not have prohibited under "service" what it specifically exempted from prohibition under "personnel." The other types of material support listed in the statute, including "lodging", "weapons", "explosives" and "transportation" are not forms of support that could be provided independently of a foreign terrorist organization. We interpret "service" along the same lines. Thus, any independent advocacy in which plaintiffs wish to engage is not prohibited by §2339B. On the other hand, a person of ordinary intelligence would understand the term "service" to cover advocacy performed in coordination with, or at the direction of, a foreign terrorist organization.

Plaintiffs argue that this construction of the statute(法律的解释) poses difficult questions of exactly how much direction or coordination is necessary for an activity to constitute a "service". The problem with these questions is that they are entirely hypothetical. Plaintiffs have not provided any specific articulation of the degree to which they seek to coordinate their advocacy with the PKK and the LTTE. They have instead described the form of their intended advocacy only in the most general terms.

Deciding whether activities described at such a level of generality would constitute prohibited "services" under the statute would require "sheer speculation"—which means that plaintiffs cannot prevail in their pre-enforcement challenge. It is apparent with respect to these claims that "gradations of fact or charge would make a difference as to criminal liability", and so "adjudication of the reach and constitutionality of the statute must await a concrete fact situation".

V

A

We next consider whether the material-support statute, as applied to plaintiffs, violates the freedom of speech guaranteed by the First Amendment. Both plaintiffs and the Government take extreme positions on this question. Plaintiffs claim that Congress has banned their "pure political speech". It has not. Under the material-support statute, plaintiffs may say anything they wish on any topic. They may speak and write freely about the PKK and LTTE, the governments of Turkey and Sri Lanka, human rights, and international law. They may advocate before the United Nations. As the Government states: "The statute does not prohibit independent advocacy or expression of any kind." Section 2339B also "does not prevent plaintiffs from becoming members of the PKK and LTTE or impose any sanction on them for doing so". Congress has not, therefore, sought to suppress ideas or opinions in the form of "pure political speech". Rather, Congress has prohibited "material support", which most often does not take the form of speech at all. And when it does, the statute is carefully drawn to cover only a narrow category of speech to, under the direction of, or in coordination with foreign groups that the speaker knows to be terrorist organizations.

For its part, the Government takes the foregoing too far, claiming that the only thing truly at issue in this litigation is conduct, not speech. Section 2339B is directed at the fact of plaintiffs' interaction with the PKK and LTTE, the Government contends, and only incidentally burdens their expression. The Government argues that the proper standard of review is therefore the one set out in *United States v. O'Brien* (1968). In that case, the Court rejected a First Amendment challenge to a conviction under a generally applicable prohibition on destroying draft cards, even though O'Brien had burned his card in protest against the draft. In so doing, we applied what we have since called "intermediate scrutiny", under which a "content-neutral regulation(内容中立的监管) will be sustained under the First Amendment if it advances important governmental interests unrelated to the suppression of free speech and does not burden substantially more speech than necessary to further those interests".

The Government is wrong that the only thing actually at issue in this litigation is conduct, and therefore wrong to argue that O'Brien provides the correct standard of review. O'Brien does not provide the applicable standard for reviewing a content-based regulation of speech, and §2339B regulates speech on the basis of its content. Plaintiffs want to speak to the PKK and the LTTE, and whether they may do so under §2339B depends on what they say. If plaintiffs' speech to those groups imparts a "specific skill" or communicates advice derived from "specialized knowledge". for example, training on the use of international law or advice on petitioning the United Nations—then it is barred. On the other hand, plaintiffs' speech is not barred if it imparts only general or unspecialized knowledge.

The Government argues that §2339B should nonetheless receive intermediate scrutiny because it generally functions as a regulation of conduct. That argument runs headlong into a number of our precedents, most prominently *Cohen v. California* (1971). Cohen also involved a generally applicable regulation of conduct, barring breaches of the peace. But when Cohen was convicted for wearing a jacket bearing an epithet, we did not apply O'Brien. Instead, we recognized that the generally applicable law was directed at Cohen because of what his speech communicated—he violated the breach of the peace statute because of the offensive content of his particular message. We accordingly applied more rigorous scrutiny and reversed his conviction.

This suit falls into the same category. The law here may be described as directed at conduct, as the law in Cohen was directed at breaches of the peace, but as applied to plaintiffs the conduct triggering coverage under the statute consists of communicating a message. As we explained in *Texas v. Johnson*: "If the Government's regulation is not related to expression, then the less stringent standard we announced in *United States v. O'Brien* for regulations of noncommunicative conduct controls. If it is, then we are outside of O'Brien's test, and we must apply a more demanding standard."

Lesson Six The Skepticism in Law and Morals

B

The First Amendment issue before us is more refined than either plaintiffs or the Government would have it. It is not whether the Government may prohibit pure political speech, or may prohibit material support in the form of conduct. It is instead whether the Government may prohibit what plaintiffs want to do—provide material support to the PKK and LTTE in the form of speech.

Everyone agrees that the Government's interest in combating terrorism is an urgent objective of the highest order. Plaintiffs' complaint is that the ban on material support, applied to what they wish to do, is not "necessary to further that interest". The objective of combating terrorism does not justify prohibiting their speech, plaintiffs argue, because their support will advance only the legitimate activities of the designated terrorist organizations, not their terrorism.

Whether foreign terrorist organizations meaningfully segregate support of their legitimate activities from support of terrorism is an empirical question. When it enacted §2339B in 1996, Congress made specific findings regarding the serious threat posed by international terrorism. One of those findings explicitly rejects plaintiffs' contention that their support would not further the terrorist activities of the PKK and LTTE: "Foreign organizations that engage in terrorist activity are so tainted by their criminal conduct that any contribution to such an organization facilitates that conduct."

Plaintiffs argue that the reference to "any contribution" in this finding meant only monetary support. There is no reason to read the finding to be so limited, particularly because Congress expressly prohibited so much more than monetary support in §2339B. Congress's use of the term "contribution" is best read to reflect a determination that any form of material support furnished "to" a foreign terrorist organization should be barred, which is precisely what the material-support statute does. Indeed, when Congress enacted §2339B, Congress simultaneously removed an exception that had existed in §2339A(a) (1994 ed.) for the provision of material support in the form of "humanitarian assistance to persons not directly involved in" terrorist activity. That repeal(法令等的废除,作废,取消,撤销,撤回;英国史上的撤销合并运动;美国废除禁酒法) demonstrates that Congress considered and rejected the view that ostensibly peaceful aid would have no harmful effects.

We are convinced that Congress was justified in rejecting that view. The PKK and the LTTE are deadly groups. "The PKK's insurgency(起义,暴动,叛变行动/性质、状态) has claimed more than 22,000 lives." The LTTE has engaged in extensive suicide bombings(自杀式轰炸) and political assassinations(政治暗杀活动), including killings of the Sri Lankan President, Security Minister, and Deputy Defense Minister. "On January 31, 1996, the LTTE exploded a truck bomb filled with an estimated 1,000 pounds of explosives at the Central Bank in Colombo, killing 100 people and injuring more than 1,400. This bombing was the most deadly terrorist incident in the world in 1996." It is not difficult to conclude as Congress did that the "taint" of such violent activities is so great that working in coordination with or at the command of the PKK and LTTE serves to legitimize and further their terrorist means.

Material support meant to "promote peaceable, lawful conduct", can further terrorism by foreign groups in multiple ways. "Material support" is a valuable resource by definition. Such support frees up other resources within the organization that may be put to violent ends. It also importantly helps lend legitimacy to foreign terrorist groups—legitimacy that makes it easier for those groups to persist, to recruit members, and to raise funds—all of which facilitate more terrorist attacks. "Terrorist organizations do not maintain organizational 'firewalls' that would prevent or deter... sharing and commingling of support and benefits." "Investigators have revealed how terrorist groups systematically conceal their activities behind charitable, social, and political fronts." "Indeed, some designated foreign terrorist organizations use social and political components to recruit personnel to carry out terrorist operations, and to provide support to criminal terrorists and their families in aid of such operations."

Money is fungible(可代替的;可互换的,可用一物代替他物偿债), and "when foreign terrorist organizations that have a dual structure raise funds, they highlight the civilian and humanitarian ends to which such moneys could be put". But "there is reason to believe that foreign terrorist organizations do not maintain legitimate financial firewalls between those funds raised for civil, nonviolent activities, and those ultimately used to support violent, terrorist operations". Thus, "funds raised ostensibly for charitable purposes have in the past been redirected by some terrorist groups to fund the purchase of arms and explosives". There is evidence that the PKK and the LTTE, in particular, have not "respected the line between humanitarian and violent activities".

The dissent argues that there is "no natural stopping place" for the proposition that aiding a foreign terrorist organization's lawful activity promotes the terrorist organization as a whole. But Congress has settled on just such a natural stopping place: The statute reaches only material support coordinated with or under the direction of a designated foreign terrorist organization. Independent advocacy that might be viewed as promoting the group's legitimacy is not covered.

Providing foreign terrorist groups with material support in any form also furthers terrorism by straining the United States' relationships with its allies and undermining cooperative efforts between nations to prevent terrorist attacks. We see no reason to question Congress's finding that "international cooperation is required for an effective response to terrorism, as demonstrated by the numerous multilateral conventions in force providing universal prosecutive jurisdiction over persons involved in a variety of terrorist acts, including hostage taking, murder of an internationally protected person, and aircraft piracy and sabotage." The material-support statute furthers this international effort by prohibiting aid for foreign terrorist groups that harm the United States' partners abroad: "A number of designated foreign terrorist organizations have attacked moderate governments with which the United States has vigorously endeavored to maintain close and friendly relations," and those attacks "threaten the social, economic and political stability" of such governments. "Other foreign terrorist organizations attack our NATO allies, thereby implicating important and sensitive multilateral security arrangements."

For example, the Republic of Turkey—a fellow member of NATO—is defending itself against a violent insurgency waged by the PKK. That nation and our other allies would react sharply to Americans furnishing material support to foreign groups like the PKK, and would hardly be mollified(使软化,缓和,减轻,使平静,平息,抚慰) by the explanation that the support was meant only to further those groups' "legitimate" activities. From Turkey's perspective, there likely are no such activities.

C

In analyzing whether it is possible in practice to distinguish material support for a foreign terrorist group's violent activities and its nonviolent activities, we do not rely exclusively on our own inferences drawn from the record evidence. We have before us an affidavit stating the Executive Branch's conclusion on that question. The State Department informs us that "the experience and analysis of the U.S. government agencies charged with combating terrorism strongly support" Congress's finding that all contributions to foreign terrorist organizations further their terrorism. In the Executive's view: "Given the purposes, organizational structure, and clandestine(秘密的,暗中的,私下的) nature of foreign terrorist organizations, it is highly likely that any material support to these organizations will ultimately inure to(有助于) the benefit of their criminal, terrorist functions—regardless of whether such support was ostensibly intended to support non-violent, non-terrorist activities."

That evaluation of the facts by the Executive, like Congress's assessment, is entitled to deference(敬意,尊敬). This litigation implicates sensitive and weighty interests of national security and foreign affairs. The PKK and the LTTE have committed terrorist acts against American citizens abroad, and the material-support statute addresses acute foreign policy concerns involving relationships with our Nation's allies. We have noted that "neither the Members of this Court nor most federal judges begin the day with briefings that may describe new and serious threats to our Nation and its people". It is vital in this context "not to substitute... our own evaluation of evidence for a reasonable evaluation by the Legislative Branch".

Lesson Six The Skepticism in Law and Morals

   Our precedents, old and new, make clear that concerns of national security and foreign relations do not warrant abdication(弃权,让位) of the judicial role. We do not defer to the Government's reading of the First Amendment, even when such interests are at stake. We are one with the dissent that the Government's "authority and expertise in these matters do not automatically trump the Court's own obligation to secure the protection that the Constitution grants to individuals". But when it comes to collecting evidence and drawing factual inferences in this area, "the lack of competence on the part of the courts is marked", and respect for the Government's conclusions is appropriate.

   One reason for that respect is that national security and foreign policy concerns arise in connection with efforts to confront evolving threats in an area where information can be difficult to obtain and the impact of certain conduct difficult to assess. The dissent slights these real constraints in demanding hard proof—with "detail", "specific facts", and "specific evidence"—that plaintiffs' proposed activities will support terrorist attacks. That would be a dangerous requirement. In this context, conclusions must often be based on informed judgment rather than concrete evidence, and that reality affects what we may reasonably insist on from the Government. The material-support statute is, on its face, a preventive measure—it criminalizes not terrorist attacks themselves, but aid that makes the attacks more likely to occur. The Government, when seeking to prevent imminent harms in the context of international affairs and national security, is not required to conclusively link all the pieces in the puzzle before we grant weight to its empirical conclusions.

   This context is different from that in decisions like Cohen. In that case, the application of the statute turned on the offensiveness of the speech at issue. Observing that "one man's vulgarity(粗俗,庸俗,下流) is another's lyric", we invalidated Cohen's conviction in part because we concluded that "governmental officials cannot make principled distinctions in this area". In this litigation, by contrast, Congress and the Executive are uniquely positioned to make principled distinctions between activities that will further terrorist conduct and undermine United States foreign policy, and those that will not.

   We also find it significant that Congress has been conscious of its own responsibility to consider how its actions may implicate constitutional concerns. First, §2339B only applies to designated foreign terrorist organizations. There is, and always has been, a limited number of those organizations designated by the Executive Branch, and any groups so designated may seek judicial review of the designation. Second, in response to the lower courts' holdings in this litigation, Congress added clarity to the statute by providing narrowing definitions of the terms "training", "personnel," and "expert advice or assistance", as well as an explanation of the knowledge required to violate §2339B. Third, in effectuating its stated intent not to abridge First Amendment rights, Congress has also displayed a careful balancing of interests in creating limited exceptions to the ban on material support. The definition of material support, for example, excludes medicine and religious materials. In this area perhaps more than any other, the Legislature's superior capacity for weighing competing interests means that "we must be particularly careful not to substitute our judgment of what is desirable for that of Congress". Finally, and most importantly, Congress has avoided any restriction on independent advocacy, or indeed any activities not directed to, coordinated with, or controlled by foreign terrorist groups.

   At bottom, plaintiffs simply disagree with the considered judgment of Congress and the Executive that providing material support to a designated foreign terrorist organization—even seemingly benign(善意的) support—bolsters(帮助,支持) the terrorist activities of that organization. That judgment, however, is entitled to significant weight, and we have persuasive evidence before us to sustain it. Given the sensitive interests in national security and foreign affairs at stake, the political branches have adequately substantiated their determination that, to serve the Government's interest in preventing terrorism, it was necessary to prohibit providing material support in the form of training, expert advice, personnel, and services to foreign terrorist groups, even if the supporters meant to promote only the groups' nonviolent ends.

We turn to the particular speech plaintiffs propose to undertake. First, plaintiffs propose to "train members of the PKK on how to use humanitarian and international law to peacefully resolve disputes". Congress can, consistent with the First Amendment, prohibit this direct training. It is wholly foreseeable that the PKK could use the "specific skills" that plaintiffs propose to impart, as part of a broader strategy to promote terrorism. The PKK could, for example, pursue peaceful negotiation as a means of buying time to recover from short-term setbacks, lulling opponents into complacency(使其对手骄傲自大), and ultimately preparing for renewed attacks. A foreign terrorist organization introduced to the structures of the international legal system might use the information to threaten, manipulate, and disrupt. This possibility is real, not remote.

Second, plaintiffs propose to "teach PKK members how to petition various representative bodies such as the United Nations for relief". The Government acts within First Amendment strictures(束缚,限制,攻击) in banning this proposed speech because it teaches the organization how to acquire "relief," which plaintiffs never define with any specificity, and which could readily include monetary aid. Indeed, earlier in this litigation, plaintiffs sought to teach the LTTE "to present claims for tsunami-related aid to mediators and international bodies", which naturally included monetary relief. Money is fungible, and Congress logically concluded that money a terrorist group such as the PKK obtains using the techniques plaintiffs propose to teach could be redirected to funding the group's violent activities.

Finally, plaintiffs propose to "engage in political advocacy on behalf of Kurds who live in Turkey", and "engage in political advocacy on behalf of Tamils who live in Sri Lanka". As explained above, plaintiffs do not specify their expected level of coordination with the PKK or LTTE or suggest what exactly their "advocacy" would consist of. Plaintiffs' proposals are phrased at such a high level of generality that they cannot prevail in this pre-enforcement challenge.

In responding to the foregoing, the dissent fails to address the real dangers at stake. It instead considers only the possible benefits of plaintiffs' proposed activities in the abstract. The dissent seems unwilling to entertain the prospect that training and advising a designated foreign terrorist organization on how to take advantage of international entities might benefit that organization in a way that facilitates its terrorist activities. In the dissent's world, such training is all to the good. Congress and the Executive, however, have concluded that we live in a different world: one in which the designated foreign terrorist organizations "are so tainted by their criminal conduct that any contribution to such an organization facilitates that conduct". One in which, for example, "the United Nations High Commissioner for Refugees was forced to close a Kurdish refugee camp in northern Iraq because the camp had come under the control of the PKK, and the PKK had failed to respect its 'neutral and humanitarian naturex'." Training and advice on how to work with the United Nations could readily have helped the PKK in its efforts to use the United Nations camp as a base for terrorist activities.

If only good can come from training our adversaries in international dispute resolution, presumably it would have been unconstitutional to prevent American citizens from training the Japanese Government on using international organizations and mechanisms to resolve disputes during World War II. It would, under the dissent's reasoning, have been contrary to our commitment to resolving disputes through "'deliberative forces'," for Congress to conclude that assisting Japan on that front might facilitate its war effort more generally. That view is not one the First Amendment requires us to embrace.

All this is not to say that any future applications of the material-support statute to speech or advocacy will survive First Amendment scrutiny. It is also not to say that any other statute relating to speech and terrorism would satisfy the First Amendment. In particular, we in no way suggest that a regulation of independent speech would pass constitutional muster(经受宪法的检查/审查), even if the Government were to show that such speech benefits foreign terrorist organizations. We also do not suggest that Congress could extend the same prohibition on material support at issue here to domestic organizations. We simply hold that, in prohibiting the particular forms of support that plaintiffs seek to provide to foreign terrorist groups, §2339B does not violate the freedom of speech.

VI

Plaintiffs' final claim is that the material-support statute violates their freedom of association under the First Amendment. Plaintiffs argue that the statute criminalizes the mere fact of their associating with the PKK and the LTTE, thereby running afoul of decisions like *De Jonge v. Oregon* (1937), and cases in which we have overturned sanctions for joining the Communist Party.

The Court of Appeals correctly rejected this claim because the statute does not penalize mere association with a foreign terrorist organization. As the Ninth Circuit put it: "The statute does not prohibit being a member of one of the designated groups or vigorously promoting and supporting the political goals of the group.... What §2339B prohibits is the act of giving material support...." Plaintiffs want to do the latter. Our decisions scrutinizing penalties on simple association or assembly are therefore inapposite.

Plaintiffs also argue that the material-support statute burdens their freedom of association because it prevents them from providing support to designated foreign terrorist organizations, but not to other groups. Any burden on plaintiffs' freedom of association in this regard is justified for the same reasons that we have denied plaintiffs' free speech challenge. It would be strange if the Constitution permitted Congress to prohibit certain forms of speech that constitute material support, but did not permit Congress to prohibit that support only to particularly dangerous and lawless foreign organizations. Congress is not required to ban material support to every group or none at all.

* * *

The Preamble to the Constitution(宪法的序言部分) proclaims that the people of the United States ordained(命运注定;法律等规定,制定,命令) and established that charter of government in part to "provide for the common defence". As Madison explained, "security against foreign danger is... an avowed and essential object of the American Union". We hold(认定,认为) that, in regulating the particular forms of support that plaintiffs seek to provide to foreign terrorist organizations, Congress has pursued that objective consistent with the limitations of the First and Fifth Amendments.

The judgment of the United States Court of Appeals for the Ninth Circuit is affirmed in part (部分维持) and reversed in part(部分推翻), and the cases are remanded for further proceedings consistent with this opinion(发回重审,并依照本院意见进入下一个程序).

It is so ordered.

Lesson Seven

Rules of Legal Interpretation

> **Learning objectives**
>
> After learning the text and having done the exercises in this lesson, you will:
>
> —familiarize with knowledge of the legal characteristics and the nature of legal interpretation in Common-Law countries;
>
> —acquire an appreciation of the vocabulary and grammar or syntax relevant to the legal interpretation;
>
> —become aware of the information required in order to understand the legal interpretation;
>
> —cultivate the practical abilities to put to use the language in the specific context;
>
> —be able to do some translation from Chinese to English and from English to Chinese.

 Text

Rules of Legal Interpretation

The interpretation of laws is confided to① courts of law. In course of time, courts have evolved a large and elaborate body of rules to guide them in construing or interpreting laws. Most of them have been collected in books on interpretation of statutes② and the draftsman would be well advised to keep these in mind in drafting Acts. Some Interpretation Acts, like the Canadian one, lay down that every Act shall be deemed remedial and shall accordingly receive such fair, large and liberal interpretation as will best ensure the attainment of the object of the Act according to its true intent,

---

① confide：作为不及物动词，可表示"吐露（秘密）；信托，交托，委托"等意思，如 confide a secret to（sb.）对（某人）吐露秘密；to confide a task to（sb.）：对（某人）托付任务；to confide in one's friend：向朋友谈个人心事。

② statute：written law passed by government or a law passed by a government and formally written down,法令，法规；成文法，制定法；也可以表示"（学校,公司等的）规则,章程,条例"等意思。

Lesson Seven Rules of Legal Interpretation

meaning and spirit.① The object of all such rules or principles as aforesaid, broadly speaking, is to ascertain the true intent, meaning and spirit of every statute. A statute is designed to be workable, and the interpretation thereof by a court should be to secure that object, unless crucial omission or clear direction makes that unattainable.

It is the duty of the courts to give effect to an Act according to its true meaning; and it is during this process that the rules or principles of interpretation have come to be evolved.

India has a written Constitution② which defines *inter alia*③ the powers of the various lawmaking authorities. The Constitution itself, quite naturally, has been the subject matter of interpretation in several decisions of the Indian courts and it would be worthwhile in the first instance to examine briefly the manner in which the subject is approached before dealing with rules of interpretation in relation to ordinary statutes.

A constitution is unlike most of the numerous statutes that the courts have to interpret, and hence is not to be construed in a narrow, static and pedantic sense. As pointed out by the Rajasthan High Court④:

The Constitution is the very framework of the body polity, its life and soul, it is the fountainhead of all its authority; the mainspring of all its strength and power... It is unlike other statutes which can be at any time altered, modified or repealed. Therefore, the language of the Constitution should be interpreted as if it were a living organism capable of growth and development if interpreted in a broad and liberal spirit, and not in a narrow and pedantic sense.

According to the Supreme Court:

Legislation, both statutory and constitutional, is enacted, it is true, from an experience of evils, but its general language should not therefore, be necessarily confined to the form that evil had taken. Time works changes, brings into existence new conditions and purposes. Therefore, a principle to be valid must be capable of wider application than the mischief which gave it birth. This is particularly true of constitutions. They are not ephemeral enactments designed to meet passing occasions. They are, to use the words of Chief Justice Marshall⑤, "designed to approach

---

① 该句可以翻译成"有些《法律解释法》,如加拿大的解释法,规定每部法律均应视为具有救济性,为此应对其进行公正、广泛、开明的解释,以期最大限度地确保按其真正意图、含义和精神来实现该法目的"。句中的 such 作为形容词使用时,such 无比较级和最高级,在句中可以作定语、表语;有时为了避免形容词使用的重复,也可以用作代词;such 还可以与 all, any, no, one, few, some 等连用,一起修饰名词;此外,such 还可以引导形容词从句在修饰名词时,一般放在这些词的前面,若放在后面时,则含有轻蔑的含义;与另一形容词一起修饰单数名词时,应该置于不定冠词之前。在本句中,such 与 as 一起使用,此时的 such 是用作关联词,于 as 相呼应,表示"像……一样的","诸如之类"。如:I am not such a fool as to believe that(我可不是那种事也相信的人);His illness was not such as to cause any anxiety(他的病不是那种让人着急的病)。such 作为 connective 时,还可以与 that 连用,构成"such...that"结构,表示"如此……以致"的意思。

② Written constitution:成文宪法。

③ Inter alia:way of saying "among other things", used for saying that there are other things apart from those that are mentioned. The usual way of saying this is "among other things"。"首先"等意思。

④ the Rajasthan High Court:拉贾斯坦高等法院。

⑤ Chief Justice Marshall:首席大法官马歇尔。美国历史上有两位著名的马歇尔大法官。一位叫 John Marshall (1755—1835),联邦最高法院首席大法官(1801—1835)(Chief Justice)。另一位是 Thurgood Marshall(瑟古德·马歇尔)大法官(associate justice),他是美国联邦最高法院第一位黑人法官,生于 Baltimore。在其任职的二十四年间,他对从堕胎到宗教等范围广泛的各种问题采取开明态度。在死刑的问题上,他坚持认为宪法禁止使用死刑。去世之后,被各报刊誉为"民权英雄"、"终止官方种族隔离制度时代的法律战略设计师"和"杰出的异议者"。

immortality as nearly as human institutions can approach it",... In the application of a Constitution, our interpretation cannot be only of what has been but of what may be. ①

In interpreting a Constitution, it must be borne in mind that it is an organic statute and therefore that construction which is most beneficial to the widest amplitude of its power will be adopted. It will not be construed with the strictness of a private contract. That is not to say that different rules of construction apply in the construction of a Constitution. If at all there is a difference, it is in the degree of emphasis that is laid upon the rules. The application of the very rules of construction regarding construction of statutes requires that the court should take into account the nature and scope of the law that it is interpreting... "to remember that it is a Constitution, a mechanism under which laws are made, and not a mere Act which declares what that law is to be".

Therefore, in the construction of a Constitution, a broad and liberal spirit will be adopted; nevertheless, this does not imply that the courts are free to stretch or pervert the language of the enactment② in the interest of any legal or constitutional theory even for the purpose of supplying omissions or of correcting supposed errors. Besides, the courts have to guard themselves against extending the meaning of the words beyond their reasonable connotation. ③

The primary principle of interpretation is that a constitutional or statutory provision should be construed "according to the intent of they that made it". ④ Normally such intent is gathered from the language of the provision. If the language or phraseology employed by the Legislature is precise and plain and this by itself proclaims the legislative intent in unequivocal terms, the same intent must be given effect to, regardless of the consequences that may follow. But if the words used in the provision are imprecise, protean, evocative or can reasonably bear meaning more than one, the rule of strict grammatical construction⑤ ceases to be a sure guide to reach at the real legislative intent. In such a case, in order to ascertain the true meaning of the terms and phrases employed, it is legitimate for the court to go beyond the arid literal confines of the provision and to call in aid other well recognized rules of construction, such as legislative history⑥, the basic scheme or framework of the statute as a whole⑦, each portion throwing light on the rest, the purpose of the legislation, the object sought to be achieved⑧, and the consequences that may flow from the adop-

---

① 本句可以翻译为："适用《宪法》时,我们的解释不得仅停留于'已有的含义',而应该含'或许有的含义'。"句中 what 引导的从句在理解过程中拟按照中国习惯,将其翻译为一个名词短语,或根据上下文具体环境进行翻译。如 what we saw and heard(所见所闻);where we are going(我们的去向);for what they are(本来面目)等等。

② the language of the enactment:立法语言,等于 language used by the legislature, enactment 指立法机关制定的法律,表示"制定(法律),颁布,法令,条例,法规"等意思。有时可以用 enactment 来表示立法机关的立法。翻译时可根据上下文酌情翻译为"立法"、"立法文件"等。

③ connotation:表示"言外之意,含蓄;(词的)涵义",注意与 denotation 之间的区别,denotation 表示"指示,表示,名称;符号,(字面)意义"等。

④ according to the intent of they that made it:依照立法者的原意,根据立法原意。句中的 they 指 those who 的意思,即制定法律者。

⑤ grammatical interpretation 语法解释法,或文义解释法。

⑥ legislative history:立法历史,作者在此处表示的乃我国所称的"历史解释法"。

⑦ 该解释方法等于我国法律中的"体系解释法",或系统解释法。

⑧ the purpose of the legislation, the object sought to be achieved:该处所指乃我国所称"目的解释法",但注意,表示目的时,我们法律解释中未就法律制定所取得的目标进行规定,故此处,我们将"立法目的以及立法拟取得的目标"统称为"目的解释法"。

Lesson Seven Rules of Legal Interpretation

tion of one in preference to the other possible interpretation. Where two alternative constructions are possible, the court will choose the one which will be in accord with the other parts of the statute and ensure its smooth, harmonious working, and eschew any other which leads to absurdity, confusion or friction, contradiction and conflict between its various provisions or undermines or tends to defeat or destroy any basic scheme or purpose of the enactment. These canons of construction① apply to the interpretation of the Constitution with greater force because the Constitution is a living, integrated organism, having a soul and consciousness of its own.

While the courts do not exercise any control over the legislatures, in a country like India with a written Constitution, they have every right to determine whether a particular Act is within the competence of the Legislature passing it or whether it offends any other provision of the Constitution. For instance, if a law infringes any of the fundamental rights guaranteed by the Constitution, article 13 would operate to render it void to the extent to which it constitutes such infringement.

In this context, it may be pointed out that courts have evolved certain rules which would be applied in testing Acts of legislatures in relation to the Constitution under which such Acts are made.

The courts will exercise their power to hold legislation *ultra vires*② wisely and with unfailing restraint, and will not sit in judgment on the wisdom of the legislature in enacting the law. If the principle underlying the law is constitutional, the court will not question the policy behind it. It does not sit to exercise a power of veto on legislation. Hardship is not a matter for consideration where the meaning is clear. There is always a presumption in favor of constitutionality of a statute.③

Words in a constitutional enactment conferring legislative powers would be construed by the courts most liberally and in their widest amplitude. The omnipotence of the sovereign legislative power will not be limited by judicial interpretation except so far as the express words of the Constitution give that authority. But in order to decide whether a particular legislation offends the provisions of the Constitution and is therefore unconstitutional, the court will examine with some strictness the substance of the legislation for determining what it is that the Legislature has really done. Where in the interpretation of the provisions of an Act two constructions are possible, one which leads towards constitutionality of the legislation would be preferred to that which has the effect of

---

① Canon of construction: The system of basic rules and maxims applied by a court to aid in its interpretation of a written document, such as a statute or contract. In the case of a statute, certain canons of construction can help a court ascertain what the drafters of the statute—usually Congress or a state legislature—meant by the language used in the law. When a dispute involves a contract, a court will apply other canons of interpretation, or construction to help determine what the parties to the agreement intended at the time they made the contract. 法律解释规范/规则,法官释法借以采纳的解释书面文件的基本规则或准则系统。在制定法下,解释规则有助于法官弄清法律文件制定者/起草者使用特定语言的意图。若产生了合同纠纷,则法官可以使用某些解释规则来确定合同各方缔约时的意图。

② ultra vires:拉丁语,越权,超出(个人、公司等的)法定权限,不在权限之内,即 beyond the legal capacity of a person, company, or other legal entity; beyond the powers or means of, beyond the scope or in excess of legal power or authority, 其反义词是 intra vires(在权限之内,职权范围内)。

③ 该句可以翻译为"应推定法律是合宪的或不违宪的"。Presumption 在法律中指"推定",事实的推断(根据已知事实作出的推断)等意思,如 presumption of innocence(无罪推定), presumption of fact(事实的推断); presumption of law(法律上的假定),(在一定情况下普遍适用的)法定推论。

destroying it.

Where two constructions are possible, the Court will adopt that which will ensure the smooth and harmonious working of the Constitution and eschew the other which will lead to absurdity or give rise to practical inconvenience or make well established provisions of existing law nugatory.

The Court, however, is not over-persuaded by the form or appearance of the legislation, because the Legislature cannot disobey the prohibitions contained in the Constitution by employing any indirect drafting or other devices. What is called *"the doctrine of colorable legislation"*[①] is based on the maxim[②] that you cannot do indirectly what you cannot do directly?

Turning now to the interpretation of Acts, if the words of the Act are precise and unambiguous the courts are not left in doubt as to the true meaning of an Act. It is a cardinal rule of interpretation that the language used by the legislature is the true repository of the legislative intent and that words and phrases occurring in an Act are to be taken not in an isolated and detached manner dissociated from the context, but are to be read together and construed in the light of the purpose and object of the Act itself.

But where an Act is drawn defectively, the courts apply certain rules or principles to aid them in carrying out the purpose and object of the Act, that is to say, the intention of the legislature. The courts generally endeavor to make sense of the Act, but if the legislature has omitted to provide for any matter the courts cannot supply the deficiency for the purpose of assisting the legislature for a supposed object it might have; unless it becomes imperative to do so where such omission having regard to the legislative intent makes a statute absurd or unreasonable or where legislative intent is clearly indicated by the context or other parts of the statute but there was an accidental slip or unintentional omission.

Courts may even go so far as to modify the grammatical and ordinary sense of the words if by doing so absurdity and inconsistency may be avoided. Courts should not be astute to defeat the provisions of an Act whose meaning on the face of it is reasonably plain. Of course, this does not mean that any Act or any part of it can be re-cast. It must be possible to spell the meaning contended for out of the words actually used.

If the language of the statute is clear and unambiguous and if two interpretations are not reasonably possible, it would be wrong to discard *the plain meaning of the words*[③] used in order to meet a possible injustice.

In case of difficulties in construing a provision of a statute, the courts must not proceed as mere grammarians of the written law, but must search for the true intention of the Legislature. But the intention of a Legislature is not to be judged by what is in its mind but by its expression of that

---

① the doctrine of colorable legislation：禁止可着色立法的原理，即看似立法机关立法，实际不属于立法或貌似立法的现象应予以禁止。

② maxim：此处等于 legal maxim，法律语言中大量的法律格言（谚语）不仅要言不烦，蕴藏法理，乃金科玉律，数量众多，通常以拉丁文做成。本句中的"you cannot do indirectly what you cannot do directly"可以翻译为"不可间接为不得直接行为之事"。

③ plain meaning of words：所使用语词的日常与普通意义，plain meaning rule 乃法官进行法律解释的一主要规则，即若无法律的另行规定，则法官释法时拟采用所使用词语的一般或普通意义。由此英美法院释法时的"黄金规则"得以发展。

mind in the relevant statute itself.

The only repository of a Legislature's intention is the language it has used and in examining that language it must be presumed that the Legislature knows the accepted vocabulary of the legislative bodies and so knows what words are required and considered apt to effect a particular result. If it has not made a provision or used words from which a particular result can properly be found, courts will not be justified in finding it, simply because a contrary decision would cause hardship to the public.

Though the courts endeavor to ascertain the intention of the Legislature, they are careful lest the search for that intention should lead them into importing provisions into an Act which were not placed there by the Legislature. The sheet anchor① is that the intention of the Legislature is to be found within the four corners of the enactment② and from such connected statements as may be considered to be a part of the Act.

When the policy of the Act is clear the court has to interpret it as it stands; if there is an anomaly in the policy itself it is for the legislature to remove the defect.

Where two provisions in a statute conflict with each other, courts will try their best to read the two harmoniously, and will reject either of them as useless only in the last resort. If two constructions are possible, one leading to sense and the other to absurdity, the courts will adopt the former. The courts will always do their best to find a reasonable interpretation of the Act and help the draftsman. They will not regard any part of a statute as superfluous or nugatory. It is always to reason that the courts will lean. ③ They will not allow a law to be defeated by the draftsman's unskillfulness or ignorance. A contention that what the Legislature intended to bring about, it has failed to do by reason of defective draftsmanship is one which can only be accepted in the last resort when there is no avenue left for escape from that conclusion.

As pointed out by Justice Krishna Iyer,

Law, being pragmatic, responds to the purpose for which it is made, cognises the current capabilities of technology and life-style of the community and flexibility, fulfills the normative rule, taking the conspectus of circumstances in the given case and the nature of the problem to solve which the statute was made. Legislative futility is to be ruled out so long as interpretative possibility permits.

No statute has ever been held to be void for uncertainty. There are a few cases where a statute has been held to be void because it was meaningless, and not because it was uncertain. As ob-

---

① sheet anchor:（航海）（船首的）副锚；紧急备用大锚；紧急时的靠山；最后的依靠；最后手段。
② the four corners of the enactment：全部法律文件，four corners：the contents of a document as interpreted without reference to or consideration of outside information; the face of a document; the face of a written document. Four corners rule：a rule holding that if a document (as a contract, deed, or will) appears on its face to be complete no outside evidence may be used to challenge it. 全部法律文件规则（若合同或契约表面看具有完整性,则不得采纳外部任何证据对其质疑）。
③ It is always to reason that the courts will lean："法官总是倾向于合理性原则"。该句乃一个强调句,被强调成分是"to reason"。强调句的基本构成形式是"It is / was ＋ 被强调成分 ＋ that ＋ 其他成分"。若被强调成分为人,则 that 可以用 who/whom/whose 或用 that 等,但若被强调成分是时间、条件、原因或方式,在剩余部分的引导词只能用 that,不用表示时间的 when、表示方式的 how 以及 how 引导的成分或表示原因的 why 等词进行强调。

served by Lord Denning①, "The duty of the court is to put a fair meaning on the terms used and not, as was said in one case, to repose on the easy pillow of saying that the whole is void for uncertainty".② When a defect appears, a judge cannot fold his hands and blame the draftsman. A judge must not alter the material of which the Act is woven but he can and should iron out the creases.

The courts will presume that the Legislature had the intention to do the best for the public. For example, legislation undertaken for the benefit of labor will not be so construed as to prejudice the rights and welfare of labor. It would be an illegitimate method of interpretation of a statute whose dominant purpose is to protect workmen to introduce by implication words of which the effect must be to reduce the protection.

Where there is ambiguity, the courts will adopt a construction which follows general principles of law, public policy and justice rather than assume that the Legislature intended to depart from those principles. The courts will, when possible, construe an Act so that the least inconvenience is caused to particular persons or a beneficial rather than a detrimental result is attained.

But there are limits to the court's assistance. The "intention of the legislature" is a common and very slippery phrase in argument which may signify any thing from intention embodied in positive enactment to speculative opinion as to what the legislature probably would have meant although there has been an omission to enact it; and to embark upon the latter speculation carried the matter outside the functions of the courts. It is not the business of the court to usurp the functions of the Legislature and remedy the defects of the law. What the Legislature intended to be done or not to be done can only be legitimately ascertained from that which it has chosen to enact. The intention of the Legislature is to be gathered only from the words used by it and no such liberties can be taken by the courts for effectuating a supposed intention of the Legislature.

So the courts put limits on their powers and the draftsman must bear these in mind. If the words of an Act are clear, the courts cannot refuse to enforce it, or allow an evasion or exception merely because of the hardship which will ensue. "Hard cases make bad law" is a warning that the endeavor to modify the law in cases where the legislature might reasonably have made a modification often leads to the illegality of going beyond the terms of the enactment. The courts have to allow an Act to cause hardship or injustice if there is no way to avoid the result by legitimate rules of construction.

Ordinarily the courts start by assuming that the Act is complete. Documents connected with the origin of the Bill are not relied on as an indication of the intention with which the legislature ul-

---

① Lord Denning:丹宁法官,但在中国多数学者将该词译为"丹宁勋爵"。本书编者认为法律英语中,将 Lord 译为"法官"较为适宜,因为在英国法律文书中,Lord 就是"法官";在具体的文书中,英国也常用 Lord 指不同的人,如 Lord Advocate(苏格兰的法院院长、大法官、检察总长)、Lord Chancellor（大法官）、Lord Chief Justice（大法官）、Lord Mayor(伦敦等大都市的市长)、Lord High Clerk(法院的助理法官)、Lord Treasurery(财务大臣)等。由此可见,Lord 一词在英国的用法不仅仅指构成 House of Lords 中的勋爵,在具体的环境中,其含义是不同的。

② "The duty of the court is to put a fair meaning on the terms used and not, as was said in one case, to repose on the easy pillow of saying that the whole is void for uncertainty":"法官的责任在于对(立法机关)所用术语做出合理的含义解释,而不得以往某案件所说那样,因不确定性而泰然宣布整部法规无效"。丹宁法官在本句中使用了比喻,使其论述更生动形象。court 在英语中,通常可以翻译成"法官",不能仅仅理解为"法院"。

timately passed the measure. Although section 57 of the Evidence Act, 1872, suggests the admissibility of evidence obtainable from the proceedings of the legislature, the courts tend to hold at arms length the Statement of Objects and Reasons①which accompany the Bill when it is introduced in the legislature and the speeches made in the House and opinions of Select Committees②, but there are cases, though exceptional, where the courts accept opinions from these sources when an enactment cannot be construed without such reference.

A statute is not passed in a vacuum; but in a framework of circumstances so as to give a remedy for a known state of affairs. To arrive at its true meaning, it is essential to know the circumstances with reference to which the words were used and what was the object appearing from those circumstances which Parliament had in mind.

Ordinarily in construing the provisions of a statute speeches made in the course of debate on the Bill should not be taken into consideration, nor the statement of objects and reasons, nor the reports of select committees, nor the subsequent omission or addition of words from or to a Bill as introduced. The acceptance or rejection of amendments to a Bill in the course of its Parliamentary career cannot be said to form part of the pre-enactment history of the statue. But in the *State of West Bengal* v. *Subodh Gopal Bose*, the status of objects and reasons was quoted possibly with a view to ascertaining the conditions prevailing at the time of passing of the Act. Such a statement may explain the object of the legislature in enacting the Act.

The history of the law as shown by previous enactment is used as a guide to a consolidating or amending Act; but only if the latter is not sufficiently clear. If the words are clear and unambiguous, it would be unreasonable to interpret them in the light of the alleged background of the statute and to attempt to see that their interpretation conforms to the said background. The previous state of the law will be relevant as part of the circumstances on which the Act was passed. The courts will presume that the Legislature knew the law, including previous enactment and rulings thereon. If words are used which have received judicial interpretation, the Legislature will be presumed to use those words in the same sense. Care is required in drafting an Act to indicate clearly any departure from existing law and decision.

 Legal Terminology

1. legal interpretation

法律解释,指由一定的国家机关、组织或个人,为适用和遵守法律,根据有关法律规定、政策、公平正义观念、法学理论和惯例对现行的法律规范、法律条文的含义、内容、概念、术语以及适用的条件等所作的说明。根据具体情况的不同,学者往往将法律解释分为:文理解释(literal interpretation),逻辑解释(logical interpretation)或系统解释(systematic interpretation)

---

① the Statement of Objects and Reasons:立法目的与原因说明。

② Select committee:(英国下院受命进行某一特别调查工作的)小型特别委员会,特别委员会,专责委员会(group of politicians examining particular subject, a small group of politicians who are chosen to find out about a particular subject and then make a report)。

等。此外,学者还根据不同的标准还作出如下的分类:

根据解释方法的不同,法律解释分为:(1) 历史解释(history of legislation);(2) 目的解释(purposive interpretation);(3) 当然解释(指在法律没有明文规定的情况下,根据现有的法律规定,某一行为当然应该纳入该规定的适用范围时,对适用该规定的说明);(4) 社会学解释(sociological interpretation)指以社会效果、社会目的为根据,对法律进行阐释和说明以及(5) 合宪性解释(whether the statute is unconstitutional)。

根据解释的尺度不同,法律解释可以分为:(1) 字面解释(literal interpretation);(2) 扩大解释(extended interpretation);(3) 限制解释(restrictive interpretation)。

根据解释的自由度不同,法律解释可分为:(1) 狭义解释(strict-sense interpretation),又称严格解释(literal interpretation);(2) 广义解释(broad sense interpretation),又称自由解释(liberal interpretation)。

此外,学习 legal interpretation 时须注意,其有时表达的概念还可以用 legal construction, statutory interpretation(注意其意不是"法定解释")或 judicial interpretation(注意区别我国所规定的司法解释)来表示,有时还可以用 construction and interpretation 来表示法律解释。

2. statute

statute 来源于古法语,statut 和拉丁语 statutum,意思是"a law, decree"。

A statute is a formal written enactment of a legislative authority that governs a state, a city or county. Typically, statutes command or prohibit something, or declare policy. The word is often used to distinguish law made by legislative bodies from case law, decided by courts, and regulations issued by government agencies. Statutes are sometimes referred to as legislation or "black letter law". As a source of law, statutes are considered primary authority (as opposed to secondary authority). 立法机关所制定的用于调整国家、城市或郡县等的正式书面法律文件,其通常规定、禁止或宣布某项政策,该词的使用,主要用于将立法机关所制定的法律(law)与法官所制定的判例法(case law)以及政府机关所指定的条例(regulations)区分开,但多数情况下,statute 所指乃国家立法机关的立法,或"black letter law"。从法律渊源看,其具有最高法律权威(对应于 secondary authority)。

学习该词时,还应该注意与英语中表示法律的其他用语,如 act, legislation, bill, law 等之间的区别。这几个词,都含有"法律或法规的"意思,但一般说来,act 所指乃立法机关所制定的法律,常常作为某单部法律的名称,如 The Theft Act(反盗窃法),而 law 则既可以指某一单部法律或法规,又可以表示具有一般抽象的含义,通常不作为某一单部法律的名称使用,但中国的法律翻译中一般都将某某法律翻译为"The Law of...",如《中华人民共和国合同法》则翻译成"the Law of Contract of the People's Republic of China",其实,最简明的翻译方法就是"The Contract Act of the People's Republic of China",外国人则一目了然,该法乃经过我国人大制定并通过的法律。Bill 与上述表示法律的词的意义不尽相同,bill 一般指提交议会或国会(中国人大)进行审议的议案或提案,只有经过议会或国会(中国人大)的全部审议程序的最后文件,才可以成为 an act。Legislation 主要指立法,也就是具有立法权力的机关或人所制定的法律,为此,常常与 statute 同义。

3. Constitution

宪法,是每一个民主国家最根本的法的渊源,其法律地位和效力是最高的。宪法一词来源于拉丁文 constitutio,本是组织、确立的意思。古罗马帝国用它来表示皇帝的"诏令"、"谕旨"。欧洲封建时代用它表示在日常立法中对国家制度的基本原则的确认。英国在中世纪建立了代议制度,确立了国王没有得到议会同意就不得征税和进行其他立法的原则。后来代议制度普及于欧美各国。中文的"宪法"一词很早就出现于春秋时期(公元前770年—公元前476年),左丘明编撰的《国语·晋语九》:"赏善罚奸,国之宪法也"。然而,现代的"宪法"的概念是从西方传入。"宪"、"宪令"、"宪法"等词在中国古代典籍中与"法"同义,日本古代"宪"也指法令、制度,都与现代"宪法"一词含义不同。19 世纪60年代明治维新时期,随着西方立宪政治概念的传入,日本才有相当于欧美的概念出现。1898年,中国戊戌变法时,以康有为为首的维新派要求清廷制定宪法,实行君主立宪。1908年清政府颁布《钦定宪法大纲》,从此"宪法"一词在中国就成为国家根本法的专用词。

　　根据世界各国制度的不同,宪法可以有为形式和实质等分类方式。形式上看,主要有以下三种:(1) 成文宪法(written constitution, codified constitution)与不成文宪法(unwritten constitution, uncodified constitution)。这种分类的依据和标准是宪法是否具有统一的法典形式。所谓成文宪法,是指由一个或者几个规定国家根本制度和根本任务的宪法性法律文件所构成的宪法典。世界上最早的成文宪法是1787年的美国宪法。现代世界上绝大多数国家的宪法是成文宪法。所谓不成文宪法,是指既有书面形式的宪法性法律文件、宪法判例,又有非书面形式的宪法惯例等构成的宪法。英国宪法是典型的不成文宪法,主要由宪法性法律文件、法院判例、宪法惯例构成。(2) 刚性宪法(rigid constitution)与柔性宪法(flexible constitution)。这种分类的依据和标准是宪法的制定修改程序的不同。所谓刚性宪法,是指制定和修改宪法的程序比普通法律严格的宪法。当今世界上绝大多数国家的宪法属于这种类别的宪法。所谓柔性宪法,是指制定和修改宪法的程序、法律效力与普通法律完全相同的宪法。如作为英国宪法的重要组成部分的宪法性法律文件是在不同历史时期,由议会以一般立法程序制定和修改的。(3) 钦定宪法(constitution by the Imperial enactments)、民定宪法(constitution by the People)和协定宪法(constitution by agreement)。这种分类的依据是制定宪法的主体。所谓钦定宪法,是指由君主自上而下地制定并颁布实施的宪法。如1889年日本明治天皇颁布的《大日本帝国宪法》及1908年中国清末的《钦定宪法大纲》等。钦定宪法是封建君主迫于社会要求民主的压力而制定的,对民权作了点缀式规定,而主要是以宪法的形式规定了至高无上的君权。所谓民定宪法,是指由民选议会、制宪会议或公民投票表决制定的宪法。当今绝大多数国家的宪法属于这种类别。所谓协定宪法,是指由君主与人民或民选议会进行协商共同制定的宪法。

　　从宪法的实质分类,马克思主义观点认为可做如下分类:(1) 资本主义类型的宪法(capitalist constitution)与社会主义类型(socialist constitution)的宪法。这是根据宪法所赖以产生和存在的经济基础的性质以及国家政权的性质所进行的分类。所谓资本主义类型的宪法,是指建立在资本主义私有制基础之上和确认资产阶级专政的宪法。资本主义类型的宪法建立在生产资料资本家私有制的基础之上,为资本主义的经济制度服务,确认和保护资产阶级专政。所谓社会主义类型的宪法,是指建立在社会主义公有制基础之上和确认由人民当家做主的宪法。社会主义类型的宪法建立在生产资料社会主义公有制基础之上,为社会主义经济制度服务,并公开确认工人阶级在整个国家中的领导作用。(2) 法定的宪法与现实的宪法。这是列宁根据马克思主义关于经济基础与上层建筑之间的关系的基本原理进行的分类。所谓法定的宪法,又称成文的宪法,是指统治阶级通过法定程序制成的书面形式的宪法。所谓现实的宪法,又称事实的宪法或真正的宪法,是指一个国家现实的社会经济和政治关系,以及现实的政治力量对比关系。列宁认为,现实的宪法决定法定的宪法的性质和内容,只有当法定的宪法真实地反映现实的经济、政治关系,与现实的宪法一致起来,才能符合社会发展要求和广大人民的愿望,法定的宪法才是真实的。

4. provision

(法律、法规以及合同等其他法律文件中的)条款、规定等。法律英语中表示"规定"一词的还有"stipulation",二者的区别在于,stipulation 多指当事人经协商达成的约定性规定,在合同以及协议中的而非法律规定,二人 provision 的使用范围更宽泛些,既可以指合同或契约中属于约定性的规定,又可以指法律或法规中属于强制行的规定。如:the provision of a contract(合同的约定内容);The statute has many provisions.(该法律有很多条文)。税务法律中,tax provision 表示"税款准备金",tax shelter provision 表示"避税规定",peculiar tax shelter provision of liquidation proceeds 表示"有关清算收益的特定避税规定"等意思。但同时注意,该词还可以表示"预备,准备,粮食,食物,供应,规定;(做动词使用时)供给,给……食物及必需品"等意思。

Justice Scalia, who has been in the vanguard of efforts to redirect statutory construction toward statutory text and away from legislative history, has aptly characterized this general approach. "Statutory construction... is a holistic endeavor. A provision that may seem ambiguous in isolation is often clarified by the remainder of the statutory scheme—because the same terminology is used elsewhere in a context that makes its meaning clear, or because only one of the permissible meanings produces a substantive effect that is compatible with the rest of the law."

(斯加利亚法官)认为:法律解释乃法官们各方所做努力,单独看来具有歧义的法律规定可以通过法律制定的其他部分得到消除,因为同样的术语在其他地方也会得到使用,且其意义清楚无误,还因为,一种可取的意义可以产生与法律其他部分相适应的实体性结果。

5. legislative intent

立法意图,立法原意。当法律在适用过程中出现含混或歧义时,需要法官就所适用的法律进行解释。通常情况下,法官可以依赖如下材料进行法律的解释:

提交给立法机关的提案或议案文本(the text of the bill as proposed to the legislative body);

经提交并予以接受或否决的议案或提案的修订情况(amendments to the bill that were proposed and accepted or rejected);

就某一主题进行听证的记录(the record of hearings on the topic);

立法记录或议事录(legislative records or journals);

提案或议案表决前的演讲或辩论(speeches and floor debate made prior to the vote on the bill);

立法机关各小组委员会的记录、事实认定和/或报告(legislative subcommittee minutes, factual findings, and/or reports);

其他用于理解制定法中的释义可用的相关法律(other relevant statutes which can be used to understand the definitions in the statute on question);

其他用以说明所讨论法律之限制的相关法律(other relevant statutes which indicate the limits of the statute in question);

州长或总统等行政机关的有关立法文件(legislative files of the executive branch, such as the governor or president);

法律制定前的判例法以及其后表明立法机关试图通过议案或提案予以解决的问题(case law prior to the statute or following it which demonstrates the problems the legislature was attempting to address with the bill);

有关宪法的某些决定,如:国会是否在得知先前法律某些部分无效后是否仍然通过所讨论法律的某些部分呢?(constitutional determinations, i.e. "Would Congress still have passed certain sections of a statute 'had it known' about the constitutional invalidity of the other portions of the statute?")

立法意图—立法原因(legislative intent-the reason for passing the law),等等。

Exercises

I Verbal Abilities

Part One

Directions: *For each of these completing questions, read each item carefully to get the sense of it. Then, in the proper space, complete each statement by supplying the missing word or phrase.*

1. In the field of contracts, we must look to the outward expression of a person as _____ his intention rather than his secret or unexpressed intention.

    A. exteriorizing   B. manifesting   C. externalizing

    D. incarnating   E. personifying

2. One of the _____ in a partnership consists of a factual relationship between two or more persons who conduct a business enterprise together.

    A. factors   B. ingroup   C. influxion

    D. opponent   E. ingredients

3. A director who is absent from the board meeting is presumed to _____ in action taken on a corporate matter, unless he files "a dissent with the secretary of the corporation within a reasonable time after learning of such action".

    A. accede   B. coincide   C. collaborate

    D. concur   E. dissent

4. All persons who assume to act as a corporation without the authority of a certificate of incorporation issued by the Corporation Commissioner, shall be jointly and _____ liable for all debts and liabilities incurred or arising from as a result thereof.

    A. severally   B. assortedly   C. particularly

    D. sepulchral   E. ascetically

5. The reinsurance business was described by an expert at trial as having "a magic _____ around it of dignity and quality and integrity".

    A. soothsaying   B. augmentation   C. aura

    D. emanation   E. odour

6. A parent corporation that controls the management and operations of its wholly owned subsidiary can be held responsible for its subsidiary's liabilities without _____ the corporate veil.

    A. penetrating   B. puncturing   C. thrilling

    D. piercing   E. pricking

7. As a general rule, the directors of a corporation may _____ a corporation only when they act as a legal meeting of the board.

    A. obligate   B. bind   C. strap

    D. encumber   E. constrain

8. No act of a partner _____ of a restriction on authority shall bind the partnership to persons having knowledge of the restriction.

    A. in violation   B. in contrariety   C. in consternation

    D. in abrogation   E. in contravention

9. Usually a director can a _____ himself from liability by informing other directors of the impropriety and voting for a proper course of action.

    A. absolve   B. abstain   C. abdicate

    D. accrue   E. acrimony

10. An agreement or mutual assent is of course essential to a valid contract, but the law of contract _____ to the person an intention corresponding to the reasonable meaning of his words and acts.

    A. accredit   B. subscribe   C. improvise

    D. impregnate   E. imputes

Part Two

Directions: *Choose the one word or phase that best keep the meaning of the original sentence if it were substituted for the underlined part.*

1. A budding barrister must first be admitted to one of the four Inns of Court and must dine at least 32 times in a period of eight terms.

    A. sprouting   B. experienced   C. developing

    D. burrowing   E. burgeoning

2. The basic contract principle rejects single-value theories of contract, such as autonomy theories, and instead accepts multiple values and even conflicting values.

    A. autocracy   B. austerity   C. authentication

    D. interdependence   E. self-governing

3. By early modern times, continental writers had concluded that, in principle, a plaintiff ought to have an action in tort whenever his rights were violated.

    A. in concert   B. in clover   C. in rapport

    D. in general   E. in abeyance

4. Notwithstanding the lack of formal agreements or treaties with any other countries, American courts—both national and state-level—have regularly enforced the judgments of foreign courts for well over 100 years.

Lesson Seven Rules of Legal Interpretation

  A. Although   B. Nevertheless   C. Despite
  D. However   E. In spite

5. A foreign judgment will not be <u>recognized</u> in the English courts if there has been a prior English judgment of the same matter.

  A. reclaimed   B. recompensed   C. reconciled
  D. recollected   E. acknowledged

6. China has <u>acceded</u> to some international conventions containing provisions on international legal cooperation since late seventies.

  A. accentuated   B. acquiesced   C. ascend
  D. consented   E. succeeded

7. Many nations today base their bilateral treaties on <u>reciprocity</u> under which a nation grants an extradition request only in exchange for the extradition or promise of future extradition of an individual it seeks from the requesting state.

  A. interchangeability   B. alternation   C. mutuality
  D. complementation   E. complimentary

8. Organized criminal groups are now expanding their activities rapidly across national frontiers, taking advantage of gaps in international cooperation, <u>diversifying</u> their activities and moving away from some of the more traditional forms of crime and into others, often using modern management techniques.

  A. branching out   B. radiating   C. altering
  D. modifying   E. diverging

9. A mental person who is unable to <u>account for</u> his own conduct shall be a person having no capacity for civil conduct and shall be represented in civil activities by his agent *ad litem*.

  A. elucidate   B. count upon   C. explain
  D. be responsible for   E. ledger

10. <u>Mercenary</u> marriages, marriages upon arbitrary decision by any third party and any other acts of interference in the freedom of marriage shall be prohibited.

  A. avaricious   B. materialistic   C. voluntary
  D. venereal   E. sordid

II Cloze Test

Directions: *For each blank in the following passage, choose the best answer from the choices given.*

The present position may be summarized in the words of the Supreme Court as ___(1)___ : Punctuation is ___(2)___ a minor element in the construction of a statute and even if the orthodox view that it forms no part of the statute is to be regarded ___(3)___ imperfect obligation and it can be looked at as *contemporanea exposltia*(按当时情况解释), it is clear that it cannot be allowed to control the plain meaning of a text.

It may be mentioned that punctuation marks are seldom subjected to amendments during the

___(4)___ of a Bill. For instance, where a proviso(附带条款,附文;条件,但书,限制性条款) comes to be added to a section during the passage of a Bill, it is not the practice to ___(5)___ an amendment for replacing the full stop at the end of the section by a colon; this is done when the final copy of the Bill as passed is ___(6)___ by the draftsman or other officer concerned.

Adding illustrations to a section is a practice which has now been happily given up. Although in one or two stray cases (example, the Companies Act of 1956) a few illustrations were allowed to ___(7)___. The draftsman should not rely on illustrations to make his intention clear as this may ___(8)___ to defective or incompetent draftsmanship.

It is outside the proper scope of an illustration or example explanatory of a legislative enactment to ___(9)___ special legislation for a particular type of case; its function, ___(10)___, is to show how the principle already enunciated in the section of the enactment (to which the illustration is appended) is to be applied or how the particular facts of the case supported by the illustration ___(11)___ the paragraph.

An illustration does not exhaust the full content of the section which it illustrates; but equally it can neither ___(12)___ nor expand its ambit.

Where, however, illustrations are given, it is the duty of the court to accept, if it can be done, the illustrations as being both of relevance and value in the construction of the text. The illustrations should ___(13)___ be rejected because they do not square with the ideas possibly derived from another system of jurisprudence as to the law ___(14)___ they or the sections deal. And it would require a very special case to warrant the rejection on the ___(15)___ of their assumed repugnancy to the sections themselves. It would be the very last resort of construction to make any such assumption. The great usefulness of the illustrations which have, *although not part of the sections*, (italics furnished) been expressly furnished by the legislature as helpful on the working and application of the statute, should not be impaired.

(1) A. follows   B. following   C. followed
     D. follow   E. has been followed

(2) A. above all   B. after all   C. in all
     D. at all   E. once and for

(3) A. as for   B. as regards   C. as is
     D. as seen   E. as of

(4) A. acceptance   B. attainment   C. adopting
     D. passage   E. pronouncement

(5) A. ask   B. propose   C. move
     D. introduce   E. apply

(6) A. verified   B. overseen   C. overhauled
     D. canvassed   E. checked

(7) A. creep in   B. creep away   C. creep on
     D. creep onto   E. creep over

(8) A. jeopardize   B. jostle   C. amount
     D. attribute   E. attenuate

(9) A. constrain   B. express   C. expostulate
    D. convey   E. conspire

(10) A. on one hand B. on the contrary C. in the opposite
     D. on delivery E. over the hill

(11) A. come across B. come over   C. come under
     D. come off   E. come about

(12) A. diminish   B. abbreviate   C. lessen
     D. subtract   E. curtail

(13) A. in any case B. in no case   C. in some way
     D. in no way   E. under no case

(14) A. with which B. in which   C. with that
     D. in that   E. of which

(15) A. proposal   B. reason   C. supposition
     D. ground   E. assumption

III Reading Comprehension

Part One

Directions: *In this section there are passages followed by questions or unfinished statements, each with several suggested answers. Choose the one you think is the best answer.*

Passage One

Assistance may be obtained from the preamble to a statute in ascertaining the meaning of the relevant enacting part, since words derive their color and content from their context. But the preamble is not to affect the meaning otherwise ascribable to the enacting part unless there be compelling reason and it is not a compelling reason that the enacting words go further than the preamble indicated. The preamble, in the words of Chief Justice Subba Rao, contains in a nutshell the ideas and aspirations of the legislation.

On the other hand, there are some difficulties which one may have to face if he has to have recourse to the preamble to construe a statute. The preamble may not be exhaustive; it may only recite some and pot all of the inconveniences or evils. The evil recited may be the motive *for* legislation, but the remedy may extent beyond the cure of the evil. Radical amendments may have been made in the Act during its passage without the preamble being touched.

Indian courts have generally followed the English precedent and have held that where the meaning of the legislation is clear in the enacting part, there is no necessity to refer to the title, long or short or to the preamble. It is only in cases where the meaning of the legislation is not dear beyond doubt that the aid of title or preamble is sought.

The, preamble of a statute has been said to be a good means of finding out its meaning and as it were a key to the understanding of the Act. The policy and purpose of an Act can be ascertained from the preamble. The recital of facts in a preamble may be taken as material for legislative clarification.

The law on the subject may be said to have been summarized by the Supreme Court in M/s *Burralcur Coal Co., Ltd., v. The Union of India*. While it is permissible to look at the preamble for understanding the import of the various clauses contained in a Bill, it is not the case that full effect should not be given to the express provisions of an Act where they go beyond the terms of the preamble. It is one of the cardinal principles of construction that where the language of an Act is clear, the preamble must be disregarded, though, when the object or meaning of an enactment is not clear, the preamble may be resorted to explain it. Again, where very general language is used in an enactment which it is clear is intended to have a limited application, the preamble must be used to indicate to what particular instances the enactment is intended to apply.

Or again, the title and preamble, whatever their value might be as aids to construction of a statute, undoubtedly throw light on the intent and design of the Legislature and indicate the scope and purpose of the legislation itself.

The present practice in India is to do away with preambles generally. The long titles are good enough substitutes for preambles in most cases, if not all. In many cases, the preambles used to be mere elaboration of the long titles. The long titles can very well be used for the purpose of interpreting an Act ascertaining its scope in the same manner as a preamble as a whole and might be used. That the policy and purpose behind an enactment may be deduced from its long title (and the preamble) has been recognized in many decisions of the Supreme Court in India. In *re Kerala Education Bill, 1957*, the Supreme Court said that the general policy of the Bill as laid down in its title and elaborated in the preamble is to "provide for the better organization and development of educational institutions, providing a varied and comprehensive educational service throughout the State" and therefore each and every one of the clauses in the Bill has to be interpreted and read in the light of this policy. A reference was made to the case of *Biswambhar Singh v. State cif Orissa*, where, while interpreting the Orissa Estate Abolition (Amendment) Act, 1952, the Court relied on the long title of the Act and its preambles.

The long title, no doubt indicates the main purpose of the enactment but cannot, obviously control the express operative provisions of the Act, nor can it limit the plain meaning of the text. Where something is doubtful or ambiguous, the long titles may be looked at to resolve the doubt or ambiguity, but in the absence of doubt or ambiguity, the passage under construction must be taken to mean what it says, so that if its meaning be clear, that meaning is not to be narrowed or restricted by reference to the long title.

Similarly, the title of a chapter cannot be legitimately used to restrict the plain meaning of an enactment.

1. What will the preamble probably do in a statute?

A. The preamble is used to ascertain the meaning of the relevant enacting part.

B. The preamble is used to contain in a nutshell the ideas and aspirations of the legislation.

C. The preamble is used to recite and pot all of the inconveniences or evils in a statute.

D. The preamble is used to indicate to what particular instances the statute is intended to apply.

2. In construing the statute, the things to be paid attention to are _____.

A. The preamble will tell the public about the legislative intention.

B. The preambles may be replaced by long titles.

C. Radical amendments have to be made so that the preamble can stick to the intent of legislators.

D. Where the statute is clear, the preamble shall be disregarded.

3. What does the word "recital" probably mean in the phrase "recitals of the facts"?

   A. relation   B. summary   C. statement   D. discourse

4. The reason that long titles of a statute can replace the preamble is that _____.

A. Long titles throw light on the intent and design of the Legislature and indicate the scope and purpose of the legislation itself in the same manner as a preamble.

B. Long titles can not interpret an Act and ascertains its scope in the same manner as a preamble.

C. Long titles can provide for the better organization and development of educational institutions, providing a varied and comprehensive educational service throughout the State.

D. Long titles indicates the main purpose of the enactment and can obviously control the express operative provisions of the Act, can limit the plain meaning of the text.

5. The main idea of the passage may probably be _____.

A. Assistance may be obtained from the preamble to a statute in ascertaining the meaning of the relevant enacting part.

B. Where very general language is used in an enactment which it is clear is intended to have a limited application, the preamble must be used to indicate to what particular instances the enactment is intended to apply.

C. The preamble or long titles throw light on the intent and design of the Legislature and indicate the scope and purpose of the legislation itself, so they can be used to construe a statute.

D. The policy and purpose of an Act can be as taken as material for legislative clarification.

Passage Two

With regard to marginal notes or cross headings, there was some amount of uncertainty as to their utility in the construction of the relevant portions of the Act. In this connection, it should be noted that marginal notes are inserted by the draftsman as a matter of convenience; they are intended to condense the section to a short and accurate phrase, not always an easy task. Such notes can never give an exhaustive picture of the sections against which they appear. They are not discussed in Parliament; nor are they voted upon as is the case with long titles (and preambles). They are often altered by the draftsman in consultation with the Parliament Secretariat when the sections against which they appear undergo a change during their passage in Parliament. As Russell has pointed out, marginal notes have no legislative authority and may be revised in a later edition though the alteration of a marginal note is a matter to be most sparingly undertaken.

What would happen if the marginal note is in conflict with the section against which it appears. Does the marginal note overrule the section or vice-versa? So far as India is concerned, it was stated by Lord Macnaghten in *Thakurain Balraj Kunwar* v. *Rae Jagar Pal Singh*:

It is well settled that marginal notes to the sections of an Act cannot be referred to for the purpose of construing the Act. The contrary opinion originated in a mistake and has been exploded long ago. There seems to be no reason for giving the marginal notes in an Indian statute any greater authority than the marginal notes to an English Act of Parliament.

It was however, observed that the marginal note, though it cannot control the meaning of the section if it is clear and unambiguous, may be of some assistance to show the drift of a section.

The reason on which the rule rests was thus stated by Baggallay J. in *Attorney-General* v. *Great Eastern Railway*, "I never knew an amendment set down or discussed upon marginal notes to a clause. The House of Commons has nothing to do with a marginal mote".

After citing the above passage, Justice Venkatrama Ayyar in the *Bengal Immunity case* added, "This reasoning applies with equal force to marginal notes to Indian statutes. In my opinion, the marginal note to article 286 (1) (of the Constitution) cannot be referred to for construing the explanation. It is clearly inadmissible for cutting down the plain meaning of the words of the Constitution". He referred in this connection to *The Commissioner of Income tax*, Bombay v. *Ahtnedbhal Umarbhai*.

Where the word "sedition" did not occur in the body of the section but only in the marginal note, the Privy Council observed that there was no justification for restricting the content of the section by the marginal note which was not an operative part of the section but merely provided the name by which the crime defined in the section was to be known.

The temptation of using the marginal note for explaining the section should, of course, be repelled by the draftsman. If any explanation is needed, the section should be redrafted.

Punctuation and other typographical aids are no doubt important items. But it is dangerous for the draftsman to rely on a comma to show the sense of a section because careless checking of the proof of the printed Act may result in altering the sense. Early draftsman of deeds avoided reliance on punctuation because of the risk of ambiguity and hence the old deeds were verbose.

Indian Acts used always to be punctuated, unlike early English Acts, but as early as 1887, the Privy Council ruled that it is an error to rely on punctuation marks in construing a statute.

They were said to be of little importance. Certain Indian cases, however, took a different view, distinguishing the Privy Council rulings as based on English precedents or as referring to old Regulations.

The present position may be summarized in the words of the Supreme Court as follows:

Punctuation is after all a minor element in the construction of a statute and even if the orthodox view that it forms no part of the statute is to be regarded as of imperfect obligation and it can be looked at as *contemporanea exposltia*(按当时情况解释), it is clear that it cannot be allowed to control the plain meaning of a text.

1. Which of the following is not true about the use of the marginal notes or cross headings?

A. Marginal notes are very often inserted by the draftsmen for convenience.

B. They are intended to co9ndense the idea of a section of a statute.

C. They are unlike the preamble.

D. They have legislative authority and can be revised by the law-makers.

2. Which of the following will the draftsmen depend on very much to construe the statute?

A. marginal notes

B. punctuation marks

C. Using the marginal notes to explain a certain section.

D. Using punctuation marks for construing the a statute.

3. The word "verbose" in the passage may probably mean _____.

A. vernacular   B. circumlocutory   C. redundant   D. veritable

Part Two True or False Questions

Direction: *In this part of the exercise, there is a passage with eight true or false questions. Read the passage carefully and mark T if it is true and F if it is false.*

It may be mentioned that the Law Commission of India in its third report on the Limitation Act has recommended the omission of illustrations as unnecessary and misleading. Similarly in its report on the Specific Relief Act, the Law Commission observes that some of the illustrations are not warranted by the terms of the relevant sections, while others have tended to prevent the development of equitable jurisprudence.

Stating that an officer "shall" perform a certain function makes the performance obligatory. If the Act says that the officer "may" do something, the matter is left to his discretion. But it is not unoften that courts are left in doubt whether the legislature meant to make the matter obligatory or otherwise.

It has been stated by the Supreme Court, when a statute used the word "shall", *prima facie* (*at first view*; *on first appearance absent other information or evidence*), it is mandatory, but the court may ascertain the real intention of the legislature by carefully attending to the whole scope of the statute. For ascertaining the real intention of the legislature, the court may consider, *inter alia* (*among other things*), the nature and design of the statute and the consequences which would follow from construing it one way or the other, the impact of other provisions whereby the necessity of complying with the provisions in question is avoided, the circumstances that the statute provides for a contingency of compliance with the provisions, the fact that non-compliance with the provisions is or is not visited by some penalty, the serious or trivial consequences that flow therefrom and above all whether the object of the legislation wilt be defeated or furthered.

The support of the auxiliary verb "shall" is inconclusive as to whether it is mandatory or otherwise and similarly the mere absence of the imperative is not conclusive either. "May" may be construed as "shall" when the existence of the purpose is established and the conditions for the exercise of the discretion are fulfilled. In other words "may" will be construed as "shall" when the thing directed to be done is for the sake of justice or public good.

Perhaps, the addition of the words "in his discretion" after the word "may" in cases where performance of the function is not obligatory, may render the intention clearer.

The phrase "it shall be lawful" means that if the law had not been enacted, there would have been no authority to do the act. The phrase is apt to express that a power is given; and as *prima facie* the donee of the power may either exercise it or leave it unused; it is not inaccurate to say that *prima facie* the words are equivalent to saying that the donee may do it but if the object for which the power is conferred is for enforcing a right, there may be a duty cast on the donee to exercise the power for the benefit of such persons.

While the word "*etc.*" should be avoided in statutes, quite often general words follow certain specific terms when the intention is to include within the general term other matters or things falling within the same category or genus. The rule of *ejusdem generis* (*a rule of construction: general words that follows specific words in a list must be construed as referring only to the types of things identified by the specific words*) applies in such cases. The true scope of the rule of *ejusdem generis* is that words of a general nature following specified and particular wards should be construed as limited to things which are of the same nature as those specified and not its reverse, that specific words which precede are controlled by the general words which follow.

The true scope of the rule of *ejusdem generis* is that words of a general nature following specific and particular words should be construed as limited to things which are of the same nature as those specified. But the rule is one which has to be applied with caution and not pushed too far. It is a rule which must be confined to narrow bounds so as not to unduly or unnecessarily limit general or comprehensive words. If a broad-based genus could consistently be discovered, there is no warrant to cut down general words to dwarf size. If giant it cannot be, dwarf it need not be.

The word "or" and the word "and" are often used interchangeably. As a result of this common and careless use of the two words in legislation, there are occasions when the court, through construction, may change one to the other. This cannot be done if the meaning of the statute is clear or if the alteration operates to change the meaning of the law. It has been said that "or" may mean "nor"—not necessarily as laying down something in the alternative. Where five conditions were laid down with an "or" at the end of the fourth condition, a question arose whether the conditions were cumulative or disjunctive.

The solicitorial conjunction "and/or" sometimes favored by draftsman (particularly of deeds) has been described as a bastard conjunction and as an elliptical and embarassing expression which endangers accuracy for the sake of brevity. It is a slipshod and blundering phrase and shows lack of draftsmanship and should be dropped from the jargon of law.

The ordinary right of recourse to the courts for the trial of any claim is one of the rights which is not to be curtailed except by clear words. So far as the jurisdiction of the High Court and the Supreme Court in respect of the issue of writs under the Constitution is concerned it cannot be taken away by any form of words. There is a presumption against retrospective effect being given to a statute. When no contrary intention is shown the courts assume that the statute deals with the future and not with the past. No statute will be construed to have retrospective operation unless such a construction appears very clearly in the terms of the Act, or arises by necessary implication.

It is a well recognized rule that a statute should be interpreted if possible, so as to respect vested rights. Where the effect would be to alter a transaction already entered into, where it would be to make that valid which was previously invalid, to make an instrument which had no effect at all, and from which the party was at liberty to depart as long as he pleased, binding, the *prima fade* construction of the Act is that it is not to be retrospective.

Where the substantive law is altered during the pendency of a suit the rights of the parties will be decided according to the law as it existed when the action was begun unless the enactment makes it clear that the contrary is intended, either expressly or by necessary intendment. A substantive right cannot be taken away retrospectively unless the law expressly states so or there is clear intendment.

A right of appeal prevailing at the time of institution of a suit is not taken away by a law passed during the pendency of the suit omitting provision for appeal. If the Legislature intends to abolish the right of appeal which has accrued by the filing of a suit, the enactment must be framed so as to make it clear. It was held by the Supreme Court in *Garikapati* v. *S. Choudhny* that the right of appeal is a vested right and such a right to enter the superior court accrues to the litigant and exists as on and from the date the *lis* commences and this vested right of appeal can be taken away only by a subsequent enactment, if it so provides expressly or by necessary intendment and not otherwise. However, in the matter of procedure, there is no vested right and a change in the law of procedure operates retrospectively and, unlike the law relating to vested right, is not prospective. Thus a person accused of the commission of an offence has no vested right to be tried by a particular court or a particular procedure except in so far as there is any constitutional objection by way of discrimination or the violation of any other fundamental right is involved.

It is a fundamental canon of construction that a court of law will not permit the sanctity of obligations or of contracts to be interfered with unless the statute, in express terms, permits a violation of that sanctity.

1. Use of illustration in the statute is new strictly prohibited in India. (　)
2. The use of "shall" in a statute often conveys the idea of "being obligatory" or "mandatory". (　)
3. The rule of *ejusdem generis* means that words of general nature can only be construed as non-specific. (　)
4. Use of "and / or" should be altogether banned by the draftsmen. (　)
5. Any statute can be construed as having recourse to the past, that is "being retrospective". (　)
6. The interpretation of the statute should respect vested rights. (　)
7. A right of appeal can be taken away by any appellant court. (　)
8. A substantive law can not alter the retrospective feature of the existing statute. (　)

IV　Translation Abilities

法律语言特征分析与法律翻译技能培养之七：

法律语言类型

法律语言受法律工作者自身职业以及工作者的对象所使用语言的影响,形成了立法、司法等部门各自独立的表达方式。同时,由于法律工作者在应用法律语言的过程中所显示的语体功能不同,法律语言可以分为口语变体和书面语变体,此外,由于使用法律语言的具体场合不同,我们还可以作出更多种类的分类,从而使得法律语言变得更加丰富,具备其独特的、与其他社团不同的特点：(1)法律专业术语在法院、检察院、公安局、律师、劳教、公证等不同性质和工作对象的执法部门和单位中所用语言各有特点；(2) 各种法律语言变体既具有通俗性，又具有简明性和庄严性等特点，因为它不仅应该为全民理解，还应该体现出法律规范和司法文书的严肃性和权威性。具体的法律语言类型可以表现如下：

法律语言类型						
书面语言体					口头语言体	
立法语言体			司法书面语体		程式化法律公务口语的表现形式	应变性司法公务口语的表现形式
义务性法律规范表达形式	禁止性法律规范表达形式	授权性法律规范表达形式	程式化司法书面语表达方式	应变性书面语表达方式	程式化法律公务口语表达方式	应变性司法公务口语表达方式
			法院、检察院、公安局、律师、劳教、公证	法院、检察院、公安局、律师、劳教、公证	调解、传令、审判、论辩、公证	调解、审判、论辩、公证、宣讲

由于上述变体的表达方式以及表现手段各异，法律语言翻译过程中，有时就需要根据具体环境选词造句。

Translation Exercises：

Part One *Put the Following into Chinese*

Where an Act creates a new or special remedy for the enforcement of a right or duty, the courts should not be left in doubt whether this remedy is intended to be exclusive of the usual remedy, although the courts have ruled in aid of the draftsman that where an Act creates a new right and also provides the remedy for enforcing it, that remedy may be presumed to be the exclusive method of enforcing that right. For example, when a special tribunal or authority is appointed to determine questions under an Act, there is a strong presumption that the Legislature intended to provide completely for the matter and that the person aggrieved is limited to the remedy so provided. This does not, of course, affect the special powers vested by the Constitution in the High Courts and the Supreme Court.

But where an Act merely provides a new mode of enforcing preexisting legal rights, then, in the absence of any clear indication in the Act to the contrary, the new remedy is deemed to be an additional remedy and the right of suit in the civil court is not taken away.

Acts which impose penalties are subject to strict construction. The courts will not read into a penal section any words which extend the operation of the section. While interpreting a penal statute, Pollock, C. B. observed, "Our constitutions were never more safe than at the present moment, but we cannot lose any of the grounds of our security; no calamity would be greater than to introduce a lax or elastic interpretation of a criminal statute to serve a special but temporary purpose".

The Supreme Court pointed out in *Motibhai Fu! a Shot Patel & Co. v. R. Prasad* that in dealing with a provision relating to forfeiture, one is dealing with a penal provision. It would not be proper for the court to extend the scope of that provision by reading into it words which are not there and thereby widen the scope of the provision relating to confiscation.

In a penal statute affecting the business of hundreds of persons, the court would construe words of ambiguous meaning in a broad and liberal sense so that they will not become traps for honest, unlearned (in the law) and unwary men.

The rule of strict construction means that the language of a statute should be so construed that no case shall be held to fall within it which does not come within the reasonable interpretation of the statute. In construing a penal statute it is a cardinal principle that in case of doubt, the construction favorable to the subject shall be preferred. The courts will give the best construction consistent with commonsense, reason and justice. In this process moral and ethical considerations have no place.

Where two Acts provide different penalties for the same act or omission, the question should not be left in doubt whether the latter enactment supersedes the former. Under article 20 of the Constitution no person accused of an offence shall be prosecuted and punished for the same offence more than once and the General Clauses Act, 1897, also contains a somewhat similar provision.

Taxing Acts are also subject to strict construction and the benefit of doubt is given to the person sought to be taxed. The Act will be construed strictly according to its terms so as not to affect persons by mere implication. But in choosing between two possible constructions of the statute, effect is to be given to the one that favors the citizen and not the one that imposes a burden on him.

There is no presumption of law against a person being taxed for the same thing under two enactments. The latter law should survey the previous enactment and render this question clear if any overlapping of the subject matter is likely to occur.

Part Two *Put the Following into English*

对法律/法规进行严格的释意解释时,回顾一下 Crawford 在他的《法律解释》一书中的话是十分有益的(参见最高法院的 *Subba Rao* v. *Commissioner of Income tax*, *Madras.*):

"为什么法规的解释应该视情况严格按意义进行解释呢? 唯一正确的答案只能是,不同类型的解释方法能够有效表明立法意图。有时为了是立法意图更加明确,就需要对法规进行释意解释,但有时这种解释又会歪曲立法意图。若此乃法律解释中应该遵循的恰当规则的话,则严格意义上的释意解释不过是一种为了表明立法意图而使得法律法规的范围得以延展或限制的方式而已。若这样做乃严格意义上进行释意解释应取的姿态,则所涉及法律法规无论是关于惩处、刑事、作为补偿、还是丧失共同权利等等都不会有多大的区别,因为基于这样的分类本身就没有任何意义。"

上述内容不过是任何关于法律解释的书籍中均极力加以阐释的较为重要的一般原则。正如加尔各答高等法院的一资深法官在 1946 年所说,法律解释的原则现已到了一种自身需要进行解释的程度;C. K. 艾伦在他的一本受人爱戴的书《法律的制定》(*Law in the Making*)中所说,有关法律法规解释的多数案例表明,"文字通常给赋予生命的精神以更大的伤害力"。为此,人们对法官解释法律的多数批评在于,法官更多关注了法律的本身,而不是所制定的法的精神。由此造成不协调。若再套用 C. K. 艾伦的话,也就是,"根本性的毛病就在于人类语言已经不足以其完美的精确性来表达人类的思想和立法意图"。

好的法律就像好法官一样,乃人们追寻的理想,事实上是无法达到的;但法律起草者的目的就在于永远追求这一理想。若他能够将模棱两可的东西减少到最低限度,那么他就大功告成。

V Interaction

Discuss with your tutor(s) or the People's judges in your locality about the methodology of construction of a statute. Then based on the discussion, you are supposed to write a composition about the method of the construction of statute. Remember that you are required to express your ideas clearly.

VI Appreciation of Judge's Opinions

(1) Case Name(案件名):*Whitman v. American Trucking Associations, Inc.*

Whitman, Administrator of Environmental
Protection Agency, et al. V. American
Trucking Associations, INC., et al.
Certiorari to the United States Court of Appeals for
The District of Columbia Circuit
No. 99—1257. Argued November 7, 2000—Decided February 27, 2001 *

Whitman v. American Trucking Associations, Inc.

Supreme Court of the United States

Argued November 7, 2000
Decided February 27, 2001

Full case name	Christine Todd Whitman, Administrator of Environmental Protection Agency, et al. v. American Trucking Associations, Inc., et al.
Citations	531 U.S. 457 (more)
Argument	Oral argument

Holding

The Clean Air Act properly delegated legislative power to the Environmental Protection Agency, but the EPA cannot consider implementation costs in setting primary and secondary national ambient air quality standards.

Lesson Seven Rules of Legal Interpretation

Court membership

Chief Justice
William Rehnquist
Associate Justices
John P. Stevens · Sandra Day O'Connor
Antonin Scalia · Anthony Kennedy
David Souter · Clarence Thomas
Ruth Bader Ginsburg · Stephen Breyer

Case opinions

Majority	Scalia, joined by Rehnquist, O'Connor, Kennedy, Ginsburg
Concurrence	Stevens, joined by Souter
Concurrence	Breyer
Concurrence	Thomas

Laws applied

Section 109 of the Clean Air Act (CAA)

(2) Case Summary(案件简介)

Whitman v. American Trucking Associations, Inc., 531 U.S. 457 (2001), was a case decided by the United States Supreme Court in which the Environmental Protection Agency's National Ambient Air Quality Standard (NAAQS) for regulating ozone and particulate matter was challenged by the American Trucking Association along with other private companies and the States of Michigan, Ohio, and West Virginia.

The Supreme Court faced the issues of whether the statute had impermissibly delegated legislative power to the agency, and whether the Administrator of the EPA, Christine Todd Whitman, could consider the costs of implementation in setting national ambient air quality standards.

Section 109(b)(1) of the CAA (Clean Air Act) instructed the EPA to set "ambient air quality standards the attainment and maintenance of which in the judgment of the Administrator, based on [the] criteria [documents of Section 108] and allowing an adequate margin of safety, are requisite to protect the public health."

The D.C. Circuit Court of Appeals had decided that the standard making procedure delegated by Congress to the EPA to set air quality was an unconstitutional delegation in contravention of Article I, Section I of the U.S. Constitution because the EPA had interpreted the statute to provide "no intelligible principle" to guide the agency's exercise of authority. It also found that the EPA could not consider the cost of implementing a national ambient air quality standard.

In an opinion written by Justice Scalia the Supreme Court affirmed in part and reversed in part the Court of Appeals' decision.

The Court affirmed that the text of Section 109(b) unambiguously barred cost considerations from the NAAQS-setting process.

The court then held, "whether the statute delegates legislative power is a question for the courts, and an agency's voluntary self-denial has no bearing upon the answer," and that the scope of discretion Section 109(b)(1) allowed was well within the outer limits of nondelegation precedents.

The court remanded the case for the Court of Appeals to reinterpret the statute that would avoid a delegation of legislative power.

(3) Excerpts of the Judgment(法官判决词)

Justice Scalia delivered the opinion of the Court.

These cases present the following questions:(1) Whether §109(b)(1) of the Clean Air Act (CAA)(《清洁空气法》)delegates(授权) legislative power to the Administrator of the Environmental Protection Agency (EPA)(美国联邦环境保护署).(2) Whether the Administrator may consider the costs of implementation in setting national ambient air quality standards (NAAQS)(全国空气质量标准)under §109(b)(1).(3) Whether the Court of Appeals had jurisdiction to review the EPA's interpretation of Part D of Title I of the CAA, with respect to implementing the revised ozone(臭氧)NAAQS.(4) If so, whether the EPA's interpretation of that part was permissible(可以允许/许可的).

I(omitted)

II(omitted)

III(omitted)

IV

The final two issues on which we granted certiorari(调卷令)concern the EPA's authority to implement the revised ozone NAAQS in areas whose ozone levels currently exceed the maximum level permitted by that standard. The CAA designates such areas "nonattainment,"(不达标地区)and it exposes them to additional restrictions over and above the implementation requirements imposed generally by §110 of the CAA. These additional restrictions are found in the five substantive subparts of Part D of Title I, 42 U.S.C. §7501—7515. Subpart 1, §§7501—7509a, contains general nonattainment regulations that pertain to every pollutant for which a NAAQS exists. Subparts 2 through 5, §§7511—7514a, contain rules tailored to specific individual pollutants(针对特定的污染物). Subpart 2, added by the Clean Air Act Amendments(《清洁空气法》(修订))of 1990, §103, 104 Stat. 2423, addresses ozone. The dispute before us here, in a nutshell(用一句话概括起来,极简单地) is whether Subpart 1 alone (as the agency determined), or rather Subpart 2 or some combination of Subparts 1 and 2, controls the implementation of the revised ozone NAAQS in nonattainment areas.

A

The Administrator first urges, however, that we vacate(上级法院废除下级法院的判决行为)the judgment of the Court of Appeals on this issue because it lacked jurisdiction to review the EPA's implementation policy. Section 307(b)(1) of the CAA, 42 U.S.C. §7607(b)(1), gives the court jurisdiction over "any... nationally applicable regulations promulgated, or final action taken, by the Administrator," but the EPA argues that its implementation policy was not agency "action," was not "final" action, and is not ripe for review. We reject each of these three contentions.

At the same time the EPA proposed the revised ozone NAAQS in 1996, it also proposed an "interim implementation policy"(临时施行政策)for the NAAQS, that was to govern until the details of implementation could be put in final form through specific "rulemaking actions." The preamble(绪言,条约等的前言) to this proposed policy declared that "the interim implementation policy... represent[s] EPA's preliminary views on these issues and, while it may include various statements that States must take certain actions, these statements are made pursuant to EPA's preliminary interpretations, and thus do not bind the States and public as a matter of law." If the EPA had done no more, we perhaps could accept its current claim that its action was not final. However, after the agency had accepted comments on its proposed policy, and on the same day that the final ozone NAAQS was promulgated(颁布,公布法令等), the White House published in the Federal Register(美国联邦公报,美国联邦日志,国会授权的联邦政府刊载总统行政命令或其他国会要求公布的文件的官方刊物)what it titled a "Memorandum for the Administrator of the Environmental Protection Agency" that prescribed implementation procedures for the EPA to follow. The EPA supplemented this memorandum with an explanation of the implementation procedures, which it published in the explanatory preamble to its final ozone NAAQS under the heading, "Final decision on the primary standard." "In light of comments received regarding the interpretation proposed in the Interim Implementation Policy," the EPA announced, it had "reconsidered that interpretation" and settled on a new one. The provisions of "subpart 1 of part D of Title I of the Act" will immediately "apply to the implementation of the new 8-hour ozone standards." Moreover, the provisions of subpart 2 "will also continue to apply as a matter of law for so long as an area is not attaining the old 1-hour standard." Once the area reaches attainment for the old standard, however, "the provisions of subpart 2 will have been achieved and those provisions will no longer apply."

We have little trouble concluding that this constitutes final agency action subject to review under §307. The bite in the phrase "final action" (which bears the same meaning in §307(b)(1) that it does under the Administrative Procedure Act (APA)) is not in the word "action," which is meant to cover comprehensively every manner in which an agency may exercise its power. It is rather in the word "final," which requires that the action under review "mark the consummation of the agency's decisionmaking process."(标志着环境署决策过程的完结) Only if the "EPA has rendered its last word on the matter" in question, is its action "final" and thus reviewable. That standard is satisfied here. The EPA's "decisionmaking process," which began with the 1996 proposal and continued with the reception of public comments, concluded when the agency, "in light of these comments," and in conjunction with a corresponding directive(指令) from the White House, adopted the interpretation of Part D at issue here. Since that interpretation issued, the EPA has refused in subsequent rulemakings to reconsider it, explaining to disappointed commenters that its earlier decision was conclusive. Though the agency has not dressed its decision with the conventional procedural accoutrements of finality, its own behavior thus belies(证明……是假的;与……相背/相反、相左) the claim that its interpretation is not final.

The decision is also ripe for our review. "Ripeness 'requires us to evaluate both the fitness of the issues for judicial decision and the hardship to the parties of withholding court consideration.'" The question before us here is purely one of statutory interpretation that would not "benefit from further factual development of the issues presented." Nor will our review "inappropriately interfere with further administrative action," ibid., since the EPA has concluded its consideration of the implementation issue. Finally, as for hardship to the parties: The respondent States must—on pain of forfeiting to the EPA control over implementation of the NAAQS—promptly undertake the lengthy and expensive task of developing state implementation plans (SIP's) that will attain the new, more stringent standard within five years. Whether or not this would suffice in an ordinary case brought under the review provisions of the APA, we have characterized the special judicial-review provision of the CAA, as one of those statutes that specifically provides for "pre-enforcement" review. Such statutes, we have said, permit "judicial review directly, even before the concrete effects normally required for APA review are felt." The effects at issue here surely meet that lower standard.

Beyond all this, the implementation issue was fairly included within the challenges to the final ozone rule that were properly before the Court of Appeals. Respondents argued below that the EPA could not revise the ozone standard, because to do so would trigger the use of Subpart 1, which had been supplanted (for ozone) by the specific rules of Subpart 2. The EPA responded that Subpart 2 did not supplant but simply supplemented Subpart 1, so that the latter section still "applies to all nonattainment areas for all NAAQS,... including nonattainment areas for any revised ozone standard." The agency later reiterated(反复,反复讲;反复做;重申) that Subpart 2 "does not supplant implementation provisions for revised ozone standards. This interpretation fully harmonizes Subpart 2 with EPA's clear authority to revise any NAAQS." In other words, the EPA was arguing that the revised standard could be issued, despite its apparent incompatibility with portions of Subpart 2, because it would be implemented under Subpart 1 rather than Subpart 2. The District of Columbia Circuit ultimately agreed that Subpart 2 could be harmonized with the EPA's authority to promulgate revised NAAQS, but not because Subpart 2 is entirely inapplicable—which is one of EPA's assignments of error. It is unreasonable to contend, as the EPA now does, that the Court of Appeals was obligated to reach the agency's preferred result, but forbidden to assess the reasons the EPA had given for reaching that result. The implementation issue was fairly included within respondents' challenge to the ozone rule, which all parties agree is final agency action ripe for review.

B

Our approach to the merits(案件实质内容) of the parties' dispute is the familiar one of *Chevron U. S. A. Inc. v. Natural Resources Defense Council, Inc.* (1984). If the statute resolves the question whether Subpart 1 or Subpart 2 (or some combination of the two) shall apply to revised ozone NAAQS, then "that is the end of the matter." ut if the statute is "silent or ambiguous"(无规定或模棱两可) with respect to the issue, then we must defer to a "reasonable interpretation made by the administrator of an agency." We cannot agree with the Court of Appeals that Subpart 2 clearly controls the implementation of revised ozone NAAQS, because we find the statute to some extent ambiguous. We conclude, however, that the agency's interpretation goes beyond the limits of what is ambiguous and contradicts what in our view is quite clear. We therefore hold the implementation policy unlawful.

The text of Subpart 1 at first seems to point the way to a clear answer to the question, which Subpart controls? Two sections of Subpart 1, 7502(a)(1)(C) and 7502(a)(2)(D), contain switching provisions stating that if the classification of ozone nonattainment areas is "specifically provided for under other provisions of Part D," then those provisions will control instead of Subpart 1's. Thus it is true but incomplete to note, as the Administrator does, that the substantive language of Subpart 1 is broad enough to apply to revised ozone standards. To determine whether that language does apply one must resolve the further textual issue(文本问题) whether some other provision, namely Subpart 2, provides for the classification of ozone nonattainment areas. If it does, then according to the switching provisions of Subpart 1 it will control.

So, does Subpart 2 provide for classifying nonattainment ozone areas under the revised standard? It unquestionably does. The backbone of the subpart is Table 1, which defines five categories of ozone nonattainment areas and prescribes attainment deadlines for each. Section 7511(a)(1) funnels(使汇集) all nonattainment areas into the table for classification, declaring that "each area designated nonattainment for ozone... shall be classified at the time of such designation, under table 1, by operation of law." And once an area has been classified, "the primary standard attainment date for ozone shall be as expeditiously as practicable but not later than the date provided in table 1." The EPA argues that this text is not as clear or comprehensive as it seems, because the title of §7511 (a) reads "Classification and attainment dates for 1989 nonattainment areas," which suggests that Subpart 2 applies only to areas that were in nonattainment in 1989, and not to areas later designated nonattainment under a revised ozone standard. The suggestion must be rejected, however, because §7511(b)(1) specifically provides for the classification of areas that were in attainment in 1989 but have subsequently slipped into nonattainment. It thus makes clear that Subpart 2 is not limited solely to 1989 nonattainment areas. This eliminates the interpretive role of the title, which may only "shed light on(使……更清楚)some ambiguous word or phrase in the statute itself".

It may well be, as the EPA argues that some provisions of Subpart 2 are ill fitted to implementation of the revised standard. Using the old 1-hour averages of ozone levels, for example, as Subpart 2 requires, would produce at best an inexact estimate of the new 8-hour averages. Also, to the extent that the new ozone standard is stricter than the old one, the classification system of Subpart 2 contains a gap, because it fails to classify areas whose ozone levels are greater than the new standard (and thus nonattaining) but less than the approximation of the old standard codified by Table 1. And finally, Subpart 2's method for calculating attainment dates—which is simply to count forward a certain number of years from November 15, 1990 (the date the 1990 CAA Amendments took force), depending on how far out of attainment the area started—seems to make no sense for areas that are first classified under a new standard after November 15, 1990. If, for example, areas were classified in the year 2000, many of the deadlines would already have expired at the time of classification.

These gaps in Subpart 2's scheme prevent us from concluding that Congress clearly intended Subpart 2 to be the exclusive, permanent means of enforcing a revised ozone standard in nonattainment areas. The statute is in our view ambiguous concerning the manner in which Subpart 1 and Subpart 2 interact with regard to revised ozone standards, and we would defer to(服从,听从,遵从;把某事交由某人决定) the EPA's reasonable resolution of that ambiguity. We cannot defer, however, to the interpretation the EPA has given.

Whatever effect may be accorded the gaps in Subpart 2 as implying some limited applicability of Subpart 1, they cannot be thought to render Subpart 2's carefully designed restrictions on EPA discretion utterly nugatory(无效的)once a new standard has been promulgated, as the EPA has concluded. The principal distinction between Subpart 1 and Subpart 2 is that the latter eliminates regulatory discretion that the former allowed. While Subpart 1 permits the EPA to establish classifications for nonattainment areas, Subpart 2 classifies areas as a matter of law based on a table. Whereas the EPA has discretion under Subpart 1 to extend attainment dates for as long as 12 years, under Subpart 2 it may grant no more than 2 years' extension. Whereas Subpart 1 gives the EPA considerable discretion to shape nonattainment programs, Subpart 2 prescribes large parts of them by law. Yet according to the EPA, Subpart 2 was simply Congress's "approach to the implementation of the [old] 1-hour" standard, and so there was no reason that "the new standard could not simultaneously be implemented under... subpart 1." To use a few apparent gaps in Subpart 2 to render its textually explicit applicability to nonattainment areas under the new standard utterly inoperative is to go over the edge of reasonable interpretation. The EPA may not construe(解释)the statute in a way that completely nullifies textually applicable provisions meant to limit its discretion.

The EPA's interpretation making Subpart 2 abruptly obsolete(已废弃的,已不用的,已失时效的)is all the more astonishing because Subpart 2 was obviously written to govern implementation for some time. Some of the elements required to be included in SIP's under Subpart 2 were not to take effect until many years after the passage of the Act. A plan reaching so far into the future was not enacted to be abandoned the next time the EPA reviewed the ozone standard—which Congress knew could happen at any time, since the technical staff papers had already been completed in late 1989. Yet nothing in the EPA's interpretation would have prevented the agency from aborting Subpart 2 the day after it was enacted. Even now, if the EPA's interpretation were correct, some areas of the country could be required to meet the new, more stringent ozone standard in at most the same time that Subpart 2 had allowed them to meet the old standard. Los Angeles, for instance, "would be required to attain the revised NAAQS under Subpart 1 no later than the same year that marks the outer time limit for attaining Subpart 2's one-hour ozone standard." An interpretation of Subpart 2 so at odds with(与……不一致) its structure and manifest purpose cannot be sustained.

We therefore find the EPA's implementation policy(实施政策)to be unlawful, though not in the precise respect determined by the Court of Appeals. After our remand, and the Court of Appeals' final disposition of this case, it is left to the EPA to develop a reasonable interpretation of the nonattainment implementation provisions insofar as they apply to revised ozone NAAQS.

* * *

To summarize our holdings(裁定)in these unusually complex cases: (1) The EPA may not consider implementation costs (实施成本)in setting primary and secondary NAAQS under §109(b) of the CAA. (2) Section 109(b)(1) does not delegate legislative power(立法授权) to the EPA in contravention of Art. I, §1, of the Constitution. (3) The Court of Appeals had jurisdiction to review the EPA's interpretation of Part D of Title I of the CAA, relating to the implementation of the revised ozone NAAQS. (4) The EPA's interpretation of that Part is unreasonable.

The judgment of the Court of Appeals is affirmed(维持原判)in part and reversed(推翻原判)in part, and the cases are remanded(发回重审)for proceedings consistent with this opinion.

It is so ordered.

Lesson Eight

U. S. Legal History on Capital Punishment
—Crime of Homicide in Chicago from 1870 to 1930

Learning objectives

After learning the text and having done the exercises in this lesson, you will be able to:

—acquire knowledge of the legal characteristics and the nature of the legal history on capital punishment in common-law countries;

—familiarize yourself with the vocabulary, grammar, or syntax concerned in this text;

—become aware of the information required to understand the legal history on capital punishment;

—cultivate practical abilities to put to use the language in the specific context; and

—translate relevant materials from Chinese to English and from English to Chinese.

U. S. Legal History on Capital Punishment
—Crime of Homicide in Chicago from *1870* to *1930*

I Introduction: Capital Punishment①, Race and Poverty

In the criminal justice system, the ultimate and final act in any homicide② case is the application of the death penalty. Of course, not all homicides result in a death sentence, and not all homicide offenders are sentenced to death. As a consequence, the question of which offenses and which offenders merit a death sentence has always been central to the concern over whether capital

---

① capital punishment: 死刑;极刑。death penalty: 死刑,极刑。principal punishment: 主刑,基本刑。accessory punishment: 从刑;附加刑。fixed term imprisonment: 有期徒刑。temporary punishment: 有期徒刑。life imprisonment: 无期徒刑。life sentence: 无期徒刑的判决。

② homicide: the deliberate and unlawful killing of one person by another; murder 谋杀,凶杀,他杀。另外,criminal homicide: 刑事上杀人;culpable homicide: 有罪杀人;unlawful homicide: 非法杀人;justifiable homicide: 正当杀人。

punishment should be used at all. On the one hand, as times change and the criminal justice system changes with them, we would expect corresponding changes in the application of the death penalty. On the other hand, if capital punishment is rooted as fundamentally in the racial and economic inequities of society as some have argued, then even over a century we might see far more similarities than differences in how many offenders are sentenced to death, who they are, and for what kinds of homicides.

Included in the file on Chicago homicides from 1870 to 1930 are a small number of cases in which the offender was sentenced to capital punishment and was executed. Certainly, the questions of the morality or the efficacy of capital punishment, as well as concerns over the fairness of its application, were as relevant and alive then as they are now. An analysis of these death penalty cases could enable us to consider whether some of the patterns we see in capital punishment over the last half of the twentieth century held true in Chicago over a century ago. We can consider what kinds of homicides and what kinds of offenders were more likely to draw a death sentence, and examine whether those patterns changed over time. We can also examine how the application of capital punishment changed in Chicago over those fifty years, and can compare the patterns in death sentences in Chicago to the patterns we see in modem America. This is interesting in its own right, a look at a piece of history in a major American city at the turn of the last century, but it may also bring more data①to bear on the fundamental moral and practical questions which have shaped the death penalty debate for decades.

II The Debate over Capital Punishment: the relevance of race and poverty

Debates on capital punishment tend to revolve around philosophical questions as to the morality of the death penalty, or pragmatic questions as to the efficacy②or effectiveness of the death penalty. In Furman v. Georgia, Justice Brennan wrote that "although pragmatic arguments... have been frequently advanced.... At bottom, the battle has been waged on moral grounds." On one extreme, there are those who argue that it is neither right nor moral for anyone to take another's life, and that "anyone" includes the state. For these opponents, the death penalty in any form or under any condition is wrong.

On the other extreme are those who adopt a rigid "eye for an eye③" belief, in which anyone who kills another person without legal justification should die. From that perspective, it makes no difference whether capital punishment "functions" to deter crime or not, it is simply something that must morally be done.

In between those extremes, however, and much more characteristic of the concerns of a majority of citizens and more representative of their position if the polls are accurate, is the argument which holds that it may be legitimate, and even moral, for the state to take a life under certain circumstances if taking that life could be shown to save the lives of others. Under this approach, the

---

① data：此处指"论据"(哲)—(Philosophy) things known or assumed as facts, making the basis of reasoning or calculation.
② efficacy：(formal) the ability to produce a desired or intended result:(正式)功效;效力;效能。
③ eye for an eye：以眼还眼,以牙还牙。

argument becomes pragmatic, and the primary focus shifts to the question of what these "certain circumstances" might be. Most citizens would support the death penalty only under the condition that it is fairly and justly applied. While any number of criteria might be used to determine what is fair and just, since the inception① of the modern debate on the death penalty two variables② have stood out as problematic or key for this determination—race and poverty. These two factors constitute one focus of our analysis. The Chicago database allows us to look more closely at the question of the application of capital punishment a hundred years ago, and to ask whether these factors were paramount then as well.

A number of factors are involved in considering who is sentenced to capital punishment and who is not. Age, gender, and even geographic location show clear associations with the occurrence of homicide, and are consequently mirrored in the death row population. Historically, however, being black and being poor have always increased any homicide offender's chance of being a death row③ statistic. These Chicago data provide us with an opportunity to look at those variables from yet another perspective, partly in the hope that they might indicate this has not always been the case, but more realistically in the expectation that they will confirm the consistency over time of poverty and race as key characteristics of whom we send to death row.

A. Race of Offender and Victim in Capital Homicides

Race stands out as the dominant factor④ that suggests the death penalty is not fairly and evenly applied across the population. Prior to the Furman decision, African Americans were more likely to be charged, sentenced, and executed than were others. Of more than 13,000 executions in the United States documented in the Espy File from 1790 to 1985, nearly half were African American. Among eleven Southern states, sixty-three percent to ninety percent of all executions during the first half of the 20th century were of blacks. In rape cases, eighty-nine percent of all the offenders executed were blacks. Jeffrey Adler has analyzed data from Chicago homicides prior to 1920, and found that African Americans were never more than 4.2% of the city's population, but comprised 12.1% of homicide offenders and 27.5% of those executed for homicide. Further, when African Americans killed a white victim, 6.8% were executed, but when they killed another African American only 1.5% were executed. And, in keeping with national data, there were no executions of a white offender for killing an African American.

There is also evidence that race plays a role at each stage of the processing of a capital punishment case. Research has shown race based differences at the points of charging or indictment⑤, sentencing, and post-sentence activities. The prosecution⑥ is more likely to seek the death penalty for cases with white victims. Also, evidence indicates that this disproportion is most pro-

---

① inception: the establishment or starting point of an institution or activity,(机构,活动) 开业,开始。
② variable: 变量;因素。
③ death row:(监狱的) 死囚区。
④ dominant factor: 主要因素;优势因子。
⑤ indictment:(Law) a formal charge or accusation of a serious crime,(律) 指控,控告,起诉;刑事起诉书;公诉书。
⑥ prosecution: the institution and conducting of legal proceedings against someone in respect of a criminal charge,(就刑事指控的) 起诉;告发,检举。

nounced①in less dramatic or brutal cases. It has been suggested that it is among these "lesser" murders, where the crime is not as brutal or as heinous, that racism on the part of the prosecutor, judge, or jury member comes into play. Also, charged blacks are more likely to receive the death penalty, and when sentenced are more likely to have that sentence carried out. In short, the effects of race have an impact throughout the process of enacting the death penalty.

B. Economic Status and the Sentence of Death

The other variable that has been associated with executions②has been poverty. However, because of the difficulties of actually measuring the wealth, or lack of the same, of many of the individuals convicted of capital murder, this has been a very difficult relationship to accurately quantify. Radelet and Vandiver note that there is little quantitative research③on the impact of socioeconomic variables④on the imposition of capital punishment. Such research is badly needed.... They also recognize that "this absence of research reflects the difficulty of accurately measuring the social class of prisoners through official records of defendant's income."

Whatever the difficulty is in measuring poverty, there is no doubt but that the inability to hire adequate private counsel is reflected in the poverty found on death row. Stephen Bright pointedly notes that, "in consequence, a large part of the death row population is made up of people who are distinguished by neither their records nor the circumstances of their crimes, but by their abject⑤poverty, debilitating mental impairments, minimal intelligence, and the poor legal representation they received." And while being defended by other than privately hired counsel certainly increases one's chances of being sentenced to death, it appears that even being defended by lawyers who are part of an established public defender program offers a better chance of avoiding the death penalty than being defended by a court appointed and paid lawyer from the private bar.

III The Chicago Database and Census Data: strengths and weakness

The major limitation on any detailed or precise statistical analysis of the file is the nature of the data themselves. Problems associated with the data make comparisons of capital and non-capital homicides something that must be interpreted with some caution. There are a number of reasons for this. The contents of the data are police records, which were originally recorded a century ago by an unknown number of different personnel over a fifty year period. The emphasis on what was important to record obviously varied by time and by recorder, and there is no way to know what errors this may have introduced. Further, the coding of the existing data from the re-cords produced some odd results. There are some cases where no sentence is recorded as being given, yet there is a code for an execution, the date of the execution, and the method.

On the one hand, this is far less perfect than we would want. But on the other hand, these

---

① pronounced:明显的;显著的。
② execution:the carrying out of a sentence of death on a condemned person:死刑的执行。
③ quantitative research:定量研究。
④ socioeconomic variables:社会和经济变数。
⑤ abject:(of a situation or condition) extremely bad, unpleasant, and degrading:(境遇,情况) 糟透了的,可怜的,凄惨的。

are the data that are available for the analysis. The best solution, it would appear, is to acknowledge the problems and then consider the findings with that acknowledgment in mind. Certainly, while we will be noting comparisons of capital punishment cases with homicides generally and will be doing some discussion of change over time, we must always keep in mind that these are always with the caveats① mentioned above.

One of the first decisions was to eliminate accidental deaths from our cases, leaving a file of "intentional death" cases, which more accurately reflects the universe from which capital cases are drawn. This "intentional victim" file was constructed by selecting only those cases from the Victim Record in which the cause of death was known, and in which the cause of death was not one of the cases coded as unintentional on the variable "Method of Killing." Even in this we must make some assumptions—drownings, for example, were left in because they were very few in number and because a drowning can be a method of murder. Abortion also posed a problem, since leaving those cases in would create a set of homicides which do not correspond to modern homicide cases. In the final analysis, the cases eliminated were those which involved being run over by a car or truck, abortions, deaths during medical procedures other than abortions, and alcohol poisonings. This left us with a total sample of 9095 "intentional victim" cases.

From the defendants② in these cases, there were 103 sentenced to death as coded in the files. In addition, there were eleven more cases in which an execution was recorded as having occurred, but there no coding of having been sentenced to death. This produced 114 cases in which a defendant was sentenced to death, whether subsequently executed or not, or was executed (with the assumption he had been so sentenced first, despite not having been so coded).

A. The Use of Occupation as a Surrogate③ for Poverty

While there is no variable measuring the income of the offender (and one would be useless given the problems discussed earlier), it is possible to at least consider the role of economic status by a consideration of the occupation in those cases in which occupation is recorded. In the past this has been less than useful because of the rarity with which this is recorded. That proved to be the case in this sample as well, with only fourteen percent of the 9095 cases having the victim's occupation listed. From among the sample of refinery four capital cases, slightly better than seventeen percent have their occupation recorded.

B. Race and the Census Data

The census data for Chicago for 1870 through 1930 were obtained from the U. S. Census reports. In these counts, the categories change so that it is impossible to do a complete consideration of ethnicity. In 1870 the only race/ethnicity categories are white, colored, and Indian. In 1880 "Chinese or Japanese" is added, in 1890 Colored becomes Negro, Indian becomes Civilized Indians, and Chinese and Japanese are split into individual categories. Among whites, a breakdown of Native Born of Native Parents, Native Born of Foreign Parents, and Foreign Born are present in

---

① caveats：附件说明；警告。
② defendant：被告，为通用语，可用于一般民事或刑事案件的初审中。accused 专指刑事被告。
③ surrogate：a substitute, esp. a person deputizing for another in a specific role or office,替代,代理。

1900 and 1910, then only Native and Foreign Born in 1920 and 1930. Despite these changes, these are census data and do appear to be reasonably accurate, at least for the overall white and black populations. The rates that can be computed reliably across the entire time frame of this analysis, then, are the total rate and the black and white rate. Given the small number of individuals (or offenders) in other categories and the dominance of race as a salient factor[①] for the system and for our concerns, this was not a problem.

IV Analysis: Homicide and Capital Punishment in Chicago

The nature of the database and the general research on capital punishment led us to seek answers to the following four basic sets of questions. Taken together, the answers to these questions should give us a broad picture of the use of capital punishment in murder cases in Chicago from 1870 to 1930.

1. What proportion of homicides in Chicago resulted in a death sentence? Do these numbers change over time, and does the percentage of homicides resulting in a death sentence change over time?

2. Are there differences in the victims and offenders in death penalty homicides along racial or economic lines? Also, are the crimes themselves different, particularly do they tend to occur in the commission of another felony?

3. Were the people sentenced actually executed? Were there racial differences in the processing of death penalty cases once the sentence had been handed down?

4. Do the victims and offenders in these death penalty homicides represent the demographic composition of Chicago at the time?

Again, specifically are the death penalty homicide rates larger for minority populations?

V Capital Cases from 1870 to 1930, Numbers, Proportions, and Changes

Not all cases of homicide, nor even all relevant or applicable cases of homicide, result in a charge, conviction, or sentence to death. As noted previously, there were 103 cases in which the offender was coded as being sentenced to death and 11 cases in which the offender was coded as being executed but without having been initially coded as sentenced to death. We reviewed each of these cases, and were able to confirm that in all 114 of these situations an offender was, in fact, sentenced to death. Of this total, we were then able to confirm that in seventy-six of these cases, at least one offender sentenced was executed.

From our set of 9095 "intentional victim" cases this suggests that about 1.2% of all of these cases resulted in a death sentence. Further, overall only about 0.96% of these cases resulted in an offender being executed. It is interesting to observe how closely these percentages match modern data.

In 1997, across the United States, 256 prisoners were received from the courts under sentence of death. That same year, there were 18,209 murders reported to the Federal Bureau of In-

---

① salient factor: 突出因素。

vestigation. Again, we must stress that the statistics we are going to derive from this are not precise, and depend upon a series of assumptions. All of those sentenced to death were obviously not offenders who committed their crime in 1997, for example. However, these numbers do give us at least a basis for making some reasoned estimates, and are instructive to consider if one keeps their limitations clearly in mind.

Assuming the numbers of homicides do not change too dramatically from one year to another (there were 18,209 in 1997 and 19,645 in 1996, for example), and assuming that in the current system it takes a few months to a year from the date of the crime to reach a capital punishment verdict, it appears that about 1.4% of the murders in any given year result in a sentence of death. It is much more suspect to compare the actual number of executions and murders in any given year, of course, since under the current system it is anywhere from three to twenty-plus years from a murder to the execution of the offender for that murder. However, again, we can make a very broad statement. There were 74 executions in 1997, and 18,209 homicides. Using only these data, we find a baseline in which the number of executions in 1997 was 0.4% of the number of homicides that year. If we assume an average of seven years from a homicide to the execution for that homicide, then these seventy-four executions in 1997 actually represent homicides that occurred in 1990. In that year, there were 23,438 homicides, so we would estimate that 0.3% of those homicides (74 of the 23,438) resulted in executions.

Review of the case files indicates that the lag from homicide to execution problem existing in the modern criminal justice system was not present during the Chicago data era. Executions commonly occurred within a year, frequently within a few months, of the crime. In these data, then, the lag problem is not an issue.

There is again remarkable consistency for most of the decades, with 0.7% to 1.7% of all homicides resulting in the death penalty. However, there is a significant decrease in the proportion of homicides which result in executions during the 1910's, which drops to an unusual low of 0.2%. This proportion begins to return to the levels seen in previous decades, and the data from the single year 1930 imply that the decline in the proportion from 1910 through the 1920's was out of the ordinary. Unfortunately, there is nothing in the data which provides any reason, or even any clues, as to why this occurred. This simply remains an anomaly[①]that will require historical research into other data sources to resolve. In general, however, it appears that the percentage of cases resulting in the death penalty is not only relatively consistent through this era, but is very similar to modern percentages as well.

VI The Nature of the Crime and the Death Sentence

The cases of those who were sentenced to death cover the range of events that lead to homicide, but the cases of those who are eventually executed are heavily concentrated in two areas: robberies and killings of peace officers.

Of the eighteen cases in which a sentence of death was handed down but later reversed or

---

① anomaly:反常;异常现象。

commuted, five involved robberies of some kind, three were domestic quarrels (or related to domestic quarrels), and the remaining ten were the result of arguments among strangers or friends, or the causes were simply not listed. Some of these arguments appear to be as trivial as those that lead to homicide today. In 1916 one fifty-five year old victim was stabbed to death (ten stab wounds) by a saloon keeper because he would not stop singing. In 1926 another victim is stabbed in a fight precipitated when he tells several men to get out of his stairway for making too much noise.

Among the cases in which the offender was executed there are two pronounced types. In twenty-two of these seventy-six cases, or twenty-nine percent, the homicide occurs in the commission of a robbery or a burglary. In another nineteen cases (twenty-five percent) the victim is a peace officer. Thus, in fully fifty-four percent of all of the cases resulting in the execution of an offender, the case either involved a robbery or a burglary, or the victim was a police officer. Further, there are three cases in which a notation is made of evidence of rape, or that the victim was "ravished," which means that in almost sixty percent of these executions the victim was a police officer, or the homicide occurred during the commission of another felony.

Clearly, and in line with its reputation on this issue, Chicago does not like the killing of its officers. Of the total of twenty-seven cases involving a robbery or burglary in which a death sentence was handed down, the cases were equally likely to result in the offender being executed (twenty-two of seventy-six, or twenty-nine percent of all those executed) or not executed (five of eighteen, or twenty-eight percent of those not executed). However, in those cases in which a death sentence was given and the victim was a peace officer, fully 100% of the offenders were subsequently executed.

In short, the descriptions of these situations from a century ago are strikingly close to the descriptions we find in current cases. Those cases in which the offender is sentenced to death are most commonly those which involve another concurrent① felony②, or in which the victim is a police officer. Of the remaining cases, there is nothing obvious in the description to suggest why one offender is given the death penalty and executed, another given the death penalty and not executed, and yet another not sentenced to death.

VII Conclusions: the consistency of race and poverty

Perhaps the most interesting single finding from the analysis of these data is the similarity of the patterns found in Chicago to the findings from all other places and times in the United States. Black life is devalued. The black homicide rate is consistently higher, and the percentage of all executions which involve blacks is higher for each decade in the 1900's except 1910 to 1920 (with no conclusion drawn for the single year 1930). Further, among all executions for which the race of the victim is known, ninety percent involve white victims, ten percent involve black victims, and in no case is a white man executed for killing a black man. And as to the economics of execution,

---

① concurrent: n. 同时发生的事件; a. 同时发生的, 一致的。
② felony: 重罪, 与 misdemeanour (轻罪) 相对应。

from what little data are available we may not be able to say that most people on death row during this time were poor, we can say with more certainty that few, if any, of them were rich.

Cases in which the offender is sentenced to death commonly involve a concurrent felony or a peace officer as a victim. It appears that if the concurrent felony involves more than one victim or the offenders are known to have engaged in a series of crimes, the offenders sentenced are more likely to be executed, although this is anecdotal and based on a very small number of cases. But if an offender kills a peace officer in Chicago and is sentenced to death, the sentence is carried out.

Even the general pattern of capital punishment for homicide remains similar over the period of time represented, and is similar to modern patterns. A surprisingly close percentage of homicide cases appear to result in a death sentence when we compare the Chicago data to present data, and a very similar number of those cases which do receive a death sentence appear to result in execution.

And finally, the reasons for those homicides for which people are executed seem to have changed little. Husbands kill wives, robbers kill their victims, and drunks kill each other. If capital punishment were having some effect, we would expect to see some change or improvement. Yet it appears that the one outstanding fact from these data is that we are entering a new century with patterns which are strikingly similar to those with which we entered the last century, and the fact that we are finally willing to execute a white person for the murder of a black person is not the evidence of humanitarian progress we might have wished over that past century.

Legal Terminology

1. homicide, killing, manslaughter 与 murder

以上这些单词均有杀人的含义。目前市面流行的英汉词典,包括一些较常用的英汉法律词典在内,对其中的一些词,如 homicide 和 manslaughter 等的译法都存在一些问题,须认真予以矫正。在这些单词中,killing 为通用词,其并非严格意义上的法律术语,其可用于指一切杀人行为,即包括 homicide(他杀,即 to kill someone)与 suicide(自杀,即 to kill oneself)两种。

homicide 为"他杀",为一正式法律术语,指一个人的作为或不作为导致或促使他人的死亡,其为中性词,并非就道德或法律判定该行为一定为犯罪或有过错。在刑法上"他杀"可分为"无罪杀人"及"有罪杀人"两种。无罪杀人(lawful homicide)包括"正当杀人"(justifiable homicide),即指合法将人致死的行为,行为人应被推定无罪,其常发生在处决死刑罪犯、罪犯拒捕、警方驱散暴民等场合;"可宽恕的杀人"(excusable homicide),指意外事故致人死亡或自卫过程中的杀人,杀人者的行为合法,且尽了应有的注意,其不应受到法律的惩处;注意的是 justifiable homicide 有时也用于指 excusable homicide。"有罪杀人"(felonious homicide),也称为 criminal homicide 或 culpable homicide,指无正当法律理由杀人而触犯刑律之情况。

普通法上的"有罪杀人"(felonious 或 criminal homicide)又包括 murder(谋杀)和 manslaughter(非预谋杀人罪)两种:murder(谋杀)常可按其情节分为一级和二级等多种等级(cf. murder),而"非预谋杀人罪"则分可为 involuntary manslaughter(无故意非预谋杀人罪,如:过失杀人,指在履行合法行为或有过错但非犯罪行为中因未尽到应有的注意或疏忽或因缺乏规定的技术等原因导致他人死亡)和 voluntary manslaughter(非预谋但故意杀人罪,如:激情杀人"heat of passion"或行为能力减退情况"diminished capacity"下杀人,指一时冲动而故意杀人,也称为 intentional manslaughter)。以往不少英汉法律词典都将 manslaughter 翻译为"过失杀人"(注:过失杀人的正译应为:negligent homicide 或 criminally negligent homicide),此种译法当然不全面,一是因 manslaughter 是与"谋杀"相对,主要指的是是否有预谋(malice),是否有作案的预备过程,而非特指是否具有过失(neglect);二是其含有"激情杀人",有杀人故意,故此时将其译为"过失杀人"肯定不妥。此外,有的法律词典还将 manslaughter in self-defense 译为"自卫杀人",这也为一错误,这是因为 manslaughter 本身的含义是一种"犯罪",故其只能译为"防卫过当致人死亡罪"。

2. aggrieved party, injured person 与 victim

乍看上去,上述单词或词组似乎均有"受害人"的含义,但究其内涵差异却极大。首先是 aggrieved party,因单词 aggrieve 在表示"伤害"或"不公正对待"时,只适用于法律场合情况下的伤害,故在法律英语中,aggrieved party(也称为 party aggrieved 或 person aggrieved)。专指在司法或准司法程序中其合法权益受到伤害或不公正对待者,即受到认为不公正的判决、命令或惩处者,按规定,此种人具有上诉或申诉之权利地位(standing as an appellant or a petitioner or a complaint)。为与其他"受害人"相区别,最好将其译为"受屈人"或"权益受侵害人"或不服判决、命令等的"上诉人"或"申诉人"。因此,the aggrieved party in a case 便应为"案件受屈人",指在案件中的受到不公正待遇者,或"案件申(上)诉人",指案件中的 plaintiff 或 petitioner,而不应是有些词典中的"案件中受害的一方"或"被害人"。injured person 和 victim 则是指其权利、财产或人身等受到其他当事人伤害者,injured party 指法律诉讼中的曾受到另一方当事人行为伤害的"受害人",即原告。victim 尤指犯罪、侵权或其他过错行为之受害人。

3. evidence

在美国,evidence(证据)之类型(types of evidence)基本可分为两种,即直接(direct evidence)和间接证据(indirect evidence)或旁证(circumstantial evidence)。

证据又可分为三种基本形式(forms of evidence),即言词证据(testimonial evidence),实物证据(tangible evidence)和司法认知(judicial notice)。其中,实物证据即案件中的"展示物品"(physical exhibit),其包括实在证据(real evidence)和示意证据(demonstrative evidence)。实在证据指案件中如凶器等"实实在在的东西",而示意证据则指能表明案件某些情况的视听材料,如现场模型和图示等。司法认知是指无须专门证明即可由法官确认的事实。

此外,证据一般有3大规则:即相关性(relevant),可采性(competent 或 admissible)和实质性(material),与之相对则为无相关性(irrelevant),不可采性(incompetent)和非实质性(immaterial)。

4. false arrest 与 false imprisonment

两个术语均有非法限制他人自由的含义。false arrest 为"非法拘捕",其等同 unlawful arrest,指用非法手段不经他人同意限制其人身自由,其多属于侵权行为,除可处以补偿性(compensatory)或名义(nominal)赔偿金外,还可处以惩罚性赔偿金(punitive damages);如被拘捕者被关押(be taken into custody),不论其时间长短即构成非法拘禁"false imprisonment"(非法拘禁),故有时 false arrest 也被认为是非法拘禁的一种形式(a species of false imprisonment)。false imprisonment 是指故意或过失地限制他人人身自由,其可属普通法上民事侵权行为,也可属于一种犯罪,如绑架罪即为非法拘禁的一种形式。

5. civil court、civil custody、civil prison 与 civil prisoner

在翻译以上术语时人们经常会犯错误,故务必要小心才行。首先应注意的是 civil court,该词组除在英、美等国指"民事法院"外,在其他地区,如在加拿大,它可用作指具有一般管辖权(包括具有简易审判程序)的刑事法院,其与民事无任何关系,civil 在此等同 ordinary,故应译为"普通刑事法院"。同样,civil custody 也是指警方或其他相关民政当局"对一般罪犯所作的拘留或关押"(普通监狱"civil prison"或教养所"penitentiary"的关押均包括在内)。civil prison 则可指任何关押由普通刑事法院(civil court)经简易审判程序(summary procedure)审判的罪行较轻、刑期在 2 年以下罪犯之监狱(包括 jail 和其他场所),故为"普通监狱"。由此可知,civil prisoner 则是指由 civil court 所判处的被 civil prison 关押的刑期为 2 年以下的"普通服刑犯"。对于 civil prisoner 而言,《英汉法律词典》的新版本更正了其第一版将该术语译为"民事犯"之谬误,将其译为"普通犯",然而该词典援引的《法窗译话》之解释,即"普通犯"是"与政治犯、国事犯、军事犯、战犯等对称时用"的解释却仍然应为谬误,这里的"普通"两字,实则应为"罪行较轻"的含义。

6. defendant、respondent、accused、defender 与 libel(l)ee

上述这些单词均有"被告"的含义。其中,defendant 为通用语,可用于一般民事或刑事案件的初审中,与其相对的原告为 plaintiff。respondent 用于上诉审(此时也称为 appellee)及申请获得特别命令或离婚、遗嘱验证等衡平法案件中,与其相对的原告(或上诉人)有 appellant, petitioner, applicant 等。accused 专指刑事被告;与之相对的原告有 plaintiff(刑事自诉人)或 prosecution(公诉方)。defender 则是苏格兰专门用语,与其相对的原告为 pursuer。libel(l)ee 则专指海事或离婚案件的原告,与其相对的原告为 libel(l)ant。

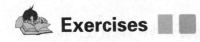
Exercises

I Verbal abilities

Part One

Directions: *For each of these questions, read each item carefully to get the sense of it. Then, in the proper space, complete each statement by supplying the missing word or phrase.*

1. The _____ must stop the infringement at once and compensate for the loss.

　　A. culprit　　　　　　B. criminal　　　　　　C. malefactor

　　D. offender　　　　　E. felon

2. The _____ source of our confidence is, of course, the solid promises of the constitutional document, our Basic Law.

　　A. ultimate　　　　　B. elementary　　　　　C. concluding

　　D. eventual　　　　　E. terminal

3. But conditions are still fragile and much more remains to be done on both the _____ and diplomatic fronts.

A. improver B. humanist C. humanistic
D. sympathetic E. humanitarian

4. That country's penchant for _____ is explained by a dictatorship which has a low regard for citizens' rights and uses violence as an instrument of the state power.

A. performance B. execution C. implementation
D. effectuation E. actualization

5. Trade growth is _____ higher on average than overall economic growth but it also tends to be more variable, dropping sharply during recessions.

A. systematically B. uniformly C. consistently
D. compatibly E. contradictorily

6. Laws bar Miss Suu Kyi from office both as the widow of a foreigner, and, under a rule that also debars many of the League's other leaders, as the holder of a criminal _____.

A. sentence B. conviction C. acquittal
D. condemnation E. confirmation

7. Most crimes involve socially unacceptable conduct that unreasonably interferes with another's interests, e. g., arson, _____, manslaughter, murder, rape, and robbery.

A. burglary B. theft C. larceny
D. pilfering E. pilferage

8. The defendant's lawyers said his trial was hasty and that, although their statements were read into evidence, _____ testifying against him did not appear in court to face cross-examination.

A. witnesses B. speculators C. informants
D. attestants E. testimony

9. Applied ethics concerns specific controversial issues, such as abortion, infanticide, animal rights, environmental concerns, homosexuality, capital _____, or nuclear war.

A. penalty B. sanction C. punishment
D. forfeiture E. deprivation

10. Thousands of Chinese-flagged merchant ships now cross the ocean each year, giving China plenty of _____ for increasing its naval presence.

A. opportunity B. occasions C. function
D. justification E. juncture

Part Two

Directions: *Choose the word or phase that best keeps the meaning of the original sentence if it substitutes for the underlined part.*

1. I think she hurt my feelings <u>deliberately</u> rather than by accidents as she claimed.

A. virtually B. intentionally C. literally
D. appropriately E. accidentally

2. As a <u>versatile</u> actor, he can perform, sing, dance and play several kinds of musical instruments.

A. flexible B. sophisticated C. talented

D. productive E. adaptable

3. There are not many teachers who are strong advocates of traditional methods in English teaching.

A. sponsors B. contributors C. counsel

D. proponent E. pleaders

4. We managed to reach the top of the mountain, and half an hour later we began to descend.

A. ascend B. decline C. plunge

D. immerse E. go down

5. Competition, they believe, intensifies the national character rather than corrupts it.

A. heightens B. enforces C. confirms

D. strengthens E. escalates

6. The reason for believing that prolonged life is an evolutionary response to starvation rather than just a weird accident is that when an animal is starving, the evolutionary calculus changes.

A. lengthy B. extended C. chronical

D. strengthened E. protracted

7. On weekends my grandma usually indulges in a glass of wine.

A. subscribes to B. engages in C. hangs on

D. feeds up with E. enjoys herself with

8. People living in these apartments have free access to that swimming pool.

A. excess B. excursion C. amusement

D. entrance E. recreations

9. At the party we found that shy girl clinging to her mother all the time.

A. depending on B. coinciding with C. adhering to

D. complying with E. holding on

10. When you put up the wallpaper, should you _____ the edges or put them next to each other?

A. coincide B. extend C. stretch

D. collide E. overlap

II Cloze

Directions: *For each blank in the following passage, choose the best answer from the choices given.*

In the immediate post-Furman years, the first executions were predominately older, white males. Today, the balance on death row reflects, in __(1)__, the levels of involvement in homicide of blacks and whites as offenders. However, a more __(2)__ racism appears to continue to exist. Probably __(3)__ what Darnell Hawkins calls the devaluation of black life, the odds (可能性) of being __(4)__ and sentenced are significantly higher if the victim of the homicide is __(5)__. Widmayer and Marquart argue that "clearly, the most salient racial __(6)__ in post-

Lesson Eight U. S. Legal History on Capital Punishment

Furman capital punishment is the frequency in which white victim cases result in death sentences. "

Certainly, the raw numbers themselves seem to __(7)__ an argument that white life is somehow valued __(8)__ in the processing of capital murder cases. Of the 598 offenders __(9)__ in the United States from 1977 to January 1, 2000, fifty-six percent were white; thirty-five percent were __(10)__. This is obviously higher than the twelve percent of the general population which is black, but on the surface appears to be much more racially __(11)__ when compared to the population of homicide offenders, of whom just under fifty percent are black. __(12)__, the current racial breakdown of offenders on death row __(13)__ execution is very close to the actual involvement in homicides, with forty-seven percent being white and forty-three percent black. __(14)__, any apparent equity disappears completely when one looks at the race of the victim of those who have been executed. Eighty-two percent of the victims of the 598 executed offenders were white, but only twelve percent were black. Thus, while we seem to be coming __(15)__ to the actual percentages of involvement in homicides in our populations on death row, it is clear that one's odds of being sentenced to death if the victim was white are significantly higher than if the victim was not.

(1) A. practice   B. theory   C. fact
    D. reality   E. general
(2) A. different   B. subtle   C. indifferent
    D. interesting   E. harmful
(3) A. reflected   B. reflects   C. reflecting
    D. reflection   E. reflective
(4) A. charged   B. fired   C. dismissed
    D. discharged   E. admitted
(5) A. black   B. white   C. different
    D. greater   E. lower
(6) A. kind   B. sort   C. requirement
    D. factor   E. variety
(7) A. discourage   B. refuse   C. support
    D. abandon   E. prove
(8) A. much   B. greater   C. fewer
    D. less   E. more
(9) A. executed   B. executing   C. executing
    D. executive   E. fulfill
(10) A. color   B. colorful   C. yellow
     D. black   E. white
(11) A. balancing   B. balance   C. balanced
     D. proportion   E. proportionate
(12) A. Farther   B. Further   C. However
     D. In addition   E. Whereas

(13) A. expecting   B. awaiting for   C. awaited
     D. waiting   E. awaiting
(14) A. Forever   B. However   C. While
     D. Further   E. Furthermore
(15) A. next   B. nearer   C. second
     D. closer   E. closest

III Reading Comprehension

Part One

Directions: *In this section there is a passage followed by questions or unfinished statements, each with suggested answers. Choose the one you think is the best answer.*

Legal history or the history of law is the study of how law has evolved and why it changed. Legal history is closely connected to the development of civilizations and is set in the wider context of social history. Among certain jurists and historians of legal process it has been seen as the recording of the evolution of laws and the technical explanation of how these laws have evolved with the view of better understanding the origins of various legal concepts, some consider it a branch of intellectual history①. Twentieth century historians have viewed legal history in a more contextualized manner more in line with the thinking of social historians. They have looked at legal institutions② as complex systems of rules, players and symbols and have seen these elements interact with society to change, adapt, resist or promote certain aspects of civil society. Such legal historians have tended to analyze case histories from the parameters of social science inquiry, using statistical methods, analyzing class distinctions among litigants, petitioners and other players in various legal processes. By analyzing case outcomes, transaction costs, number of settled cases they have begun an analysis of legal institutions, practices, procedures and briefs③ that give us a more complex picture of law and society than the study of jurisprudence, case law④ and civil codes⑤ can achieve.

Ancient world

Ancient Egyptian law, dating as far back as 3000 BC, had a civil code that was probably broken into twelve books. It was based on the concept of Ma'at, characterized by tradition, rhetorical speech, social equality and impartiality. By the 22nd century BC, Ur-Nammu, an ancient Sumerian⑥ ruler, formulated the first law code, consisting of casuistic⑦ statements ("if... then..."). Around 1760 BC, King Hammurabi further developed Babylonian⑧ law, by codifying and inscri-

---

① intellectual history:文化史。
② legal institution:纪纲;法律制度。
③ brief:(律)(供出庭律师用的)案情摘要,诉讼要点。(美)案情申述(呈交法庭的书面材料)。
④ case laws:判例法。
⑤ civil code:民法典。
⑥ Sumerian:闪族人(语)的;(与)苏美尔语(有关)的。
⑦ casuistic:决疑的;诡辩的。
⑧ Babylonian:巴比伦的,与巴比伦有关的。

bing it in stone. Hammurabi①placed several copies of his law code throughout the kingdom of Babylon as stelae, for the entire public to see; this became known as the Codex Hammurabi. The most intact copy of these stelae was discovered in the 19th century by British Assyriologists②, and has since been fully transliterated and translated into various languages, including English, German and French. The Torah③from the Old Testament④is probably the oldest body of law still relevant for modern legal systems, dating back to 1280 BC. It takes the form of moral imperatives⑤, like the Ten Commandments⑥and the Noahide Laws, as recommendations for a good society. Ancient Athens, the small Greek city-state, was the first society based on broad inclusion of the citizenry, excluding women and the slave class. Athens had no legal science, and Ancient Greek has no word for "law" as an abstract concept, retaining instead the distinction between divine law (thémis), human decree (nomos) and custom (díkē). Yet Ancient Greek law contained major constitutional innovations in the development of democracy.

Southern Asia

Ancient India and China represent distinct traditions of law, and had historically independent schools of legal theory and practice⑦. The Shastra⑧, dating from the 400 BC, and the Smriti⑨from 100 AD were influential treatises⑩in India, texts that were considered authoritative legal guidance. Manu's⑪central philosophy was tolerance and pluralism, and was cited across South East Asia. But this Hindu tradition, along with Islamic law, was supplanted by the common law when India became part of the British Empire. Malaysia, Brunei, Singapore and Hong Kong also adopted the common law.

Eastern Asia

The eastern Asia legal tradition reflects a unique blend of secular and religious influences. Japan was the first country to begin modernizing its legal system along western lines, by importing bits of the French, but mostly the German Civil Code. This partly reflected Germany's status as a rising power in the late nineteenth century. Similarly, traditional Chinese law gave way to westernization towards the final years of the Qing dynasty in the form of six private law codes based mainly on the Japanese model of German law. Today Taiwanese "law" retains the closest affinity to the

---

① Hammurabi：汉谟拉比（死于公元前 1750 年，巴比伦王国第一个王朝的第六个国王，统治时期为公元前 1792—前 1750 年，扩大了巴比伦帝国并制定了迄今所知的最早的法典）。
② Assyriologist：亚述研究者，亚述专家。
③ Torah：（犹太教的）律法书，托拉；上帝向摩西启示的律法，记录于《旧约》首五卷，即《摩西五经》。
④ Old Testament：《旧约全书》（基督教《圣经》的第一部分，由 39 卷组成，大致相当于希伯来《圣经》；写于约公元前 1200—前 100 年，其中大部分是用希伯来语写的，部分用阿拉姆语写成，构成了古以色列人主要的法律、历史、预言和智慧文献）。
⑤ moral imperatives：道德规则。
⑥ Ten Commandments：《圣经》十诫：根据《出埃及记》20：11，上帝在西奈山上向摩西吐露的十条有关生活和礼拜的法规。
⑦ independent schools of legal theory and practice：法律理论与实践的独立学派。
⑧ Shastra：印度教经典。
⑨ Smriti：传承；印度教传统宗教教义经籍，如《摩诃婆罗多》。
⑩ treatises：专题著作。
⑪ Manu：摩奴：印度神话中人的原型，大洪水的幸存者和人类的祖先；传说他还是最著名的印度宗教法典之一—《摩奴法典》的制定者，该法典用梵语写成，今本可追溯到公元前 1 世纪。

codifications from that period and the current legal infrastructure in the People's Republic of China was heavily influenced by soviet Socialist law, which essentially inflates administrative law at the expense of private law rights. Today, however, because of rapid industrialization China has been reforming, at least in terms of economic (if not social and political) rights. A new contract code in 1999 represented a turn away from administrative domination. Furthermore, after negotiations lasting fifteen years, in 2001 China joined the World Trade Organization.

1. Legal history is the study of _____.

A. the evolution of law and reasons for the changes of law

B. the development of civilizations

C. the context of social history

D. the recording of the evolution of laws and the technical explanation of how

2. Historians in the twentieth century viewed legal history as _____.

A. the process of interactions with social changes

B. something contextualized more in line with the thinking of social historians

C. complex systems of rules, players and symbols

D. the adaptation, resistance, or promotion of certain aspects of civil society

3. Which of the following is true of Ancient Egyptian law?

A. it has a history of over 3000 years.

B. it was written in twelve volumes.

C. it has a history of over 5000 years with the form of a civil code based on the concept of Ma'at, advocating social equality and impartiality.

D. it is a kind of speech written by Ma'at.

4. Which of the following statement is **NOT** true of Hammurabi?

A. he was a king and in about 1760 he codified Babylonian law and inscribed it in stone.

B. he spread the law code inscribed in stelae throughout his kingdom with the purpose that all the public could see it.

C. he had the law code inscribed in stone and it later became known as Codex Hammurabi.

D. he had the law code fully transliterated and translated into various languages, including English, German and French.

5. As to ancient laws, which of the following is true?

A. The Ten Commandments takes the form of moral imperatives written in the Old Testament.

B. The Old Testament has in it something that is law in the modern sense.

C. In the small Greek city-state, ancient Athens formed the first society, with all people in it regarded as citizenry.

D. Athens' legal science contained major constitutional innovations in the development of democracy.

6. According to the passage, which of the following statements is **NOT** true?

A. The legal tradition in eastern Asia was uniquely influenced by both secular customs and religious doctrines.

B. The reason why Japan imported mostly the German Civil Code was partly that Germany was rising as a power in the late nineteenth century.

C. In the later years of the Qing dynasty, traditional Chinese law absorbed western law spirit and formed private law codes mainly based on the German law after the Japanese model.

D. Both the mainland's and Taiwan's legal infrastructure was heavily influenced by Soviet socialist law.

7. According to the author, which of the following is true?

A. Today Taiwanese "law" retains the closest affinity to the codifications from the period of the later Qing dynasty.

B. The PRC's law has administrative law and private law, with the latter more powerfully enforced than the former.

C. China has been equally reforming its citizenry's economic, social, and political rights.

D. A new contract code in 1999 represented that the administrative law was no longer dominative in China compared with other branches of law.

Part Two   True or False Questions

Direction: *In this part of the exercise, there is a passage with true or false questions. Read the passage carefully and mark T if it is true and F if it is false.*

One of the major legal systems developed during the Middle Ages was Islamic law and jurisprudence. A number of important legal institutions were developed by Islamic jurists during the classical period of Islamic law and jurisprudence. One such institution was the Hawala, an early informal value transfer system, which is mentioned in texts of Islamic jurisprudence as early as the 8th century. Hawala itself later influenced the development of the Aval in French civil law and the Avallo in Italian law.

Roman law was heavily influenced by Greek teachings. It forms the bridge to the modern legal world, over the centuries between the rise and decline of the Roman Empire. Roman law, in the days of the Roman republic and Empire, was heavily procedural and there was no professional legal class. Instead a lay person, index, was chosen to adjudicate. Precedents were not reported, so any case law that developed was disguised and almost unrecognized. Each case was to be decided afresh from the laws of the state, which mirrors the (theoretical) unimportance of judges' decisions for future cases in civil law systems today. During the 6th century AD in the Eastern Roman Empire, the Emperor Justinian codified and consolidated the laws that had existed in Rome so that what remained was one twentieth of the mass of legal texts from before. This became known as the Corpus Juris Civilis[①]. As one legal historian wrote, "Justinian consciously looked back to the golden age of Roman law and aimed to restore it to the peak it had reached three centuries before."

During the Byzantine Empire the Justinian Code was expanded and remained in force until the Empire fell, though it was never officially introduced to the West. Instead, following the fall of the Western Empire and in former Roman countries, the ruling classes relied on the Theodosian Code

---

① Corpus Juris Civilis: 《民法法典》。

to govern natives and Germanic customary law for the Germanic incomers—a system known as folk-right—until the two laws blended together. Since the Roman court system had broken down, legal disputes were adjudicated according to Germanic custom by assemblies of learned law speakers in rigid ceremonies and in oral proceedings that relied heavily on testimony. After much of the West was consolidated under Charlemagne, law became centralized so as to strengthen the royal court system, and consequently case law, and abolished folk-right. However, once Charlemagne's kingdom definitively splintered, Europe became feudalistic, and law was generally not governed above the county, municipal or lordship level, thereby creating a highly decentralized legal culture that favored the development of customary law founded on localized case law. However, in the 11th century, Crusaders, having pillaged the Byzantine Empire, returned with Byzantine legal texts including the Justinian Code, and scholars at the University of Bologna① were the first to use them to interpret their own customary laws. Medieval European legal scholars began researching the Roman law and using its concepts and prepared the way for the partial resurrection of Roman law as the modern civil law in a large part of the world. There was, however, a great deal of resistance so that civil law rivaled customary law for much of the latter medieval period. After the Norman conquest of England, which introduced Norman legal concepts into medieval England, the English King's powerful judges developed a body of precedent that became the common law. In particular, Henry II instituted legal reforms and developed a system of royal courts administered by a small number of judges who lived in Westminster and traveled throughout the kingdom. Henry II also instituted the Assize of Clarendon in 1166, which allowed for jury trials and reduced the number of trials by combat. Louis IX of France also undertook major legal reforms and, inspired by ecclesiastical② court procedure, extended Canon-law evidence and inquisitorial-trial systems to the royal courts. Also, judges no longer moved on circuits becoming fixed to their jurisdictions, and jurors were nominated by parties to the legal dispute rather than by the sheriff. In addition, by the 10th century, the Law Merchant, first founded on Scandinavian trade customs, then solidified by the Hanseatic League, took shape so that merchants could trade using familiar standards, rather than the many splintered types of local law. A precursor to modern commercial law, the Law Merchant emphasized the freedom of contract and alienability of property.

The two main traditions of modern European law are the codified legal systems of most of continental Europe, and the English tradition based on case law.

As nationalism grew in the 18th and 19th centuries, lex③ mercatoria was incorporated into countries' local law under new civil codes. Of these, the French Napoleonic Code and the German Bürgerliches Gesetzbuch became the most influential. As opposed to English common law, which consists of massive tomes of case law, codes in small books are easy to export and for judges to apply. However, today there are signs that civil and common law are converging. European Union law is codified in treaties, but develops through the precedent sat down by the European Court of

---

① Bologna：博洛尼亚；意大利北部城市，艾米利亚罗马涅区首府，1990 年人口 411,800；该市有欧洲最古老的大学，建于 11 世纪。
② ecclesiastical：基督教的；与教会有关的。
③ lex：(拉)法；法律；法律体系。

Justice.

The United States legal system developed primarily out of the English common law system (with the exception of the state of Louisiana, which continued to follow the French civilian system after being admitted to statehood). Some concepts from Spanish law, such as the prior appropriation doctrine and community property①, still persist in some U.S. states, particularly those that were part of the Mexican Cession in 1848. Under the doctrine of federalism②, each state has its own separate court system, and the ability to legislate within areas not reserved to the federal government.

1. Islamic jurists developed plenty of important legal institutions during the classical period of Islamic law and jurisprudence. (   )

2. Greek teachings greatly influenced Roman law which was heavily procedural and there was no professional legal class. (   )

3. In Roman law, a professional person was chosen to adjudicate the case but precedents were not reported, so any case law was almost unrecognized. (   )

4. The Justinian Code was officially introduced to the West, expanded and remained in force until the fall of the Byzantine Empire. (   )

5. After much of the West was consolidated under Charlemagne, to strengthen the royal court system, law became centralized. (   )

6. The modern civil law in a large part of the world is based on Roman law whose concepts remain unchanged because of the research of Medieval European legal scholars. (   )

7. The Norman Conquest introduced Norman legal concepts into medieval England, and English judges developed a body of precedent that became the common law. (   )

8. The codified legal systems of most of continental Europe and case law legal system of the U.K. are two main traditions of modern European law. (   )

9. The reason why civil and common law are converging is that English common law that consists of massive tomes of case law makes it easier for judges to apply and codes that are written in small books are easy to export. (   )

10. All the fifty states in the U.S. have their legal system developed out of the English common law system. (   )

IV Translation Abilities

法律语言特征分析与法律翻译技能培养之八：

立法语言与翻译

立法语言指规范性法律文件使用的语言。宪法、各种法律、法规、决定、命令、条例、立法解释以及司法解释等法律文件均可称为规范性法律文件。这类文件具有规范性和约束力。立法语言由于具有上述特点，为此各国均十分重视这种语言的表现形式，总是用特定的方式来表明公民的权利和义务、确定人们行为规范准则。具体地说，这些规范可以分为义务性规

---

① community property：夫妻共有财产。
② federalism：联邦政治；联邦制度。

范、授权性规范和禁止性规范。各种规范若用汉语和英语两种语言进行表述,大致分为:

(1) 表示义务性规范的语言:义务性规范是"规定法律关系主体必须依法作出一定行为的法律规范",其汉语的表达方式是"有……的义务"、"必须"等;英语的表达方式是"It is the duty of..."、"have the duty of..."、"shall"、"must"等。如:"中华人民共和国公民有依照法律纳税的义务",可以翻译成:"It is the duty of citizens of the People's Republic of China to pay taxes in accordance with the law.""All foreign enterprises, other foreign organizations as well as Chinese-foreign joint venture companies within Chinese territory shall abide by the law of the People's Republic of China."可以翻译成:"在中国境内的外国企业和其他外国经济组织以及中外合资的企业,都必须遵守中华人们共和国的法律。"

(2) 表示禁止性规范的语言表示方法:禁止性规范是指禁止法律关系主体为某种行为的法律规范。汉语的表达方通常是"严禁"、"禁止"、"不得"、"不能"等,而英语的表达方式表示禁止意义的"prohibit"词外,还可以 使用"shall not"、"may not"、"must not"、"not allowed"等方式表示。如:"禁止对任何民族的歧视和压迫,禁止破坏民族团结和制造民族分裂的行为"可以译为:"Discrimination against and oppression of any nationality are prohibited; any act which undermines the unity or instigates division between or among any nationality is prohibited.""All judgements and orders of the Supreme People's Court, as well as judgements and orders that may not be appealed according to law or have not been appealed within the prescribed time limit, shall be legally effective."可以翻译成:"最高人民法院的判决、裁定以及依法不准上诉或者超过上诉期没有上诉的判决、裁定,是发生法律效力的判决、裁定。"

(3) 表示授权性规范的语言:授权性规范指的是"规定法律关系主体依法有权自己权为某种行为以及要求他人为或不为某种行为的法律规范"。其汉语的表达方式为"享有……的权利"、"有权……"等等,而英语的表达方式是"have the right to..."、"enjoy the rights of..."、"be entitled to..."、"may"等。如:"中华人们共和国公民有受教育的权利和义务"可以翻译为:"Citizens of the People's Republic of China have the duty as well as the right to receive education.""Citizens who makes discoveries shall be entitled to the rights of discovery."可以翻译为:"公民对自己的发现享有发现权。"

此外,shall一词在立法语言中的使用频率也极高,它在条约、规章、法令等文献中常常可以表示责任、义务、命令、禁止等意思。翻译时,常常可以译为"必须"、"应当"等意思,而其否定形式译成"不得"。如:

"The people's court shall, in accordance with the prescribed procedures, collect and examine evidence comprehensively and objectively."(译文:"人民法院应当按照法定程序,全面、客观地搜集和调查证据。")

"The user of a trademark shall be responsible for the quality of the goods on which the trademark is used."(译文:"商标使用人应当对其使用商标的商品质量负责。")

Translation Exercises:

Part One *Put the Following into Chinese*

However, the number of executions has increased to over 100 in 2000. If we assume about 100 executions in 2002, based on the 21,606 homicides that occurred in 1995, then around 0.5% of homicides may eventually result in an actual execution. These are approximations, and varying the assumptions made, first, about length of time from murder to execution and, and second, about the average number of executions to be expected in any given year, this percentage can easily vary from 0.3% to 0.8%. If, for example, we assume the increase in the number of executions continues, and we reach 150 executions a year by 2004, those executions being from the 18,209 homicides in 1997, then 0.8% of homicides will result in executions. In fact, this estimated range of 0.3% to 0.8% is a calculated best guess. But even with this range, and given the assumptions that have to be made, these figures closely match the data from Chicago of a century ago.

Further, with the changes in society that occurred over the fifty years represented in this database, it is reasonable to consider whether the proportion of all homicides which resulted in a death penalty has changed. Again, we must caution that the calculation of these changes rests upon assumptions as to the validity of the early data.

Part Two *Put the following into English*

最终导致死刑判决的杀人行为的其他主要类别是那些涉及另外一种类型的犯罪行为,最常见的是抢劫或者入室盗窃。在检查每个案件里所能得到的有限数据时,有趣的是看到了罪犯最终被执行死刑的杀人抢劫案与罪犯被判处死刑但却并未执行死刑的案件并没有什么明显的区别。在罪犯被执行死刑的22起案件中,4起发生在大厅或台球房,6起发生在街上,11起发生在企业(只有一起发生在家里)。在5个没有执行死刑的案件中,2起发生在大厅,一起在街上,另外2起在企业。卷宗描述的情况似乎类似。1901年一个11岁的受害者"在台球房……,被拦路抢劫(holdup)的三人中的一个人在抢劫该地时枪杀",最后罪犯被执行死刑。在某些案件中存在可以解释为什么执行死刑的差异。最常见的差异是案件中受害者不止一人或者查明罪犯之作案方式似乎已为警方熟知,且本案为一系列抢劫案中的一个。但决定生死之差起作用的显然还有其他因素,然而这些在数据中似乎没有出现。

V Interaction

Discuss with your tutor(s) or the People's judges in your locality about China's or the world's main countries' legal history. Then based on the discussion, you are supposed to write a composition about the legal history of a certain country or a certain part of the world. Remember that you are required to express your ideas clearly.

VI Appreciation of the Judge's Opinions

(1) Case Name(案件名):*Furman v. Georgia*

Furman v. Georgia

Supreme Court of the United States

Argued January 17, 1971
Decided June 29, 1972

Full case name	William Henry Furman v. State of Georgia
Citations	408 U. S. 238 (more)
	92 S. Ct. 2726; 33 L. Ed. 2d 346; 1972 U.S. LEXIS 169
Prior history	Certiorari granted (403 U. S. 952)
Subsequent history	Rehearing denied (409 U. S. 902)

Holding

The arbitrary and inconsistent imposition of the death penalty violates the Eighth and Fourteenth Amendments, and constitutes cruel and unusual punishment.

Court membership

Chief Justice
Warren E. Burger
Associate Justices
William O. Douglas · William J. Brennan, Jr.
Potter Stewart · Byron White
Thurgood Marshall · Harry Blackmun
Lewis F. Powell, Jr. · William Rehnquist

Case opinions

Majority	none
Concurrence	Douglas
Concurrence	Brennan
Concurrence	Stewart
Concurrence	White
Concurrence	Marshall
Dissent	Burger, joined by Blackmun, Powell, Rehnquist
Dissent	Blackmun
Dissent	Powell, joined by Burger, Blackmun, Rehnquist
Dissent	Rehnquist, joined by Burger, Blackmun, Powell

Laws applied

U. S. Const. amends. VIII, XIV

U. S. Supreme Court
FURMAN v. GEORGIA, 408 U. S. 238 (1972)
408 U. S. 238
FURMAN v. GEORGIA

Lesson Eight U.S. Legal History on Capital Punishment

CERTIORARI TO THE SUPREME COURT OF GEORGIA

No. 69-5003.

Argued January 17, 1972

Decided June 29, 1972．

(2) Case Summary(案件简介)

Furman v. Georgia, 408 U.S. 238 (1972) was a United States Supreme Court decision that ruled on the requirement for a degree of consistency in the application of the death penalty. The case led to a de facto(拉丁语,实际上的) moratorium(延期偿付权,延期履行权,行动暂停) on capital punishment throughout the United States, which came to an end when *Gregg v. Georgia* was decided in 1976. The Supreme Court consolidated(合并) *Jackson v. Georgia* and *Branch v. Texas* with the Furman decision, and thus also invalidated the death penalty for rape. The Court had also intended to include the case of *Aikens v. California*, but between the time Aikens had been heard in oral argument and a decision was to be issued, the Supreme Court of California decided in *California v. Anderson* that the death penalty violated the state constitution(死刑违反了州宪法), thus the Aikens case was dismissed as moot(无实际意义的) since all death cases in California were overturned.

Background

In the case, the victim awoke in the middle of the night to find William Henry Furman burgling(入室盗窃,破门行盗) in his house. At trial, in an unsworn statement(未经宣誓的陈述) allowed under Georgia criminal procedure, Furman said that while trying to escape, he tripped and the weapon he was carrying fired accidentally, killing the victim. This contradicted his prior statement to police that he had turned and blindly fired a shot(盲目开枪) while fleeing. In either event, because the shooting occurred during the commission of a felony, Furman would have been guilty of murder and eligible for the death penalty under then-extant(当时尚存的/现存的) state law. Furman was tried for murder and was found guilty based largely on his own statement. He was sentenced to death. Although he was sentenced to death, the punishment was never carried out.

Holding

In a 5-4 decision, the Court's one-page per curiam opinion(法院全席意见) held that the imposition of the death penalty in these cases constituted cruel and unusual punishment and violated the Constitution. Each of the justices filed their own concurrences(法官赞同判决但理由各异书面意见) and dissents; none were able to gather more than three other justices to support them. Only Justices Brennan and Marshall believed the death penalty to be unconstitutional in all instances. Other concurrences focused on the arbitrary nature with which death sentences have been imposed, often indicating a racial bias against black defendants(针对黑人被告的种族偏见). The Court's decision forced states and the national legislature to rethink their statutes for capital offenses to assure that the death penalty would not be administered in a capricious or discriminatory manner.

Concurrences

Justices Byron White and William O. Douglas expressed similar concerns about the apparent arbitrariness(任意性,武断性) with which death sentences were imposed under the existing laws.

Justices Brennan and Marshall concurred on the grounds that the death penalty was "cruel and unusual punishment" proscribed by the Eighth Amendment(第八修正条款所禁止的) as incompatible with the evolving standards of decency of a contemporary society. Because the opinions of Justices Stewart and White were the narrowest, finding only that the death penalty as applied under the statutes in existence at the time was cruel and unusual; theirs are often considered the controlling majority opinions.

Dissents

Chief Justice Burger and Justices Harry Blackmun, Lewis F. Powell, and William H. Rehnquist, each appointed by President Richard Nixon, dissented. They argued that capital punishment had always been regarded as appropriate under the Anglo-American legal tradition(英美法系) for serious crimes and that the text of the Constitution implicitly authorized United States death penalty laws because of the reference in the Fourteenth Amendment to the taking of "life."

(3) **Excerpts of the Judgment**(法官判决词)

PER CURIAM(拉丁语,依法院的,由法庭共同议决的(指的是整个法庭的判决意见,而不是其中某一法官的意见);Latin for "by the court." An opinion from an appellate court that does not identify any specific judge who may have written the opinion)

The Court holds that the imposition and carrying out of the death penalty(判处与执行死刑) in these cases constitute cruel and unusual punishment in violation of the Eighth and Fourteenth Amendments(违反了第八和第十四修正条款). The judgment in each case is therefore reversed(推翻原判) insofar as it leaves undisturbed the death sentence imposed, and the cases are remanded(发回重审) for further proceedings.

MR. JUSTICE DOUGLAS, MR. JUSTICE BRENNAN, MR. JUSTICE STEWART, MR. JUSTICE WHITE, and MR. JUSTICE MARSHALL have filed separate opinions in support of the judgments. THE CHIEF JUSTICE, MR. JUSTICE BLACKMUN, MR. JUSTICE POWELL, and MR. JUSTICE REHNQUIST have filed separate dissenting opinions.

MR. JUSTICE DOUGLAS, concurring.

In these three cases the death penalty was imposed, one of them for murder, and two for rape. In each the determination of whether the penalty should be death or a lighter punishment was left by the State to the discretion of the judge or of the jury. In each of the three cases the trial was to a jury. They are here on petitions for certiorari(申请调卷令) which we granted limited to the question whether the imposition and execution of the death penalty constitute "cruel and unusual punishment" within the meaning of the Eighth Amendment as applied to the States by the Fourteenth. I vote to vacate each judgment(取消各案件的判决), believing that the exaction of the death penalty(强行执行死刑) does violate the Eighth and Fourteenth Amendments.

It has been assumed in our decisions that punishment by death is not cruel, unless the manner of execution can be said to be inhuman and barbarous(惨无人道和野蛮之极). It is also said in our opinions that the proscription of cruel and unusual punishments "is not fastened to the obsolete but may acquire meaning as public opinion becomes enlightened by a humane justice." A like statement was made in *Trop v. Dulles* that the Eighth Amendment "must draw its meaning from the evolving standards of decency(不断演变的礼仪标准) that mark the progress of a maturing society."

The generality of a law inflicting capital punishment is one thing. What may be said of the validity of a law on the books and what may be done with the law in its application do, or may, lead to quite different conclusions.

It would seem to be incontestable(毋庸置疑) that the death penalty inflicted on one defendant is "unusual" if it discriminates against him by reason of his race, religion, wealth, social position, or class, or if it is imposed under a procedure that gives room for the play of such prejudices. . . .

But the debates of the First Congress on the Bill of Rights throw little light on its intended meaning. All that appears is the following:

"Mr. SMITH, of South Carolina, objected to the words 'nor cruel and unusual punishments;' the import(意义,重要性) of them being too indefinite."

"Mr. LIVERMORE: The clause seems to express a great deal of humanity, on which account I have no objection to it; but as it seems to have no meaning in it, I do not think it necessary. What is meant by the terms excessive bail? Who are to be the judges? What is understood by excessive fines? It lies with the court to determine. No cruel and unusual punishment is to be inflicted; it is sometimes necessary to hang a man, villains(坏人,坏蛋;村夫,庄稼汉;隶农,半自由的农奴) often deserve whipping, and perhaps having their ears cut off; but are we in future to be prevented from inflicting these punishments because they are cruel? If a more lenient mode of correcting vice and deterring others from the commission of it could be invented, it would be very prudent in the Legislature to adopt it; but until we have some security that this will be done, we ought not to be restrained from making necessary laws by any declaration of this kind."

The words "cruel and unusual" certainly include penalties that are barbaric. But the words, at least when read in light of the English proscription against selective and irregular use of penalties, suggest that it is "cruel and unusual" to apply the death penalty—or any other penalty—selectively to minorities whose numbers are few, who are outcasts(被驱逐的人,被抛弃的东西;废物;无家可归的人,流浪者;流氓,无赖) of society, and who are unpopular(不受欢迎的;不得人心的;不流行的), but whom society is willing to see suffer though it would not countenance(支持,赞助,鼓动;纵容,默认) general application of the same penalty across the board.

There is increasing recognition of the fact that the basic theme of equal protection is implicit in "cruel and unusual" punishments. "A penalty... should be considered 'unusually' imposed if it is administered arbitrarily or discriminatorily." The same authors add that "the extreme rarity with which applicable death penalty provisions are put to use raises a strong inference of arbitrariness." The President's Commission on Law Enforcement and Administration of Justice recently concluded:

"Finally there is evidence that the imposition of the death sentence and the exercise of dispensing power by the courts and the executive follow discriminatory patterns. The death sentence is disproportionately imposed and carried out on the poor, the Negro, and the members of unpopular groups."

Those who wrote the Eighth Amendment knew what price their forebears(先祖,前辈,祖宗) had paid for a system based, not on equal justice, but on discrimination. In those days the target was not the blacks or the poor, but the dissenters(持异议者), those who opposed absolutism in government(专制政府), who struggled for a parliamentary regime, and who opposed governments' recurring efforts to foist a particular religion on the people(将宗教硬塞给他人). But the tool of capital punishment was used with vengeance(报仇,复仇,报复) against the opposition and those unpopular with the regime. One cannot read this history without realizing that the desire for equality was reflected in the ban against "cruel and unusual punishments" contained in the Eighth Amendment.

In a Nation committed to equal protection of the laws(法律的平等保护) there is no permissible "caste"(种姓制度,等级制度) aspect of law enforcement. Yet we know that the discretion of judges and juries in imposing the death penalty enables the penalty to be selectively applied, feeding prejudices against the accused if he is poor and despised, and lacking political clout(政治影响力,权势), or if he is a member of a suspect or unpopular minority, and saving those who by social position may be in a more protected position. In ancient Hindu law a Brahman was exempt from capital punishment, and under that law, "generally, in the law books, punishment increased in severity as social status diminished." We have, I fear, taken in practice the same position, partially as a result of making the death penalty discretionary and partially as a result of the ability of the rich to purchase the services of the most respected and most resourceful legal talent in the Nation.

The high service rendered by the "cruel and unusual" punishment clause of the Eighth Amendment is to require legislatures to write penal laws that are evenhanded(公平的, 公平无私的), nonselective, and nonarbitrary, and to require judges to see to it that general laws are not applied sparsely, selectively, and spottily to unpopular groups.

A law that stated that anyone making more than \$50,000 would be exempt from the death penalty would plainly fall, as would a law that in terms said that blacks, those who never went beyond the fifth grade in school, those who made less than \$3,000 a year, or those who were unpopular or unstable should be the only people executed. A law which in the overall view reaches that result in practice has no more sanctity than a law which in terms provides the same.

Thus, these discretionary statutes are unconstitutional in their operation. They are pregnant with(充满着) discrimination and discrimination is an ingredient not compatible with the idea of equal protection of the laws that is implicit in the ban on "cruel and unusual" punishments.

I concur in the judgments of the Court.

MR. JUSTICE BRENNAN, concurring.

The punishment challenged in these cases is death. Death, of course, is a "traditional" punishment, one that "has been employed throughout our history," and its constitutional background is accordingly an appropriate subject of inquiry.

There is, first, a textual consideration raised by the Bill of Rights itself. The Fifth Amendment declares that if a particular crime is punishable by death, a person charged with that crime is entitled to certain procedural protections. We can thus infer that the Framers(制宪者) recognized the existence of what was then a common punishment. We cannot, however, make the further inference that they intended to exempt this particular punishment from the express prohibition of the Cruel and Unusual Punishments Clause. Nor is there any indication in the debates on the Clause that a special exception was to be made for death. If anything, the indication is to the contrary, for Livermore specifically mentioned death as a candidate for future proscription under the Clause. Finally, it does not advance analysis to insist that the Framers did not believe that adoption of the Bill of Rights would immediately prevent the infliction of the punishment of death; neither did they believe that it would immediately prevent the infliction of other corporal punishments that, although common at the time, are now acknowledged to be impermissible.

There is also the consideration that this Court has decided three cases involving constitutional challenges to particular methods of inflicting this punishment. In *Wilkerson v. Utah* (1879), and In re Kemmler (1890), the Court, expressing in both cases the since-rejected "historical" view of the Clause, approved death by shooting and death by electrocution. In *Wilkerson*, the Court concluded that shooting was a common method of execution; in *Kemmler*, the Court held that the Clause did not apply to the States. In *Louisiana ex rel. Francis v. Resweber*, the Court approved a second attempt at electrocution after the first had failed. It was said that "the Fourteenth Amendment would prohibit by its due process clause execution by a state in a cruel manner," but that the abortive attempt did not make the "subsequent execution any more cruel in the constitutional sense than any other execution." These three decisions thus reveal that the Court, while ruling upon various methods of inflicting death, has assumed in the past that death was a constitutionally permissible punishment. Past assumptions, however, are not sufficient to limit the scope of our examination of this punishment today. The constitutionality of death itself under the Cruel and Unusual Punishments Clause is before this Court for the first time; we cannot avoid the question by recalling past cases that never directly considered it.

The question, then, is whether the deliberate infliction of death is today consistent with the command of the Clause that the State may not inflict punishments that do not comport with human dignity(人的尊严). I will analyze the punishment of death in terms of the principles set out above and the cumulative test to which they lead: It is a denial of human dignity for the State arbitrarily to subject a person to an unusually severe punishment that society has indicated it does not regard as acceptable, and that cannot be shown to serve any penal purpose more effectively than a significantly less drastic punishment. Under these principles and this test, death is today a "cruel and unusual" punishment.

Death is a unique punishment in the United States. In a society that so strongly affirms the sanctity of life, not surprisingly the common view is that death is the ultimate sanction. This natural human feeling appears all about us. There has been no national debate about punishment, in general or by imprisonment, comparable to the debate about the punishment of death. No other punishment has been so continuously restricted, nor has any State yet abolished prisons, as some have abolished this punishment. And those States that still inflict death reserve it for the most heinous crimes. Juries, of course, have always treated death cases differently, as have governors exercising their commutation powers. Criminal defendants are of the same view. "As all practicing lawyers know, who have

Lesson Eight U. S. Legal History on Capital Punishment

defended persons charged with capital offenses, often the only goal possible is to avoid the death penalty." Some legislatures have required particular procedures, such as two-stage trials and automatic appeals, applicable only in death cases. "It is the universal experience in the administration of criminal justice that those charged with capital offenses are granted special considerations." This Court, too, almost always treats death cases as a class apart. And the unfortunate effect of this punishment upon the functioning of the judicial process is well known; no other punishment has a similar effect.

The only explanation for the uniqueness of death is its extreme severity. Death is today an unusually severe punishment, unusual in its pain, in its finality, and in its enormity. No other existing punishment is comparable to death in terms of physical and mental suffering. Although our information is not conclusive, it appears that there is no method available that guarantees an immediate and painless death. Since the discontinuance of flogging(鞭打, 笞打) as a constitutionally permissible punishment, death remains as the only punishment that may involve the conscious infliction of physical pain. In addition, we know that mental pain is an inseparable part of our practice of punishing criminals by death, for the prospect of pending execution exacts a frightful toll during the inevitable long wait between the imposition of sentence and the actual infliction of death. As the California Supreme Court pointed out, "the process of carrying out a verdict of death is often so degrading and brutalizing to the human spirit as to constitute psychological torture." Indeed, as Mr. Justice Frankfurter noted, "the onset of insanity while awaiting execution of a death sentence is not a rare phenomenon."

The unusual severity of death is manifested most clearly in its finality and enormity. Death, in these respects, is in a class by itself. Expatriation(脱离原国籍,脱籍), for example, is a punishment that "destroys for the individual the political existence that was centuries in the development," that "strips the citizen of his status in the national and international political community," and that puts "his very existence" in jeopardy. Expatriation thus inherently entails "the total destruction of the individual's status in organized society." "In short, the expatriate(被逐出国外的人,移居国外的人) has lost the right to have rights." Yet, demonstrably, expatriation is not "a fate worse than death." Although death, like expatriation, destroys the individual's "political existence" and his "status in organized society," it does more, for, unlike expatriation, death also destroys "his very existence." There is, too, at least the possibility that the expatriate will in the future regain "the right to have rights." Death forecloses even that possibility.

Death is truly an awesome punishment. The calculated killing(故意致死) of a human being by the State involves, by its very nature, a denial of the executed person's humanity. The contrast with the plight of a person punished by imprisonment is evident. An individual in prison does not lose "the right to have rights." A prisoner retains, for example, the constitutional rights to the free exercise of religion, to be free of cruel and unusual punishments, and to treatment as a "person" for purposes of due process of law and the equal protection of the laws. A prisoner remains a member of the human family. Moreover, he retains the right of access to the courts. His punishment is not irrevocable. Apart from the common charge, grounded upon the recognition of human fallibility(易错;易受骗;虚妄) that the punishment of death must inevitably be inflicted upon innocent men, we know that death has been the lot of men whose convictions were unconstitutionally secured in view of later, retroactively applied, holdings of this Court. The punishment itself may have been unconstitutionally inflicted, yet the finality of death precludes relief. An executed person has indeed "lost the right to have rights." As one 19th century proponent of punishing criminals by death declared, "When a man is hung, there is an end of our relations with him. His execution is a way of saying, 'You are not fit for this world, take your chance elsewhere.'"

In comparison to all other punishments today, then, the deliberate extinguishment of human life by the State is uniquely degrading to human dignity. I would not hesitate to hold, on that ground alone, that death is today a "cruel and unusual" punishment, were it not that death is a punishment of longstanding usage and acceptance in this country. I therefore turn to the second principle—that the State may not arbitrarily inflict an unusually severe punishment.

The outstanding characteristic of our present practice of punishing criminals by death is the infrequency with which we resort to it. The evidence is conclusive that death is not the ordinary punishment for any crime....

When a country of over 200 million people inflicts an unusually severe punishment no more than 50 times a year, the inference is strong that the punishment is not being regularly and fairly applied. To dispel it would indeed require a clear showing of nonarbitrary infliction.

Although there are no exact figures available, we know that thousands of murders and rapes are committed annually in States where death is an authorized punishment for those crimes. However the rate of infliction is characterized—as "freakishly" or "spectacularly" rare, or simply as rare—it would take the purest sophistry(诡辩法,诡辩法的应用;似是而非的推理/论证) to deny that death is inflicted in only a minute fraction of these cases. How much rarer, after all, could the infliction of death be?

When the punishment of death is inflicted in a trivial number of the cases in which it is legally available, the conclusion is virtually inescapable that it is being inflicted arbitrarily. Indeed, it smacks of little more than a lottery system. The States claim, however, that this rarity is evidence not of arbitrariness, but of informed selectivity: Death is inflicted, they say, only in "extreme" cases.

Informed selectivity, of course, is a value not to be denigrated. Yet presumably the States could make precisely the same claim if there were 10 executions per year, or five, or even if there were but one. That there may be as many as 50 per year does not strengthen the claim. When the rate of infliction is at this low level, it is highly implausible that only the worst criminals or the criminals who commit the worst crimes are selected for this punishment. No one has yet suggested a rational basis that could differentiate in those terms the few who die from the many who go to prison. Crimes and criminals simply do not admit of a distinction that can be drawn so finely as to explain, on that ground, the execution of such a tiny sample of those eligible. Certainly the laws that provide for this punishment do not attempt to draw that distinction; all cases to which the laws apply are necessarily "extreme."

Although it is difficult to imagine what further facts would be necessary in order to prove that death is, as my Brother STEWART puts it, "wantonly and... freakishly" inflicted, I need not conclude that arbitrary infliction is patently obvious. I am not considering this punishment by the isolated light of one principle. The probability of arbitrariness is sufficiently substantial that it can be relied upon, in combination with the other principles, in reaching a judgment on the constitutionality of this punishment.

When there is a strong probability that an unusually severe and degrading punishment is being inflicted arbitrarily, we may well expect that society will disapprove of its infliction. I turn, therefore, to the third principle. An examination of the history and present operation of the American practice of punishing criminals by death reveals that this punishment has been almost totally rejected by contemporary society.

I cannot add to my Brother MARSHALL's comprehensive treatment of the English and American history of this punishment. I emphasize, however, one significant conclusion that emerges from that history. From the beginning of our Nation, the punishment of death has stirred acute public controversy. Although pragmatic arguments for and against the punishment have been frequently advanced, this longstanding and heated controversy cannot be explained solely as the result of differences over the practical wisdom of a particular government policy. At bottom, the battle has been waged on moral grounds. The country has debated whether a society for which the dignity of the individual is the supreme value can, without a fundamental inconsistency, follow the practice of deliberately putting some of its members to death. In the United States, as in other nations of the western world, "the struggle about this punishment has been one between ancient and deeply rooted beliefs in retribution, atonement(补偿;赎罪) or vengeance on the one hand, and, on the other, beliefs in the personal value and dignity of the common man that were born of the democratic movement of the eighteenth century, as well as beliefs in the scientific approach to an understanding of the motive forces of human conduct, which are the result of the growth of the sciences of behavior during the nineteenth and twentieth centuries. " It is this essentially moral conflict that forms the backdrop for the past changes in and the present operation of our system of imposing death as a punishment for crime. . . .

Thus, although "the death penalty has been employed throughout our history," in fact the history of this punishment is one of successive restriction. What was once a common punishment has become, in the context of a continuing moral debate, increasingly rare. The evolution of this punishment evidences, not that it is an inevitable part of the American scene, but that it has proved progressively more troublesome to the national conscience. The result of this movement is our current system of administering the punishment, under which death sentences are rarely imposed.

The progressive decline in, and the current rarity of, the infliction of death demonstrate that our society seriously questions the appropriateness of this punishment today. The States point out that many legislatures authorize death as the punishment for certain crimes and that substantial segments of the public, as reflected in opinion polls and referendum votes(全民公决), continue to support it. Yet the availability of this punishment through statutory authorization, as well as the polls and referenda, which amount simply to approval of that authorization, simply underscores the extent to which our society has in fact rejected this punishment. When an unusually severe punishment is authorized for wide-scale application but not, because of society's refusal, inflicted save (except) in a few instances, the inference is compelling that there is a deep-seated reluctance to inflict it. Indeed, the likelihood is great that the punishment is tolerated only because of its disuse (废止,废弃). The objective indicator of society's view of an unusually severe punishment is what society does with it, and today society will inflict death upon only a small sample of the eligible criminals. Rejection could hardly be more complete without becoming absolute. At the very least, I must conclude that contemporary society views this punishment with substantial doubt.

The final principle to be considered is that an unusually severe and degrading punishment may not be excessive in view of the purposes for which it is inflicted. This principle, too, is related to the others. When there is a strong probability that the State is arbitrarily inflicting an unusually severe punishment that is subject to grave societal doubts, it is likely also that the punishment cannot be shown to be serving any penal purpose that could not be served equally well by some less severe punishment.

The States' primary claim is that death is a necessary punishment because it prevents the commission of capital crimes more effectively than any less severe punishment. The first part of this claim is that the infliction of death is necessary to stop the individuals executed from committing further crimes. The sufficient answer to this is that if a criminal convicted of a capital crime poses a danger to society, effective administration of the State's pardon and parole laws can delay or deny his release from prison, and techniques of isolation can eliminate or minimize the danger while he remains confined.

The more significant argument is that the threat of death prevents the commission of capital crimes because it deters potential criminals who would not be deterred by the threat of imprisonment. The argument is not based upon evidence that the threat of death is a superior deterrent. Indeed, as my Brother MARSHALL establishes, the available evidence uniformly indicates, although it does not conclusively prove, that the threat of death has no greater deterrent effect than the threat of imprisonment. The States argue, however, that they are entitled to rely upon common human experience, and that experience, they say, supports the conclusion that death must be a more effective deterrent than any less severe punishment. Because people fear death the most, the argument runs, the threat of death must be the greatest deterrent.

It is important to focus upon the precise import (意义,重要性) of this argument. It is not denied that many, and probably most, capital crimes cannot be deterred by the threat of punishment. Thus the argument can apply only to those who think rationally about the commission of capital crimes. Particularly is that true when the potential criminal, under this argument, must not only consider the risk of punishment, but also distinguish between two possible punishments. The concern, then, is with a particular type of potential criminal, the rational person who will commit a capital crime knowing that the punishment is long-term imprisonment, which may well be for the rest of his life, but will not commit the crime knowing that the punishment is death. On the face of it, the assumption that such persons exist is implausible.

In any event, this argument cannot be appraised in the abstract. We are not presented with the theoretical question whether under any imaginable circumstances the threat of death might be a greater deterrent to the commission of capital crimes than the threat of imprisonment. We are concerned with the practice of punishing criminals by death as it exists in the United States today. Proponents of this argument necessarily admit that its validity depends upon the existence of a system in which the punishment of death is invariably and swiftly imposed. Our system, of course, satisfies neither condition. A rational person contemplating a murder or rape is confronted, not with the certainty of a speedy death, but with the slightest possibility that he will be executed in the distant future. The risk of death is remote and improbable; in contrast, the risk of longterm imprisonment is near and great. In short, whatever the speculative validity of the assumption that the threat of death is a superior deterrent, there is no reason to believe that as currently administered the punishment of death is necessary to deter the commission of capital crimes. Whatever might be the case were all or substantially all eligible criminals quickly put to death, unverifiable possibilities are an insufficient basis upon which to conclude that the threat of death today has any greater deterrent efficacy than the threat of imprisonment.

There is, however, another aspect to the argument that the punishment of death is necessary for the protection of society. The infliction of death, the States urge, serves to manifest the community's outrage at the commission of the crime. It is, they say, a concrete public expression of moral indignation that inculcates（反复灌输；谆谆劝导）respect for the law and helps assure a more peaceful community. Moreover, we are told, not only does the punishment of death exert this widespread moralizing influence upon community values, it also satisfies the popular demand for grievous condemnation of abhorrent crimes and thus prevents disorder, lynching（私刑）, and attempts by private citizens to take the law into their own hands.

The question, however, is not whether death serves these supposed purposes of punishment, but whether death serves them more effectively than imprisonment. There is no evidence whatever that utilization of imprisonment rather than death encourages private blood feuds（私人间的血亲复仇）and other disorders. Surely if there were such a danger, the execution of a handful of criminals each year would not prevent it. The assertion that death alone is a sufficiently emphatic denunciation（指责，弹劾；控诉，告发，揭发；声讨檄文；废约通告）for capital crimes suffers from the same defect. If capital crimes require the punishment of death in order to provide moral reinforcement for the basic values of the community, those values can only be undermined when death is so rarely inflicted upon the criminals who commit the crimes. Furthermore, it is certainly doubtful that the infliction of death by the State does in fact strengthen the community's moral code; if the deliberate extinguishment of human life has any effect at all, it more likely tends to lower our respect for life and brutalize our values. That, after all, is why we no longer carry out public executions. In any event, this claim simply means that one purpose of punishment is to indicate social disapproval of crime. To serve that purpose our laws distribute punishments according to the gravity of crimes and punish more severely the crimes society regards as more serious. That purpose cannot justify any particular punishment as the upper limit of severity.

There is, then, no substantial reason to believe that the punishment of death, as currently administered, is necessary for the protection of society. The only other purpose suggested, one that is independent of protection for society, is retribution. Shortly stated, retribution in this context means that criminals are put to death because they deserve it.

Although it is difficult to believe that any State today wishes to proclaim adherence to "naked vengeance," the States claim, in reliance upon its statutory authorization, that death is the only fit punishment for capital crimes and that this retributive purpose justifies its infliction. In the past, judged by its statutory authorization, death was considered the only fit punishment for the crime of forgery, for the first federal criminal statute provided a mandatory death penalty for that crime. Obviously, concepts of justice change; no immutable moral order requires death for murderers and rapists. The claim that death is a just punishment necessarily refers to the existence of certain public beliefs. The claim must be that for capital crimes death alone comports with society's notion of proper punishment. As administered today, however, the punishment of death cannot be justified as a necessary means of exacting retribution from criminals. When the overwhelming number of criminals who commit capital crimes go to prison, it cannot be concluded that death serves the purpose of retribution more effectively than imprisonment. The asserted public belief that murderers and rapists deserve to die is flatly inconsistent with the execution of a random few. As the history of the punishment of death in this country shows, our society wishes to prevent crime; we have no desire to kill criminals simply to get even with them.

In sum, the punishment of death is inconsistent with all four principles: Death is an unusually severe and degrading punishment; there is a strong probability that it is inflicted arbitrarily; its rejection by contemporary society is virtually total; and there is no reason to believe that it serves any penal purpose more effectively than the less severe punishment of imprisonment. The function of these principles is to enable a court to determine whether a punishment comports with human dignity. Death, quite simply, does not.

IV

When this country was founded, memories of the Stuart horrors(斯图亚特王朝时代的恐怖) were fresh and severe corporal punishments(肉体惩罚) were common. Death was not then a unique punishment. The practice of punishing criminals by death, moreover, was widespread and by and large acceptable to society. Indeed, without developed prison systems, there was frequently no workable alternative. Since that time, successive restrictions, imposed against the background of a continuing moral controversy, have drastically curtailed(缩减,减少) the use of this punishment. Today death is a uniquely and unusually severe punishment. When examined by the principles applicable under the Cruel and Unusual Punishments Clause, death stands condemned as fatally offensive to human dignity. The punishment of death is therefore "cruel and unusual," and the States may no longer inflict it as a punishment for crimes. Rather than kill an arbitrary handful of criminals each year, the States will confine them in prison. "The State thereby suffers nothing and loses no power. The purpose of punishment is fulfilled, crime is repressed by penalties of just, not tormenting, severity, its repetition is prevented, and hope is given for the reformation of the criminal."

I concur in the judgments of the Court.

MR. JUSTICE STEWART, concurring.

The penalty of death differs from all other forms of criminal punishment, not in degree but in kind. It is unique in its total irrevocability. It is unique in its rejection of rehabilitation of the convict as a basic purpose of criminal justice. And it is unique, finally, in its absolute renunciation(放弃;抛弃,废弃;弃权;否认状;放弃声明书) of all that is embodied in our concept of humanity.

For these and other reasons, at least two of my Brothers have concluded that the infliction of the death penalty is constitutionally impermissible in all circumstances under the Eighth and Fourteenth Amendments. Their case is a strong one. But I find it unnecessary to reach the ultimate question they would decide.

The opinions of other Justices today have set out in admirable and thorough detail the origins and judicial history of the Eighth Amendment's guarantee against the infliction of cruel and unusual punishments, and the origin and judicial history of capital punishment. There is thus no need for me to review the historical materials here, and what I have to say can, therefore, be briefly stated.

Legislatures—state and federal—have sometimes specified that the penalty of death shall be the mandatory punishment for every person convicted of engaging in certain designated criminal conduct. Congress, for example, has provided that anyone convicted of acting as a spy for the enemy in time of war shall be put to death. The Rhode Island Legislature has ordained the death penalty for a life term prisoner who commits murder. Massachusetts has passed a law imposing the death penalty upon anyone convicted of murder in the commission of a forcible rape. An Ohio law imposes the mandatory penalty of death upon the assassin of the President of the United States or the Governor of a State.

If we were reviewing death sentences imposed under these or similar laws, we would be faced with the need to decide whether capital punishment is unconstitutional for all crimes and under all circumstances. We would need to decide whether a legislature—state or federal—could constitutionally determine that certain criminal conduct is so atrocious (dreadful) that society's interest in deterrence and retribution wholly outweighs any considerations of reform or rehabilitation of the perpetrator, and that, despite the inconclusive empirical evidence, only the automatic penalty of death will provide maximum deterrence.

On that score I would say only that I cannot agree that retribution is a constitutionally impermissible ingredient in the imposition of punishment. The instinct for retribution is part of the nature of man, and channeling that instinct in the administration of criminal justice serves an important purpose in promoting the stability of a society governed by law. When people begin to believe that organized society is unwilling or unable to impose upon criminal offenders the punishment they "deserve," then there are sown the seeds of anarchy—of self-help, vigilante justice (民团正义), and lynch law(私刑).

The constitutionality of capital punishment in the abstract is not, however, before us in these cases. For the Georgia and Texas Legislatures have not provided that the death penalty shall be imposed upon all those who are found guilty of forcible rape. And the Georgia Legislature has not ordained that death shall be the automatic punishment for murder. In a word, neither State has made a legislative determination that forcible rape and murder can be deterred only by imposing the penalty of death upon all who perpetrate those offenses. As MR. JUSTICE WHITE so tellingly puts it, the "legislative will is not frustrated if the penalty is never imposed."

Instead, the death sentences now before us are the product of a legal system that brings them, I believe, within the very core of the Eighth Amendment's guarantee against cruel and unusual punishments, a guarantee applicable against the States through the Fourteenth Amendment. In the first place, it is clear that these sentences are "cruel" in the sense that they excessively go beyond, not in degree but in kind, the punishments that the state legislatures have determined to be necessary. In the second place, it is equally clear that these sentences are "unusual" in the sense that the penalty of death is infrequently imposed for murder, and that its imposition for rape is extraordinarily rare. But I do not rest my conclusion upon these two propositions alone.

These death sentences are cruel and unusual in the same way that being struck by lightning is cruel and unusual. For, of all the people convicted of rapes and murders in 1967 and 1968, many just as reprehensible as these, the petitioners are among a capriciously selected random handful upon whom the sentence of death has in fact been imposed. My concurring Brothers have demonstrated that, if any basis can be discerned for the selection of these few to be sentenced to die, it is the constitutionally impermissible basis of race. But racial discrimination has not been proved, and I put it to one side. I simply conclude that the Eighth and Fourteenth Amendments cannot tolerate the infliction of a sentence of death under legal systems that permit this unique penalty to be so wantonly(放肆地,胡作非为地,肆无忌惮地)and so freakishly(反复无常地) imposed.

For these reasons I concur in the judgments of the Court.

MR. JUSTICE WHITE, concurring.

The facial constitutionality of statutes requiring the imposition of the death penalty for first-degree murder, for more narrowly defined categories of murder, or for rape would present quite different issues under the Eighth Amendment than are posed by the cases before us. In joining the Court's judgments, therefore, I do not at all intimate that the death penalty is unconstitutional per se or that there is no system of capital punishment that would

Lesson Eight U. S. Legal History on Capital Punishment

comport with the Eighth Amendment. That question, ably argued by several of my Brethren(同行法官们), is not presented by these cases and need not be decided.

The narrower question to which I address myself concerns the constitutionality of capital punishment statutes under which (1) the legislature authorizes the imposition of the death penalty for murder or rape; (2) the legislature does not itself mandate the penalty in any particular class or kind of case (that is, legislative will is not frustrated if the penalty is never imposed), but delegates to judges or juries the decisions as to those cases, if any, in which the penalty will be utilized; and (3) judges and juries have ordered the death penalty with such infrequency that the odds are now very much against imposition and execution of the penalty with respect to any convicted murderer or rapist. It is in this context that we must consider whether the execution of these petitioners would violate the Eighth Amendment.

I begin with what I consider a near truism(自明之理;明明白白的事情;起码的常识;老套语) that the death penalty could so seldom be imposed that it would cease to be a credible deterrent or measurably to contribute to any other end of punishment in the criminal justice system. It is perhaps true that no matter how infrequently those convicted of rape or murder are executed, the penalty so imposed is not disproportionate to the crime and those executed may deserve exactly what they received. It would also be clear that executed defendants are finally and completely incapacitated from again committing rape or murder or any other crime. But when imposition of the penalty reaches a certain degree of infrequency, it would be very doubtful that any existing general need for retribution would be measurably satisfied. Nor could it be said with confidence that society's need for specific deterrence justifies death or so few when for so many in like circumstances life imprisonment or shorter prison terms are judged sufficient, or that community values are measurably reinforced by authorizing a penalty so rarely invoked.

Most important, a major goal of the criminal law—to deter others by punishing the convicted criminal—would not be substantially served where the penalty is so seldom invoked that it ceases to be the credible threat essential to influence the conduct of others. For present purposes I accept the morality and utility of punishing one person to influence another. I accept also the effectiveness of punishment generally and need not reject the death penalty as a more effective deterrent than a lesser punishment. But common sense and experience tell us that seldom-enforced laws become ineffective measures for controlling human conduct and that the death penalty, unless imposed with sufficient frequency, will make little contribution to deterring those crimes for which it may be exacted(勒索钱财等,强要、强制,逼使服从等;急需,需要).

The imposition and execution of the death penalty are obviously cruel in the dictionary sense. But the penalty has not been considered cruel and unusual punishment in the constitutional sense because it was thought justified by the social ends it was deemed to serve. At the moment that it ceases realistically to further these purposes, however, the emerging question is whether its imposition in such circumstances would violate the Eighth Amendment. It is my view that it would, for its imposition would then be the pointless and needless extinction of life with only marginal contributions to any discernible social or public purposes. A penalty with such negligible returns to the State would be patently excessive and cruel and unusual punishment violative of the Eighth Amendment.

It is also my judgment that this point has been reached with respect to capital punishment as it is presently administered under the statutes involved in these cases. Concededly(众所周知,明白地,众所承认地), it is difficult to prove as a general proposition that capital punishment, however administered, more effectively serves the ends of the criminal law than does imprisonment. But however that may be, I cannot avoid the conclusion that as the statutes before us are now administered, the penalty is so infrequently imposed that the threat of execution is too attenuated to be of substantial service to criminal justice.

I concur in the judgments of the Court.

MR. JUSTICE MARSHALL, concurring.

The Eighth Amendment's ban against cruel and unusual punishments derives from English law. In 1583, John

Whitgift, Archbishop of Canterbury, turned the High Commission into a permanent ecclesiastical court, and the Commission began to use torture to extract confessions from persons suspected of various offenses. Sir Robert Beale protested that cruel and barbarous torture violated Magna Carta(大宪章), but his protests were made in vain.

Cruel punishments were not confined to those accused of crimes, but were notoriously applied with even greater relish(嗜好,兴趣;食欲,胃口;玩味,赏玩) to those who were convicted. Blackstone described in ghastly detail the myriad of inhumane forms of punishment imposed on persons found guilty of any of a large number of offenses. Death, of course, was the usual result.

The treason trials of 1685—the "Bloody Assizes(巡回裁判开庭期/开庭地)"—which followed an abortive rebellion by the Duke of Monmouth, marked the culmination of the parade of horrors, and most historians believe that it was this event that finally spurred the adoption of the English Bill of Rights containing the progenitor(祖先;先驱;前辈) of our prohibition against cruel and unusual punishments. The conduct of Lord Chief Justice Jeffreys at those trials has been described as an "insane lust for cruelty" which was "stimulated by orders from the King" (James II). The assizes received wide publicity from Puritan pamphleteers and doubtless had some influence on the adoption of a cruel and unusual punishments clause. But, the legislative history of the English Bill of Rights of 1689 indicates that the assizes may not have been as critical to the adoption of the clause as is widely thought. After William and Mary of Orange crossed the channel to invade England, James II fled. Parliament was summoned into session and a committee was appointed to draft general statements containing "such things as are absolutely necessary to be considered for the better securing of our religion, laws and liberties." An initial draft of the Bill of Rights prohibited "illegal" punishments, but a later draft referred to the infliction by James II of "illegal and cruel" punishments, and declared "cruel and unusual" punishments to be prohibited. The use of the word "unusual" in the final draft appears to be inadvertent(出于无心的,非故意的,无意中的).

This legislative history has led at least one legal historian to conclude "that the cruel and unusual punishments clause of the Bill of Rights of 1689 was, first, an objection to the imposition of punishments that were unauthorized by statute and outside the jurisdiction of the sentencing court, and second, a reiteration of the English policy against disproportionate penalties," and not primarily a reaction to the torture of the High Commission, harsh sentences, or the assizes.

Whether the English Bill of Rights prohibition against cruel and unusual punishments is properly read as a response to excessive or illegal punishments, as a reaction to barbaric and objectionable modes of punishment, or as both, there is no doubt whatever that in borrowing the language and in including it in the Eighth Amendment, our Founding Fathers intended to outlaw torture and other cruel punishments.

The precise language used in the Eighth Amendment first appeared in America on June 12, 1776, in Virginia's "Declaration of Rights," §9 of which read: "That excessive bail ought not to be required, nor excessive fines imposed, nor cruel and unusual punishments inflicted." This language was drawn verbatim from the English Bill of Rights of 1689. Other States adopted similar clauses, and there is evidence in the debates of the various state conventions that were called upon to ratify the Constitution of great concern for the omission of any prohibition against torture or other cruel punishments.

The Virginia Convention offers some clues as to what the Founding Fathers had in mind in prohibiting cruel and unusual punishments. At one point George Mason advocated the adoption of a Bill of Rights, and Patrick Henry concurred, stating:

"By this Constitution, some of the best barriers of human rights are thrown away. Is there not an additional reason to have a bill of rights?... Congress, from their general powers, may fully go into business of human legislation. They may legislate, in criminal cases, from treason to the lowest offence—petty larceny(盗窃罪,非法侵占他人财产). They may define crimes and prescribe punishments. In the definition of crimes, I trust they will be directed by what wise representatives ought to be governed by. But when we come to punishments, no latitude ought to be left, nor dependence put on the virtue of representatives. What says our bill of rights? — 'that excessive bail ought not to be required, nor excessive fines imposed, nor cruel and unusual punishments inflicted.' Are you not, therefore, now calling on those gentlemen who are to compose Congress, to prescribe trials and define punishments without this control? Will they find sentiments there similar to this bill of rights? You let them loose; you do more— you depart from the genius of your country...."

"In this business of legislation, your members of Congress will loose the restriction of not imposing excessive fines, demanding excessive bail, and inflicting cruel and unusual punishments. These are prohibited by your declaration of rights. What has distinguished our ancestors? —That they would not admit of tortures, or cruel and barbarous punishment. But Congress may introduce the practice of the civil law, in preference to that of the common law. They may introduce the practice of France, Spain, and Germany—of torturing, to extort a confession of the crime. They will say that they might as well draw examples from those countries as from Great Britain, and they will tell you that there is such a necessity of strengthening the arm of government, that they must have a criminal equity, and extort(强取豪夺,强夺;敲诈,勒索;强求,逼迫) confession by torture, in order to punish with still more relentless severity. We are then lost and undone."

Henry's statement indicates that he wished to insure that "relentless severity" would be prohibited by the Constitution. Other expressions with respect to the proposed Eighth Amendment by Members of the First Congress indicate that they shared Henry's view of the need for and purpose of the Cruel and Unusual Punishments Clause.

Thus, the history of the clause clearly establishes that it was intended to prohibit cruel punishments. We must now turn to the case law to discover the manner in which courts have given meaning to the term "cruel...."

II

The Court used the same approach seven years later in the landmark case of *Weems v. United States* (1910). Weems, an officer of the Bureau of Coast Guard and Transportation of the United States Government of the Philippine Islands, was convicted of falsifying a "public and official document." He was sentenced to 15 years' incarceration at hard labor with chains on his ankles, to an unusual loss of his civil rights, and to perpetual surveillance. Called upon to determine whether this was a cruel and unusual punishment, the Court found that it was. The Court emphasized that the Constitution was not an "ephemeral" enactment, or one "designed to meet passing occasions." Recognizing that "time works changes, and brings into existence new conditions and purposes," the Court commented that "in the application of a constitution... our contemplation cannot be only of what has been but of what may be."

In striking down the penalty imposed on Weems, the Court examined the punishment in relation to the offense, compared the punishment to those inflicted for other crimes and to those imposed in other jurisdictions, and concluded that the punishment was excessive. Justices White and Holmes dissented and argued that the cruel and unusual prohibition was meant to prohibit only those things that were objectionable at the time the Constitution was adopted.

Weems is a landmark case because it represents the first time that the Court invalidated a penalty prescribed by a legislature for a particular offense. The Court made it plain beyond any reasonable doubt that excessive punishments were as objectionable as those that were inherently cruel. Thus, it is apparent that the dissenters' position in O'Neil had become the opinion of the Court in Weems.

Then came another landmark case, *Louisiana* ex el. *Francis v. Resweber* (1947). Francis had been convicted of murder and sentenced to be electrocuted(电刑处死). The first time the current passed through him, there was a mechanical failure and he did not die. Thereafter, Francis sought to prevent a second electrocution on the ground that it would be a cruel and unusual punishment. Eight members of the Court assumed the applicability of the Eighth Amendment to the States. The Court was virtually unanimous in agreeing that "the traditional humanity of modern Anglo-American law forbids the infliction of unnecessary pain," but split 5-4 on whether Francis would, under the circumstances, be forced to undergo any excessive pain. Five members of the Court treated the case like

In re Kemmler and held that the legislature adopted electrocution for a humane purpose, and that its will should not be thwarted(反对;阻挠;挫败对方意图等) because, in its desire to reduce pain and suffering in most cases, it may have inadvertently increased suffering in one particular case. The four dissenters felt that the case should be remanded for further facts.

As in Weems, the Court was concerned with excessive punishments. Resweber is perhaps most significant because the analysis of cruel and unusual punishment questions first advocated by the dissenters in O'Neil was at last firmly entrenched in the minds of an entire Court.

Trop v. Dulles (1958), marked the next major cruel and unusual punishment case in this Court. Trop, a native-born American, was declared to have lost his citizenship by reason of a conviction by court-martial for wartime desertion. Writing for himself and Justices Black, DOUGLAS, and Whittaker, Chief Justice Warren concluded that loss of citizenship amounted to a cruel and unusual punishment that violated the Eighth Amendment.

Emphasizing the flexibility inherent in the words "cruel and unusual," the Chief Justice wrote that "the Amendment must draw its meaning from the evolving standards of decency that mark the progress of a maturing society." His approach to the problem was that utilized by the Court in Weems: he scrutinized the severity of the penalty in relation to the offense, examined the practices of other civilized nations of the world, and concluded that involuntary statelessness was an excessive and, therefore, an unconstitutional punishment. Justice Frankfurter, dissenting, urged that expatriation(移居国外,脱离原国籍) was not punishment, and that even if it were, it was not excessive. While he criticized the conclusion arrived at by the Chief Justice, his approach to the Eighth Amendment question was identical.

Whereas in *Trop* a majority of the Court failed to agree on whether loss of citizenship was a cruel and unusual punishment, four years later a majority did agree in *Robinson v. California*, that a sentence of 90 days' imprisonment for violation of a California statute making it a crime to "be addicted to the use of narcotics"(麻醉药品,麻醉剂,麻药;安眠药;起麻痹作用的东西) was cruel and unusual. MR. JUSTICE STEWART, writing the opinion of the Court, reiterated what the Court had said in Weems and what Chief Justice Warren wrote in *Trop*—that the cruel and unusual punishment clause was not a static concept, but one that must be continually re-examined "in the light of contemporary human knowledge." The fact that the penalty under attack was only 90 days evidences the Court's willingness to carefully examine the possible excessiveness of punishment in a given case even where what is involved is a penalty that is familiar and widely accepted.

We distinguished Robinson in *Powell v. Texas* (1968), where we sustained a conviction for drunkenness in a public place and a fine of $20. Four Justices dissented on the ground that Robinson was controlling. The analysis in both cases was the same; only the conclusion as to whether or not the punishment was excessive differed. Powell marked the last time prior to today's decision that the Court has had occasion to construe the meaning of the term "cruel and unusual" punishment.

Several principles emerge from these prior cases and serve as a beacon(号所,望楼;灯塔,信标;警告,指南) to an enlightened decision in the instant cases.

III

Perhaps the most important principle in analyzing "cruel and unusual" punishment questions is one that is reiterated again and again in the prior opinions of the Court: i. e., the cruel and unusual language "must draw its meaning from the evolving standards of decency that mark the progress of a maturing society." Thus, a penalty that was permissible at one time in our Nation's history is not necessarily permissible today.

The fact, therefore, that the Court, or individual Justices, may have in the past expressed an opinion that the death penalty is constitutional is not now binding on us....

Faced with an open question, we must establish our standards for decision. The decisions discussed in the previous section imply that a punishment may be deemed cruel and unusual for any one of four distinct reasons.

Lesson Eight U. S. Legal History on Capital Punishment

First, there are certain punishments that inherently involve so much physical pain and suffering that civilized people cannot tolerate them, e. g. , use of the rack(拉肢拷问;扭伤), the thumbscrew(拇指夹), or other modes of torture. Regardless of public sentiment with respect to imposition of one of these punishments in a particular case or at any one moment in history, the Constitution prohibits it. These are punishments that have been barred since the adoption of the Bill of Rights.

Second, there are punishments that are unusual, signifying that they were previously unknown as penalties for a given offense. In light of the meager history that does exist, one would suppose that an innovative punishment would probably be constitutional if no more cruel than that punishment which it superseded. We need not decide this question here, however, for capital punishment is certainly not a recent phenomenon.

Third, a penalty may be cruel and unusual because it is excessive and serves no valid legislative purpose. . . .

Fourth, where a punishment is not excessive and serves a valid legislative purpose, it still may be invalid if popular sentiment abhors it. For example, if the evidence clearly demonstrated that capital punishment served valid legislative purposes, such punishment would, nevertheless, be unconstitutional if citizens found it to be morally unacceptable. A general abhorrence on the part of the public would, in effect, equate a modern punishment with those barred since the adoption of the Eighth Amendment. There are no prior cases in this Court striking down a penalty on this ground, but the very notion of changing values requires that we recognize its existence.

It is immediately obvious, then, that since capital punishment is not a recent phenomenon, if it violates the Constitution, it does so because it is excessive or unnecessary, or because it is abhorrent(跟……不投合的) to currently existing moral values.

We must proceed to the history of capital punishment in the United States.

IV

. . . .

The foregoing history demonstrates that capital punishment was carried from Europe to America but, once here, was tempered considerably. At times in our history, strong abolitionist movements have existed. But, they have never been completely successful, as no more than one-quarter of the States of the Union have, at any one time, abolished the death penalty. They have had partial success, however, especially in reducing the number of capital crimes, replacing mandatory death sentences with jury discretion, and developing more humane methods of conducting executions.

This is where our historical foray(侵略, 掠夺; 摧残, 践踏) leads. The question now to be faced is whether American society has reached a point where abolition is not dependent on a successful grass roots movement in particular jurisdictions, but is demanded by the Eighth Amendment. To answer this question, we must first examine whether or not the death penalty is today tantamount to excessive punishment.

V

In order to assess whether or not death is an excessive or unnecessary penalty, it is necessary to consider the reasons why a legislature might select it as punishment for one or more offenses, and examine whether less severe penalties would satisfy the legitimate legislative wants as well as capital punishment. If they would, then the death penalty is unnecessary cruelty, and, therefore, unconstitutional.

There are six purposes conceivably served by capital punishment: retribution(报应), deterrence(威慑), prevention of repetitive criminal acts(预防反复性犯罪行为), encouragement of guilty pleas and confessions(利于认罪和供述), eugenics(仿生学), and economy(经济). These are considered seriatim below.

A. The concept of retribution is one of the most misunderstood in all of our criminal jurisprudence. The principal source of confusion derives from the fact that, in dealing with the concept, most people confuse the question "why do men in fact punish?" with the question "what justifies men in punishing?" Men may punish for any number of reasons, but the one reason that punishment is morally good or morally justifiable is that someone has broken the law. Thus, it can correctly be said that breaking the law is the sine qua non(必要条件，要素) of punishment, or, in other words, that we only tolerate punishment as it is imposed on one who deviates from the norm established by the criminal law.

The fact that the State may seek retribution against those who have broken its laws does not mean that retribution may then become the State's sole end in punishing. Our jurisprudence has always accepted deterrence in general, deterrence of individual recidivism, isolation of dangerous persons, and rehabilitation as proper goals of punishment. Retaliation, vengeance, and retribution have been roundly condemned as intolerable aspirations for a government in a free society.

Punishment as retribution has been condemned by scholars for centuries, and the Eighth Amendment itself was adopted to prevent punishment from becoming synonymous with vengeance.

It is plain that the view of the Weems Court was that punishment for the sake of retribution was not permissible under the Eighth Amendment. This is the only view that the Court could have taken if the "cruel and unusual" language were to be given any meaning. Retribution surely underlies the imposition of some punishment on one who commits a criminal act. But, the fact that some punishment may be imposed does not mean that any punishment is permissible. If retribution alone could serve as a justification for any particular penalty, then all penalties selected by the legislature would by definition be acceptable means for designating society's moral approbation(disapproval) of a particular act. The "cruel and unusual" language would thus be read out of the Constitution and the fears of Patrick Henry and the other Founding Fathers(国父们) would become realities.

To preserve the integrity of the Eighth Amendment, the Court has consistently denigrated(污蔑,诽谤) retribution as a permissible goal of punishment. It is undoubtedly correct that there is a demand for vengeance on the part of many persons in a community against one who is convicted of a particularly offensive act. At times a cry is heard that morality requires vengeance to evidence society's abhorrence(嫌恶,厌恶,痛恨;极其讨厌的人/物) of the act. But the Eighth Amendment is our insulation from our baser selves. The "cruel and unusual" language limits the avenues through which vengeance can be channeled. Were this not so, the language would be empty and a return to the rack and other tortures would be possible in a given case.

Mr. Justice Story wrote that the Eighth Amendment's limitation on punishment "would seem to be wholly unnecessary in a free government, since it is scarcely possible that any department of such a government should authorize or justify such atrocious conduct"(凶暴的,残忍的,万恶的).

I would reach an opposite conclusion—that only in a free society would men recognize their inherent weaknesses and seek to compensate for them by means of a Constitution.

The history of the Eighth Amendment supports only the conclusion that retribution for its own sake is improper.

B. The most hotly contested issue regarding capital punishment is whether it is better than life imprisonment as a deterrent(威慑) to crime.

While the contrary position has been argued, it is my firm opinion that the death penalty is a more severe sanction than life imprisonment. Admittedly, there are some persons who would rather die than languish in prison for a lifetime(在监狱中惨死). But, whether or not they should be able to choose death as an alternative is a far different question from that presented here, i. e., whether the State can impose death as a punishment. Death is irrevocable(不可逆转,无法挽回的); life imprisonment is not. Death, of course, makes rehabilitation(恢复,复兴,改善)impossible; life imprisonment does not. In short, death has always been viewed as the ultimate sanction, and it seems perfectly reasonable to continue to view it as such.

It must be kept in mind, then, that the question to be considered is not simply whether capital punishment is a deterrent, but whether it is a better deterrent than life imprisonment.

There is no more complex problem than determining the deterrent efficacy of the death penalty. "Capital punishment has obviously failed as a deterrent when a murder is committed. We can number its failures. But we cannot

Lesson Eight U.S. Legal History on Capital Punishment

number its successes. No one can ever know how many people have refrained from murder because of the fear of being hanged." This is the nub of the problem and it is exacerbated(使病等更重/恶化，加深痛苦等；激怒，使烦恼) by the paucity of useful data. The United States is more fortunate than most countries, however, in that it has what are generally considered to be the world's most reliable statistics.

The two strongest arguments in favor of capital punishment as a deterrent are both logical hypotheses devoid of evidentiary support, but persuasive nonetheless. The first proposition was best stated by Sir James Stephen in 1864:

"No other punishment deters men so effectually from committing crimes as the punishment of death. This is one of those propositions which it is difficult to prove, simply because they are in themselves more obvious than any proof can make them. It is possible to display ingenuity in arguing against it, but that is all. The whole experience of mankind is in the other direction. The threat of instant death is the one to which resort has always been made when there was an absolute necessity for producing some result.... No one goes to certain inevitable death except by compulsion. Put the matter the other way. Was there ever yet a criminal who, when sentenced to death and brought out to die, would refuse the offer of a commutation(算，交换，变换；减刑；抵偿；抵偿金；划拨)of his sentence for the severest secondary punishment? Surely not. Why is this? It can only be because 'All that a man has will he give for his life.' In any secondary punishment, however terrible, there is hope; but death is death; its terrors cannot be described more forcibly."

Statistics also show that the deterrent effect of capital punishment is no greater in those communities where executions take place than in other communities. In fact, there is some evidence that imposition of capital punishment may actually encourage crime, rather than deter it. And, while police and law enforcement officers are the strongest advocates of capital punishment, the evidence is overwhelming that police are no safer in communities that retain the sanction than in those that have abolished it.

There is also a substantial body of data showing that the existence of the death penalty has virtually no effect on the homicide rate in prisons. Most of the persons sentenced to death are murderers, and murderers tend to be model prisoners.

In sum, the only support for the theory that capital punishment is an effective deterrent is found in the hypotheses with which we began and the occasional stories about a specific individual being deterred from doing a contemplated criminal act. These claims of specific deterrence are often spurious, however, and may be more than counterbalanced by the tendency of capital punishment to incite(煽动，唆使；激励；刺激)certain crimes.

The United Nations Committee that studied capital punishment found that "it is generally agreed between the retentionists(保留死刑者)and abolitionists(废除死刑者), whatever their opinions about the validity of comparative studies of deterrence, that the data which now exist show no correlation between the existence of capital punishment and lower rates of capital crime."

Despite the fact that abolitionists have not proved non-deterrence beyond a reasonable doubt, they have succeeded in showing by clear and convincing evidence that capital punishment is not necessary as a deterrent to crime in our society. This is all that they must do. We would shirk(逃避；躲避；规避义务、责任等；怠忽；偷懒)our judicial responsibilities if we failed to accept the presently existing statistics and demanded more proof. It may be that we now possess all the proof that anyone could ever hope to assemble on the subject. But, even if further proof were to be forthcoming, I believe there is more than enough evidence presently available for a decision in this case.

In 1793 William Bradford studied the utility of the death penalty in Pennsylvania and found that it probably had no deterrent effect(威慑效果)but that more evidence was needed. Edward Livingston reached a similar conclusion with respect to deterrence in 1833 upon completion of his study for Louisiana. Virtually every study that has since been undertaken has reached the same result.

In light of the massive amount of evidence before us, I see no alternative but to(不得不)conclude that capital punishment cannot be justified on the basis of its deterrent effect.

C. Much of what must be said about the death penalty as a device to prevent recidivism is obvious—if a murderer is executed, he cannot possibly commit another offense. The fact is, however, that murderers are extremely unlikely to commit other crimes either in prison or upon their release. For the most part, they are first offenders, and when released from prison they are known to become model citizens. Furthermore, most persons who commit capital crimes are not executed. With respect to those who are sentenced to die, it is critical to note that the jury is never asked to determine whether they are likely to be recidivists. In light of these facts, if capital punishment were justified purely on the basis of preventing recidivism, it would have to be considered to be excessive; no general need to obliterate(消灭) all capital offenders could have been demonstrated, nor any specific need in individual cases.

D. The three final purposes which may underlie utilization of a capital sanction—encouraging guilty pleas and confessions, eugenics, and reducing state expenditures—may be dealt with quickly. If the death penalty is used to encourage guilty pleas and thus to deter suspects from exercising their rights under the Sixth Amendment to jury trials, it is unconstitutional. Its elimination would do little to impair the State's bargaining position in criminal cases, since life imprisonment(终身监禁) remains a severe sanction which can be used as leverage for bargaining for pleas or confessions in exchange either for charges of lesser offenses or recommendations of leniency(仁慈).

Moreover, to the extent that capital punishment is used to encourage confessions and guilty pleas, it is not being used for punishment purposes. A State that justifies for the same purposes.

In light of the previous discussion on deterrence, any suggestions concerning the eugenic benefits of capital punishment are obviously meritless. As I pointed out above, there is not even any attempt made to discover which capital offenders are likely to be recidivists(累犯), let alone which are positively incurable. No test or procedure presently exists by which incurables can be screened from those who would benefit from treatment. On the one hand, due process would seem to require that we have some procedure to demonstrate incurability before execution; and, on the other hand, equal protection would then seemingly require that all incurables be executed. In addition, the "cruel and unusual" language would require that life imprisonment, treatment, and sterilization(绝育) be inadequate for eugenic(优生学的) purposes. More importantly, this Nation has never formally professed eugenic goals, and the history of the world does not look kindly on them. If eugenics is one of our purposes, then the legislatures should say so forthrightly and design procedures to serve this goal. Until such time, I can only conclude, as has virtually everyone else who has looked at the problem, that capital punishment cannot be defended on the basis of any eugenic purposes.

As for the argument that it is cheaper to execute a capital offender than to imprison him for life, even assuming that such an argument, if true, would support a capital sanction, it is simply incorrect. A disproportionate amount of money spent on prisons is attributable to death row(监狱的死囚区). Condemned men are not productive members of the prison community, although they could be, and executions are expensive. Appeals are often automatic, and courts admittedly spend more time with death cases.

At trial, the selection of jurors is likely to become a costly, time-consuming problem in a capital case, and defense counsel will reasonably exhaust every possible means to save his client from execution, no matter how long the trial takes.

During the period between conviction and execution(定罪与执行死刑), there are an inordinate(过度的,无限制的;不规则的,紊乱的) number of collateral(附属的,附随的,间接的,附带的) attacks on the conviction and attempts to obtain executive clemency(仁慈,宽厚), all of which exhaust the time, money, and effort of the State. There are also continual assertions that the condemned prisoner has gone insane. Because there is a formally established policy of not executing insane persons, great sums of money may be spent on detecting and curing mental illness in order to perform the execution. Since no one wants the responsibility for the execution, the condemned man

Lesson Eight U. S. Legal History on Capital Punishment

is likely to be passed back and forth from doctors to custodial officials to courts like a ping-pong ball. The entire process is very costly.

When all is said and done, there can be no doubt that it costs more to execute a man than to keep him in prison for life.

E. There is but one conclusion that can be drawn from all of this—i. e., the death penalty is an excessive and unnecessary punishment that violates the Eighth Amendment. The statistical evidence is not convincing beyond all doubt, but it is persuasive. It is not improper at this point to take judicial notice of the fact that for more than 200 years men have labored to demonstrate that capital punishment serves no purpose that life imprisonment could not serve equally well. And they have done so with great success. Little, if any, evidence has been adduced to prove the contrary. The point has now been reached at which deference to the legislatures is tantamount to(同等价值/效力的,与……相等的) abdication(弃权;让位;辞职) of our judicial roles as factfinders(事实裁判者), judges, and ultimate arbiters of the Constitution. We know that at some point the presumption of constitutionality accorded legislative acts gives way to a realistic assessment of those acts. This point comes when there is sufficient evidence available so that judges can determine, not whether the legislature acted wisely, but whether it had any rational basis whatsoever for acting. We have this evidence before us now. There is no rational basis for concluding that capital punishment is not excessive. It therefore violates the Eighth Amendment.

VI

In addition, even if capital punishment is not excessive, it nonetheless violates the Eighth Amendment because it is morally unacceptable to the people of the United States at this time in their history.

In striking down(取消) capital punishment, this Court does not malign(诬蔑,诽谤,中伤) our system of government. On the contrary, it pays homage to(效忠,尊敬) it. Only in a free society could right triumph in difficult times(只有在自由社会里,权利才会战胜艰难时期) and could civilization record its magnificent advancement. In recognizing the humanity of our fellow beings, we pay ourselves the highest tribute. We achieve "a major milestone in the long road up from barbarism" and join the approximately 70 other jurisdictions in the world which celebrate their regard for civilization and humanity by shunning(躲开,避开) capital punishment.

I concur in the judgments of the Court.

(dissenting opinions: omitted)

Lesson Nine

Judicial Discipline and Judicial Independence

Learning objectives

After learning the text and having done the exercises in this lesson, you will:

—familiarize with knowledge of the legal characteristics and the nature of judicial discipline and judicial independence;

—acquire an appreciation of the vocabulary and grammar or syntax relevant to judicial discipline and judicial independence;

—become aware of the information required in order to understand judicial discipline and judicial independence;

—cultivate the practical abilities to put to use the language in the specific context;

—be able to do some translation from Chinese to English and from English to Chinese.

Text

Judicial Discipline and Judicial Independence

Discipline, Independence, and State Courts

The question of judicial accountability① and independence arises primarily in the context of state courts. Federal judges, however they might be criticized or berated, are protected by the Constitutions provision for life tenure during good behavior②. Hence, even the most concerted political or editorial attack on a federal judge cannot truly threaten the judge's independence. While

---

① judicial accountability:司法问责制,法官问责制,即实施对法官过错责任的追究; judicial independence:司法独立,该翻译得到普遍的使用,但在当前背景下,本书编者认为翻译为"法官独立"或"法院独立"会更好一些。因为在英文中,judicial 一词主要指"司法的,法官的,与法院有关的"等意思。而在我国背景下,"司法"的意思会更广泛一些。

② for life tenure during good behavior:只要品行良好将终身任职。

Lesson Nine   Judicial Discipline and Judicial Independence

Circuit Judicial Councils[①] are now authorized to investigate complaints of judicial misconduct, their disciplinary powers are narrowly circumscribed. When it comes to accountability, it is state judges—many of whom face the additional burden of running for retention or reelection—who must be concerned about threats to their independence.

In 1960, California became the first state to establish a permanent commission charged with the *regulation* of judges' conduct. By 1981, all fifty states and the District of Columbia had created judicial conduct organizations empowered to investigate, prosecute, and adjudicate allegations of judicial misbehavior. Though the commissions vary widely in structure, composition, and procedure, they are typically authorized either to recommend or impose sanctions on a continuum that extends from private reprimand to removal from office. Moreover, nearly every state has also adopted a version of the Model Code of Judicial Conduct[②], which sets mandatory standards for both official and off-the-bench conduct[③].

Both phenomena—the establishment of commissions and the promulgation of the Judicial Code—were motivated by a perceived need to increase the *accountability* of judges. In this they have succeeded. State court judges are subject to regulation of conduct involving the management of their personal finances, civic and charitable activities, public speaking or writing, and social activity. In recent years, judges have actually faced discipline for the use of racial slurs, sexual harassment, improper business activity, fund raising, offensive conduct, and substance abuse.

To be sure, judicial independence does not require absolute immunity, so it is hardly threatened when judges are called to account for personal transgressions. It is not controversial to expect judges to refrain from sexual assault, racial slurs, financial coercion, and similar conduct. No one worries that the independence of the judiciary is threatened by enforceable standards of dignity, respect for others, and non-exploitation of office[④].

Judicial Independence in Theory and Practice

The abstract principal of judicial independence ranks high on the scale of democratic values. Without an independent judiciary, many of our rights and liberties would amount to little more than hollow promises. But what are the components of judicial independence?

---

①　Circuit Judicial Councils:巡回法院法官行为委员会,该委员会的主要责任是在其辖区内通过对保证整个巡回法院内部运行有关联的事项进行处理,从而进一步改进法律实施,其依法可以发出"为进一步有效及时地处理整个辖区内法律实施有关的适当的且必要的命令"。其主要由巡回法院首席法官以及巡回法院其他法官及相等数量的地区法院的法官组成。英文表达:The primary function of the Circuit Judicial Council is to improve the administration of justice within the circuit by acting on issues that affect the internal operations of the entire circuit. The Council is empowered by statute to "... make all necessary and appropriate orders for the effective and expeditious administration of justice within its circuit" (28 U.S.C. §§332 (d)(1)). Within this broad grant of supervisory power, the Council has two important mandates: formulation of circuit policy and implementation of policy directives received from the United States Judicial Conference and, in some instances, the Congress. The law provides that councils must consist of the Chief Judge of the Court of Appeals and an equal number of circuit and district court judges.

②　the Model Code of Judicial Conduct:《法官行为示范法典》,有的学者翻译为《标准司法行为规范》,美国律师协会制定的有关法官行为的准则,几乎得到各州接受,或被各州纳入其法律。

③　official and off-the-bench conduct:法官职务行为和非职务行为。其中,off-the-bench 指离开法官席,没开庭审案的意思。

④　non-exploitation of office:not abuse of office,不得渎职。

Though he did not use term explicitly, we can learn much about the meaning and value of judicial independence from a little known passage by the late Justice Robert Jackson. Writing in the midst of the Cold War, and deep in the throes of the McCarthy ear, Justice Jackson observed:

Severe substantive laws can be endured if they are fairly and impartially applied. Indeed, if put to the choice, one might well prefer to live under Soviet substantive law applied in good faith by our common-law procedures than under our substantive law enforced by Soviet *procedure* practices.

Justice Jackson's pointed disdain was for Soviet procedural *practices*, not necessarily for their formal law of procedure. His point, in other words, was that Soviet judges were known to be influenced by considerations other than the merits of a particular case①. They decided cases as the government wanted them decided—they were not independent.

Parsing further, we may conclude that the details of independence are fairness, impartiality, and good faith. Thus, an independent judge gives every party a full and fair opportunity to be heard without regard to the party's identity or position in society. An independent judge presides impartially, free from extraneous influences and immune to outside pressure. An independent judge rules in good faith, determined to follow the law as she understands it, unmindful of possible personal, political, or financial repercussions.

There are, no doubt, other components or definitions of judicial independence, but Justice Jackson's conception surely provides us with a useful starting point. What is the potential impact of accountability upon a judge's capacity to be fair and impartial and to rule in good faith?

Independence Notwithstanding Accountability

Why should judges be "accountable", and for what? While a survey of the law and philosophy of judicial discipline is beyond the scope of this essay, it is probably safe to say that a broad consensus of the public expects judges to be answerable, one way or another, for broad categories of misconduct that include misuse of office, undignified behavior, bias or prejudgement, harmful or offensive conduct, dereliction of duty, or disrespect for the law (including, of course, lawbreaking).

It is striking note how little threat to independence is implicit in most instances that seem to call for accountability. Looking only at the events of the past few years, there can be no serious argument that independence is compromised when a judge faces reprimand or suspension for using his office to coerce the payment of a debt to his daughter, fixing traffic tickets (or attempting to)②, or attempting to recruit litigants as Amway sales representatives③ to the judge's own financial benefit. Nor would fairness and impartiality be threatened when a judge faces discipline for vulgar

---

① to be influenced by considerations other than the merits of a particular case:受到除具体案件事实之外其他种种考虑因素的影响。other than 等同 except for;merits of a case 为案件的实体部分,案件事实。

② fixing traffic tickets (or attempting to):摆平(或企图摆平)交通违章传票事件。其中,fixing 是指非法买通或操纵,其主要见于 to fix the jury 以贿赂等不当方式买通陪审团等,故在我国,"律师与法官勾兑"的说法,可以翻译为 to fix the judge。

③ Amway sales representatives:安利公司的销售代理商。Amway 是美国一家公司,以直销日化商品著名。

sexual harassment (or worse), public intoxication, or interference with law enforcement.

The preceding examples are easy for two reasons: The judges' conduct was outrageous and their interest in pursuing the conduct was trivial. If accountability calls for a balancing test, harassment and intoxication place negative weight on the scale.

There are other situations, however, where judicial discipline does collide with important rights and interests. It may well be that judges are over-regulated in certain areas, resulting in an unnecessary diminution of personal freedom. Nonetheless, it does not follow that all improvident restrictions impinge upon independence.

For example, there has been much litigation in recent years over the scope of judges' campaign speech. The clear trend has been toward broadening the range of permitted speech, but some restrictions still remain. There are good arguments on both sides of this issue. Restrictionists want to keep judging out of politics; campaigning judges want to inform the electorate. For the time being, it appears that the balance will tip in favor of speech, although it is possible that a series of excesses might swing the pendulum back toward constraint.

For present purposes, however, it is sufficient to note that even the more rigid limits on campaign speech do not threaten judicial independence. A recent controversy in Georgia illustrates this point. In a 1998 election for a position on the Georgia Supreme Court, candidate George Weaver made a series of abrasive attacks on the incumbent, Justice Leah Sears. A special panel of the state's Judicial Qualifications Commission ("GJQC") determined that Mr. Weaver's campaign materials were misleading, as defined by the Georgia Code of Judicial Conduct, and issued a "cease and desist request." When Mr. Weaver continued to run his television spots, the GJQC issued a formal rebuke branding Mr. Weaver's materials "false, deceptive, and misleading." The GJQC faxed its finding to twelve major news carriers, adding that "all appropriate media outlets are requested and urged to prominently publicize this Notice at the earliest practical date." Mr. Weaver responded by filing a federal court lawsuit, which is unresolved as of this writing.

Mr. Weaver's campaign rhetoric was rough by any standard. He claimed that Justice Sears believed traditional moral standards to be "pathetic and disgraceful," that she favored licensing same-sex marriage, and that she had called the electric chair "silly." The GJQC panel, however, believed that Mr. Weaver had taken all of his references far out of context—hence the reprimand. Of course, the constitutional issues are clearly framed: Is there a compelling public interest in confining the terms of debate in judicial campaigns? Does a public reprimand amount to a prior restraint?

But it is equally clear that whatever the outcome of Mr. Weaver's litigation, whether or not the GJQC continues to vet campaign ads for deception, there will be no discernible impact on judicial independence. Returning to our touchstones of fairness, impartiality, and good faith, we can conclude rather safely that the extent of Mr. Weaver's ability to criticize his opponent would not cause him to be more or less fair and impartial upon taking the bench. The reprimand of Mr. Weaver—that is, the GJQC's assertion of accountability—had little capacity to affect the manner in which he would have judged had he won the election. Mr. Weaver campaigned as a conservative. Can there be any doubt he would have judged as a conservative, with or without the GJQC's cease and desist request? Indeed, both candidates' views predated the election, as did their qualifications, and the only real question posed by the GJOC's reprimand was how much information would be shared with the public.

The same can be said of non-campaign related speech. While the issues are important and in need of serious attention, judicial independence is not compromised by restrictions—even by unacceptable restrictions—on judges' First American rights.

In *In re Sanders*①, a specially constituted *pro tempore* panel② of the Washington Supreme Court considered disciplinary charges against Justice Richard Standards, an elected member of that court. The Washington Commission on Judicial Conduct ("WCJC") had earlier reprimanded Justice Sanders for addressing a "March for Life" held on the steps of the state capitol. In a prepared statement, delivered shortly following his induction to his court, Justice Sanders told the assembled marchers:

I want to give all of you my best wishes in this celebration of human life. Nothing is, nor should be, more fundamental in our legal system than the preservation and protection of innocent human life. By coincidence, or perhaps by providence, my formal induction to the Washington State Supreme Court occurred about an hour ago. I owe my election to many of the people who are here today and I'm here to say thank you very much and good luck. Our mutual pursuit of justice requires a lifetime of dedication and courage. Keep up the good work.

The WCJC concluded that these remarks, in the context of a rally that also included the endorsement of political candidates, violated-several sections of the Washington Code of Judicial Conduct, primarily because the political nature of the event (in their view) "diminished public confidence in the judiciary".

The Washington Supreme Court disagreed, holding that Justice Sanders's short speech did not "rise to a level permitting sanction." The court analyzed the issue as a conflict between the "government's interest in a fair and impartial judiciary (and) a judge's interest in the right to express his or her views". On balance, the court decided that Justice Sander's "words and actions" had not "called into question the integrity and impartiality of the judge." Consequently, the reprimand was reversed.

Many, obviously including the Washington Commission on Judicial Conduct, believe this to have been a close case③. The court itself, while reversing the sanction, limited its ruling to the facts of the case, observing that "the principle of impartial justice under law is strong enough to entitle government to restrict the freedom of speech of participants in the judicial process." Thus, the question is sure to arise again in other states and in other contexts.

It is important to note that the Washington Supreme Court consistently characterized Justice Sanders's interest as "the right to express [his] views" and the need for "free expression" and

---

① *In re Sanders*:桑德斯有关事项案。*in re* 多用作指无对方当事人的对物诉讼,或由单方当事人提起的案件,此处其是指由法官桑德斯因不满"华盛顿州法官行为委员会"(the Washington Commission on Judicial Conduct)所作出的谴责(reprimand)裁定而代表自己单方提起的要求废除谴责裁定之诉。

② *pro tempore* panel:临时审判庭。pro tempore:拉丁语,暂时的,临时的。

③ close case:势均力敌的,无胜负之分的案件。

"the interest of a judge in exercising his or her rights under the First Amendment." In other words, freedom of speech is a personal right; it is precious and not easily abridged, hut it is not an essential element of independent judging. The Washington court did not conclude, nor does it appear that Justice Sanders argued, that restrictions on speech would impinge upon judicial independence.

Thus, we may conclude, in turn, that the WCJC reprimand (read: order of accountability), had it been upheld, would have been bad for Justice Sanders and his colleagues, but that it would not have compromised the fairness, impartiality, and good faith of the Washington judiciary.

I do not mean to trivialize restrictions on judges' speech. Rather, my point is that the impact of such limitations is personal and not institutional. We could have a perfectly independent judiciary even if they had to function under severe—even unjustified and unnecessary—constraints on individual expression. Other incidents of accountability do, however, threaten judicial independence.

Accountability and independence are not mutually exclusive: most often, we can have both. But there are situations in which the possibility of discipline most definitely does endanger the independence of the judiciary. The most serious threat arises when sanctions are imposed based upon the content of a judge's decision. Consider a series of fairly recent cases in California, Alaska, and Illinois.

Perhaps the most troubling and controversial matter is the pending case against Justice J. Anthony Kline of the California Appellate Court. In 1997, Justice Kline issued a dissenting opinion in *Morrow v. Hood Communications, Inc.* In which he stated that he declined, "as a matter of conscience" to follow a state supreme court precedent that allows parties to use so-called stipulated reversals as a settlement device. Several months later, the California Commission on Judicial Performance ("CCJP") filed a formal charge against Justice Kline, accusing him of "willful misconduct" in office, based on his dissent in *Marrow*. This may well be the very first time that a state judicial conduct organization has pursued disciplinary charges solely on the basis of the substance of a judge's written ruling.

The threat to judicial independence is made all the more palpable by the moderate and reasoned nature of Justice Kline's position. First, it must be noted that Justice Kline wrote in dissent. The majority of his court actually entered the requested reversal, though noting that they agreed with Justice Kline's objections to the procedure. Consequently, the most that can be said of Justice Kline's action is that he expressed his opinion about a matter of California law. Although he refused to sign an order, that refusal had no consequence to any party or any court. Moreover, Justice Kline detailed his reasons, making it clear that he acted in good faith, According to Justice Kline, the "stipulated reversal" process can damage the adjudicative function of trial court by turning their decisions into "commodities that may be bought and sold." Stating that he would "of course comply with an order of the California Supreme Court to grant a particular request for a stipulated reversal," he went on to implore that court to reexamine its precedent and explained that his dissent could provide them with an opportunity to do so, which might not arise in the ordinary course of litigation:

It is an unwise and even dangerous decision that warrants reconsideration by our Supreme Court. However, because motions for stipulated reversal are by nature collaborative and almost never opposed, and because the Courts of Appeal have little discretion to deny them, petitions for review to the Supreme Court are unlikely. That court will therefore have few opportunities to reconsider the precedent unless it exercises its power to review on its own motion. This case provides an excellent opportunity for the exercise of that power.

Thus, Justice Kline faces punishment—in theory, the penalty could include removal from the bench—because he stated his views while attempting to follow the law in good faith. Indeed, his dissent served a purposeful legal function, in that it created a path for the Supreme Court to reconsider a ruling that might other "rules in good faith, determined to follow the law as [he] understands it, unmindful of possible personal... repercussions". The CCJP's action threatens precisely that concept of independence. In a regime where judges are punished for speaking their minds, the judiciary will necessarily become timid and unimaginative. In the worst case, the disciplinary authorities may use such power to enforce a judicial orthodoxy, limiting the way in which the law may be interpreted or understood. Judges who must rule in the shadow of personal jeopardy are the very antithesis of independent, as fear and doubt may cause them to steer a safe course rather than a true one.

The Kline inquiry turns out to be an easy case for almost everyone except the California Commission on Judicial Performance. Judges, lawyers, academics, and even legislators have rallied behind Justice Kline. It is safe to say that there is very little support for punishing judges under such circumstances (though as of this writing the CCJP continues to pursue Justice Kline). Other cases, however, are harder. The judge may not be so articulate or sympathetic; the ruling may be less principled, it may be wrong, it my even be intolerable. The true test of our commitment to judicial independence comes in more difficult circumstances.

While everyone believes in judicial independence, it turns out to be much harder to appreciate independent judges—especially when their rulings are objectionable or ill-conceived. But independence is intended to protect a judge's freedom of conscience, not to guarantee popular, or even uniformly appropriate, outcomes.

In an unreported[①]Alaska case, a trial court judge was charged by that state's judicial commission with having violated the due process rights of a criminal *defendant*. The judge, on his own motion, had ordered an *ex parte* "security hearing" in which he considered various precautions to be taken in the courtroom against the possibility that the defendant might attempt to escape. The prosecutor was asked to propose security measures to the court, but the defendant and his counsel were excluded from the hearing.

It was later determined, at least to the satisfaction of the disciplinary panel, that the judge had indeed violated the defendant's right to be present. In other words, the ruling was wrong. Moreover, it had few of the saving graces of Justice Kline's dissent. The Alaska judge acted alone: his order was not merely advisory, but actually imposed severe conditions on a defendant who had

---

① unreported:未收入判例汇编的。

Lesson Nine Judicial Discipline and Judicial Independence

no input at the hearing. The judge did not write an opinion aimed at obtaining review from a higher court, but rather pushed ahead over the defendant's objection. It was not alleged that the judge acted other than in good faith, but his alleged disregard for the defendant's rights resulted in a disciplinary charge.

In a far more notorious and widely-reported case, Judge Howard Broadman of California's trial court created a national controversy when he ordered a female defendant to submit to an implanted birth control device as a condition of probation. Women's groups and civil liberties organizations protested that the judge had trampled on the defendant's right to bodily integrity. Judge Broadman refused to relent, stating his position that his "Norplant condition"① enabled him to sentence her to probation rather than the penitentiary. He did, however, stay his order pending appeal. The order thereafter became moot when the defendant violated her probation and _was sentenced to_ prison by another judge.

In a similar case, Judge Broadman placed a woman on probation for five years subject to the condition that she "not get pregnant" during that time. Convicted on drug charges, the woman had previously lost custody of all five of her children. Said Judge Broadman, "I'm afraid that if you get pregnant we're going to get a cocaine or heroin addicted baby". The "no pregnancy" condition was later reversed on appeal because it impinged upon the exercise of the fundamental right to privacy.

The California Commission on Judicial Performance served a formal complaint on Judge Broadman, charging him with willful misconduct in office on the ground that he had abused the rights of defendants and acted in excess of his judicial authority. Without full rehearsing the facts, which have been thoroughly reported in the legal and mainstream press, suffice it to say that this aspect of the Broadman case place the issue of judicial independence in sharp contrast. On one hand, the CCJP, supported by many civil liberties and women's groups, charged that Judge Broadman had flouted clear legal mandates, in the process violating the most intimate rights of several defendants.

On the other hand, Judge Broadman, supported by an *amicus* brief from the California Judges Association, argued that the disciplinary charge itself impinged upon his own exercise of judicial independence. He pointed out that his efforts at creative sentencing (even if misguided) had allowed him to place two women on probation who otherwise would have been sentenced to the penitentiary and that future defendants would be ill-served if judges were to become wary of creative sentencing alternatives, lest they subject themselves to charges of misconduct.

As matters developed, the "improper sentencing" charges against Judge Broadman were both dismissed, as was the "security hearing" charge against the Alaska judge, though not until after lengthy hearings. In each case, the respondent-judge② was required to retain counsel③ at personal expense and was subjected to an extended public review. While neither was ultimately punished for the content of his rulings, the potential for intimidation nonetheless seems clear.

---

① "Norplant condition": Norplant 是法官 Howard Broadman 审理案件中的女被告,她因虐待子女被定罪,在判刑时又怀有身孕,判决待她分娩后才能生效。
② respondent-judge:作为被告的法官。
③ retain counsel:雇佣律师。注意的是雇佣律师通常不用 employ 而用 retain。

Legal Terminology

1. regulations 与 ordinance

regulations 作为"条例"来讲时,与 ordinance 为同义词,不过,尽管在词典中它们均被译为"条例",但两者的区别却较大。Ordinances 多指由自治市或其他地方立法机关所颁布的一种地方性法规(of municipal and other local legislative bodies),其也称为 bylaw 或 municipal ordinance。而 regulations 则主要指由行政机构(executive agencies)所制定和颁布的规则,故其应为"行政条例"。

2. accountability, responsibility 与 liability

accountability 在法律英语中译为"责任",同时还具有此意的单词有 responsibility, liability。尽管均有"责任"之意,但在实际的使用当中却有极大的差别。Accountability 含有下级对上级的责任之意,譬如官员对人民负有的责任则用 accountability,类似我国的问责制;而 responsibility 则是指上级对下级的事前的责任, liability 侧重指事后的责任, e. g. the defendant's liability to the plaintiff still has to be determined.

3. procedure, action, litigation, suit 与 proceedings

procedure 有诉讼的含义。其近义词有 action, litigation, suit, proceedings。action, litigation 和 proceedings 都为一般术语,可指各种诉讼案件。但 action 则逐渐演变,现在多用于指民事诉讼了,因而有 action is a mode of proceeding 的说法。如果要表示刑事诉讼,多应在 action 前面加 criminal 予以区分。Litigation 除了指诉讼之外,还有诉讼程序的含义,如 Civil Litigation 便为《民事诉讼程序》,是一本有关英国民事诉讼程序的专著。Suit 是 lawsuit 的简略形式,主要用于指民事诉讼。传统上,action 和 suit 之间的差异在于 action 指普通法法院的诉讼,其程序到法院判决(judgment)即终止;而 suit 则为衡平法法院的用语,其程序包括判决和执行(judgment and execution)。在美国,这两个单词的差异因衡平法院和普通法院的合并已经不再存在。Procedure 主要是指诉讼程序,如 criminal procedure code(刑事诉讼法典)等。

4. defendant, respondent, accused, defender 与 libel(l)ee

五词均有"被告"的含义。其中,defendant 为通用语,可用于一般民事或刑事案件的初审中,与其相对的原告为 plaintiff。Respondent 用语上诉审(此时也称为 appellee)及申请获得特别命令或离婚、遗嘱验证等衡平法案件中,与其相对的原告(或上诉人)有 appellant, petitioner, applicant 等。Accused 专指刑事被告,与之相对的原告有 plaintiff(形式自诉人)或 prosecution(公诉方)。Defender 则是苏格兰专门用语,与其相对的原告为 pursuer。libel(l)ee 则专指海事或离婚案件的原告,与其相对的原告为 libel(l)ant。

5. sentence, decision, award, finding, judgment 与 verdict

sentence 译为判决、裁定。常见的含有此意的还有 decision, award, finding, judgment, verdict 等。Decision 为通用词汇,可指任何类别的裁决或判决,如 arbitral decision(仲裁判决)或 judicial decision(司法判决)等。Award(也称 arbitrament)专指仲裁裁决或陪审团有关损害赔偿金的裁决。Finding(finding of fact 也常简称为 finding)多用于指对事实的裁定。Judgment 多指法院对诉讼案件的最终判决(final decision),可指民事判决,也可用于指刑事判决,尤其是指结果为赦免、撤销原判、驳回上诉等不科处刑罚之判决。而与之相对, sentence 的中心含义为科刑(inflicting punishment on the convicted),故其只限于指刑事判决,且为处以刑罚之目的的判决；如无罪开释则应用其他词，如 decision 或 judgment 等来表示。Verdict 是指陪审团作出的有关事实等的陪审判决。

Exercises

I Verbal Abilities

Part One

Directions: *For each of these completing questions, read each item carefully to get the sense of it. Then, in the proper space, complete each statement by supplying the missing word or phrase.*

1. He was _____ for his abuse of office.
   A. amortized   B. berated   C. indicted
   D. enervated   E. protracted

2. Judges should, in my opinion, refrain from sexual assault, racial slurs, financial _____, and similar conduct.
   A. coercion   B. extraction   B. plunder
   D. robbery   E. smuggling

3. _____ further, one can find that many economics blame the decline of inner city on "structural changes".
   A. Departing   B. Accounting   C. Going
   D. Alleging   E. Parsing

4. While giving his ruling, an independent judge should be unmindful of personal, political, or financial _____.
   A. effects   B. backgrounds   C. capacities
   D. repercussions   E. millenaries

5. Misuse of office, undignified behavior, bias or _____, harmful or offensive conduct should be considered misconduct of judges.
   A. burglar   B. prejudgement   C. threatening
   D. slurs   E. precondition

6. Any judge who is _____ in his duty should be disciplined by the Washington Commission on Judicial Conduct.
   A. ignore   B. misuse   C. derelict
   D. inferential   E. garrulous

7. It is incumbent _____ you to warn the boy of the danger of smoking.
   A. to   B. up to   C. of
   D. upon   E. for

8. Don't try to _____ on another's rights.
   A. violate   B. breach   C. impinge
   D. fringe   E. restrain

9. The justice was _____ a subordinate for being imprudent.

   A. denouncing
   B. illustrating
   C. ill-treating
   D. under-valuing
   E. rebuking

10. While most politicians will cheerfully or angrily critique any story in which their name has appeared, Justices rarely respond to public comment, or even to _____ error.

   A. rank
   B. dogmatic
   C. replenished
   D. soporific
   E. millinery

Part Two

Directions: *Choose the one word or phase that best keep the meaning of the original sentence if it were substituted for the underlined part.*

1. Many people really believed that this to have been a <u>close</u> case.

   A. difficult
   B. ended
   C. even
   D. arid
   E. proximate

2. Judges who must rule in the shadow of personal jeopardy are the very <u>opposition</u> of the independent, as fear and doubt may cause them to steer a safe course rather than a true one.

   A. opponent
   B. preposition
   C. minimum
   D. antithesis
   E. circumvention

3. When the Supreme Court <u>affirms</u> a lower court it is approving the decision made and leaving it unchanged.

   A. supports
   B. holds
   C. upholds
   D. backs
   E. retains

4. The Commission shall establish for appropriate cases an <u>expedited procedure</u> for consideration and determination of the question of a stay.

   A. special proceeding
   B. extra procedure
   C. ad hoc formality
   D. accelerated procedure
   E. delayed process

5. However, in our <u>opinion</u>, this is not the issue.

   A. submission
   B. idea
   C. redolence
   D. dipsomania
   E. knowledge

6. It involves conduct that causes injury and fails to <u>meet</u> some standard set by society.

   A. come up to
   B. measure up to
   C. bring line with
   D. get compatible to
   E. account for

7. Such a document is known as a <u>self-written</u> will, and it must be written by hand by the testator, the person whose will it is.

   A. calligraphic
   B. panoramic
   C. photographic
   D. heterodesmic
   E. holographic

8. The judge had <u>flouted</u> clear legal mandates.

   A. mocked at
   B. violated
   C. looked up to
   D. blew dirty words at
   E. made slurs upon

9. He was charge of having violated the most <u>intimate</u> rights of several defendants.

A. close   B. imminent   C. urgent
D. private   E. valuable

10. Especially the error is not <u>flagrant</u> or part of a prolonged pattern.

A. notorious   B. marked   C. scandalous
D. blazing   E. evident

II Cloze Test

Directions: *Fill in each blank in the following passage with an appropriate word.*

Few judicial decisions in recent Illinois history have created as much outcry as the case of "Baby Richard," _____ birth father, Otakar Kirchner, spent three years attempting to undo an adoption _____ which he had never consented. During the extended litigation, "Richard" continued to live with his would-be adoptive parents, developing the close emotional ties attendant to every nurturing and loving relationship.

The Illinois Supreme Court, in an _____ written by Justice James Heiple, eventually ruled in favor of Mr. Kirchner, holding that "the father's parental interest was improperly terminated" and ordering that the child _____ returned to his birth-father notwithstanding the ties he had formed with his adoptive parents.

To many observers of the case, Mr. Kirchner's efforts were cruel and heartless, an attempt to sever Richard's loving connection to the only _____ he had ever known. Critics castigated the Illinois Supreme Court and Justice Heiple in particular. One highly respected legal commentator observed:

No state should be allowed to _____ a child the love and support and affection of his patents without even considering the child's interests. That is what the Illinois Supreme Court did. It held that a father had a right to be with his child _____ ignored the rights of a child to be with his [adoptive] _____.

Illinois Governor Jim Edgar took the same position, stating it even more bluntly:

[The case] is about a young boy whom the _____ has decreed should be brutally, tragically torn away from the only parents he has ever known—parents who by all accounts loved and nurtured him from the second he joined their family.

This young child should have found a champion—a protector—in the highest court of the state. Instead, he found justices who betrayed their obligations to him and to the people who placed them in their _____ positions.

III Reading Comprehension

Directions: *In this section there are passages followed by questions or unfinished statements, each with suggested answers. Choose the one you think is the best answer.*

Passage One

Most noticeably, *Chicago Tribune* columnist Bob Greene declared virtual war on Justice Heiple, devoting column after column to personal attacks on the judge. Walter Jacobson, a television newscaster, went so far as to announce Justice Heiple's home telephone number, urging his viewers to call the judge and voice their complaints. Justice Heiple no doubt made matters worse when he responded to the attacks in the body of a judicial opinion, referring to them as "journalistic terrorism."

Criticism in the press is a fact of life for judges. In extreme situations, it is possible that such criticism may actually threaten judicial independence, but there is no solution to that problem—the press must be free. The same cannot be said of politicians, however, who may seize upon press reports to launch their own attacks on unpopular judges. This is precisely what happened in the case of Justice Heiple, who seems to have done all he could to make himself as unpopular as possible.

Justice Heiple, it turns out, was a confirmed highway speeder, in consequence of which he often found himself stopped by the Illinois State Police. On at least three occasions, he used (or attempted to use) his position as a supreme court justice as a means of avoiding a citation. Once, when that method failed, he resorted to physical resistance, resulting in his arrest. The arrest led to a disciplinary charge, which led, in turn, to a formal censure. None of this, of course, remotely threatens judicial independence—but the next installment in the saga does.

By the time his speeding exploits became public knowledge, many state legislators had had quite enough of Justice Heiple. Fueled beyond question by disgust with his "Baby Richard" ruling, the Illinois House of Representatives began an investigation of possible impeachment. The impeachment inquiry was officially limited to the traffic incidents and several administrative matters, but many believed that this was simply a convenient hook on which to hang an extraordinarily unpopular judge. Other Illinois judges had done worse, in some cases much worse, without facing impeachment. Indeed, there was little doubt at the time that a significant part of the motive for impeachment inquiry could be found in the outcome of the "Baby Richard" case.

In the end, the investigation was terminated and impeachment was not pursued. The legislature's special investigative committee closed its file, announcing that "[t]o impeach for anything less than the most serious offenses would send a chilling message to once and future judges." But even in the absence of an actual impeachment, it cannot have escaped the notice of every judge in Illinois that Justice Heiple had made himself a large and easy target by applying the law as he understood it in the case of "Baby Richard."

1. Justice Heiple was attacked _____.

A. because he was a speeder

B. with his opinion in the case of "Baby Richard"

C. for he responded to the journalists in the body of a judicial opinion

D. simply because he acted unduly in dealing with his traffic breaches

E. for he bluntly treated people's critics

2. Which of the following is true?

A. Justice Heiple did not respond to the attacks.

B. *Chicago Tribune* columnist Bob Greene stroke violently with Justice Heiple.

C. People cared nothing about the war declared by *Chicago Tribune* columnist Bob Greene on

Justice Heiple.

   D. Walter Jacobson was a television viewer.

   E. Justice Heiple did not deal with reporters' attacks properly.

3. Because of highway speeding, Heiple _____.

   A. was imprisoned

   B. was fined

   C. received a formal censure

   D. was impeached

   E. was held guilty of immorality

4. According to this passage, the impeachment _____.

   A. was initiated by the Illinois justices

   B. went through by the Illinois House of representatives

   C. came to an end with the Judge's loss of office

   D. did not go through

   E. was not welcomed by justices and legislators

Passage Two

The point of the preceding discussion was to make evident the potentially corrosive effect of imposing, or even threatening discipline on the basis of a judge's good faith decision. In each of the cases reviewed, the judge attempted to apply the law to a difficult situation, perhaps correctly and perhaps in error, but always in apparent sincerity. In each case, however, the controversial or unpopular nature of the decision resulted in severe personal consequences for the judge: threatened loss of office, damage to reputation, extreme personal inconvenience and expense. While most judges are responsible and some are even courageous, it is safe to assume that few would choose to venture repeatedly into such a hazardous situation. The result, therefore, can only be timidity with no guarantee against its steady spread throughout an entire state judiciary.

One could press the case for independence too far. There is some conduct, even "decisional" conduct, that must merit punishment if for no other reason than to preserve the honor and integrity of the judiciary. Judges have been known to use ethnic slurs in the course of their judgments and even to announce cruel stereotypes as the basis for a ruling. Some judges have demonstrated utter ignorance of the law, or sheer disregard for it, some going so far as to decide cases on the basis of "coin flips". Absolute immunity for all decision-making behavior would surely go too far. Still, some method must be found that will draw the correct line between actual misconduct and mere error of unpopularity.

To my knowledge, neither any commentator nor any court has yet devised a bright-line test that will solve this problem in all circumstances. Even a pure "good faith" standard—protective as it would be of independence—is insufficient, because it would preclude the removal of a sincere-but-incompetent judge who repeatedly misapplies the law and damages the rights of litigants. While it may never be possible to fashion a comprehensive rule, the following factors describe situations in which the content of a judicial ruling may warrant discipline. And, in the absence of some unforeseen hut compelling circumstance, it seems fair to say that no discipline should ordinarily lie in the absence of at least one of the considerations.

First, as noted above, a pattern of repeated and uncorrected legal error is obviously more serious than an isolated instance. Judges who fail to learn and apply the law fall into a distinctly different category from those who simply hold minority—or innovative—opinions. The commission of multiple errors, or unacceptable judging that continues over a period of years, may indicate that the judge has not maintained professional competence in the law.

A second distinguishing criterion might be called something like the "egregiousness quotient" of the error. Serious misrulings are obviously more likely to amount to misconduct, though such a standard is admittedly inexact. There seems to be some agreement, however, that legal error becomes serious enough to warrant discipline when judges deny individuals their basic or fundamental procedural rights, as when a judge proceeds to adjudication without advising a defendant of the right to counsel, declines to hold a full hearing, or coerces a guilty plea. The same may occur when judges act beyond their lawful jurisdiction, as by sentencing defendants to jail when only a fine is authorized by law or sentencing defendants to incarceration for a period longer than the maximum allowed by statute. One formulation holds that discipline is appropriate only where "a reasonably prudent and competent judge would consider [the ruling] obviously and seriously wrong in all the circumstances."

Of course, the motive of the judge must always be considered—is he or she acting in good faith? A willful refusal to follow the law, as distinct from an honest and acknowledged difference of opinion or interpretation, may manifest unfitness for judicial office. In the same vein, a judge may be sanctioned for intemperate or abusive rulings: such discipline being imposed because of the *manner* in which the judge ruled, rather than the substance of the decision. In *In re King*, for example, it was evident that the judge had ruled on the basis of racial animus when he set an unusually high bail for four African-American defendants. Shortly after imposing the high bail, the judge said to a court clerk, "That's what blacks get for voting against my brother." (Apparently, the judge's brother had done poorly in minority precincts in a recent gubernatorial election.) Although setting bail is a judicial act, it did not threaten independence when Judge King was subsequently censured by the Supreme Judicial Court of Massachusetts—the punishment was invoked for his bad faith and ill motive in reaching a decision, not for the content of the decision itself.

A third factor is the availability of appeal. A number of cases have held that discipline is unnecessary in situations where legal errors can be corrected on appeal, especially when the error is not flagrant or part of a prolonged pattern. This principle could not be used as a *per se* rule, since the appellate process and the disciplinary process serve markedly different functions. Appealability, if only as an indicator of the judge's good faith and the "ordinary" nature of the perceived error, is nonetheless an appropriate consideration. It is widely understood that disciplinary complaints should not be misused as an alternative to appeals by disgruntled litigants; this value is well served by considering the availability of appeal as a factor when determining whether to discipline a judge.

Finally, there is the astonishing problem of the "coin-flip" cases—that is, instances where a judge made a decision by flipping it coin in open court or by asking bystanders for their opinions.

Lesson Nine Judicial Discipline and Judicial Independence

Though such behavior is "decisional" in the crudest sense, it obviously constitutes a complete abdication of the judicial function, which is, after all, the duty to make reasoned decisions according to law. However broadly one interprets judicial independence, it cannot possibly extend to throwing darts.

1. Because of their decisions, judges even in good faith may also confront such personal consequences as _____.

   A. damage to reputation
   B. extreme personal inconvenience
   C. personal expense
   D. threatened loss of office
   E. arrest

2. In the author's opinion, _____.

   A. judges' decisional conduct should not be blamed
   B. Judges have been known to be always in good faith and will not use ethnic slurs in the course of their judgments
   C. all judges are good at laws
   D. while making their decisions, not all the judges faithfully perform their obligations
   E. judges should not be disciplined for their slurs

3. Judge King was censured _____.

   A. for his in reaching an ill-motive decision
   B. for his not reaching a good faith decision
   C. because the he had ruled on the basis of racial animus
   D. due to his setting an unusually high bail for four African-American defendants
   E. because he did perform his duty in good faith

IV Translation Abilities

法律语言特征分析与法律翻译技能培养之九：
法律文本的分类

1. 以文字为特征的划分

以文字为特征进行划分，法律语言可以分为口头（oral）语言和书面（written）语言。法律口头语言包括法庭用语、警方对嫌疑犯的调查和审讯、罪犯彼此的交流、律师和被代理人之间的对话等，其具有动态性（dynamic）和互动性（interactive）特征。书面法律语言属于静态（static）符号，主要包括立法和其他法律文本文件，如公约、章程、协议、合同等。鉴于英、美等国习惯于详尽仔细（detail），力求规定面面俱到，因而不少法律文本的篇幅都较长（monologic）。

正如 Olsson（2004:5）所说：法律语言是包含无限学科领域的科学（John Olsson, 2004），隶属于法律范畴的文本也包罗万千。从某种意义上讲，任何文本，只要其与法律或犯罪语境相关，都可能成为法律语言学研究相关文本，如车票、信函、收据、股票、论文、书籍等。事实上，作为一新兴学科，法律语言学的研究对象文本正在无限递增，越来越多的文本已被国际法律语言学家学会(International Association of Forensic Linguistics,简称为 IAFL)的网站(www.thetext.co.uk)所搜集和认可,承认它们是法律语言学研究的对象。

2. 从文体学的角度

从文体学的角度,人们可以按体裁(style)将法律文本分为"规范性法律语言类"(normative language of law)和"法学著述"(literature)。

(1) 规范性法律语言类

"规范性法律语言类"指为各级法院所接受和/或某特定司法管辖区的法规所体现的基本原则(basic principles accepted by courts and/or embodied in the statutes of a particular jurisdiction)。其多为明确的(positive)、强制性的(obligatory)法律文件。其中又分为:

- 制定法(statute)、惯例(customs)、司法学说(judicial doctrines)等。具体则可分为议会法律(act)、命令(order)、先例(precedent)、条例(ordinance)、地方法规(by-laws)、规定(regulations)、指示(direction)、行政法规(decree)、令状(warrant)等。

- 公民在日常事务和商事活动中经双方意愿而订立的各种合同(contract)、协议(agreement)以及证券(securities)、发票(invoice)、信用证(letter of credit)等中的条款规定等也应当算做属于"规范性法律语言"类别的文件。

(2) 法学著述

"法学著述"也称为"法学家语言"(language of jurist)。它包括法律评论文章(law review articles)、法学论文(treaties)、专著(monograph)、法官意见(judge's opinion)等。这种著述深奥莫测,经常充满不为非法律人理解的行话(legalese)。在国外,法学著述(包括论文、专著等)具有"说服性法律渊源"(persuasive legal resource)的功能,因而可以将其视为是一种特殊的法律文本,按其内容和风格可分为"教义型"(doctrinal)和"理论型"(或纯理论型)(theoretical)两大类。"教义型"著述属于传统型,主要以分析具体案例、阐述和理论法律条文及其适用情况等为主要内容。尽管"纯理论"研究的著述迅速增长,但"教义型"类别的著述数量仍然占到目前法学著述出版和发行份额的中的 70% 左右,主要读者群体是广大法律工作者及法律专业的学生等。国外的"理论型"或"纯理论型"论文或著述主要起源于 20 世纪 60 年代,多属于抽象理论解析类型。作者一般站在交叉学科,即边缘性学科的视角对法学等学科进行诠释、剖析、解构和建构。涉及领域十分广泛,包括心理学和法律学、法律哲学、社会学和法学、法律和语言学、语言法学、法律逻辑学等,以后逐渐发展到女性法学、工会法学等五花八门的类别。其中还不乏法学内部的学科交叉,如宪法刑法学、刑法环境法学等,鉴于这类型的著述内容十分抽象和高深,其迎合的对象一般都限制在具有相同志趣的法律或相关领域理论研究者之狭小范围中,属于曲高和寡之另类。目前其数量大略占到法学论著的 30% 左右。我国法律界的"理论型"研究始于 20 世纪 80 年代,而今也已达到非常可观的数量。然而遗憾的是此类著述(包括法律语言学在内)多以国外作品为模式,缺乏创建和个性思维。由于鲜有独创性,故其价值难免会大打折扣。

Haggard(2003)将法律文本分为"论证性文件"(discoursive writing)(即"法学著述")、"诉讼类文件"(litigation writing)(包括诉状、答辩状、动议书、证据开示申请等诉讼文书)和"规范性文件"(normative writing)(即"法律")三类文本。但这种三分法与前面的两分法并无本质上的差异。在法律翻译中,文体的区分对翻译标准的掌握显得比较重要。总体说来,"规范性语言"对译者的约束性更大,即译者自由发挥的余地很小。而"法学著述"或"论证性文件"和"诉讼类文件"对译者的约束则相对要小,即译者所受到的原文文字的约束要小于前者的约束。

美国法律语言学家 Tiersma（1999）则将法律文本分为：

（1）实施性文件（Operative documents）：起创制或修饰法律关系的作用（create or modify legal relations），即创制法律框架体系的语言，包括：立法（acts, orders, statutes）、司法文件，如诉辩状（pleadings, petitions）、判决书（judgment）等以及私人法律文件，如合同、遗嘱等。

（2）阐述性文件（Expository documents）：具有客观解释法律的功能和作用，包括：律师给被代理人的信函（letter to a client）、律师事务所备忘录（office memorandum）、法学著述和法学教育类材料（writing and educational material about the law）。

（3）说服性文件（Persuasive documents）：主要律师的辩护意见（submissions to convince a court）。

Tiersma 认为后两种在语言上并非"特别正式的法律语言"。

Translation Exercises

Part One *Put the Following into Chinese*

The need for explicit attention to the relationship between fiscal costs and political incentives is nicely illustrates be recent controversies surrounding unfunded mandates and the constitutional prohibition against federal commandeering of state legislatures and executive officials. In *New York v. United States*, the Supreme Court struck down a federal regulatory provision requiring states that were unable to provide for the disposal of their radioactive waste by a certain date to take title to the waste. This, explained the Court, amounted to unconstitutional "commandeering" of state governments by "directly compelling them to enact and enforce a federal regulatory program." In *Printz v. United States*. the Court extended the anti-commandeering rule from state legislatures to state and local government executive officials by striking down the Brady Act's interim conscription of local law enforcement officers to conduct background checks on prospective handgun purchasers.

Part Two *Put the Following into English*

法是统治阶级意志的体现，但并不是凡体现统治阶级意志的都是法。法所体现的不是一般的统治阶级意志，而是统治阶级的国家意志，即由国家制定或认可的、以国家强制力保证实施的那一部分统治阶级意志。因此，法离不开国家，没有国家就没有法。有什么性质的国家，就有什么性质的法。任何阶级只有掌握了国家权力，才有可能把自己的意志制定为法，使之成为国家意志，得到普遍的遵守。

V Interaction

Directions：*In this passage there are 5 underlined sentences, each of which contains a mistake. Try to find the mistakes and correct them. After you have read the passage, discuss with your tutor or people's judge about the judge's conduct and judicial independence. Then write a short passage of "Judicial Independence in China". Remember that you are to write clearly.*

It may well turn out that judicial independence is easier to protect than define. Perhaps it is best to think of independence as applying solely to the content or substance of a judicial opinion or act. Thus, independent judges are all liberty to judge—to interpret and apply the law—as free as possible in external constraints, influences, and pressures. There are many other attributes that make for good judging—attentiveness, engagement, empathy, broad-mindedness, to name a few—that are not directly related to independence.

Thus, there are circumstances which the possibility of discipline may actually damage the quality of judging without threatening independence. For example, restrictions on civic and charitable involvement may have the effect of isolating judges from their communities, thereby making them less attuned to life on the street and ultimately less able to judge wisely. Such limitations may be ill-advise, perhaps even self-defeating, but they do not impinge on independence.

Ultimately, the most important issue is the protection of "decisional" integrity. When does accountability threaten judicial discipline? What is the distinction between misconduct and error? In this regard, the availability of appeal, the nature of the judge's conduct, the extent of the courts jurisdiction, the motive of the judge, and the egregiousness and frequency of legal error are important factors that mediate the sensitive line between judicial misconduct and simple mistake.

VI Appreciation of Judge's Opinions

(1) **Case Name**(案件名): *Linda A. Watters v. Wachovia Bank*

550 U. S. _____ (2007)

SUPREME COURT OF THE UNITED STATES

No. 05.1342

LINDA A. WATTERS, COMMISSIONER, MICHIGAN
OFFICE OF INSURANCE AND FINANCIAL SERVICES, PETITIONER

v.

WACHOVIA BANK, N. A., ET AL.
ON WRIT OF CERTIORARI TO THE UNITED STATES COURT OF
APPEALS FOR THE SIXTH CIRCUIT

[April 17, 2007]

(2) **Case Summary**(案件简介)
Facts of the Case:

Under 12 U. S. C. Section 484(a), states do not have regulatory powers(监管权) over national banks. In 2001 the federal Office of the Comptroller of Currency (OCC) issued federal regulation 12 C. F. R. 7.4006, which applied 12 U. S. C. Section 484(a) to state-chartered operating subsidiaries of national banks. Wachovia Mortgage was an operating subsidiary of the national bank Wachovia Bank, and was registered with the state of Michigan.

When Michigan attempted to exercise its regulatory powers over Wachovia Mortgage, Wachovia Bank sued Watters, a Michigan official, seeking a judgment that Michigan's laws on operating subsidies of national banks were superseded(代替,接替,更替,继任) by 12 U. S. C Section 484(a). Michigan argued that the OCC had exceeded the authority given it by Congress by extending the definition of "national bank" to cover state-registered operating subsidiaries. Michigan also argued that the extension of federal authority over state entities like Wachovia Mortgage violates the Tenth Amendment, which reserves to states all powers not delegated to the federal government.

The District Court rejected these arguments and ruled for Wachovia, and the U.S. Court of Appeals for the Sixth Circuit affirmed. The Circuit Court found that the decision of the OCC to apply rules for national banks to their operating subsidiaries was a reasonable interpretation of Congress's intent, and therefore entitled to deference under *Chevron U.S.A. v. Natural Resources Defense Council*. The Sixth Circuit also held that Congress had the power to regulate operating subsidiaries of national banks under the Commerce Clause, so the Tenth Amendment did not reserve that power to the states.

Question(s):

1) Is the decision of the Comptroller of Currency that federal authority over national banks extends to state-chartered operating subsidiaries of national banks entitled to judicial deference under *Chevron U.S.A. v. Natural Resources Defense Council*?

2) Does 12 CFR 7.4006 violate the Tenth Amendment by treating a state-chartered operating subsidiary the same as a national bank for purposes of federal regulation?

Conclusion:

Unanswered and no. The Court ruled 5-3 that state-chartered operating subsidiaries of national banks are subject to regulation by the federal Office of the Comptroller of Currency and not by the states in which they are located. The opinion by Justice Ruth Bader Ginsburg held that "... the level of deference owed to the regulation is an academic question," because "Section 7.4006 merely clarifies and confirms what the National Bank Act already conveys: A national bank has the power to engage in real estate lending through an operating subsidiary, subject to the same terms and conditions that govern the national bank itself; that power cannot be significantly impaired or impeded by state law." The Court interpreted the statute broadly, as a shield against burdensome state regulation of national banks and their subsidiaries, so the OCC's regulation preempting Michigan's regulatory laws was firmly grounded in the statute. The Court briefly and definitively disposed of Watters's Tenth Amendment argument, holding that the regulation of subsidiaries of national banks is a legitimate application of Congress's Commerce Power and therefore is not reserved to the states.

Decisions

Decision: 5 votes for Wachovia Bank, 3 vote(s) against.

(3) Excerpts of the Judgment(法官判决词)

JUSTICE GINSBURG delivered the opinion of the Court.

Business activities of national banks are controlled by the National Bank Act (NBA or Act)(全国银行法), and regulations promulgated thereunder by the Office of the Comptroller of the Currency (OCC)(美国货币监理署). As the agency charged by Congress with supervision of the NBA, OCC oversees the operations of national banks and their interactions with customers. The agency exercises visitorial powers(查视权), including the authority to audit the bank's books and records(审计银行簿记和记录), largely to the exclusion of other governmental entities, state or federal.

The NBA specifically authorizes federally chartered banks(联邦特许银行) to engage in real estate lending(房地产的借贷).

It also provides that banks shall have power "to exercise... all such incidental powers(附带权力) as shall be necessary to carry on the business of banking." Among incidental powers, national banks may conduct certain activities through "operating subsidiaries", discrete entities authorized to engage solely in activities the bank itself could undertake, and subject to the same terms and conditions as those applicable to the bank.

Respondent Wachovia Bank, a national bank, conducts its real estate lending business through Wachovia Mortgage Corporation, a wholly owned, state-chartered entity, licensed as an operating subsidiary by OCC. It is uncontested in this suit that Wachovia's real estate business, if conducted by the national bank itself, would be subject to OCC's superintendence(管理;监督,监管), to the exclusion of state registration requirements and visitorial authority. The question in dispute is whether the bank's mortgage lending activities remain outside the governance of state licensing and auditing agencies when those activities are conducted, not by a division or department of the bank, but by the bank's operating subsidiary. In accord with the Courts of Appeals that have addressed the issue, we hold that Wachovia's mortgage business(按揭业务,抵押业务), whether conducted by the bank itself or through the bank's operating subsidiary, is subject to OCC's superintendence, and not to the licensing, reporting, and visitorial regimes of the several States in which the subsidiary operates.

I

Wachovia Bank is a national banking association chartered by OCC. Respondent Wachovia Mortgage is a North Carolina corporation that engages in the business of real estate lending in the State of Michigan and elsewhere. Michigan's statutory regime exempts banks, both national and state, from state mortgage lending regulation, but requires mortgage brokers(经纪人), lenders, and servicers that are subsidiaries of national banks to register with the State's Office of Insurance and Financial Services (OIFS)(州保险与金融服务局) and submit to state supervision. From 1997 until 2003, Wachovia Mortgage was registered with OIFS to engage in mortgage lending. As a registrant, Wachovia Mortgage was required, *inter alia*, to pay an annual operating fee, file an annual report, and open its books and records to inspection by OIFS examiners.

Petitioner Linda Watters, the commissioner of OIFS, administers the State's lending laws(负责实施和履行州借贷法律). She exercises "general supervision and control" over registered lenders, and has authority to conduct examinations and investigations and to enforce requirements against registrants. She also has authority to investigate consumer complaints(消费者投诉) and take enforcement action if she finds that a complaint is not being adequately pursued by the appropriate federal regulatory authority..

On January 1, 2003, Wachovia Mortgage became a wholly owned operating subsidiary of Wachovia Bank. Three months later, Wachovia Mortgage advised the State of Michigan that it was surrendering its mortgage lending registration. Because it had become an operating subsidiary of a national bank, Wachovia Mortgage maintained, Michigan's registration and inspection requirements were preempted. Watters responded with a letter advising Wachovia Mortgage that it would no longer be authorized to conduct mortgage lending activities in Michigan.

Wachovia Mortgage and Wachovia Bank filed suit against Watters, in her official capacity as commissioner, in the United States District Court for the Western District of Michigan. They sought declaratory and injunctive relief (确权式和禁止令式的救济方法) prohibiting Watters from enforcing Michigan's registration prescriptions against Wachovia Mortgage, and from interfering with OCC's exclusive visitorial authority.

The NBA and regulations promulgated thereunder, they urged, vest supervisory authority in OCC and preempt the application of the state-law controls at issue. Specifically, Wachovia Mortgage and Wachovia Bank challenged as preempted certain provisions of two Michigan statutes—the Mortgage Brokers, Lenders, and Services Licensing Act(《按揭经纪人、借贷人和服务许可法》) and the Secondary Mortgage Loan Act(《次级按揭贷款法》). The challenged provisions (1) require mortgage lenders—including national bank operating subsidiaries but not national banks themselves—to register and pay fees to the State before they may conduct banking activities in Michigan, and authorize the commissioner to deny or revoke registrations; (2) require submission of annual financial statements to the commissioner and retention of certain documents in a particular format; (3) grant the commissioner inspection and enforcement authority over registrants; and (4) authorize the commissioner to take regulatory or enforcement actions against covered lenders.

In response, Watters argued that, because Wachovia Mortgage was not itself a national bank, the challenged Michigan controls were applicable and were not preempted. She also contended that the Tenth Amendment to the Constitution of the United States prohibits OCC's exclusive superintendence of national bank lending activities conducted through operating subsidiaries.

The District Court granted summary judgment to the banks in relevant part. Invoking the two-step framework of

Chevron U. S. A. Inc. v. *Natural Resources Defense Council, Inc.* (1984), the court deferred to the Comptroller's determination that an operating subsidiary is subject to state regulation only to the extent that the parent bank would be if it performed the same functions. The court also rejected Watters' Tenth Amendment argument.

II

A

Nearly two hundred years ago, in *McCulloch* v. *Maryland* (1819), this Court held federal law supreme over state law with respect to national banking. Though the bank at issue in *McCulloch* was short-lived, a federal banking system reemerged in the Civil War era. In 1864, Congress enacted the NBA, establishing the system of national banking still in place today. The Act vested in nationally chartered banks enumerated powers and all such incidental powers as shall be necessary to carry on the business of banking. To prevent inconsistent or intrusive state regulation from impairing the national system, Congress provided: "No national bank shall be subject to any visitorial powers except as authorized by Federal law...."

In the years since the NBA's enactment, we have repeatedly made clear that federal control shields national banking from unduly burdensome and duplicative state regulation. Federally chartered banks are subject to state laws of general application in their daily business to the extent such laws do not conflict with the letter or the general purposes of the NBA. For example, state usury laws(反高利贷法) govern the maximum rate of interest national banks can charge on loans, contracts made by national banks "are governed and construed by State laws," and national banks' "acquisition and transfer of property are based on State law." However, "the States can exercise no control over national banks, nor in any wise sense affect their operation, except in so far as Congress may see proper to permit. Any thing beyond this is an abuse, because it is the usurpation of power which a single State cannot give."

We have "interpreted grants of both enumerated and incidental 'powers' to national banks as grants of authority not normally limited by, but rather ordinarily preempting, contrary state law." States are permitted to regulate the activities of national banks where doing so does not prevent or significantly interfere with the national bank's or the national bank regulator's exercise of its powers. But when state prescriptions significantly impair the exercise of authority, enumerated or incidental under the NBA, the State's regulations must give way.

The NBA authorizes national banks to engage in mortgage lending, subject to OCC regulation. The Act provides:

"Any national banking association may make, arrange, purchase or sell loans or extensions of credit secured by liens on interests in real estate, subject to 1828(o) of this title and such restrictions and requirements as the Comptroller of the Currency may prescribe by regulation or order..."

Beyond genuine dispute, state law may not significantly burden a national bank's own exercise of its real estate lending power, just as it may not curtail or hinder a national bank's efficient exercise of any other power, incidental or enumerated under the NBA. In particular, real estate lending, when conducted by a national bank, is immune from state visitorial control: The NBA specifically vests exclusive authority to examine and inspect in OCC.

Harmoniously, the Michigan provisions at issue exempt national banks from coverage. This is not simply a matter of the Michigan Legislature's grace. For, as the parties recognize, the NBA would have preemptive force, *i. e.*, it would spare a national bank from state controls of the kind here involved. State laws that conditioned national banks' real estate lending on registration with the State, and subjected such lending to the State's investigative and enforcement machinery would surely interfere with the banks' federally authorized business: National banks would be subject to registration, inspection, and enforcement regimes imposed not just by Michigan, but by all States in which the banks operate. Diverse and duplicative superintendence of national banks' engagement in the business of banking, we observed over a century ago, is precisely what the NBA was designed to prevent: "The legislation has in view the erection of a system extending throughout the country, and independent, so far as powers conferred are concerned, of state legislation which, if permitted to be applicable, might impose limitations and restrictions as various and as numerous as the States." Congress did not intend, we explained, "to leave the field open for the States to attempt to promote the welfare and stability of national banks by direct legislation... Confusion would necessarily result from control possessed and exercised by two independent authorities."

Recognizing the burdens and undue duplication state controls could produce, Congress included in the NBA an express command: "No national bank shall be subject to any visitorial powers except as authorized by Federal law...." "Visitation," we have explained "is the act of a superior or superintending officer, who visits a corporation to examine into its manner of conducting business, and enforce an observance of its laws and regulations." Michigan, therefore, cannot confer on its commissioner examination and enforcement authority over mortgage lending, or any other banking business done by national banks.

B

While conceding that Michigan's licensing, registration, and inspection requirements cannot be applied to national banks, Watters argues that the State's regulatory regime(州监管机制/制度) survives preemption with respect to national banks' operating subsidiaries. Because such subsidiaries are separately chartered under some State's law, Watters characterizes them simply as "affiliates" of national banks, and contends that even though they are subject to OCC's superintendence, they are also subject to multistate control. We disagree.

Since 1966, OCC has recognized the "incidental" authority of national banks under §24 Seventh to do business through operating subsidiaries. That authority is uncontested by Michigan's commissioner. OCC licenses and oversees national bank operating subsidiaries just as it does national banks.

In 1999, Congress defined and regulated "financial" subsidiaries; simultaneously, Congress distinguished those national bank affiliates from subsidiaries—typed "operating subsidiaries" by OCC—which may engage only in activities national banks may engage in directly, "subject to the same terms and conditions that govern the conduct of such activities by national banks." For supervisory purposes, OCC treats national banks and their operating subsidiaries as a single economic enterprise. OCC oversees both entities by reference to "business line," applying the same controls whether banking "activities are conducted directly or through an operating subsidiary."

As earlier noted, Watters does not contest the authority of national banks to do business through operating subsidiaries. Nor does she dispute OCC's authority to supervise and regulate operating subsidiaries in the same manner as national banks. Still, Watters seeks to impose state regulation on operating subsidiaries over and above regulation undertaken by OCC. But just as duplicative state examination, supervision, and regulation would significantly burden mortgage lending when engaged in by national banks, so too would those state controls interfere with that same activity when engaged in by an operating subsidiary.

We have never held that the preemptive reach of the NBA extends only to a national bank itself. Rather, in analyzing whether state law hampers the federally permitted activities of a national bank, we have focused on the exercise of a national bank's *powers*, not on its corporate structure. And we have treated operating subsidiaries as equivalent to national banks with respect to powers exercised under federal law (except where federal law provides otherwise).

In *NationsBank of N. C., N. A.*, 513 U. S., for example, we upheld OCC's determination that national banks had "incidental" authority to act as agents in the sale of annuities(年金销售). It was not material that the function qualifying as within "the business of banking," was to be carried out not by the bank itself, but by an operating subsidiary, i. e., an entity "subject to the same terms and conditions that govern the conduct of the activity by national banks themselves."

Security against significant interference by state regulators is a characteristic condition of the "business of banking" conducted by national banks, and mortgage lending is one aspect of that business. That security should adhere whether the business is conducted by the bank itself or is assigned to an operating subsidiary licensed by

OCC whose authority to carry on the business coincides completely with that of the bank.

Watters contends that if Congress meant to deny States visitorial powers over operating subsidiaries, it would have written §484(a)'s ban on state inspection to apply not only to national banks but also to their affiliates. She points out that §481, which authorizes OCC to examine "affiliates" of national banks, does not speak to state visitorial powers. This argument fails for two reasons. *First*, one cannot ascribe any intention regarding operating subsidiaries to the 1864 Congress that enacted §§481 and 484, or the 1933 Congress that added the provisions on examining affiliates to §481 and the definition of "affiliate" to §221a. That is so because operating subsidiaries were not authorized until 1966. Over the past four decades, during which operating subsidiaries have emerged as important instrumentalities of national banks, Congress and OCC have indicated no doubt that such subsidiaries are "subject to the same terms and conditions" as national banks themselves.

Second, Watters ignores the distinctions Congress recognized among "affiliates". The NBA broadly defines the term "affiliate" to include "any corporation" controlled by a national bank, including a subsidiary. An operating subsidiary is therefore one type of "affiliate". But unlike affiliates that may engage in functions not authorized by the NBA, e. g., financial subsidiaries, an operating subsidiary is tightly tied to its parent by the specification that it may engage only in "the business of banking" as authorized by the Act. Notably, when Congress amended the NBA confirming that operating subsidiaries may "engage solely in activities that national banks are permitted to engage in directly," it did so in an Act, the GLBA, providing that other affiliates, authorized to engage in nonbanking financial activities, e. g., securities and insurance, are subject to state regulation in connection with those activities.

C

Recognizing the necessary consequence of national banks' authority to engage in mortgage lending through an operating subsidiary "subject to the same terms and conditions that govern the conduct of such activities by national banks," OCC promulgated 12 CFR §7.4006 (2006): "Unless otherwise provided by Federal law or OCC regulation, State laws apply to national bank operating subsidiaries to the same extent that those laws apply to the parent national bank". Watters disputes the authority of OCC to promulgate this regulation and contends that, because preemption is a legal question for determination by courts, §7.4006 should attract no deference. This argument is beside the point, for under our interpretation of the statute, the level of deference owed to the regulation is an academic question. Section 7.4006 merely clarifies and confirms what the NBA already conveys: A national bank has the power to engage in real estate lending through an operating subsidiary, subject to the same terms and conditions that govern the national bank itself; that power cannot be significantly impaired or impeded by state law.

The NBA is thus properly read by OCC to protect from state hindrance a national bank'是 s engagement in the "business of banking" whether conducted by the bank itself or by an operating subsidiary, empowered to do only what the bank itself could do. The authority to engage in the business of mortgage lending comes from the NBA, as does the authority to conduct business through an operating subsidiary. That Act vests visitorial oversight in OCC, not state regulators. State law (in this case, North Carolina law), all agree, governs incorporation-related issues, such as the formation, dissolution, and internal governance(内部治理)of operating subsidiaries. And the laws of the States in which national banks or their affiliates are located govern matters the NBA does not address. But state regulators cannot interfere with the business of banking by subjecting national banks or their OCC-licensed operating subsidiaries to multiple audits and surveillance under rival oversight regimes.

III

Watters' alternative argument, that 12 CFR §7.4006 violates the Tenth Amendment to the Constitution, is unavailing(无益的,无用的,无效的). As we have previously explained, "If a power is delegated to Congress in the Constitution, the Tenth Amendment expressly disclaims any reservation of that power to the States". Regulation of national bank operations is a prerogative of Congress under the Commerce and Necessary and Proper Clauses.

The Tenth Amendment, therefore, is not implicated here.

* * *

For the reasons stated, the judgment of the Sixth Circuit is
Affirmed.

JUSTICE THOMAS took no part in the consideration or decision of this case.

Lesson Ten

Investor Protection and Corporate Governance[①]

> **Learning objectives**
>
> After learning the text and having done the exercises in this lesson, you should be able to:
> —familiarize yourself with the knowledge of investor protection and corporate governance;
> —acquire an appreciation of the vocabulary and grammar and/or syntax relevant to investor protection;
> —become aware of the supplementary information required to understand investor protection;
> —enhance your practical language skills in writing, reading and listening under specific context; and
> —manage Chinese-English translations with similar contexts.

Investor Protection and Corporate Governance

Recent research on *corporate governance* around the world has established a number of empirical regularities[②]. Such diverse elements of countries' financial systems as the breadth and depth of their capital markets, the pace of new *security* issues, corporate ownership structures, dividend policies[③], and the efficiency of investment allocation appear to be explained both conceptually and empirically by how well the laws in these countries protect outside investors. According to this re-

---

① 本文摘自美国哈佛大学经济系的 Rafael La Porta 和 Andrei Shleifer 教授、肯尼迪政府学院的 Florencio Lopez-de-Silanes 教授和芝加哥大学商学研究院的 Robert Vishny 教授于1999年共同合作发表的论文 *Investor Protection and Corporate Governance*。

② empirical regularities:经验性规律。本句可译为"全球范围内关于公司治理的最新研究发现了许多经验性的规律"。

③ dividend policies:股息政策。

search, the protection of *shareholders and creditors* by the legal system is central to understanding the patterns of corporate finance in different countries.

Investor protection turns out to be crucial because, in many countries, expropriation① of minority shareholders and creditors by the controlling shareholders is extensive. When outside investors finance firms, they face a risk, and sometimes near certainty, that the returns on their investments will never materialize because the controlling shareholders or managers expropriate them. (We refer to both managers and controlling shareholders as "the insiders.") Corporate governance is, to a large extent, a set of mechanisms through which outside investors protect themselves against expropriation by the insiders.

Expropriation can take a variety of forms. In some instances, the insiders simply steal the profits. In other instances, the insiders sell the output, the assets, or the additional securities in the firm they control to another firm they own at below market prices. Such transfer pricing②, asset stripping③, and investor dilution④, though often legal, have largely the same effect as theft. In still other instances, expropriation takes the form of diversion of corporate opportunities from the firm, installing possibly unqualified family members in managerial positions, or overpaying executives. In general, expropriation is related to the agency problem described by Jensen and Meckling, who focus on the consumption of "perquisites⑤" by managers and other types of empire building. It means that the insiders use the profits of the firm to benefit themselves rather than return the money to the outside investors.

When investors finance firms, they typically obtain certain rights or powers that are generally protected through the enforcement of regulations and laws. Some of these rights include *disclosure and accounting rules*⑥, which provide investors with the information they need to exercise other

---

① expropriation:"没收,征用"的意思,有时也有"侵占和非法占有"的意思。在本句中 expropriation 的含义取的是后者的意思,这个词组连起来可以理解为"具有控制权的股东对小股东和债权人的(利益)侵害"。Expropriation 做"征用"讲时,略有别于美国的 eminent domain。根据美国《联邦宪法》第五修正案的规定,政府或其授权部门或个人需征用个人财产以作公用时,需要对征用财产作合理的补偿,这种情况被称为 eminent domain。condemnation 和 expropriation 则是指对 eminent domain 这种权利的实施程序,但在路易斯安那州,expropriation 的含义则等同 eminent domain。

② transfer pricing 内部转让定价,国际转拨计价等,指关联公司(related parties)交易的定价方法,有些跨国公司为减轻纳税负担,可有意把高税率国家分公司产品成本定得很高,借此将利润转移到低税率国家的分公司。由于这种交易不符合公平独立交易原则(arm's length principle),不少国家通过立法将其列为逃税行为。

③ asset stripping:资产剥离(referring to the process of buying an undervalued company with the intent to sell off its assets for a profit)。

④ investor dilution:投资者收益稀释。风险投资人(venture capitalists)对某公司进行投资时,通常是购买公司某类优先股(A、B、C...系列)(Series A Preferred),这些优先股在一定条件下可以按照约定的转换价格(conversion price)转换成普通股(common stock)。为了防止其手中的股份贬值(stock depreciation),投资人一般会在投资协议中加入防稀释条款(anti-dilution provision)。Dilution 的本意是"冲淡,稀释"。在金融领域表示"商标价值降低,产权平均值的减低,证券价值耗减,股权收益减损"等。常用的搭配词组有:dilution doctrine 防止商标价值降低原则,dilution of labor 劳动稀释(即用生手或半生手代替熟手的方式),dilution of ownership(股东的)股权削弱。

⑤ Perquisites: An incidental emolument, fee or profit over and above fixed income, salary, or wages or alternatively any bonus or fringe benefit granted to an employee n. (薪金外的)额外补贴(常略为 perk),津贴,奖金,额外优惠。

⑥ disclosure and accounting rules:信息披露和审计规则。这是被国际社会广为接受的几大公司治理原则之一,其他几项基本原则包括:董事会及公司治理结构和程序(board and management structure and process)、公司责任和服从(Corporate responsibility and compliance)、所有人结构和控制权实施(Ownership structure and exercise of control rights)。

rights. Protected shareholder rights include those to receive dividends on pro-rata① terms, to vote for directors, to participate in shareholders' meetings, to *subscribe* to new issues of securities on the same terms as the insiders, to sue directors or the majority for suspected expropriation, to call extraordinary shareholders' meetings②, etc. Laws protecting creditors largely deal with bankruptcy and reorganization procedures, and include measures that enable creditors to repossess *collateral*, to protect their seniority, and to make it harder for firms to seek court protection in reorganization.

In different jurisdictions, rules protecting investors come from different sources, including company, security, bankruptcy, takeover③, and competition laws, but also from stock exchange regulations and accounting standards. Enforcement of laws is as crucial as their contents. In most countries, laws and regulations are enforced in part by market regulators, in part by courts, and in part by market participants themselves. All outside investors, be they large or small, shareholders or creditors, need to have their rights protected. Absent effectively enforced rights, the insiders would not have much of a reason to repay the creditors or to distribute profits to shareholders, and external financing mechanisms would tend to break down.

The emphasis on legal rules and regulations protecting outside investors stands in sharp contrast to the traditional "law and economics" perspective on financial contracting.④ According to that perspective, most regulations of financial markets are unnecessary because financial contracts take place between sophisticated issuers and sophisticated investors. On average, investors recognize a risk of expropriation, penalizing firms that fail to contractually disclose information about themselves and to contractually bind themselves to treat investors well. Because entrepreneurs bear these costs when they issue securities, they have an incentive to bind themselves through contracts with investors to limit expropriation. As long as these contracts are enforced, financial markets do not require regulation.

This point of view, originating in the Coase theorem⑤, crucially relies on courts enforcing elaborate contracts. In many countries, such enforcement cannot be taken for granted. Indeed,

---

① pro-rata:有时也写作 pro rata,来源于拉丁语,in proportion to 的意思。该词被广泛应用于法律及经济领域。在美国和加拿大,这个词已经被本地化为 prorated 这个词。例如:Should the borrowing not be able to be obtained in the way referred to above, the Board shall separately request funds from each Party hereto pro rata its capital contribution to the Joint Venture/in proportion to its capital contribution to the Joint Venture/its capital contribution to the Joint Venture on prorated terms. 如果不能按上述方式获得借款,董事会将按合同各方各自在合资公司中的资本比例向合同各方另外征集资金。

② Extraordinary shareholders' meetings:临时股东大会,也可以写作 extraordinary shareholders' general meetings,是股东大会(shareholders' meetings)的一种。

③ Takeover:购并;the acquisition by a company ("transferee company") of all the shares, or all the shares of any class or classes, not already held by it in another company ("transferor company") 任何公司(受让人公司),收购另一公司(出让人公司)中尚未被持有的不分类别的全部股份。

④ 在对待外部投资者保护的问题上,对法律原则和规则的强调与传统的从"法律经济学"角度来考量金融合同这一做法形成了鲜明的对比。

⑤ Coase theorem:科斯定理,这是由诺贝尔经济学奖得主罗纳德·科斯(Ronald Coase)提出的一种观点。科斯定理其实并非是一个定理,而是 Ronald Coase 本人的一种观点,他认为在某些条件下,经济的外部性(externality, or transaction spillover)或曰非效率是一种成本消耗或收益,它不会随着价格的浮动而变动,可以通过当事人的谈判而得到纠正。如果这种外部性是一种收益,那么该外部性被称为 positive externality 或者 eternal benefit,反之,如是成本损耗,则被称为 negative externality 或者 external cost。

courts are often unable or unwilling to invest the resources necessary to ascertain the facts pertaining to complicated contracts. They are also slow, subject to political pressures, and at times corrupt. When the enforcement of private contracts through the court system is costly enough, other forms of protecting property rights, such as judicially-enforced laws or even government-enforced regulations, may be more efficient. It may be better to have contracts restricted by laws and regulations that are enforced than unrestricted contracts that are not.① Whether contracts, court-enforced legal rules, or government-enforced regulations are the most efficient form of protecting financial arrangements is largely an empirical question. The evidence rejects the hypothesis that private contracting is sufficient. Even among countries with well functioning judiciaries, those with laws and regulations more protective of investors have better developed capital markets.

La Porta, Lopez-de-Silanes, Shleifer, and Vishny discuss a set of key legal rules protecting shareholders and creditors and document the prevalence of these rules in 49 countries around the world. They also aggregate these rules into shareholder (antidirector) and creditor rights indices for each country, and consider several measures of enforcement quality, such as the efficiency of the judicial system and a measure of the quality of accounting standards. La Porta, Lopez-de-Silanes, Shleifer, and Vishny use these variables as *proxies* for the stance of the law toward investor protection to examine the variation of legal rules and enforcement quality across countries and across legal families.②

Legal scholars such as David and Brierley show that commercial legal systems of most countries derive from relatively few legal "families," including the English (common law), the French, and the German, the latter two derived from the Roman Law. In the 19th century, these systems spread throughout the world through conquest, colonization, and voluntary adoption. England and its former colonies, including the U.S., Canada, Australia, New Zealand, and many countries in Africa and South East Asia, have ended up with the common law system. France and many countries Napoleon conquered are part of the French civil law tradition. This legal family also extends to the former French, Dutch, Belgian, and Spanish colonies, including Latin America. Germany, Germanic countries in Europe, and a number of countries in East Asia are part of the German civil law tradition. The Scandinavian countries form their own tradition.③

La Porta, Lopez-de-Silanes, Shleifer, and Vishny has developed a Table illustrating the percentage of countries in each legal family that give investors the rights as well as the mean for that family antidirector and creditor rights scores. How well legal rules protect outside investors varies systematically across legal origins. Common law countries have the strongest protection of outside investors—both shareholders and creditors—whereas French civil law countries have the weakest

---

① 受具有强制执行力的法律法规约束的合同可能要比不受任何具有强制执行性的法律法规约束的合同要好。"...that are not"是一个省略结构,省略的内容是"that are not enforced"。这句话强调的是:相比起 contracts 本身,具有强制执行力的法律和法规能够对投资者的权益起到更有效的保护作用。

② legal family:法系,注意与法律体系的区别。在法律英语中,西方学者使用 legal system 既可以表示"法系"之意,也可以表示"法律制度"的意思。

③ 社会主义国家的法律制度很大程度上是建立在原苏联法律制度基础上的,但是社会主义阵营从成立之初到现在经历了剧烈的政治及法律制度变迁,La Porta, Lopez-de-Silanes, Shleifer, and Vishny (1998)申明:在分析研究数据时,他们未将这种变迁作为考虑的变量。

Lesson Ten Investor Protection and Corporate Governance

protection. German civil law and Scandinavian countries fall in between, although comparatively speaking they have stronger protection of creditors, especially secured creditors.① In general, differences among legal origins are best described by the proposition that some countries protect all outside investors better than others, and not by the proposition that some countries protect shareholders while other countries protect creditors.

In addition, the developed Table also points to significant differences among countries in the quality of law enforcement as measured by the efficiency of the judiciary, (lack of) corruption, and the quality of accounting standards. Unlike legal rules, which do not appear to depend on the level of economic development, the quality of enforcement is higher in richer countries. In particular, the generally richer Scandinavian and German legal origin countries receive the best scores on the efficiency of the judicial system. The French legal origin countries have the worst quality of law enforcement of the four legal traditions, even controlling for per capita income.

Because legal origins are highly correlated with the content of the law, and because legal families originated before financial markets had developed, it is unlikely that laws were written primarily in response to market pressures. Rather, the legal families appear to shape the legal rules, which in turn influence financial markets. But what is special about legal families? Why, in particular, is common law more protective of investors than civil law? These questions do not have accepted answers. However, it may be useful here to distinguish between two broad kinds of answers: the "judicial" explanations that account for the differences in the legal philosophies using the organization of the legal system, and the "political" explanations that account for these differences using political history.

The "judicial" explanation of why common law protects investors better than civil law has been most recently articulated by Coffee and Johnson, La Porta, Lopez-de-Silanes, and Shleifer. Legal rules in the common law system are usually made by judges, based on precedents and inspired by general principles such as fiduciary duty② or fairness. Judges are expected to rule on new situations by applying these general principles even when specific conduct has not yet been described or prohibited in the statutes. In the area of investor expropriation, also known as self-dealing, the judges apply what Coffee calls a "smell test," and try to sniff out whether even unprecedented conduct by the insiders is unfair to outside investors. The expansion of legal precedents to additional violations of fiduciary duty, and the fear of such expansion, limit the expropriation by the insiders in common law countries. In contrast, laws in civil law systems are made by legislatures, and judges are not supposed to go beyond the statutes and apply "smell tests" or fairness opinions. As a consequence, a corporate insider who finds a way not explicitly forbidden by

---

① secured creditors:担保债权人。
② Fiduciary duty:诚信责任,信托责任,fiduciary 一词来自于拉丁语 fiduciarius,意为"(守住)诚信",也有学者认为该词来源于 fides 一词,即"信用",指真诚行事,以真诚的职业信用对待他人的衡平法责任(equity duty)。这种信托责任主要产生于信托关系中,这种关系可以体现在以下类别中:受托人与受益人之间(trustee and beneficiary)、委托人和代理人之间(agent and principal)、公司董事会成员和公司之间(directors of a company)、卖主和拍卖人之间(vendor and auctioneer)、律师和当事人之间(solicitor and client)。受 fiduciary duty 约束的一方在履行自己的工作职责时,不得在工作上寻求不当得利,不得将自己置于个人利益和信托责任相冲突的位置。

the statutes to expropriate outside investors can proceed without fear of an adverse judicial ruling. Moreover, in civil law countries, courts do not intervene in self-dealing transactions as long as these have a plausible business purpose. The vague fiduciary duty principles of the common law are more protective of investors than the bright line rules of the civil law, which can often be circumvented by sufficiently imaginative insiders.

The judicial perspective on the differences is fascinating and possibly correct, but it is incomplete. It requires a further assumption that the judges have an inclination to protect the outside investors rather than the insiders. In principle, it is easy to imagine that the judges would use their discretion in common law countries to narrow the interpretation of fiduciary duty and to sanction expropriation rather than prohibit it. Common law judges could also in principle use their discretion to serve political interests, especially when the outside investors obstruct the government's goals. To explain investor protection, it is not enough to focus on judicial power; a political and historical analysis of judicial objectives is required. From this perspective, important political and historical differences between mother countries shape their laws. This is not to say that laws never change, but rather to suggest that history has persistent effects.

La Porta, Lopez-de-Silanes, Shleifer and Vishny argue that an important historical factor shaping laws is that the state has a relatively greater role in regulating business in civil law countries than in common law ones. One element of this view, suggested by Finer and other historians, points to the differences in the relative power of the king and the property owners across European states. In England from the seventeenth century on, the crown partially lost control of the courts, which came under the influence of the parliament and the property owners who dominated it. As a consequence, common law evolved to protect private property against the crown. Over time, courts extended this protection of property owners to investors. In France and Germany, by contrast, parliamentary power was weaker. Commercial Codes were adopted only in the nineteenth century by the two great state builders, Napoleon and Bismarck①, to enable the state to better regulate economic activity. Over time, the state maintained political control over firms and resisted the surrender of that power to financiers.② Perhaps as importantly, the state in civil law countries did not surrender its power over economic decisions to courts, and hence maintained the statutory approach to commercial laws. As we noted above, however, fairness assessments of self-dealing transactions, for which judicial power and discretion are essential, may be central to limiting expropriation.

Recent research supports the proposition that civil law is associated with greater government intervention in economic activity and weaker protection of private property than common law. La Porta, Lopez-de-Silanes, Shleifer, and Vishny examine the determinants of government performance in a large number of countries. To measure government interventionism, they consider prox-

---

① Bismarck：俾斯麦（1815—1898），德国政治家，德意志帝国第一任首相（German statesman under whose leadership Germany was united）。

② Cameron（1961年）曾经在自己的著作中提到过，由于法国政府在政策上的让步以及对投资者、所有权、经济补贴方面的支持和保护，以至于法国在19世纪曾经一度拥有十分繁荣的股票市场。

ies for the amount and quality of regulation, the prevalence of corruption and of red tape①, and bureaucratic delays②. As a general rule, they find that civil law countries, particularly French civil law countries, are more interventionist than common law countries. The inferior protection of the rights of outside investors in civil law countries may be one manifestation of this general phenomenon. This evidence provides some support for interpreting the differences in legal families based on political history.

Legal Terminology

1. security

常用复数 securities 来表示"证券"的意思,即可替换、可转让并具有一定的经济价值的票据。美国的证券可以分为**债权证券**(debt security)和**股权证券**(equity security)两大类。债券证券指证券持有者为公司或政府机构债权人的证券,如:汇票(draft)、本票(promissory note)、支票(check)、公司债券(debenture)等,股权证券指作为对有限公司(corporation)拥有部分所有权证明的有价证券,通常包括普通股票(common stock)和优先股票(preferred stock),还包括衍生工具合约(derivative contracts),如期货合约(futures)、期权合约(options)、远期合同(forwards)和互换合同(swaps)。发证证券的公司或其他实体机构被称为发行人(issuer)。

根据到期日和其他一些特征的差异,债权证券可以分为公司(无担保)债券(debentures)、债券(常指公债)(bonds)、存款证(deposits)、本票(promissory notes, notes, notes payable)和商业票据(commercial papers)。债权证券的持有者有权收取利息(interest)和本金(principal),并同时享有与发行人签订合同时约定的其他相关权利,如某些知情权。此类债券通常具有一个特定的发行期限,并且在该期限到期时,发行人有权对其赎回(redeemable)。债券证券同时又可分为担保债券(secured securities)和无担保债权(unsecured securities),而无担保债券可以进一步根据具体的合约或协议规定将其认定为优先于列后偿付债券(subordinated securities)之前的优先债券(senior securities)。

股权证券指在一个实体机构的股本如公司中股本中占有一定的股票份额。股权最通常的表现形式便是普通股(common stock),当然也包括优先股(preferred stock)这种特殊形式。股权的持有者被称为股东(shareholder)。与债权证券不同的是,股权证券的收益体现不是从发行者手中获得定期的利息回报(interest payment),而是体现在公司破产和资产收益方面的。

公司破产时,股权所有人即股东有权与其他股东分享公司债务清偿完毕后的剩余资产价值。而在公司正常运营的一般情况下,股东的权利主要体现在按照占有公司股份的比例(pro-rata portion of the control of the company),对公司享有相应的控制权,即一个公司股份的主要持有人对公司通常都享有对公司(股票发行人)的主要控制权。股权所有人同时对公司收益(profits)和资本的增值(capital gain)享有分享权,而债权证券持有者则不同:无论发行人的金融业绩有多好,此类持有者也无权分享其收益,只能按照规定的协议定时收取利息和

---

① red tape:繁琐和拖拉的公事程序;官样文章;繁文缛节。
② bureaucracy delays:官僚作风造成的办事效率低下。

协议到期时的本金。除此以外,债权证券和股权证券的区别还在于,股权证券持有者有投票权(voting rights),而债权证券所有者则没有。

一个公司的规范管理架构决定了其是否具有发行证券的资格,比方说,某些私人投资联营(private investment pools)的经营模式可能具有一些证券发行的特点,但由于他们未正式登记或经过规范化管理,他们仍无法满足证券发行的条件。

有些证券是经过美国证券交易委员会(Securities and Exchange Commission,简称SEC)认证的证券(certificated securities),另一类未经认证的证券则被称为非经授权认证的证券(non-certificated securities)。经认证的证券亦可分为两类,一种是不记名证券(bearer (securities)),另外一种是记名证券(registered securities)。不记名证券持有者仅凭手中持有的证券证明即可享有持有者应有的一切权利,而记名证券持有者若想实现自己的权利,需要在证券发行者或一个中间商内进行注册登记才行。

2. corporate governance

公司治理,又名**公司管治**、**企业管治**,具体指的是一套完整的程序、惯例、政策、法律及机构,它影响和控制着公司的经营管理模式。公司治理方法也包括公司内部利益相关人士(stakeholders)及公司治理的众多目标之间的关系。公司主要外部利益相关人士包括股东、持债人(debt holders)、贸易债权人(trade creditors)、供应商(suppliers)、客户(customers)以及其他一些与受公司经营活动影响的社会团体。公司内部主要利益相关人士有董事会(board of directors)、行政管理人员(executives)以及其他公司内部员工(employees)。

公司治理的模式主要分为两种:一种是普通法国家流行的以股东经济利益最大化为目标的模式,即Shareholder Wealth Maximization Model(SWM),另外一种是公司整体经济利益最大化为目标的模式,即Corporate Wealth Maximization Model(CWM)。这种以公司整体经济利益为目标的模式包含了含股东在内的所有利益相关人士(stakeholder)的经济利益,这些利益相关人士包括公司里有/无专业技能的劳动者(labor with or without special skills)、管理人员和借贷资本供应商(suppliers of debt capital)。

目前被国际上广为接受的公司治理原则包括以下五大类:审计(auditing)、董事会及公司治理结构和程序(Board and management structure and process)、公司责任和服从(Corporate responsibility and compliance)、财务透明度和信息披露度(Financial transparency and information disclosure)、所有人结构和控制权实施(Ownership structure and exercise of control rights)。

3. shareholders and creditors

股东和债权人。shareholder和creditor既有共同点,又有区别。二者本质上都是公司的投资人,目的都是通过对公司进行资本投资,以从其中获得投资回报。shareholder指那些合法拥有上市公司或股票未上市公司(public or private corporation)股票(shares/stocks)的个人或机构;而creditor来源于credit(信用)这个词,该词做"债权人"的含义讲时,既可以使用在个体或机构与个体之间的债务关系(debt-creditor relationship),又可以指个体或机构与公司之间的债务关系(debenture-creditor relationship)。在公司进行破产清算时,creditor相对于shareholder较先获得清偿权,而对creditor的不同分类,决定了不同类别的creditor中获得赔偿的顺序也不同。senior creditor(指持有优先债券即senior security的个体或机构)较subordinated creditor(指持有列后偿付债券即subordinated securities的个人或机构)在获得清偿方面更有优先权。

share和stock的区别:两者均可指公司的股份或股票,两个单词常交替使用,通常情况

Lesson Ten Investor Protection and Corporate Governance

差别不大。如在美国,只在某些情况两者稍微有些差异,即 share 常指所有公司,包括 company 和 corporation 的股份,而 stock 则指 corporation 中的股份。如一个 company 的股东可称为 shareholder 或 shareowner;而一个 corporation 的股东则称为 shareholder 或 stockholder,即 stockholder 不用在 company 中。此外,如两单词用在一起时,share 更多的是指"股份";而 stock 则指"股票",即一种票据。在遇到将 share 改变为 stock 的时候,则是指将公司"股份"转为上市公司的"股票"。

4. subscribe

该词的含义很广泛,在法律英语中也广泛使用于不同的场合。subscribe 的本意是"同意"的意思,来源于拉丁语 subscribere,从词组成的角度来看是由 sub 和 scribere 两部分构成的,scribere 的意思是 to write,sub 是 underneath, below 的意思,所以该词连起来的字面意思是"to write beneath",该词有以下几个含义:(1) offer to buy, as of stocks and shares,即"认购(股票)",如:The subscriber subscribed 500 shares.(那个(股票)经纪人买了 500 股股份。)(2) to pay or promise to pay or contribute money to a charity or service (radio stations, magazines, etc),especially at regular intervals,即"捐款、订阅杂志、订购服务"的意思,如:He subscribes to a lot of charities.(他在慈善方面捐出了很多钱。)又如:I subscribed to my favorite radio station at $10 a month.(我以每个月十美元的价格订购了我最喜欢的收音机频道。)(3) to feel or express hearty approval,即"表达自己诚心诚意的赞同",如:I subscribe to your view on abortion.(在堕胎这一点上,我完全同意你的观点。)(4) to sign one's name (to a document, contract, testimony, etc.) in attestation, testimony, or consent,即在(文件、合同、证词等)上签署自己的名字,表示赞同,如:He subscribed the will which he has been preparing for three years.(他在他花了三年时间准备的遗嘱上签上了自己的名字。)又如:She subscribed the letter and sent it off.(她在信件上签署了自己的名字,然后将其邮寄了出去。)

5. collateral

"抵押品"的意思,通常是由诸如股票、债券(collateral bonds)、可流通票据这类金融凭证以及具有实际价值的物品(设备、机器等)组成。在债务人无法履行债务或不能履行债务时,债权人可将抵押品变卖并以所得价款来抵冲债务。英美法中表示抵押的词很多,应用的场合有严格的限制,现就几个常用词语进行一下辨析。

mortgage 其实指的是英美法上的抵押,而 hypothec 才指的是与我国民法体系相近的大陆法系上的抵押。hypothec 是指当抵押人将符合我国《担保法》规定的财产抵押给抵押权人时,抵押权人并不占有该财产,但在抵押人不履行债务时,抵押权人依法享有的就该财产变价并优先受偿的权利或在无法变价时占有此财产。

pledge(质押)也是一种担保物权。它与抵押的一个显著的不同点就是抵押不转移占有而质押则需临时转移占有。在质押中,物品的所有权并不转移,出质人仍享有质押财产的所有权,质权人只是在出质人履行完义务前占有质押财产。但当出质人不能履行义务或清偿债务时,质权人可变卖质押财产。不过在质押期间,质权人有保护质押财产安全的义务,同时质权人不得未经出质人同意擅自使用质押财产。擅自使用(conversion)所造成的损失由质权人承担。

如上文所说,mortgage(抵押)是指英美法上的"抵押",与我国的"抵押"是有区别的。英美法的"抵押"通常有两种形式:转移的抵押(mortgage by demise)和法定押记的抵押(mortgage by legal charge)。转移的抵押是指在债务没有清偿(redemption)前,债权人临时成为抵押财产的所有人。在债务清偿完后,抵押财产应当返还。法定押记的抵押是指债务人仍旧是抵押财产的法律意义上的所有人,但债权人为了确保其债权的实现,有权占有或变卖抵押财产。

6. proxy

该词有两层含义,除了表示文中所应用的"测算指标"以外,还表示"代理人"的意思,指受公司员工或股东指派,代替自己行使在公司大会或股东大会上的表决权或其他权利的人(a person (not necessarily a company member) appointed by a company member or shareholders to attend and vote instead of him at a company meeting or shareholders' meetings)。Proxy 在表达"代理人"的意思时,与 power of attorney 有着一定的区别。两者均有"授权委托书"的含义。区别在于 power of attorney 指向具有律师资格者授权;而 proxy(也称为 the instrument appointing a proxy)则一般无此含义,即 proxy 指定的代理人不必一定是律师。此外,power of attorney 的用途较广,而 proxy 则多指如公司法中授权替其他股东表决者。

7. disclosure 与 discovery

disclosure 在经济领域表示"信息披露",而在诉讼法领域表示"证据披露"的意思,而该词的应用应与 discovery 有所区别。以上两单词在诉讼法中均有让对方知晓证据的含义。discovery("证据开示")(等同 documentary discovery)主要适用民事诉讼程序,其具有强制性,为法院主持进行,主要形式包括:interrogatories(书面询问对方当事人)、depositions(书面诘问证人)、requests for admissions(事实确认请求)以及 requests for production(出示证据请求)。disclosure("证据披露")过去多用于刑事案件,由控方向被告方展示某些情况,特定情况下被告方也会向控方披露情况,此种披露多不带强制性;但如控方所占有的证据能帮助被告人进行辩护,根据正当程序规则,该证据必须向被告方披露。在当今的民事程序改革浪潮中,英国大法官(Lord Woolf)在其"司法审判参与权"(access to Justice)报告中建议在民事诉讼程序中用 disclosure 替换 discovery,以避免无限制地要求证据开示而导致诉讼的拖延。总体说来,民事诉讼中的 disclosure 应比其在刑事诉讼中的原含义更具强制性,披露的事项由法律规定而不是像证据开示那样由当事人随意要求。

Exercises

I Verbal Abilities

Part One

Directions: For each of the following multiple choice questions, there will be only one best answer for each of these blanks. Please read each item carefully and fill in each of the blanks with the best answer by marking the corresponding choices at the proper place.

1. The 2008 bankruptcy of financial firm Lehman Brothers Inc. was the largest _____ bankruptcy in United States history.

  A. corporate   B. corporal   C. empirical

  D. incorporated   E. company

Lesson Ten Investor Protection and Corporate Governance

2. In 1952, faced with an impending strike by steelworkers, President Truman signed executive order No. 10340, 17 Fed. Reg. 3139, _____ eighty-eight steel mills across the country.

A. converting B. expropriating C. embezzling
D. misappropriating E. confiscating

3. It is so required by Kansas Wills Law that the number of witnesses must be attested and _____ in presence of testator by two or more competent witnesses who saw testator sign his name or heard him acknowledge same.

A. described B. ascribed C. scribed
D. subscribed E. prescribed

4. According to a recent study, states that do not allow or put drastic limitations on a _____'s ability to garnish the wages of debtors have lower rates of bankruptcy filings—42 percent lower according to the study

A. principal B. security holder C. shareholder
D. creditor E. obligor

5. The defendants argued it was a violation of their Fourteenth Amendment right to due process for jurors to have unrestricted _____ in deciding whether the defendants should live or die, and such discretion resulted in arbitrary and capricious sentencing.

A. access B. discretion C. arbitrariness
D. option E. discreetness

6. According to the Financial Industry Regulatory Authority (FINRA), an independent regulator of securities firms conducting business in the U.S., many people who seek to _____ investors attempt to build their credibility by claiming association with a reputable firm or having a special credential.

A. beguile B. falsify C. deceit
D. feign E. defraud

7. For someone in this position, _____ stripping, which is a process of reducing a secured claim to the value of the underlying collateral, may be an effective way to address the situation without losing the property to foreclosure.

A. lien B. mortgage C. pledge
D. security E. impawn

8. Your debts will likely not be _____ if the creditor objects and can demonstrate your prior act (usually through a prior court conviction).

A. exonerated B. exempted C. discharged
D. eliminated E. wiped out

9. A good tip for the purchase of a vehicle is to check with sources that you know from experience to be reliable—in this case, your owner's manual, your original _____, the dealer who sold you the car, and the car manufacturer.

A. promise B. warranty C. security
D. collateral E. guaranty

10. A junior creditor is one whose right to collect money from a debtor is _____ to that of

another individual who also has a right to collect payment of a different debt from the same debtor.

A. subordinate B. inferior C. subsidiary
D. correlated E. accessory

Part Two

Directions: *Choose the word or phrase that best keep the meaning of the original sentence if it were substituted for the underlined part.*

1. E-commerce businesses might have concerns about their ordinary online sales transactions, in light of a new court ruling limiting the effect of email receipts.

A. in between B. in commemoration of C. in conjunction with
D. in consideration of E. in concordance with

2. In the early stages of development, the Commission has put out a request for public comments, seeking information on how it can adapt its online advertising rules to better comport with the technological and legal advances of the last 11 years.

A. compete with B. compact with C. accord with
D. agree with E. govern with

3. According to the Supreme Court, federal law does not preempt Arizona's statute, which punishes infractions by revoking and suspending state and local business licenses.

A. in concert B. in clover C. prioritize
D. in general E. in abeyance

4. Proponents of the bill believe that it will result in lower rates and a fairer system for everyone.

A. Protagonists B. Advocators C. Antagonists
D. Litigators E. Aspirators

5. At the moment, very few states have imposed their own employer sanctions and/or E-Verify mandates; however, this is unlikely to remain unchanged.

A. enforcements B. assignments C. consignments
D. commissions E. commands

6. However, if the changes made by a state are any more than cosmetic surface level changes, the purpose of the UCC may be undermined.

A. excavated B. countermined C. counteracted
D. sabotaged E. ruined

7. An illegal contract thus must clearly and definitively be deemed illegal from one of the terms built into the contract in order to be considered unenforceable.

A. construed B. conveyed C. convicted
D. appraised E. coerced

8. Fortunately the letter sent to Securities and Exchange Commission (SEC) signed by multiple law firms was in support of its proposal to beef up shareholder rights.

A. expatiate B. elaborate C. fortify
D. diminish E. distinguish

9. Assignor and Assignee will use their respective reasonable best efforts to obtain any consent, approval or amendment required to <u>novate</u> and/or assign the Third Party Products

A. supplement   B. substitute   C. complement

D. amend   E. alter

10. The SEC Rule would <u>entail</u> increased accountability on a company in selecting a fitting board of directors by creating a transparent election process in which shareholders get a say.

A. impart   B. impact   C. entangle

D. impose   E. infer

II Cloze

Directions: *For each blank in the following passage, choose the best answer from the choices given in the opposite column.*

The focus on expropriation of investors and its prevention has a number of implications for the ownership structures of firms. Consider first the concentration of control rights in firms (as _____ to the dividend or cash flow rights). At the most basic level, when investor rights are poorly protected and expropriation is feasible on a _____ scale, control acquires enormous value because it gives the _____ the opportunity to expropriate efficiently. When the insiders actually do expropriate, the so called private benefits of control become a substantial share of the firm's value. This observation raises a question: will control in such an environment be _____ in the hands of an entrepreneur or dispersed among many investors?

The research in this area originates in the work of Grossman and Hart (1988) and Harris and Raviv (1988), who examine the _____ allocation of voting and cash flow rights in a firm. The specific question of how control is likely to be allocated has not received a clear answer.

For several reasons, _____ may wish to keep control of their firms when investor protection is poor. La Porta, Lopez-de-Silanes, and Shleifer (1999) note that if expropriation of investors requires secrecy, sharing control may restrain the entrepreneur beyond his wishes. Zingales (1995), La Porta, Lopez-de-Silanes, and Shleifer (1999), and Bebchuk (1999) argue that if entrepreneurs _____ control between many investors, they give up the "private benefits" premium in a takeover. In Bebchuk's (1999) model, diffuse control structures are unstable when investors can concentrate control without fully paying for it. Finally, an entrepreneur or his family may need to _____ control of the firm because the family's reputation is needed to raise external funds when the legal protection of outside investors is poor.

Bennedsen and Wolfenzon (2000) make a _____ argument. When investor protection is poor, dissipating control among several large investors may serve as a commitment to limit expropriation. When there is no single controlling shareholder, and the agreement of several large investors (the board) is needed for major _____ actions, these investors might together hold enough cash _____ rights to choose to limit expropriation of the remaining shareholders and pay the profits out as efficient dividends. When the dissipation of control _____ inefficient expropriation, it may emerge as an optimal policy for a wealth-maximizing entrepreneur. An entrepreneur has a number of ways to retain control of a firm. He can sell _____ with limited voting rights to the outsiders and still retain control by holding on to the shares with _____ voting rights. He can also use a pyramidal structure, in which a holding company he controls sells shares in a _____ that it itself controls.

III Reading Comprehension

Part One

Directions: *In this section, there are passages followed by questions or unfinished statements, each with five suggested answers. Choose the one you think best answers each of the following questions.*

Passage One

Last week, the German Constitutional Court (the "Bundesverfassungsgericht") published a decision that may have far-reaching implications for how law is practiced in Germany. The Court decided that a law barring contingency fees in all cases was unconstitutional. It held that, under certain narrow circumstances, there was a constitutional right to be able to bring a civil action by means of a contingency fee contract with a lawyer.

The Facts behind the Suit

The case arose as a result of a lawsuit brought by a woman the court referred to as "Frau Hanna N." She is a descendant of a German Jew who wished to sue to receive compensation for the expropriation by the German government of an estate near Dresden. In 1990, a lawyer, "Frau Dr. T." offered to litigate the suit for a 33% contingency fee. In 1998, Frau Dr. T. prevailed and received compensation on behalf of her client of DM 312,000 (about $204,000), of which she took DM 104,000 (about $68,000).

According to statute, that was illegal: In Germany, lawyers may work for clients on an hourly basis, or they may be paid according to a legally-set schedule which links the amount of their compensation to the value of the amount in dispute. Under the schedule for example, in 1998, Frau Dr. T. would have received DM 3,300 (about $2,175) for her work. Today, she would receive about $4000.

For employing a contingent fee, Frau Dr. T was fined EUR 5,000 (about $6,590 dollars), and forced to return all but the fee she was allowed by statute to retain. She then appealed.

The Court's Decision: A Balance of State Interest versus Individual Rights

On appeal, the Court voted 5-3 to overturn the law but not the civil penalty. Using an analysis similar to that which is used in American constitutional law, the German Court identified the state's interest in regulating legal fees, and weighed it against the rights or freedoms burdened by such a regulation.

The state's interest, the Court noted, is to protect clients from their lawyers' greed. The Court pointed out that where a lawyer's own "business interest" is introduced into a case, she might—albeit perhaps unconsciously—pursue her own goals over that of her client.

Against this evil, the Court weighed two rights, or freedoms: the client's right to access to the courts in civil cases, and the lawyer's right to freely practice her profession. The absolute bar on contingency fees interfered with both these rights.

The First Right: Hanna N.'s Right to Access to the Courts

First, let's look at Frau Hanna N's right to access to the courts. Like most American states, and the federal courts, Germany guarantee access to the court in civil cases against unreasonable limitations on the kind of claims that can be brought and the procedures under which those claims must be brought. Moreover, in Germany, there is legal aid for the poor in civil cases. (In the U.S., of course, there is not.)

But Hanna N. was not poor. She just did not want to pay Dr. T. by the hour. Nor did Dr. T. want to take the case for the statutory amount that would apply if she did not charge an hourly rate. Furthermore, Hanna N. was also concerned about the cost of potentially paying her opponent's attorney's fees if she lost. (Germany follows the "English Rule"—loser pays.)

The Court held that Hanna N.'s access to the courts in this restitution case was burdened in this case, because although she believed she had a strong case, she was neither rich enough to risk losing it, nor poor enough to qualify for legal aid.

The Second Right: Dr. T's Right to Practice Her Profession

The Court also held that Dr. T.'s right to practice her profession was burdened by the ban on contingency fees. Dr. T., after all, did believe in Hanna N.'s case. Indeed, she was willing to invest her own money in the case. Like contingency fee lawyers in the U.S., she offered to work for nothing if Hanna N. lost. Moreover, she also offered something contingency fee lawyers in the U.S. do not offer (since we in the U.S. do not follow the English Rule): She also offered to pay the legal fees of Hanna N.'s opponent's lawyers if she lost.

The Court noted that the German Constitution guarantees German lawyers the right to practice their profession without undue interference from the state (a right that has a particular significance given the history of German lawyers under the Third Reich). In this case, a lawyer claimed she could bring a meritorious case only if she was able to carry the cost of the litigation for her client, and only if she were able to receive a share of her client's award if she won.

The ban on that contract, held the Court, could have interfered with Dr. T.'s ability to bring a certain set of cases which the courts ought to hear. Thus, Dr. T's right was burdened too.

The Outcome, and its Possible Implications for Law Practice in Germany

In the end, the Court decided that neither of these rights was unconstitutionally burdened (perhaps because the case was in fact brought). However, it held that the prospect of future violations of these rights was so substantial that it required the German Parliament, within a year, to amend the law banning contingency fees.

It is not clear what the future will bring. The Court suggested at the very conclusion of its decision that the German government could <u>repeal</u> the law prohibiting contingency fees in its entirety, but it is unlikely that will happen. The more likely scenario is that the new law will create exceptions for persons who can credibly claim that, absent the availability of a contingency fee, they could not find a lawyer willing to take their case.

Of course, it is hard to know how this exception could be written into law. As one German lawyer told me, "What is to prevent a lawyer and a client from colluding to say that the lawyer would not take the case but for a contingent fee?"

Many American tort reformers would argue, I imagine, that the fact that no lawyer would take a case except for the existence of the contingent fee is the best evidence that the case should never be brought at all. I do not want to enter this debate now, except to point out the ways in which the current German situation helps us better understand the problems caused or cured by contingent fees.

1. What is the main idea about the passage?

A. Barring the law prohibiting contingency fees is not constitutional and therefore it is likely in the future that the adaptations to the statute would be made by the German government.

B. It is not likely to happen that the statute governing contingency fees would be repealed.

C. The balance of the state's interest and the lawyer's constitutional right is ranked the highest in all the problems encountered in order to bring the reform to the statute on contingency fees

D. The German Constitutional Court and the appellate court hold different opinion toward the case Frau Hanna N. vs. Frau Dr. T..

2. Which of the followings is correct about the appellate court's decision on the case Frau Hanna N. *vs.* Frau Dr. T.?

A. It ruled that both the client's and the lawyer's rights in the case were burdened and that the statute ruling the unconstitutionality of contingency fees was barred.

B. It ruled that both the client's and the lawyer's rights in the case were not burdened and that contingency fees were not in all cases unconstitutional.

C. It ruled that the state's interest prioritizes individual rights and that contingency fees were unconstitutional.

D. It ruled that the states' interest and individual rights should be weighed against each other and the law barring contingency fees were thus upheld constitutional.

3. How did the court recognize Dr. T's rights in the case according to the passage?

A. The court recognizes that Dr. T's right to perform her lawyer's profession without any interference by the state was burdened because of the banning of her contract with Frau Hanna N. on contingency fee arrangement issues.

B. The court recognizes that Dr. T's right to collect the contingency fees was denied and that the state interest is overweighed against lawyers' individual rights.

C. The court recognizes that Dr. T's right to practice his profession without any undue interference should be placed above the state's right protecting the plaintiff's access to the court.

D. The court recognizes that Dr. T's right to practice her profession was unduly burdened and she was severely underpaid by Frau. Hanna N.

4. What does the underlined word "repeal" probably mean in the passage (Para. 15).

  A. violate   B. supplement

  C. amend   D. revoke

5. What is the most likely scenario about the possible adaptation to the law governing contingency fee collections?

A. It is very likely that the German government would repeal the law prohibiting contingency fees entirely because the law is unconstitutional.

B. As long as the plaintiff establishes sufficient proof that lawyers will be not available unless paying certain amount of contingency fees, it will be justified to have a legal/ constitutional cause.

C. Laws governing the prohibition of contingency fees should be amended and special legal occasions justifying the collection of contingency fees should be specified by laws.

D. Creating exceptions justifying contingency fees is almost impossible because it is hard to list all likely scenarios into the law.

Passage Two

It looks like the punishing sentence handed down on Bernie Madoff may just have been one cellhouse door closing, while others may be opening up to take in new crooks. An AP source indicates that authorities are looking at charging ten more people, although a Reuters story indicates that the investigation is closer to its beginning rather than its conclusion.

The source told Reuters:

"There will probably be more people charged," the law enforcement source said. "It is likely to be 10 or more, but it is going to be a lengthy process that could take months or more."

Speculation has been rampant for months about who, if anyone, else was involved in Madoff's scheme, which by "conservative estimates" cost investors $13.2 billion. Considering both the enormity and complexity of the fraud perpetrated in the case, it certainly has seemed unlikely to many that others besides Madoff were not in on the massive Ponzi scheme, or at least aspects of it. But so far the only other person who has been charged was his outside accountant.

As far as Madoff's family goes, it should be noted that Madoff's own sons turned him in back in December of 2008 after he revealed the existence of the scheme. Still, questions have remained over whether they, and perhaps especially whether Bernie's wife Ruth Madoff, knew about the fraudulent scheme. However, it is unclear from today's reports whether any of them are included amongst those whom authorities are scrutinizing. Notably, Ruth Madoff has relinquished (quite conspicuously) her prior asserted claims to millions that were supposedly not tied in to Madoff's crookery.

In the meantime, efforts to <u>recoup</u> investor losses from the Ponzi scheme continue. A court-appointed trustee reportedly has recovered only $1.2 billion of the aforementioned $13.2 billion figure representing losses. According to the Wall Street Journal piece, most of the funds that are expected to be recovered in the future will now come from "clawback" lawsuits against investors who withdrew money from the Madoff firm in recent years. Bankruptcy laws allow for recovery of payments made by Madoff's now-defunct firm to others for a brief window of time (90 days) prior to the bankruptcy filing. This could apply even to those who were paid and had no knowledge of any of the Madoff misdeeds.

Further, as noted by the WSJ, "state statutes are broader when it comes to recovering money that the courts deem to be fraudulently conveyed as part of the Ponzi scheme", sometimes allowing for recovery of payments made years ago.

1. Which of the following is TRUE about Madoff's Ponzi scheme?

A. Bernie Madoff and Ruth alone have cost the investors a $1.2 billion loss, among the $13.2 billion figure representing loss estimated as in the entire fraudulent scheme.

B. There have been solid sources confirming that almost Madoff's entire family has been involved into the case.

C. It is admitted that the enormity and complexity of the fraud in the case indicate that people other than Madoff and his wife must have been involved in the case.

D. Bankruptcy laws allow investors in Madoff's corporation to have a 90-day period to recover payment made by Madoff's now-defunct firm even including those investors who were paid but had no knowledge of the Madoff's scheme.

2. What's the main idea of the passage?

A. Bernie Madoff's case is toward its ending and Madoff himself is facing a long sentence in prison.

B. Bernie Madoff's family, including his sons and wife, was suspected to have involved into Madoff's fraudulent scheme.

C. Efforts are being made to recover the financial losses in Ponzi scheme and it is very likely that all financial losses could be recovered.

D. Investigations have gone beyond Bernie Madoff to see who else has involved into Ponzi scheme and efforts are made to recoup investor losses.

3. The word "recoup" (para.6) in the passage may probably mean _____.

A. take back   B. distribute
C. compensate   D. estimate

Part Two   True or False Questions

Direction: *In this part of the exercise, there is a passage with ten true or false questions. Read the passage carefully and mark T if it is true and F if it is false.*

Foreign trade law's international roots extend at least as far back as the Renaissance Italian city-states, with modern antecedents dating from efforts around the beginning of the twentieth century to address customs cooperation and discrimination in international trade. The culmination of government regulation of imports and exports was reached in 1947 with the General Agreement on Tariffs and Trade (GATT). GATT forbids governments to discriminate against member countries (this is the most-favored-nation principle), to assess tariffs in excess of levels agreed on, to act to benefit domestic products over imports (the national treatment principle), or to restrict imports or exports. The GATT also contains limits on antidumping and countervailing duties—charges designed to neutralize sales of especially low priced and governmentally subsidized imports—and it contains various exceptions. The 1994 "Uruguay Round" agreements clarified certain GATT commitments, extending many beyond goods to services and intellectual property, and established the World Trade Organization (WTO).

Regionally, the North American Free Trade Agreement (NAFTA) joined Canada, Mexico, and the United States in a liberal trade alliance in 1993. Among other things, it phases out tariffs,

Lesson Ten Investor Protection and Corporate Governance

opens up investment opportunities, establishes special dispute settlement processes for antidumping and countervailing-duty matters, and contains a side accord to address environmental consequences of NAFTA.

On trade law's domestic side, the United States has many legislative and regulatory measures implementing GATT/WTO commitments. These include amendments to the 1930 Tariff Act and legislation like the Uruguay Round Agreements Implementation Act. However, departures such as the 1974 Trade Act's section 301, which can be used to respond to what the U.S. considers unfair practices of foreign governments, do exist. NAFTA commitments are also implemented in U.S. law, principally through the NAFTA Implementation Act.

The contractual relationship between private parties involved in international sales is regulated through the 1980 UN Convention on Contracts for International Sale of Goods (CISG). The antecedents of CISG reside in efforts of UNIDROIT (International Institute for Unification of Private Law) in the 1930s and 1950s, of certain European states in the 1960s, and of UNCITRAL (UN Commission on International Trade Law) in the 1970s to unify private-trade transaction law. CISG speaks to issues of contract formation, buyer and seller obligations and remedies, and risk bearing in cases of loss or injury to goods in international trade. It applies when the contract is between businesses in countries party to CISG, though even then it may be escaped by specific contract terms. It also applies when choice-of-law (i.e., private international law) rules favor the law of a CISG party. As permitted, the United States has declared it will not use CISG in the latter situation. When CISG is otherwise inapplicable, conflict-of-law rules may then result in relevant U.S. state versions of the Uniform Commercial Code being used. CISG is considered a "self-executing" treaty in U.S. constitutional law, and has required no implementing domestic legislation.

Foreign investment law is represented by two branches, both far less developed than their trade law counterparts. The first is reflected in certain bilateral treaties, regional agreements, and multilateral standards; the second, in domestic law affecting foreign nationals interested in investing within the borders of the United States.

The modern Bilateral Investment Treaty, assuring nondiscrimination and relief against expropriation, has antecedents in older treaties of friendship, commerce, and navigation. NAFTA's chapter 11 is the chief regional agreement. It requires nondiscrimination, security from expropriation, free conversion and transfer of currency, and a special claims process for NAFTA investors wronged by actions of a party state. Multilateral investment standards date from the Organization for Economic Cooperation and Development (OECD) efforts in the 1960s and 1970s to develop conventions on foreign property protection and the conduct of multinational enterprises. Though the International Monetary Fund's Guidelines on the Treatment of Foreign Investment and the UN Code of Conduct on Transnational Corporations reveal current thinking, their merely recommendatory nature leaves unresolved the shortcomings plaguing most multilateral efforts. Prominent exceptions, however, include the convention of the International Centre for Settlement of Investment Disputes and the World Bank's multilateral investment guarantee agreement.

The domestic branch of foreign investment law aims at an open-door policy, but various national and state laws limit foreigners' investment opportunities. Nationally, limitations exist in the transportation, communication, and natural resources sectors. In addition, the 1988 Exon-Florio Amendment prohibits, or compels divestment of, acquisitions of U. S. businesses when national security concerns are present. The 1978 Agricultural Foreign Investment Disclosure Act establishes a reporting requirement in connection with foreign-owned U. S. agricultural land. On the state level, an interesting example of such limitations exists in Oklahoma's restriction on foreign ownership of land.

1. Modern efforts on Foreign Trade Law focused on domestic cooperation and discrimination. ( )

2. One of the achievements reached in "Uruguay Round" agreements is "national treatment principle". ( )

3. Under NAFTA, member countries agreed to call off each other's tariffs through different stages. ( )

4. Uruguay Round Agreements Implementation Act is one of the regulatory measures taken by the U. S. for implementing GATT/WTO regulations. ( )

5. International Institute for Unification of Private Law and UN Commission on International Trade Law are both antecedents of CISG. ( )

6. When CISG is inapplicable, most countries would otherwise adopt conflict-of-law rules to settle the contractual dispute. ( )

7. The modern Bilateral Investment Treaty, assuring nondiscrimination and relief against expropriation, has antecedents in older treaties of friendship, commerce, and navigation. ( )

8. Open-door policy helped foreign investment a lot, so do various national and state laws, all of which helped many foreigners to gain their investment opportunities. ( )

IV Translation Abilities

法律语言特征分析与法律翻译技能培养之十：

法律英语中古词、旧词的使用和外来词语的借用

法律英语中,旧词、古词和十分学究气、正式的词的使用远非其他任何文体之语言所能及。在用词方面,常常使用一些源于法语和拉丁语、词义范围明确的词。对于那些在使用过程中弹性较大的词一般都避免使用,而上述这些词在日常口语中通常不为人应用,否则让人觉得说话人很生硬,有装腔作势之嫌。如：aforementioned(= previously mentioned,括号内英语是当代英语的表现方式,以下同),aforesaid(= above),behoove(= to be necessary/to be proper),foregoing,forthwith(= immediately),henceforth(= from now on),hitherto(= until this time/up to now),pursuant to(= under /according to),thence(= from there/from that place,time or source /for that reason,从那里起；从那时起；因为那样的原因),henceforth(= from that time on,after that,自那以后),to wit(= namely/that is to say,即,也就是说),whence(= from where),whensoever(= whenever),此外在法律英语中还有很多与 here-,there-,和 where-连用的一些古英语或中世纪英语,如：

hereabouts 在这附近　　　　　　　　hereafter 此后
herebefore 此前　　　　　　　　　　hereby 特此

Lesson Ten Investor Protection and Corporate Governance

herein 于此处	hereinabove(= above)在上文
hereinafter 以下,在下文中	hereof 关于这个的,于本文件中
hereunder 在下面,据此,在下文	hereupon 于此,因此
herewith(eg. enclosed herewith = enclosed) 与此一道	
thereabout (地点、时间、数量等)大约;上下;附近;左右	
thereafter(from that time on) 因此,据此	
therefore 因此	therefrom 从那里,从此;从中;由此
therein 在此文中	thereof 关于,于是
thereon 就此	thereto 又,及
thereunto 到那里	
whereas(= because/considering that/while on the contrary/inasmuch as)然而,尽管	
whereby 借此	wherefore 为什么
wheresoever,无论何时	whereon 在什么上面,(关系副词)在那上面
whereonto 到那里	whereupon 于是;因此

古词、旧词在法律英语中使用得较多,而在日常口语中,上述词语一般都不会使用,即使使用,其频率也很低。

由于历史的原因,当代法律英语中外来词语的借用十分普遍,首先,法律英语中存在有大量的、日常生活中已经很难见到人们使用的拉丁词汇。比如说:"actus legitimus"(合法行为),"ad hoc"(特别,特定;临时;特殊),"ad referendum"(尚待核准,待进一步审议),"amicus curiae"(协助法庭解释某类法律问题的人,"法庭之友"),"animus"(意愿,意图;心素),"arguendo"(for the sake of argument 在争辩中),"bancus"(法院;法官席),"cadit quaestio"(辩论终结),"capias"(拘票,拘捕令;令状),"certiorari"(上级法院向下级法院调取案卷复审的令状),"coemptio"(买卖婚),"coram"(在某人面前),"corpus juris"(法典,法令大全),"de jure"(法律上,按照法律的,合法的),"dies cedit"(权利义务成立期,债权发生日期),"dolus antecedens"(事前犯意),"en banc"(全体出庭法官听审),"et alii"(以及其他事项,以及其他等等),"fieri facias"(财物扣押令,扣押债务人动产令),"habeas corpus"(人身保护令状),"ipso facto"(根据事实本身/依事实),"jus criminale"(刑法),"lex situs = lex rei sitae"(物所在地法),"modus operandi"(惯技;作案手法;办事方法,做法),"nexus"(关系,联系;结合),"nota bene"(注意,留心),"null and void"(无效),"per curiam"(by the court 依法院/由法院所定/引用法官判词),"prima facie"(初步的;表面的),"quorum"(法定人数),"res judicata"(既决案件;已判决的事项/事件),"seriatum"(in turn/ serially/one after another 依次/逐条),"supersedeas"(中止执行令;中止诉讼令状),"stare decisis"(遵循先例原则,因循先例原则;根据判例),"vis major"(不可抗力;不能抵抗的力量),和其他许多拉丁词语,这些词汇有的已经成了英语的一部分,拉丁词汇的使用无碍信息的交流,法官、律师们认为此乃理所当然;有的虽然对于一般当事人需要一些作出解释但接受良好教育的人均能理解,并认为这才是法律中的行话(the shop talk of the law);有些拉丁词语是法律工作者必不可少的内容,如"res judicata"(既决案件;已判决的事件/事项)是民事诉讼程序中一个基本规定,虽然对部分非法律专业工作者存在一定的难度,但即使是普通的法律读者都不愿意弃绝该词语的使用。

外来词语的借用不仅是拉丁语的应用,由于1066年的诺曼征服以及其后对英国语言的影响,法语在法律英语中亦起到十分重要的作用,英语中已经被接受为其当然语言的词或词汇大多数来自法语,这些词或词语的使用不会造成英国人交往中的错误,如"appeal"、"assault"、"contract"、"damages"、"defendant"、"heir"、"larceny"、"lien"、"mortgage"、"plaintiff"、"pleadings"、"reprieve"、"tort"、"treason"、"trespass"、"verdict"等,但也有一些法语词可能会给读者或非法律专业人员造成一定的麻烦,如:

alien or aliene 作为动词使用时等于当代英语中的"to convey or to transfer"(转让,让与所有权);

cestui que trust = beneficiary(信托收益人)

cy-pres = as near as possible(尽可能地,力求近似;近似原则)

en ventre sa mere = in its mother's womb(腹中胎儿,待生胎儿)

feme covert = married woman(有夫之妇,已婚女子)

save = except(除……之外)

seisin/seizin = possession or ownership(占有物;占有土地,土地的占有;依法占有的财产)

上述这些法语词大都为英国人民所接受,特别是法律工作者更是认为其工作中必然会涉及这些词汇。如下列法语词汇仍然普遍应用到法律英语中,"estoppel"(禁止翻供/不得反悔/禁止改口/不许否认),"laches"(对行使权利的疏忽/懈怠;迟延,迟误),"voir dire"(预备询问/预先审核),等等。

Translation Exercises:

Part One *Put the Following into Chinese*

Traditional comparisons of corporate governance systems focus on the institutions financing firms rather than on the legal protection of investors. Bank-centered corporate governance systems, such as those of Germany and Japan, are compared to market-centered systems, such as those of the United States and the United Kingdom. Relatedly, relationship-based corporate governance, in which a main bank provides a significant share of finance and governance to each firm, is contrasted with market-based governance, in which finance is provided by large numbers of investors and in which takeovers play a key governance role.

The most basic prediction of the legal approach is that investor protection encourages the development of financial markets. When investors are protected from expropriation, they pay more for securities, making it more attractive for entrepreneurs to issue these securities. This applies to both creditors and shareholders. Creditor rights encourage the development of lending, and the exact structure of these rights may alternatively favor bank lending or market lending. Shareholder rights encourage the development of equity markets, as measured by the valuation of firms, the number of listed firms (market breadth), and the rate at which firms go public.

For both shareholders and creditors, protection includes not only the rights written into the laws and regulations but also the effectiveness of their enforcement. Consistent with these predictions, the research also indicates that countries that protect shareholders have more valuable stock markets, larger numbers of listed securities per capita, and a higher rate of IPO (initial public offering) activity than do the unprotective countries.

Lesson Ten Investor Protection and Corporate Governance

Part Two *Put the Following into English*

(1) 投资者在本协议签订之日起7(七)个工作日内向原股东及目标公司提供下述资料,并保证其真实性、有效性、完整性:其上溯至最终控制人的股权结构图、营业执照(或商业登记证)、公司章程、本次交易的内部决策文件;

(2) 实际控制人承诺函主要内容包括:承诺在本次交易完成日之日起3(三)年内,不转让其直接或间接持有的投资者股权;并且,在目标公司上市前,不变更股权结构;承诺并保证其自身、其控制的直接或间接持有投资者股份的主体以及投资者(视股权结构图的情况,可具体列举公司的名称)是符合中国法律法规规定和中国证监会要求的拟上市公司股东或间接股东条件的主体。

V Interaction

Hold a group discussion or consulting with your professors or other people working with expertise knowledge under the topic "how investment expropriation could be avoided in business", then write up a paper based on the discussion. Good article structure and solid grounds are needed to clarify your points.

VI Appreciation of Judge's Opinions

(1) Case Name(案件名): *Reilly v. Greenwald & Hoffman*

COURT OF APPEAL, FOURTH APPELLATE DISTRICT

DIVISION ONE

STATE OF CALIFORNIA

REILLY V. GREENWALD & HOFFMAN, LLP (2011), CAL. APP. 4TH
MARK S. REILLY, PLAINTIFF AND APPELLANT, V. GREENWALD &
HOFFMAN, LLP, ET AL., DEFENDANTS AND RESPONDENTS.
(SUPERIOR COURT OF SAN DIEGO COUNTY, NO.
37-2009-00056073-CU-BT-NC, JACQUELINE M. STERN, JUDGE.)
[No. D057299. Fourth Dist., Div. One. May 23, 2011.]

---

(2) Case Summary(案件简介)

In March 2003 Reilly and Brion agreed to operate Brion Reilly, Inc. (BRI), to provide architectural and design services(建筑设计服务). Reilly's and Brion's interests in the corporation were 49 and 51 percent, respectively, but they agreed to equal compensation and profit sharing. Brion was the president, director and chief financial officer(首席财务官) of BRI. Reilly was also an officer(高级职员) and director(董事) of BRI.

In April 2004 Reilly and Brion agreed to terminate their business relationship and dissolve BRI(解散BRI公司). In August 2009 Reilly filed an amended complaint (hereafter complaint) against BRI; Brion and an entity of hers, Brion Design, Inc. (BDI); Greenwald, who was BRI's outside counsel(外聘律师,独立董事,外部董事); a bank, an officer of the bank, and two successor banks; and a certified public accountant (CPA)(注册会计师) firm and an individual CPA. The first cause of action, titled "Shareholder Derivative Action(股东衍生/派生诉讼)", names all defendants. It alleges that between June 2006 and the end of 2008, Brion excluded Reilly from BRI's premises "and converted and misappropriated(转移侵占) to herself the monies, receivables(应收款项/票

据), personal property, and work in progress of BRI"; Brion engaged in this conduct with the cooperation and assistance of defendants; and as a result of defendants' misconduct BRI has suffered damages.

The seventh through ninth causes of action are solely against Greenwald. The seventh cause of action, for constructive fraud(推定诈欺,指某种行为不一定有诈欺故意,但产生诈欺的后果,法律上应以诈欺论) and negligent misrepresentation(过失性陈述), alleges Greenwald, while acting as BRI's counsel, "advised BRI that... Brion and BDI had no duty or obligation, in connection with the termination of the business and dissolution of BRI, to account for the monies, receivables, personal property and work in progress of BRI as of the date of the termination of the business by BRI." Further, it alleges Greenwald "counseled and advised BRI that defendants Brion and BDI were entitled to appropriate(占用) such assets of BRI to their own use without any duty... to distribute to plaintiff his proportionate share of such assets." The eighth cause of action, for legal malpractice, alleges Greenwald breached the standard of care(注意标准) owed BRI, and violated rules of professional conduct, by facilitating Brion's misconduct. The ninth cause of action, for breach of contract, alleges Greenwald's conduct was a breach of his written agreement with BRI for legal services.

The fourteenth cause of action, for conspiracy(合谋,共谋,同谋) is against Brion, BDI, and Greenwald. It alleges they conspired to exclude Reilly from the business premises of BRI, and misappropriated to their own use the monies, receivables and work in progress of BRI, and as a consequence BRI was damaged.

Greenwald demurred(抗辩) to the complaint, arguing it is barred as to him under *McDermott*, because BRI has not waived the attorney-client privilege(律师—当事人特权规则) covering communications between him and Brion during his representation of BRI, and thus he cannot mount any meaningful defense. Additionally, Greenwald argued the fourteenth cause of action is barred because plaintiff did not comply with the procedural requirements of Civil Code section 1714.10, subdivision (b).

On March 12, 2010, the court issued a tentative ruling sustaining the demurrer(支持抗辩) on the basis of the opinion in *McDermott*. After a hearing on the same date, the court confirmed its ruling. A judgment of dismissal was entered on April 13, 2010.

(3) Excerpts of the Judgment(法官判决词)

McCONNELL, P. J.

This is a shareholder derivative action(股东代表诉讼) by minority shareholder(少数股东) Mark S. Reilly against a corporation and its majority shareholder, Lena Brion, and as relevant here, the corporation's outside counsel(公司外聘律师,独立董事), Greenwald & Hoffman, LLP, and Paul E. Greenwald (together, Greenwald). The complaint(诉辩状) alleges causes of action against Greenwald for negligent and tortious conduct(过失与侵权行为) for facilitating the majority shareholder's conversion of corporate funds to her own use after she and Reilly agreed to dissolve the corporation.

Reilly appeals a judgment for Greenwald entered after the trial court(一审法院) sustained without leave(许可,同意) to amend his demurrer to the amended complaint. Reilly contends the court erred by finding that under *McDermott, Will & Emery v. Superior Court* (2000), the claims against Greenwald are barred(禁止起诉) because the corporation has not waived the attorney-client privilege covering communications between Brion and Greenwald that are the subject matter of the claims, and thus Greenwald cannot adequately defend himself. Reilly asserts *McDermott* is inapplicable to a dissolved corporation, but that argument was recently rejected in *Favila v. Katten Muchin Roseman LLP* (2010) which we find persuasive. We affirm the judgment.

DISCUSSION

I *Standard of Review*

We treat the demurrer(法律上不生效的答辩,妨碍诉讼的抗辩;抗辩) as admitting all material facts properly pleaded, but not contentions, deductions or conclusions of fact or law. We also consider matters which may be judicially noticed. Further, we give the complaint a reasonable interpretation. "The judgment of dismissal must be affirmed if any ground for demurrer is well taken, but it is error for a trial court to sustain a demurrer when the plaintiff has stated a cause of action under any possible legal theory. Further, it is an abuse of discretion(滥用自由裁量权) to sustain a demurrer without leave to amend when the plaintiff shows there is a reasonable possibility an identified defect can be cured by amendment." "While the decision to sustain or overrule a demurrer is a legal ruling subject to de novo review on appeal(上诉时重新审查), the granting of leave to amend involves an exercise of the trial court's discretion."

II *Applicability of Attorney-Client Privilege in Shareholder Derivative Action Against Corporate Outside Counsel*
A

"A shareholder has the same right as anyone else to sue the corporation or its officers to enforce the shareholder's personal claims. However, a shareholder may only bring or defend an action on behalf of the corporation in exceptional cases where the directors fail to act. In these cases, the shareholder's suit is called a 'derivative action' because the wrong to be redressed is one against the corporation, and normally the corporation would bring the suit. However, when the corporation fails or refuses to act after proper demand, the shareholder's ultimate interest in the corporation is sufficient to justify bringing a 'propulsive' action, 'designed to set in motion the judicial machinery for the redress of the wrong to the corporation.'"

"A *derivative* action...does not transfer the cause of action from the corporation to the shareholders. Rather, the cause of action in a shareholder derivative suit belongs to and remains with the corporation.... Though it is named as a defendant, the corporation is 'the real plaintiff and it alone benefits from the decree; the stockholders derive no benefit therefrom except the indirect benefit resulting from a realization upon the corporations' assets'.(公司资产的变现)"

McDermott notes "a derivative lawsuit for malpractice against corporate outside counsel raises unique attorney-client privilege issues". The purpose of the attorney-client privilege "is to promote full and open discussion between clients and their attorneys".

"A client has a privilege to refuse to disclose, and to prevent another from disclosing, a confidential communication between the client and his or her lawyer unless the privilege is waived.... Once a party establishes that a privilege applies, the burden shifts to the party opposing the privilege to demonstrate that the privilege did not apply, that an exception existed, or that there was an express or implied waiver."

In *McDermott*, the court explained that while shareholders "stand in the shoes"(处于某人的位置,站在某人的立场上) of the corporation for most purposes, "the one notable exception is with respect to the attorney-client privilege." "It is the corporation, and not the shareholder, who is the holder of the privilege. Shareholders do not enjoy access to such privileged information merely because the attorney's actions also benefit them. Nor do shareholders obtain the right to waive the privilege simply by virtue of filing the action on the corporation's behalf. This distinction makes a derivative malpractice action far different from a direct malpractice action. Generally, the filing of a legal malpractice action against one's attorney results in a waiver of the privilege, thus enabling the attorney to disclose, to the extent necessary to defend against the action, information otherwise protected by the attorney-client privilege. However, because a derivative action does not result in the corporation's waiver of the privilege, such a lawsuit against the corporation's outside counsel has the dangerous potential for robbing the attorney defendant of the only means he or she may have to mount any meaningful defense. It effectively places the defendant attorney in the untenable position of having to 'preserve the attorney client privilege (the client having done nothing to waive the privilege) while trying to show that his representation of the client was not negligent.'"

McDermott adds: "California courts have refused to carve out a shareholder exception to the attorney-client privilege, even in a derivative action. We simply cannot conceive how an attorney is to mount a defense in a shareholder derivative action alleging a breach of duty to the corporate client, where, by the very nature of such an action, the attorney is foreclosed, in the absence of any waiver by the corporation, from disclosing the very communications which are alleged to constitute a breach of that duty." *McDermott* holds "the creation of any shareholder right to waive the privilege in a derivative action should be left to the California Legislature. And, in the absence of such a right, this derivative action, necessarily brought in equity, cannot go forward."

In *McDermott*, the court declined to apply the case-by-case approach some federal courts have adopted, which allows a shareholder access to privileged information in a shareholder derivative action on a "finding of good cause, including a likelihood that the corporate decision would be outside the protections of the business judgment rule." The court explained, "Longstanding California case authority has rejected this application of the federal doctrine, noting it contravenes the strict principles set forth in the Evidence Code of California which precludes any judicially created exceptions to the attorney-client privilege."

B

In his opening brief, Reilly contends *McDermott* is inapplicable because a *dissolved* corporation such as BRI may not assert the attorney-client privilege. Shortly before he filed the brief, however, the *McDermott* court issued *Favila*, which rejects the same argument. *Favila* explains: "A dissolved corporation continues to exist for various purposes. Because it continues in existence... it would appear the persons authorized to act on the dissolved corporation's behalf during the windup process—its ongoing management personnel—should be able to assert the privilege, at least until all matters involving the company have been fully resolved and no further proceedings are contemplated. Indeed, if the lawyer-client privilege is simply extinguished upon dissolution, then the corporation's ability to effectively prosecute or defend actions is eviscerated(取出,去除); and the shareholders who may be responsible for their pro rata(按比例地,成比例地)portions of any claims are unfairly disadvantaged."

We agree with *Favila*'s analysis. Corporations Code section 2010, subdivision (a) provides: "A corporation which is dissolved nevertheless continues to exist for the purpose of winding up its affairs, prosecuting and defending actions by or against it and enabling it to collect and discharge obligations, dispose of and convey its property and collect and divide its assets, but not for the purpose of continuing business except so far as necessary for the winding up thereof." "Courts have repeatedly construed [Corporations Code] section 2010 and its predecessors... as permitting parties to bring suit against dissolved corporations." "Under our statutory scheme, the effect of dissolution is not so much change in the corporation's status as a change in its permitted scope of activity.... Thus, a corporation's dissolution is best understood not as its death, but merely as its retirement from active business."

Indeed, Reilly is able to bring this action because BRI's existence continues for purposes of litigation. It is only logical that if a dissolved corporation continues to exist for litigation, it remains the holder of the attorney-client privilege during the litigation. A dissolved corporation would be at just as great a disadvantage as an active corporation by having to disclose confidential communications with its outside counsel. Moreover, the status of a corporation does not affect corporate counsel's inability to adequately defend himself or herself against malpractice and related claims in a shareholder derivative suit absent the corporation's waiver of the privilege.

In his reply brief, Reilly asserts that notwithstanding *Favila*, BRI cannot assert the attorney-client privilege because there is "no functioning management of the corporation" to assert the privilege on its behalf. The complaint, however, does not allege BRI lacks current management, and Reilly does not seek leave to amend. To the contrary, the complaint effectively concedes(承认,认可)Brion is managing BRI post-dissolution. For instance, the complaint alleges "Brion is now... the owner of fifty-one... shares of stock of BRI and an officer and a director of BRI." Further, it alleges Reilly "did not make any effort to secure action from the Board of Directors of BRI in pursuing this action since any such effort would have been futile for the reasons that... Brion, on June 15, 2006 and continuing thereafter, was the President, Chief Financial Officer and owner of fifty-one... of the shares of BRI, representing fifty-one percent... of the voting power of BRI, and would have obviously refused to comply with any request or demand for such action. " The complaint also alleges that as president, chief financial officer and majority shareholder of BRI, Brion has a *current* duty to "account to BRI for all of the assets of BRI... as of June 15, 2006. " "The board of directors and officers of the dissolved corporation have the authority to act on the corporation's behalf to wind up its affairs. "

Even if Brion were not following procedures set forth in the Corporations Code during the windup period, as Reilly suggests, absent a waiver of the attorney—client privilege by *someone* authorized to make it on BRI's behalf, *Greenwald* is duty-bound to claim the privilege. "An attorney cannot, without the consent of his client, be examined as to any communication made by the client to him, or his advice given thereon in the course of professional employment. "Evidence Code section 955 provides, "The lawyer who received or made a communication subject to the privilege under this article shall claim the privilege whenever he is present when the communication is sought to be disclosed and is authorized to claim the privilege under subdivision (c) of Section 954. "The complaint does not allege BRI's waiver of the attorney-client privilege, and Reilly does not seek leave to amend. Absent waiver, Greenwald cannot adequately defend himself against claims he facilitated Brion's wrongdoing.

Reilly's reliance on Evidence Code section 953, subdivision (d) for the proposition that only the successor to a dissolved corporation holds the attorney-client privilege is misplaced. The statute provides that the holder of the attorney-client privilege is a "successor, assign, trustee in dissolution, or any similar representative of a... corporation... *that is no longer in existence.* "BRI remains in existence to wind up its affairs, including to litigate the instant action. Under subdivision (a) of section 953, the client is the holder of the privilege.

Reilly also cites Evidence Code section 958, which states, "There is no privilege under this article as to a communication relevant to an issue of breach, by the lawyer or by the client, of a duty arising out of the lawyer-client relationship. "The statute does not apply, however, to a derivative malpractice action.

Additionally, *City of Rialto v. United States Department of Defense*(2007) is inapt. *Rialto* was not a shareholder derivative action against corporate outside counsel. *Rialto* was a discovery dispute in which the court concluded a corporation (Kwikset) that dissolved and transferred its assets to a successor company about 50 years earlier did not retain the attorney-client privilege. Rather, the privilege transferred to the successor company, and then again to that company's successor. Under those facts, the court upheld a special master's finding that "Kwikset, as a dissolved corporation, cannot assert the attorney-client privilege in this litigation. "The court concluded the ultimate successor waived the right to assert the privilege by not timely objecting to discovery requests. Here, BRI has no successor to whom the privilege was transferred, and it is still in the windup period. Further, *Rialto* acknowledges that when it was decided, there was no California law determining whether a corporation loses the attorney-client privilege on dissolution. Now we have the opinion in *Favila*.

C1

Reilly contends the privilege issue here should not be decided at the pleading stage. He cites this court's opinion in *Dietz v. Meisenheimer & Herron* (2009). In *Dietz*, we concluded there are several factors a court must consider, under *General Dynamics Corp. v. Superior Court* (1994) (General Dynamics) and its progeny (子孙;结果), before it "may dismiss a case on the ground that a defendant attorney's due process right to present a defense would be violated by the defendant's inability to disclose a client's confidential information if the action were allowed to proceed. "To dismiss a case at the pleading stage, a court must determine whether (1) the evidence at issue is the client's confidential information, and the client insists that it remain confidential; (2) given the nature of plaintiff's claim the confidential information is highly material to the defendants' defenses; (3) there are "ad hoc" measures available to avoid dismissal such as " ' sealing and protective orders, limited admissibility of evidence, orders restricting the use of testimony in successive proceedings, and, where appropriate, in camera (秘密地;私下地;不公开审讯地) proceedings"; and (4) it would be fundamentally unfair to proceed.

In *Dietz*, we acknowledged that the McDermott court "relied heavily on the fact that the confidential information at issue there was highly material to the defendants' defenses. In *McDermott*, the court held that dismissal was proper in a case in which the plaintiff brought a claim that, by its very nature, necessitated that the defendant disclose privileged or confidential information in order to present 'a meaningful defense'. "Here, the situation is the same. The complaint alleges Greenwald's negligence and tortious conduct facilitated Brion's conversion of BRI's assets to her own use. Obviously, his confidential communications with her are highly material to his defenses. Further, the complaint does not allege any waiver by BRI, and thus the client insists on confidentiality. Under the circumstances, it would be fundamentally unfair to proceed against Greenwald.

2

As to the propriety of dismissal at this stage, we also acknowledge the approach the court adopted in *Favila*. In *Favila*, the court reversed a judgment of dismissal entered after the sustaining of corporate outside counsels' demurrer to a shareholder derivative action. The court remanded the matter to the trial court for its further consideration of whether under McDermott the attorneys' inability to disclose privileged information barred the action. The court concluded the propriety (礼仪,规矩) of the trial court's ruling "depends on the resolution of several difficult questions involving the lawyer-client privilege in the context of an asset sale followed immediately by corporate dissolution."

The court explained "a demurrer based on McDermott... is unlike most pleading motions; for it asks the trial court to speculate about matters in the future (can the lawyer-defendant adequately defend the case if privileged information cannot be disclosed), rather than to evaluate the legal sufficiency of the complaint actually before it. Accordingly, if a demurrer to a derivative complaint against outside counsel would otherwise be overruled but for the *McDermott*... issue and there appears to be a realistic possibility that litigation of the remainder of the action against corporate insiders will result in a waiver of the corporation's privilege or produce additional evidence supporting an exception to that privilege, the trial court should not sustain the demurrer and dismiss the action. Rather, under these circumstances, the appropriate action is for the court to conditionally stay further proceedings against outside counsel, including discovery as to the causes of action against them, and defer consideration of any demurrer or judgment on the pleadings based on counsel's inability to defend because of the lawyer-client privilege."

Greenwald criticizes the conditional stay approach as requiring factual findings on demurrer, implementing a vague procedure without legislative approval or sufficient guidelines, and prejudicing corporate outside counsel in the event of the lifting of a stay after discovery and trial against other defendants proceeded, and by counsels' inability to represent the corporation without a prompt ruling on the demurrer. In his reply brief, Reilly addresses *Favila*, but he does not assert there is any realistic possibility BRI will waive the privilege or that any evidence may develop to show an exception to the privilege, or that the ruling on the demurrer should be conditionally stayed under *Favila*. Accordingly, Reilly has forfeited review of the issue and we need not decide if we agree with Favila's conditional stay approach.

DISPOSITION

The judgment is affirmed. Greenwald is entitled to costs on appeal.

Nares, J., and O'Rourke, J., concurred(同意判决结果,但理由不一致).

Lesson Eleven

Using Theory to Study Law: A Company Law Perspective

> **Learning objectives**
>
> After learning the text and having done the exercises in this lesson, you will:
>
> —familiarize with the development of the US legal scholarship;
>
> —acquire an appreciation of the vocabulary and grammar or syntax relevant to the legal scholarship;
>
> —become aware of the information required in order to understand the legal scholarship;
>
> —cultivate the practical abilities to put to use the language in the specific context;
>
> —be able to do some translation from Chinese to English and from English to Chinese.

 Text

Using Theory to Study Law: A Company Law Perspective

A much-remarked upon feature of British legal literature is its "descriptive" and "doctrinal" orientation①. This characterization is at least in some measure misleading. Plenty of anecdotal evidence now exists which demonstrates that British legal scholarship does not consist entirely of doctrinal work and has been influenced by theoretical analysis. Indeed, it has been suggested that "legal studies are experiencing a mini-renaissance"②. This trend is certainly not unique to the United Kingdom. In the United States, for example, theorizing about law has flourished. This has

---

① A much-remarked upon feature of British legal literature is its "descriptive" and "doctrinal" orientation:句中的 mach-remarked 是惯用法,意为"讲述或讨论得很多的",如,much-touted(renowned,有名的)。句中的 doctrinal 和 descriptive 与 theoretic 相对,指英国法学研究多基于以 case law 以及 statutes 中的原理和规则为基础,而非纯理论的抽象理论研究,意为"原理性的"和"阐述性的"。故全句可译为:"英国法律著述一显著特征是其阐述性和原理性。"

② legal studies are experiencing a mini-renaissance:法学研究正在经历着一次微型复兴。句中的 mini-renaissance 指的是"小的复兴运动"。Renaissance 本义指的是中世纪后在意大利等国发生的"文艺复兴"运动。

caused considerable disquiet in American legal circles. Fears have been expressed that the move towards theory has reduced the practical utility of legal scholarship and could be having adverse side-effects in the classroom.

The controversy which has arisen in the United States concerning the relationship between law and theory has, as of yet①, attracted little attention in Britain. Since theoretical scholarship has begun to grow in prominence in the United Kingdom. The situation could change. As a result, this is a suitable occasion to assess whether theoretical analysis can make a valuable contribution both with respect to research and teaching. This essay will begin by outlining the basic parameters of the debate. It will then advance the thesis that continued use of theory will have a beneficial influence on academic writing and should lead to improvements in the classroom. This will be done primarily by focusing on a particular subject area, company law.

Defining Theoretical Legal Scholarship

In order to discuss the role which theory can and should play in the study of law, defining what constitutes theoretical legal scholarship is a good point of departure. According to the Butterworths Australian Legal Dictionary②, legal theory refers "to any academic analysis of the law which requires a degree of abstraction from the principles stated in case and statute-based law". Under this definition, jurisprudence, which is concerned with questions regarding the nature of law, its general structure, its sources and so on, should qualify as theoretical analysis. For present purposes, however, the focus will be on a different use to which the term legal theory is put. Theoretical scholarship will be defined as the study of law from the "outside". This implies the use of intellectual disciplines external to law, to carry out research on its economic, social or political implications. Typically, the techniques and approaches are in fact borrowed from the social sciences and the humanities. The ultimate objective of this sort of interdisciplinary exercise is to secure a deeper and broader understanding of the legal system by placing it in its proper context.

Scholarship characterized as "doctrinal" or "descriptive" does not qualify as theory under the foregoing definition③. With legal research of this nature, the author typically seeks to organize and categorize legal rules ("doctrine") in a systematic fashion. Social and economic context have little role to play with such an exercise. Doctrinal or descriptive scholarship instead involves an "internal" account of the legal rules that govern particular subject matter and tends to reflect a general preference for the coherence of law. Hence, in circumstances where a legal problem does not fall neatly within④ the purview of an existing rule, a doctrinal analyst will take into account related cases and from them inductively determine the most suitable way to resolve the uncertainty.

An important distinction between theoretical and doctrinal scholarship is the audience to

---

① as of yet:到目前为止(多用于肯定句),而 as yet 也为此意,但多用于否定句。
② Butterworths Australian Legal Dictionary:《巴特沃兹澳大利亚法律词典》。
③ Scholarship characterized as "doctrinal" or "descriptive" does not qualify as theory under the foregoing definition:句中的 qualify as 表示"把……叫做或当做;取得做……的资格;宣誓做……"的意思。"以'原理性'和'阐述性'为特征的学术成就按上述界定不配称为理论之资格。"
④ fall within:属于……的范围/范畴;属于……之列,与其对应的乃 fall without,意思是"不属于……之内"。

which the writing is directed①. Research of a doctrinal character is often written with the objective of helping members of the legal profession, such as judges and the lawyers who argue before them, to "find" the existing law. Such scholarship might take the form of an article addressing a knotty doctrinal problem that is already or soon likely to be, before the courts. Alternatively and more ambitiously, an author might write a book mapping an area of law so as to identify basic principles and provide a systematic exposition of the relevant legal rules.

Doctrinal scholarship, as well as serving the practical needs of the legal profession, can find an audience among law students. Students, in most of the courses they take, will need to learn the relevant "black letter" law②. A text which supplies essential background material and discusses legal rules in a convenient, accessible and lucid manner is likely to be a popular source of assistance. A classic example familiar to British company lawyers is Cower's *Principles of Modern Company Law*.

Those who approach legal scholarship from an interdisciplinary perspective tend to think of their audience in much different terms from their doctrinal counterparts. Ultimately, those who "do theory" seek to contribute to debates about law and its relationship to society, culture and the economy. Often, such work has no obvious or immediate connection to actual law practice, which reduces the likelihood that it will be of potential interest to practicing lawyers or judges. Also, much of the literature is too abstract or specialized to be popular with law students. For many of those who carry out interdisciplinary research, the fact that "theory" does not have the same sort of immediate practical value to the legal profession or law students as does doctrinal scholarship is not a critical problem. This is because their most important constituency is their fellow scholars: for them, legal theory is for legal theoreticians.

Theory and Legal Scholarship in the United Kingdom

Academic legal writing in the United Kingdom is often said to have a strongly doctrinal, descriptive character③. The trend manifests itself in a number of ways. Articles in academic journals are commonly constructed as commentary upon the decisions of the courts or upon legislative measures. There is a wide variety of texts available to students to enable them to learn about the "black letter" law in their courses and law teachers monopolize this market. Many of the books which the legal profession uses to "find" the law are written by academics or by combined teams of academics and practitioners.

A number of academics have said that, because legal literature in Britain is primarily descrip-

---

① An important distinction between theoretical and doctrinal scholarship is the audience to which the writing is directed:句中的 direct to 表示"把……指向;把……针对"的意思。故整个句子可以译为:理论法学与原理性学术研究之区别就在其著述所针对的读者之不同。

② "black letter" law:指严谨的应按字面解释的法律原则,众所周知且无争议的法律原则。

③ Academic legal writing in the United Kingdom is often said to have a strongly doctrinal, descriptive character:句中的 doctrinal 和 descriptive 与 theoretic 相对,指英国法学研究多基于以 case law 以及 statutes 中的原理和规则为基础,而非纯理论的抽象理论研究,意为"原理性的"和"阐述性的"。故整句话可译为:"联合王国的法学学术著述常被人说成具有浓郁的原理性和阐述性性质。"

tive in orientation, it is and, uncreative, tedious and lacking in "vision"①. The prescription typically offered is a shift towards theoretical scholarship.

The case in favor of theory can be summarized as follows. Doctrinal scholarship no doubt provides necessary information to those who act within the legal system. On the other hand, since the focus is "internal", the social consequences of law are ignored. This is of importance because the legal system is not marked off neatly from other systems in society. Instead, the subject-matter of law is relevant to most aspects of public and private life and legal institutions are human constructs embodying political, economic and moral choices.

Since the legal order is not isolated from the social order of which it is a part, to understand fully the role of law it is necessary to borrow methodologies that are exterior to conventional legal discourse. Fields outside law provide analytical and conceptual techniques which can be used to broaden perspectives on experience through systematic observation and, theoretical reflection. Increased use of interdisciplinary approaches should therefore help to unlock the legal system's animating principles, provide a better understanding of the probable impact of legal rules on behavior and improve comprehension of law as a social practice.

Pleas in favor of theoretical legal scholarship have in fact yielded a positive response in the United Kingdom. There is currently a growing interest in interdisciplinary analysis and increased curiosity about how the law works in practice rather than merely on paper. The "mini-renaissance" in legal studies referred to earlier reflects this. Despite the intellectual ferment and diversification in the United Kingdom, British academics who have studied developments in the United States have acknowledged that matters have progressed considerably further in American law schools than has been the case inBritain. To obtain guidance, therefore, on the future prospects for interdisciplinary approaches to law, it is helpful to consider what has taken place in the United States.

Theory and Legal Scholarship in the United States

Although the main trends in theoretical Legal scholarship are currently being set in the United States, theory did not always occupy a preeminent position there. Until 1960s, American law professors strongly identified themselves with the legal profession and their writing was in most instances designed to guide judges and practicing lawyers in the path of sound legal reasoning. The result was that legal scholarship consisted primarily of law review articles which took a relatively narrow problem and addressed it doctrinally, together with some systematic expositions of substantive law set out in the form of treatises.

Beginning in the 1960s, however, the character of legal literature began to change, as conceptual approaches drawn from the social sciences and the humanities were imported into and made the basis of legal analysis. Theorizing about the law ultimately became a "growing industry"②, with academics increasingly producing general, abstract accounts of legal topics which departed

---

① lacking in "vision":缺乏远见。句中的 lack 作为动词使用时,其使用方式和作为名词使用时的用法不同,故常常有 for lack of 与 be lacking in 的区别,其意义均可以指"缺乏,缺少"。

② Theorizing about the law ultimately became a "growing industry":法律理论化最终成了一个"新兴的产业"。

substantially from the ways in which law had been conceptualized previously. Tangible manifestations of the intellectual shift abound. There has been an increase in the "market share" of theoretically oriented articles in leading law reviews[①], a proliferation of specialized journals devoted to interdisciplinary approaches to law and much more frequent citation of theoretical scholarship in legal literature.

Within the new theoretical literature, a number of leading schools of thought[②] have emerged. These include "law and economics"[③] which entails the application of economic methodologies to legal subjects, and "feminism", which involves the study of law from an angle that emphasizes the perspective of women and is animated by the objective of exposing inequality. Also notable have been "law and society"[④], which is a scholarly enterprise that explains or describes legal phenomena in social and cultural terms, and "critical legal studies", which is dedicated to exposing the indeterminacy and value-laden qualities of legal decision-making.

The rise of theoretical, interdisciplinary study in US law schools has been praised as a "very good thing" which has "increased and refined our understanding of law far beyond what generations of doctrinalists had achieved". Hence, according to some, "the last quarter century has been a golden age for American legal scholarship". Such views are not, however, held unanimously. Instead, the interdisciplinary movement in legal thought has prompted a strong backlash. Judge Harry T. Edwards of the US Court of Appeals for the District of Columbia Circuit[⑤] energized the debate with a provocative article published in 1992.

Judge Edwards, who served on the law faculties at Harvard and Michigan, argued in his 1992 article that a regrettable disjunction was growing between law schools and the legal profession. He placed much of the balance on academics, deploring their choice to pursue "abstract" theory at the expense of engaging in analysis of legal doctrine. Judge Edwards said that because law professors were choosing not to focus on cases, statutes and related sources of law, the judiciary and practicing lawyers were getting less and less help from legal scholarship. He made his case in part by quoting a lawyer who had previously acted as a clerk for him:

"I look for articles and treatises containing solid doctrinal analysis of a legal question; comprehensive summaries of an area of law; and well-argued and supported positions on specific legal issues. Theory wholly divorced from cases has been of no use to me in practice".

Also troubling for Judge Edwards was that Harvard and some other "elite" US law schools[⑥] had acquired significant contingents of "impractical" scholars who preferred to forget that they

---

① leading law reviews:主要的法律评论。在美国,多数法学院均有其学报或专门的杂志,对法律问题进行细致而深刻的分析和研究。另一种最为常见的称之为"law journals"(法律期刊)。

② Within the new theoretical literature, a number of leading schools of thought have emerged:句中的 school 为学派、流派。全句可译为:在新的理论文献中,涌现出了许多重要的思想流派。

③ "law and economics":法律经济学;法经济学。

④ Also notable have been "law and society":句中的"law and society"指"法律社会学"或"法社会学"。整个句子为完全倒装句。可以译为:法律社会学同样惹人注目。

⑤ the U.S. Court of Appeals for the District of Columbia Circuit:美国哥伦比亚特区巡回上诉法院。

⑥ Harvard and some other "elite" US law schools:哈佛和其他一些美国"精英"法学院。"elite"为法语单词,为"精华、杰出"之意。

were in a professional faculty and who were disdainful of the practice of law. He feared that such attitudes were carrying over into the classroom, which meant students were being taught by professors who not only lacked practical legal experience but had little interest in legal doctrine. Law school graduates were therefore in danger of not acquiring the fluency with legal texts and concepts they required for practice. As well, they were prone to feel alienated from their chosen field, which in turn was tending to produce an increasingly cynical and unethical legal profession.

Judge Edwards' appraisal of law schools and the legal profession elicited a strong reaction. Many expressed support for his views. Certainly, there are examples of legal scholarship which seem to bear out his fears, as a sampling of recent titles in US law journals illustrates: "Never Confuse Efficiency with a Liver Complaint", "A Feminist Theory of Malebashing" and "Foucault, Gadamer and the Law: Hermeneutics[①] in Postmodern Legal Thought[②]". Judge Edwards' comments were also met by a torrent of rebuttals. Those who stepped forward to address his arguments typically sympathized with some or many of his concerns but suggested he had overstated his case against theory in various ways. First, while many lawyers in the United States may indeed feel alienated from their profession, law school teaching is unlikely to be the primary cause. Of greater importance is the development of increasingly rigorous competition within the legal services industry, which has fostered accelerated commercialization and has created new business pressures for practitioners.

Second, while interdisciplinary legal scholarship often may not have an immediate connection to the day-to-day life of a lawyer, links do exist between theory and the legal profession. Various attempts have been made, for example, to harness theoretical advances from the social sciences (primarily economics and sociology) to explain how lawyers create value for their clients (e.g. by employing their connections in the business community to link compatible parties and by implementing system to resolve disputes without recourse to expensive litigation). Also, interdisciplinary legal writing can matter to lawyers since it can have a significant impact on the development of the law in important areas. In the United States, feminist jurisprudence has influenced debates over rape law, sexual harassment and the legal protection of pornography. As well, the application of economics to law is generally believed to have transformed that country's antitrust law and contributed significantly to its deregulation movement, which affected fields such as transportation law, communication law and even the regulation of the legal profession itself.

Third, while there is a growing number of interdisciplinary academics in US law faculties, in no sense has doctrine been forsaken. With legal scholarship, the change in approach has occurred primarily in law journals linked with the most prestigious law schools and specialized journals devoted to an interdisciplinary approaches to law. Otherwise, the dominance of doctrinal analysis remains unquestioned. Indeed, since there has been a proliferation of law reviews in the United States in recent years, the total output of articles which are "practical" is probably greater at pres-

---

① Hermeneutics:(圣经)解释学;释经学;注释学。根据哲学解释学的基本原理,法学研究中借用 Legal hermeneutics 来表示"法律解释学",但该词在中国法学研究中,通常被翻译为"法律阐释学"。本书编者倾向于使用"法律解释学"。

② Postmodern Legal Thought:后现代法律思想。

ent than it ever has been. In addition, the interdisciplinary movement has not had a revolutionary effect in the classroom. Even in elite law schools, the core curriculum continues to be doctrinal and the dominant form of teaching remains the analysis of cases.

Fourth, while law students might well suffer if they only received instruction from "impractical" scholars who said little about cases and legislation, theory in fact can play a valuable role in law teaching. Lawyers, in order to do their job well, must know more than the rules. Instead, they must be mindful of how the law in action can diverge from the law in books①. For example, they should develop a sense of the social context in which lawmaking occurs and regulatory bodies operate since a judge or regulator acting in a particular institutional setting may apply a rule in a manner quite different from a counterpart operating in a different milieu. Lawyers also should be able to reason their way to a sensible conclusion in the absence of case law on point, must be able to apply rules to facts and must be able to argue contrary interpretations. These skills in turn require some grasp of principles and policies and a sense of the importance of contextual variation. Since lawyers face such challenges, law students should benefit from being exposed to the insights which interdisciplinary approaches to law can provide. Resistance in the classroom can be expected since students usually are most comfortable when a course is taught as a clear, well-organized presentation of legal rules. Nevertheless, it should be possible for them to recognize the importance of theory and social context if this is done in the setting of concrete legal problems.

Judge Edwards and British Legal Scholarship

Judge Edwards' plea for a return to doctrinal legal analysis has provoked relatively little comment in the United Kingdom. One reason might be that British judges and lawyers pay less attention to what academics write than do their American counterparts and thus are indifferent to trends in the literature. Since academic law apparently does have an audience within Britain's legal profession, a more likely explanation is that theoretical writing has not proliferated to the same extent in the United Kingdom as it has in the United States. Nevertheless, if interdisciplinary scholarship continues to grow in prominence in Britain, concerns could arise about the practical value of academic law, both inside and outside the classroom. Legal scholars who do theory will then need to work harder to make the utility of their type of scholarship apparent.

If the issues brought up by Judge Edwards do become the subject of debate in the United Kingdom, law teachers should in fact be well prepared to present the case in favor of theory. This is because they have already raised arguments on the point similar to those brought up here. Various British academics have stressed, for instance, that using interdisciplinary approaches improves in a general way our understanding of law. Also, while there has been some reluctance to defend theory on the grounds that it is relevant to the legal profession, the existence of a link between theory and practice has been recognized. It has been argued that efforts must be made to address con-

---

① they must be mindful of how the law in action can diverge from the law in books:句中的 law in action 表示"实践中的法律"、"现实生活中的法律",而 law in books 表示"书本上的法律"、"法律理论"的意思。故全句可译为:他们必须注意到实践中的法律和书本上法律的区别。

crete legal issues. This is because, if academics simply pursue theory for its own sake, the relevance and value of their work will be questioned and their voice will be confined to an ever diminishing band of listeners.

A number of British law-teachers have also asserted that interdisciplinary analysis has a role to play in the classroom. Support exists for the proposition that "good theory makes good practice", in the sense that the quality of a law student's professional training should improve as a result of injections of theory. Still, those who speak in favor of adding an interdisciplinary element to legal education have not relied solely on vocational relevance to make their case. They say instead that exposure to theory helps to provide the sort of liberal education① which a university should be offering. This is particularly relevant for British law students since, unlike their counterparts in the United States, they typically have not had prior experience in a university setting and frequently have not settled on a career in practice when attending law school.

If the sort of concerns expressed by Judge Edwards is raised in earnest in the United Kingdom, the foregoing suggests that the exchange of views on the role of legal theory should be a lively one. On balance, however, theoretical analysis should be able to make a valuable contribution both with respect to research and teaching. The fact that this is the case② can be illustrated by considering a field often thought to be primarily technical and "vocational" in nature, namely company law.

Theory and Company Law Scholarship—Recent Developments

The movement towards theory which has influenced law in a general way has also affected company law. As was the case with legal scholarship overall, until fairly recently there was little theoretical work done on the laws regulating the company. In 1984, Roberta Romano, a US law professor, characterized corporate law as "an uninspiring field for research" and said that the last major work of original scholarship had been published in 1932. Two years later, Mary Stokes, a British academic, said that "company lawyers lack an intellectual tradition which places the particular rules and doctrines of their discipline within a broader theoretical framework which gives meaning and coherence to them".

Things soon changed rapidly as theory began to play a considerably more prominent role. Dan Prentice, a leading British company law scholar, said in 1993 that "legal scholarship in the field of company law has been a growth industry over the past decade", Deborah DeMott, a US law professor, wrote similarly in 1996 about "the current vigor of scholarly writing about corporate law" and denounced suggestions that corporate law is "a presently or prospectively moribund field". The development of an expanded intellectual range was an important cause for the new optimism.

According to Professor DeMott, whereas company law scholarship formerly was "uninspiring" and "parochial" in scope, "the introduction of perspectives grounded in non-legal academic disciplines has demonstrably invigorated discussion and deepened analysis."

---

① liberal education:通才教育。
② this is the case:此乃千真万确。句中 be the case 的意思为"be true, be the truth"(的的确确、千真万确,真实的)。

Lesson Eleven Using Theory to Study Law: A Company Law Perspective

The emergence of theoretical company law scholarship has not been restricted to any one country. Australian, British and Canadian academics have all carried out important interdisciplinary work. Nevertheless, as has been the case with legal scholarship generally, the move towards theory has been most dramatic in the United States. An important characteristic of the US literature is that one school of thought, law and economics, dominates the academic study of corporate law. A significant feature of the economic approach is the treatment of corporate personality①. Those writing from an economic perspective attach little significance to the fact that as a matter of legal formality a company is a separate entity. They emphasize instead that a business firm is a focal point for bargaining relationships entered into voluntarily and thus operates as a "nexus of contracts"②. As such, a company resembles a market, which is a medium where buyers and sellers engage in free and willing exchange.

Law and economics scholars, having established the parallel between the company and exchange relations elsewhere in the economy, seek to describe fundamental features of corporate activity in terms of economic logic. For instance, the limited liability enjoyed by those who own shares in companies is characterized as distributing the risk associated with business failure in a manner which is mutually advantageous for investors and creditors. Similarly, vesting the power to run companies in the hands of the board of directors and executives appointed by the board is said to be a sensible delegation in favor of individuals who have the special skills required to make managerial and entrepreneurial decisions.

The bargaining relationships which exist in companies do not necessarily yield optimal outcomes. For instance, the delegation of managerial power to executives creates the danger that investors will suffer "agency costs"③ as a result of self-serving behavior by those in charge. Still, law and economics scholars are skeptical whether government regulation is a suitable solution for such possible market failure④. They say that defects in the law-making process and problems with the administration and enforcement of legal rules can often render state intervention counterproductive.

The fact that law and economics has mounted a largely successful takeover of the corporate legal academy in the United States means that scholars who take a different interdisciplinary approach tend to be more firmly united in what they oppose—unjustified reliance on economic analysis—than by what they support. These skeptics say the relevant theories go too far in attributing materialistic motives to people and thus fail to account adequately for key human traits such as altruism and an underlying sense of social justice. Furthermore, they denounce the nexus of contracts concept, saying it is unrealistic to characterize relations as contractual when parties such as shareholders and employees often become involved in a company on a "take it or leave it"⑤ basis

---

① corporate personality:公司人格。
② nexus of contracts:合同关系说。
③ agency costs:代理成本。
④ market failure:市场失灵,与此对应,经济法中经常涉及另一个概念,即"政府失灵",其英文表达是"government failure"。
⑤ "take it or leave it":"不接受则走人"。指股东或雇员只有两种选择,要么接受公司(购股或雇佣)条件,要么离开公司。

instead of engaging in any sort of meaningful negotiations before acting. As well, law and economics scholars stand accused of being thinly disguised apologists for the rich and powerful who are pursuing a deregulatory agenda in order to perpetuate the existing distribution of wealth and influence in our society.

Theoretically-oriented academics① who are skeptical of economic analysis have not focused solely on criticizing economics. Instead, both in the United States and elsewhere, they have also begun to use conceptual approaches in an affirmative fashion in order to analyze corporate behavior. For example, feminist corporate law literature is beginning to appear. Feminist academics have sought to explore issues of gender and male domination hidden by the basic concepts of corporate law. They have drawn attention to the lack of women in the boardrooms of public companies, have sought to explore women's involvement in family-owned companies and have criticized limited liability on the grounds that it diminishes personal responsibility by allowing shareholders to impose risks others must bear.

In addition to feminist scholarship, there is a substantial body of theoretical literature for which it is difficult to provide a satisfactory label but which does seem to be defined by a common set of ideas. One possible designation is "institutionalism"②, since an aspect of the line of thinking in question is that companies should be thought of as institutions reflecting an independent and distinct reality rather than merely a nexus of contracts. It is said that relations between those involved in companies have an important social component and therefore are not the sort of "arm's length" arrangements one normally associates with market activity. For instance, in a well-run business enterprise, a key source of success can be that all those involved share a strong sense of mutual trust and a deep commitment to the firm and thus are keen to work effectively on an interdependent basis. The existence of this sort of pattern illustrates that the organizational life of a company is more than the sum of the actions of those associated with the business enterprise.

Another aspect of the line of thinking in question is that there must be recognition of the whole community of interests who contribute to or are affected by the corporate entity. Since various constituencies are integrally involved in corporate enterprise, the classic view that a company is to be run for the benefit of the owners of the company —the shareholders—must be replaced by a new paradigm. A company should instead be thought of by reference to its employees and others potentially having a "stake" in the business, such as suppliers, customers and perhaps society at large. The fact that stress is placed on the need to recognize the multilateral community of interests affected by corporate behavior has led some to refer to the set of ideas involved as "communitarian" or "stakehohderism".③

---

① theoretically-oriented academics:理论朝向的学者们,以理论研究为主的学者们,类似结构较多,如,market-oriented reform(面向市场的改革)。

② "institutionalism":制度主义,该词来源于 institutional economics(制度经济学),由此出现 legal institutionalism,即"法律制度主义"或"制度法学"。但应注意,该制度非规章制度的意思。

③ "communitarian" or "stakehohderism":"社群式或公有制社会制度"或"风险共担主义",stakeholder 主要源自 shareholder(公司股东),指公司中涉及的关系不再局限于"股东",还必须包括雇员、供应商、顾客乃至整个社会等。

An additional feature of "institutionalist", "communitarian" or "stakeholder" thinking is a favorable disposition towards regulation. Reforms proposed have included restructuring the duties of directors to ensure that a company's various constituencies are taken into account by those in charge, fostering increased consultation with stakeholder groups (e. g. by providing representation in the boardroom) and deterring transactions that pose threats to key corporate relationships (e. g. corporate acquisitions motivated primarily by the objective of cutting costs by firing staff). The case in favor of state intervention has been made in part on a pragmatic basis. Again, a characteristic of a well-run business can be that relations between the company and its stakeholders are supported by a strong sense of trust and commitment. Laws which provide a suitable framework for the creation and survival of such ties should in turn foster corporate success.

Those who think of companies in communitarian or stakeholder terms also say that public scrutiny and control of corporate activity is justified because companies are sufficiently crucial for the economy as a whole to be categorized as quasi-public entities. As institutions of this character, companies should not exist for the benefit of a single constituency, such as the shareholders or management. Regulation which secures fair treatment for potentially vulnerable stakeholder groups is therefore justifiable, even if the measures in question may reduce corporate profits or restrict the latitude available to executive.

Legal Terminology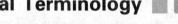

1. hermeneutics

阐释学(hermeneutics)作为理解和解释法律的学科,在西方已有漫长的历史。20世纪60年代出现的哲学阐释学,更将阐释学理论推向新的巅峰,对人文社会学科产生了不可磨灭的影响。源于德文 *hermeneutik* 的 hermeneutics 除具有"阐释"(construction)这一含义外,其另外一个义项即是"翻译"(translation)。从某种意义上,这或许能说明阐释与解释之间的密切关系。无独有偶的是,与 hermeneutics 相对应且属于非"舶来"的英文单词 interpretation 也同时具有"阐释"和"翻译"(尽管多指口译)的双重意义。当然,在法律语境中,interpretation 除被翻译为"阐释"外,还可以译为"诠释"或"解释"(尽管笔者认为在法理学上最好将该单词译为"阐释"或"诠释",即学者或法学家对法律的"阐释"或"诠释";而在司法实践中则适宜将其译为"解释",即法官对"法律解释")。对比研究,人们不难发现法律"翻译"和法律"阐释"具有很多共性,在许多层面上两者其实并无实质性差异。其中不同的只是,法律翻译的模式是使一条信息经过改造,由源语过渡到目标语的过程,换句话说,法律翻译即是一种双语(bilingual)转换过程,即从一种法律语言到另一种法律语言;而法律阐释则多是使法律信息经过改造,由源语的一种形式过渡到源语的另一种形式,是一种单一语言(monolingual)的信息转换过程。法律之所以需要阐释或解释,关键在于法律的不确定性(indetermination 或 uncertainty)。事实上,任何法律都具有模糊性,容易产生歧义。文本产生后,在适用过程中因地域和时空以及语境的变化,也需要阐释或解释。这就涉及法律与语言的关系问题,因为"法律问题实际就是语言问题"。而语言本身便具有多义性,模糊性以及语言文化歧义性。对于任何符号文字,不同文化领域中人们思维和表达的差异都可能会导致不同结果的产生。

同样,法律翻译也是为了解决法律交际活动中人们对不同法律语言的疑惑和不解,把一种法律语言文字的意义用另一种语言文字表达出来。而翻译转换过程中的一个关键问题也是解决法律语言含义的不确定性问题。

事实上,法律阐释学是介于法学和法律社会学之间的中介科学,是在规范与事实之间架起的一座桥梁。期间,法官、律师等法律人将日常生活事实"翻译"成具有法律意义的事实。这些法官、律师间要进行"法人法语"的交流,探讨规范与事实之间的互动关系,为合法,公正地解决案件寻求方案。法律阐释学是以实在世界的一部分,即法律现象为认识对象的。这里的法律现象包括两种:作为社会统治的符号技术(symbolic technique)的法(即法律规范总体)与从依法进行统治之立场出发被认为是重要的人的社会行为。法律阐释学不是纯粹逻辑理论,而是一种实践能力,它的任务是对现实生活所提出的各种命题,假说进行逻辑分析研究(归纳,演绎等),得出一定的概念,观点,理论,然后再放入实践中验证,获得科学的认识(陈金钊等,2003:20)。从某种意义上讲,法律阐释学与法律翻译学在许多层面上,如对待作者、译者以及译文读者的态度,对原文本的理解,对原文本的处理规则和方法等方面均具有共性,因而研究法律阐释学无疑会极大有助于对英汉对比法律语言学的研究。当然,尽管法律翻译可以而且应当借鉴或参考法律阐释学的许多原理和规则,然而法律翻译绝不等同于法律阐释。在法律翻译过程中,译者的主动性和创制性远比阐释者小,换句话说,法律翻译主体要更多地受到来自原文本的羁绊和制约。尽管如此,对法律阐释学的立场、目标、特征、本体和方法、原则等诸多方面深入研究必定会赋予英汉对比法律语言学研究以新鲜动力和能量。

2. legislation

有法律或法规的含义,但主要是指"立法",即具有立法权力的机关或人所颁布的法律,在这个意义上讲,其与 statute 相似,一般来说,legislation 又可分为本位立法和次位立法两种(primary and secondary legislations)。Act 主要是指由立法机关所制定的法律(the formal product of a legislative body),该单词常用作单一的法律的名称,翻译时可以译为××法,如 Criminal Law Act(《刑法》),Anti-competitive Act(《反不正当竞争法》)等。相比之下,Law 可用作指单部法律或法规,如:a law 或 laws,又可用作表示一般和抽象的含义(the law),但它一般不用做某个特定的法律命令的名称,如 Uniform Law of the International Sale of Goods 则不应译为《统一国际商品销售法》,而只能译为《国际商品销售统一法规编纂》,这样可避免人们将其误以为是一部具有具体的法规(事实上,它是欧共体的一部示范性发典)。同理,如《中华人民共和国婚姻法》不应译为"Marriage Law of the People's Republic of China"(此种译法容易被人误认为其是一部论述我国的婚姻法的论著,或一部涵盖所有有关婚姻的法律法规的法规汇纂),而应译为"Marriage Act of the People's Republic of China"。Statute 主要指"制定法",与判例法相对,因而,作为立法机关制定的 act 既可以称作 a law,也可以为 a statute。Bill 除有时可指"颁布的成文法"(an enacted statute)之外(如在 Bill of Rights 中),其主要指提交议会审议的"议案"或"提案",一般情况下,a bill 经议会通过生效后,即成为 an act(A legislative proposal offered for debate before its enacted),因而,act 只能译为"法"、"法律"、"法令"等,而绝不能译为本应由 bill 表示的"法案"。

3. litigation, action 和 proceedings

三词均有诉讼的含义,且都为一般术语,可指各种诉讼案件。但 action 则逐渐演变,现在多用于指民事诉讼了,因而有 action is a mode of proceeding 的说法。如果要表示刑事诉讼,多应在 action 前面加 criminal 予以区分。Litigation 除了指诉讼之外,还有诉讼程序的含义,如 Civil Litigation 便为《民事诉讼程序》,是一本有关英国民事诉讼程序的专著。Suit 是 lawsuit 的简略形式,主要用于指民事诉讼。传统意义上,action 和 suit 之间的差异在于 action 指普通法院的诉讼,其程序到法院判决(judgment)即终止;而 suit 则为衡平法院的用语,其程序包括判决和执行(judgment and execution)。在美国,这两个单词的差异因衡平法院和普通法院的合并已经不再存在。Procedure 主要是指诉讼程序,如 criminal procedure code(刑事诉讼法典)等。

4. corporation, company 和 firm

三词均有"公司"的含义。鉴于在英国公司法被称作 company law,因此在英国,company 常用作指已经登记注册的正式公司,包括大公司在内,而在美国,公司法常被称作 corporation law 或 corporate law,因而美国人多视 corporation 为按公司法注册登记成立的大公司,而视 company 为规模较小或不甚正式的公司,故我们对 company 和 corporation 的理解应依照英美两国不同的国情而定。以往,firm 多指合伙企业或未按公司法规定的程序而正式成立的商事实体或企业,其多不是具有完全法人资格的独立实体,这在破产法上尤为重要,尽管现在其也常被用于指 company。在法律字典中,corporation 和 legal person 均被称为法人,它们之间实际存在一定差异,legal person(也称为 artificial person, fictitious person, juristic person, moral person)为一通用语,指民事权利主体之一,其与自然人(natural person)相对,指按照法定程序设立,有一定的组织机构和独立的(或独立支配的)财产,并能以自己的名义享有民事权利,承担民事义务的社会组织。其可指企业、事业、社团等各种性质的法人机构。相比之下,corporation(也称为 corporation aggregate, aggregate corporation, body corporate, corporate body)则是专门用语,即我们所说的企业公司法人,其属于 legal person 所包含的范畴。

5. legal doctrine

法律规范,其法律原理的概括性最强,常表示实质性的法律规范,包括带共同主题的、系统的一套处理特殊情况、典型事例和法律秩序的原则、规则和准则,它们在逻辑上相互关联,结合为有机的统一体,可从基础和逻辑前提进行法律推理,如英美法系中的合同对价原理以及公共政策原理等。Legal principle(法律原则)多指对较具体的简单陈述,法律适用进行论证,统一和解释,并作为更进一步的法律推理的权威前提的普遍性规范。Legal rule(法律规则)则多指比较专门和具体的规范,用以规定某种法律事实的特定法律后果,如必须有两人或两人以上者证明遗嘱方能生效规则等。

6. lawyer

除指律师外,可泛指取得法律专业资格有权从事法律工作者。在英国,其可包括法官、开业律师、法学教师等。在美国,其可指参与法庭诉辩或提供法律咨询的任何人,该单词有时也用于专指开业律师。现有人将其译为"法律人"(与"非法律人"(layman)相对)。在英国,attorney 最初是指在普通法法院执业的律师(与其相对,solicitor 在衡平法法院,Proctor 在宗教法法院),即指由当事人指定,以委托人名义行使职责、代写诉讼文书、财产转让书等的法律代理人,后被 solicitor 取代,现代英国 attorney 已鲜用。在美国,attorney 广泛用来指行使英格兰的巴律师、沙律师和代理人等全部职能的律师,其比 lawyer 正式,范围窄,多仅限于法律事务代理律师。Attorney-at-law 为美国用语,通常在名片上使用。Barrister 和 solicitor 多用于英国或一些英联邦国家或地区,这与美国和加拿大等国的律师不分类别的情况不同。这两个单词的译法很多,前者有出庭律师、高级律师、专门律师、大律师等,后者有诉状律师、初级律师等,这些译法均不太准确,易误导读者。事实上,这两种律师的职能各有差异,根本不能简单用高级和低级区分。此外,solicitor 也常常在高等法院之外的其他法庭上出庭辩护,故也不能用出庭律师或不出庭律师加以区别,至于专门、大小、诉状等词也不适当。鉴于 barrister 和 solicitor 的培养,职责和区别等决非能用一两个字准确表达,笔者推崇上海陈忠诚教授的音译法,即将前者译为"巴律师",后者译为"沙律师",然后加上适当的注释,如:沙律师:通过律师事务所实践(practice)培养,与代理人直接交往,负责接案和收取诉讼费,只可在 high court 以外的初级法庭出庭辩护,遇到再 high court 的案件,得恳请巴律师替其出庭辩护(solicit the services of a barrister to plead his case, solicitor 也因此而得名);巴律师:学院派律师(由四大律师学院培养),不与当事人直接交往,从沙律师出分得诉讼费,应沙律师请求负责案件相关法律问题和出庭辩护。Counsel 为"顾问律师",在英国多指为沙律师提供意见或建议的巴律师,有时也指成为王室法律顾问的巴律师,即 Queen's(或 King's) Counsel。在美国,其多指为公司或政府担当法律顾问的律师,如 in-house counsel。Counselor 在英国已经被废弃,其在爱尔兰和美国等地有时仍在使用,基本等同 counsel,但比 counsel 正式。主要是指提供法律咨询,处理各种法律事务,出庭进行诉、辩等的法律代理人,也应译为"顾问律师"。Conveyancer 主要指从事不动产转让事务的专门律师,故为"不动产转让律师",在英国,巴律师和沙律师均可从事。advocate 为"出庭律师"(a lawyer who works and argues in support of another's cause, esp. in court)。此外,苏格兰的巴律师也被称为 advocate,而沙律师则被称为 law agent。Proctor 现指宗教法院的教堂的辩护律师或宗教事务律师(an advocate of a religious house, one who represents a religious society in its legal affairs),其也称为 procurator。

7. district-court

指法院的一种级别,美国各州的审判级法院的名称各异,如地方法院(district-court),高级法院(superior court),县法院(county court),巡回法院(circuit court)等,但其职能却几乎相同。Trial court 为"原审级别的法院,原审法院",多为案件提起之法院,故常被当做初审法院(court of first instance)理解。美国联邦地区法院(United States district courts)。Appellant court 为"上诉级法院",职能是复审审判级法院(或低级上诉法院)移送的上诉案件,对原审法院的判决作出诸如维持(affirm),撤销(reverse)或发回重审(remand)等裁决。在美国联邦法院体系的上诉级法院为联邦上诉法院(United States courts of appeal)和联邦最高法院(US Supreme Court);州法院体系则有州中级上诉法院(intermediate appellate courts)和州高级法院(state high courts,不少州称为 supreme court)。Inferior court 为"低级法院",其等级在 trial court 之下,一般不属于记录法院(court of record),州法院体系的低级法院有市镇法院(municipal court),州法院体系的低级法院有市镇法院(municipal court)、违警法院(police court)、治安法院(justices of the peace)等,其上诉首先移送审判级法院复审。联邦体系的低级法院则有联邦破产法院(United States bankruptcy courts)等,不服此种法院判决之上诉多先由联邦审判级法院,即联邦地方法院(US district court)受理。

Lesson Eleven Using Theory to Study Law: A Company Law Perspective

 Exercises

I Verbal Abilities

Part One

Directions: *For each of these completing questions, read each item carefully to get the sense of it. Then, in the proper space, complete each statement by supplying the missing word or phrase.*

1. This characterization is at least _____ misleading.

   A. in some measure   B. in measure   C. at a sense
   D. as for   E. for good

2. The _____ objective of this sort of interdisciplinary exercise is to secure a deeper and broader understanding of the legal system by placing it in its proper context.

   A. finally   B. ultimate   C. unite
   D. unique   E. certain

3. Scholarship _____ "doctrinal" or "descriptive" does not qualify as theory under the foregoing definition.

   A. acted as   B. established as C. referred to
   D. regarded for   E. characterized as

4. Such scholarship might take the form of an article addressing a _____ doctrinal problem that is soon likely to be before the courts.

   A. indefinite   B. hard-nut   C. knotty
   D. enterprising   E. unchallenging

5. Ultimately, those who "do theory" seek to _____ debates about law and its relationship to society, culture and the economy.

   A. grant leave to   B. lend hand to   C. donate to
   D. contribute to   E. be subjugated to

6. Pleas in favor of theoretical legal scholarship have in fact _____ a positive response in the United Kingdom.

   A. bought through   B. provided for   C. acquiesced in
   D. rendered important   E. yielded

7. Judge Edwards' appraisal of law schools and the legal profession _____ a strong reaction.

   A. effectuated   B. solicited   C. elevated
   D. elicited   E. elucidated

8. While many lawyers in the United States may indeed feel _____ from their profession, law school teaching is unlikely to be the primary cause.

   A. alienated   B. remote   C. far
   D. detached   E. separated

9. Certainly, there are examples of legal scholarship which seem to _____ his fears.

A. bear up for B. bear off C. bear away

D. bear down E. bear out

10. The method of enquiry again needs to be interdisciplinary, _____ political theory, studies of managerial behavior, economies and history.

A. drawing in B. drawing back C. drawing forth

D. drawing upon E. drawing from

Part Two

Directions: *Choose the one word or phase that best keep the meaning of the original sentence if it were substituted for the underlined part.*

1. This is of importance because the legal system is not <u>marked off</u> neatly from other systems in society.

A. divided into B. produced C. characterized

D. fortified E. hedged

2. As well, lawyers were <u>prone to</u> feel alienated from their chosen field.

A. reliable B. subjected C. optional

D. original E. successive

3. Even in <u>elite</u> law schools, the core curriculum continues to be doctrinal.

A. superior B. ordinary C. identified

D. anonymous E. unknown

4 Instead, they must be mindful of how the law in action can <u>diverge from</u> the law in books.

A. react to B. reason for C. increase by

D. impress on E. differ from

5. If the issues <u>brought up</u> by Judge Edwards do become the subject of debate in the United Kingdom, what do you think of it?

A. incriminated B. impeached C. renewed

D. posed E. inflicted

6. Such scholarship might take the form of an article addressing a <u>knotty</u> doctrinal problem.

A. problematical B. considerable C. profound

D. challenging E. political

7. Judge Edwards' plea for a return to doctrinal legal analysis has <u>provoked</u> relatively little comment in the United Kingdom.

A. aggravated B. enraged C. occasioned

D. irritated E. denounced

8. The trend <u>manifests</u> itself in a number of ways.

A. monopolizes B. brings to the open C. lays barely

D. summarizes E. holds up to view

9. This theory did not occupy a <u>preeminent</u> position in the United States.

A. predominant B. premeditated C. systematic

Lesson Eleven Using Theory to Study Law: A Company Law Perspective

  D. preoccupied   E. surpassing

10. Laws which provide a suitable framework for the creation should in turn <u>foster</u> corporate success.

  A. forsake   B. promote   C. formulate
  D. neglect   E. disnurture

II Cloze

Directions: *For each blank in the following passage, choose the best answer from the choices given.*

  As part of a general "mini-renaissance" in __(1)__ in the United Kingdom, company law __(2)__ have been developing an expanded intellectual range. Together with their counterparts in other countries, they have begun to carry __(3)__ important interdisciplinary work. To this __(4)__, the rise of theory has been fairly uncontroversial. The situation, however, could change. In the United States, where theorizing about law has __(5)__, the interdisciplinary movement in legal thought has __(6)__ a strong backlash, fears have been expressed that "impractical" scholars are doing the legal profession and law students a disservice by pursuing "abstract" theory at the __(7)__ of engaging in analysis of legal doctrine.

  The criticism of interdisciplinary work which has occurred in the United States should not be accepted at face value. Theory can have practical relevance and can be valuable in the classroom. These are points which are salient with __(8)__ the regulation of corporate activity in the same way they generally are. The fact that the Department of Trade and Industry, in its current wide-ranging review of company law, has implicitly put stakeholding on the __(9)__ illustrates that matters which have noteworthy theoretical dimensions can have significant implications for practicing lawyers. With respect to teaching, students are never going to learn about all aspects of company law in one course. As a result, sacrificing discussion of some topics in order to provide an improved understanding of how the law __(10)__ in the context of business and legal practice is probably a sensible trade-off. The upshot is that even if the development of an expanded intellectual range within British company law ultimately provokes disapproval, academics who use theory have recourse to persuasive arguments they can use to defend their efforts inside and outside the classroom.

(1) A. legal studies   B. legal literature   C. legal researching
    D. legal discussion   E. legal work
(2) A. enforcement officials   B. officers   C. practitioners
    D. professors   E. academics
(3) A. away   B. out   C. through
    D. over   E. on
(4) A. way   B. degree   C. sense
    D. point   E. extent
(5) A. prosper   B. impregnate   C. doom

    D. flourish   E. boom

(6) A. called forth   B. reminded   C. prompted

    D. instigated   E. stimulated

(7) A. danger   B. stake   C. peril

    D. mercy   E. expense

(8) A. regard to   B. respect to   C. a view to

    D. the intention of   E. concerns of

(9) A. view   B. timetable   C. agenda

    D. schedule   E. aftermath

(10) A. operates   B. ministers   C. maneuvres

    D. superintends   E. effectuates

III　Reading Comprehension

Part One　Short Answer Questions

Directions: *In this section, there is one passage followed by questions or unfinished statements. Read carefully and answer the given questions or finish the incomplete parts.*

Reaction to the Move towards Theory in Company Law Scholarship

  Since the rise of theoretical, interdisciplinary study in the legal academy has prompted criticism from people such as Judge Harry Edwards, the emergence of new approaches to company law might have been expected to prompt some form of backlash. As of yet, however, there is little evidence of concern that changing trends are causing company law academics to neglect practical issues unduly. Admittedly, there have been warnings that new approaches to company law should not operate wholly at the level of theory; academics instead should deal with concrete contemporary legal issues (e.g. the implications of the growing influence of institutional investors in publicly quoted companies). Also, in a 1993 law review article an influential Delaware judge pointed out that, while there are matters which have an obvious theoretical dimension, there are technical questions where the link may not be important. For instance, it should not be surprising if the validity of terms in the corporate constitution, the need for a vote by a class of shareholders and the tabulation of votes at meetings are dealt with as matters of form according to pre-existing rules rather than by reference to contestable assertions of social meaning. Despite the expression of such reservations, overall the move towards theory in company law has not prompted the same degree of controversy as it has in the legal academy generally.

  There is a variety of possible explanations for the absence of a hostile reaction to the emergence of new approaches in company law. First, indifference and ignorance might have played a role. Lawyers and judges who choose not to pay attention to the academic literature are unlikely to react in a adverse manner to new trends. A second possible answer is that practitioners who do follow academic writing are unconcerned by the change in approach because plenty of doctrinal scholarship is still being produced. In Britain, for example, both academics and practicing lawyers continue to contribute to a rich body of company law literature devoted to the analysis of cases and

Lesson Eleven Using Theory to Study Law: A Company Law Perspective

the description of statutory measures.

Third, those members of the legal profession who are familiar with theoretical company law literature may be favorably impressed with the work which is being done. There is in fact some anecdotal evidence which supports this proposition and it probably should not be surprising that this is so. This is because, according to Professor DeMott, "the recent literature eagerly embraces as topics for study all manner of current developments in business and financial practice". Perhaps the strongest evidence of receptivity to theoretical scholarship is in the United States, where judicial opinions and practitioner publications are filled with the jargon of law and economics. No such trends have emerged in the United Kingdom, but the Insolvency Service provided an endorsement of interdisciplinary scholarship by referring to economic literature in a 1993 report on the restructuring of financially distressed companies and the Law Commission did likewise in 1998 by securing a contribution from law and economics experts as part of its examination of the duties of directors of companies.

Fourth, even when theoretical company law literature has not been of a sufficiently practical nature to be of direct interest to those in the legal profession, the fact that the focus has often been on issues which are significant from a public policy perspective may have served to deflect criticism. Consider "stakeholding", which has proved to be a popular theme in recent-company law literature in the United Kingdom. Most legal practitioners do not have to worry on any sort of regular basis whether a proper balance of duties, rights and responsibilities exists for those constituencies which have a stake in companies. Still, "stakeholder" has emerged as a key term in British political debate, in large part because Labor politicians fell into the practice of relying on it when discussing policy issues.

While those who practice company law currently do not have to follow debates about stakeholding for any sort of pragmatic reason, in the future they may have to increase their awareness of the status of the various constituencies affected by corporate activity. The Department of Trade of Industry (DTI) announced in a discussion paper released in 1998 that it was carrying out a fundamental review of the framework of core company law and in so doing implicitly placed stakeholding on the agenda. The DTI said its review could lead to the enactment of legislation redefining the duty of directors to act in a company's best interests so as to compel them to take into account employees, creditors, customers, the environment and the wider community. A change of this nature would serve to ensure that stakeholder issues took on immediate practical relevance for lawyers who advise those managing companies.

1. Possible reasons for an absence of hostile reaction to the emergence of new approaches in company law might be _____, _____, _____, _____, _____, _____.

2. What will the Department of Trade of Industry (DTI) be supposed to do in the future?

Part Two True or False Questions

Direction: *In part of the exercise, there is a passage with eight true or false questions. Read the passage carefully and mark T if it is true and F if it is false.*

Theoretical Analysis of Company Law: Future Directions for the United Kingdom

While interdisciplinary company law scholarship is becoming more common and there has, as yet, not been an adverse reaction to this trend, this does not mean complacency is justified. Since the use of theory by legal scholars has prompted a backlash in the United States, the possibility remains that the same could occur with respect to British company law. In such an event, the case will have to be made that continued emphasis should be placed on theoretical work. We have already considered in a general sense the arguments in favor of interdisciplinary research, but points which are of particular relevance with company law deserve mention.

To start, the law is only one factor which influences corporate activities, and in many circumstances it is not the key one. This means it is impossible to assess the impact of company law rules by addressing only the subtleties of legal doctrine. It is necessary, in addition, to take into account the manner in which business enterprises operate in practice. This will be an enquiry of an interdisciplinary nature, with fields such as economics, management theory (including accountancy) and sociology providing potentially crucial guidance.

Also noteworthy is that company law changes rapidly. For instance, in the United Kingdom during the present decade, the law governing insider dealing has been revised, the regulations governing disclosure of financial information by smaller companies have been changed, a new scheme regulating public offers of securities has been introduced and the rules of the London Stock Exchange have been amended to enhance disclosure of corporate governance and executive pay practices. Since the rules governing corporate activity tend to be in a state of flux, knowledge of the law as it is now should be accompanied by an understanding of the forces which determine its current form and its ongoing development. The method of enquiry again needs to be interdisciplinary, drawing upon political theory, studies of managerial behavior, economies and history.

A final consideration is that while British company law academics have begun to carry on important interdisciplinary work, scope nevertheless remains for future research and writing. In various areas, the theoretical literature has developed in a promising fashion. This is the case, for instance, with "stakeholder" issues, shareholder remedies, corporate governance and corporate acquisitions (including takeover bids). With other significant topics, however, relatively little has been written from an interdisciplinary perspective. Examples include executive pay, closely held companies and the rules regulating self-serving conduct by directors. Furthermore, the forces which determine the nature and content of British company law have, generally speaking, escaped serious theoretical scrutiny.

Current developments in fact provide an ideal opportunity for academics to gain a better understanding of the forces which influence the development of company law. The DTI acknowledged in its 1998 discussion paper that British companies legislation suffers from difficulties such as over-formal language, excessive detail, over-regulation and complex structure. This suggests that there have been serious problems with past efforts at law reform. The DTI has promised that its fundamental review of core company law will yield better results. Academics can use the DTI's current efforts at reform as an opportunity to evaluate whether obstacles to effective change can be relatively easily addressed or are deep-seated and endemic.

The DTI's review of company law should act as a catalyst for theoretical scholarship in another respect. The Department has said that the terms of reference for the exercise include designing a framework for carrying out business activity which permits the maximum amount of freedom and flexibility to those organizing and directing companies. At the same time, the interests of shareholders, creditors and employees are to be properly protected, through regulation where necessary. Academics will likely seek to assets possible changes to the law in accordance with the terms the DTI has set down and when they do so they will probably find that conventional legal discourse is not adequate for the purpose. It will not be sufficient, for instance, to rely on an intuitive sense of what is good and bad in company law. Doctrinal analysis will also not be of much assistance since carrying out an exposition of principles from an internal standpoint offers little scope for critical reflection, except perhaps in terms of the intrinsic coherence of the set of rules in question.

Since conventional legal discourse is unlikely to be adequate, academics seeking to evaluate the DTI's current efforts at reform should make explicit use of theory. By taking into account how business enterprises operate and by assessing the impact which legal rules are having on existing patterns of behavior, it should be possible to gain a sense of whether a legislative regime is placing undue restrictions on beneficial corporate activity or is exposing various constituencies affiliated with companies to excessive risks. As we have seen, interdisciplinary methodology can be used to gain a sense of how legal rules affect corporate activity. Theoretical analysis therefore should provide academics with the means required to evaluate current and proposed legislation in accordance with the terms set down in the DTI's 1998 discussion paper.

If British company law academics in fact do respond to the challenges posed by the DTI's review by increasing their use of theory, the prospects for company law research look bright. It is more difficult to be optimistic with teaching. Traditionally, company law instructors in the United Kingdom have not made extensive use of theory. Furthermore, skepticism is likely to persist, even if progress is made with research and writing. For someone who has not followed recent developments in the literature and is not planning to write about company law in the future, taking the time to learn about unfamiliar interdisciplinary theories is unlikely to be all appetizing prospect. Since the presence of a huge mass of company law raises the conundrum of what to leave out of the syllabus, even a law teacher who, has an open mind about theory will become concerned about "overload" and will wonder whether it is possible to discuss the issues raised and still "cover the field".

Also potentially significant is negative feedback in the classroom. Since students are most comfortable when a course is taught as a well-organized presentation of legal doctrine, attempts to introduce abstract theoretical notions may well be met by resistance. Such a reaction seems particularly likely to occur with company law. Students can perceive it to be a "vocational" subject where thorough knowledge of the rules will provide them with better prospects of success in a lucrative area of practice.

Though teaching company law from an interdisciplinary perspective poses difficulties, the possibility of progress should not be dismissed out-of-hand. There may be some law teachers for whom change will be more than they wish to contemplate. For those with an open mind. however further consideration is worthwhile. Theory can play a valuable role in the classroom, and this should be the case with company law as much as with any other field. Since the law is only one of the factors which influence corporate activities, if students only learn about cases and statutory rules, there is a mismatch of business law education and business law practice. A law teacher, by drawing upon interdisciplinary research, should be able to introduce students to some of the key aspects of corporate reality. This, in turn, will allow them to understand better the facts of the cases they are reading and provide them with a sense of how they would use the rules they are learning about in the real world.

Increased use of theory should also improve the quality of analysis of policy issues in the classroom. Few teachers of company law adopt a purely "black letter" approach; they instead make some attempt to evaluate and criticize the law they describe. Students are likely to find such normative critiques to be more coherent and intelligible if they are made aware of the theoretical premises which underlie the arguments being advanced. Given this, and given that the use of theory may increase in some ways the practical utility of a company law course, student resistance to interdisciplinary analysis may in fact not pose as much of a problem as might be anticipated.

Concerns about "overload" also might not pose as serious an obstacle to the use of theory in the classroom as would seem to be the case at first glance. It is becoming increasingly obvious that academic company lawyers cannot teach the whole subject. A law teacher's reflex reaction might be to continue to try to cover as many topics as possible, but an alternative approach is available which can readily accommodate the use of theoretical perspectives. The aim will be to enable students to grasp the basic formal principles of company law while ensuring they understand in outline how the law operates in the context of business and legal practice. A course taught in this manner should convey the intellectual excitement of company law while establishing a conceptual framework students can rely upon if they continue with the subject in future life. Since they should be well prepared to expand their expertise outside the classroom, dispatching particular topics to the quiet place where laws go that are no longer worth teaching ultimately should not be a cause for great concern.

1. Continued emphasis should be placed on theoretical work in the analysis of company law. ( )

2. In Great Britain, the law governing insider dealing has been revised, the regulations governing disclosure of financial information by smaller companies changed, a new scheme regulating public offers of securities introduced and the rules of the London Stock Exchange amended to enhance disclosure of corporate governance and executive pay practices. ( )

3. British company law academics have begun to take on important interdisciplinary work, directing all their attention to the scope of the work. ( )

4. Executive pay, closely held companies, the rules regulating self-serving conduct by direc-

tors, the forces which determine the nature and content of British company law, generally speaking, deserved world attention for British academics' serious theoretical scrutiny. (   )

5. Since interdisciplinary methodology can be used to gain a sense of how legal rules affect corporate activity, theoretical analysis therefore should provide academics with the means required to evaluate current and proposed legislation in accordance with the terms set down in the DTI's 1998 discussion paper. (   )

6. Traditionally, company law instructors in the United Kingdom have not made extensive use of theory and skepticism is likely to persist, even if no progress is made with research and writing. (   )

7. Students are most comfortable when a course is taught as a well-organized presentation of legal doctrine, so, attempts to introduce abstract theoretical notions may be fervently resisted. (   )

8. A law teacher, drawing upon interdisciplinary research in company law, should be able to introduce students to some of the key aspects of corporate reality, which, in turn, will allow the students to understand better the facts of the cases they are reading and provide them with a sense of how they would use the rules they are learning about in the real world. (   )

IV Translation Abilities

法律语言特征分析与法律翻译技能培养之十一：
以-ee 结尾的法律英语词汇及其翻译

法律词汇中许多动词词尾加上-ee,可以用以表示某一类人,作为动作的承受者。在翻译成为汉语时,一般可以译为"被……","受……"等,或表示被动意义的词,这一类词在法律英语中的使用极为普遍,常见的有：

abandonee 被遗弃者;弃物受领人;受委付人(对应于 abandoner)

absentee 不在住所的人;缺席者;居住国外者;外住者;失踪人;(不居于产权所在地的)不在地主

addressee 收件人;收信人(对应于 addresser/or)

adpoptee 被收养人(对应于 adopter)

alienee 受让人(对应于 alienor)

allotee 领受人;接受分配者;接受配给者;接受拨给物资的人或机构(对应于 alloter)

appellee 应诉人;被申诉者(对应于 appelant,控诉人;上诉人;请求人)

appointee 被指定人;被委任者(对应于 appointor/er 指定人)

arrestee 被捕者;被拘押者

assessee 收入价值或财产价值已被估定的人(对应于 assessor)

assignee 财产收让人;财产管理人;受托人;代理人;被指定人(对应于 assignor)

bailee 收寄托人;受托人(对应于 bailor)

bargainee 买主(对应于 bargainor)

blackmailee 被勒索者/人(对应于 blackmailer)

detainee 被扣押者;被拘留者(对应于 detainer)

deportee 被驱逐出境者;被判处流放者
designee 被指名者(对应于 designator)
devisee 接受捐赠不动产者;受遗赠者(对应于 deviser)
devotee 热爱者;皈依者(对应于 devoter)
disinheritee 被剥夺继承权者
distrainee 财物被扣押者(对应于 distrainer/or)
disseisee 被强占地产者;被强夺者,被侵占者;被强占状态(对应于 dissesor/disseizor)
distributee 被分配到财产的人(对应于 distributor)
divorcee 被离婚者;离了婚的人
donee 受赠人;收遗赠人(对应于 denator/donor)
draftee 应征入伍者(对应于 drafter)
drawee 受票人;付款人;汇票付款人(对应于 drawer)
employee 雇员,雇工;受雇人(对应于 employer)
endorsee 被背书人;受让人 = indorsee(对应于 endorser)
enrollee 被征入伍者;如会者;入学者
escapee 越狱犯人;逃犯;逃脱者
evacuee 撤退者;被疏散者
evictee 被驱逐者;被没收者(对应于 evictor)
examinee 受审查的人;接受审查者;参加考试者,考生(对应于 examiner)
expellee 被驱逐出境者;被驱逐出国者;被开除者(对应于 expeller)
expiree 刑满出狱者;服满刑期者(= emancipist)
garnishee (接扣押令后的)第三债务人;财产受托人(对应于 garnisher,通知扣押债权者)
grantee 被授予人;受让人;受补助者(对应于 grantor)
hijackee 被劫持者(对应于 hijacker)
indemnitee 接受赔偿者
indictee 被告;被起诉者(对应于 indicte/ror,起诉者)
inductee 就任者;入会者;应征入伍者(美国)
internee (战争期间的)被拘留者;拘留民,拘留犯
legatee 遗产受赠人,遗产继承人,受遗赠者(对应于 legator)
lessee 承租人;租户;租界人(对应于 lessor)
libellee 被诽谤者;(在海事或宗教裁判所起诉的)被控告者(对应于 libellor/libellist)
licencee(licensee)许可证接受者;被许可者;领有许可者/执照者(对应于 licensor/licenser)
loanee 借入者;债务人(对应于 loaner)
mergee 合并的一方;被合并的公司等(对应于 merger)
mortgagee 接受抵押人;受押人;质权人;抵押权人(对应于 mortgagor/mortgager)
muggee 行凶抢劫的受害者;被行凶抢劫者(对应于 mugger)
murderee 被谋杀者(对应于 murderer)
nominee 被提名的候选人;被任命者(对应于 nominator)
obligee 债权人,权利人;债主;受惠人(与 obliger 相对)

Lesson Eleven　Using Theory to Study Law: A Company Law Perspective

offeree 受要约人;被发价人;受盘人(对应于 offerer/or)
parolee 获假释者
patentee 专利权人,专利获得者,专利权所有人;专利权获得者(与 patentor 相对)
pawnee 承典人,收当人;质权人;出典人,典当人;接受抵押品的人(与 pawner/or 相对)
payee 受款人;提款人;收款人;收票人(与 payer/ payor 相对)
persecutee 受迫害者(对应于 persecutor)
pledgee 接受质押者;抵押权人;受质人,质权人(与 pledger/pledgor 对应)
presentee 受赠人;被推荐者
promisee 受约人(与 promisor 对应)
recoveree 被追索财产者
referee 受法庭委托的鉴定人;仲裁人,公断人
refugee 避难者,逃亡者,难民,流亡者
releasee 被免除债务者;权利、财产等的受让人(对应于 releasor)
remittee 汇票的收款人(对应于 remitter /remittor,汇款人)
retiree 退休者;退职者
returnee 流放或服刑后释放归来者;从国外回来者;海外服役归来的军人
testee 测试/测验对象;接受测试者;被试验者(对应于 tester)
transferee 财产等的受让人;买者,承买人;被调动的人,被调职者(与 transferor 对应)
transportee 被放逐者
trustee 受托人,受托管理人;保管人,保管委员;受托管国
vouchee 被担保者(对应于 voucher)
warrantee 被保证人(对应于 warrantor/er)

Translation Exercises:

Part One　*Put the Following into Chinese*

If cyberspace is a type of community, a giant neighborhood made up of networked computer users around the world, then it seems natural that many elements of a traditional society can be found taking shape as bits and bytes. With electronic commerce comes electronic merchants, plugged-in educators provide network education, and doctors meet with patients in offices on-line. It should come as no surprise that there are also cybercriminals committing cybercrimes.

As an unregulated hodgepodge of corporations, individuals, governments, educational institutions, and other organizations that have agreed in principle to use a standard set of communication protocols, the Internet is wide open to exploitation. There are no sheriffs on the Information Superhighway waiting to zap potential offenders with a radar gun or search for weapons if someone looks suspicious. By almost all accounts, this lack of "law enforcement" leaves net users to regulate each other according to the reigning norms of the moment. Community standards in cyberspace appear to be vastly different from the standards found at the corner of Main Street and Elm in Any City, USA. Unfortunately, cyberspace is also a virtual tourist trap where faceless, nameless con tourists can work the crowds.

Mimicking real life, crimes and criminals come in all varieties on the Internet. The FBI's National Computer Crime Squad is dedicated to detecting and preventing all types of computer-related crimes. Some issues being carefully studied by everyone from Net veterans and law enforcement agencies to radical pundits include: computer network break-ins; industrial espionage; software piracy; child pornography; e-mail bombing; password sniffers; spoofing; credit card fraud.

Part Two *Put the following into English*

各种数据保护法律中有关侵犯他人隐私之罪的主要区别在我们详细分析刑事法律规定时会更加清楚。要对此进行比较分析，人们就应区分四种有关侵犯隐私的刑事法律规定，而这种规定在欧洲有关隐私的法律中较为常见。

（1）侵犯有关隐私的第一种犯罪与侵犯实质性隐私权利有关，这包括非法披露、传播、获取和/或访问数据；非法使用数据；旨在造成破坏的非法进入、修改和/或篡改数据；收集、录制或储存数据，这样做有悖于实质性政策，因此违法；或储存错误数据。对有关刑事法律规定进行细致分析发现，上述实质性侵犯隐私权的规定不仅在所涉及的数据方面不同，而且在应受惩处的行为方面的规定也是不一样的。此外，在法律许可的行为方面，也存在着差距。由于刑事法律规定既可以指侵犯隐私权的民事侵权方面的一般规定，又可以指根据一般条款不够有权利用个人资料的例外，这一点与行政规定有许多相似之处，为此，行政法律中的诸多异常性、不准确性和不确定性均可以在有关刑事法律规定中找到。

（2）由于实体法律规定的不确定性问题，无数法律制度在很大程度上都指望靠第二种有关犯罪的规定，并致力于履行各种形式法律要求或实施监督机构的命令。这些包含在隐私保护法中的犯罪情况，通常比实体性犯罪规定要包括更多对禁止行为的准确描述。但这些形式规定也因各国法律不同而各异。各国刑事法律所规定的形式要件构成包括开始处理私人数据的法律要求（如，注册登记、通知、注册登记申请、告示或许可等）。在欧洲许多国家有关隐私法律中规定的不同的犯罪情况主要有：违反某种规定、管理机关禁止或决定的行为；拒绝提供信息或向管理机关提供虚假信息；拒绝允许进入其财产或拒绝同意由管理机关检查；阻碍授权执行的情况；拒绝为公司指定数据保护控制员；拒绝揭示传播私人数据的理由或方式等。

（3）侵犯隐私权的刑事法律规定的第三种情况是侵犯进入法律，如，个人接触信息的权利（信息自由）。就某一当事人的接触信息的权利而言，欧洲许多国家将提供虚假信息或拒绝通知登记注册的一方当事人或拒绝作出答复的行为视为犯罪。

（4）有些国家还更激进，用行政罚款或刑事制裁等方式来处罚对安全措施的忽视。此乃第四种犯罪方式。

V Interaction

1. Write a piece of composition to illustrate the relationship between Law and Theory.

2. Make a comment on what the writer in this text offered to you and report it to your classmates.

VI Appreciation of Judge Opinions

(1) Case Name(案件名): *Global-Tech Appliances, Inc. v. SEB S. A.*

Global-Tech Appliances, Inc. v. SEB S. A.

Supreme Court of the United States

Argued February 23, 2011
Decided May 31, 2011

Full case name   Global-Tech Appliances, Inc., et al., Petitioners v. SEB S. A.
Docket nos.   10-6
Citations   563 U. S. _____

Court membership

Chief Justice
John G. Roberts
Associate Justices
Antonin Scalia · Anthony Kennedy
Clarence Thomas · Ruth Bader Ginsburg
Stephen Breyer · Samuel Alito
Sonia Sotomayor · Elena Kagan

Case opinions

Majority   Alito, joined by Roberts, Scalia, Thomas, Ginsburg, Breyer, Sotomayor, Kagan
Dissent   Kennedy

GLOBAL-TECH APPLIANCES, INC., ET AL. v. SEB S. A.
CERTIORARI TO THE UNITED STATES COURT OF APPEALS FOR
THE FEDERAL CIRCUIT
No. 10-6. Argued February 23, 2011—Decided May 31, 2011

---

(2) Case Summary(案件简介)

After respondent(被告) SEB invented an innovative deep fryer(油炸锅), obtained a U. S. patent for its design(外观设计专利), and began selling its fryer in this country, Sunbeam Products, Inc., asked petitioner(原告) Pentalpha Enterprises, Ltd., a Hong Kong home appliance maker(家用电器制造商) and wholly owned subsidiary(全资子公司) of petitioner Global-Tech Appliances, Inc., to supply Sunbeam with deep fryers meeting certain specifications(详细说明书,规格). Pentalpha purchased an SEB fryer that was made for sale in a foreign market and thus lacked U. S. patent markings, copied all but the fryer's cosmetic features, and retained an attorney(聘请律师) to conduct a right-to-use study without telling him it had copied directly from SEB's design. Failing to locate SEB's patent, the attorney issued an opinion letter stating that Pentalpha's deep fryer did not infringe any of the patents that he had found. Pentalpha then started selling its fryers to Sunbeam, which resold them in this country under its own trademarks at a price that undercut SEB's. SEB then sued Sunbeam for patent infringement. Though Sunbeam notified Pentalpha of the lawsuit, Pentalpha went on to sell its fryers to other companies, which resold them in the U. S. market under their respective trademarks. After settling the Sunbeam lawsuit, SEB sued Pentalpha, asserting, as relevant here, that it had contravened(违反,违背,违法) 35 U. S. C. §271(b) by actively inducing Sunbeam and the other purchasers of Pentalpha fryers to sell or offer to sell them in violation of SEB's patent rights. The jury found for SEB on the induced infringement theory, and the District Court entered judgment for SEB(作出有利于 SEB 的判决). Affirming, the Federal Circuit stated that induced infringement(诱使侵权,引诱侵权) under §271(b) requires a showing that the alleged infringer(被控侵权人) knew or should have known that his actions would induce actual infringements; declared that this showing includes proof that the alleged infringer knew of the patent; held that, although there was no direct evidence that Pentalpha knew of SEB's patent before it received notice of the Sunbeam suit, there was adequate proof that it deliberately disregarded a known risk that SEB had a protective patent; and said that such disregard is not different from, but a form of, actual knowledge.

(3) Excerpts of the Judgment(法官判决词)

JUSTICE ALITO delivered the opinion of the Court.

We consider whether a party who "actively induces infringement of a patent" under 35 U. S. C. §271(b) must know that the induced acts constitute patent infringement(专利侵权).

I

This case concerns a patent for an innovative deep fryer(油炸锅) designed by respondent SEB S. A., a French maker of home appliances. In the late 1980's, SEB invented a "cool touch" deep fryer, that is, a deep fryer for home use with external surfaces that remain cool during the frying process. The cool-touch deep fryer consisted of a metal frying pot surrounded by a plastic outer housing. Attached to the housing was a ring that suspended the metal pot and insulated(绝缘)the housing from heat by separating it from the pot, creating air space between the two components. SEB obtained a U. S. patent for its design in 1991, and sometime later, SEB started manufacturing the cool-touch fryer and selling it in this country under its well-known "T-Fal" brand. Superior to other products in the American market at the time, SEB's fryer was a commercial success.

In 1997, Sunbeam Products, Inc., a U. S. competitor of SEB, asked petitioner Pentalpha Enterprises, Ltd., to supply it with deep fryers meeting certain specifications. Pentalpha is a Hong Kong maker of home appliances and a wholly owned subsidiary(全资子公司) of petitioner Global-Tech Appliances, Inc. In order to develop a deep fryer for Sunbeam, Pentalpha purchased an SEB fryer in Hong Kong and copied all but its cosmetic features(外部特征,外表特征). Because the SEB fryer bought in Hong Kong was made for sale in a foreign market, it bore no U. S. patent markings. After copying SEB's design, Pentalpha retained an attorney(请律师)to conduct a right-to-use study, but Pentalpha refrained from telling the attorney that its design was copied directly from SEB's. The attorney failed to locate SEB's patent, and in August 1997 he issued an opinion letter stating that Pentalpha's deep fryer did not infringe any of the patents that he had found. That same month, Pentalpha started selling its deep fryers to Sunbeam, which resold them in the United States under its trademarks. By obtaining its product from a manufacturer with lower production costs, Sunbeam was able to undercut SEB in the U. S. market. After SEB's customers started defecting to Sunbeam, SEB sued Sunbeam in March 1998, alleging(诉称)that Sunbeam's sales infringed SEB's patent. Sunbeam notified Pentalpha of the lawsuit the following month. Undeterred, Pentalpha went on to sell deep fryers to Fingerhut Corp. and Montgomery Ward & Co., both of which resold them in the United

States under their respective trademarks. SEB settled the lawsuit with Sunbeam, and then sued Pentalpha, asserting two theories of recovery: First, SEB claimed that Pentalpha had directly infringed SEB's patent in violation of 35 U. S. C. §271(a), by selling or offering to sell its deep fryers; and second, SEB claimed that Pentalpha had contravened §271(b) by actively inducing Sunbeam, Fingerhut, and Montgomery Ward to sell or to offer to sell Pentalpha's deep fryers in violation of SEB's patent rights. Following a 5-day trial, the jury found for(作出支持……的裁决) SEB on both theories and also found that Pentalpha's infringement had been willful. Pentalpha filed post-trial motions seeking a new trial or judgment as a matter of law on several grounds. As relevant here, Pentalpha argued that there was insufficient evidence to support the jury's finding of induced infringement under §271(b) because Pentalpha did not actually know of SEB's patent until it received the notice of the Sunbeam lawsuit in April 1998. The District Court rejected Pentalpha's argument, as did the Court of Appeals for the Federal Circuit, which affirmed the judgment. Summarizing a recent en banc(全席,全体法官的审判) decision, the Federal Circuit stated that induced infringement under §271(b) requires a "plaintiff [to] show that the alleged infringer knew or should have known that his actions would induce actual infringements" and that this showing includes proof that the alleged infringer knew of the patent. Although the record contained no direct evidence that Pentalpha knew of SEB's patent before April 1998, the court found adequate evidence to support a finding that "Pentalpha deliberately disregarded a known risk that SEB had a protective patent." Such disregard, the court said, "is not different from actual knowledge, but is a form of actual knowledge." We granted certiorari(调卷令,上级法院向下级法院发出的要求调取案卷进行复审的法院令).

II

Pentalpha argues that active inducement liability under known risk that the induced acts may violate an existing patent. Instead, Pentalpha maintains, actual knowledge of the patent is needed.

A

In assessing Pentalpha's argument, we begin with the text of §271(b)—which is short, simple, and, with respect to the question presented in this case, inconclusive(证据不完全). Section 271(b) states: "Whoever actively induces infringement of a patent shall be liable as an infringer."(任何积极诱使侵害专利的人得作为侵权人承担责任)Although the text of §271(b) makes no mention of intent, we infer that at least some intent is required. The term "induce" means "[t]o lead on; to influence; to prevail on; to move by persuasion or influence." *Webster's New International Dictionary* 1269 (2d ed. 1945). The addition of the adverb "actively" suggests that the inducement must involve the taking of affirmative steps to bring about the desired result. When a person actively induces another to take some action, the inducer obviously knows the action that he or she wishes to bring about. If a used car salesman induces a customer to buy a car, the salesman knows that the desired result is the purchase of the car. But what if it is said that the salesman induced the customer to buy a damaged car? Does this mean merely that the salesman induced the customer to purchase a car that happened to be damaged, a fact of which the salesman may have been unaware? Or does this mean that the salesman knew that the car was damaged? The statement that the salesman induced the customer to buy a damaged car is ambiguous. So is §271(b). In referring to a party that "induces infringement," this provision may require merely that the inducer lead another to engage in conduct that happens to amount to infringement, i. e., the making, using, offering to sell, selling, or importing of a patented invention. §271(b) requires more than deliberate indifference to a §271(a). On the other hand, the reference to a party that "induces infringement" may also be read to mean that the inducer must persuade another to engage in conduct that the inducer knows is infringement. Both readings are possible.

B

Finding no definitive answer in the statutory text, we turn to the case law that predates the enactment of §271 as part of the Patent Act of 1952. As we recognized in *Aro Mfg. Co. v. Convertible Top Replacement Co.* (1964) (Aro II), "the section was designed to 'codify in statutory form principles of contributory infringement' which had been 'part of our law for about 80 years.'" Unfortunately, the relevant pre-1952 cases are less clear than one might hope with respect to the question presented here. Before 1952, both the conduct now covered by §271(b) (induced infringement) and the conduct now addressed by §271(c) (sale of a component of a patented invention) were viewed as falling within the overarching concept of "contributory infringement." Cases in the latter category—i.e., cases in which a party sold an item that was not itself covered by the claims of a patent but that enabled another party to make or use a patented machine, process, or combination—were more common. The pre-1952 case law provides conflicting signals regarding the intent needed in such cases. In an oftcited decision, then-Judge Taft (当时还是法官的塔夫特(塔夫特,1909—1913年间为美国第二十七任总统,1921—1930年间为美国联邦最高法院首席大法官)) suggested that it was sufficient if the seller of the component part intended that the part be used in an invention that happened to infringe a patent. He wrote that it was "well settled that where one makes and sells one element of a combination covered by a patent with the intention and for the purpose of bringing about its use in such a combination he is guilty of contributory infringement." On the other hand, this Court, in *Henry v. A. B. Dick Co.*, (1912), overruled on other grounds, *Motion Picture Patents Co. v. Universal Film Mfg. Co.* (1917), stated that "if the defendants [who were accused of contributory infringement] knew of the patent and that [the direct infringer] had unlawfully made the patented article... with the intent and purpose that [the direct infringer] should use the infringing article... they would assist in her infringing use." Our decision in *Metro-Goldwyn-Mayer Studios Inc. v. Grokster, Ltd.* (2005), which looked to the law of contributory patent infringement for guidance in determining the standard to be applied in a case claiming contributory copyright in fragment, contains dicta that may be read as interpreting the pre-1952 cases this way. In *Grokster*, we said that "the inducement rule... Premises liability on purposeful, culpable expression and conduct." While both the language of §271(b) and the pre-1952 case law that this provision was meant to codify are susceptible to conflicting interpretations, our decision in Aro II resolves the question in this case. In Aro II, a majority held that a violator of §271(c) must know "that the combination for which his component was especially designed was both patented and infringing," and as we explain below, that conclusion compels this same knowledge for liability under §271(b).

* * * * * *

The Court is correct, in my view, to conclude that 35 U.S.C. §271(b) must be read in tandem(一前一后,纵列地) with §271(c), and therefore that to induce infringement a defendant must know "the induced acts constitute patent infringement." Yet the Court does more. Having interpreted the statute to require a showing of knowledge, the Court holds that willful blindness will suffice. This is a mistaken step. Willful blindness is not knowledge; and judges should not broaden a legislative proscription by analogy. In my respectful submission, the Court is incorrect in the definition it now adopts; but even on its own terms the Court should remand to the Court of Appeals to consider in the first instance whether there is sufficient evidence of knowledge to support the jury's finding of inducement. The Court invokes willful blindness to bring those who lack knowledge within §271(b)'s prohibition. The Court's definition of willful blindness reveals this basic purpose. One can believe that there is a "high probability" that acts might infringe a patent but nonetheless conclude they do not infringe. The alleged inducer who believes a device is non-infringing cannot be said to know otherwise. The Court justifies its substitution of willful blindness for the statutory knowledge requirement in two ways, neither of which is convincing. First, the Court appeals to moral theory by citing the "traditional rationale" that willfully blind defendants "are just as culpable as those who have actual knowledge." But the moral question is a difficult one. Is it true that the lawyer who knowingly suborns perjury is no more culpable than the lawyer who avoids learning that his client, a criminal defendant, lays when he testifies that he was not the shooter? The answer is not obvious. Perhaps the culpability of willful blindness depends on a person's reasons for remaining blind. Or perhaps only the person's justification for his conduct is relevant. This is a question of morality and of policy best left to the political branches. Even if one were to accept the substitution of equally blameworthy mental states in criminal cases in light of the retributive purposes of the criminal law, those purposes have no force in the domain of patent law that controls in this case. The Constitution confirms that the purpose of the patent law is a utilitarian one, to "promote the Progress of Science and useful Arts." Second, the Court appeals to precedent, noting that a "similar concept" to willful blindness appears in this Court's cases as early as 1899. But this Court has never before held that willful blindness can substitute for a statutory requirement of knowledge. *Spurr v. United States* (1899), explained that "evil design may be presumed if the bank officer purposefully keeps himself in ignorance of whether the drawer has money in the bank or not, or is grossly indifferent to his duty in respect to the ascertainment of that fact." The question in *Spurr* was whether the defendant's admitted violation was willful, and with this sentence the Court simply explained that wrongful intent may be inferred from the circumstances. It did not suggest that blindness can substitute for knowledge. Neither did *Turner v. United States* (1970), or *Leary v. United States* (1969). As the Court here explains, both cases held only that certain statutory presumptions of knowledge were consistent with due process. And although most Courts of Appeals have embraced willful blindness, counting courts in a circuit split is not this Court's usual method for deciding important questions of law. The Court appears to endorse the willful blindness doctrine here for all federal criminal cases involving knowledge. It does so in a civil case where it has received no briefing or argument from the criminal defense bar, which might have provided important counsel on this difficult issue. There is no need to invoke willful blindness for the first time in this case. Facts that support willful blindness are often probative of actual knowledge. Circumstantial facts like these tend to be the only available evidence in any event, for the jury lacks direct access to the defendant's mind. The jury must often infer knowledge from conduct, and attempts to eliminate evidence of knowledge may justify such inference, as where an accused inducer avoids further confirming what he already believes with good reason to be true. The majority's decision to expand the statute's scope appears to depend on the unstated premise that knowledge requires certainty, but the law often permits probabilistic judgments to count as knowledge. The instant dispute provides a case in point. Pentalpha copied an innovative fryer. The model it copied bore no U.S. patent markings, but that could not have been a surprise, for Pentalpha knew that a fryer purchased in Hong Kong was unlikely to bear such markings. And Pentalpha failed to tell the lawyer who ran a patent search that it copied the SEB fryer. These facts may suggest knowledge that Pentalpha's fryers were infringing, and perhaps a jury could so find.

But examining the sufficiency of the evidence presented in the 5-day trial requires careful review of an extensive record. The trial transcript alone spans over 1,000 pages. If willful blindness is as close to knowledge and as far from the "knew or should have known" jury instruction provided in this case as the Court suggests, then reviewing the record becomes all the more difficult. I would leave(允许,许可) that task to the Court of appeals in the first instance on remand(发回重审).

For these reasons, and with respect, I dissent(持异议,不同意).

Lesson Twelve

Ethical Implications of Energy for Sustainable Development

Learning objectives

After learning the text and having done the exercises in this lesson, you will:

—familiarize with knowledge of the legal characteristics and the nature of the energy for sustainable development;

—acquire an appreciation of the vocabulary and grammar or syntax relevant to the energy for sustainable development;

—become aware of the information required in order to understand the energy for sustainable development;

—cultivate the practical abilities to put to use the language in the specific context;

—be able to do some translation from Chinese to English and from English to Chinese.

Text

Ethical Implications of Energy for Sustainable Development

In 1999, the UNESCO World Commission① on the Ethics of Scientific Knowledge and Technology (COMEST②) set up a Sub-Commission on the Ethics of Energy③, Two years later, the Sub-Commission presented its first report. The report begins with the following sentence:

---

① UNESCO:联合国教育、科学及文化组织(United Nations Educational, Scientific and Cultural Organization)是联合国(UN)专门机构之一,简称联合国教科文组织(UNESCO)。该组织1946年成立,总部设在法国巴黎。其宗旨是促进教育、科学及文化方面的国际合作,以利于各国人民之间的相互了解,维护世界和平。2011年10月31日,联合国教科文组织正式接纳巴勒斯坦。

② COMEST:Acronym taken from the French name 'Commission mondiale d'éthique des connaissances scientifiques et des technologies'. The World Commission on the Ethics of Scientific Knowledge and Technology (COMEST),即联合国教科文组织世界科学知识和技术伦理委员会。

③ Sub-Commission on the Ethics of Energy:能源伦理委员会。

Lesson Twelve Ethical Implications of Energy for Sustainable Development

"Sustainable development, meaning the use of our planetary resources for the well-being of all its present and future inhabitants, has become the concept which must guide both individual and collective action at every level and national and international policies."

This is a remarkable statement as it contains challenges of energy for sustainable development:

First, the concept of sustainable development is to guide energy decision-making at all levels, personal and collective, national and international. This calls for a broadening our ethical concerns for energy. Energy is no longer a matter of maximizing supplies for more and more people, it is also a matter of social, environmental and future equity.

Second, sustainable development is concerned with the well-being of "all", not just human inhabitants of the planet. The inclusion of nonhuman beings poses important ethical challenges to the concept of sustainable development.

Third, the guidance of sustainable development is seen as a "must", not a more consideration for our actions. This raises the question of ethical guidance for energy policy and law.

1. Difference between energy ethics[①] and ethics of sustainable energy[②]

The report of the COMEST Sub-Commission gives an excellent introduction to energy ethics in the age of sustainable development. In comparison to the general and fairly well-established field of "energy ethics", sustainable energy ethics is relatively new and more focused.

In the age of industrialism, energy has been promoted as a prerequisite for development: the more energy, the more economic prosperity. The various forms of energy were assessed in terms of their short-term, not long-term efficiency and largely dictated by available technologies. Long-term environmental effects were either ignored altogether or dealt with in separate environmental policies and laws.

A reflection of this focus on short-term efficiency is energy law's emphasis on ensuing adequate supply. Energy law has developed fairly isolated from environmental concerns. Until today, energy law appears as an addendum to public administrative law with little regard to the principles that have shaped environmental law. In a similar way, energy ethics has been concerned with social justice issues such as access to, and fair distribution of, energy. Environmental concerns were of little importance. A typical question of this nature was whether the government or the corporate sector is better equipped to meet ever-growing energy demands.

The 1987 WCED[③] Report and the 1992 Rio-Summit[④] have shifted the environment from the periphery closer to the center of economic development. With this shift the links between energy

---

① energy ethics:能源伦理学。
② ethics of sustainable energy:可持续发展伦理学。
③ WCED:世界环境与发展委员会(World Commission on Environment and Development)。
④ 1992 Rio-Summit:1992 年里约热内卢地球峰会, 也称 The United Nations Conference on Environment and Development (UNCED)(联合国环境与发展大会), 又叫 Rio Conference, Earth Summit (葡萄牙文: Eco'92), 于 1992 年 6 月 3—14 日在里约热内卢举行。2012 年,6 月 20—22 日,联合国环境与发展大会再次在里约热内卢举行, 又被称为 Rio + 20 或 Rio Earth Summit 2012。

and greenhouse gases were disclosed, in the light of climate change, some forms of energy production appear favorable over others. There is now an ethical divide between objectionable forms (coal, oil and natural gas) and desirable forms of energy (solar, wind) with some indifference on nuclear and hydropower. At the same time, the importance of energy conservation and efficient use is without any dispute.

In the age of sustainable development, energy becomes accountable to economic, social and environmental objectives. That makes ethical considerations a lot more complex and, in a true sense, political. Should energy equally meet economic, social and environmental needs, or are there certain hierarchies? Is, for example, economic prosperity prerequisite for environmental protection or, other way round, is the environment basis of all human (i.e. economic and social) activities?

The COMEST report does not attempt to define these relationships, but makes some recommendations that can help clarifying them. An important starting-point are the introductory remarks of the Sub-Commission's Chair, Professor *Hamish Kimmins*.[①] When considering ethical approaches to energy, we must not deal with them in isolation, but realize that all human activities are linked with energy. This calls for a broader approach based on relevant space and time factors. Considering that sustainable development requires the broadening of space (to include global dimensions) and time (to include future generations) in decision-making, energy ethics need to address issues of ecological justice[②] as well as social justice. As an ethical concept sustainable development raises questions beyond inequalities in access to affordable energy. The new and more fundamental questions concern inequalities in environmental security and the perpetuation of human life. Now the planet's ecology becomes our home and not just the country we happen to live in.

Ethical considerations of this nature require a new approach. Simply adding environmental concerns to the list of economic and social concerns of energy supply would not be enough. A short list of today's supply problems shows us why:

- there is a huge degree of inequality in the distribution of energy, with about 4 billion people in the world having no access or very limited access to electricity;
- by contrast, the richest countries use nearly 25 times as much energy *per capita* as the poorest countries, with demand steadily increasing;
- certain sources of energy are facing imminent rarefaction and exhaustion.
- more than half of greenhouse gas emissions are generated from the use of fossil fuels.

All these problems are inconsistent with sustainable development and none of them can be solved without fundamentally addressing issues of how we organize our lives, especially in the rich countries. The framework for dealing with these issues is the ethics of sustainable development.

The COMEST Report identifies a number of principles that are part of this new framework. Among these are:

---

① Hamish Kimmins:哈梅斯·克敏斯,不列颠哥伦比亚大学森林生态学教授。
② ecological justice:生态正义,指个人或社会集团的行为符合生态平衡原理,符合生物多样性原则,符合世界人民保护环境的愿望和全球意识,符合"只有一个地球"的全球共同利益,特别是符合为子孙万代保护环境的可持续发展观。

Lesson Twelve Ethical Implications of Energy for Sustainable Development

- Sustainability and intergenerational equity①

Energy sources should be sustainable, thus equitably meeting the needs of the present without impairing the ability of future generations to meet their own foreseeable needs. In this regard, energy sources should ideally be risk- and pollution-free and available in perpetuity;

- Environmental responsibility

Active measures should be taken to reduce the environmental impact of energy production and use. This involves reductions in the negative environmental consequences of energy exploration, production, storage and distribution. In the short run, particular emphasis should be put on:

* the establishment of an effective global framework to limit the release of gases into the atmosphere, inducing the greenhouse effect, in recognition of the dangers associated with global warming;

* the problem of storage of nuclear waste products;

* the environmental impact of unmanaged and unsustainable biomass energy use. ②

While these principles and recommendations are relevant to the promotion of sustainable energy, they cannot substitute a much wider investigation into the ethics of sustainable development. The Report itself says "it is disappointing and alarming" how little progress has been made since the 1992 Rio Earth Summit "on issues fundamental to human safety, environmental quality and the future of humanity. Perhaps the most tangible indication of this neglect is the increasing global climate change...." Such criticism hints to the systemic failure underpinning current energy policies.

An ethic of sustainable energy cannot be dealt with in isolation from its wider context. Recommendations to move towards sustainable forms of energy are meaningless if the causes for current unsustainable forms are not addressed. These causes lie in the way the economy works and in the way people define their needs and aspirations.

To start with, energy has no intrinsic value. It is a mere means to satisfy certain needs. Such needs may include heating and cooling, lighting, transportation and other goods and services. None of these needs are so fundamental as, for example, food or water. And while they may be important they have to be put into the context of concerns for justice and fairness.

Together with the indirect impacts of energy development on biodiversity (mainly through climate change), the world's 45,000 large dams contribute directly and significantly to the loss of biodiversity. This raises the issue of justice in relation to the nonhuman world.

Examples like these highlight the complexity of justice issues associated with energy. Each form of energy use poses challenges for justice and fairness, both at national and international level. There are four levels of fair distributions:

- among nations,
- within nations,

---

① intergenerational equity:代际公平:是可持续发展原则的一个重要内容,主要是指当代人为后代人类的利益保存自然资源的需求。这一理论最早由美国国际法学者爱迪·B.维丝提出。

② the environmental impact of unmanaged and unsustainable biomass energy use:此句可以翻译为"无法控制的不可持续的生物量能源使用对环境的影响"。biomass:生物量,即某一地域或单位面积内存在的生物的总量。

- between generations, and
- between human needs and the environment per se

Addressing such multifaceted issues of justice is only the possible broader ethical framework that captures all human activities. Such a framework can be found in the ethics of sustainable development.

2. The ethics of sustainable development

The 2002 World Summit on Sustainable Development (WSSD)[①] focused on energy as one of the key areas for sustainable development. The importance of access to energy for human dignity was noted in the Johannesburg Declaration[②] and further explained in the Johannesburg Plan of Implementation[③]. The Plan of Implementation details eight recommendations for improved access to energy services and resources, cleaner use of fossil fuels and the development of regulatory and institutional frameworks, however, it says very little about the principles to guide these issues.

On the other hand, the entire Plan of Implementation is based on the concept of sustainable development. It is significant; therefore, that Article 5 acknowledges the importance of ethics for sustainable development. This is the first time that states express their commitment to ethics for the implementation of sustainable development. Given the fact, that sustainable development is essentially an ethical concept, this late commitment could be read as an admission of failure. However, it also reflects renewed ethical awareness among states.

The practical importance of Article 5 has yet to be seen. Much will depend on whether there is, in fact, a genuine desire among states to address the basic ethical issues. It is clear, however, that any such desire can rely on a body of principles that already exists in international and municipal law[④].

Some basic principles for sustainable development and sustainable energy are readily available. They are part of international environmental law.

Among the principles relevant here are:
- the precautionary approach;
- the "polluter-pays" principle;
- the principle of common but differentiated responsibility; and
- the principle of public participation.

In addition to these general legal principles, there are further concepts that make up the framework of international environmental law.

Among such concepts are:
- common heritage of humanity;
- common concern of humanity; and
- sustainable development.

---

① World Summit on Sustainable Development (WSSD): 世界可持续发展峰会。
② Johannesburg Declaration:《约翰内斯堡宣言》。
③ Johannesburg Plan of Implementation: 约翰内斯堡实施计划。
④ international and municipal law: 国际法和国内法。

Lesson Twelve Ethical Implications of Energy for Sustainable Development

There is a compelling reason why the concept of sustainable development cannot be broken down to existing principles of international law: it is the very basis of legal principles and not just an addition to them. Sustainable development sets the tone for interpreting, applying and developing the law, is a key benchmark for all nations and the fabric for "weaving the rules for our common future".

Such fundamental importance clearly points to the need of defining sustainable development in line and beyond the principles and concepts already mentioned, As Article 5 of the Johannesburg Plan of Implementation implies there is now a need to identify the ethics underlying sustainable development.

The most popular approach to capture the essence of sustainable development is the idea of integrating environmental protection and social economic development. This integrative approach was proclaimed in Article 4 of the Rio Declaration[①] and has been promoted in national and regional strategies for sustainable development around the world. It is perceived as bridging environmental protection and socio-economic development in line with each other. But is this really the essence? The assumption of states and some doctrines seems to be that integrating existing policies is all that is needed to achieve sustainable development. If that was true we could just as well hope for world peace on the basis of integrating the nations' domestic and foreign policies. Obviously, further guidance is needed to define purpose and content of such policy integration.

It does not help to describe social, economic and environmental three policies as being of equal importance. The assumption of equal importance (commonly expressed as "three pillars" or "triple-bottom line"[②]) may be politically convenient, but is neither supported by international law nor reflective of the ethical debate surrounding sustainable development. The key issue is one of priority: on what basis should conflicts between the three policy areas be solved?

a. Recognition of ecological sustainability in international documents

At the level of international law, this issue was first addressed in the World Conservation Strategy (1980) prepared by IUCN[③], UNEP[④] and WWW. Ecological sustainability is defined there as a precondition to development. Two years later the UN World Charter for Nature[⑤] set out the principles "by which human conduct affecting nature is to be guided and judged." Although the Charter does not specifically refer to sustainable development, it defines nature conservation as prerequisite for all forms of resource use and development planning. Notably, the Charter describes humanity as "part of nature" and states: "Every form of life is unique, warranting respect

---

① Rio Declaration:《里约宣言》,全称是《里约热内卢环境与发展宣言》。1992 年,在巴西里约热内卢召开的联合国环境与发展大会上,183 个国家、102 位国家元首和政府首脑、70 个国际组织、2400 多名非政府组织的代表等就可持续发展的道路达成共识,正式通过了《里约宣言》,旨在为各国在环境与发展领域采取行动和开展国际合作提供指导原则,规定一般义务。

② three pillars or triple-bottom line:三根支柱或三角形基线。

③ IUCN:International Union for Conservation of Nature(IUCN),世界自然保护联盟,是目前世界上最大的、最重要的世界性保护联盟,是政府及非政府机构都能参与合作的少数几个国际组织之一,成立于 1948 年 10 月。

④ UNEP:United Nations Environment Programme, 联合国环境规划署,成立于 1972 年, 总部设在肯尼亚首都内罗毕,是全球仅有的两个将总部设在发展中国家的联合国机构之一。

⑤ the UN World Charter for Nature:《联合国世界自然宪章》,联合国于 1982 年 10 月 28 日(111 票赞成,美国 1 票反对,18 票弃权)通过,制定了影响人类行为需予以遵守的五项保护原则。

regardless of its worth to man". The World Conservation Strategy was revised in 1991 under the title "Caring for the Earth: a Strategy for Sustainable Living" to further define sustainable development. Its essence is described as improving the quality of human life while living within the carrying capacity of the Earth's ecosystems? Its two principles are firstly, the commitment to a new ethic based on respect and care for each other and the Earth, and secondly, the integration of conservation and development.

By comparison, the famous definition of the World Commission on Environment and Development (WCED) is less outspoken by merely referring to "development that meets the needs of the present without compromising the ability of future generations to meet their own needs". The WCED then gives an explanation to this definition: "It contains within it two key concepts: the concept of 'needs', in particular the essential needs of the world's poor, to which the overriding priority should be given, and the idea of limitations imposed by the state of technology and social organization on the environment's ability to meet present and future needs." The two key concepts became known as the principle of intergenerational justice It is notable; however, that hidden between these principles is the reference to the "environment's ability" requiring limitations to technology and social organization. Essentially, this contains a call for self-restrictions within the limits of the planet's ecosystem.

b. The Earth Charter① as the defining framework

Like the Draft Covenant, the Earth Charter does not define sustainable development, but rather assumes the validity of the WCED definition. The Earth Charter aims, however, for a more complete elaboration on the guiding ethical principles.

The key is Principle I ("Respect Earth and life in all its diversity") with its definition for respect for life: "Recognize that all beings are interdependent and every form of life has value regardless of its worth to human beings."

The principles of respect for life (in all its forms) is diametrically opposed to utilitarian, anthropocentric② ethics of sustainable development, in the centre of development is ecological sustainability described as the "community of life".

The WCED definition contains two ethical elements that are widely accepted as being essential to the idea of sustainable development:

—concern for the poor (intragenerational justice or equity); and

—concern for the future (intergenerational justice or equity).

However, these two elements leave us with a "missing link". What do they mean with respect to the planetary ecosystem? If we are to share environmental goods and burdens fairly among us living today and also with future generations, what do we have to leave? The integrity of the planetary ecosystem, i.e. the "natural stock", or our knowledge to control it, i.e. the "capital stock"?

---

① The Earth Charter:《地球宪章》，一国际咨询机构所作的在21世纪建构一个公平、可持续的和平社会的关于基本价值和原则的国际宣言,该宪章旨在激发全世界人民认识到全球相互依赖和国际大家庭共同福利的重要性,在伦理上提出"环境保护、人权、人类公平发展以及和平既相互依赖,又不可或缺"。

② Anthropocentric: 以人类为宇宙中心的,按人类标准判断宇宙万物的;anthropocentrism: 人类中心说,人类本位说。

Lesson Twelve Ethical Implications of Energy for Sustainable Development

As we are unable to determine the needs of future generations, the reasonable choice would be a duty to pass on the integrity of the planetary ecosystem as we have inherited it. Uncertainty requires precaution, and there seems no better choice than assuming that future generations would like the planetary ecosystem as bountiful as we have found it.

And yet, such an obvious duty is neither suggested by the WCED definition nor favored by governments. As the dominant morality of the industrialized world is confined to social ethics, the importance of an environmental ethic to incorporate nature is widely ignored. Instead, the standard view is that society, economy and environment are of equal importance. As a result, sustainable development is perceived as balancing act between economic, social and environmental goals with trade-offs as a necessary outcome. There is no guidance that could ensure, for example, a preference for ecological sustainability or the needs of future generations. Without such guidance, policies may become more integrated, but they will not make a difference to existing unsustainable patterns of production and consumption.

This business-as-usual approach is commonly known as "weak sustainability". If associated with moral obligations to the future; weak sustainability policies consider it our sovereign decision what kind of assets, "stock" or legacy we wish to leave for future generations. It could be the "natural stock," but it also could be the technology-based altering the natural stock, for example, through excessive use of fossil fuels or climate change.

To preserve the integrity of the planetary ecosystem is the only reliable alternative and may, in fact, be a desirable goal for most people. However, only if we give this goal moral significance, we have the guidance needed for a policy of sustainable development. Only then the "weak" will become the "strong"; and the missing link in the WCED definition is found. A third element, therefore, needs to be added to the two mentioned above:

· concern for the planetary ecosystem (interspecies justice or equity).

The Earth Charter reflects this element with the first set of principles I:1 to 4 on ("respect and care for the community of life") and principles II:5 to 8 ("Ecological integrity"). They outline the environmental ethic that has, so far, been missing in the states' discourse on sustainable development.

The essence of sustainability ethics is to see the "community of life" in the centre of concerns for sustainable development, as Principle I of the Earth Charter states, and not just "human beings" as Principle 1 of the Rio Declaration proclaimed.

From a legal perspective the Earth Charter's three ethical principles of sustainable development appear as aspects of ecological justice with its three elements intragenerational, intergenerational and interspecies justice. While the first two elements are fairly established in international and national jurisdictions, the notion of "interspecies justice" is less familiar. The ethical debate surrounding "justice for the nonhuman world" and "interspecies justice" has not yet entered the legal debate. Fundamentally, we have to ask whether the nonhuman world can be part of the *juatitia comrnunis* or whether is it bound to stay excluded?

Obviously, this question goes to the heart of how we perceive justice and fairness. Western legal tradition has always maintained its anthropocentric stance. The leading theorist of justice,

John Rawls[①], has been quite clear about the exclusion of the nonhuman world from the *justitia communis*: "(the) status of the natural world and our proper relation to it is not a constitutional essential or a basic question of justice". While Rawls acknowledges "duties" in this regard, he describes them as "duties of compassion and humanity" rather than duties of justice. Any "considered beliefs" to morally include the nonhuman world "are outside the scope of the theory of justice." His "original position" cannot assume such a morality.

Contemporary (Western) legal theories of justice all suffer from avoiding the moral debate. That is why no legal theory has ever addressed ecological justice. And yet, the ethics of sustainable development demand no less than the recognition that the environment is of intrinsic value. Only then thinking about justice and the law will be informed by ecological ethics. It remains an open question whether international and domestic law will progress in this respect.

International law theory may be at a crossroads now. Either it reinforces the state-centred model of international law assuming that each international agreement limits state sovereignty. Or it deliberately follows a community-based model of international law made up by both, states and global civil society[②]. Such broader approach is visible in the moves towards new world order, a fundamental obligation of co-operation and strengthening the role of non-state actors. However, underlying these moves is the awareness of globalization. In a globalized world values and ethics are no longer a national affair.

It seems appropriate, therefore, to take the search for globally shared ethics very seriously. And while the search for a universally shared set of values and principles may be difficult, it cannot be left to states and governments alone. They are likely to reinforce their own paradigm of state sovereignty. There is no reason why the emerging global civil society should not be able to identify universally shared ethics.

With respect to sustainable development the relevant principles and values can reliably be found in the Earth Charter.

The importance of the Earth Charter for the international law and policy can hardly be underestimated. At the beginning of last year's World Summit in Johannesburg President Mbeki cited the Earth Charter as a significant expression of "human solidarity" and as part of "the serial base from which the Johannesburg World Summit must proceed." In the closing days of the Summit, the first draft of the Johannesburg Declaration on Sustainable Development included in paragraph 13 recognition of "the relevance of the challenges posed in the Earth Charter." On the last day of the Summit in closed-door negotiations the reference to the Earth Charter was deleted from the Political Declaration, however, the final version of the Political Declaration included, in paragraph 6, wording almost identical to the concluding words of the first paragraph of the Earth Charter Preamble, which states that "it is imperative that we, the peoples of Earth, declare our responsibility to one another, to the greater community of life, and to future generations." Furthermore, the mentioned

---

① John Rawls:约翰·罗尔斯,美国政治哲学家、伦理学家、普林斯顿大学哲学博士,哈佛大学教授,写过《正义论》、《政治自由主义》、《作为公平的正义:正义新论》、《万民法》等名著,是20世纪英语世界最著名的政治哲学家之一。
② global civil society:全球公民社会。

Lesson Twelve Ethical Implications of Energy for Sustainable Development

Article 5 of the Plan of Implementation is a reflection of the Summit's appreciation of the Earth Charter.

A few weeks ago, the UNESCO General Conference adopted a resolution to "recognize the Earth Charter as an important ethical framework for sustainable development, and acknowledge its ethical principles, its objectives and its contents, as an expression that coincides with the vision that UNESCO has with regard to their new Medium-Term Strategy for 2002—2007". The resolution calls on Member States to utilize the Charter for their education for sustainable development.

Earlier this year, the IUCN Council resolved to present the Earth Charter to the World Conservation Congress in Bangkok, November 2004, for endorsement as a guide to policy and program. Such endorsement would be a further significant step towards recognition in international Law.

Since the 1980s international documents have consistently promoted an ethic that puts ecological sustainability into the centre of sustainable development. The Earth Charter is a culmination of this process as it describes the entire ethical framework for sustainable development around respect and responsibility for the community of life. At the same time, the Charter represents a consensus of emerging global civil society. With the increasing acceptance of the Earth Charter by international organizations and individual states, the ethical framework for sustainable development can now be seen as forming part of international law.

 ## Legal Terminology

1. inhabitant 与 resident

两词均有居民的含义。其区别在于 inhabitant 所指的居住状态比 resident 更稳定和长久,由此 inhabitant 比 resident 所拥有的权利和义务要多,故相对说来,inhabitant 的界定也严格一些,如一个法人(corporation)只有在其注册登记州(state of its incorporation)才能成为 inhabitant。

2. judge, justice 与 court

三者均可做"法官"之义。其主要区别在于 justice 多指较高等级法院的法官,如美国的州高级法院(state supreme court)、联邦巡回法院(circuit court)、联邦最高法院(US supreme Court)以及英国的王座法院(King's Bench or Queen's Bench)、上诉法院(Court of Appeals)的法官。而 judge 则为一般级别法院的法官。当文章涉及案例分析以及案件的上诉,且上下文中交替使用 judge 和 justice 时,读者应注意 judge 多指 trial judge,即一审法官或初审法官,且其多数是独任审理案件,而 justice 则常指 appellant court justice,即上诉法院法官,且多为合议庭审案。Court 既可以替代 judge,又可用于替换 justice。

3. admission, confession 与 statement

三词均与被告招认违法或犯罪事实有关。confession 限于刑事犯罪领域,指罪犯完全承认其被指控的犯罪以及有关定罪所需的所有事实,或至少是主要事实,并承认有罪(acknowledgement of guilt),有供认不讳的含义,陪审团据此可作出有罪裁定,故为"供认"。相比之下,admission 则用于指对民事责任行为以及对无犯罪故意的刑事责任行为的招认,多表示承认一个或多个事实,此种招认远没有达到足以定罪和供认不讳的程度,故为"供述"。Statement 则是指警方在侦破犯罪过程中对某人,尤指疑犯的招供所作的记述和报告(account of a suspect's acknowledgement of a crime),故为"供述记录"。

4. resolution

决定,决议。决议是官方机构或组织,尤其是指立法机关正式表达的意见、旨意或决定,作为议会决议,其是议会所通过的文件,虽常不具备法律效力,但其已经不是"案",故不宜将其译为"议案"或"决议案"。

5. regulation 与 ordinance

均可译为"条例"。区别在于 ordinance 多指由自治市或其他地方立法机关所颁布的一种地方性法规(of municipal and other local legislative bodies),其也称为 bylaw 或 municipal ordinance;而 regulation 则主要是由行政机构(executive agencies)所制定和颁布的规则。

Exercises

I Verbal Abilities

Part One

Directions: *For each of these completing questions, read each item carefully to get the sense of it. Then, in the proper space, complete each statement by supplying the missing word or phrase.*

1. Against the background of international documents existing at the time, the 1992 Rio Declaration on Environment and Development marked a _____ step backwards.

    A. significant   B. important   C. insignificant

    D. signify   E. significance

2. In direct response to the Rio Declaration, the Global Forum of NGO's negotiated an Earth Charter that _____ the Declaration's human-centered concept and placed ecological sustainability into the centre of development.

    A. negative   B. rejected   C. refuse

    D. inferior   E. ingredients

3. What is more, it is _____ with the vast literature on sustainability ethics and its reflection in the international documents preceding Rio.

    A. inconsiderable   B. inconstant   C. increment

    D. incompetent   E. incredulous

4. The 1995 IUCN Draft Covenant on Environment and Development sets out "an integral Legal framework, _____ to those existing in other fields of international law, such as the law of the sea and the international protection of human rights".

    A. cognate   B. comparable   C. particularly

    D. compatible   E. similar

5. In doing so the Draft Covenant "provides ecological and ethical guidance" _____ legal norms.

Lesson Twelve   Ethical Implications of Energy for Sustainable Development   355

A. in accordance   B. in addition   C. in addition to
D. on the side   E. on top of

6. A reaction to former _____ approaches which limited legal protection to forms of life perceived to be immediately useful to economic interests, ignoring the functions of different species in ecosystems and even their future or potential usefulness.

A. utilitarianism   B. utilitarian   C. functional
D. uterine   E. utility

7. Process and content of the Earth Charter make it the most suitable document to-date to identify the ethics of _____ development.

A. further   B. healthy   C. educational
D. sustainable   E. commercial

8. It is the result of a decade-long, worldwide, multicultural, multisectoral consultation process reflecting the "_____ of a global civil society".

A. violation   B. emergence   C. egression
D. outgrowth   E. emerge

9. The critique of the Rio Declaration was already _____ during the Rio Summit.

A. projecting   B. distinguished   C. celebrated
D. popular   E. prominent

10. Ever since the Rio Declaration the public image not necessarily content! —of sustainable development _____ the idea that what needs to be sustained is human use, especially agricultural use and industrial production.

A. intensify   B. reinforced   C. strengthen
D. fortify   E. imputed

Part Two

Directions: *Choose the one word or phase that best keep the meaning of the original sentence if it were substituted for the underlined part.*

1. The 2000 Earth Charter is closely related to the Draft Covenant, both <u>in terms of</u> its origins and content.

A. in accordance with   B. in addition to   C. besides
D. according   E. in line

2. No other international document has been drafted in such a comprehensive and <u>inclusive</u> manner.

A. contain   B. exclusive   C. conclusive
D. embody   E. include

3. Such reductionism is <u>incapable</u> to perceive the environment as anything different from traditional instrumental values.

A. imperfect   B. unable   C. ineffective
D. capable   E. ample

4. However, underlying these moves is the <u>awareness</u> of globalization. In a globalized world

values arid ethics are no longer a national affair.

  A. realization   B. cognizance   C. acknowledge

  D. cognisance   E. concern

 5. The importance of the Earth Charter for the international law and policy can hardly be <u>underestimated</u>.

  A. overestimated   B. disappreciation   C. underrated

  D. disappointment   E. calculation

 6. Opposition leaders were wondering about whether she would <u>abide by</u> the election results if they went against her.

  A. in accordance with   B. comply with   C. respect

  D. in light of   E. agree

 7. Basically the developing countries as a whole have not been able to <u>accelerate</u> their food production growth rates enough to keep up with their rapidly increasing populations.

  A. retard   B. alternation   C. speed up

  D. impede   E. acceleration

 8. The power of a god or demon to transform a <u>concept</u> into an element of the sensible world

  A. conceptual   B. understand   C. notion

  D. construct   E. sensible

 9. One such compact, involving the states of New York, New Jersey, and Connecticut, created the Interstate Sanitation Commission to <u>abate</u> pollution in the waters of the New York harbor area.

  A. decrease   B. calm down   C. raise

  D. strengthen   E. augment

 10. Except for some of the <u>exotic</u> equipment on the 11th floor, nothing he saw in the Residency surprised him very much.

  A. indigenous   B. extraneous   C. voluntary

  D. endemic   E. outside

II Blank-filling

Directions: *Fill in the blanks in the following sentences with the words or phrases taken from the text.*

 1. In the age of industrialism, energy has been promoted as a _____ for development: the more energy, the more economic _____. The various forms of energy were _____ in terms of their short-term, not long-term efficiency and largely dictated by available technologies.

 2. To start with, energy has no _____ value. It is a mere means to satisfy certain _____. Such needs may include heating and cooling, lighting, transportation and other goods and services. None of these needs are so fundamental as, for example, food or water. And while they may be important they have to be put into the context of concerns for justice and _____.

 3. There is a compelling reason why the concept of _____ development cannot be broken

Lesson Twelve   Ethical Implications of Energy for Sustainable Development   357

down to existing principles of international law: it is the very basis of _____ principles and not just an addition to them. Sustainable development sets the tone for interpreting, applying and developing the law, is a key _____ for all nations and the fabric for "weaving the rules for our common future".

4. It does not help to describe social, economic and environmental three _____ as being of equal importance. The assumption of equal importance (commonly expressed as "three _____" or "triple-bottom line") may be politically convenient, but is neither supported by international law nor reflective of the _____ debate surrounding sustainable development.

5. The essence of _____ ethics is to see the "community of life" in the centre of concerns for sustainable development, as Principle I of the Earth _____ states, and not just "human beings" as Principle 1 of the Rio _____ proclaimed.

6. While there is no _____ in all respects of sustainable development, two _____ elements can be relied on, i. e. concern for equity among the people living today (intragenerational justice) and the concern for equity between present and future _____ (intergenerational justice).

7. Examples for this broader expression can be found in the environmental _____ of New Zealand. The Resource Management Act 1991 (RMA) is guided by the principle of "_____ management" which is not _____ with sustainable development, but nevertheless related to it.

8. The National Sustainability _____ (Nationaler Nachhaltigkeiterat) and independent Environmental Advisory Council (Sachverstgndigenrat fgr Umweltfragen-SRU) have also _____ for the adoption of a stronger, more ecologically focused concept of _____ energy.

9. While he sees the emphasis still on supply and _____, he also notes "a change from reliance on non-renewable fossil fuels to _____ oriented energy" and calls for a "long-term public participatory process" including the business sector. "Without the _____ of business circles, the ethics of energy will still be a word on paper".

10. Availability and _____ of energy should always be seen as an expression of respect for human life. But energy does more, it can also pose _____ to future generations and to the environment. Therefore, we should also be able to see production and use of energy as a _____ risk to future generations and life as a whole.

III Reading Comprehension

Part One

Directions: *In this section there are passages followed by questions or unfinished statements, each with five suggested answers. Choose the one you think is the best answer.*

Passage One

Environmental justice(EJ) is "the fair treatment and meaningful involvement of all people regardless of race, color, sex, national origin, or income with respect to the development, implementation and enforcement of environmental laws, regulations, and policies." In the words of Bunyan Bryant, "Environmental justice is served when people can realize their highest potential".

Environmental justice emerged as a concept in the United States in the early 1980s; its proponents generally view the environment as encompassing "where we live, work, and play" (some definitions also include "pray" and "learn") and seek to redress inequitable distributions of environmental burdens (such as pollution, industrial facilities, and crime). Root causes of environmental injustices include "institutionalized racism; the co-modification of land, water, energy and air; unresponsive, unaccountable government policies and regulation; and lack of resources and power in affected communities."

The United States Environmental Protection Agency defines Environment Justice as follows:

"Environmental Justice is the fair treatment and meaningful involvement of all people regardless of race, color, national origin, or income with respect to the development, implementation, and enforcement of environmental laws, regulations, and policies. EPA has this goal for all communities and persons across this Nation. It will be achieved when everyone enjoys the same degree of protection from environmental and health hazards and equal access to the decision-making process to have a healthy environment in which to live, learn, and work".

In the early 1980s, environmental justice emerged as a concept in the United States, fueled by a mounting disdain within African-American, Hispanic and indigenous communities that were subject to hazardous and polluting industries located predominantly in their neighborhoods. This prompted the launch of the environmental justice movement, which adopted a civil rights and social justice approach to environmental justice and grew organically from dozens, even hundreds, of local struggles, events and a variety of other social movements. By many accounts, the environmental justice movement began in 1982 in Warren County, North Carolina. The state selected the Shocco Township to host a hazardous waste landfill containing 30,000 cubic yards of polychlorinated biphenyl (PCB)-contaminated soil. Sixty-nine percent of the Shocco Township's population is non-white and 20 percent of the residents have incomes below the poverty level. The Shocco Township has the third lowest per capita income in the state. The publication of two studies, one by the government and the other by the United Church of Christ's Commission for Racial Justice (1987), provided empirical support for the claims of environmental racism. Robert D. Bullard's Dumping in Dixie (1990) added further support for the disproportionate burden of toxic waste on minority communities.

In January 1990, the University of Michigan's School of Natural Resources sponsored a conference on race and the incidence of environmental hazards. Later the same year, the United States Environmental Protection Agency established its Workgroup on Environmental Equity. By September 1991, the First National People of Color Environmental Leadership Summit took place, organized and attended by more than 650 grassroots and national leaders representing more than 300 environmental groups. The Second National People of Color Environmental Leadership Summit (also called Summit II) was also held in Washington DC, from October 23—26, 2002. Materials produced at the summit included a timeline for Environmental Justice milestones.

By 1992, the EPA established its Office of Environmental Equity and the Work group on Environmental Equity had finished its report. Critics of the report contend that EPA did not go far enough in examining its current activities, including its own role in reinforcing environmental inequalities. Legislatively, a number of bills were introduced into Congress, including the Environmental Justice Act 1992. President Clinton signed Executive Order 12898 (federal actions to address environmental justice in minority populations and low-income populations) into law on February 11, 1994.

Historically, minorities have been absent from the rank and file membership of mainstream environmental associations. At the same time, these organizations have not taken on environmental justice issues. In the 1990s, mainstream environmental organizations such as the Sierra Club, the Audubon Society, Friends of the Earth, and Greenpeace all began to recruit minorities both among their membership and to serve in staff and decision making positions. A few, including the Sierra Club and Greenpeace have participated in the environmental justice struggle by filing briefs or providing informational and organizational resources. Others assert that since the 1990s, an international Environmental Justice Movement is flourishing, having emerged out of various struggles, events and social movements worldwide.

1. Which of the following statements is true according to the passage?

A. Environment Justice is served when people can realize their highest potential.

B. Environment Justice was subject to hazardous and polluting industries located predominantly in their neighborhoods.

C. Environment Justice has been absent from the rank and file membership of mainstream environmental associations.

D. Environmental justice emerged as a concept in the United States in the early 1960s

2. In the definition of Environment Justice, it can be described as _____.

A. It is only a concept which is widely used.

B. Environmental Justice is the fair treatment and meaningful involvement of all people

C. Environmental justice movement began in 1982 in Warren County, North Carolina.

D. These organizations have not taken on environmental justice issues.

3. What does the word "hazardous" probably mean in the phrase "a hazardous waste landfill"?

A. unharmed   B. damage   C. risky   D. safe

4. The reason of Environment Justice is _____.

A. Institutionalized racism and he co-modification of land, water, energy and air.

B. Unresponsive, unaccountable government policies and regulation.

C. Lack of resources and power in affected communities.

D. All of the above.

5. The main idea of the passage may probably be _____.

A. United States Environmental Protection Agency established its Workgroup on Environmental Equity.

B. Environmental Justice emerged as a concept in the United States.

C. Environmental Justice Movement is flourishing, having emerged out of various struggles, events and social movements worldwide.

D. Environment Justice is important in our modern lives.

Passage Two

It shouldn't cause much difficulty to define ethics for sustainable energy as reflecting ethics for sustainable development, if sustainable development is the overarching concept for future energy policies, both need to be guided by the same ethical framework. Thus, the ethics of sustainable development provide the ethical framework for sustainable energy. All ethical considerations on energy should start from there.

A first task for these considerations is to explore the ethical contents of sustainable development. They can be found in a multitude of books, reports and articles, but most reliably so in documents reflecting (a certain degree of) international consensus.

While there is no consensus in all respects of sustainable development, two core elements can be relied on, i.e. concern for equity among the people living today (intragenerational justice) and the concern for equity between present and future generations (intergenerational justice). Manifestations of these two elements are, for example, equitable access and affordability of energy, conservation of energy and the precautionary approach to energy policy and law.

A third core element of sustainable development is the concern for equity towards the nonhuman, natural world (interspecies justice). This element is not recognized in international law. Promoted by global civil society and supported by international documents, states have yet to acknowledge the central role of ecological sustainability. They tend to overlook the simple truth that economic systems depend on the functioning of ecological systems—not the other way round.

International organizations such as the IUCN, the Earth Council and UNESCO have accepted this ecological wisdom. With respect to energy ethics, this can be demonstrated in UNESCO's approach to defining the role of science and education. UNESCO is a task manager in the United Nations system of Chapters 15 (Science) and 36 (Education) of Agenda 21. The Sub-Committee on the Ethics of Energy of UNESCO's World Commission on the Ethics of Scientific Knowledge and Technology describes its ethical considerations as follows:

"The preservation of the environment is a key condition for the perpetuation and prosperity of human rife. If this environment is to continue to provide what is needed for sustaining and developing the human species, it is imperative to fully understand the importance of preserving and improving its ecological functions at local, regional and global levels." Quoting the World Energy Council, the Sub-Commission's Report states that over the past 40 years there has been an increase of 300% global energy consumption with a further increase of between 50 to 225% predicted for the next 40 years. For this reason, the way in which energy demands are satisfied needs to be modified. Referring, in particular, to global climate change as an environmental problem largely generated by fossil fuels consumption, the Report expresses deep concerns for the environment to sustain itself.

With the recent adoption of the Earth Charter UNESCO has stepped up its recognition of ecological sustainability as the key prerequisite for sustainable development. Principle II:5 of the Earth Charter reads: "Protect and restore the integrity of Earth's ecological systems, with special concern for biologics diversity and the natural processes that sustain life". Sub-principle 5 e. calls for management of the use of renewable resources within the capacity of ecosystems and sub-princi-

Lesson Twelve Ethical Implications of Energy for Sustainable Development

ple 5 f. calls for management of extraction and use of non-renewable resources such as fossil fuels in ways that minimize harm to the environment. These and a number of other principles and sub-principles related to energy all assume the overarching importance of ecological sustainability.

If UNESCO's activities can be seen as supporting the case for strong sustainability, they are in line with the relevant literature and some key international documents advocating that "the natural sphere is paramount and cannot be compromised".

Essentially this would mean, that energy must be generated and used in a way that does not compromise ecological integrity.

The three ethical principles for sustainable energy are, therefore:

1. The principle of ecological sustainability (or interspecies justice):

Energy must be generated and used in a way that does not compromise the integrity of the Earth's ecological systems.

2. The principle of social and economic equity (or intergenerational justice):

Energy must be available to individuals on an equitable basis and at an adequate level, allowing them to meet their needs.

3. The principle of responsibility for future generations (or intergenerational justice):

The first of these principles distinguishes strong sustainability from weak sustainability. It ensures that all human needs, present and future, can only be met within the limits of ecological systems. Principle I guides both following principles and is, in this sense, superior to them.

It should be recognized that a strict application of principle I is difficult to achieve. As long as there are inequalities between nations as well as within nations, a total ban of fossil fuels, for example, could create new inequalities, thus violating principle 2. So, there needs to be room for flexibility to meet the requirements of principle 2. That does, however, not diminish the importance of preserving the natural capital as a prime goal. The ecological focus of sustainable development is the only way to prevent excessive use of natural resources, Without it, trade-offs would be inevitable and business-as-usual policies likely.

As note above, there is a range of legal principles and concepts supporting these ethical principles for sustainable energy. The application of the precautionary principle, for example, helps to implement the principle of ecological sustainability as well as the principle of future generations responsibility. Quite obviously, sustainable energy policies must take a precautionary approach.

It is also possible to formulate a number of more specific requirements for sustainable energy derived from existing legal principles and the ethics of sustainable development: Such requirements could, for example, include:

• protection of the natural environment without compromise, including the avoidance of irreversible impacts on the ecosystem and the maintenance of biodiversity;

• minimization, or preferably avoidance, of greenhouse gas emissions and other contaminants to the environment;

• use of all energy from all sources in an as efficient manner as possible;

• maximum possible use of renewable energy sources within the capacity of the ecosystem to allow natural regeneration;

• investment in, and research into, energy issues, including methods to improve energy efficiency and new sources of energy, particularly renewable sources;

• responsibility of all members of society to conserve energy and use it in an efficient way;

• provision of ambitious and binding targets alongside the provision of incentives to meet such targets;

• promotion of public awareness of and involvement in energy issues.

These or similar requirements can be found in energy policies of countries implementing the Kyoto Protocol.

It is crucial, however, to not overlook the basic ethics of sustainable development. As said before, the ethics of sustainable energy reach wider than any existing principles of environmental law. They are more fundamental and should be expressed accordingly.

1. The ethical principles for sustainable energy are:

A. The principle of ecological sustainability (or interspecies justice).

B. The principle of social and economic equity (or intergenerational justice).

C. The principle of responsibility for future generations (or intergenerational justice)

D. All of the above.

2. Which is the concept of specific requirements for sustainable energy?

A. Use all energy from all sources in an as efficient manner as possible.

B. Have no responsibility for all members of society to conserve energy and use it in an efficient way.

C. Promotion of private awareness of and involvement in energy issues.

D. Protection of the natural environment with compromise.

3. The word "imperative" in the passage may probably mean _____.

A. inevitable   B. important

C. voluntary   D. crucial

Part Two True or False Questions

Direction: *In this part of the exercise, there is a passage with ten true or false questions. Read the passage carefully and mark T if it is true and F if it is false.*

Examples for broader expression of sustainable management can be found in the environmental legislation of New Zealand. The Resource Management Act 1991 (RMA) is guided by the principle of "sustainable management" which is not identical with sustainable development, but nevertheless related to it. Section 5 (2) of the RMA reads:

"Sustainable management means managing the use, development and protection of natural and physical resources in a way, or at a rate, which enables people and communities to provide for their social, economic and cultural wellbeing and for their health and safety while:

a. Sustaining the potential of national and physical resources to meet the reasonably foreseeable needs of future generations; and

Lesson Twelve   Ethical Implications of Energy for Sustainable Development

b. Safeguarding the life-supporting capacity of air, water, soil, and ecosystems; and

c. Avoiding, remedying or integrating any adverse effects of activities on the environment."

The elements of this definition are compatible with the three ethical principles of sustainable development. The recognition of intrinsic values and the reference to the ethic of guardianship are consistent with the legal principle of interspecies justice.

The approach of the RMA has, however, not yet been translated into energy policies based on strong sustainability, in January 2003, the Government issued a document called "Sustainable Development for New Zealand: Programme of Action". Its "overarching goal" for energy is "to ensure the delivery of energy services to all classes of consumer in an efficient, fair, reliable and sustainable manner." To achieve this the Programme then lists three "desired outcomes":

- Energy use in New Zealand becomes progressively more efficient and less wasteful;
- Renewable sources of energy are developed and maximized;
- New Zealand consumers have a secure supply of electricity.

The second chapter of the Program is entitled "Sustainable Development In Policy and Decision Making". That section gives a list of principles for policy and decision-making. Some of those principles suggest a move towards strong sustainability, including the following:

- Considering the long-term implications of decisions;
- Seeking innovative solutions that are mutually reinforcing; rather than accepting that gain in one area will necessarily be achieved at the expense of another;
- Addressing risks and uncertainty when making choices and taking a precautionary approach when making decisions that may cause serious or irreversible damage.

This Program now awaits implementation. New Zealand's current energy law and policy is based on weak sustainability but subject to criticism within Government and civil society. The Parliamentary Commissioner for the Environment in particular, has repeatedly called for a strong sustainability approach to energy. An example is this definition:

"A sustainable energy system, like a natural ecosystem, is characterized by its ability to deliver required energy services within available resource and waste sink constraints."

Looking at Germany's energy law a similar pictures emerges. The German Energy Report 2001 states the three objectives (or pillars) of sustainable energy as follows:

"Energy is sustainable when it meets the equal goals of supply security, economy and environmental protection."

However, the current review of energy law to meet the Kyoto targets is surrounded by the controversy between strong and weak sustainability. While most Federal ministries prefer the 3-pillar approach, the Environmental ministry favors a strong sustainability model. The National Sustainability Council (Nationaler Nachhaltigkeiterat) and independent Environmental Advisory Council (Sachverstgndigenrat fgr Umweltfragen-SRU) have also pleaded for the adoption of a stronger, more ecologically focused concept of sustainable energy:

"Although it has to be acknowledged that a strict concept of strong sustainability is difficult to realize, the principle, to keep the natural capital constant over time, should be the guideline for the interpretation of sustainability."

At the level of the European Union, the EU Strategy for Sustainable Development contains a number of energy-related measures including a phase-out of subsidies for fossil fuel production and consumption by 2010. There is a plethora of Directives regulating electricity and gas, energy efficiency, renewable energy and energy taxes. However, the overall approach is based on weak sustainability. Calls for a strong sustainability approach came, in particular, from the European Environmental Agency and the European Consultative Forum on Environment and Development.

With respect to current energy policies in China, Professor Yonglong Lu has commented on ethical challenges. He resumes that "China is now on the track of Rule by Law" with over thirty laws and regulations being adopted. While he sees the emphasis still on supply and distribution, he also notes "a change from reliance on non-renewable fossil fuels to renewable oriented energy" and calls for a "long-term public participatory process" including the business sector. "Without the participation of business circles, the ethics of energy will still be a word on paper".

Perhaps the best way to advance strong sustainable energy ethics is to promote them at the level of international law. So far, international energy law has not been guided by sustainability ethics despite the fact that roost international agreements since the 1992 Rio Summit aim for contributions to sustainable development. Nicholas Robinson makes the point, for example, "that the objectives of the 1992 United Nations Framework Convention on Climate Change could not be achieved without building the sustainability policies adopted at the UN Conference on Environment and Development (UNCED) in 1992 into the energy laws of each nation." These sustainability policies have been developed through the UN Commission on Sustainable Development, the energy related paragraph 8 of the WSSD Plan of Implementation and the various activities of international agencies. The core of such sustainability policies, however, has yet to be discovered. If policies are not informed by ethical principles they are in danger of reinforcing business-as-usual.

An example of this is the Energy Charter Treaty (ECT) 98 and its accompanying Energy Charter Protocol on Energy Efficiency and Related Environmental Aspects (Protocol). Article 19 ('Environmental Aspects') of the ECT requires each contracting party.

"in pursuit of sustainable development and taking into account its obligations under those international agreements concerning the environment to which it is party... to strive to minimize in an economically efficient manner harmful environmental impacts occurring either within or outside the Area from el/ operations within the energy cycle in its area taking proper account of safety."

Such vagueness still allows for a priority of economic concerns over environmental concerns, thus does not even meet the minimum standards for sustainable development. The Protocol could, therefore, be expected to give some further guidance. Instead, the Protocol provides a menu of good practices that may be good enough for states with transitional economies, but merely reflect OECD practices. It certainly does not add to the understanding of sustainable development and its importance for energy law and policy.

Most promising are efforts that formulate an international consensus and translate it to codes of conduct, guidelines or similar documents of "soft international law". Soft law allows states to take an interest without having to commit. It makes a lot of sense, therefore, to promote a "statement of principles for a global consensus on sustainable energy production and consumption", as drafted by *Adrian Bradbreok* and *Ralph Wahnschafft*. The purpose of such a statement on sustainable energy principles is to reinforce established principles and develop new ones. This way existing international law—whether "hard" or "soft"—can be taken a step further to the next level.

True or False:

1. The elements of this definition are compatible with the three ethical principles of sustainable development. (　　)

2. Energy use in New Zealand becomes progressively less efficient and more wasteful (　　)

3. At the level of the European Union, the EU Strategy for Sustainable Development contains a number of energy-related measures including a phase-out of subsidies for fossil fuel production and consumption by 2012. (　　)

4. Without the participation of business circles, the ethics of energy will still be a word on paper. (　　)

5. The Protocol could, therefore, be expected to give some further guidance. (　　)

6. Most promising are efforts that formulate an international consensus and translate it to codes of conduct, guidelines or similar documents of "hard international law". (　　)

7. These sustainability policies have been developed through the UN Commission on Sustainable Development. (　　)

8. If policies are informed by ethical principles they are in danger of reinforcing business-as-usual. (　　)

IV　Translation Abilities

法律语言特征分析与法律翻译技能培养之十二：
法律英语中表达主观感情之形容词或副词的限制使用问题

法律语言对于形容词和副词的使用十分严格。一般地说,法律语言中极少使用描绘性质的形容词,立法语言中,更是如此。立法语言中的形容词大多表示性质和程度。对于表示时间、程度、范围、状态、语气等副词的使用也极为慎重。如 legitimate gains（合法收入）、"犯罪分子违法所得的一切财物,应当予以追缴或责令退赔;对被害人的合法财产,应当及时返还;违禁品和供犯罪所用的本人财物,应当予以没收。没收的财物和罚金,一律上缴国库,不得挪用和自行处理"就翻译成:"All money and property illegally obtained by a criminal shall be recovered, or compensation shall be ordered; the lawful property of the victim shall be returned without delay; and contrabands and possessions of the criminal that are used in the commission of the crime shall be confiscated. All the confiscated money and property and fines shall be turned over to the State Treasury, and no one may misappropriate or privately dispose of them."再如:"以暴力或其他方法公然侮辱他人或捏造事实诽谤他人,情节严重的,处三年以下有期徒刑、拘

役或剥夺政治权利"可以翻译成:"Whoever, by violence or other methods, publicly humiliates another person or invent stories to defame him, if the circumstances are serious, shall be sentenced to fixed-term imprisonment of not more than three years, criminal detention, public surveillance or deprivation of political rights."

此外,法律语言中还限制使用具有主观感情色彩的形容词和副词,究其原因,是因为此类形容词和副词容易混淆视听,往往造成不必要的争议或争执。国外许多法律工作者在签订合同或者草拟法律条文时,常常规定有专门条款以限制人们使用像 splendid, happy, 或者 rather, quite 等之类的形容词、副词等,其目的在于,尽量避免法官和律师或者各方当事人发生理解上的困难或造成歧义,从而避免了争议的产生,从而达到了法律语言追求用词严谨的目的,使表意更加周密、无懈可击。

但在使用该类形容词时,应特别注意该类形容词所表达的与一般用语不同的意思,如:在 adverse possession(逆权占有制度)中,其一构成要件是 notorious possession,翻译该词时,就要特别注意此处的 notorious 不再是"臭名昭著的"意思,而是"公开的,公然的"意思,即该种占有是大家都知晓的。同理,在翻译 infamous crime 时,也要注意到 infamous 在此处不是"臭名昭著的"意思,而是"可处以监禁刑的犯罪"或者在普通法上,因为犯叛逆、重罪、伪证、欺诈等罪行在被判处监禁的同时,剥夺犯罪者的信誉、使其丧失权利的行为。

总之,法律语言中对于形容词和副词的使用较名词或动词的使用要少,但其地位是不可忽视的,每个形容词和副词均具有其特定的语境意义,绝非可有可无的东西,在翻译过程中,翻译者必须慎重,应充分考虑应使用形容词和副词的具体场合和使用范围。

Part One *Translate the following into Chinese*

We stand at a critical moment in Earth's history, a time when humanity must choose its future. As the world becomes increasingly interdependent and fragile, the future at once holds great peril and great promise. To move forward we must recognize that in the midst of a magnificent diversity of cultures and life forms we are one human family and one Earth community with a common destiny. We must join together to bring forth a sustainable global society founded on respect for nature, universal human rights, economic justice, and a culture of peace. Towards this end, it is imperative that we, the peoples of Earth, declare our responsibility to one another, to the greater community of life, and to future generations.

Part Two *Translate the following into English*

人类是不断演化的宇宙的组成部分。地球——我们的家园是独特的生命群落。大自然的力量使生存成为一种强迫的和不定的冒险,不过,地球提供了生命演化所必需的条件。生命群落的恢复力和人类的福祉依赖于:保护一个拥有所有生态系统、种类繁多的动植物、肥沃的土壤、纯净的水和清洁的空气的健全的生物圈。资源有限的全球环境是全人类共同关心的问题。保护地球的生命力、多样性和美丽是一种神圣的职责。

V Interaction

Discuss with your tutor(s) or the People's judges in your locality about the environmental protections. Then based on the discussion, you are supposed to write a composition about how the judges handled the environmental cases. Remember that you are required to express your ideas clearly.

VI   Appreciation of Judge's Opinions

(1) Case Name(案件名): *Friends of the Earth, Inc., et al. v. Laidlaw Environmental Services, Inc.*

Friends of the Earth, Inc., et al. v. Laidlaw Environmental Services, Inc.

Supreme Court of the United States

Argued October 12, 1999
Decided January 12, 2000

Full case name	*Friends of the Earth, Incorporated, et al. v. Laidlaw Environmental Services (TOC), Incorporated*
Citations	528 U.S. 167 (more)
	120 S. Ct. 693; 145 L. Ed. 2d 610; 2000 U.S. LEXIS 501; 49 ERC (BNA) 1769; 163 A. L. R. Fed. 749; 2000 Cal. Daily Op. Service 289; 2000 Daily Journal DAR 375; 30 ELR 20246; 1999 Colo. J. C. A. R. 142; 13 Fla. L. Weekly Fed. S 37
Prior history	On writ of certiorari to the United States Court of Appeals for the Fourth Circuit

Holding

The Court held that plaintiff residents in the area of South Carolina's North Tyger River had standing to sue an industrial polluter against whom various deterrent civil penalties were being pursued.

Court membership

Chief Justice
William Rehnquist
Associate Justices
John P. Stevens · Sandra Day O'Connor
Antonin Scalia · Anthony Kennedy
David Souter · Clarence Thomas
Ruth Bader Ginsburg · Stephen Breyer

Case opinions

Majority	Ginsburg, joined by Rehnquist, Stevens, O'Connor, Kennedy, Souter, Breyer
Concurrence	Stevens
Concurrence	Kennedy
Dissent	Scalia, joined by Thomas

Laws applied

U. S. Const.

(2) Case Summary(案情简介)

Facts of the Case

After Laidlaw Environmental Services, Inc. bought a wastewater treatment plant(废水处理厂), it was granted a National Pollutant Discharge Elimination System (NPDES) permit(全国污染物排放消减系统许可证). The permit authorized Laidlaw to discharge treated water(排放经处理的废水) and limited pollutants(部分污染物). Laidlaw's discharge of mercury(水银,汞)into the North Tyger River repeatedly exceeded the limits set by the permit. Ultimately, Friends of the Earth(地球之友,致力于更安全和更公平世界的一家环境保护组织)and others (FOE) filed a citizen suit(环境法上的公民诉讼) under the Clean Water Act against Laidlaw, alleging noncompliance(不遵循,未遵守)with the NPDES permit, seeking injunctive relief(禁止令)and an award of civil penalties(民事处罚金). Laidlaw moved for summary judgement(简易判决) on the ground that FOE lacked standing to bring the lawsuit(缺乏提起诉讼的资格). The District Court denied the motion. Ultimately, the District Court found that Laidlaw violated the mercury discharge limitation. In issuing its judgment, the District Court concluded that a civil penalty of $405,800 would be adequate to forestall(阻止)future violations, given that Laidlaw would have to reimburse(补偿)the plaintiffs for a significant amount of legal fees and had itself incurred significant legal expenses. The court declined to order injunctive relief because Laidlaw, after the lawsuit began, had achieved substantial compliance with the terms of its permit. FOE appealed(上诉)to the amount of the District Court's civil penalty judgment, but did not appeal the denial of declaratory or injunctive relief(确权性或禁止令类的救济). The Court of Appeals ordered the case to be dismissed. The appellate court held that the case had become moot(n. 诉由消失之事项; adj. 失去实际意义的,未决的)once Laidlaw complied with the terms of its permit. The court reasoned that the only remedy currently available to FOE, civil penalties payable to the Government, would not redress any injury FOE had suffered.

Question: Does an environmental group's citizen suit for civil penalties under the Clean Water Act become moot when the defendant, after commencement of the litigation, has come into compliance with its National Pollutant Discharge Elimination System permit?

Conclusion

Decision: 7 votes for Friends of the Earth, 2 vote(s) against

Legal provision: Federal Water Pollution Control (Clean Water), plus amendments

No. In a 7-2 opinion delivered by Justice Ruth Bader Ginsburg, the Court held that a citizen suitor's claim for civil penalties need not be dismissed as moot when the defendant, after commencement of the litigation(诉之始), has come into compliance with its NPDES permit. "A defendant's voluntary cessation(休止,中止)of allegedly unlawful conduct ordinarily does not suffice to moot a case," Justice Ginsburg wrote for the Court. "Congress has found that civil penalties in the Clean Water Act cases do more than promote immediate compliance... they also deter future violations," concluded Justice Ginsburg. The Court also ruled that FOE had standing to bring the suit on behalf on its members.

(3) Excerpts of the Judgment(法官判决词)

JUSTICE GINSBURG delivered the opinion of the Court.

This case presents an important question concerning the operation of the citizen-suit(公民诉讼) provisions of the Clean Water Act. Congress authorized the federal district courts to entertain Clean Water Act suits initiated by "a person or persons having an interest which is or may be adversely affected." To impel future compliance with the Act, a district court may prescribe injunctive relief in such a suit; additionally or alternatively, the court may impose civil penalties(民事处罚) payable to the United States Treasury(美国财政部). In the Clean Water Act citi-

Lesson Twelve Ethical Implications of Energy for Sustainable Development

zen suit now before us, the District Court determined that injunctive relief(禁止令) was inappropriate because the defendant, after the institution of the litigation, achieved substantial compliance with the terms of its discharge permit. The court did, however, assess a civil penalty of $405,800. The "total deterrent effect" of the penalty would be adequate to forestall future violations, the court reasoned, taking into account that the defendant "will be required to reimburse plaintiffs for a significant amount of legal fees and has, itself, incurred significant legal expenses."

The Court of Appeals vacated(使作废,取消契约等) the District Court's order. The case became moot, the appellate court declared, once the defendant fully complied with the terms of its permit and the plaintiff failed to appeal the denial of equitable relief. "Civil penalties payable to the government," the Court of Appeals stated, "would not redress any injury Plaintiffs have suffered." Nor were attorneys' fees in order, the Court of Appeals noted, because absent relief on the merits, plaintiffs could not qualify as prevailing parties.

We reverse the judgment of the Court of Appeals. The appellate court erred in concluding that a citizen suitor's claim for civil penalties must be dismissed as moot when the defendant, albeit after commencement of the litigation (诉讼伊始), has come into compliance. In directing dismissal of the suit on grounds of mootness, the Court of Appeals incorrectly conflated(混杂,合并) our case law on initial standing to bring suit, with our case law on postcommencement mootness. A defendant's voluntary cessation of allegedly unlawful conduct ordinarily does not suffice to moot a case. The Court of Appeals also misperceived the remedial potential of civil penalties. Such penalties may serve, as an alternative to an injunction, to deter future violations and thereby redress the injuries that prompted a citizen suitor to commence litigation.

I A

In 1972, Congress enacted the Clean Water Act (Act), also known as the Federal Water Pollution Control Act(《联邦水污染控制法》). Section 402 of the Act, provides for the issuance, by the Administrator of the Environmental Protection Agency (EPA)(环境保护署) or by authorized States, of National Pollutant Discharge Elimination System (NPDES) permits. NPDES permits impose limitations on the discharge of pollutants, and establish related monitoring and reporting requirements(监控与报告要求), in order to improve the cleanliness and safety of the Nation's waters. Noncompliance with a permit constitutes a violation of the Act.

Under §505(a) of the Act, a suit to enforce any limitation in an NPDES permit may be brought by any "citizen," defined as "a person or persons having an interest which is or may be adversely affected." Sixty days before initiating a citizen suit, however, the would-be plaintiff must give notice of the alleged violation to the EPA, the State in which the alleged violation occurred, and the alleged violator. "The purpose of notice to the alleged violator is to give it an opportunity to bring itself into complete compliance with the Act and thus... render unnecessary a citizen suit." Accordingly, we have held that citizens lack statutory standing under §505(a) to sue for violations that have ceased by the time the complaint is filed. The Act also bars a citizen from suing if the EPA or the State has already commenced, and is "diligently prosecuting," an enforcement action.

The Act authorizes district courts in citizen-suit proceedings to enter injunctions and to assess civil penalties, which are payable to the United States Treasury. In determining the amount of any civil penalty, the district court must take into account "the seriousness of the violation or violations, the economic benefit (if any) resulting from the violation, any history of such violations, any good-faith efforts to comply with the applicable requirements, the economic impact of the penalty on the violator, and such other matters as justice may require." In addition, the court "may award costs of litigation (including reasonable attorney and expert witness fees) to any prevailing or substantially prevailing party, whenever the court determines such award is appropriate."

B

In 1986, defendant-respondent(作为被告的被上诉人) Laidlaw Environmental Services (TOC), Inc., bought a hazardous waste incinerator facility(有毒废物垃圾焚化设施) in Roebuck, South Carolina, that included a wastewater treatment plant. (The company has since changed its name to Safety-Kleen (Roebuck), Inc., but for simplicity we will refer to it as "Laidlaw" throughout.) Shortly after Laidlaw acquired the facility, the South Carolina Department of Health and Environmental Control (DHEC)(南加州卫生与环境监管局), acting under 33 U.S.C. §1342(a)(1), granted Laidlaw an NPDES permit authorizing the company to discharge treated water into the North Tyger River. The permit, which became effective on January 1, 1987, placed limits on Laidlaw's discharge of several pollutants into the river, including-of particular relevance to this case-mercury, an extremely toxic pollutant. The permit also regulated the flow, temperature, toxicity(毒性), and pH of the effluent(排出物,流出物) from the facility, and imposed monitoring and reporting obligations.

Once it received its permit, Laidlaw began to discharge various pollutants into the waterway; repeatedly, Laidlaw's discharges exceeded the limits set by the permit. In particular, despite experimenting with several technological fixes, Laidlaw consistently failed to meet the permit's stringent 1.3 ppb (parts per billion) daily average limit on mercury discharges. The District Court later found that Laidlaw had violated the mercury limits on 489 occasions between 1987 and 1995.

On April 10, 1992, plaintiff-petitioners Friends of the Earth (FOE) and Citizens Local Environmental Action Network, Inc. (CLEAN)(公民地方环境行动网络公司)(referred to collectively in this opinion, together with later joined plaintiff-petitioner Sierra Club(塞拉俱乐部,台湾地区翻译为"山峦协会或山峦俱乐部"), as "FOE") took the preliminary step necessary to the institution of litigation(起诉). They sent a letter to Laidlaw notifying the company of their intention to file a citizen suit against it under §505(a) of the Act after the expiration of the requisite 60-day notice period, i.e., on or after June 10, 1992. Laidlaw's lawyer then contacted DHEC to ask whether DHEC would consider filing a lawsuit against Laidlaw. The District Court later found that Laidlaw's reason for requesting that DHEC file a lawsuit against it was to bar FOE's proposed citizen suit through the operation of 33 U.S.C. §1365(b)(1)(B). DHEC agreed to file a lawsuit against Laidlaw; the company's lawyer then drafted the complaint for DHEC and paid the filing fee. On June 9, 1992, the last day before FOE's 60-day notice period expired, DHEC and Laidlaw reached a settlement requiring Laidlaw to pay $100,000 in civil penalties and to make "'every effort'" to comply with its permit obligations.

On June 12, 1992, FOE filed this citizen suit against Laidlaw under §505(a) of the Act, alleging noncompliance with the NPDES permit and seeking declaratory and injunctive relief and an award of civil penalties. Laidlaw moved for summary judgment on the ground that FOE had failed to present evidence demonstrating injury in fact, and therefore lacked Article III standing to bring the lawsuit. In opposition to this motion, FOE submitted affidavits(宣誓书) and deposition testimony(庭外取证获得的证言证词) from members of the plaintiff organizations. The record before the District Court also included affidavits from the organizations' members submitted by FOE in support of an earlier motion for preliminary injunctive relief. After examining this evidence, the District Court denied Laidlaw's summary judgment motion, finding-albeit "by the very slimmest of margins"-that FOE had standing to bring the suit.

Laidlaw also moved to dismiss the action(中止诉讼) on the ground that the citizen suit was barred under 33 U.S.C. §1365(b)(1)(B) by DHEC's prior action against the company. The United States, appearing as amicus curiae(拉丁语,法院之友,法庭之友), joined FOE in opposing the motion. After an extensive analysis of the Laidlaw-DHEC settlement and the circumstances under which it was reached, the District Court held that DHEC's action against Laidlaw had not been "diligently prosecuted"; consequently, the court allowed FOE's citizen suit to proceed. The record indicates that after FOE initiated the suit, but before the District Court rendered judgment, Laidlaw violated the mercury discharge limitation in its permit 13 times. The District Court also found that Laidlaw had committed 13 monitoring and 10 reporting violations during this period. The last recorded mercury discharge violation occurred in January 1995, long after the complaint was filed but about two years before judgment was rendered.

Lesson Twelve Ethical Implications of Energy for Sustainable Development

On January 22, 1997, the District Court issued its judgment. It found that Laidlaw had gained a total economic benefit of $1,092,581 as a result of its extended period of noncompliance with the mercury discharge limit in its permit. The court concluded, however, that a civil penalty of $405,800 was adequate in light of the guiding factors listed in 33 U. S. C. §1319(d). In particular, the District Court stated that the lesser penalty was appropriate taking into account the judgment's "total deterrent effect." In reaching this determination, the court "considered that Laidlaw will be required to reimburse plaintiffs for a significant amount of legal fees." The court declined to grant FOE's request for injunctive relief, stating that an injunction was inappropriate because "Laidlaw has been in substantial compliance with all parameters in its NPDES permit since at least August 1992."

FOE appealed the District Court's civil penalty judgment, arguing that the penalty was inadequate, but did not appeal the denial of declaratory or injunctive relief. Laidlaw cross-appealed(反诉), arguing, among other things, that FOE lacked standing to bring the suit and that DHEC's action qualified as a diligent prosecution precluding FOE's litigation. The United States continued to participate as amicus curiae in support of FOE.

On July 16, 1998, the Court of Appeals for the Fourth Circuit issued its judgment. The Court of Appeals assumed without deciding that FOE initially had standing to bring the action, but went on to hold that the case had become moot. The appellate court stated, first, that the elements of Article III standing-injury, causation, and redressability-must persist at every stage of review, or else the action becomes moot. Citing our decision in Steel Co., the Court of Appeals reasoned that the case had become moot because "the only remedy currently available to FOE—civil penalties payable to the government—would not redress any injury FOE has suffered." The court therefore vacated the District Court's order and remanded with instructions to dismiss the action. In a footnote, the Court of Appeals added that FOE's "failure to obtain relief on the merits of its claims precludes any recovery of attorneys' fees or other litigation costs because such an award is available only to a 'prevailing or substantially prevailing party.'"

According to Laidlaw, after the Court of Appeals issued its decision but before this Court granted certiorari, the entire incinerator facility in Roebuck was permanently closed, dismantled, and put up for sale, and all discharges from the facility permanently ceased.

We granted certiorari, to resolve the inconsistency between the Fourth Circuit's decision in this case and the decisions of several other Courts of Appeals, which have held that a defendant's compliance with its permit after the commencement of litigation does not moot claims for civil penalties under the Act.

II A

The Constitution's case-or-controversy limitation on federal judicial authority, underpins both our standing and our mootness jurisprudence, but the two inquiries differ in respects critical to the proper resolution of this case, so we address them separately. Because the Court of Appeals was persuaded that the case had become moot and so held, it simply assumed without deciding that FOE had initial standing. But because we hold that the Court of Appeals erred in declaring the case moot, we have an obligation to assure ourselves that FOE had Article III standing at the outset of the litigation. We therefore address the question of standing before turning to mootness.

In *Lujan v. Defenders of Wildlife*, we held that, to satisfy Article III's standing requirements, a plaintiff must show (1) it has suffered an "injury in fact" that is (a) concrete and particularized and (b) actual or imminent, not conjectural(推测的,猜想的,臆测的)or hypothetical(假设的); (2) the injury is fairly traceable to the challenged action of the defendant; and (3) it is likely, as opposed to merely speculative, that the injury will be redressed by a favorable decision. An association has standing to bring suit on behalf of its members when its members would otherwise have standing to sue in their own right, the interests at stake are germane to(恰当的,贴切的,切题的,关系密切的) the organization's purpose, and neither the claim asserted nor the relief requested requires the participation of individual members in the lawsuit.

Laidlaw contends first that FOE lacked standing(起诉。诉讼资格)from the outset even to seek injunctive relief, because the plaintiff organizations failed to show that any of their members had sustained or faced the threat of any "injury in fact" from Laidlaw's activities. In support of this contention Laidlaw points to the District Court's finding, made in the course of setting the penalty amount, that there had been "no demonstrated proof of harm to the environment" from Laidlaw's mercury discharge violations.

The relevant showing for purposes of Article III standing, however, is not injury to the environment but injury to the plaintiff. To insist upon the former rather than the latter as part of the standing inquiry is to raise the standing hurdle higher than the necessary showing for success on the merits in an action alleging noncompliance with an NPDES permit. Focusing properly on injury to the plaintiff, the District Court found that FOE had demonstrated sufficient injury to establish standing. For example, FOE member Kenneth Lee Curtis averred(证明) in affidavits that he lived a half-mile from Laidlaw's facility; that he occasionally drove over the North Tyger River, and that it looked and smelled polluted; and that he would like to fish, camp, swim, and picnic in and near the river between 3 and 15 miles downstream from the facility, as he did when he was a teenager, but would not do so because he was concerned that the water was polluted by Laidlaw's discharges. Curtis reaffirmed these statements in extensive deposition testimony. For example, he testified that he would like to fish in the river at a specific spot he used as a boy, but that he would not do so now because of his concerns about Laidlaw's discharges.

Other members presented evidence to similar effect.

CLEAN member Angela Patterson attested that she lived two miles from the facility; that before Laidlaw operated the facility, she picnicked, walked, birdwatched, and waded in and along the North Tyger River because of the natural beauty of the area; that she no longer engaged in these activities in or near the river because she was concerned about harmful effects from discharged pollutants; and that she and her husband would like to purchase a home near the river but did not intend to do so, in part because of Laidlaw's discharges. CLEAN member Judy Pruitt averred that she lived one-quarter mile from Laidlaw's facility and would like to fish, hike, and picnic along the North Tyger River, but has refrained from those activities because of the discharges. FOE member Linda Moore attested that she lived 20 miles from Roebuck, and would use the North Tyger River south of Roebuck and the land surrounding it for recreational purposes were she not concerned that the water contained harmful pollutants. In her deposition, Moore testified at length that she would hike, picnic, camp, swim, boat, and drive near or in the river were it not for her concerns about illegal discharges. CLEAN member Gail Lee attested that her home, which is near Laidlaw's facility, had a lower value than similar homes located farther from the facility, and that she believed the pollutant discharges accounted for some of the discrepancy. Sierra Club member Norman Sharp averred that he had canoed(划独木舟) approximately 40 miles downstream of the Laidlaw facility and would like to canoe in the North Tyger River closer to Laidlaw's discharge point, but did not do so because he was concerned that the water contained harmful pollutants.

These sworn statements, as the District Court determined, adequately documented injury in fact. We have held that environmental plaintiffs adequately allege injury in fact when they aver that they use the affected area and are persons "for whom the aesthetic and recreational values(美学与娱乐价值) of the area will be lessened" by the challenged activity.

Our decision in *Lujan v. National Wildlife Federation* (1990), is not to the contrary. In that case an environmental organization assailed(指责,谴责) the Bureau of Land Management's(土地管理局) "land withdrawal review program," a program covering millions of acres, alleging that the program illegally opened up public lands to mining activities. The defendants moved for summary judgment, challenging the plaintiff organization's standing to initiate the action under the Administrative Procedure Act, 5 U.S.C. §702. We held that the plaintiff could not survive the summary judgment motion merely by offering "averments which state only that one of the organization's members uses unspecified portions of an immense tract of territory, on some portions of which mining activity has occurred or probably will occur by virtue of the governmental action."

Lesson Twelve Ethical Implications of Energy for Sustainable Development

In contrast, the affidavits and testimony presented by FOE in this case assert that Laidlaw's discharges, and the affiant members' reasonable concerns about the effects of those discharges, directly affected those affiants' recreational, aesthetic, and economic interests. These submissions present dispositively more than the mere "general averments" and "conclusory allegations" found inadequate in National Wildlife Federation. Nor can the affiants' conditional statements—that they would use the nearby North Tyger River for recreation if Laidlaw were not discharging pollutants into it—be equated with the speculative "'some day' intentions" to visit endangered species halfway around the world that we held insufficient to show injury in fact in Defenders of Wildlife.

Los Angeles v. Lyons (1983), relied on by the dissent, does not weigh against standing in this case. In Lyons, we held that a plaintiff lacked standing to seek an injunction against the enforcement of a police chokehold policy(掐脖子政策)because he could not credibly allege that he faced a realistic threat from the policy. In the footnote from Lyons cited by the dissent, we noted that "the reasonableness of Lyons' fear is dependent upon the likelihood of a recurrence of the allegedly unlawful conduct," and that his "subjective apprehensions"(忧虑,不安) that such a recurrence would even take place were not enough to support standing. Here, in contrast, it is undisputed (毋庸置疑)that Laidlaw's unlawful conduct—discharging pollutants in excess of permit limits—was occurring at the time the complaint was filed. Under Lyons, then, the only "subjective" issue here is "the reasonableness of the fear" that led the affiants to respond to that concededly ongoing conduct by refraining from use of the North Tyger River and surrounding areas. Unlike the dissent, we see nothing "improbable" about the proposition that a company's continuous and pervasive illegal discharges of pollutants into a river would cause nearby residents to curtail their recreational use of that waterway and would subject them to other economic and aesthetic harms. The proposition is entirely reasonable, the District Court found it was true in this case, and that is enough for injury in fact.

Laidlaw argues next that even if FOE had standing to seek injunctive relief, it lacked standing to seek civil penalties. Here the asserted defect is not injury but redressability(可救济性). Civil penalties offer no redress to private plaintiffs, Laidlaw argues, because they are paid to the Government, and therefore a citizen plaintiff can never have standing to seek them.

Laidlaw is right to insist that a plaintiff must demonstrate standing separately for each form of relief sought. But it is wrong to maintain that citizen plaintiffs facing ongoing violations never have standing to seek civil penalties.

We have recognized on numerous occasions that "all civil penalties have some deterrent effect." More specifically, Congress has found that civil penalties in Clean Water Act cases do more than promote immediate compliance by limiting the defendant's economic incentive to delay its attainment of permit limits; they also deter future violations. This congressional determination warrants judicial attention and respect. "The legislative history of the Act reveals that Congress wanted the district court to consider the need for retribution and deterrence, in addition to restitution, when it imposed civil penalties... The district court may seek to deter future violations by basing the penalty on its economic impact."

It can scarcely be doubted that, for a plaintiff who is injured or faces the threat of future injury due to illegal conduct ongoing at the time of suit, a sanction that effectively abates(取消法令,中止诉讼;排除障碍) that conduct and prevents its recurrence provides a form of redress. Civil penalties can fit that description. To the extent that they encourage defendants to discontinue current violations and deter them from committing future ones, they afford redress to citizen plaintiffs who are injured or threatened with injury as a consequence of ongoing unlawful conduct.

The dissent argues that it is the availability rather than the imposition of civil penalties that deters any particular polluter from continuing to pollute. This argument misses the mark(迷失目标/方向)in two ways. First, it overlooks the interdependence of the availability and the imposition; a threat has no deterrent value unless it is credible that it will be carried out. Second, it is reasonable for Congress to conclude that an actual award of civil penalties does in fact bring with it a significant quantum（量，额；定量，定额；份；总量） of deterrence over and above what is achieved by the mere prospect of such penalties. A would-be polluter may or may not be dissuaded by the existence of a remedy on the books, but a defendant once hit in its pocketbook will surely think twice before polluting again.

We recognize that there may be a point at which the deterrent effect of a claim for civil penalties becomes so insubstantial or so remote that it cannot support citizen standing. The fact that this vanishing point is not easy to ascertain does not detract from the deterrent power of such penalties in the ordinary case. Justice Frankfurter's observations for the Court, made in a different context nearly 60 years ago, hold true here as well:

"How to effectuate policy—the adaptation of means to legitimately sought ends—is one of the most intractable of legislative problems. Whether proscribed conduct is to be deterred by qui tam action（拉丁语，要求取得罚金的起诉/此项罚金由起诉人与官方均分）or triple damages or injunction, or by criminal prosecution, or merely by defense to actions in contract, or by some, or all, of these remedies in combination, is a matter within the legislature's range of choice. Judgment on the deterrent effect of the various weapons in the armory of the law can lay little claim to scientific basis."

In this case we need not explore the outer limits of the principle that civil penalties provide sufficient deterrence to support redressability. Here, the civil penalties sought by FOE carried with them a deterrent effect that made it likely, as opposed to merely speculative, that the penalties would redress FOE's injuries by abating current violations and preventing future ones-as the District Court reasonably found when it assessed a penalty of $405,800.956.

Laidlaw contends that the reasoning of our decision in Steel Co. directs the conclusion that citizen plaintiffs have no standing to seek civil penalties under the Act. We disagree. Steel Co. established that citizen suitors lack standing to seek civil penalties for violations that have abated by the time of suit. We specifically noted in that case that there was no allegation in the complaint of any continuing or imminent violation, and that no basis for such an allegation appeared to exist. In short, Steel Co. held that private plaintiffs, unlike the Federal Government, may not sue to assess penalties for wholly past violations, but our decision in that case did not reach the issue of standing to seek penalties for violations that are ongoing at the time of the complaint and that could continue into the future if undeterred.

B

Satisfied that FOE had standing under Article III to bring this action, we turn to the question of mootness.

The only conceivable basis for a finding of mootness in this case is Laidlaw's voluntary conduct—either its achievement by August 1992 of substantial compliance with its NPDES permit or its more recent shutdown of the Roebuck facility. It is well settled that "a defendant's voluntary cessation of a challenged practice does not deprive a federal court of its power to determine the legality of the practice." "If it did, the courts would be compelled to leave 'the defendant... free to return to his old ways.'" In accordance with this principle, the standard we have announced for determining whether a case has been mooted by the defendant's voluntary conduct is stringent: "A case might become moot if subsequent events made it absolutely clear that the allegedly wrongful behavior could not reasonably be expected to recur." The "heavy burden of persuading" the court that the challenged conduct cannot reasonably be expected to start up again lies with the party asserting mootness.

The Court of Appeals justified its mootness disposition by reference to Steel Co., which held that citizen plaintiffs lack standing to seek civil penalties for wholly past violations. In relying on Steel Co., the Court of Appeals confused mootness with standing. The confusion is understandable, given this Court's repeated statements that the doctrine of mootness can be described as "the doctrine of standing set in a time frame: The requisite personal interest that must exist at the commencement of the litigation (standing) must continue throughout its existence (mootness)."

Lesson Twelve Ethical Implications of Energy for Sustainable Development

Careful reflection on the long-recognized exceptions to mootness, however, reveals that the description of mootness as "standing set in a time frame" is not comprehensive. As just noted, a defendant claiming that its voluntary compliance moots a case bears the formidable burden of showing that it is absolutely clear the allegedly wrongful behavior could not reasonably be expected to recur. By contrast, in a lawsuit brought to force compliance, it is the plaintiff's burden to establish standing by demonstrating that, if unchecked by the litigation, the defendant's allegedly wrongful behavior will likely occur or continue, and that the "threatened injury is certainly impending." Thus, in Lyons, as already noted, we held that a plaintiff lacked initial standing to seek an injunction against the enforcement of a police chokehold policy because he could not credibly allege that he faced a realistic threat arising from the policy. Elsewhere in the opinion, however, we noted that a citywide moratorium(行动、活动等的暂停/暂禁；延期偿付权；延缓偿付期) on police chokeholds—an action that surely diminished the already slim likelihood that any particular individual would be choked by police—would not have mooted an otherwise valid claim for injunctive relief, because the moratorium by its terms was not permanent. The plain lesson of these cases is that there are circumstances in which the prospect that a defendant will engage in (or resume) harmful conduct may be too speculative to support standing, but not too speculative to overcome mootness.

Furthermore, if mootness were simply "standing set in a time frame," the exception to mootness that arises when the defendant's allegedly unlawful activity is "capable of repetition, yet evading review," could not exist. When, for example, a mentally disabled patient files a lawsuit challenging her confinement in a segregated institution, her postcomplaint transfer to a community-based program will not moot the action, despite the fact that she would have lacked initial standing had she filed the complaint after the transfer. Standing admits of no similar exception; if a plaintiff lacks standing at the time the action commences, the fact that the dispute is capable of repetition yet evading review will not entitle the complainant to a federal judicial forum.

We acknowledged the distinction between mootness and standing most recently in Steel Co.:

"The United States... argues that the injunctive relief does constitute remediation (补习,辅导) because 'there is a presumption of future injury when the defendant has voluntarily ceased its illegal activity in response to litigation,' even if that occurs before a complaint is filed... This makes a sword out of a shield. The 'presumption' the Government refers to has been applied to refute the assertion of mootness by a defendant who, when sued in a complaint that alleges present or threatened injury, ceases the complained-of activity... It is an immense and unacceptable stretch to call the presumption into service as a substitute for the allegation of present or threatened injury upon which initial standing must be based."

Standing doctrine functions to ensure, among other things, that the scarce resources of the federal courts are devoted to those disputes in which the parties have a concrete stake. In contrast, by the time mootness is an issue, the case has been brought and litigated, often (as here) for years. To abandon the case at an advanced stage may prove more wasteful than frugal. This argument from sunk costs(沉积成本) does not license courts to retain jurisdiction over cases in which one or both of the parties plainly lack a continuing interest, as when the parties have settled or a plaintiff pursuing a non surviving claim has died.

In its brief, Laidlaw appears to argue that, regardless of the effect of Laidlaw's compliance, FOE doomed its own civil penalty claim to mootness by failing to appeal the District Court's denial of injunctive relief. This argument misconceives the statutory scheme. Under §1365(a), the district court has discretion to determine which form of relief is best suited, in the particular case, to abate current violations and deter future ones. "A federal judge sitting as chancellor is not mechanically obligated to grant an injunction for every violation of law."

Denial of injunctive relief does not necessarily mean that the district court has concluded there is no prospect of future violations for civil penalties to deter. Indeed, it meant no such thing in this case. The District Court denied injunctive relief, but expressly based its award of civil penalties on the need for deterrence. As the dissent notes, federal courts should aim to ensure "'the framing of relief no broader than required by the precise facts.'"

In accordance with this aim, a district court in a Clean Water Act citizen suit properly may conclude that an injunction would be an excessively intrusive remedy, because it could entail continuing superintendence of the permit holder's activities by a federal court—a process burdensome to court and permit holder alike.

Laidlaw also asserts, in a supplemental suggestion of mootness, that the closure of its Roebuck facility, which took place after the Court of Appeals issued its decision, mooted the case. The facility closure, like Laidlaw's earlier achievement of substantial compliance with its permit requirements, might moot the case, but—we once more reiterate—only if one or the other of these events made it absolutely clear that Laidlaw's permit violations could not reasonably be expected to recur. The effect of both Laidlaw's compliance and the facility closure on the prospect of future violations is a disputed factual matter. FOE points out, for example-and Laidlaw does not appear to contest—that Laidlaw retains its NPDES permit. These issues have not been aired in the lower courts; they remain open for consideration on remand.

C

FOE argues that it is entitled to attorneys' fees on the theory that a plaintiff can be a "prevailing party" for purposes of 33 U. S. C. §1365(d) if it was the "catalyst" that triggered a favorable outcome. In the decision under review, the Court of Appeals noted that its Circuit precedent construed our decision in *Farrar v. Hobby*, o require rejection of that theory.

Farrar acknowledged that a civil rights plaintiff awarded nominal damages may be a "prevailing party" under 42 U. S. C. § 1988. The case involved no catalytic effect. Recognizing that the issue was not presented for this Court's decision in Farrar, several Courts of Appeals have expressly concluded that Farrar did not repudiate the catalyst theory. Other Courts of Appeals have likewise continued to apply the catalyst theory notwithstanding Farrar.

It would be premature, however, for us to address the continuing validity of the catalyst theory in the context of this case. The District Court, in an order separate from the one in which it imposed civil penalties against Laidlaw, stayed the time for a petition for attorneys' fees until the time for appeal had expired or, if either party appealed, until the appeal was resolved. In the opinion accompanying its order on penalties, the District Court stated only that "this court has considered that Laidlaw will be required to reimburse plaintiffs for a significant amount of legal fees," and referred to "potential fee awards." Thus, when the Court of Appeals addressed the availability of counsel fees in this case, no order was before it either denying or awarding fees. It is for the District Court, not this Court, to address in the first instance any request for reimbursement of costs, including fees.

* * *

For the reasons stated, the judgment of the United States Court of Appeals for the Fourth Circuit is reversed, and the case is remanded for further proceedings consistent with this opinion.

It is so ordered.

Lesson Thirteen

Virtual Civil Litigation: A Visit to John Bunyan's Celestial City

Learning objectives

After learning the text and having done the exercises in this lesson, you will:

—familiarize with knowledge of the legal characteristics and the nature of virtual civil litigation;

—acquire an appreciation of the vocabulary and grammar or syntax relevant to the virtual civil litigation;

—become aware of the information required in order to understand the virtual civil litigation;

—cultivate the practical abilities to put to use the language in the specific context;

—be able to do some translation from Chinese to English and from English to Chinese.

 Text

Virtual Civil Litigation: A Visit to John Bunyan's Celestial City

The law's cost and delay are causes of chronic dissatisfaction with every legal system. The federal Civil Justice Reform Act 1990① recently exhibited our inability to solve these eternal difficulties; it reflected both the ambition of Congress to reduce cost and delay and its authors' lack of a realistic idea how that might be done. We now have the meager results of the initiatives. While some of the innovations in local plans promulgated under the Act yielded modest redemptive benefits, none made serious dent in cost and delay②.

---

① 《1990年联邦民事司法改革法》,本法要求美国所有的94个联邦地区法院执行"降低司法诉讼成本和拖延之计划"以"促进民事案件依据案情谨慎裁决,指导证据开示,促进诉讼管理,确保民事纠纷公正、快速和低成本地解决"。

② to make a dent in sth.:这一短语表示的意思是"减少(特指金钱)的数量"。此句的意思是:根据本法令之规定:各地制定的相关改革措施并未取得预期的回报,没有大幅度地降低诉讼成本,解决案件裁决的拖延。

The institutions of civil litigation are, however, headed for fundamental change caused by the invention of the computer chip①. The digitization of information offers technical solutions to problems that have long defied us. Indeed, technologies deploying digitization undercut many, perhaps most, of the premises of civil procedure as it has been practiced, not merely in America, but everywhere since the beginning of time; The law of unintended consequences decrees that the resolution of current problems will create or reveal new ones; for this reason, unqualified optimism is always inappropriate. But it is now a reasonable hope that radical reform might achieve radical benefits.

It pleases our politicians to speak of the twenty-first century as if it were a different place than the twentieth. For our courts, it just might be. A half century hence, the futility of the Civil Justice Reform Act of 1990 may be recognized as a passage through a Slough of Despond that we pilgrims were doomed to experience on our way to the Celestial City, where *Legality* resides.② This Essay is a speculation on how the Celestial City might appear when at last we leave our present mire and progress to that place.

I Three Centuries of Judicial Law Reform in a Nutshell

To put the effects of digitization in perspective, one might say that in the history of our Republic, there have been perhaps six ideas about civil procedure that matter. First, there was the idea, brought to us in the eighteenth century by the Enlightenment, that cases should be decided on the facts and the law, and not as a consequence of the skill or luck of the parties' representatives in jousting or sumo③, a sport initially devised as a method of dispute resolution, or in a word game such as common law pleading: That idea of the Enlightenment has been notably celebrated by Max Weber.

Second, there was the mid-nineteenth century reform denoted as fact pleading and advanced in this country by David Dudley Field and other Jacksonians who hoped to simplify civil procedure by identifying the factual issues quickly, thereby reducing cost and delay. That reform was soon frustrated by the evasions of lawyers who made fact pleading just another word and an instrument of cost and delay. Despite the information gained from an adversary's pleading, many litigants experienced surprise④ at trial, while others encountered difficulties in getting to trial.

Third, there was the twentieth century extension of the discovery⑤ devices employed in English equity⑥ to investigate and reveal evidence before trial. The movement for that reform was led

---

① Computer chip:计算机芯片。
② 此比喻源自 John Bunyan 1678 年创作的作品:The Pilgrim's Progress From This world to That Which is to Come: Delivered under the Similitude of a Dream wherein is Discovered。"合法"(*Legality*)是 Bunyan 给一个"具有良好品行公正无私的有能力帮助人们解决困难负担的人"取的名字。在 John Bunyan 去寻找"合法"(*Legality*)所在的天堂的路上,他历经了千辛万难。首当其冲的就遇到了许多其他的清教徒深陷失望痛苦的沼泽之地。
③ joust:指(中古骑士的)马上长枪比武。Sumo:相扑运动,日本的一种传统摔跤运动。此句表达的意思是:案件应当按照事实和法律规定予以裁决,而非像这两种源于解决纠纷的运动依赖参与者的技能或运气来决定。
④ surprise:突袭。
⑤ discovery:证据开示。
⑥ equity:衡平法。

by Charles Clark and his associates, who drafted the Federal Rules of Civil Procedure① promulgated in 1938. Their hope was to reduce cost and delay by revealing the proof in advance of trial, thus encouraging early settlements based on better predictability of the outcomes of trials. That reform also underestimated the gamesmanship of lawyers, who found diverse ways to misuse discovery. In 1980, Justice Powell strongly criticized discovery on that account. While his assessment seems overdrawn to me, there is wide-spread dissatisfaction because some lawyers refuse to play by the rules and others overuse the process to impose needless costs on adversaries.

Fourth in sequence came the idea of juridical case management emerging since 1970. The idea has been that judges, by involving themselves in pretrial preparation, can restrain the costly and dilatory gamesmanship. The role of the managerial judge more clearly resembles that of judges on the continent of Europe. Management can entail more work for counsel as well as the judge, and may therefore elevate cost. As Judith Resnik has observed, it often seems that our judges are more occupied in managing lawyers than in managing cases. Like fact pleading and discovery, it works sometimes, but the net benefit is at best modest②.

Two other ideas having ancient origins recur and are put to use from time to time in the hope of reducing cost and delay. One is privatized case management, requiring parties to engage in preliminary mediation or non-binding arbitration. Such court-annexed ADR③ may cause some cases to settle earlier, and the overall settlement rate may increase marginally, while some parties may be better prepared for trial. But these benefits come at the cost of introducing an additional step in the process that can itself cause cost and delay. In addition to the added expense of the lawyer time invested in the additional step, someone has to pay the mediator or arbitrator. Again, savings have been achieved in some case but the net benefit of mandatory mediation is not easily demonstrated.

Finally, there is the other idea—long employed elsewhere—of cost-shifting to deter wasteful litigation. In simple terms, the concept is to apply market economics to litigants, forcing them to take a harder look at their prospects and to back away from causing unnecessary expense they will themselves have to bear if the costs are not justified by the prospective effect on the outcome. The problem with this strategy is that some litigants are more vulnerable to the deterrent effect than others, and therefore operates independently of the merits of their claims or defenses. Nevertheless, this idea, too, has had some positive uses. I have recently proposed that it be used on a limited scale to correct the overuse of discovery.

Another ancient idea now in vogue is an idea not for improving the judicial process, but for avoiding it altogether by employing alternative forums created by contract. Of course, for parties who freely choose arbitration, there may be real savings resulting from their cooperation. That has likely always been true. But a current trend is to compel arbitration by enforcing arbitration clauses

---

① Federal Rules of Civil Procedure：联邦民事诉讼规则。
② but the net benefit is at best modest：在此句中指自 20 世纪 70 年代开始的案件程序管理这一理念实际上产生的效果并不显著。
③ ADR：指的是 Alternative Dispute Resolution，翻译为"替代性纠纷解决方法"，或"任择性纠纷解决方法"。有些国家，如澳大利亚又称为"External Dispute Resolution"。尽管历史上很多当事人及其律师一直抵制反对这种解决纠纷的方法，但近来这种理念获得了大众和法律人士的广泛认同。事实上，有些法庭现在要求当事人双方须先采用某种方法。

in contracts of adhesion that may result in actual increases in cost and delay. Adhesive arbitration clauses are now widely used to diminish the value of any claims individuals might later make against the "repeat player" who drafted them.

Reviewing these alternatives, one cannot be encouraged about the prospect for materially improving our methods of litigating civil cases by any means in use at the end of the twentieth century. So far, digital technologies have been applied to law chiefly by resourceful publishers and private counsel seeking to enhance the effectiveness of their trial advocacy. There is little reason for the public to cheer the results of these applications. Lawyers and judges have easier access to more legal authorities, and triers of fact are sometimes dazzled by multi-media presentations. But there is no evidence that these achievements have resulted in more accurate discernment of fact, more faithful enforcement of law, or the reduction of cost or delay.

Courts have been properly cautious in making use of electronic communications. Not until 1993 was there a right to videotape a deposition for use in a federal court[①]. Occasional use is now made of live testimony transmitted by satellite. A few courts are now experimenting with electronic filing of court papers[②]. There is, however, still no duty of parties to accept service of papers by facsimile transmission or e-mail. Such caution is necessary because judicial systems must accommodate counsel who may not be the most resourceful and must meet expectations of service entrenched in the minds of lawyers and litigants. Also, judicial systems must be administered by judges of mature years who are naturally unreceptive to new technologies and modes of conduct. For these reasons, courts must inevitably be among the last institutions to accommodate new circumstances. Yet there will come a time when the utility of technology is so visible that the natural and proper institutional inertia will have to yield.

II Assumptions Regarding Future Reform

In this thought experiment, I assume no fundamental changes in our legal culture other than those wrought by technology. Thus, I assume that a purpose of our civil procedure will continue to be the enforcement of rights. One can now hear expressions of despair about this Enlightenment vision of the function of courts. It is sometimes assumed that the business of courts is merely dispute resolution, by whatever means may be effective to bring repose; that is the premise of many who are promoting ADR, or of those who favor mass settlements of mass tort claims[③] without regard for the merits of individual claims. I assume that this pre-Enlightenment purpose will not become the norm, and that we will continue to expect courts to decide cases by applying law to fact.

I also assume no fundamental change in the roles of parties and counsel. As noted in Part I, those roles have changed at a glacial pace. The primitive impulse to make law a tournament is still visible in some current practice, and this ludic element of litigation can probably never be alto-

---

① 《联邦民事诉讼规则》第30条b节第2款规定:取证可通过录音、声像或速记等方法记录下来,进行取证的一方应当承担取证记录的所有费用。但于1993年进行的改革未完全包含体现现代记录技术的优势,迄今仍要求有书面材料。
② electronic filing of court papers:指法院文件的电子报送、送达与归档等。
③ mass tort claims:侵权集团诉讼。

Lesson Thirteen Virtual Civil Litigation: A Visit to John Bunyan's Celestial City

gether eliminated. But paeans① to the adversary tradition notwithstanding, good government dictates the need to continue to reduce—insofar as is feasible—the opportunities of advocates to evade the lash of the law on their clients by obstructing civil justice, and that aim will continue to conflict with the impulses of some lawyers to engage in unrestrained combat like knights in armor or sumo champions.

I also assume that our courts will continue to perform political functions, and that we will continue to insist on their sharing the juridical power with he communities in which they sit by means of trial by jury.

I will not pause to consider the manifest political difficulties with the future radical reform of judicial institutions. Any program to reduce cost and delay will threaten entrenched interests, both of those within the legal profession having intellectual, emotional, and professional investments in existing practices, and of those outside the law whose interests are sometimes well-served by cost and delay. There will necessarily be compromises fashioned to protect the rotten boroughs of the law②. I disregard these difficulties to focus on longer term possibilities.

There may also be questions appropriately addressed to social psychologists that I am here neglecting. I have no doubt that the process I am about to depict will appall some, perhaps many, readers; indeed, it rather appalls me, and 1 take comfort that I personally will not be called upon to participate in virtual litigation such as one might expect to find in the Celestial City. But a future generation more accustomed to digitized transmissions may find some such legal process more congenial, and may even damaged that its courts embrace at least some of the changes I forecast.

These assumptions and disclaimers stated, I proceed. But not in what might be described as a chronological order of the stages of virtual litigation. In these matters, the jawbone is ultimately connected to the anklebone, yet the trial is the heart of the process. I therefore first consider how digitization might modify the trial of an issue of fact. I then consider the impact of digitization on the appeal as a means of preventing (and not merely correcting) errors at trial, on preparation for the virtual trial, and finally on territorial jurisdiction. At each stage, the availability of digitization suggests radical transformation. In a world traveling at the speed of light, trial advocacy will more closely resemble the work of the Hollywood film producer and less that of the Hollywood actor. Among the possible implications are the elimination of (1) the distinction between summary judgment and pretrial judgment as a matter of law, (2) the final decision as a precondition to appeal, (3) physical access to the courthouse as a factor in the determination of jurisdiction over the person of the defendant, and (4) the office of local clerk of court. Also in prospect is a reduction in the sweep of the trial judge's discretion. Trials will be shorter and cheaper. Appeals will be quicker and cheaper. Pretrial maneuvering will be less extensive and cheaper. Territorial jurisdiction will be contested less frequently.

---

① paeans:古希腊对太阳神的赞歌;凯歌,欢乐歌,赞美歌。
② "rotten borough"意思是"腐败选区"。这是18世纪英国的一个政治术语,指1832年英国改革法令通过之前,人们发现有些选区腐化之极,即有投票权的人数甚少,却可以选出议会议员的选区。

A. Virtual Trials

The traditional trial is becoming obsolete. My wife and I are now equipped to hold video conferences with our grandchildren in four distant cities. The system is far from perfect, but its perfection is plainly within reach inside a decade or so. The hardware needed for the conduct of virtual litigation is already partly in place and will soon be completely so, at least in the United States. The software is improving rapidly and there appear to be no insurmountable problems to perfecting it without large financial investments by courts or lawyers. What is suggested here will therefore require no substantial expenditure not likely to be made anyway.

Given easy, almost costless, preservation of images in digitized form, and their instantaneous transmission over long distances, there will no longer be sufficient reason to require, expect, or even permit much, if any, evidence to be presented in the form of personal testimony by witnesses in a room in which the judge, jury and counsel are all present. A trial will normally be a movie presentation.

To be sure, there will be something lost in spontaneity and in the interpersonal contact between witnesses and triers of fact, but those costs will be outweighed by the savings in money, time, and convenience attainable by means of digitized communication of testimony. People will not be willing to travel distances at a particular time to await the presence and availability of others when images can be made at almost ally place or time, preserved, and transmitted as and when needed, painlessly, and almost without cost to any place.

Perhaps it will always be desirable to preserve the authority of the court on special occasions to allow a party to appear and testify in a traditional courtroom, or perhaps even to compel a witness to do so. That might be appropriate where two observation witnesses are engaged in a swearing match on a crucial issue in a case involving stakes large enough to warrant the increased cost; on such occasions, demeanor evidence that is conveniently available may arguably be worth the cost. But jurors will always have the opportunity to observe demeanor in file recorded testimony when it is screened. It seems at least possible that what is left out when testimony is observed on the cool screen is the part of demeanor evidence that is positively misleading, for those radiations of the spirit that cause us to be irrationally attracted to a witness or irrationally repelled by him or her may then be less intense. It may actually be harder to lie effectively on a screen than in person.

On the assumption that testimony in the future will be presented electronically, we can see that trial counsel become co-producers of a multi-media presentation. Testimony will be recorded in advance of trial and reviewed by adversary counsel, much as documentary exhibits presently are. All evidentiary issues not resolved by agreement of the parties will be resolved by the court at a pretrial conference. Because all the proof is unalterably recorded before any of it is presented to a trier of fact, every evidentiary issue can be resolved in limine[①]. This will result in a clean visual recording of all the testimony and arguments of counsel to be presented, with no distractions from

---

[①] in limine: (Latin: at the beginning or on the threshold, not an expression in common current use, it means simply preliminary) 拉丁语,日常用语少见,表示"预备的,初步的,起初的"意思。

bickering lawyers. The bickering will have occurred before trial and will have been recorded, but not as part of the trial tape to be seen by the trier of fact. The possibility of surprise at trial will be completely eliminated, and quickness of wit as a professional trait of trial counsel will be much devalued, being displaced by traits valued in television announcers and theater directors.

The pretrial conference will also afford an occasion to consider whether the material supplied by counsel is, as a whole, worthy of consideration by a trier of fact. The question of whether a genuine issue or fact is presented will be raised by a motion for judgment as a matter of law. Granting the motion at this point has the same effect as the "old-fashioned" directed verdict① or summary judgment②. Given that the entire trial can be previewed with complete confidence that nothing can later be added or subtracted, if a party's factual contentions are legally deficient, there is no reason to summon jurors, schedule a trial, and conduct an actual submission of the proof before aborting the proceeding. Thus, summary judgment, directed verdict, and judgment as a matter of law become one, and the ruling can be most efficiently made at the pretrial stage.

Given the opportunity of counsel to edit the evidence, long trials should seldom be required. There will be no interruptions for objections, exceptions, or sidebar conferences③ of any kind. A long movie will be interrupted for bathroom and lunch breaks, but will otherwise run from eight to five. It should in most cases be possible to return to the time when almost all jury trials were conducted in a single day, or at most two. Something like a shot clock④, but hopefully less rigid and mechanical, could be employed to encourage and even require close editing by counsel. Such rulings are not unknown to present practices. Because the value of evidence can be accurately appraised in advance of trial, there is no reason to allow lawyers to use valuable court time with rambling presentations. It will seldom be in the interests of lawyers or their clients to overstay the court's welcome or risk stretching the attention span of jurors.

Given this change in the mode of presenting evidence and the resulting ability of parties to know for certain the contentions of their adversaries, the use of opinion testimony could be reduced. Courts could more readily and more wisely make in limine rulings on the merit and pertinence of scientific or technical proof. This would be so in part because the court would not in every instance be required to speculate on what the experts might say at trial, for judges would know this precisely at the time of the in limine ruling. This reality might in turn be expected to lead to more prudent and effective use of independent, disinterested scientists or technicians to advise the court in determining the utility of opinion testimony.

Closer, better scrutiny of expert opinion evidence⑤ could have another advantage as well. If attorneys know before trial what the expert evidence will look like, they might be more likely to agree on which opinion evidence is worth acquiring and what the nature and compass of that evidence should be. Adversaries would, of course, still need to consult retained experts to assess the

---

① directed verdict:指令裁决,在原告举证不力的情况下,法官指示陪审团所作的有利于被告的裁决。
② summary judgment:简易判决,不经过陪审团听审而作的判决。
③ sidebar conferences:法庭审理过程中,法官将双方当事人的律师叫到审判席前小声讨论某些事件的情况。
④ a shot clock:时限钟,秒钟装置,进攻时间钟,秒计时器。
⑤ expert opinion evidence:专家证人证据。

likelihood that scientific or technical evidence could be presented that might be useful to the client and persuasive to the trier of fact. Closer pretrial scrutiny of opinion evidence① ought to reduce the incentives for parties to align a series of carefully prepared experts presenting divergent and equally unpersuasive opinions, an impulse too often turning the contemporary trial into the spectacle of a barking seal contest.

It also seems likely that, in some cases, the competing experts might be wisely replaced by the single disinterested witness appointed by the court pursuant to Evidence Rule 706. Such disinterested testimony would be more readily available because the experts would never need to leave their offices or laboratories to testify, and their consultations could be scheduled to fit their reasonable convenience. Use of such disinterested testimony in lieu of a battle of experts could abbreviate and reduce the cost of many trials.

Once the digitized trial has been produced by counsel and all issues between them resolved by the court in limine, the court in a case to be tried by jury would prepare a charge to the jury that would be presented in both written and video form. Opening and closing arguments would also be recorded in video form, diminishing somewhat the influence of the theatrical flamboyance of counsel. The trial would then be a screening of the complete and edited tape for the jury. There would be no particular reason for a judge to be present during that screening. A judge would be needed to preside over the selection of jurors -and event that would likely occur in the courtroom on the eve of trial—and to provide an appropriate ceremony at the start and end of the trial, but it would not need to be the same judge for all the events. Counsel and the parties would likely wish to be present (at least virtually present), if for no other reason than to observe the jurors as the jurors observed the screening of the proof and returned their verdict.

Because few trials would extend over more than two days, jury service would be much less onerous, making it possible for more citizens to participate. Such trials would also be less burdensome to the public fisc②. It is not difficult to imagine that the jurors could remain at their home or workplace and become a virtual jury. As Boris Bittker bas suggested, "panels of couch potatoes"③ could quickly announce their verdicts "on everyone's electronic bulletin board." But if trials are to be as brief as I suggest, this would seem to be unnecessary as well as impolitic and imprudent. A virtual jury would not provide the same satisfaction to litigants that live jurors do, at least to those who seek emotional gratification from the resolution of the dispute. Moreover, the deliberation of the jury would be seriously impeded by the absence of social contact. By retaining the public rendering of a verdict, the virtual trial retains some elements of drama and the involvement of real people. Therefore, the courtroom of the future might do without a witness box or a bench, but it would need a live audience in front of the screen.

The virtual non-jury trial would, of course, closely resemble the virtual jury trial. But the formal screening of the prepared tape might almost as efficiently be seen by a judge other than the

---

① opinion evidence：意见证据。
② fisc：本意指"古罗马的皇室财库，国库，王室的财库"，此处与public一起表示"公共，人们大众"的意思。
③ couch potatoes：成天看电视的人，电视迷；闲人，懒散的人，终日懒散在家的人。

one who ruled on the pretrial issues. This change of judges would avoid any prejudice that might have been aroused by the pretrial bickering and the judge's familiarity with evidence that was excluded. In lieu of the recorded instructions to the jury and closing arguments, counsel would prepare proposed findings and conclusions.

Whether before a jury or judge, the virtual trial will not only be shorter, but it will greatly facilitate firm scheduling. The precise length of each trial will be known long in advance. And because of the limited function of the presiding judge, the trial will not materially interfere with the scheduling of other necessary conferences with judges. Greatly reduced, if not almost eliminated, will be the time lost by lawyers and witnesses waiting around the courthouse for their turn to be heard.

B. Virtual Review

The digitized trial lends itself to expeditious review. Roscoe Pound long ago proposed that post-trial motions be consolidated with the first level appeal, thereby eliminating a redundant stage in the process. Digital technology allows us to go Pound one better. If there is to be a jury trial, it would be most efficient to conduct the appeal before the jury is summoned. Because almost all the court's rulings will have been made in limine, interlocutory review of the pretrial rulings would be feasible and more efficient.

Pound envisioned that the post-trial review would be conducted by a panel of three lower court judges specialized in the conduct of trials. That panel as he envisioned it would review the record of the trial and order a new trial if that seemed warranted for any reason, including the ground that the verdict was against the weight of the evidence. In the exercise of that power, the panel might reduce an excessive verdict. Pound's panel would also enter judgment as a matter of law if that was warranted by the record. These actions having been taken by three judges rather than one, Pound thought further review of determinations of facts would be unnecessary and unworthy of the expense. Further review would be permitted only at the discretion of the court of last resort[①], which would be the only high court in his system.

With digitized records of the pretrial conference and trial, Pound's vision becomes even more efficient. The review panel can with relative ease achieve the same familiarity with the case as that possessed by the judge who made the pretrial rulings. There is little reason to confer the large discretionary powers of the trial judge on a single individual, with the added hazards of human failings that such confidence entails. The jury could be deployed only after the trial tape had been cleansed of error by the court of usual last resort consisting not of one, but of three judges.

A useful feature of the traditional appeal is that it is heard by judges who are remote from the trial judge. This reduces the possibility of mutual deference among peers, which could be expected to occur if the appellate jurisdiction were regularly conferred on three judges chambered in the same building as the trial judge or otherwise sharing common duties. But digitization eliminates any need for that. The virtual review panel could consist of any three judges in the state or in the federal judicial systems. They could be randomly selected and could perform their duties from

---

① the court of last resort: 终审法院。

chambers in three widely separated courthouses.

The only issues concerning the trial that could be raised after a verdict would be possible jury misconduct—a very rare event—or excessive damages. Perhaps even the latter issue might be resolved at a preliminary stage, as will be suggested below.

One advantage in reviewing the pretrial rulings before the jury trial is that it would eliminate many trials. The mistrial① would be eliminated entirely, as would those trials conducted for the purpose of delay. A second advantage is that the jury trail would become a climactic event in which the citizen-jurors were almost always given the final word, thus giving new meaning in federal courts to the final clause of the Seventh Amendment.

The problem of arguably excessive verdicts is not solved, but is made more prominent, by digitization. Because other traditional grounds for a new trial will have been resolved before the trial is conducted, the need to consider that issue on appeal becomes especially bothersome. There is another way to address the problem of extreme verdicts, and the other reforms suggested by digitization provide an occasion to consider it. In keeping with the aim to make the publicly announced verdict terminal, the parties might be required to bargain over limits on verdicts that assess unliquidated damages②. A variation on a technique used in summary jury practice conducted pursuant to agreement of the parties might be adapted for general use. That device requires adversaries to predict the award for unliquidated compensation or the punitive award with the understanding that the prediction closest to the number selected by the jury will be the one on which the judgment will be entered. This effectively forecloses outlying verdicts and forces the awards for unliquidated sums into reckonable bounds. It is superior to the motion for new trial or for remittitur③ because it leaves the parties in control of their own fates and eliminates the need for any judge to guess at the proper amount.

If no jury were demanded, a single judge could conduct the public event at which the trial tape was screened, but there would be no reason to rely upon that individual to make findings of fact given the deference presently required by the clear error rule④. The judicial findings could as well be made in the first instance by a panel of three judges, perhaps including one member of the appellate court. All three non-jury-trial panelists might then receive from counsel proposed findings of fact and trial briefs and hear virtual oral argument. They might normally be expected to decide the case from their virtual bench, deliberating openly and rendering their decisions seriatim, in the traditional English manner. If two of the three review panelists regarded the legal questions as doubtful; they could say so and certify the questions to the appropriate higher court. But review by a higher court would otherwise be discretionary to that court and limited to review for errors embedded in the conclusions of law employed by the review panel.

---

① mistrial:失审或流审,指陪审团达不成一致意见,无法作出裁决的一种情况。该词常被人翻译成"误审"。
② unliquidated damages: 未经算定损害赔偿,未清算的损失,未确定的损害赔偿额。
③ Remittitur:减少损害赔偿金(指法官减少或建议减少陪审团裁定中的损害赔偿金),源自法语。
④ clear error rule:于上级法院而言,一审法院法官判决/裁决中的明显错误无规则。

This practice of seriatim opinions① would yield few decisions of a court purporting to serve as precedent authority; It would thus reduce the load of "infoglut"② burdening the practice of law in the United States. Because three judges would participate in the findings, the role of the appellate court would, as Pound saw, be substantially reduced. In the federal system, or the larger states, there would still be an intermediate appellate function③ to perform, but it would be needed in a minor fraction of the cases now heard at the appellate level. The number of courts and judges engaged in performing that function could surely be reduced. On the other hand, to secure stability and "reckonability" in the law made through their interpretative work, it would be useful, as well as feasible, to eliminate the practice of sitting in small panels. A court publishing an opinion of the court ought perhaps to consist of at least seven members. Thus, the role and responsibility of the individual member of the appellate judiciary, like that of the judge and counsel at trial, would be diminished.

C. Preparation and Production of the Virtual Trial

The virtual trial also makes it possible to place increased responsibility on the parties and counsel to conduct the preparation and production of the trial record. Competent counsel will have less need of a judge before trial to manage their cases.

Attorney case management can be done efficiently in stages. The plaintiff might be allowed a period of discovery in which to assemble her case. The defendant could await a preliminary presentation of the plaintiff's case before commencing preparation of the defense. Viewing the plaintiff's proposed presentation in the privacy and convenience of his office, defense counsel④ could notify plaintiff of any objections made to the evidence proffered. If persuaded, the plaintiff might voluntarily delete objectionable material. Other objections might be marked for later resolution by the court. Or, in appropriate circumstances, the court might entertain an early motion for judgment as a matter of law.

Assuming no such motion were granted, it would then be the defendant's turn to conduct discovery. The plaintiff's counsel could view the defendant's preliminary presentation of the defense and record objections, perhaps resulting in the withdrawal of some of the defense material, with remaining objections to be marked for resolution by the court. The plaintiff might also move for judgment as a matter of law, or might renew her discovery efforts to record additional material rebutting that offered by the defense. The defense might then again review the material and respond to the rebuttal. The plaintiff might then be given the last word, with the possibilities of another round if authorized by the court upon a showing of reasonable need.

In many cases, this staging of the trial preparation might result in very substantial savings of costs. The defendant would need to defend only against the case actually made by the plaintiff and not against all the claims that might be imagined to appear in an unpredictable real trial. The

---

① seriatim opinions: 分别陈述的意见(指合议庭审理案件后法官分别陈述己见,而非以合议庭集体的名义陈述一个意见)。
② Infoglut: 资讯超载,复合词,由 information 和 glut 构成。
③ intermediate appellate function: 中级上诉的职能。
④ defense counsel: 被告律师,也称为 defense attorney。

plaintiff would likewise be freed of any need to anticipate defenses and gather evidence to refute those that were never effectively asserted in the form of credible proof.

The interrogation of witnesses for a virtual trial could be managed with incomparably greater efficiency. They would be interrogated under oath by video conference, at a time and place convenient to the witness, generally at the witness's home or workplace. The interrogator could be thousands of miles away. The only person possibly needed to be present would be the designated officer of the court administering an oath① and recording the testimony. And even that person could be elsewhere if counsel agreed. The videotaped record of the testimony would itself be the material used at trial. There would be no rehearsal deposition.

Moreover, because of the reduced inconvenience, the interrogation of a witness could be conducted discontinuously. Thus, a defendant might elect to wait until he had seen the plaintiff's tentative presentation at trial before beginning to erect a defense by conducting cross-examinations that might be used in the defense's presentation. A re-direct examination② might then follow later, when it was again the adversary's turn to rebuild her case: This discontinuity is feasible because neither the witness nor counsel would need to leave their offices to reopen an interrogation. The earlier testimony of the witness would be readily available for review by the witness as well as by counsel. Discontinuity thus allows all counsel to be better prepared, making the examination of witnesses more effective and more efficient. Furthermore, inconsequential witness examinations could be deleted from the tape presented at trial, so that there was no useless testimony consuming the time of the trier of fact. Counsel would co-produce the trial tape, assembling sequentially that part of the testimony of each witness that either counsel wished to have presented at trial.

The elimination of the rehearsal deposition suggests a reason to enlarge somewhat the duties of counsel to disclose material such as adopted and recorded statements of witnesses. A statement to a lawyer that is recorded or made in writing and signed may, under present law, be viewed as protected trial preparation material. But such material is non-replicable, and the interest of protecting work product by withholding shared access to that kind of material is outweighed by the efficiency gained in sharing such statements.

Because digitization makes retrieval so easy, parties could have full access to statements made by their adversaries in earlier, similar litigation in order to discover possible evidence, especially prior inconsistent statements. All examinations of witnesses and examined documents would be filed with the court in digitized form. The problem of storage disappears because all the testimony given in all cases in the United States in a year could be stored in a single computer occupying very little space. A national index of testimony by any citizen in any court could be maintained so that material could be retrieved with modest effort by counsel. The functions of the local clerk of court would thus be substantially reduced, for if all records of all proceedings can be kept in a single digitized file comprehending all actions in the system, there is no need for autonomous local filings and records.

---

① administer an oath：监视。

② re-direct examination：再直诘，指对方当事人在对己方证人询问后进行的直接询问，有时用 reexamination 表示。

Lesson Thirteen Virtual Civil Litigation: A Visit to John Bunyan's Celestial City

To make this system fully effective and to avoid the taking of useless testimony, parties who are employers would also be obliged to make their employees available for preliminary interviews by adversary counsel. An employee causing a fruitless formal examination by refusing an informal preliminary interview would be liable, and would expose his employer to liability, for the resulting economic waste.

Document searches are today a major cost in big cases. That cost cannot be eliminated, but it will be reduced as categories of documents are produced in digitized form facilitating word searches. By that means, the proverbial needle in the haystack① will often be executed as if by a magnet, by a secretary rather than a paralegal②, and in minutes or hours rather than weeks or months. It will be more difficult to hide a "smoking gun."

Finally, counsel would be obliged to participate in a continuing discourse with one another regarding the pretrial investigation of facts at issue. This duty, would be performed digitally (e.g., by email) and recorded. This electronic conversation (or is it a bulletin board or a chat room?) would contain or replace formal notices and requests, interrogatories, answers to interrogatories, and case management conferences with the judge. Because the communications would be part of the record in the case, there would be meager opportunity to engage in off-the-record incivilities. As now, timely responses to any questions or requests for information would be required, and either party or counsel could at any time seek sanctions against others for causing unjustified cost or delay. The record on which such a motion rests would be readily available at the movement of a switch in the judge's chambers, but case management could otherwise be conducted by counsel rather than by the court.

A similar form of communication would generally replace the service of a summons as the means of initiating litigation. Every government or public agency—federal, state, or local—and ever), corporation engaged in commerce or owning property would be required to register its electronic address for the receipt of service of process. Individuals would remain free to register such address or not, but if they failed to do so, they would be required to bear the cost of service and, if they were familiar with litigation, would be liable for a penalty for delay.

CONCLUSION

I cannot estimate the dimensions of the savings to be achieved by means of virtual litigation, but they might be substantial. One can say with confidence that the benefits would fall directly to those plaintiff and defendants having the most meritorious claims and defenses. Those asserting hopeless claims or defenses would be diminished in their ability to impose burdens on their adversaries.

The secondary consequences of a dramatic reduction in cost and delay are not easily visualized. One must assume that such reductions would lower the threshold of restraint and result in increased filings. To those presently preoccupied with the alleged litigation explosion, this may be

---

① needle in the haystack: 就像在草堆里找一根针, 如同在稻草堆里找一根针, 大海捞针。
② paralegal: 辅助律师业务的人, 律师的专职助手, 律师助理, 律师专职助手。

the ultimate horror.

On the other hand, properly deployed, digitization promises to revitalize our appreciation of litigation as an exercise of individual rights and a means of private law enforcement. One might also suppose that the facilitation of discovery will result in closer observation of the law by those with duties whose defaults will be more exposed to public light. Ours will indeed be a city wherein Legality resides.

Although more interesting and gratifying for jurors, virtual civil litigation will be relatively undramatic and impersonal for the parties. It will suppress the importance of individual judges and trial counsel, but will elevate the importance of the professional craft of organizing the presentation at trial. Those who value litigation as entertainment and as a means of venting spleen will be less gratified. But virtual litigation will be more civil, more predictable, more in control of the parties and their lawyer, and more likely to result in the application of law to fact.

Virtual litigation is not yet on our doorstep. Neither the profession, nor the courts, nor the litigants—certainly not this author—are ready for it, nor can they be made ready soon. Nevertheless, the prospective benefits appear to be so substantial, and the process so much in step with the rest of social life in the information age, that some of what bas been described here will happen in due course. Meanwhile, those who make rules and laws today may make themselves more useful if they have in mind a sense of the direction of change such as I have tried to supply.

Legal Terminology

1. discovery

披露；证据开示（程序）。这是民事诉讼中的一种审前程序，一方当事人可以通过该程序从对方当事人处获得与案件有关的事实与信息，以助于准备庭审。根据美国《联邦民事诉讼规则》(Federal Rules of Civil Procedure)的规定，要求披露的方式有：书面证词(deposition)、书面质询(written interrogatories)、请求承认(requests for admissions)、请求出示文件(requests for production)等。在英国，任何一方当事人经法庭许可并预交诉讼费用保证金后，可以书面质询的方式要求对方披露有关事实和文件，对方应经宣誓后作出回答，其回答的内容在庭审时可作为证据使用。刑事诉讼中的披露程序侧重于强调辩护方有权获得对其辩护所必要的证据，如美国《联邦刑事诉讼规则》(Federal Rules of Criminal Procedure)规定，被告人可以通过披露程序获得其所作的书面或被记录下来的陈述或有罪供认、检查与测试的结果、在大陪审团面前所作的证词、控诉方的专家证人的证词，并有权查阅控方的文件、照片、证物等。

2. the adversary system

对抗制，抗辩制，辩论式的诉讼制度，为英美法上的诉讼制度。在这种诉讼程序中，奉行当事人主义，强调双方当事人的对抗性，当事人有很大的主动性，且基本不受阻碍，通过双方当事人及其律师询问和交叉询问证人，相互争辩，来推进诉讼进程，揭示案件真相。法官作为中立的裁判者，听取双方的陈述和辩论，而不是积极介入。与之相对的是大陆法系国家采用的纠问式或审问式诉讼制度(the inquisitorial system)。

3. summary judgment

简易程序判决,指当当事人对案件中的主要事实(material facts)不存在真正的争议(genuine issue)或案件仅涉及法律问题时,法院不经开庭审理而及早解决案件的一种方式。根据美国《联邦民事诉讼规则》,在诉讼开始 20 天后,如果经诉答程序(pleadings)、披露(discovery)以及任何宣誓书(affidavit)表明当事人对案件的主要事实不存在真正的争议,认为自己在法律上应当胜诉的一方当事人可随时申请法庭作出简易判决。简易判决可就全部案件也可就案件中的部分事实作出。英国《最高法院规则》第 14 条规定:在由宣誓书(affidavit)支持的传票(summons)签发后,该宣誓书证实了原告诉因的真实性并说明被告不会作答辩或提不出有争论性(arguable)的答辩,原告可向法院申请不经过开庭审理而对案件作出判决。原告的申请应在其起诉状(statement of claim)送达并且被告接受了送达(acknowledgment of service)、声明出庭应诉之后提出,但是对书面诽谤(libel)、口头诽谤(slander)、恶意控告(malicious prosecution)、欺诈所提起的诉讼、海事对物诉讼(admiralty action in rem)或对国家提起的诉讼(claim against the Crown)不得申请简易判决。在郡法院进行的诉讼中也有类似的程序。也称为 summary disposition; judgment on the pleadings。

4. verdict

(陪审团)裁断。陪审团就提交其审理的事项所作的正式裁决。通常可分为概括裁断(general verdict),即确定原告胜诉还是被告胜诉(民事案件中)或被告人有罪还是无罪(刑事案件中)的裁断;和特别裁断(special verdict),即陪审团进对案件中的特定事项作出裁决,而将对该事实适用法律的问题留给法官解决。在英国,根据 1974 年《陪审团法》(Juries Act),民事案件中的陪审团裁断必须是一致裁断(unanimous verdict),除非当事人双方同意接受多数裁断(majority verdict);刑事案件中在某些情况下,法庭可以接受多数裁断。在苏格兰,民事诉讼中的裁断可以是一般裁断或特别裁断,且接受多数裁断;刑事诉讼中的裁断则包括有罪裁断(guilty)、罪证不足的裁断(not proven)和无罪裁断(not guilty),其中后两者都具有宣告无罪的效力。在美国,传统上要求陪审团裁断须是一致裁断,但现在已有改变。在刑事案件中,若所涉罪行轻微,有些州允许陪审团作出多数裁断;在民事案件中,许多州已放弃了对一致性的要求,允许作出 12 人陪审团中有 10 人同意的裁断,联邦法院则允许当事人约定将一定多数陪审员同意的裁断作为陪审团的裁断。

5. opinion evidence

意见证据,指证人就争议问题陈述的自己的观点、看法或推论,区别于证人就自己所了解的案件事实而做的客观性陈述。证据规则通常不允许普通证人以其对案件事实的意见或推论作证,但是有例外,如因具有相应的科学技术或其他专业知识而具备专家资格的专家证人(expert witness)的意见可以作为证据采信;普通证人的意见证词一般只有在符合法律规定的少数例外情况下才可予以采信,如美国《联邦证据规则》(Federal Rules of Evidence)规定,对普通证人以意见或推论形式作出的证词只有在符合:(1)合理建立在证人的感觉之上,和(2)对清楚理解该证人的证词或确定争议中的事实有益时,才可被采纳。相关的术语有:expert opinion evidence 专家意见证据。expert testimony 专家证言,指专家提供的意见证据。在法律上,如果科学、技术或其他专业知识能够帮助陪审团理解证据或确定争议事实,那么,在知识、技能、经验或教育等方面具有专家资格的证人可以用意见或其他方式作证。expert witness 专家证人,指具有专家资格,并被允许帮助陪审团理解某些普通人难以理解的复杂的专业性问题的证人。expert evidence 专家证据,指具有专门知识或技能的人,如医生、药物学家、建筑师、指纹专家等,依其知识或技能对案件中的有关问题提供的意见证据。专家不一定是该专业方面的权威,但在该专业方面必须具备一定的经验和资格。在只有专家意见才能帮助法官或陪审团解决争议问题的情况下,专家意见是可以被采纳为证据的。

6. cross-examination

交叉询问;反询问 指在听审或开庭审理程序中,一方当事人对对方提供的证人进行的询问。反询问应在提供证人的本方对该证人进行主询问(examination-in-chief)之后进行,目的在于核查证人的证言或质疑证人或其证言的可信性,如指出证言与证人先前所作证言中的矛盾之处,向证人提出疑问,诱使证人承认某些事实以削弱证言的可信性等。在交叉询问中允许提诱导性问题(leading question),但通常只能限于主询问中涉及的事项以及证人的可信性问题。

7. forum non conveniens

(拉丁语)不方便法院,如法院认为案件由另一法院审理对双方当事人更为方便且更能达到公正的目的,可不予受理。法院在作出这项决定时,必须综合考虑:取得证据的方便程度、减少证人到庭的困难和费用、勘验现场的可行性以及其他各种使审判方便、快捷、节约的实际问题。此外,要有至少两个法院对案件有管辖权,即原告可任择其一起诉时,法院才能行使这项裁量权。类似的术语有 forum conveniens:适于审理案件的地点,指考虑到双方当事人和公众的最大利益,最适于审理案件的地点。change of venue:审判地的变更,指将在一地已经开始的案件移至另一地审判,也指在同一地域内将案件从一个法院移至另一法院审判。

Exercises

I Verbal Abilities

Part One

Directions: *For each of these completing questions, read each item carefully to get the sense of it. Then, in the proper space, complete each statement by supplying the missing word or phrase.*

1. A long-arm statute is codified law that permits state or federal courts to exercise personal _____ over nonresident defendants.

    A. forum   B. right   C. interference

    D. jurisdiction   E. judgment

2. Service in the courts of the United States and of the States shall be made upon an agency or instrumentality of a foreign state as directed by order of the court _____ with the law of the place where service is to be made.

    A. compromise   B. related   C. against

    D. reliance   E. consistent

3. _____ is a pleading in a lawsuit that objects to or challenges a pleading filed by an opposing party.

    A. dismissing   B. demurrer   C. deviating

Lesson Thirteen Virtual Civil Litigation: A Visit to John Bunyan's Celestial City

D. disputing E. dissenting

4. The first thing that must be done for a jury-trial is to _____ a jury. This is done by means of the voir dire prior to the actual trial on the issues.

A. impanel B. form C. organize
D. choose E. select

5. Pleadings are the documents filed with the court by plaintiff and defendant that detail the facts _____, and possible defenses to the action.

A. claims B. legal resources C. charges
D. evidence E. prosecutions

6. _____ is essential to litigation to clarify the issues in dispute and to identify facts and evidence to assist the Court to determine the appropriate outcome.

A. debating B. evidence C. interrogation
D. discovery E. argument

7. The action commences with the filing of a complaint (also called a petition or a declaration) by the plaintiff that states the _____ wrongdoing of the defendant.

A. charged B. prosecuted C. ostensible
D. alleged E. convicted

8. Federal Rule 403 allows relevant evidence to be _____ "if its probative value is substantially outweighed by the danger of unfair prejudice", if it leads to confusion of the issues, if it is misleading or if it is a waste of time.

A. considered B. included C. admitted
D. granted E. excluded

9. Besides damages, alternative civil _____ include restitution or transfer of property, or an injunction to restrain or order certain actions.

A. restoration B. remedies C. compensation
D. panacea E. judgment

10. It is generally accepted that the desirability of fact-finding arrangements in the legal _____ cannot be measured solely in terms of their capacity to generate accurate outcomes.

A. action B. proceeding C. process
D. procession E. practices

Part Two

Directions: *Choose the one word or phase that best keep the meaning of the original sentence if it was substituted for the underlined part.*

1. <u>Interrogatories</u> are a series of written questions for which written responses are then prepared and signed under oath.

A. Debriefs B. Interviews C. Grills
D. Askings E. Examinations

2. The growth in use of computers and contracting via the Internet creates an added <u>dimension</u> to the questions of personal jurisdiction.

A. aspect	B. scale	C. significance
D. decision	E. difficulty

3. The adversarial system is the two-sided structure under which criminal trial courts operate that pits the prosecution against the defense.

A. resist	B. beat	C. contest
D. cushion	E. protect

4. In some jurisdictions the litigant in person is restricted from cross-examining the alleged victim in rape and other serious sexual offences.

A. sins	B. insults	C. wrongs
D. transgressions	E. crimes

5. For the most part, discovery takes place outside the courtroom, with parties exchanging written information and sitting through face-to-face questioning sessions (called "depositions").

A. seasons	B. periods	C. forums
D. plenary	E. symposiums

6. A "motion to dismiss" asks the court to decide that a claim, even if true as stated, is not one for which the law offers a legal remedy.

A. movement	B. motive	C. motivation
D. proposal	E. gesture

7. A party that fails to comply with an injunction faces criminal or civil penalties and may have to pay damages or accept sanctions.

A. warrants	B. sanatives	C. punishments
D. restriction	E. discipline

8. The defendant can file an answer in response to plaintiff's complaint denying some or all of the allegations set forth in the complaint and setting forth affirmative defenses.

A. presented	B. started	C. set out
D. laid down	E. brought forth

9. Depositions function as mini-trials and are the most expensive and perhaps most useful of the discovery devices.

A. regard as	B. serve as	C. is like
D. equal to	E. enforce as

10. In every jurisdiction based on the English common law tradition, evidence must conform to a number of rules and restrictions to be admissible.

A. comply with	B. confront to	C. accord to
D. respond to	E. adjust to

II Blank Filling

Directions: *Choose the appropriate word to fill in each of the blanks from the provided words. Change the forms if necessary.*

purpose	interact	subject	due	proprietor
remote	infringe	border	principle	hale
Internet	contact	assert	change	national

Personal jurisdiction in Internet cases refers to a growing set of judicial precedents in American courts where personal jurisdiction has been __(1)__ upon defendants based solely on their Internet activities. Personal jurisdiction in American civil procedure is premised on the notion that a defendant should not be __(2)__ to the decisions of a foreign or out of state court, without having "__(3)__ availed" himself of the benefits that the forum state has to offer. Generally, the doctrine is grounded on two main __(4)__: courts should protect defendants from the __(5)__ burden of facing litigation in an unlimited number of possibly __(6)__ jurisdictions (in line with the Due Process requirements of the U. S. Constitution), and courts should prevent states from __(7)__ on the sovereignty of other states by limiting the circumstances under which defendants can be "__(8)__" into court.

In the __(9)__ context, personal jurisdiction cases often involve __(10)__ of websites or Internet-based services that either advertise or actively promote their businesses __(11)__, but argue that they do not have sufficient __(12)__ within a particular state to subject them to litigation in that state. With the growth of the Internet, courts have faced the challenge of applying long-standing principles of personal jurisdiction to a __(13)__ communication medium that enables businesses and individuals all over the world to instantaneously __(14)__ across state boundaries. This is a rapidly __(15)__ area of law without a U. S. Supreme Court precedent. There is however, a growing consensus among Federal District Courts as to how to determine when personal jurisdiction may be asserted in an Internet context.

III Reading Comprehension

Part One

Directions: *In this section there are passages followed by questions or unfinished statements, each with suggested answers. Choose the one you think is the best answer.*

Much of the law on the limits of territorial jurisdiction was formed around considerations of physical access to the courthouse. The virtual courthouse is equally accessible everywhere.

Thus, the doctrine of forum non conveniences becomes obsolete. Perhaps Judge Oakes was premature twenty years ago when he proclaimed it to be so as a consequence of the relative ease and safety of transport. But parties will soon be able to participate in litigation in Fairbanks, Alaska, without leaving their offices in Durham, North Carolina. To the extent that convenience of access is a consideration in applying a due process standard to limit "long arm" jurisdiction, that factor is almost eliminated. The right of the defendant conveniently to attend the screening event of trial can be readily observed by digitizing and transmitting it to the defendant anywhere.

Considerations of sovereignty would abide. The fact that a courthouse is conveniently accessible to everyone on the planet does not entitle it to rule the world. Moreover, if physical access and convenience are no longer factors, there is less reason to respect the plaintiff's choice of forum. A plaintiff choosing a forum in a jurisdiction other than the one whose law governs the issues in dispute lacks a justification for his or her choice. Accordingly, the principle of due process limiting the territorial jurisdiction of courts merges with the constitutional limits on the territorial reach of legislation. Courts should have jurisdiction to enforce their own laws if applicable, and should be presumptively disabled from taking jurisdiction to enforce the law of a foreign sovereign. In other words, choice of law would become the issue of judicial jurisdiction, and the conflict of laws disappears as a separate topic.

There would remain a problem with respect to the plaintiff's right to choose among the courts of the jurisdiction whose law is applicable to the events. There is no reason to allow the plaintiff to forum shop among such courts for sympathy or influence. An appropriate response to this problem might be to select the judge presiding over the virtual trial preparation from among the whole roster of judges available in the system, much as might be done to assemble a virtual review panel. This would effectively forestall shopping for that judge. This suggests that the local court as an administrative unit managing judicial personnel is as obsolete as its clerk's office or as the doctrine of forum non convenience.

It might even be proposed that the federal judiciary implement the idea advanced by the American Bar Association in 1909 that there be only one court in each system, sitting throughout the jurisdiction and containing its own internal forums for correcting error. But the jury and the judges presiding over the selection of the jury or sitting without a jury need to have reasonable access to the courthouse at which the screenings will be conducted. This indicates a continuing need for some local administration.

Even if judge-shopping were eliminated, digitization suggests no answer for jury-shopping. These considerations suggest the need for more tightly drafted venue requirements designating a place of trial for every kind of case, leaving the plaintiff little room for shopping. Proximity to events in dispute would seem to be the most suitable basis on which to legislate such requirements.

1. What would be the best title for this passage based on the structure of the text?

   A. Virtual Jurisdiction

   B. Virtual Forum

   C. Virtual Situs

   D. Virtual Court

2. What would be the benefit for the plaintiff and defendant if virtual civil litigation were applied with respective to the jurisdiction?

   A. They would not take the trouble in travailing to meet the requirement of jurisdiction.

   B. They could choose the law as they like if it is applicable.

   C. They could save time in choosing the court.

D. Both A and C.

3. Which would be more important if virtual litigation were applied?

A. the courthouse selected by the parties

B. the presiding judge

C. the law governs the issue

D. the jury

4. Why should jury-shopping be kept even digitization is applied?

A. Because the jury cannot make the fundamental decision.

B. Because the jury must be kept for the purpose of justification.

C. Because the plaintiff may have more room to select the court without the jury.

D. Because digitization could not provide a better solution to get rid of jury.

5. According to the passage, if digitization were realized, it could be a prospect EXCEPT.

A. sovereignty would not be in the consideration of the judge when they make the the decision.

B. "Long arm" would become longer in dealing with personal jurisdiction over a particular defendant.

C. there would be only one court in each system, together with some local administrative units.

D. conflict of law would not be in the consideration of the judge.

Part Two True or False Questions

Direction: *In this part of the exercise, there is a passage with ten true or false questions. Read the passage carefully and mark T if it is true and F if it is false.*

Limits on What can be Discovered

Virtually any bit of information that might have even a slight connection to the lawsuit is fair game for discovery. But this enormous latitude sometimes leads to abuse. Lawyers might try to pry into subjects that have no legitimate significance for the lawsuit, or that are private and confidential, serving only to annoy or embarrass the parties. Fortunately, there are some legal limits on this kind of probing, and some protections to keep private material from being disclosed to the public.

Confidential conversations. Conversations between people engaged in certain relationships are given a special legal protection known as privilege. Courts and legislatures have decided that the free flow of confidential information in these relationships is so important that it must be protected, even though that information might be important to others in a lawsuit. Under the law, no one can be required to disclose any information, whether verbal or written, that was confidentially exchanged within the following relationships:

- husband and wife
- lawyer and client
- doctor and patient, and
- religious advisor and advisee (although this privilege is often referred to as "priest-peni-

tent," it applies more generally to any confidential conversation between a member of the clergy of a recognized religion and a person seeking spiritual counsel).

Private matters. In recent years, courts have increasingly recognized that some aspects of personal life should remain private, beyond the reach even of lawyers. But the right to privacy is a fairly recent and still-developing legal notion. As a result, there is no clear definition of precisely what it covers—and the extent of its protection varies considerably from state to state. Roughly, the right to privacy protects a person from having to divulge information that is not obviously relevant to the lawsuit and is a matter that a person would not normally discuss or reveal to anyone outside of immediate family and intimate friends. This might include issues such as:

- health or body issues
- sexuality, sexual practices, or sexual partners
- spiritual or religious beliefs, and
- immediate family relationships.

Privacy rights of third parties. Courts are more willing to protect the privacy of third parties—for example, witnesses, co-workers, or family members of a party—than the privacy of parties to a lawsuit. Courts often put limits on how much a party can find out about someone who isn't involved in a lawsuit, reasoning that it isn't fair to invade the privacy of someone who was dragged into a dispute.

Keeping discovery information from the public. Even if a party is required to disclose certain information to the other side in a lawsuit, that information can be treated confidentially by the court—that is, the party who receives it can be prevented from revealing it to anyone else, and the court can keep it out of the public record. This might be done to protect, for example, sensitive financial information, confidential information belonging to a business, or personal medication information that is relevant to the lawsuit. For this to happen, a judge must usually order that information be kept confidential, in what's often called a "protective order."

Discovery Procedures

There are four types of formal discovery tools that are frequently used in lawsuits. They are:

- **Depositions.** In a deposition, one party or that party's lawyer conducts face-to-face questioning of the other party or a witness to the dispute. The person being questioned (the "deponent") must answer under oath, and the answers are recorded for later use at trial. If the deponent cannot testify at trial, the questions and answers might be read to the jury as evidence. If the deponent does testify and gives different answers at trial from those he gave during the deposition, the questions and answers can be used to show the jury that the witness changed his story.

- **Requests for production of evidence.** In a request for production of evidence, one party asks the other for physical evidence related to the dispute. Requests for production are usually used to gather pertinent documents, such as contracts, employment files, billing records, or documents related to real estate. However, these requests can also be used to inspect physical objects or property—for example, in a dispute about whether a contractor properly repaired a homeowner's roof, the contractor's lawyer might ask to have a roofing expert inspect the work.

- **Interrogatories.** Interrogatories are written questions one party sends to the other to be answered under oath. The answers can be used at trial in the same way as deposition answers—to challenge a party who changes her story later.

- **Requests for admission.** In a request for admission, one party asks the other party to admit, under oath, that certain facts are true or certain documents are genuine. These requests are generally used to save time and to narrow the issues that have to be proved at trial.

1. Lawyers have the right to investigate any issue of the parties which is related to the litigation. (   )

2. Courts and legislatures should protect the private information, even it is important to others in a lawsuit. (   )

3. The right to privacy has not been well developed since its extent has not be defined. (   )

4. The conversation between the doctor and his patient can be applied as the evidence in the litigation. (   )

5. The reason for the court to protect the privacy of the third party is to keep fairness. (   )

6. The protective order issued by the court can reveal the private information to public for the purpose of the lawsuit. (   )

7. The purpose of the deposition is to challenge the deponent who changes his words at trial. (   )

8. Interrogatories are carried out in the same way as the deposition. (   )

9. Request for production of evidence includes the production of the physical evidence and the expert opinion evidence. (   )

10. One party of a lawsuit can ask the other party to admit that certain facts are true or certain documents are genuine in order to speed up the process. (   )

IV Translation Abilities

法律语言特征分析与法律翻译技能培养之十三：

法律术语和行话的使用

作为正式文体的法律英语，其一大特点就是对于法律术语和行话(terms of art and argot)的使用。法律术语根据大卫·麦林科夫(David Melinkoff)的解释，是"具有特定意义的专门化词"(a technical word with a specific meaning)，根据布赖恩. A. 加纳的解释，是"在某一特定专业中具有特定、准确意义的词集(words having specific, precise significance in a given specialty)"，也就是说，法律术语是作为科学的法律中特有的术语，仅出现在或者多数情况下出现在法律文件中，如，"certiorari"就是一个法律术语，它出现在法律文件之中，意思是"上级法院向下级法院发出的调取案卷进行复审的令状"，但实际法律生活中，人们都会从文化背景范围内去了解该词的确切含义。现在人们使用该词时都会明白法律工作中上诉程序的运行情况、上级法院的自由裁量权的大小，也明白一国最高法院到底是如何选择它来听审案件的。

然而，在法律生活实践中，法律术语不能仅仅局限于上述意义，这是因为，上述法律术语在法律文体中的数量不多，为此，术语还包含有另外一种，即，出现于其他各种文体中的词语在法律文体中被赋予了特定的法律意义，如：

例词	一般语体词义	法律语体意义	范例
Action	行为、行动	诉讼、起诉权	Action in chief（主诉，本诉）；action at law（法律诉讼，诉讼行为）
Adopt	采纳，采用，采取	收养；正式通过	to adopt a resolution（通过一项决议）
Advance	前进，进行，进展	预付；预付款，贷款	Advance sb. money（预付某人一些钱）
Appeal	呼吁，号召；请求	上诉；控诉；上诉状	To appeal against a finding（不服裁决的上诉）
Arm	臂；前肢；扶手；臂状物	权力；效力	Arm of the law（法律效力/威力）；Justice has long arms.（法网恢恢，疏而不漏）
Bar	（铁、木等）条，杆，棒；栅；（光、色等）线，条	法庭的围栏；阻碍，阻止；	Bar association（律师协会）；be called the bar（取得律师资格）；the Bar（法庭、审判席、律师界）；to bar sb. from stationing a trial（阻止某人起诉）
Challenge	挑战；要求决斗；质问，怀疑	对表决或投票资格提出质问/怀疑；	Challenge of juror（要求陪审员回避、反对某人作陪审员）；to challenge for cause（有正当理由要求某陪审员回避）
Circuit	环行；周线；范围	巡回审判；巡回法庭；巡回审判区	Circuit trial system（巡回审判制度）
Discovery	发现，看出	（证据等的）开示	Discovery process（开示程序）
Exhibit	展览，陈列，展出；表示，显示；展览会	物证，证物；证据；证件	Exhibit register（物证登记册）
Instrument	仪器/器械；手段；工具；乐器，	证券；契约；文件	Negotiable instrument（流通票据）；legal instrument（法律文件）
Minor	较轻微的；较次要的；次要学科；	未成年人，未成年	Minor offender（未成年罪犯）
Party	党，党派，政党；社交性或娱乐性的宴会	诉讼有关的一方/当事人	Both parties（双方当事人）
Sentence	句子；乐句	判决，判刑；科刑	Sentenced offender（已决犯）；sentence of life imprisonment（无期徒刑）

此外，行话的使用也是非常普遍的。所谓"行话"（argot），就是法律出现的一些为少数人、特别是律师们相互之间所使用的一种特定语言（lawyer's shop talk），为此，行话的使用在平常人之间不应加以提倡，但如果使用得当，将会起到意想不到的作用。如" case on all fours"，"adhesion contract"（附意合同/格式合同/订不订由你的合同）"，"attractive nuisance"（诱惑性危险物），"case at bar"（在审案件），"clean hands"（清白无瑕），"cloud on title"（所有权的缺陷），"court below"（下级法院），"four corners of the document"（全部文件），"instant case"（在审案件，或曰 case at bar 正在由法院进行审理的案件），"off the record"（不公开的/非正式的），"pierce the corporate veil"（揭开公司面纱），"reasonable man"（有理性的人），"res ipsa loquitur"（事情不言自明），"sidebar conference"（法官当庭召集双方当事人律师的会议），等等。

Lesson Thirteen Virtual Civil Litigation: A Visit to John Bunyan's Celestial City

Translation Exercises:

Part One *Put the Following into Chinese*

On the Power of Judging in the Roman Government

The power of judging was given to the people, to the senate, to the magistrates, and to certain judges. Its distribution must be seen. I begin with matters of civil business.

After the kings, the consuls judged, and the praetors judged after the consuls. Servius Tullius had divested himself of judging civil suits; the consuls did not judge them people consented to it, except in very rare cases that were called, for this reason, *extraordinary*. They were satisfied to name the judges and to form the tribunals that were to judge. It seems, according to the discourse of Appius Claudius, in Dionysius of Halicarnassus, that as early as the Roman year 259 (495 B.C.) this was regarded as an established custom among the Romans, and tracing it back to Servius Tullius is not going very far back.

Each year, the praetor made a list or table or those he chose to perform the function of judges during the year of his magistracy. A number sufficient for each suit was taken from it. The English practice is quite similar. And, what was very favorable to liberty is that the praetor selected the judges with the consent of both parties. That many objections to judges may be made in England today amounts to approximately this usage.

These judges decided only questions of fact; for example, if a sum had bee paid or not, if an action had been committed or not. But because questions of right required a certain ability, these were taken to the tribunal of the centumvirs.

The kings kept for themselves the judgment of criminal suits, and the consuls succeeded them in this. As a consequence of this authority the consul Brutus had his children put to death as well as all who had conspired on behalf of the Tarquins. This power was exorbitant. The consuls, who already held military power, carried it exercise even into the public business of the town, and their proceedings, devoid of the forms of justice, were violent actions rather than judgments.

Part Two *Put the Following into English*

人民法院作出的发生法律效力的判决、裁定,如果被执行人或者其财产不在中华人民共和国领域内,当事人请求执行的,可以由当事人直接向管辖权的外国法院申请和执行,也可以由人民法院依照中华人民共和国缔结或者参加的国际条约的规定,或者按照互惠原则,请求外国法院承认和执行。

中华人民共和国涉及仲裁机构作出的发生法律效力的仲裁裁决,当事人请求执行的,如果被执行人或者其财产不在中华人民共和国领域内,应当由当事人直接向有管辖权的外国法院申请承认和执行。

人民法院对申请或者请求承认和执行的外国法院作出的发生法律效力的判决、裁定,依照中华人民共和国缔结或者参加的国际条约,或者按照互惠原则进行审查后,任务不违反中华人民共和国法律的基本原则或者国际主权、安全、社会公共利益的,裁定承认其效力,需要执行的,发出执行令,依照本法的有关规定执行。违反中华人民共和国法律的基本原则或者国际主权、安全、社会公共利益的,不予承认和执行。

V. Interaction

1. Discuss with your tutor(s) or the People's judges in your locality about the application of the information technology in the courtrooms. Then based on the discussion, you are supposed to write a composition about how the IT technology can improve the judicial efficiency. Remember that you are required to express your ideas clearly.

VI Appreciation of Judge's Opinions

(1) Case Name(案件名): *Panavision International v. Toeppen*

PANAVISION INTERNATIONAL, L. P., a Delaware Limited Partnership,

Plaintiff,

v.

Dennis TOEPPEN, an individual, Network Solutions, Inc., a District of Columbia Corporation, and Does 1-50, Defendants.

No. 96-3284 DDP (JRX).

United States District Court, C. D. California.

Sept. 19, 1996.

(2) Case Summary(案件简介)

This case presents two novel issues. We are asked to apply existing rules of personal jurisdiction(属人管辖) to conduct that occurred, in part, in "cyberspace."(网络空间) In addition, we are asked to interpret the Federal Trademark Dilution Act(联邦商标反淡化法) as it applies to the Internet.

Panavision accuses Dennis Toeppen of being a "cyber pirate"(网络海盗)who steals valuable trademarks and establishes domain names(域名) on the Internet using these trademarks to sell the domain names to the rightful trademark owners(合法商标所有权人).

The district court(联邦地区法院)found that under the "effects doctrine," Toeppen was subject to personal jurisdiction in California. The district court then granted summary judgment in favor of Panavision, concluding that Toeppen's conduct violated the Federal Trademark Dilution Act of 1995, 15 U.S.C. §1125(c), and the California Anti-dilution statute, California Business & Professions Code §14330.

Toeppen appeals(提起上诉). He argues that the district court erred in exercising personal jurisdiction over him because any contact he had with California was insignificant, emanating solely from his registration of domain names on the Internet, which he did in Illinois. Toeppen further argues that the district court erred in granting summary judgment because his use of Panavision's trademarks on the Internet was not a commercial use(非商业用途) and did not dilute those marks.(为构成对商标的淡化)

We have jurisdiction under 28 U.S.C. §1291 and we affirm. The district court's exercise of jurisdiction was proper and comported with the requirements of due process. Toeppen did considerably more than simply register Panavision's trademarks as his domain names on the Internet. He registered those names as part of a scheme to obtain money from Panavision. Pursuant to that scheme, he demanded $13,000 from Panavision to release the domain names to it. His acts were aimed at Panavision in California, and caused it to suffer injury there.

We also conclude Panavision was entitled to summary judgment under the federal and state dilution statutes. Toeppen made commercial use of Panavision's trademarks and his conduct diluted those marks.

(3) Excerpts of the Judgment(法官判决词)

PREGERSON, District Judge.

Defendant Dennis Toeppen's Motion to Quash(撤销,宣布无效) the Summons and Dismiss(驳回) for Lack

Lesson Thirteen Virtual Civil Litigation: A Visit to John Bunyan's Celestial City

of Personal Jurisdiction, brought pursuant to Federal Rules of Civil Procedure 12(b)(2), came before the Court on September 16, 1996. After reviewing and considering the materials submitted by the parties and hearing oral argument, the Court denies Toeppen's Motion to Quash.

I BACKGROUND

Plaintiff Panavision International, L. P. ("Panavision") is a Delaware limited partnership(有限合伙) with its principal place of business in Los Angeles, California. Panavision owns several federally registered trademarks, including "Panavision" and "Panaflex," which it uses in connection with its theatrical motion picture and television camera and photographic equipment business.

Defendant Dennis Toeppen ("Toeppen") is an individual residing in Illinois. Toeppen owns several web sites, including the two at issue in this case, "panavision.com" and "panaflex.com."

Defendant Network Solutions, Inc. ("NSI") is a District of Columbia corporation with its principal place of business in Herndon, Virginia. NSI registers Internet domain names.

The Internet is an international computer "super-network" of over 15,000 computer networks used by about 30 million individuals, corporations, organizations, and educational institutions worldwide. In recent years, businesses have begun to use the Internet to provide information and products to consumers and other businesses.

Every Internet user has a unique address consisting of one or more address components. This address is commonly referred to as the "domain" or "domain name."(域名) On the Internet, domain names serve as the primary identifier of the Internet user. Businesses on the Internet commonly use their business names (e.g., IBM) with the designation ".com" (e.g., IBM.com) as their domain names. The designation ".com" identifies the name holder as a commercial entity(商业性实体机构). NSI does not make an independent determination of an applicant's right to use a domain name. However, since at least November 23, 1995, NSI has required applicants, including Toeppen, to make certain representations and warranties, including: (1) that the applicant's statements in the application are true and the applicant has the right to use the requested domain name; (2) that the use or registration of the domain name does not interfere with or infringe the rights of any third party with respect to trademark, service mark, trade name, company name or any other intellectual property right; and (3) that the applicant is not seeking to use the domain name for any unlawful purpose, including tortious interference with contract or prospective business advantage, unfair competition, injuring the reputation of another, or for the purpose of confusing or misleading a person, whether natural or incorporated.

In December of 1995, Toeppen applied for registration of the Internet domain name "Panavision.com" and NSI registered the domain name. Toeppen is not, and never has been, authorized to use the Panavision Marks.

After registering the "Panavision.com" domain name, Toeppen established a "web site" displaying aerial views of Pana, Illinois. At no time did Toeppen use the "Panavision.com" name in connection with the sale of any goods or services.

Like many businesses, Panavision has decided to do business via the Internet. When Panavision attempted to establish a web site under its own name, however, it discovered that Toeppen had registered domain names using the Panavision trademarks.

By registering the "Panavision.com" domain name with NSI, Toeppen has prevented Panavision from registering and using its own trademark, Panavision, as an Internet domain name. After Panavision notified Toeppen of its intent to use the "Panavision.com" domain name, Toeppen demanded $13,000 to discontinue use of the domain name. Toeppen subsequently registered Panavision's "Panaflex" trademark as the domain name "Panaflex.com." Panavision asserts, based on conversation with an attorney for American Standard, Inc., that Toeppen is also a defendant in trademark actions (商标诉讼中的被告) brought by American Standard, Inc. and Intermatic, Inc. because of Toeppen's registration of "americanstandard.com" and "intermatic.com" as domain names and subsequent demands for money to relinquish control of the names. Toeppen is also the registered owner of several other domain names that are similar to trademarked names, including: aircanada.com; anaheimstadium.com; arriflex.com (Arriflex is Panavision's main competitor); australiaopen.com; camdenyards.com; deltaairlines.com; eddiebauer.com; flydelta.com; frenchopen.com; lufthansa.com; neiman-marcus.com; northwestairlines.com; and yankeestadium.com.

Panavision asserts that Toeppen's sole purpose in registering the domain names at issue was to extort(敲诈) money from Panavision. On May 7, 1996, Panavision brought claims against Toeppen and NSI in the Central District of California for: 1) federal dilution of trademark; 2) state dilution of trademark; 3) federal trademark infringement; 4) federal unfair competition; 5) unfair competition; 6) intentional interference with prospective economic advantage; 7) negligent interference with prospective economic advantage; and 8) breach of contract. On August 21, 1996, Toeppen filed this Motion to Quash the Summons and Dismiss the Complaint for Lack of Personal Jurisdiction pursuant to Federal Rule of Civil Procedure 12(b)(2). Toeppen alleges(声称) that the Court lacks personal jurisdiction because Toeppen resides in Illinois and the allegations concern Toeppen's actions in Illinois.

II DISCUSSION

It is the plaintiff's burden to establish personal jurisdiction. The plaintiff need only make a *prima facie* showing of jurisdiction where, as here, the court did not hear testimony or make factual findings. This showing can be based on the affidavits(宣誓书,誓章) of knowledgeable witnesses.

Where there is no applicable federal statute governing personal jurisdiction, federal courts must apply the law of the state in which the district court sits. California's "long-arm" statute permits courts to assert jurisdiction over a nonresident defendant whenever permitted by the state and federal Constitutions. Therefore, the Court "need only determine whether personal jurisdiction in this case would meet the requirements of due process."

A. General Jurisdiction

General jurisdiction(一般管辖) permits a court to exercise personal jurisdiction over the defendant as to any cause of action arising in any jurisdiction. General jurisdiction exists when the defendant is domiciled in the forum state(管辖地所在州) or its activities there are "substantial" or "continuous and systematic." The Court does not have general jurisdiction over Toeppen. First, he is domiciled in Illinois, not California. Second, his activities in California are not substantial, systematic, or continuous. In 1996, Toeppen was in California twice, which he asserts is representative of his yearly contacts with this state.

B. Specific Jurisdiction(特别管辖)

Specific jurisdiction arises in circumstances where the defendant's contacts with the forum state are insufficient to establish general jurisdiction but the defendant's activities in the forum are sufficient to establish jurisdiction for the purposes of the litigation. The defendant need not ever have been physically present in the forum state for specific jurisdiction to apply. The Court holds that it has specific jurisdiction over Toeppen.

The Ninth Circuit uses a three part test for specific jurisdiction:

(1) "the nonresident defendant must do some act or consummate some transaction with the forum or perform some act by which he purposefully avails himself of the privilege of conducting activities in the forum, thereby invoking the benefits and protections of its laws; (2) the claim must be one which arises out of or results from the defendant's forum-related activities; and (3) exercise of jurisdiction must be reasonable."

1. The "Purposeful Availment" Prong

The "purposeful availment"(有意接受)(美国民事诉讼法中,一方当事人针对另一州所为之故意行为,从而使得该州可以对其主张宪法上的属人管辖权) prong assures that a nonresident defendant will be aware that it could be sued in the forum state. In other words, this requirement protects a nonresident from being haled before a court solely because of "random, fortuitous or attenuated" contacts over which it has no control. To pass this part of the test, it must be foreseeable that the defendant's conduct and connection with the forum state are such that the defendant should reasonably anticipate being haled into court there.

Lesson Thirteen Virtual Civil Litigation: A Visit to John Bunyan's Celestial City

The "purposeful availment" test differs depending upon the underlying cause of action. For example, in cases arising from contract disputes, merely contracting with a resident of the forum state is insufficient to confer specific jurisdiction. In the tort setting, however, jurisdiction "can be predicated on (1) intentional actions (2) expressly aimed at the forum state (3) causing harm, the brunt(压力,影响力) of which is suffered—and which the defendant knows is likely to be suffered—in the forum state." This doctrine is known as the "effects test."

Therefore, the court's initial analysis must be directed towards determining the nature of the underlying cause of action. Panavision's allegations may be summarized as follows: Panavision and Panaflex are valuable trademarks associated with Panavision's business. A domain name is the primary way businesses are located on the Internet. The registration of its trademarks as domain names is valuable to Panavision because it allows Internet users who are familiar with the trademarks to easily search the Internet, locate Panavision's web site, and review any information that Panavision has posted. Toeppen identified Panavision (and other businesses), as a business whose trademarks were not registered as domain names. Toeppen then registered Panavision's trademarks as his domain names. Toeppen registered Panavision's trademarks because he believed that Panavision would eventually decide to create its own web address using its trademarks, that Panavision would discover that Toeppen had previously registered the trademarks as domain names, and that Panavision would pay Toeppen to relinquish his domain registrations rather than incur the expense and delay inherent in suing him. In short, Panavision alleges that Toeppen is not "doing business" in the traditional sense—he is not a competitor. His "business" is to act as a "spoiler," preventing Panavision and others from doing business on the Internet under their trademarked names unless they pay his fee. Assuming the truth of Panavision's allegations for purposes of this motion, the Court finds that the tort analysis provides the proper analytical framework. At the very least, this action is "more akin to a tort claim than a contract claim." *Ziegler*, 64 F. 3d at 474 (holding that a Section 1983 claim was "more akin to a tort claim than a contract claim" and using the "effects test" to analyze the "purposeful availment" prong of the jurisdiction test). The "effects test" was established in *Calder v. Jones*, 465 U.S. 783 (1984). In *Calder*, the Court held that a reporter and an editor, both Florida residents, were subject to personal jurisdiction in California for an allegedly defamatory article(毁谤文章) that they had written for publication in a national magazine. The Court held that jurisdiction in California was proper because California was "the focal point of both the story and of the harm suffered."

The Court emphasized that "petitioners were not charged with mere untargeted negligence... but with intentional, and allegedly tortious, actions... expressly aimed at California." In such circumstances, "an individual injured in California need not go to Florida to seek redress from persons who, though remaining in Florida, knowingly cause injury in California." Under the "effects doctrine," Toeppen is subject to personal jurisdiction in California. Toeppen allegedly registered Panavision's trademarks as domain names with the knowledge that the names belonged to Panavision and with the intent to interfere with Panavision's business. Toeppen expressly aimed his conduct at California. Finally, Toeppen has harmed Panavision, the brunt of which Panavision has borne in California, which Toeppen knew would likely happen because Panavision's principal place of business and the heart of the theatrical motion picture and television camera and photographic equipment business are in California. Toeppen's actions are anything but "random, fortuitous(偶然的,意外的) or attenuated(减弱的,衰减的,衰耗的)." He has not engaged in "untargeted negligence" but has "expressly aimed" his tortious activities at California. Jurisdiction is proper because Toeppen's out of state conduct was intended to, and did, result in harmful effects in California. Panavision should not now be forced to go to Illinois to litigate its claims. It is important to note that the Court does not hold that Toeppen is "doing business" in California via the Internet. Accordingly, cases such as *Bensusan Restaurant Corp. v. King*, *CompuServe. Inc. v. Patterson*, 89 F. 3d 1257 (6th Cir. 1996), and *Pres-Kap. Inc. v. System One*, 636 So. 2d 1351 (Fla. Dist. Ct. App. 1994) are not analogous(类比) to the case before the Court. The issue in those cases was whether contacts with the forum state via the Internet (or, in *Pres-Kap*, via a computerized airline and hotel reservation system) were sufficient to confer specific jurisdiction.

Although at first blush(乍一看来)the cases seem similar to the case at bar, the semblance(外观,外貌,外表,样子;类似,相似)is superficial only. In each of those cases, the parties had legitimate businesses and legitimate legal disputes. Here, however, Toeppen is not conducting a business but is, according to Panavision, running a scam(诓骗,诈骗) directed at California.

2. The "arises out of or results from" prong

Courts in the Ninth Circuit follow a "but for" analysis of this prong of the test. That is, if the plaintiff would not have suffered loss "but for" the defendant's forum-related activities, courts hold that the claim arises out of the defendant's forum-related activities. Here, "but for" Toeppen's conduct in registering Panavision's trademarks as domain names, Panavision would be able to establish an easily located web site and thus would not have been injured.

3. The "reasonableness" prong

This prong requires that the court's exercise of jurisdiction comport with(与……一致,相称,相适应) "fair play and substantial justice." The factors that the court must consider are: (1) the extent of defendant's "purposeful" interjection; (2) the burden on defendant in defending in the forum(法院地); (3) the extent of conflict with the sovereignty of the defendant's state; (4) the forum state's interest in adjudicating the dispute; (5) the most efficient judicial resolution of the controversy; (6) the importance of the forum to plaintiff's interest in convenient and effective relief; and (7) the existence of an alternative forum. No one factor is dispositive(决定性的,decisive): the court must balance all seven.

In the tort setting(侵权环境下), "if a nonresident, acting outside the state, intentionally causes injuries within the state, local jurisdiction is presumptively not unreasonable: 'Where a defendant who purposefully has directed his activities at forum residents seeks to defeat jurisdiction, he must present a compelling case that... would render jurisdiction unreasonable.'"

The Court finds that Toeppen has not presented a compelling case that jurisdiction is unreasonable. After balancing the seven factors from *Burger King*, it is clear that jurisdiction over Toeppen comports with "fair play and substantial justice." "In this era of fax machines and discount air travel," (在一个传真机遍地和机票打折的年代) requiring Toeppen to litigate in California is not constitutionally unreasonable.

III CONCLUSION

The Court finds that Defendant Dennis Toeppen meets the due process requirements for personal jurisdiction. Therefore, the Court denies Defendant Dennis Toeppen's Motion to Quash the Summons and Dismiss for Lack of Personal Jurisdiction.

It is so ordered.

Lesson Fourteen

Successive Confessions and the Poisonous Tree

> **Learning objectives**
>
> After learning the text and having done the exercises in this lesson, you will:
> —familiarize with knowledge of the legal characteristics and the nature of successive confessions;
> —acquire an appreciation of the vocabulary and grammar or syntax relevant to the successive confessions;
> —become aware of the information required in order to understand the successive confessions;
> —cultivate the practical abilities to put to use the language in the specific context;
> —be able to do some translation from Chinese to English and from English to Chinese.

 Text

Successive Confessions and the Poisonous Tree

"A principal reason why a suspect might make a second or third confession is simply that, *having* already confessed *once or* twice, he might think he has little to lose by repetition. If a first confession is not shown to be voluntary①, I do not think that a later confession that is merely a direct product of the earlier one should be held to he voluntary. It would be neither conducive to good police work, nor fair to a suspect, to allow the erroneous impression that he has nothing to lose to play the major role in a defendant's decision to speak a second or third time." (*per* Justice Harlan②).

---

① If a first confession is not shown to be voluntary:句中的 voluntary 指"任意性"自白或招供,即 voluntary statement 或 voluntary confession,故此句话的意思是:如不能证明第一次招供为任意性自白。

② Justice Harlan:哈伦法官(注:本段话引自其在 *Darwin v. Connecticut* 一案中的意见),391 US 346(1968) at 350—351。

Introduction

It is a well-known feature of the English common law of evidence that it refuses to recognize the doctrine often described, following United States nomenclature, as the "fruit of the poisonous tree".① The issue with which that doctrine is concerned can arise in a number of different ways, though its essential form is always the same. Where evidence has been obtained (the primary evidence) in a way which renders it inadmissible, should other evidence (the secondary evidence) itself be inadmissible where acquired in consequence of the primary evidence? The poisonous tree metaphor is straightforward; the secondary evidence is the fruit of the tree which the primary evidence constitutes.

The most obvious way in which the issue arises is where a confession has been extracted from the accused by improper means and the detail of that confession leads the police to some incriminating item②. Application of the "fruits" doctrine would lead to the exclusion of that item. However, over 200 years ago, in *warickshall* the common law adopted a robust stance, rejecting the application of the doctrine in just that situation. There, the accused had been led, by promises of favor, to confess to receiving stolen goods. In consequence of her confessions, those goods were found concealed in her lodgings. It was held permissible for evidence to be given of where the goods had been found, since:

"a fact if it exist at all, must exist invariably in the some manner, whether the confession from which it derived be in other respects true or false."

Section 76(4)(a) of the Police and Criminal Evidence Act 1984③ puts this decision into statutory form.

There are many variations on the theme. Thus, in the leading Supreme Court case④, it was held that a confession was inadmissible because the fruit of an unlawful arrest by the police. Another example is provided by a case in which the tree was the accused's own statements to the police, the fruit the testimony of a person to whose existence the accused had referred in those statements.

Rather more prosaic, perhaps, is the focus of this article. It is very common for the police to *allege* that the accused confessed more than once. The circumstances may be such that the later confession is a fuller version of the earlier one; but it is perfectly possible for the content of the two to be essentially the same. In either of those circumstances, the defense may argue that, if the judge has decided that the earlier confession is inadmissible under section 76(2)(a) or (b) of

---

① "fruit of the poisonous tree":其和 cat out of the bag 均为证据法则中的术语,fruit of the poisonous tree 为"毒树之果",主要指以非法程序手段所获证据,根据证据排除原则此种证据不可被采信;cat out of the bag 则为"无意泄露之秘密"(或直译为"出袋之猫"),其与"毒树之果"密切相关,主要指被告在非法程序手段下,如刑讯逼供之下招供后,又安排被告在合法的取证程序中进行供述,此次供述尽管程序合法,但因此次供述可能会受"毒果"的影响(因被告可能认为秘密已经无意泄露或"猫已经跑了",再次重复供述也无关紧要,故再次予以供述),因而此次供述所得证据也不能予以采信。

② incriminating item:evidence that can prove someone guilty of a crime(犯罪证据)。

③ Police and Criminal Evidence Act:《1984 年警察和刑事证据法》,在英语中简称为 PACE1984。

④ leading Supreme Court case:句中的 leading case 为"指导性判例",指经充分辩论而裁定的判例,因其重要性而常被以后的法官引用作为解决同类案件的"guide"而得名。

the 1984 Act, he ought also to exclude the later one as flowing therefrom.①Equally, where the earlier one has been excluded under section 78(1) as a discretionary matter, it may argue that the later one ought also to be excluded under that subsection because its admission too would have an adverse effect on the fairness of the proceedings.

There is a considerable body of material, both empirical and anecdotal②, suggesting that it is common for suspects to be interviewed more than once, and not only where the earlier interviews have proved fruitless. Much of the research evidence concerns the situation where informal interviews or exchanges have preceded the formal, recorded interview. Mosron and Stephenson, in a study of the questioning and interviewing of suspects outside the police station, found there to be a very close relationship between the outcomes of earlier exchanges outside the police station and later ones inside it. Of 34 suspects who made an earlier admission, 30 repeated that admission at a later stage. There is also evidence that exchanges inside the station may be used as precursors③to formal interviews. Dixon *et al.* found that 53 per cent of a sample of officers whom they interviewed said that they always or often sought to clarify a suspect's account before the interview began, while only 28 per cent said that they did so rarely or never. In one example they give of this kind of softening-up process,④a suspect was first asked a series of questions. Then, he was cautioned⑤, and the recorded interrogation began with the officer going over things previously discussed. When the suspect protested that he had already told the officer about those things, the officer replied that he had now to get it on to the formal record.

In addition, it is a feature of many of the reported cases, a number of which will be dealt with later in this article, that they demonstrate a similar police practice of building the confessional case against the accused through a series of exchanges, culminating in a set-piece, contemporaneously recorded interview.

The common law position

The decision in Smith

The leading common law case concerned with successive confessions is *Smith*. Three soldiers had received stab wounds during a fight with other soldiers. One of them later died. A regimental sergeant major⑥put a company on parade and told them that they would stay there until be found out who had been involved in the fighting. Eventually, Smith stepped forward and confessed, apparently to all three stabbings. On the following morning, a (military) sergeant from the Special

---

① he ought also to exclude the later one as flowing therefrom：句中的 therefrom 等同 from the earlier confession，因此本句话应为：他也应当排除源于先前招供的以后的供述。

② both empirical and anecdotal：relying on facts or on the anecdotes，"不论是基于事实或基于传闻"。

③ precursors：rehearsal，预演，排练。

④ In one example they give of this kind of softening-up process：句中的 they give 和 of this kind...一个是定语从句,另一个是介词短语,均是修饰 example 的成分。softening-up process 则是指警方从精神或肉体上降伏疑犯的所谓"软化处理程序",故该句话可译为:在他们(指警方)所列举的一个此种软化处理程序范例中。

⑤ cautioned：be given warnings,"告诫",为刑事司法上一重要程序,指警方在审讯疑犯前须用"米兰达告诫"(Miranda Warning)警告嫌疑犯,告诉他有权保持沉默,他所说的一切均可用作对他不利的证据等。

⑥ A regimental sergeant major：在团部工作的准尉。

Investigation Branch①saw Smith. He cautioned him, referred to what had happened the night before, and then told Smith that he understood him to have confessed to the stabbings. The reply was, "Yes, I am not denying it, I stabbed three of them all right." He later made a written statement to the same effect. The judge-advocate, at Smith's trial for murder, allowed evidence to be called of both the earlier and the later confession.②

The Courts-Martial Appeal Court③agreed with counsel for Smith that the earlier confession was inadmissible, for it had been obtained by a threat. As far as the later confession was concerned, counsel argued and argued only that it must be excluded unless the effect of the earlier threat had been dissipated and the fear which had brought about the first admission no longer persisted in any way. The Court agreed with counsel as to the basis for exclusion, saying:

"Only if the time-limit between the two statements, the circumstances existing at the time and the caution are such that it can be said that the original threat or inducement has been dissipated can the second statement be admitted as a voluntary statement."

On the facts, the Court concluded that the effect of the original threat was spent. It pointed out that nine hours had elapsed since the parade had ended. In doing so, it refused to take the point of counsel fir Smith that the order to confess given by the regimental sergeant-major, someone clearly in authority over Smith,④remained in effect.

What is entirely missing from *Smith* is the very different argument that, once Smith had confessed the night before, he might think there little point in refusing to repeat that confession the morning after. This is particularly surprising, for the circumstances of the case were especially suitable for such an argument. The sergeant had begun by reminding Smith that he had already confessed to his regimental sergeant-major. Smith might well take this as pointing up the uselessness of a denial now, indeed, Lord Parker C. J.⑤suggested that this reminder "put the appellant in a difficulty" and was "no doubt introduced...in the hope that thereby he might get a continued confession." It must follow that the case involves the most radical inconsistency possible with what is known, in the United States cases, as the "cat out of the bag"⑥argument.

The earlier authorities

Three of the four cases cited in *Smith* as supporting the principle there relied upon are certainly consistent with it. In *Meynell*, *Sherrington* and *Doherty*, the second confession was excluded because it had not been shown that the direct effect of the original inducement was entirely dissipated. Therefore, in none was it necessary to consider whether or not there might have been the more

---

① Special Investigation Branch:特别调查组。

② The judge-advocate, at Smith's trial for murder, allowed evidence to be called of both the earlier and the later confession:句中的 judge-advocate 为"军法官",而 of both the...是修饰 evidence 的定语,只是在它前面插入了另一个作为宾语补足语的不定式短语 to be called。故该句子应当译为:审判史密斯谋杀案的军法官采信了前后两次供认的证据。

③ the Courts-Martial Appeal Court:军事上诉法庭,经国会通过于1950年成立,受理不服 court-martial 判决的刑事上诉案件。

④ regimental sergeant-major, someone clearly in authority over Smith:其中的 in authority over 等同上文中的 threat,故该句的意思是:团部下来的准尉长官,明显对史密斯造成威逼。

⑤ Lord Parker C. J.:大法官帕克阁下。

⑥ "cat out of the bag":"无意泄露之秘密"(或直译为"出袋之猫"),参见相关前注。

Lesson Fourteen Successive Confessions and the Poisonous Tree

indirect, "cat out of the bag" effect. There is a number of other nineteenth century authorities consistent with *Smith*. More directly supportive is *Howes*, where counsel for the accused put to the judge, Denman C. J.①, that the second confession should be excluded precisely because, "[t]he magistrate does not seem to have gone to the full extent of telling the prisoner that his former confession would have no effect". His Lordship② rejected the argument because he could not say,③ "that this statement [resulted] from the same influence as the first." Relying upon this case and many of the other authorities, Joy, in his famous work on confessions, expressed the firm view that:

"where a confession has been obtained, or inducement been held out under circumstances which would render a confession inadmissible, a confession subsequently made is not admissible in evidence, unless from the length of time intervening, from proper warning of the consequences, or from other circum stances, there is reason to presume that the hope or fear which influenced the first confession is dispelled."

However, the authority was not all one way. In *Nute*, decided in 1800, the jury had expressly found the first confession to have been made under a hope of favor, and the second under the influence of having made the first. On a case reserved, the judges held that these were not properly jury matters, but that, if the trial judge agreed with the jury, neither confession was receivable. In a case at assizes, *Sexton*, the accused had agreed to tell a police officer all about the offence in question in return for a glass of gin. He was given two glasses and then confessed. Having been later cautioned by the magistrate, who knew nothing of the gin episode, he admitted the truth of his confession to the officer. In the view of Best J.④:

"Had the magistrate known that the officer had given the prisoner gin, he would no doubt, have told the prisoner that what he had already said could not be given in evidence against him, and that it was for him to consider whether he would make a second confession. If the prisoner had been told this, what he afterwards said would be evidence against him; but for want of this information, he might think that he could not make his case worse than he had already made it,⑤ and under this impression might sign the confession before the magistrate."

Not the least interesting feature of *Sexton* is the reason which Best J. went on to give for his ruling:

"If a confession, so obtained, were allowed to be proved at the trial of a prisoner, however careful a magistrate might be that a prisoner should not be entrapped into a confession, an over zealous constable might defeat the humane provisions of the law, by so practicing on the hopes and fears of a prisoner⑥ just before he came into the magistrates' presence, as to make him, when be-

---

① Denman C. J.：邓曼大法官。
② His Lordship：法官大人，指 Denman C. J.。
③ because he could not say："因为他未能证明"，其中的"he"指上文中的 counsel for the accused。
④ Best J.：贝斯特法官，尔后成为普通法院首席法官（Chief Justice of Common Pleas）。
⑤ but for want of this information, he might think that he could not make his case worse than he had already made it："但因为不知道该信息，他可能认为反正已经招供，再坏也就是那样了"，其中，for want of 为一词组，意思是"缺乏"。
⑥ practicing on the hopes and fears of a prisoner：taking advantage of the hopes and fears，意思是"利用罪犯的希望和恐惧"，此处的利用"希望"是指警方的"诱供"，而利用"恐惧"则是指"逼供"。

fore the magistrate, appear to make an uninfluenced and voluntary confession, when every sort of trick had been made use of."

Plainly, the concern is that the police might soften up the prisoner, persuading him to confess before them, then take him quickly before the magistrate to repeat the confession, at a time when he might consider all to be lost. Though the situation of successive confessions to the police themselves is somewhat different, the following comment of Moston and Stephenson, concerning their study of the relationship between the (untaped) questioning of the suspect before arrival at the police station and the (taped) questioning after arrival, seems apposite:

"The taped interview represents only a partial picture of a suspect's exchanges with police officers and could be a stage-managed and sanitized version of police interviewing procedures taken as a whole."

A final point about the nineteenth century authority is that the fourth case relied upon in *Smith*, that of *Rue*, turns out, on closer inspection, not to be clearly in favor of what might be termed the "undissipated taint" view of the law. Rue was a servant suspected by her mistress of having murdered the latter's infant child. The mistress held out to her certain inducements, as a result of which she confessed. A neighbor was then summoned. She apprised him of Rue's confession, though it is unclear whether or not this was done in Rue's presence. The neighbor questioned her in her mistress's absence, the result being that she also confessed to him. Denman J. excluded the first confession without difficulty. It seems clear that his main concern about the second was that the case was not one of successive confessions to the person who held out the original inducement, but one where the second had been made to a third party who had held out no fresh inducement. He had no doubt that the first confession could not he retrospectively validated by having been repeated to the third party but he saw fit to consult Kelly L. C. B.① before giving his ruling as to whether or not the second confession was itself to be excluded. Having done so, he ruled that, in this particular case, the second confession must also be rejected:

"... upon the ground that it was so connected under the circumstances with the inducement held out by [the mistress] as to be inadmissible in law."

This does, at first blush, seem to support the undissipated taint view. In other words, the *reason* for exclusion seems to be that the original taint had not been dissipated, but remained directly operative. Yet the actual decision is not inconsistent with the *Mute/Sexton* view, for that view simply adds a second basis for exclusion where the taint *has* been dissipated, namely that the original *confession*, rater than the original *taint*, is an operative cause of the later confession—the cat out of the bag. Furthermore, it is not at all clear that the reason for exclusion in *Rue* was that the original taint had not been dissipated. No reference is made in *Smith* to the nub of the objection to the second confession, as described by Denman J.:

"... it would not have been made but for the previous involuntary statement②, and it is made

---

① Kelly L. C. B.：理财法院首席法官凯利阁下，L. C. B. 乃 Lord Chief Baron 的缩写形式。

② ... it would not have been made but for the previous involuntary statement：句中的 it 指的是 later statement，即以后的自白，but for 为词组，等同 if there had not been，故该句子应译为："如果没有前面的非任意性自白，就不可能作出第二次自白"。

in answer to questions put by the person to whom it was made, which questions were induced by the information obtained from the person to whom shortly before a confession had been made under an inducement."

The stress here is upon the way in which the second confession grew out of the first and the neighbor's knowledge of it, so Denman J.'s reasoning smacks of the *Nute/Sexton* view.① It can, at the very least, be said that the ease fails to provt e unequivocal support for the undissipated taint view of the common law.

The post-1984 Act law

In general

Under both the oppression and unreliability heads of section 76(2) of the 1984 Act, there is a general requirement of a causal link between the item of conduct in question (oppression, or thing said or done) and the confession. Taking the case of oppression, it will be clear that, if that oppression remains operative at the time of the later confession, it will have retained causative potency. Where the argument is put in terms of the earlier confession having led to the later one, the issue of causation may seem to be more problematical, for it might appear that the original oppression is not a cause of the later confession. However, this may be thought too simplistic a view of causation. It seems entirely tenable to argue that, though the oppression has ceased to be directly operative, it remains indirectly operative through the medium of the earlier confession. It must be added that this aspect of the issue under consideration does not seem to have been discussed in the authorities.

In general terms, the argument for exclusion of the later confession under section 78(1) would seem even stronger than that for exclusion under section 76(2). The basis for exclusion under section 78(1) is that admission of the evidence "would have such an adverse effect on the fairness of the proceedings that the court ought not to admit it." We do not have to worry about continuing, but indirect, causes in this situation, for there is no reason why the unfairness should not consist in making the accused suffer the evidential disadvantage of having the later confession, obtained from him at a time when he would have assumed he was already condemned from his own mouth, used against him. Of course, it would remain an integral part of this argument that the original confession was itself to be excluded, *i.e.* that he had been *inadmissibly* led so to condemn himself.②

Inadmissible confessions

There are three post-Act appeal level cases, all of which are inconsistent with the undissipated taint view of the law. Before they are dealt with, it should be pointed out that in none of them

---

① smacks of the *Nute/Sexton* view: smack of 的意思是"带有某种味道",指近似或接近,故此句话为:"近似 *Nute* 和 *Sexton* 案例中的观点"。

② it would remain an integral part of this argument that the original confession was itself to be excluded, *i.e.* that he had been *inadmissibly* led so to condemn himself: 其中, integral part 指不可分割的部分,即指必要前提条件; condemn himself: incriminated himself, 即"自证其罪", 故该句子应译为: "最初的供认本身应予以排除,即,他由此被诱导而自证其罪的证据不应被采信,这一点应作为该论证必要的前提条件"。

was any reference at all made to *Smith*. This may seem a remarkable omission, though it is to be remembered that the Court of Appeal laid down in *Fulling* that the 1984 Act, being a codifying statute, was to be interpreted, in the first instance, according to its natural meaning and uninfluenced by considerations derived from the previous state of the law.①

The leading post-Act case is *McGovern*. The accused was suspected of having participated in a particularly brutal murder. She was aged 19, was six months' pregnant and had an I.Q. of 73. Immediately before she was first interviewed, she had been vomiting in her cell. The police decided to deny her access to legal advice.② At interview, after initial difficulty in understanding the caution, she began by denying that she had been present, then admitted her presence but said that the death had been accidental, and finally confessed to having stabbed the victim. By this time, the accused was weeping uncontrollably. Having ruled the denial of legal advice unlawful, the Court of Appeal concluded that this confession ought to have been excluded under section 76(2)(b) as not having been shown to be unlikely to be unreliable.

After the first interview, the police allowed her access to a solicitor. He must, it seems, have been apprised of what had transpired at the first interview, but had not been informed that the accused's request for a solicitor before that interview had been denied. He was present at a second interview, conducted entirely properly, at which his client made a full confession.

Crown counsel③ argued that evidence of the second interview was admissible because "not tarnished by the shortcomings of the first." His argument was rejected by the Court, which preferred counsel for the appellant's contention that, "the subsequent confession was a direct consequence of the fruit." Farquharson L. J. specifically endorsed the "cat out of the bag" argument as follow:

"One cannot refrain from emphasizing that when an accused person has made a series of admissions as to his or her complicity in a crime at a first interview, the very fact that those admissions have been made are (sic.) likely *to* have an effect upon her during the course of the second interview."

The relevance of the solicitor's ignorance of the earlier denial of access was said to be that, had he been told, he would have realized that the first confession was suspect and would, in all probability, not have allowed the second interview to go ahead.

Gloves seems inexplicable except on the same basis as *McGovern*. The accused, aged only 16, was suspected of a number of burglaries, one of which had involved the death of an old lady. The investigating officers, who seem to have been inexperienced and certainly of junior rank, had, by what the Court of Appeal described as "improper questioning", obtained from Gloves a damaging admission implicating him in the homicide. Evidence of this admission had been excluded at trial, apparently under section 76(2)(b).

---

① according to its natural meaning and uninfluenced by considerations derived from the previous state of the law:其中，natural meaning 为自然或惯常含义，即法律的本意；previous state of the law 中的 state of the law，在此上下文情况中，指的是适用法律的情况，即指的是判例法，故该句子的意思是："(对成文法的解释首先应)根据其自然本意，而不应受衍生自以往判例法的种种考虑因素的影响"。

② to deny her access to legal advice:不准她接触法律咨询，即不准她会见律师而得到法律咨询意见。

③ Crown counsel:public prosecutor,检察官。

Fully eight days later, Gloves was interviewed again, but this time by more senior officers who asked him only about the homicide. The sole criticism made by counsel of this interview was that no "appropriate adult" had been present. However, this apparent breach of paragraph 13.1 of Code C was not an element of the Court's decision that the second confession, no less than the first, should have been excluded under section 76(2)(B).

The language of Owen J.'s judgment suggests that the ruling was based on the notion that the taint affecting the earlier interview was still operative. Thus, his justification for the Court's conclusion was that, "that which had led him to make the remarks which he had made earlier continued until (the later interview)".①This is difficult to follow, for the questioning at the second interview was certainly not improper. The case resembles *Smith*, in this respect. The taint was specific to the first interview; the manner of the earlier questioning could no more persist for eight days than could the threat of being kept indefinitely on parade persist once it have been withdrawn.

One point stressed by the Court may give the clue to what really led it to rule the later confession inadmissible. The trial judge had reasoned that it might fairly be assumed that Gloves had had the opportunity of taking legal advice during the eight days in question. Owen J. said that the real issue was whether or not he had actually taken advice. The evidence before the Court was that he had not. It is hard to see what significance such advice could have, other than that it would tell him that the slate was clean② and that he should put out of his mind what he had said at the earlier interview, starting afresh in relation to the later one. It is in that context that one should view Owen J.'s remark that:

"We do not take the view, which was urged to us at one time, that in circumstances like this there must inevitably be a continuing blight on any subsequent confessions."

In the third case, *Wood*, though the argument for exclusion of the later confession was put in terms of both section 76 and section 78, it is clear that the *Court of Appeal* finally relied upon the former section in overturning the trial judge's decision③ to admit it. The facts presented a particularly strong case for exclusion. Wood, suspected of manslaughter, had, at a first interview, admitted delivering a blow to the infant victim, but had denied delivering, a day later, what the forensic evidence④ showed must have been the fatal blow or blows. Though Wood was mentally handicapped, he had not, before that interview, been either cautioned or informed of his right to legal advice. In addition, the police had breached the contemporaneous recording requirement. At a second interview, there were no such breaches; indeed, a solicitor was present throughout. However, the Court pointed out that, though Wood had consulted his solicitor before that interview, there was no evidence that the police had told the solicitor the nature of the charges or what had transpired earlier. The police began the interview with a detailed recapitulation of what had been

---

① that which had led him to make the remarks which he had made earlier continued until (the later interview):导致他作出他先前已经作过的供述的因素在(以后的审讯中)依旧存在。

② the slate was clean:此处的"slate"有 record 的含义,指记录是清白的,即前面的招供并非一定记录在案的意思。

③ trial judge's decision:此处的 trial judge 指的是"初审法官",即 judge in the court of first instance。

④ forensic evidence:法医证据。

said at the first one. Once again, Wood admitted the earlier blow, but denied delivering the fatal blow or blows on the following day.

The Court's principal reason for allowing the appeal was that the case should have been withdrawn from the jury, but it went on to deal with the successive confessions point because it had been "fully argued". In overturning the judge,① the Court pointed out that the breaches had not been merely technical, but also stressed that the two interviews "were closely linked, both in time and content, since the second interview started by a recapitulation of what had occurred in the first". In other words, it took the point not taken in *Smith*. Furthermore, this was a mentally handicapped man who had not had the opportunity, before the second interview, of *a full* discussion with his solicitor, by which the Court must have meant one dealing with the infirmities of the first. Crown counsel had pressed the point, accepted by the judge, that it was significant that Wood had maintained throughout his denial of having delivered the later blow or blows. That point was rejected② in the following terms:

"The fact that he resolutely refused to admit any other blow does not mean that he felt able to retract what he had already said, which the police reminded him of at the outset."

Though neither *McGovern* nor *Gloves* was referred to, and, indeed, though the cases which were referred to, *Gillard and Barret* and *Yeoman v. DPP* are both concerned with exclusion under section 78(1), where, as we shall see, a rather different line has been taken, it seems clear that *Wood* is entirely at one with the other two section 76(2) decisions.

Legal Terminology

1. confession, admission 与 statement

这三个单词均与被告招认违法或犯罪事实有关。confession 多限于刑事犯罪领域(在加拿大民事诉讼程序中,其可等同于 formal admission),指刑事被告完全承认其被指控的犯罪及有关定罪所需的所有事实,或至少是主要事实,并承认有罪(acknowledgement of guilt),有供认不讳的含义,陪审团根据其招供则可作出有罪裁定,故为"供认"。相比之下,admission 常用作指对民事责任行为的承认。在刑事领域,admission 常用作指对民事责任行为的招认,多表示承认一个或数个事实,此种招供远没有达到足以定罪的程度;与 confession 相比,admission 主要的区别在于被告无认罪表示(an *admission* is a confession that an allegation or factual assertion is true without any acknowledgement of guilt with respect to the criminal charges, whereas a *confession* involves an involves an acknowledgement of guilt as well as of the true of predicate factual allegations),故 admission 应译为"供述",而不能译为"供认",因其没有"认",即认罪的含义。在刑事诉讼中,statement 主要是指警方在侦破犯罪过程中对某人,尤指疑犯的招供所作的记录和报告(an account of a person's (usually a suspect's) acknowledgement of a crime, taken by the police pursuant to their investigation of the offense),故应译为"供述记录"。

---

① In overturning the judge:In reversing the trial judge's judgement(在推翻初审法官的判决时)。

② That point was rejected:此处是指"该论点(在上诉时)被驳回",而在初审时其被初审法官,即 judge 所接受。

Lesson Fourteen Successive Confessions and the Poisonous Tree

2. evidence

在美国,evidence(证据)之类型(types of evidence)基本可分为两种,即直接(direct evidence)和间接证据(indirect evident),间接证据也称为旁证(cirumstantial evidence)。证据又可分为三种基本形式(forms of evidence),即言词证据(testimonial evidence)、实物证据(tangible evidence)和司法认知(judicial notice)。其中,实物证据即案件中的展示物品(physical exhibit),其包括实在证据(real evidence)和示意证据(demonstrative evidence)。实在证据指案件中如凶器等"实实在在的东西",而示意证据则指能表明案件某些情况的视听材料,如现场模型和图示等。司法认知是指无须专门证明可由法官确认的事实。此外,证据一般有三大规则,即相关性(relevant)、可采性(competent 或 admissible)和实质性(material),与之相对则为无相关性(irrelevant)、不可采性(incompetent)和非实质性(immaterial)。

3. accused

与 convicted 两者(加上定冠词 the)均用于刑事案件中,指被告或罪犯。其区别在于 the accused 是指因违法行为而受到指控者,在此阶段,按无罪推定原理其还不应被称为罪犯,只有在被定罪,即 convicted of guilty 时,其才可被称为罪犯,故 the accused 只应为"刑事被告"。而 the convicted 指被法院裁定有罪者(a person to be found guilty of a criminal offense),其自然便可被译为"罪犯",至于其是否被判刑、翻案或被赦免等则是后话。此外,在外国法中,the convicted 一般不包括犯藐视法庭罪(contempt of court)而被指控和受罚者,而 the accused 则包括此类人员。

4. assert, affirm, allege, aver, avouch, avow, maintain 与 testify

以上词汇均有"宣称"或"断言"等含义。其中,assert 指有力地且具有说服力地陈述和要求,以求得(法庭等的)认可。affirm 指主动、庄严和正式地宣称或陈述某事属实,故主要表示确认,如上级法院对下级法院判决的确认,以及声称其没有宗教信仰,或声称合同有效,某诉辩事实属实等。allege 表示在尚未提供证据的情况下的声称,其声称的事实需要经过证实或得到否决,故其经常具有"指控"的含义;此外,其还可用作等同 aver。aver 指在诉辩状(pleading)之辩护中引例证明,用简短事实说明,故为"立证"。avouch 指一种提保或确认,尤指确认或证明一行为。avow 指在诉辩状中公开宣称或承认,或证明已实施的行为正当等,如 avow one's guilt。maintain 多指违背事实对以前的陈述进行坚持,或就事实作相反争辩,如:In spite of circumstantial evidence printing to his guilt, the accused maintained that he was innocent。testify 主要指作为证人以提供证据的方式陈述和确认。

5. decision, award, finding, judgment, sentence, verdict, decree, ruling 与 disposition

以上词汇均有裁定、裁决或判决的含义。它们之间的区别在于:decision 为通用词汇,可指任何类别的裁决或判决,如 arbitral decision(仲裁裁决)或 judicial decision(司法裁决)等。award(也称为 arbitrament)专指仲裁裁决或陪审团有关损害赔偿金的裁决。finding(finding of fact 也常简称为 finding)多用于指对事实的裁定。judgment 多指法院对诉讼案件的最终判决(final decision),可指民事判决,也可用于指刑事判决,尤其是指结果为赦免、撤销原判、驳回上诉等不科处刑罚之判决。而与之相对,sentence 的中心含义为科刑(inflicting punishment on the convicted),故其只限于指刑事判决,且为处以刑罚之目的的判决;如无罪开释应用其他词,如 decision 或 judgment 等来表示。verdict 是指陪审团作出的有关事实等的陪审裁决。decree 是指法院根据衡平法上的权利所作的裁定,故多用于指衡平法院、海事法院以及继承和离婚法院所作的判决或裁定。ruling 多指在诉讼中就动议所作出的裁决,以及为解释法律、法令、法规、条例等而作出裁定。disposition 在民事上多指法官就某事项或动议的裁定,等于 judge's ruling;其更多用于刑事案件方面,指科刑,如 probation is often a desirable disposition;此外,其还常用作对未成年罪犯的判决,指科刑或给予其他所规定的对等和处理。

6. act, law, statute, bill 与 legislation

以上词汇均有法律法规的含义。act 主要是指由立法机关所制定的法律(the formal product of a legislative body),该单词常用作单一的法律的名称,翻译时可译为××法,如 Criminal Law Act(《刑法》)、Anti-competitive Act(《反不正当竞争法》)等。相比之下,law 可用作指单部法律或法规,如:a law 或 laws,又可用作表示一般和抽象的含义(the law),但它一般不用作某个特定的法律命令的名称,如 Uniform Law on the International Sale of Goods 则不应译为《统一国际商品销售法》,而只能译为《国际商品销售统一法规编纂》,这样可避免人们将其误认为是一部具体的法规(事实上,它是欧共体的一部示范性法典)。同理,如《中华人民共和国婚姻法》不应翻译为 Marriage Law of the People's Republic of China(此种译法容易被人误认为其是一部论述我国的婚姻法的论著,或一部涵盖所有有关婚姻的法律法规的法规汇纂),而应译为 Marriage Act of the People's Republic of China。statement 主要指"制定法",与判例法相对,因而,作为立法机关制定的 act 既可称作 a law,也可称为 a statute。bill 除有时可指"颁布的成文法"(an enacted statute)之外(如在 Bill of Rights 中),其主要指提交议会审议的"议案"或"法案",一般情况下,a bill 经议会通过生效后,即成为 an act(A legislative proposal offered for debate before its enacted),因而,act 只能译为"法"、"法律"、"法令"等,而决不能译为应由 bill 表示的"法案"。legislation 主要指"立法",即具有立法权力的机关或人所颁布的法律,在这个意义上讲,其与 statute 相似,一般说来,legislation 又可分为本位立法和次位立法两种(primary and secondary legislation)。

7. court of Appeal

在美国,court of appeals(在有些州也称为 court of appeal)可指联邦中级法院或州中级法院。如在加州和路易斯安那州,其是指中级法院,这些州的高级法院称为 supreme court;而在哥伦比亚特区、马里兰和纽约州,court of appeal 是指州高级,即州最高法院,这些州的 supreme court 反而成了州的中级法院。在英格兰,court of appeal 是最高司法法院"Supreme Court of Judicature"的一个分院,译为"上诉法院"。

Exercises

I Verbal Abilities

Part One

Directions: For each of these completing questions, read each item carefully to get the sense of it. Then, in the proper space, complete each statement by supplying the missing word or phrase.

1. The mistress held out to her certain _____, as a result of which she confessed.

 A. inducements   B. incrimination   C. stance

 D. nomenclatures   E. interviews

Lesson Fourteen Successive Confessions and the Poisonous Tree

2. Where a confession _____ the warning requirements provided for by Miranda v. Arizona, it shall be deemed inadmissible.
   A. shackles of
   B. falls foul of
   C. inconsistent with
   D. bear against
   E. relies upon

3. All eight were convicted, with one given a prison sentence, one a suspended sentence, two being fined and four being _____ to keep the peace.
   A. punished
   B. confined
   C. bound over
   D. restrained
   E. forced

4. The victims' initial reasons for not reporting included fear of _____ from the offenders.
   A. assaults
   B. reprisals
   C. poundings
   D. milieu
   E. fouls

5. Robberies in which a number of victims were threatened or assaulted, as in a _____, were not included.
   A. company damage
   B. firm disaster
   C. general catastrophe
   D. sex harassment
   E. bank raid

6. _____ of a compensation scheme is obvious a prerequisite for an application to that scheme.
   A. Knowledge
   B. Eligibility
   C. Assessment
   D. Comprehensibility
   E. Indifference

7. Reference must of course be made to the statutes and decisions of each particular _____.
   A. court
   B. country
   C. region
   D. jurisdiction
   E. tribunal

8. But the English original act received a very strict construction at the hand of a court alarmed at the difficulty of evaluating the _____ injuries to sentiments and affections.
   A. onerous
   B. controversial
   C. spontaneous
   D. fetid
   E. impalpable

9. This necessarily involves a large element of speculation, turning on such matters as life expectancy, income, character, and his past contributions to his family, together with the _____ of an uncertain future.
   A. insouciance
   B. incubus
   C. optimum
   D. insipidity
   E. vicissitudes

10. Particularly _____ misconduct must be deterred through particularly stern action.
    A. famous
    B. set-piece
    C. positive
    D. egregious
    E. salient

Part Two

Directions: Choose the one word or phase that best keep the meaning of the original sentence if it were substituted for the underlined part.

1. On the radar screen appears <u>an unidentified</u> plane.
   A. an unknown
   B. an anonymous
   C. a vague

D. a suspicious   E. a unwarranted

2. No reference is made in Smith to the nub of the objection to the second confession.

A. tip   B. view   C. nip

D. point   E. knob

3. A recent plethora of studies on police effectiveness has, however, confirmed the small role that traditional police investigation plays.

A. overfullness   B. evidence   C. compilation

D. complement   E. morbid

4. It is also consistent with Howley's finding on the stress place by police officers on technical efficiency in their dealing with suspects.

A. loquacious   B. congruent   C. pertaining

D. agreement   E. compliance

5. The Court of Appeal attached more credence to his account, but did not expressly overturn the judge's ruling of fact.

A. attack   B. credit   C. deposit

D. amount   E. belief

6. This is most unlikely to be because they are keen to deter, as such, future behavior of an egregious kind, for the law shies away here from a disciplinary approach.

A. shields from   B. avoids   C. shuffles away from

D. objects to   E. rejects against

7. It is almost free from the intrusion of non-juristic elements, confusing casuistry and sterile abstraction.

A. supernatural ideas   B. doctrines   C. false but clever argument

D. advanced methodology   E. mixed metaphrase

8. Many of America's quaint customs, spawned by the exigencies of pioneer days, have fallen into the state of being quite forgotten.

A. oblivion   B. desuetude   C. concatenation

D. chasm   E. favor

9. Now the legal language of the Romans is a model of terseness, perspicuity and precision.

A. conciseness   B. particularity   C. lucidity

D. meaningfulness   E. succinctness

10. They were called upon from time to time to reduce to writing the rules of law in vogue in the community at any given point of time.

A. fantasy   B. obsolescence   C. practice

D. favor   E. operation

II Cloze

Directions: *For each blank in the following passage, choose the best answer from the choices given.*

Confessions excluded by discretion

Here, there are two possible situations. More obviously, the earlier confession having been excluded under section 78(1), the question which arises is whether or not the later one should equally be excluded under that subsection. However, it is also possible for the earlier confession to be excluded under section 76(2), but the later one under section 78(1).

Ismail appears *to* be an example of the latter situation. There, a whole ___(1)___ of breaches had occurred during the first five ___(2)___. Only the sixth and last had been conducted properly. The judge excluded evidence of the third interview, apparently on the basis of ___(3)___. The Court of Appeal ruled that she should equally have excluded evidence of the last three interviews, but that Court did not place reliance on oppression. Rather, to admit them would be to ___(4)___ the flouting of provisions designed to guard against non genuine confessions, thus having an adverse effect on the possibility of a fair trial for the accused.

It might be suggested that this section 78(1) analysis, in relation to the later confession, would be the better way of explaining *McGovern*, *Glaves* and *Wood*. However, this would be to ___(5)___ in the face of the Court of Appeal's reasoning in all three cases, for in each it was made absolutely clear that the later confession, no less than the earlier, was properly to be excluded under section 76(2).

Somewhat surprisingly, where the ___(6)___ for exclusion has turned entirely on section 78(1), some of the cases are inconsistent with the view taken, as regards section 76(2), in the line of cases beginning with *McGovern*.

Canale seems, at first glance, to favor the *McGovern* view, but turns out, on closer inspection, to be ___(7)___. There, police ___(8)___ of initial interviews in which Canale had made admissions were excluded because they had deliberately made no contemporaneous record and had committed various breaches of Code C. Two later interviews were properly recorded, with no other breach present, yet the Court of Appeal held that evidence of these was also to be excluded. The central matter of dispute between the parties was whether or not Canale's initial admissions, which he accepted he had made, had resulted from certain police ___(9)___. Therefore, the failure to record the initial interviews disabled the court from deciding what was leading Canale to make further admissions at the later stage. Thus, the original taint remained directly operative, for "the initial breaches...affected the whole series of ___(10)___ admissions."

  (1) A. mob   B. lot   C. raft
     D. package   E. pile
  (2) A. interviews   B. entertains   C. confessions
     D. hearings   E. trials
  (3) A. inducement   B. promise   C. seduce

D. horror	E. oppression	
(4) A. agree	B. opposite	C. conducive
D. sedative	E. condone	
(5) A. poke	B. fly	C. flint
D. blow	E. draw	
(6) A. argument	B. point	C. expounding
D. plea	E. motion	
(7) A. controversial	B. questionable	C. equivocal
D. arid	E. tedious	
(8) A. interviews	B. stories	C. addresses
D. accounts	E. remarks	
(9) A. decisions	B. rulings	C. coercing
D. breaches	E. promises	
(10) A. viewed	B. reported	C. recorded
D. purported	E. bound	

III Reading Comprehension

Part One

Directions: *In this section there are passages followed by questions or unfinished statements, each with five suggested answers. Choose the one you think is the best answer.*

Passage one

The undissipated taint line of approach gains support from *Gillard and Rarrett* and from *Yeoman v. DPP*. Both cases were decided after *McGovern* but before *Gloves*, though reference is made to *Mcgovern*,, only in *Yeoman*. In *Gillard and Barrett*, the breaches before the earlier interview with Gillard were a failure to caution her or inform her of her legal rights, while that concerning Barrett was a failure to make a contemporaneous record. The trial judge in each case had excluded evidence of these interviews, but had allowed evidence of the properly conducted ones to be adduced. The Court of Appeal pointed out that:

"there can be no universal rule that whenever the Code has been breached in one or more interviews, all subsequent interviews must be tainted and should therefore be excluded by the trial judge."

It distinguished *Canale* on the basis just suggested. However, it drew the unwarranted conclusion therefrom that it was only if the elements which had led to exclusion of the earlier confessions were still directly operative that it would be proper to exclude later ones. It appears that in the case of neither appellant was legal advice taken between the two sets of interviews. Nor does it seem that a lawyer was present at the later interviews themselves. It is hard to believe, then, that either appellant was in a position to know that the slate against them might well be clean.

In *Yeoman v. DPP* the Divisional Court seems to have adopted a position very similar to that of the Court of Appeal in *Gillard and Barrett*. It is noteworthy that, in relation to the properly-conducted interview, counsel for Yeoman relied strongly on the indirect taint point or, as Rougier J. described it, "a sort of knock-on effect," yet the Court upheld the magistrates' decision to exclude only evidence of the earlier exchanges which had been conducted in breach of various Code C requirements. There were three features of the case which may help to explain this ruling. First, the initial confession seems to have been entirely spontaneous, and it may be that many courts would have admitted it in evidence notwithstanding that it had not been recorded contemporaneously. Secondly, as Taylor L. J. pointed out, a solicitor had been present at the properly-conducted interview. Finally, at a fifth and final interview, Yeoman had both denied his guilt and given a reason for his earlier confessions. This may suggest that, at the immediately preceding interview, he had not felt borne down by the weight of his earlier remarks, especially given that he had the support of a lawyer.

A view more consonant with the *McGovern* line of approach seems to have been taken in *Neil*. In that case, *Canale*, *Gillard and Barrett*, *Yeoman* and *Gloves* were all referred to, though not *McGovern* itself. The trial judge had excluded Neil's first statement under section 78(1) for "numerous breaches" of the codes. The Court of Appeal overturned his decision to allow evidence to be given of a second, properly-conducted interview on the following day. Describing the issue as one of fact and degree, the Court explained that Neil would have considered himself bound by his admissions in the first statement. It referred to the need for him to be given a sufficient opportunity to exercise an "informed and independent choice" as to whether to repeat or retract his earlier admissions, a need not met in Neil's case. The Court does also seem to have said that this test applied only where the objections leading to the exclusion of the earlier statement were of a "fundamental and continuing nature". It is not entirely clear whether any of the earlier code breaches remained directly operative. It seems unlikely that they did, for it must have been the case that the earlier breaches had not been repeated, and the essence of breaches of most code requirements is that they cease to have any direct effect when remedied by later being met. For example, a suspect not cautioned the first time will be the second.

Finally in *Conway*, officers had made at least one visit to the accused in his cell—he said more than one—but had failed to record its contents. Only about 20 minutes after the admitted visit, he made a tape-recorded confession, which confession alone the prosecution sought to rely upon. Conway alleged that, during the unrecorded exchanges, he had been promised that, if he confessed, he could go home to care for his sick mother. Having heard evidence on the *voire dire*, the judge had rejected Conway's account. As a result, she had decided not to exclude his confession under either section 76(2) or section 78(1). The Court of Appeal attached more credence to Conway's account, but did not expressly overturn the judges finding of fact. It relied on *Canale* as showing that earlier breaches may remain relevant even when followed by properly-recorded interviews under caution. It pointed out that one of the earlier breaches had been a failure to caution. Given all this, it is unclear whether or not the Court thought that there might have been an earlier inducement and that, if there had been, it would remain directly operative. Its final conclusion was that:

"the nexus between [the first] interview and that which followed was such that the second could not be safely divorced from the first. No more than 20 minutes separated them in point of time. If the first could not properly be admitted, that told strongly against the admission of the second."

Though no reference is made to the slate not having been wiped clean and no express reliance is placed upon section 78(1) as the basis for exclusion, it seems entirely possible that the Court did intend to exclude for tat reason and under that subsection.

1. In *Gillard and barrett*, the Court of Appeal _____.

   A. reversed the judge's ruling

   B. insisted that the later confession should not be admitted

   C. might have ruled that the appellants prevailed

   D. remanded the case

   E. affirmed the ruling made by the trial judge

2. Which of the following statements is NOT true in respect of *Yeoman v. DPP*?

   A. *Yeoman v. DPP* did not succeed in the appeal.

   B. The author suggests that the lawyer for the appellant wrongly relied on the indirect taint as his ground.

   C. DPP may stand for Director of Public Prosecutions.

   D. In *Yeoman* was interviewed for five times

   E. Some of the evidences were not excluded by the Court.

3. From this passage, we can infer that in *Neil* _____.

   A. the trial judge absolutely excluded Neil's later confession

   B. the Court of Appeal reversed the trial's decision to exclude the evidence received on the following day

   C. the Court of Appeal held that the second confession would be the fruit of the poisonous tree

   D. the suspect was not allowed to get access to legal advise

   E. the case was treated with the well-known cat out of the bag argument.

4. In this passage, *voire dire* means _____.

   A. a formal trial

   B. an oral test

   C. a properly held interview

   D. a preliminary examination

   E. a controversial exchange

Passage two

We may conclude, first, that where the original reason for exclusion of the initial confession remains directly operative, the later one will also be excluded, and this applies whether the exclusionary rule or the exclusionary discretion has been invoked. This at least is consistent with *Smith*. Secondly, as far as the indirect, "cat out of the bag" effect on the later confession is concerned, the authorities are in some disarray. Though in none of them has it been suggested that there is any

Lesson Fourteen Successive Confessions and the Poisonous Tree

basis, in principle, for accepting the indirect ground where section 76(2) is invoked but rejecting it where section 78(1) is invoked, that may be the effect of the law. Part of the problem is that the issue has nowhere been explicitly considered as a whole. In addition, relevant authority has not been cited in several of the cases. Nonetheless, it does seem clear that, where the earlier confession has failed to clear the section 76(2) hurdle, the defense may employ the argument that the accused confessed a second time at least partly because he had confessed a first time. Then, the later confession may be excluded either under section 76(2) itself or, relying on *Ismail*, because its admission would, for the purposes of section 78(1), have an adverse effect on the fairness of proceedings. Finally, where the earlier confession was itself excluded under section 78(1), the cases clash, though the leading case, *Gillard and Barrett*, which says that only a continuing, undisstpated, direct taint will suffice, has never been doubted.

A clear decision, with full discussion of all relevant authorities, whether it be in the Court of Appeal or the House of Lords, is urgently needed, no less for practical reasons than for doctrinal ones. It will probably be clear from the foregoing that this writer's view is that the *McGovern* line of authority is to be preferred, not least because of the encouragement which would otherwise be given to police use of off-the-record softening-up tactics.

United States Supreme Court jurisprudence exhibits a similarly bifurcated approach. The poisonous tree doctrine applies firmly to the situation where the earlier confession has failed to meet the Fifth Amendment's voluntariness requirement. However, where the earlier confession has fallen foul only of the warning requirements provided for by *Miranda v. Arizona*, it is established by *Oregon v. Elstad* that, as long as those warnings have been administered in full before the later confession is forthcoming, that confession will, subject to the other elements of *Miranda* being satisfied, be admissible in evidence.

Justice Brennan, dissenting in *Oregon v. Elstad*, suggested that certain factors were most frequently relied upon by lower courts in arguing that the indirect taint had been removed. In his view, the most effective way of disposing of the taint would be for the law enforcement authorities to advise the suspect that his earlier admissions may not be admissible and that, therefore, he need not speak solely out of a belief that the cat is out of the bag. It is noteworthy that the limitation of the terms of the advice to what *may* be the case is quite deliberate. A second factor was the proximity in time and space of the two confessions. Where there is a considerable time gap and/or different officers conduct the two interviews, this will strengthen the inference that the accused was released from the shackles of his earlier confession. Thirdly, he thought it would be significant that "a meaningful intervening event actually occurred". He gave as examples, consultation with a lawyer, or with family or friends. What he no doubt had in mind was that the accused might thereby be persuaded that his situation had not been rendered hopeless by his earlier confession. Indeed, in a case which Justice Brennan cited as supporting the significance of that factor, the accused had, by the time he confessed a second time, already appeared in court with counsel in order to seek to have the earlier confession suppressed.

1. The issue of the indirect taint _____.

   A. has been well decided

   B. has not been decided because of the clash of laws

   C. has resulted in the inconsistency of the authorities

   D. is resulted form the invocation of Section 76(2)

   E. is resulted from the invocation of Section 78 (1)

2. We may infer that _____.

   A. the author dislike the police softening-up practice

   B. Section 76(2) and Section 78 (1) are sharply contradicted

   C. the Court of Appeal and the House of Lords disagree with each other

   D. case law is inconsistent with statute in the issue of exclusion of the tainted confessions

   E. the appellants did not fare well

3. The passage implies that _____.

   A. the *Miranda* requirements are regularly observed in the United States

   B. where the *Miranda* requirements are not complied with, the evidence collected so shall be excluded

   C. the United States Supreme Court jurisprudence exhibits a multiple approaches in the exclusion of evidence

   D. *McGovern* line of authority is to be preferred by the United States Supreme Court

   E. *Smith* line of authority is to be preferred by the United States Supreme Court

4. According to the passage, we know that _____.

   A. Justice Brennan is a lower court judge

   B. Justice Brennan disagreed with his colleagues in the case *Oregon v. Elstad*

   C. where the indirect taint had been removed the evidence derived from the confession should be admissible

   D. proximity in time and space of the two confessions are not closely linked

   E. consultation with a lawyer, or with family or friends is not preferred by Justice Brennan

IV Translation Abilities

法律语言特征分析与法律翻译技能培养之十四：

法律术语翻译注意事项

法律语言学(Legal Language)是法学领域长期实践的一种产物，其之所以能成为专门的学科独立存在，法律术语起到了十分重要的作用。除源于拉丁、法文等外来语的术语之外，法律术语主要可分为由一般术语演变的专门术语和纯专业术语(words of art)两种。翻译法律术语时，常需注意的事项有：

1. "法人法话"

所谓"法人法话"即尽量做到译成语符合法律习惯和用法，成为地道的法律术语，如将overlapping of laws 翻译为"法规竞合"而非"法律的重叠"等，adverse possession 最好法翻译成"逆权占有"，而不是多数词典中所说"时效占有"或"非法占有"。

2. 准确

要做到取意的准确,最重要的依据是按上下文取意。如 due care and diligence 在民法中多翻译为"应有的注意",而在海商法中则常翻译为"恪尽职守";又以 access 为例,其一般指接触、交流等的权利,在地役权中指通行权,在婚姻法中其既可指夫妻的性权利,也可指离婚父母对子女的探视权。至于含义的取舍,则主要由上下文决定。

3. 切忌望文生义

翻译时最忌讳望文生义,如将 construction of law(法律解释)译为"法律建设",cold-blooded murder(故意谋杀)译为"残忍的谋杀";infamous crime(处以剥夺公民权利的犯罪)译为"丑恶无耻罪"或"丑行罪"等。

4. 注意法律文化和习俗的差异

鉴于英美法系在文化和习俗上与我国的现行法律差异较大,故很多术语不能与我国常用的法律术语完全等值和几乎等值,因而译者不能一味用我国的法律术语与貌似相同的英语术语作对等翻译。为满足翻译的需要,译者有时可生造一定的术语,如将 bilateral contract 译为"双诺合同"而非"双务合同",将 discovery 译为"证据开示程序"等。

5. 同义词的区分

与基础英语相同,就某一概念而言,法律术语除存在一个一般术语之外,多还有一些特殊和具体含义的术语,翻译时应注意它们的差异。如 decision 为一般术语,表示"判决"、"裁决"等。此外,judgment 多指民事判决,sentence 多指刑事判决的量刑,ruling 多指裁定或裁决,而 verdict 则指陪审团的裁决,award 多指仲裁裁决等。

Translation Exercises

Part One *Put the Following into Chinese*

Finally Justice Brennan referred to the purpose and flagrancy of the illegality. In his view, "particularly egregious misconduct must be deterred through particularly stern action". Also, a blatant failure to advise the suspect of his constitutional rights would make it fair to assume that the officers pursued their strategy precisely in order to weaken his ability knowingly and willingly to exercise those rights. We have seen that English courts too have considered the flagrancy of the breach, or its technical nature, as a factor-in the argument one way or the other. This is must unlikely to be because they are keen to deter, as such, future behavior of an egregious kind, for the law shies away here from a disciplinary approach. However, where doubt is cast upon the genuineness of the earlier confession and/or where the provisions breached are designed to guard against non-genuine confessions, *Ismail* suggests that the courts will be more willing also to exclude the later confession, whether because unreliability of the earlier suggests unreliability of the later on because police practices conducive to the generation of unreliable confessions should be discouraged. It remains to be seen what view will be taken where the courts conclude that the earlier police treatment of the suspect may have been designed to soften him up in order to have him confess, in the belief that he might be expected to repeat his confession at a later, set-piece interview.

Part Two *Put the Following into English*

那么,究竟何为社会责任?换言之,社会责任的意蕴何在?纽曼所言社会责任论主张"罪犯之所以应该对一种犯罪行为负责任,仅仅因为(1)他实施了它;(2)他是社会的一员",道出了社会责任论的底蕴。据此,社会责任论实际上是一种存在决定论。在有些人看来,个人是作为社会的份子而存在,其天然便具有不危害社会的义务。

V Interaction

Discuss with your tutor(s) or the People's judges in your locality about the doctrine of the fruit of poisonous tree. Then based on the discussion, you are supposed to write a composition about "The Fruit of Poisonous Tree & Successive Confessions in China". Remember that you are required to express your ideas clearly.

VI Appreciation of Judge's Opinions

(1) Case Name(案件名): *Missouri v. Seibert*

Missouri v. Seibert

Supreme Court of the United States

Argued December 9, 2003
Decided June 28, 2004

Full case name	Missouri, Petitioner v. Patrice Seibert
Citations	542 U. S. 600 (more)
	124 S. Ct. 2601; 159 L. Ed. 2d 643; 2004 U.S. LEXIS 4578; 72 U.S.L.W. 4634; 2004 Fla. L. Weekly Fed. S 476
Prior history	Defendant convicted of second-degree murder, Circuit Court, Pulaski County; affirmed, State v. Seibert, 2002 WL 114804 (Mo. App. S. D.); reversed and remanded for a new trial, State v. Seibert, 93 S.W.3d 700 (Mo. 2002); certiorari granted, Missouri v. Seibert, 538 U. S. 1031 (2003)

Holding

Missouri's practice of interrogating suspects without reading them a Miranda warning, then reading them a Miranda warning and asking them to repeat their confession is unconstitutional.

Court membership

Chief Justice
William Rehnquist
Associate Justices
John P. Stevens · Sandra Day O'Connor
Antonin Scalia · Anthony Kennedy

David Souter · Clarence Thomas
Ruth Bader Ginsburg · Stephen Breyer

Case opinions	
Plurality	Souter, joined by Stevens, Ginsburg, Breyer
Concurrence	Breyer
Concurrence	Kennedy
Dissent	O'Connor, joined by Rehnquist, Scalia, Thomas

Laws applied
U.S. Const. amends. V, XIV

MISSOURI v. SEIBERT
CERTIORARI TO THE SUPREME COURT OF MISSOURI
No. 02-1371. Argued December 9, 2003-Decided June 28, 2004

(2) **Case Summary**(案件简介)

Respondent Seibert feared charges of neglect when her son, afflicted with cerebral palsy(脑性瘫痪;婴儿脑性瘫痪;大脑性麻痹;先天性运动障碍综合征;脑性麻痹;痉挛性两侧麻痹), died in his sleep. She was present when two of her sons and their friends discussed burning her family's mobile home to conceal the circumstances of her son's death. Donald, an unrelated mentally ill 18-year-old living with the family, was left to die in the fire, in order to avoid the appearance that Seibert's son had been unattended. Five days later, the police arrested Seibert, but did not read her her rights under *Miranda* v. *Arizona*. At the police station, Officer Hanrahan questioned her for 30 to 40 minutes, obtaining a confession that the plan was for Donald to die in the fire. He then gave her a 20-minute break, returned to give her *Miranda* warnings, and obtained a signed waiver. He resumed questioning, confronting Seibert with her prewarning statements and getting her to repeat the information. Seibert moved to suppress both her prewarning and postwarning statements. Hanrahan testified that he made a conscious decision to withhold *Miranda* warnings, question first, then give the warnings, and then repeat the question until he got the answer previously given. The District Court suppressed the prewarning statement but admitted the postwarning one, and Seibert was convicted of second-degree murder. The Missouri Court of Appeals affirmed, finding the case indistinguishable from *Oregon* v. *Elstad*, in which this Court held that a suspect's unwarned inculpatory statement made during a brief exchange at his house did not make a later, fully warned inculpatory statement inadmissible. In reversing, the State Supreme Court held that, because the interrogation was nearly continuous, the second statement, which was clearly the product of the invalid first statement, should be suppressed; and distinguished *Elstad* on the ground that the warnings had not intentionally been withheld there. The judgment is affirmed.

(3) **Excerpts of the Judgment**(法官判决词)

Justice Souter announced the judgment of the Court and delivered an opinion, in which Justice Stevens, Justice Ginsburg, and Justice Breyer join.

This case tests a police protocol(议定书;调查书,始末记;草案,草约;教皇诏书等的首尾程序) for custodial interrogation that calls for giving no warnings of the rights to silence and counsel until interrogation has produced a confession. Although such a statement is generally inadmissible(不予采信), since taken in violation of *Miranda* v. *Arizona* (1966), the interrogating officer follows it with *Miranda* warnings and then leads the suspect to cover the same ground a second time. The question here is the admissibility of the repeated statement. Because this midstream recitation(详述,叙述;口头答问) of warnings after interrogation and unwarned confession could not effectively comply with *Miranda*'s constitutional requirement, we hold that a statement repeated after a warning in such circumstances is inadmissible.

I

Respondent Patrice Seibert's 12-year-old son Jonathan had cerebral palsy, and when he died in his sleep she feared charges of neglect(被指控无视孩子) because of bedsores(褥疮) on his body. In her presence, two of her teenage sons and two of their friends devised a plan to conceal the facts surrounding Jonathan's death by incinerating his body in the course of burning the family's mobile home, in which they planned to leave Donald Rector, a mentally ill teenager living with the family, to avoid any appearance that Jonathan had been unattended. Seibert's son Darian and a friend set the fire, and Donald died.

Five days later, the police awakened Seibert at 3 a.m. at a hospital where Darian was being treated for burns. In arresting her, Officer Kevin Clinton followed instructions from Rolla, Missouri, officer Richard Hanrahan that he refrain from giving *Miranda* warnings. After Seibert had been taken to the police station and left alone in an interview room(审问室) for 15 to 20 minutes, Hanrahan questioned her without *Miranda* warnings for 30 to 40 minutes, squeezing her arm and repeating "Donald was also to die in his sleep." After Seibert finally admitted she knew Donald was meant to die in the fire, she was given a 20-minute coffee and cigarette break. Officer Hanrahan then turned on a tape recorder, gave Seibert the *Miranda* warnings, and obtained a signed waiver of rights from her. He resumed the questioning with "Ok, 'trice, we've been talking for a little while about what happened on Wednesday the twelfth, haven't we?," and confronted her with her prewarning statements:

Hanrahan: "Now, in discussion you told us, you told us that there was a[n] understanding about Donald."

Seibert: "Yes."

Hanrahan: "Did that take place earlier that morning?"

Seibert: "Yes."

Hanrahan: "And what was the understanding about Donald?"

Seibert: "If they could get him out of the trailer(拖车式活动房屋), to take him out of the trailer."

Hanrahan: "And if they couldn't?"

Seibert: "I, I never even thought about it. I just figured they would."

Hanrahan: "'Trice, didn't you tell me that he was supposed to die in his sleep?"

Seibert: "If that would happen, 'cause he was on that new medicine, you know...."

Hanrahan: "The Prozac? And it makes him sleepy. So he was supposed to die in his sleep?"

Seibert: "Yes."

After being charged with first-degree murder for her role in Donald's death, Seibert sought to exclude both her prewarning and postwarning statements. At the suppression hearing, Officer Hanrahan testified that he made a "conscious decision" to withhold *Miranda* warnings, thus resorting to an interrogation technique he had been taught: question first, then give the warnings, and then repeat the question "until I get the answer that she's already provided once." He acknowledged that Seibert's ultimate statement was "largely a repeat of information... obtained" prior to the warning.

The trial court(一审法院) suppressed the prewarning statement but admitted the responses given after the *Miranda* recitation. A jury convicted Seibert of second-degree murder. On appeal, the Missouri Court of Appeals affirmed, treating this case as indistinguishable from *Oregon* v. *Elstad* (1985).

The Supreme Court of Missouri reversed(推翻原判), holding that "in the circumstances here, where the interrogation was nearly continuous,... the second statement, clearly the product of the invalid first statement, should have been suppressed." The court distinguished *Elstad* on the ground that warnings had not intentionally been withheld there, and reasoned that "Officer Hanrahan's intentional omission of a *Miranda* warning was intended to deprive Seibert of the opportunity knowingly and intelligently to waive her *Miranda* rights". Since there were "no circumstances that would seem to dispel the effect of the *Miranda* violation," the court held that the postwarning confession was involuntary and therefore inadmissible. *Ibid*. To allow the police to achieve an "end run"(迂回战术,躲避的技巧,常以欺骗或狡诈而躲过阻碍物的战术或技巧) around *Miranda*, the court explained, would encourage *Miranda* violations and diminish *Miranda*'s role in protecting the privilege against self-incrimination(保护其不自证其罪). One judge dissented, taking the view that *Elstad* applied even though the police intentionally withheld *Miranda* warnings before the initial statement, and believing that "Seibert's unwarned responses to Officer Hanrahan's questioning did not prevent her from waiving her rights and confessing.".

We granted certiorari, 538 U. S. 1031 (2003), to resolve a split in the Courts of Appeals.

II

"In criminal trials, in the courts of the United States, wherever a question arises whether a confession is incompetent because not voluntary, the issue is controlled by that portion of the Fifth Amendment(第五修正案条款)... commanding that no person 'shall be compelled in any criminal case to be a witness against himself.' " A parallel rule governing the admissibility of confessions(供述可否接受为证据) in state courts emerged from the Due Process Clause of the Fourteenth Amendment, which governed state cases until we concluded in *Malloy* v. *Hogan* (1964), that "the Fourteenth Amendment secures against state invasion the same privilege that the Fifth Amendment guarantees against federal infringement—the right of a person to remain silent unless he chooses to speak in the unfettered exercise of his own will(其个人意志不受约束), and to suffer no penalty... for such silence." In unifying the Fifth and Fourteenth Amendment voluntariness tests, *Malloy* "made clear what had already become apparent—that the substantive and procedural safeguards(实体与程序的保障) surrounding admissibility of confessions in state cases had become exceedingly exacting(严格的), reflecting all the policies embedded in the privilege" against self-incrimination.

In *Miranda*, we explained that the "voluntariness doctrine in the state cases... encompasses all interrogation practices which are likely to exert such pressure upon an individual as to disable him from making a free and rational choice,". We appreciated the difficulty of judicial enquiry *post hoc*(拉丁文,在此之后,因此) into the circumstances of a police interrogation, and recognized that "the coercion inherent in custodial interrogation blurs the line between voluntary and involuntary statements, and thus heightens the risk" that the privilege against self-incrimination will not be observed. Hence our concern that the "traditional totality-of-the-circumstances" test posed an "unacceptably great" risk that involuntary custodial confessions would escape detection.

Accordingly, "to reduce the risk of a coerced confession and to implement the Self-Incrimination Clause," this Court in *Miranda* concluded that "the accused must be adequately and effectively apprised of his rights and the exercise of those rights must be fully honored," *Miranda* conditioned the admissibility at trial of any custodial confession on warning a suspect of his rights: failure to give the prescribed warnings and obtain a waiver of rights before custodial questioning generally requires exclusion of any statements obtained. Conversely, giving the warnings and getting a waiver has generally produced a virtual ticket of admissibility; maintaining that a statement is involuntary even though given after warnings and voluntary waiver of rights requires unusual stamina(毅力,持久力;精力,体力), and litigation over voluntariness tends to end with the finding of a valid waiver. To point out the obvious, this common consequence would not be common at all were it not that *Miranda* warnings are customarily given under circumstances allowing for a real choice between talking and remaining silent.

III

There are those, of course, who preferred the old way of doing things, giving no warnings and litigating the voluntariness of any statement in nearly every instance. In the aftermath of *Miranda*, Congress even passed a statute seeking to restore that old regime, although the Act lay dormant for years until finally invoked and challenged in *Dickerson* v. *United States*. *Dickerson* reaffirmed *Miranda* and held that its constitutional character prevailed against the statute.

The technique of interrogating in successive, unwarned and warned phases raises a new challenge to *Miranda*. Although we have no statistics on the frequency of this practice, it is not confined to Rolla, Missouri. An officer of that police department testified that the strategy of withholding *Miranda* warnings until after interrogating and drawing out a confession was promoted not only by his own department, but by a national police training organization and other departments in which he had worked. Consistently with the officer's testimony, the Police Law Institute, for example, instructs that "officers may conduct a two-stage interrogation.... At any point during the pre-*Miranda* interrogation, usually after arrestees have confessed, officers may then read the *Miranda* warnings and ask for a waiver. If the arrestees waive their *Miranda* rights, officers will be able to repeat any *subsequent* incriminating statements later in court." The upshot of all this advice is a question-first practice of some popularity, as one can see from the reported cases describing its use, sometimes in obedience to departmental policy.

IV

When a confession so obtained is offered and challenged, attention must be paid to the conflicting objects of *Miranda* and question-first. *Miranda* addressed "interrogation practices...likely...to disable an individual from making a free and rational choice" about speaking, and held that a suspect must be "adequately and effectively" advised of the choice the Constitution guarantees. The object of question-first is to render *Miranda* warnings ineffective by waiting for a particularly opportune time to give them, after the suspect has already confessed.

Just as "no talismanic(护符的,法宝内的,有神奇魔力的)incantation(咒语,咒文,妖术,念咒) is required to satisfy *Miranda*'s strictures," t would be absurd to think that mere recitation of the litany(启应祷文,枯燥、重复的说明或叙述)suffices to satisfy *Miranda* in every conceivable circumstance. "The inquiry is simply whether the warnings reasonably 'convey to a suspect his rights as required by *Miranda*.'" The threshold issue when interrogators question first and warn later is thus whether it would be reasonable to find that in these circumstances the warnings could function "effectively" as *Miranda* requires. Could the warnings effectively advise the suspect that he had a real choice about giving an admissible statement at that juncture? Could they reasonably convey that he could choose to stop talking even if he had talked earlier? For unless the warnings could place a suspect who has just been interrogated in a position to make such an informed choice, there is no practical justification for accepting the formal warnings as compliance with *Miranda*, or for treating the second stage of interrogation as distinct from the first, unwarned and inadmissible segment.

There is no doubt about the answer that proponents of question-first give to this question about the effectiveness of warnings given only after successful interrogation, and we think their answer is correct. By any objective measure, applied to circumstances exemplified here, it is likely that if the interrogators employ the technique of withholding warnings until after interrogation succeeds in eliciting a confession, the warnings will be ineffective in preparing the suspect for successive interrogation, close in time and similar in content. After all, the reason that question-first is catching on is as obvious as its manifest purpose, which is to get a confession the suspect would not make if he understood his rights at the outset; the sensible underlying assumption is that with one confession in hand before the warnings, the interrogator can count on getting its duplicate, with trifling additional trouble. Upon hearing warnings only in the aftermath of interrogation and just after making a confession, a suspect would hardly think he had a genuine right to remain silent, let alone persist in so believing once the police began to lead him over the same ground again. A more likely reaction on a suspect's part would be perplexity about the reason for discussing rights at that point, bewilderment being an unpromising frame of mind for knowledgeable decision. What is worse, telling a suspect that "anything you say can and will be used against you," without expressly excepting the statement just given, could lead to an entirely reasonable inference that what he has just said will be used, with subsequent silence being of no avail. Thus, when *Miranda* warnings are inserted in the midst of coordinated and continuing interrogation, they are likely to mislead and "deprive a defendant of knowledge essential to his ability to understand the nature of his rights and the consequences of abandoning them." By the same token(同样), it would ordinarily be unrealistic to treat two spates of integrated and proximately conducted questioning as independent interrogations subject to independent evaluation simply because *Miranda* warnings formally punctuate them in the middle.

V

Missouri argues that a confession repeated at the end of an interrogation sequence envisioned in a question-first strategy is admissible on the authority of *Oregon* v. *Elstad* (1985), but the argument disfigures(毁损……的外形/外貌,使破相,使变丑;毁损……的优点/价值) that case. In *Elstad*, the police went to the young suspect's house to take him into custody on a charge of burglary. Before the arrest, one officer spoke with the suspect's mother, while the other one joined the suspect in a "brief stop in the living room,", where the officer said he "felt" the young man was involved in a burglary. The suspect acknowledged he had been at the scene. This Court noted that the pause in the living room "was not to interrogate the suspect but to notify his mother of the reason for his arrest," and described the incident as having "none of the earmarks of coercion,". The Court, indeed, took care to mention that the officer's initial failure to warn was an "oversight" that "may have been the result of confusion as to whether the brief exchange qualified as 'custodial interrogation' or... may simply have reflected... reluctance to initiate an alarming police procedure before an officer had spoken with respondent's mother." At the outset of a later and systematic station house interrogation going well beyond the scope of the laconic(文章、说话等简洁的,简短的;精练的) prior admission, the suspect was given *Miranda* warnings and made a full confession. In holding the second statement admissible and voluntary, *Elstad* rejected the "cat out of the bag" theory that any short, earlier admission, obtained in arguably innocent neglect of *Miranda*, determined the character of the later, warned confession, on the facts of that case, the Court thought any causal connection between the first and second responses to the police was "speculative and attenuated". Although the *Elstad* Court expressed no explicit conclusion about either officer's state of mind, it is fair to read *Elstad* as treating the living room conversation as a good-faith *Miranda* mistake, not only open to correction by careful warnings before systematic questioning in that particular case, but posing no threat to warn-first practice generally.

The contrast between *Elstad* and this case reveals a series of relevant facts that bear on(影响) whether *Miranda* warnings delivered midstream could be effective enough to accomplish their object: the completeness and detail of the questions and answers in the first round of interrogation, the overlapping content of the two statements, the timing and setting of the first and the second, the continuity of police personnel, and the degree to which the interrogator's questions treated the second round as continuous with the first. In *Elstad*, it was not unreasonable to see the occasion for questioning at the station house as presenting a markedly different experience from the short conversation at home; since a reasonable person in the suspect's shoes could have seen the station house questioning as a new and distinct experience, the *Miranda* warnings could have made sense as presenting a genuine choice whether to follow up on the earlier admission.

At the opposite extreme are the facts here, which by any objective measure reveal a police strategy adapted to undermine the *Miranda* warnings. The unwarned interrogation was conducted in the station house, and the questioning was systematic, exhaustive, and managed with psychological skill. When the police were finished there was little, if anything, of incriminating potential left unsaid. The warned phase of questioning proceeded after a pause of only 15 to 20 minutes, in the same place as the unwarned segment. When the same officer who had conducted the first phase recited the *Miranda* warnings, he said nothing to counter the probable misimpression that the advice that anything Seibert said could be used against her also applied to the details of the inculpatory(使负罪的,使担责任的) statement previously elicited. In particular, the police did not advise that her prior statement could not be used. Nothing was said or done to dispel the oddity of warning about legal rights to silence and counsel right after the police had led her through a systematic interrogation, and any uncertainty on her part about a right to stop talking about matters previously discussed would only have been aggravated by the way Officer Hanrahan set the scene by saying "we've been talking for a little while about happened on Wednesday the twelfth, haven't we?". The impression that the further questioning was a mere continuation of the earlier questions and responses was fostered by references back to the confession already given. It would have been reasonable to regard the two sessions as parts of a continuum, in which it would have been unnatural to refuse to repeat at the second stage what had been said before. These circumstances must be seen as challenging the comprehensibility and efficacy of the *Miranda* warnings to the point that a reasonable person in the suspect's shoes would not have understood them to convey a message that she retained a choice about continuing to talk.

VI

Strategists dedicated to draining the substance out of *Miranda* cannot accomplish by training instructions what *Dickerson* held Congress could not do by statute. Because the question-first tactic effectively threatens to thwart(反对;阻挠;挫败对方意图等) *Miranda*'s purpose of reducing the risk that a coerced confession would be admitted, and because the facts here do not reasonably support a conclusion that the warnings given could have served their purpose, Seibert's postwarning statements are inadmissible(不予采信). The judgment of the Supreme Court of Missouri is affirmed(维持原判).

It is so ordered.

Lesson Fifteen

Due Process and Targeted Killing of Terrorists

> **Learning objectives**
>
> After learning the text and having done the exercises in this lesson, you will be able to:
> —acquire knowledge of legal characteristics and the nature of due process and its application in practice in the U.S.A.;
> —familiarize yourselves with the vocabulary, grammar, or syntax concerned in this text;
> —become aware of the information required to understand due process;
> —cultivate practical abilities to put to use the language in the specific context; and
> —translate relevant materials from Chinese to English and from English to Chinese.

Due Process and Targeted Killing① of Terrorists

Introduction

Suppose President Obama decides to kill a suspected terrorist②. The President might use a marvel called the—"Predator drone"③, a small, unmanned aircraft④ equipped with surveillance cameras⑤. By Hellfire missiles⑥ launched from the drone, he can kill people thousands of miles away from the White House. The target does not see or hear the weapon as it is fired. The hit, from far enough away, has the tidiness of a video game.

---

① Targeted Killing:定点清除。
② suspected terrorist:恐怖疑犯。
③ Predator drone:捕食者无人机。drone: a remote-controlled pilotless aircraft or missile,(遥控)无人驾驶飞机,导弹。
④ unmanned aircraft:无人驾驶飞机。
⑤ surveillance cameras:监控探头;监控摄影机。
⑥ Hellfire missiles:地狱之火导弹。

"Targeted killing" is extrajudicial①, premeditated killing② by a state of a specifically identified person not in its custody③. States have used this tool, secretly or not, throughout history. In recent years, targeted killing has generated new controversy as two states in particular—Israel and the United States—have struggled against opponents embedded in civilian populations④. As a matter of express policy⑤, Israel engages in targeted killing of persons it deems members of terrorist organizations involved in attacks on Israel. The United States, less expressly, has adopted a similar policy against al Qaeda⑥—particularly in the border areas of Afghanistan and Pakistan, where the CIA has used unmanned Predator drones to fire Hellfire missiles to kill al Qaeda leaders and affiliates. This campaign of Predator strikes has continued into the Obama Administration⑦.

I Reflection on the Attack of the Drone

The United States government has used the Predator with considerable success since 9/11. One important attack occurred in 2002, when a Predator killed a group of al Qaeda members driving in the Yemeni desert. Their remote location ruled out⑧ capture or conventional attack. So the President or one of his delegates gave an order. Then somebody pushed a button that fired a missile, killing all the suspects. Among the dead was an American citizen. Did our government mean to kill an American this way? No one outside the cone of silence⑨ knows, and the CIA will neither confirm nor deny.

Targeted killing by any state poses frightening risks of error and abuse. The fears are heightened by American mistakes at Guantanamo Bay⑩ and by the use of coercive techniques on detainees held outside the full protections of the criminal justice system⑪. It is therefore not surprising that targeted killing has generated a wide range of commentary about its legality. Some condemn targeted killing as extrajudicial execution. Others accept it as a legitimate aspect of armed conflict against determined, organized terrorists from al Qaeda and other groups.

From the technical stance⑫ of the law, much of the controversy over targeted killing stems from the fact that it does not fit comfortably into either of two models that generally control the state's use of deadly force: human rights law and international humanitarian law⑬ (IHL). The human rights model controls law enforcement operations generally, and it permits the state to kill a person

---

① extrajudicial:(Law) (of a sentence) not legally authorized,(律)(判决)无法律效应的,非经法律许可的。另外,(of a settlement, statement, or confession) not made in court; out-of-court(法庭职权以外的)。
② premeditated killing:预先策划的杀人行为。
③ in its custody:被该国监禁;in custody:被监禁。its 代替前面的 state's (国家的)。
④ civilian populations:平民。
⑤ express policy:明确的政策。
⑥ al Qaeda:基地组织。
⑦ Obama Administration:奥巴马政府。
⑧ ruled out:宣布……不可能;排除……的可能性。
⑨ cone of silence:静锥区;盲区。本文指"政府权力中心"。
⑩ Guantanamo Bay:关塔那摩湾。
⑪ criminal justice system:刑事司法制度。
⑫ stance: the attitude of a person or organization towards something; a standpoint(态度;立场;观点)。
⑬ international humanitarian law:国际人道主义法。

not in custody only if necessary to prevent him from posing a threat of death or serious injury to others. IHL is that part of the laws of war that enforces minimum standards of humane treatment of individuals. As part of the *lex specialis*① of war, IHL displaces the human rights model during armed conflicts, granting the state broad authority to kill opposing combatants as well as civilians who are directly taking part in hostilities. Under this two-model dichotomy, extrajudicial, targeted killing of a person who is not an imminent threat can be legal only as permitted under IHL. However, conceding that IHL—as part of the laws of war—can apply to targeted killing might seem to grant the executive too much power to categorize suspected terrorists as combatants and then kill them off② without a shred of process.

II Reasons for the Predator Program

From the perspective of common sense, there are many reasons why the President might keep the trigger authority③ to himself. First, the fewer people involved in a secret decision, the less likely it will leak to the public. Second, launching a missile into a foreign country might be perceived as the making of war④, an activity at the core of the Commander-in-Chief power. Third, if the United States notifies or seeks the permission of the foreign country into which the missile will be fired, diplomatic protocol⑤ suggests that the American head of state be involved. Fourth, related to the other three reasons, the President might trust his own judgment more than that of his advisers.

There are countervailing reasons why the President may choose to delegate the trigger authority. First, the President may not want to dirty his own hands. The making of war against a foreign country, along with dramatic announcements from the Oval Office⑥, may carry an air of dignity. By contrast, the selective killing of individuals, even if well justified, seems more the business of a Mafioso⑦ than a statesman. Second, if something goes wrong with the strike, the President might be able to pass the blame to subordinates⑧ whom he would claim, rightly or wrongly, did not carry out the delegation as he intended. It would be a return to the era of "plausible deniability⑨" when Presidents had their dirty work done on the basis of winks and nods. Third, if the trigger authority is delegated closer to the personnel who operate the Predator drone, the time between spotting the target and deciding to fire the missile would be measured in minutes. On the other hand, if the President pulls the trigger, the time it would take for the intelligence⑩ from the field to be passed to him would be measured in hours, if not days.

---

① *Lex specialis*:特别法。
② kill...off:消灭;把……一个接一个地杀死。
③ trigger authority:本文指"无人机导弹发射授权"。
④ making of war:开战。
⑤ diplomatic protocol:外交礼节。
⑥ Oval Office:美国总统办公室。
⑦ Mafioso:黑手党成员,秘密政党成员。
⑧ subordinates: a person under the authority or control of another within an organization (部属,下级)。
⑨ plausible deniability:(官员等的)能说会道的否认本领;推诿于不知情的本事。
⑩ intelligence:情报。

III Targeted Killing and International Humanitarian Law

Due process depends on the severity of the potential deprivation①as well as the substantive grounds that might justify that deprivation. The procedures suited for determining whether a student should be suspended because she has violated school rules are not suited for determining whether a person should be killed because he has committed murder. Therefore, to assess the due process②of targeted killing, we begin by identifying the circumstances under which this practice has been justified under substantive law.

As a threshold matter, the legality of one form of targeted killing is relatively clear. Recall that the human rights model for law enforcement permits targeted killing where necessary to prevent a person from posing an imminent threat of death or serious injury to others. Here, the human rights model and IHL overlap.

More difficult is the scope of legal authority to kill persons who do not pose an imminent threat. It is commonly (but not universally) accepted that for such killing to be legal, it must comply with IHL. This body of law includes various international treaties and customary international law that can interact in complex ways with American domestic law. In theory, domestic law could bar practices that would otherwise be legal under IHL. As Professors Raven-Hansen and Banks have ably demonstrated, however, American domestic law does not bar③the President from using the tool of targeted killing under some circumstances. Alternatively, domestic authorities might purport to legalize④practices that IHL proscribes. In this regard, scholars have debated the degree to which customary international law binds the executive. Some have gone so far as to claim that the President can, pursuant to his Commander-in-Chief power, override treaties limiting his authority to wage war. For the present purpose, however, we will not wade into this dispute about executive power. As we will show, a reasonable construction of IHL grants the executive considerable power to kill the state's enemies. So for the sake of argument, we accept that the substantive legality of targeted killing depends on its consistency with IHL.

For IHL to apply, an armed conflict must exist as a matter of fact. An armed conflict is something more than sporadic violence—for example, putting down a riot does not constitute an armed conflict. Rather, armed conflict requires protracted armed violence to which the parties may be states or organized armed groups. The applicability of IHL thus does not depend on whether Congress has formally declared war or otherwise announced the existence of an armed conflict. Facts on the ground drive the analysis.

Armed conflicts can be either "international" or "non-international." In *Hamdan v. Rumsfeld*, the Supreme Court held that the conflict with al Qaeda is of the latter type. We take as given that the Court's characterization is correct—a non-international armed conflict does in fact exist between al Qaeda and the United States, which leaves room for IHL to apply. The law of non-inter-

---

① deprivation：本文指"剥夺生命"。
② due process：正当程序；法定诉讼程序。
③ bar：(Law) prevent or delay (an action) by objection (禁止；阻止)。
④ legalize：使有法律效力。

national armed conflicts, however, is best understood in light of the much better developed law of international armed conflicts—to which we now turn.

The law of international armed conflicts grants states broad authority to kill opposing "combatants" but sharply limits their authority to kill "civilians." The category of lawful combatant includes members of the armed forces of an opposing state as well as members of other organized armed groups of the state that satisfy the following four conditions: (a) they are commanded by responsible authority; (b) they wear a fixed, distinctive emblem recognizable at a distance; (c) they carry their arms openly; and (d) they comport with the laws and customs of war.

It is often asserted that a combatant can legally kill opposing combatants provided they have not made plain that they are *hors de combat*① by, for instance, surrendering with the proverbial② white flag. Unlike the law enforcement model, this assertion leaves room to kill persons without regard to whether they pose any immediate threat at all—think of bombing soldiers while they sleep in their barracks. Some, however, maintain that this room to kill opposing combatants③ is not so absolute given a proper understanding of "military necessity", which requires that "the kind and degree of force resorted to must be actually necessary for the achievement of a legitimate military purpose." This limits "senseless slaughter of combatants where there manifestly is no military necessity to do so, for example where a group of defenseless soldiers has not had the occasion to surrender, but could clearly be captured without additional risk to the operating forces." In the archetypical battle zone in which well-matched adversaries fight each other in real time, the choice between these models does not much matter. Often, opposing forces have not clearly surrendered or been incapacitated④. But, as applied to targeted killing, one might argue that the principle of military necessity blocks killing an isolated enemy combatant who can be captured without risk to his captors or bystanders. On this view, neither the CIA nor the military could kill an unarmed al Qaeda operative who could easily be captured. They could not, for instance, shoot Jose Padilla at O'Hare Airport rather than arrest him. This view of military necessity suggests that apart from other legal and diplomatic concerns, it is more difficult to justify targeted killing in locations the United States or its allies control than elsewhere; it is just easier to capture a terrorist in Chicago or London than in the mountains of Pakistan. Given that executive officials have every incentive to capture al Qaeda members to interrogate them, a limited approach to military necessity—which allows killing only where capture is risky—is presumably consistent with United States policy toward terrorists.

Consistent with military necessity, attacks must be designed to reduce an adversary's military strength and force submission rather than to punish in a reprisal⑤. Of course, in the context of the war on terror, a suspected terrorist's past actions such as prior attacks on civilians, prior assembly

---

① *hors de combat*: (法)adj. 失去战斗力的。
② proverbial: 出名的, 众所周知的; 谚语的, 谚语所表达的。
③ opposing combatants: 地方战斗人员。
④ incapacitated: 丧失战斗能力。
⑤ reprisal: 报复行为。

of bombs, and prior financial support to terrorist cells①will inevitably be factored into decisions about future intent and dangerousness. Moreover, the higher the suspected terrorist is within the hierarchy②of his group, the greater the need for self-defense against that terrorist. A Predator strike on Osama bin Laden has a greater claim on necessity than a strike on his driver Salim Hamdan.

Also, the laws of war bar treachery or perfidy. This does not bar a surprise attack on a legitimate military target by a Predator strike—at least if the attacker has not unfairly tricked the target into thinking he is safe. It does, however, bar attackers from posing as members of the Red Cross to lure targets into an ambush. Similarly, it would be treacherous, and a violation of the laws of war, to hoist a white flag and shoot at the people who then attempt to capture you.

"Civilians" are shielded from direct attack except when they are taking a direct part in the hostilities. To give effect to the crucial combatant-civilian distinction, plans of attack must discriminate between lawful and unlawful targets, and planners must use feasible precautions to avoid harming civilians. Attacks also must be proportionate, i.e., they must not cause excessive "collateral damage" to persons or property that the laws of war do not permit to be directly targeted. Thus, it would be a war crime to drop a nuclear bomb on Tehran to kill one suspected terrorist.

To summarize, where IHL applies, the United States may kill terrorists either as civilians who are directly participating in hostilities or, possibly, as "combatants" provided their commitment to terrorism is sufficiently active and deep. In practice, the difference between these two approaches may be more theoretical than real because what is needed to show direct participation in hostilities may also show active and deep support. On either approach, the legality of an attempt to kill would depend on many factors—for example, the attack would need to be part of an armed conflict, satisfy the requirement of military necessity (which in this context may preclude the possibility of safe arrest), target a person not protected from direct attack, honor the rules against treachery and perfidy③, avoid disproportionate civilian casualties, etc.

IV Due Process and Enemy Combatants

In our age of terror, one challenge is to determine whether the Constitution's Due Process Clause imposes procedural controls on how the government goes about killing suspected terrorists. A conclusion that no limits exist might allow the government to engage in extra-judicial, targeted killing with impunity. Limits that are too constrictive, by contrast, might prevent the from protecting the nation from attacks more catastrophic than 9/11.

Similar concerns about the balance between oversight and discret al cases discussing detention of "enemy combatants." Two blockbu first is Hamdi v. Rumsfeld—arguably still the most important decision handed down relating to due process in the war on terror. In Hamdi, a con Court invoked the Due Process Clause to sketch a framework for deciding whether a

---

① cell：(喻) 政治活动核心小组(通常为颠覆性的秘密组织)。
② hierarchy：统治集团；领导层。
③ perfidy：背信弃义；背叛。
④ blockbusters：重磅炸弹，了不起的人或事。

izen could be detained as an enemy combatant. The second is Boumediene v. Bush, in which the Court ruled that prisoner sat Guantanamo Bay had a constitutional right to habeas corpus[①]in the federal courts. For purposes of this discussion, Boumediene is especially important for what it says and suggests about extraterritorial[②]application of the Due Process Clause.

A. *Hamdi v. Rumsfeld* Sketches a Due Process Framework for Detention

Yaser Esam Hamdi, an American citizen by virtue of his birth in Louisiana to Saudi parents, was plucked from the battlefield in Afghanistan after 9/11. The government claimed the authority to designate him an enemy combatant, and, given this designation, to detain him for the duration of the war on terror. It claimed constitutional authority from the President's inherent power to protect national security. It also claimed congressional support from the Authorization for the Use of Military Force (AUMF), which granted the President authority to use all necessary and appropriate force against those nations, organizations, or persons he determines planned, authorized, committed, or aided the terrorist attacks.

Even on the assumption that the government has the power to detain persons like Hamdi as enemy combatants, what procedures must the government provide? As an answer to this question, the Bush Administration argued that either: (a) courts should play no role whatsoever in determining whether a given person was an enemy combatant; or, at most, (b) courts should confine themselves to determining whether "some evidence" proffered by the government supported the designation—a standard the government said it satisfied in Hamdi's case by a hearsay affidavit[③]from a Defense Department official.

In deciding these intertwined questions of power and process, the Supreme Court broke into four groups. One group, including Justices Scalia and Stevens, dissented based upon a hard-line of protecting civil liberties. They insisted that the traditional and proper means for detaining a citizen accused of treason or similar crimes was via criminal prosecution. The government could avoid this process only if Congress had used its constitutional authority to suspend the writ of habeas corpus, which it had not done. The choice confronting the government was therefore simple: Bring criminal charges such as treason against Hamdi and honor the Bill of Rights, or release him.

Justice Thomas, writing solely for himself, dissented based on a hard-line of protecting executive discretion during an armed conflict. He conceded that it was a proper judicial function to determine whether the executive possessed the power to detain enemy combatants. The answer to this question was a straightforward "yes", because detaining the enemy for the duration of a conflict is a fundamental incident of war.

B. *Boumediene v. Bush* and the Worldwide Reach of Due Process

On a crabbed reading, one might think that Hamdi should have little relevance to the broader war on terror because it addressed the executive's power to detain as an enemy combatant an American citizen in the United States. The overwhelming majority of detainees in the war on terror are

---

① habeas corpus:人身保护权。
② extraterritorial:治外法权的;在疆界以外的;不受管辖的。
③ affidavit:(Law) a written statement confirmed by oath or affirmation, for use as evidence in court (律)(经宣誓或确认在法庭作为证据的)附誓书面陈述,宣誓书。

not Americans, and the group that has attracted the most attention languishes in Guantanamo, technically not American soil. The detainees were shipped to Guantanamo Bay when the Bush Administration was under the mistaken impression that federal courts would not interfere with military detentions outside of American sovereign territory. Even so, on the same day it issued Hamdi, the Supreme Court also issued *Rasul v. Bush*, which extended the statutory right of habeas corpus to Guantanamo.

The Court's decisions triggered reactions from the other branches. Given Rasul, the military concluded that it would be wise to grant hearings of the sort suggested in Hamdi to Guantanamo detainees. These hearings were held by entities called Combatant Status Review Tribunals (CSRTs). They determined whether each detainee was such a threat to national security that he should remain imprisoned as an enemy combatant. Consistent with Hamdi's template, the rules for CSRTs departed from the criminal justice model by, among other things, presuming the government's evidence to be valid and allowing CSRTs to base their conclusions on hearsay and classified① evidence kept secret from the detainee.

Congress responded to Rasul and Hamdi by passing the Detainee Treatment Act② of 2005 (DTA). The DTA contained strong language that seemed to strip federal courts of jurisdiction on habeas petitions from Guantanamo detainees. Plus, the DTA funneled review of CSRT determinations to the D.C. Circuit③, but with unclear limits on that court's scope of review.

V Due Process and Targeted Killing

Where the paradigm of war applies, the executive dominates in deciding who lives or dies. Justice O'Connor nonetheless claimed in Hamdi that the war on terror does not give the executive a blank check④ to do as it pleases in the name of security. If one accepts this premise, then the question becomes how to control the executive's war power without unduly hampering it. Under a Mathews-style approach, to determine whether due process demands a particular procedural control over targeted killing, one should: (a) identify the range of legitimate interests that the procedure might protect; (b) assess the degree to which adoption of the procedure actually would protect these interests; and (c) weigh these marginal benefits against the damage the procedure may cause other legitimate interests.

Judicial control of targeted killing could increase the accuracy of target selection, reducing the danger of mistaken or illegal destruction of lives, limbs, and property. Independent judges who double-check targeting decisions could catch errors and cause executive officials to avoid making them in the first place.

More broadly, judicial control of targeted killing could serve the interests of all people—targets and non-targets—in blocking the executive from exercising an unaccountable, secret power to kill. If possible, we should avoid a world in which the CIA or other executive officials have unbe-

---

① Classified:(信息)归入机密的,保密的。
② Detainee Treatment Act:《被监禁者待遇法》。
③ D. C. Circuit:华盛顿哥伦比亚特区联邦巡回法院。D. C. = District of Columbia.
④ blank check:空白支票。本文中指自由处理权。

lievable power to decide who gets to live and who dies in the name of a shadow war that might never end. Everyone has a cognizable interest in stopping a slide into tyranny.

Yet—in favor of executive autonomy—we live in an imperfect world where judicial obstacles to killing could hinder national security. It would be silly, for instance, to require the military to use the full procedures of the law enforcement model to decide what to bomb in the midst of a war. Likewise, given the conflict with al Qaeda, it may be silly to judicialize① the process for killing its committed members. Moreover, not only does judicialization threaten national security, it might not deliver countervailing benefits because courts lack the competence to improve military and national security decisions.

Reasonable minds can and do differ on how to balance such concerns. That said, one possible balance is to reject virtually all judicial control of targeted killing, a position that comports with② Justice Thomas's treatment of executive detentions in his Hamdi dissent. A hands-off③ approach, however, is impossible to square with④ the historical fact that courts can and do judge whether military actions constitute war crimes. Indeed, the Geneva Conventions⑤ require states to prosecute or extradite persons who have committed grave breaches, a category that includes, among other crimes; willful, wanton, unjustified killing or infliction of great suffering. The United States has codified this requirement in the War Crimes Act.

Besides legal barriers, there are many practical barriers to prosecutions under the laws of war. Primary among them, a prosecuting authority must see enough evidence to conclude that a war crime occurred. Such information will often be buried under the rubble of war or surrounded in secrecy. Also, the prosecuting authority must have the political will to bring an action. As a general rule, no government wishes to prosecute one of its own officials for war crimes. Still, a war criminal from one country—especially a weak or defeated one—just might find himself facing prosecution in the courts of another country or an international authority.

For these and related reasons, it is beyond doubt that many more war crimes occur than are prosecuted. Nonetheless, even if a CIA official who authorizes a Predator strike faces little threat of criminal liability, the potential for criminal prosecution proves our point: It is common—indeed, obvious—that courts do have a role to play in identifying the limits of acceptable warfare.

But might due process require courts to play a more expansive role in controlling targeted killing than adjudicating a war crime prosecution that may never come? Justice Thomas mocked this possibility in Hamdias leading to the conclusion that executive officials must give notice and an opportunity to be heard⑥ to a person before killing him with a missile. This *reductio ad absur*

---

① judicialize:使司法化;使履行司法程序。
② comport with:一致,相符。
③ hands-off:(adj.) 不插手的;不干涉的。比较:hand-off (n.),传球给队友。
④ square with:(使)与……相符。
⑤ Geneva Conventions:日内瓦各公约(规定战时被俘及受伤军事人员和平民的地位和待遇的国际协议,1864 年初订于日内瓦,后有修改)。
⑥ hear:此处不是"听见"之意,而是"听审"或"审理"。

dum① does not stand up to scrutiny, however, for the simple reason that due process does not always demand notice and an opportunity to be heard before a deprivation occurs. Where such pre-deprivation procedures would be impracticable, due process may take the form of post-deprivation procedures. North American Cold Storage Co. v. City of Chicago provides a canonical② example. In this case, local authorities seized and destroyed meat they had determined was putrid and unfit for sale. The Court③ held that, because of health concerns, immediate destruction was acceptable to prevent the meat from being sold on the sly④ during the pendency of any hearings. The owners of the meat were not left without a remedy, though; they were free to sue the local officials in tort for the value of their destroyed meat.

No matter the variations between internal and external oversight, we stand by our central point: Under the Due Process Clause, the executive must conduct some kind of serious investigation of any targeted killing. In keeping with the purpose and the pragmatism of Mathews v. Eldridge, this investigation should be as thorough, independent, and public as possible without damage to national security.

Striking the balance between openness and security requires nuance. Even so, failing to develop any investigatory program for Predator strikes is not an option under law. Since executive officials swear to uphold the Constitution, they should, if they have not done so already, develop a solid review of the Predator program without waiting for a court order which is unlikely to come.

Conclusion

This Article has explored the implications of the due process model that the Supreme Court developed in Hamdi v. Rumsfeld and Boumediene v. Bush for targeted killing—particularly Predator strikes by the CIA. Contrary to Justice Thomas's charge, this model does not break down in the extreme context of targeted killing but, instead, suggests useful means to control this practice and heighten accountability. One modest control is for appropriate plaintiffs to bring Bivens-style actions to challenge the legality of targeted killings, no matter where they may have occurred in the world. Resolution of any such action that surmounted all the practical and legal obstacles in its way—including the state-secrets privilege and qualified immunity—would enhance accountability without causing substantial risk to national security. Yet as a practical matter, this role for the courts is vanishingly small. It is therefore all the more important that the executive branch itself develop fair, rational procedures for its use of targeted killing. Under Boumediene, it has a constitutional obligation to do so. To implement this duty, the executive should, following the lead of the Supreme Court of Israel and the European Court of Human Rights, require an independent, intra-executive investigation of targeted killing by the CIA. Even in a war on terror, due process demands at least this level of accountability for the power to kill suspected terrorists.

---

① reductio ad absurdum: 拉丁语，归谬法，间接证明法；反证法（说明某一命题的反面为不可能或荒谬，以证明该命题为正确）。
② canonical: 按照教规的；权威的；公认的。
③ Court: 法院、法官、裁判所。本文里应理解为"法官"。
④ on the sly: 秘密地。

Lesson Fifteen Due Process and Targeted Killing of Terrorists

Legal Terminology

1. legislator 与 lawmaker

两个术语均有"立法者"的含义。区别在于 legislator 与 legislature 相关,故其多指属于立法机关成员(member of a legislature)者。而 law-maker 则范围较广,除包括 legislator 之外,通过判例制定法律的法官,甚至缔结合同的双方当事人,在某种意义上都可以称为 law maker。

Legislator: a person who makes laws, esp. a member of a legislative body.

Lawmaker: Although historically lawmaker was thought to be equivalent to legislator, the advent of legal realism made it apply just as fully to a judge as to a legislator.

2. admission、confession 与 statement

三个术语均与被告招认违法或犯罪事实有关。confession 多限于刑事犯罪领域(在加拿大民事诉讼程序中,其可用于等同 formal admission),指刑事被告完全承认其被指控的犯罪及有关定罪所需的所有事实,或至少是主要事实,并承认有罪(acknowledgement of guilt),有供认不讳的含义,陪审团根据其招供则可作出有罪裁定,故为"供认"。相比之下,admission 常用作指对民事责任行为的承认。在刑事领域,admission 多指对无犯罪故意的刑事责任行为的招认,多表示承认一个或数个事实,此种招供远没有达到足以定罪程度;与 confession 相比,admission 主要的区别在于被告无认罪表示(an *admission* is a confession that an allegation or factual assertion is true without any acknowledgement of guilt with respect to the criminal charges, whereas a *confession* involves an acknowledgement of guilt as well as of the true of predicate factual allegations.),故 admission 应译为"供述"而不能是"供认",因其没有"认",即认罪的含义。在刑事诉讼中,statement 主要是指警方在侦破犯罪过程中对某人,尤指疑犯的招供所作的记录和报告:an account of a person's (usually a suspect's) acknowledgement of a crime, taken by the police pursuant to their investigation of the offense,故应译为"供述记录"。

3. affidavit 与 deposition

两者均有口供书的含义。其区别在于 affidavit(宣誓证明书)是一种宣誓文件,为不经盘问而自愿所作的口供的笔录,当证人无法亲自出庭时,affidavit 可被法庭作为证言接受。deposition(证明笔录)则是宣誓后在正式质询下所作口头证明的笔录,是接受诘问的一种产物。在法律程序中,按规定,向法庭提供 deposition 的当事人必须向另一方当事人通知,并给予另一方当事人对证人进行盘诘(cross-examination)的机会;相比之下,affidavit 则无如此之规定。

4. apprehension、arrest、attachment 与 seizure

这些单词均有逮捕或拘捕的含义。其中,apprehension 和 arrest 都是指刑事拘捕,可互换使用,apprehension 是指将罪犯抓获并以拘禁。arrest 则指对正在实施犯罪的人或被怀疑实施了犯罪的人进行的实际管束,尤指将某人拘押以送警察局进行刑事指控。attachment 多用于民事上的拘押,常指对债务人的人身进行拘捕以迫使其到庭解决债务纠纷。seizure 所指的拘捕有两种含义,一是达到 arrest 的程度,另一种则是短时间拘捕以讯问或调查(等同 stop)。根据宪法规定,两种情况对逮捕令(warrant)的要件要求也就不同。

5. argue、debate、dispute 与 reason

这些单词均有争辩或辩论的含义。argue 为最常用单词,主要在于说服他人接受某项结论或支持、证明某项结论,其有时措辞较激烈,有接近争吵之嫌;argue 也可指在法庭上陈述案情。debate 通常指正式的 argue,双方陈述观点,过程受裁决人的控制,且按一定的规则进行,尤指议会对议案进行讨论等,如:The House of Representatives debate the proposal for two days。dispute 则常指感情多于理性的 argue,且常带有一种派系观点。reason 多指谨慎和煞费苦心进行的争辩,目的在于劝导或作某课题上深层次的探讨。

Exercises

I Verbal Abilities

Part One

Directions: *For each of these questions, read each item carefully to get the sense of it. Then, in the proper space, complete each statement by supplying the missing word or phrase.*

1. Senior executives should drill down decision-rights and _____ to operating managers who handle the capital.

 A. capability   B. potentiality   C. competency

 D. incapability   E. accountability

2. Once registered, a trade union becomes a body corporate and enjoys _____ from certain civil suits.

 A. exemption   B. resistance   C. immunity

 D. infection   E. susceptibility

3. The Bear funds had borrowed to _____ returns, and in doing so had to post collateral with lenders, known as prime brokers.

 A. combat   B. uplift   C. enrich

 D. enhance   E. develop

4. Where such action constitutes a crime, criminal _____ shall be pursued in accordance with the law.

 A. accountability   B. liability   C. incredibility

 D. capability   E. fatigability

5. The U. S. government especially the department of Justice on its failing on its basic responsibility to investigate and _____ contractors who are implicated in Iraq and Afghanistan.

 A. prosecute   B. execute   C. discharge

 D. represent   E. defend

6. The public interest provides the _____ basis for the administrative behavior such as administrative requisition.

 A. legalized   B. discriminative   C. legally

 D. legitimate   E. rightful

7. Charges against a sixth detainee were _____ last month without explanation, but experts note he has claimed some of the evidence against him was obtained through torture.

 A. withdrawn   B. disengaged   C. deposited

Lesson Fifteen Due Process and Targeted Killing of Terrorists

D. adjourned   E. secluded

8. British _____ government pattern in the Middle Ages is the judicature, and authority of the king gets certain limit in the judicial field, but in the political field.

A. constitutionality   B. unconstitutional   C. constitutional
D. constitutionally   E. contradictory

9. Currency, credit and interest rate risks at some monetary authorities are now such that specific market movements would generate _____ losses.

A. moderate   B. catastrophic   C. harmful
D. calamity   E. institutional

10. The bulk of China's growing peacekeeping mission, which reflects its desire to become a big power, lacks one _____: good English skills.

A. necessity   B. essential   C. requirement
D. opportunity   E. potential

Part Two

Directions: *Choose the word or phase that best keeps the meaning of the original sentence if it substitutes for the underlined part.*

1. In a modern war both <u>combatant</u> and noncombatant are killed in air attack.

A. belligerent   B. combat   C. soldier
D. civilian   E. bomber

2. Their <u>customary</u> rights are recognized locally, but often not accepted in law, or in the terms of a foreign-investment deal.

A. accustomed   B. unusual   C. conventional
D. habitual   E. established

3. This research has obvious <u>implication</u> for law enforcement and is being used by Salt Lake county sheriffs to help identify a murdered woman.

A. significance   B. deduction   C. entailment
D. incapacity   E. implementation

4. Given the recent release of economic data, inflation has been persistently an <u>imminent</u> threat.

A. prominent   B. outstanding   C. impending
D. distinguishing   E. distinguished

5. We will never allow any change to the history, reality and universally-recognized legal status of Taiwan, that is, it has been an <u>inalienable</u> part of China/'s territory since ancient times.

A. indefensible   B. inviolable   C. unforgettable
D. insupportable   E. indefeasible

6. The Meat Cutters decision expanded the range of procedural safeguards that are considered relevant to the <u>delegation</u> question.

A. commission   B. deputation   C. relegation
D. authorization   E. delegacy

7. For the female, the greatest challenge from an evolutionary perspective is to ensure that her genetic investment flourishes.
  A. position   B. prospect   C. prospective
  D. promising   E. prosperity

8. Most analysts reckon that Russia's fleet is more frightening on paper than in reality, and that it is too stretched to upset the balance of power in the Mediterranean.
  A. terrorization   B. alarming   C. weird
  D. speculative   E. risky

9. In the United States more recently, controversy has centered on state-owned companies rather than acquisitive sovereign-wealth funds.
  A. quarrelsome   B. contestant   C. argumentation
  D. controversial   E. consistency

10. But to fully explain the origin of life, the remarkable trend toward complexity and the invention of intelligence requires more than addition.
  A. stupidity   B. intellect   C. intellectual
  D. information   E. intellection

II Cloze

Directions: *For each blank in the following passage, choose the best answer from the choices given.*

  If the journalists are correct, the Bush ___(1)___ chose speed over accountability on Predator strikes. America's ghost warriors, men and ___(2)___ at the CIA, were trusted to do the right thing in protecting America's national ___(3)___. Any formal process that preceded a CIA strike was ___(4)___. Determinations that the target had been properly ___(5)___ and that collateral damage would be acceptable may have occurred solely at Langley without any input from the National Security Council, the White House, or other parts of the ___(6)___ branch. Participation by the other ___(7)___ branches, if any, appears to have been limited to the provision of notice to the heads of Intelligence Committees in the ___(8)___ and Senate.

  We know less about the Obama Administration in its early days. To start, it attempted a clean break from some of the Bush Administration's counterterrorism policies. In his first week in ___(9)___, President Obama signed executive ___(10)___ that required closure of Guantanamo Bay as a detention center within a year and precluded the CIA from conducting interrogations using methods beyond those outlined in the Army Field Manual. Predator strikes ___(11)___ suspected terrorists, however, have continued.

  All in all, it is not clear as a matter of common ___(12)___ whether during the Bush Administration, the President or a ___(13)___ was the person on the trigger of the Predator drone. The public record, however, presents some clues. Jane Mayer, Dana Priest, and other investigative ___(14)___ have reported that soon after 9/11, President Bush delegated trigger authority to the Director of the Central Intelligence Agency (DCIA), and in turn, the DCIA delegated his authority

Lesson Fifteen Due Process and Targeted Killing of Terrorists

to the head of the CIA's Counterterrorist Center. That means that two men who garnered their own controversy on other stories, Cofer Black and Jose Rodriguez, had the power to kill or not kill. These two were neither elected nor subject to Senate confirmation. They also were not part of the Pentagon's chain-of-command① or, so far as is publicly known,　　(15)　　to the extensive body of rules that the Department of Defense has developed to ensure its compliance with the laws of war.

(1) A. government   B. executive   C. Administration
    D. office   E. branch
(2) A. people   B. children   C. human beings
    D. women   E. peoples
(3) A. defense   B. safety   C. danger
    D. risk   E. security
(4) A. secret   B. mystery   C. enigma
    D. hidden   E. private
(5) A. discovered   B. identified   C. described
    D. designated   E. distinguised
(6) A. governmental   B. administrative C. judicial
    D. legislative   E. executive
(7) A. two   B. three   C. four
    D. security   E. national
(8) A. Senate   B. House   C. Hall
    D. Office   E. Camera
(9) A. work   B. job   C. assignment
    D. office   E. task
(10) A. ordinations   B. edicts   C. commands
     D. orders   E. dictations
(11) A. upon   B. for   C. against
     D. with   E. toward
(12) A. sense   B. meaning   C. appreciation
     D. practice   E. authorization
(13) A. superior   B. peers   C. subordinate
     D. counterpart   E. equal
(14) A. reporters   B. journalists   C. writers
     D. dramatists   E. plumbers
(15) A. aim   B. intend   C. object
     D. subject   E. oppose

---

① chain-of-command:指挥系统;行政管理系统。

III Reading Comprehension

Part One

Directions: *In this section there a passage followed by questions or unfinished statements, each with suggested answers. Choose the one you think is the best answer.*

Amendment XIV to the United States Constitution was adopted on July 9, 1868 as one of the Reconstruction Amendments.

Its Citizenship Clause① provides a broad definition of citizenship that overruled the Dred *Scott v. Sandford* (1857) holding that blacks could not be citizens of the United States.

Its Due Process Clause② prohibits state and local governments from depriving persons of life, liberty, or property without certain steps being taken to ensure fairness. This clause has been used to make most of the Bill of Rights③ applicable to the states, as well as to recognize substantive and procedural rights.

Its Equal Protection Clause④ requires each state to provide equal protection under the law to all people within its jurisdiction. This clause was the basis for Brown v. Board of Education (1954), the Supreme Court decision which precipitated⑤ the dismantling⑥ of racial segregation in the United States.

The amendment also includes a number of clauses dealing with the Confederacy⑦ and its officials.

Section 1. All persons born or naturalized⑧ in the United States, and subject to the jurisdiction thereof, are citizens of the United States and of the State wherein they reside. No State shall make or enforce any law which shall abridge⑨ the privileges or immunities⑩ of citizens of the United States; nor shall any State deprive any person of life, liberty, or property, without due process of law; nor deny to any person within its jurisdiction the equal protection of the laws.

...

Section 5. The Congress shall have power to enforce, by appropriate legislation, the provisions of this article.

Due Process Clause

Beginning with Allgeyer v. Louisiana (1897), the Court interpreted the Due Process Clause of the Fourteenth Amendment as providing substantive protection to private contracts and thus pro-

---

① Citizenship Clause:公民的权利和义务条款。
② Due Process Clause:正当程序条款。
③ Bill of Rights:权利宣言:美国宪法前十条修正条款。
④ Equal Protection Clause:平等保护条款。
⑤ precipitate:促成;使发生。
⑥ dismantle:废除;取消。
⑦ the Confederacy:美国(南北战争时的)南部邦联(正式名称为 the Confederate States of America)。
⑧ naturalize:接收(外国人)入籍。
⑨ abridge:剥夺。
⑩ immunities:保护。

hibiting a variety of social and economic regulation, under what was referred to as "freedom of contract①". Thus, the Court struck down② a law decreeing maximum hours for workers in a bakery in Lochner v. New York (1905) and struck down a minimum wage law in Adkins v. Children's Hospital (1923). However, the Court did uphold some economic regulation such as state prohibition laws (Mugler v. Kansas), laws declaring maximum hours for mine workers (Holden v. Hardy, 1898), laws declaring maximum hours for female workers (Muller v. Oregon, 1908), President Wilson's intervention in a railroad strike (Wilson v. New, 1917), as well as federal laws regulating narcotics (United States v. Doremus, 1919).

The Court repudiated③ the "freedom of contract" line of cases in West Coast Hotel v. Parrish (1937). In the past forty years it has recognized a number of "fundamental rights" of individuals, such as privacy, which the states can regulate only under narrowly defined circumstances. The Court has also significantly expanded the reach of procedural due process, requiring some sort of hearing before the government may terminate civil service employees, expel a student from public school, or cut off a welfare recipient's benefits.

The Court has ruled that in certain circumstances, the Due Process Clause requires a judge to recuse④ himself on account of concern of there being a conflict of interest⑤. For example, in Caperton v. A. T. Massey Coal Co. (2009) the Court ruled that a justice of the Supreme Court of Appeals of West Virginia had to recuse himself from a case that involved a major contributor to his campaign for election to that court.

The Due Process Clause has been used to apply most of the Bill of Rights to the states.

1. Which of the following is true according to the Citizenship Clause of the US Constitution?

A. Blacks in the U.S.A. were not regarded as American citizens prior to 1857.

B. Blacks in the U.S.A. were not regarded as American citizens prior to 1868.

C. Following the year 1868 Blacks and Whites became equal.

D. Following the year 1857 Blacks and Whites became equal.

2. The correct understanding of the due process is that _____.

A. the due process is a series of steps that must be followed to legally and justly correct or answer a contested issue.

B. the aim of the due process is to deprive states and local governments of their rights to take people's life, liberty, or property.

C. the aim of due process is to ensure people's life, liberty, or property from taken away by state and local governments.

D. the due process is to ensure the application of the Bill of Rights to states, thus ensuring citizens' life, liberty, or property.

① freedom of contract:订约自由。
② strike down:取消。
③ repudiate:拒绝接受;拒绝履行。
④ recuse:要求撤换。
⑤ conflict of interest:违背公众利益的行为;利益冲突。

3. Which of the following best interprets Section 1 in this passage?

   A. It tells us who are U.S. citizens and what rights they enjoy.

   B. It defines the scope of U.S citizenship and further clarifies citizens' rights.

   C. It aims to protect a citizen's rights and at the same time prohibits states or local governments from depriving citizen's rights.

   D. It formally defines citizenship and protects a person's civil and political rights from being abridged or denied by any state.

4. The reason why the Court struck down a law decreeing maximum hours for workers in a bakery is that _____.

   A. the Due Process Clause prohibits a variety of social and economic regulation.

   B. the Due Process Clause provides substantive protection to private contracts.

   C. the law decreeing maximum hours for workers is not constitutional.

   D. under "freedom of contract", the law decreeing maximum hours for workers is inappropriate.

5. Some sort of hearing is required before the termination by the government of terminate civil service employees and things like that because _____.

   A. to expel a student from public school, or cut off a welfare recipient's benefits is not lawful.

   B. the Due Process Clause has been used to apply most of the Bill of Rights to the states.

   C. the Court has significantly expanded the reach of procedural due process.

   D. the Due Process Clause requires a judge to recuse himself on account of concern of there being a conflict of interest.

Part Two   True or False Questions

Direction: *In this part of the exercise, there is a passage with ten true or false questions. Read the passage carefully and mark T if it is true and F if it is false.*

The following are two pages of the Fourteenth Amendment in the National Archives of the USA.

Section 1 formally defines citizenship and protects a person's civil and political rights from being abridged or denied by any state. This represented the Congress's overruling of the Dred Scott decision's ruling that black people were not, and could not become, citizens of the United States or enjoy any of the privileges and immunities of citizenship. The Civil Rights Act of 1866 had already granted U.S. citizenship to all persons born in the United States, as long as those persons were not subject to a foreign power; the framers of the Fourteenth Amendment added this principle into the Constitution to prevent the Supreme Court from ruling the Civil Rights Act of 1866 to be unconstitutional for lack of congressional authority to enact such a law and to prevent a future Congress from altering it by a mere majority vote.

This section was also in response to the Black Codes① that southern states had passed in the

---

①　the Black Codes:"黑人法典"（奴隶制取消前南部某些州的奴隶法）。

wake of the Thirteenth Amendment, which ended slavery in the United States. Those laws attempted to return freed slaves to something like their former condition by, among other things, restricting their movement, forcing them to enter into year-long labor contracts, prohibiting them from owning firearms, and by preventing them from suing or testifying in court.

Finally, this section was in response to violence against black people within the southern states. A Joint Committee on Reconstruction[①] found that only a Constitutional amendment could protect black people's rights and welfare within those states.

Citizenship Clause

There are varying interpretations of the original intent of Congress, based on statements made during the congressional debate over the amendment. During the original debate over the amendment Senator Jacob M. Howard of Michigan—the author of the Citizenship Clause—described the clause as having the same content, despite different wording, as the earlier Civil Rights Act of 1866, namely, that it excludes Native Americans who maintain their tribal ties and "persons born in the United States who are foreigners, aliens, who belong to the families of ambassadors or foreign ministers." According to historian Glenn W. LaFantasie of Western Kentucky University, "A good number of his fellow senators supported his view of the citizenship clause." Others also agreed that the children of ambassadors and foreign ministers were to be excluded. However, concerning children born in the United States to parents who are not U. S. citizens (and not foreign diplomats), three Senators, including Senate Judiciary Committee Chairman Lyman Trumbull, the author of the Civil Rights Act, as well as President Andrew Johnson, asserted that both the Civil Rights Act and the Fourteenth Amendment would confer citizenship on them at birth, and no Senator offered a contrary opinion.

Senator James Rood Doolittle of Wisconsin asserted that all Native Americans were subject to the jurisdiction of the United States, so that the phrase "Indians not taxed" would be preferable, but Trumbull and Howard disputed this, arguing that the U. S. government did not have full jurisdiction over Native American tribes, which govern themselves and make treaties with the United States.

In *Elk v. Wilkins*, 112 U. S. 94 (1884), the clause's meaning was tested regarding whether birth in the United States automatically extended national citizenship. The Supreme Court held that Native Americans who voluntarily quit their tribes did not automatically gain national citizenship.

The clause's meaning was tested again in the case of *United States v. Wong Kim Ark* 169 U. S. 649 (1898). The Supreme Court held that under the Fourteenth Amendment a man born within the United States to Chinese citizens who have a permanent domicile and residence in the United States and are carrying on business in the United States—and whose parents were not employed in a diplomatic or other official capacity by a foreign power—was a citizen of the United States. Subsequent decisions have applied the principle to the children of foreign nationals of non-Chinese descent.

---

① Reconstruction:美国南部重建时期:美国南北战争后(1865—1877),原南部邦联诸州在联邦政府控制下进行社会立法,包括给予黑人新的权利。

Loss of citizenship

Loss of national citizenship is possible only under the following circumstances:

Fraud in the naturalization(外国人入美国籍;入籍) ***process***

Technically, this is not loss of citizenship but rather a voiding of the purported naturalization and a declaration that the immigrant never was a United States citizen.

Voluntary relinquishment of citizenship. This may be accomplished either through renunciation procedures specially established by the State Department or through other actions that demonstrate desire to give up national citizenship.

For much of the country's history, voluntary acquisition or exercise of a foreign citizenship was considered sufficient cause for revocation of national citizenship. This concept was enshrined in a series of treaties between the United States and other countries (the Bancroft Treaties). However, the Supreme Court repudiated this concept in *Afroyim v. Rusk*, 387 U.S. 253 (1967), as well as *Vance v. Terrazas*, 444 U.S. 252 (1980), holding that the Citizenship Clause of the Fourteenth Amendment barred the Congress from revoking citizenship.

1. So long as persons were not subject to a foreign power, the Civil Rights Act of 1866 granted U.S. citizenship to all persons born in the United States. (　)

2. Some southern states passed the Black Codes so as to end slavery in the United States. (　)

3. Native Americans who maintain their tribal ties and persons born in the United States who are foreigners are excluded from American citizens. (　)

4. Native Americans who voluntarily quit their tribes did not automatically gain national citizenship. (　)

5. Although there are varying interpretations of the original intent of Congress concerning the citizenship clause, the real intent of the said clause is something definite. (　)

6. Under the Fourteenth Amendment, a man born within the United States to Chinese citizens who have a permanent domicile and residence in the United States and are carrying on business in the United States is a citizen of the United States. (　)

7. Fraud in the naturalization process itself technically indicates that as a United States citizen, the immigrant concerned will have his or her citizenship lost. (　)

8. An American citizen can give up his or her national citizenship through renunciation procedures or through other actions that demonstrate such a desire. (　)

9. Voluntary acquisition or exercise of a foreign citizenship is definitely considered sufficient cause for revocation of national citizenship. (　)

IV Translation abilities

法律语言特征分析与法律翻译技能培养之十五：

判例名称、引证的翻译

1. 判例的名称及其翻译

按习惯，判例的名称应用斜体字（或底下加横线）写出，且都用当事人的姓名来表示，一般是原告在前，被告在后。如当事人是法人而非自然人，则需写出其全称（可以缩写），如：Orkin Exterminating Co., inc. v. Pestoco of Canada Ltd, et. al（译为：奥肯杀虫剂有限责任公司诉加拿大佩斯特有限公司等一案）。为简略起见，在第二次引证时，则可用一个当事人（原告）的名字来称呼该案，如将上述案件简称为 Orkin（奥肯案）。但当事人是官方机构时则不能作此种简略，如 US v. White（美国联邦政府诉怀特案）便不能简称为 US 一案。

此外还有在案件名字中加拉丁词的情况：

（1）在当事人姓名之后（或前面）In re，如：White, In re（或 In re White），译为"怀特有关事项案"。这表明该案件无对立的当事人，原告仅就某物或事所提起的诉讼，如有关破产（bankruptcy）、遗嘱检验（probate）、监护权（guardianship）、藐视法庭（contempt）、律师黜名（disbarment）、人身保护令（habeas corpus）等事项的案件。

（2）在当事人姓名后加 ex parte，如 ex parte White（译为：怀特单方提起之诉）。

（3）又如 State ex rel. White v. Green，其等同 State on the relation of White v. Green，表明此是一桩以州的名义按受害人 White 的控告对 Green 提起的公诉案，其事由可涉及要求法院签发命令、制止令、复审令、收回特权或签发人身保护令等，可译为：州政府就怀特事由诉格林案。

刑事案件由国家机关公诉，案名含国家机构，如：State v. White（州政府诉怀特案）；有的州也写作：People v. White（以人民名义诉怀特案）或 Commonwealth v. White（州政府诉怀特案）等（注：美国的 Kentucky, Massachusetts, Pennsylvania 和 Virginia 4 个州，commonwealth 等同 state 的含义）。

按海商法的规定，船舶也可以作为被告，因此便有以船舶名作案名的情况。此外，在没收货物的案件中，商品名称也可用作案名，如：US v. 45 Barrels of Whisky（译为：美国联邦政府没收 45 桶威士忌案）。

2. 引证及翻译

判例汇编名称前的数字用于表明汇编的卷数，如 3 Pacific Reporter（《太平洋地区判例汇编》第 3 卷）。此外，有些汇编分辑（series）出版，引证时用 2d（第 2 辑）、4d（第 4 辑）等符号表示，放在汇编名称之后。

至于判例汇编的名称，美国多加上 reports、reporter、cases 或 bulletin（公报）等词来表示。在引证和脚注中，经常用这些单词的缩略形式。一般来说，reports 可缩略为 R 或 Rep，如：A. C. R（American Criminal Reports，《美国刑事判例汇编》）、A. L. R.（American Law Reports，《美国判例注释汇编》）以及 A. B. A. Rep.（American Bar Association Reports，《美国律师协会判例汇编》）等；reporter 则缩略为 Rptr，如：All India Rptr.（All India Reporter《全印第安判例汇编》）；cases 缩略为 cas. 如：Bell Cr. Cas（Bell Criminal Cases，《贝尔刑事判例汇编》）；Bulletin 缩略为 Bull，如：Cri. L. Bull.（Criminal Law Bulletin，《刑事判例公报》）。

此外,有时还有将上述单词省略的情况,如:A.(Atlantic Reporter,《大西洋地区判例汇编》)、Alaska(Alaska Reports,《阿拉斯加判例汇编》)。

在美国,判例汇编一般分为官方和非官方两种,此外,其还可按法院的类别,地区或案件类型进行分类汇编。

(1)联邦法院判例汇编

联邦法院的判例汇编分为联邦最高法院判例汇编和联邦地方法院以及上诉法院判例汇编两大类。

A. 常见的联邦最高法院判例汇编:

United States Reports(U.S.):《美国联邦判例汇编》,官方汇编;

United States Supreme Court Reports(L. Ed)或(L. Ed. ad.):《美国联邦最高法院判例汇编》律师版第1辑或第2辑,非官方汇编;

United States Law Week(U.S.L. Week):《美国联邦判例周刊》,非官方汇编;

United States Supreme Court Bulletin(U.S.S.Ct.Bull):《美国联邦最高法院公告》,非官方汇编;

Supreme Court Reporter(Sup. Ct 或 S. Ct.):《联邦法院判例汇编》,非官方汇编。

B. 美国联邦地方法院和上诉法院的判例无专门的官方汇编,一般只登载在如 West 出版公司出版的非官方判例汇编中。如联邦地方法院的判例多收在《联邦判例补编》(Federal Supplement)(F. Supp.),联邦上诉法院的判例一般则收在《联邦判例汇编》(Federal Reports)(F.)中。有关联邦法院程序规则的裁决则收录在《联邦程序规则裁决汇编》(Federal Rules Decisions)(F. R. D.)中。

(2)州法院的判例汇编

州法院的判例汇编也分为官方和非官方两种。官方汇编多用州名命名,引证时可只用州名的缩写,如:Wisconsin Reports(Wis.,《威斯康星州法院判例汇编》),Virginia Reports(Va. R.,《弗吉尼亚州法院判例汇编》)等。

Translation Exercises

Part One　*Put the following into Chinese*

The Yemeni strike provides a dramatic example of targeted killing. In recent years, targeted killing has generated new controversy in two states, Israel and the United States. In January 2009, a U.S. official claimed that an intensified campaign of CIA Predator strikes into Pakistan had killed eight out of al Qaeda's top twenty leaders. President Obama, on his third full day of office, authorized two more strikes, embracing President Bush's policies at least to some degree. Since then, many additional Predator strikes have been reported. Targeted killings, whether ordered by Republicans or Democrats, provide a demoralized public with some tangible evidence that democracies are tough enough to strike at suspected terrorists, to kill before we are killed. Any backlash overseas is a different story.

Disinclined to issue a general hunting license, much of the scholarship that accepts the potential legitimacy of targeted killing also seeks to prevent abuse. To this end, some scholars have argued that IHL imposes stricter controls on killing than is commonly thought. Others have suggested that the law should control targeted killing by developing a mixed model that combines elements of the human rights model and IHL. Yet most of this scholarship shies away from examining the legality of targeted killing under American law, preferring instead to focus on this practice's legality under international law.

Part Two *Put the following into English*

Boumediene 和 Mathews 两个案例之间的关系表明正当程序条款在全球范围内勉强适用于政府行为的模式。这与《美国联邦宪法》第五修正案之纯文本是一致的。该修正案禁止政府在没有任何明显地域限制的情况下,未经正当法律程序剥夺任何人的生命、自由或财产。正当程序之核心内涵在于要求政府公正,即要求政府使用合理程序以确保政府不会任意剥夺人们的生命、自由或财产。无论对关塔那摩湾的被监禁者来说还是对捕食者无人机攻击的目标而言,仅因为他们是非居民外国人就表明政府可以任意伤害他们,这样做非常令人厌恶。

大法官 Harlan 在 Reid 一案和大法官 Kennedy 在 Boumediene 一案中都认为,宪法之某一规定——无论是陪审团审理的权利还是人身保护令权利在海外都适用——如果这执行起来并非不可行或者并非破例的话。因而我们发现了正当程序(包括合理待遇问题)中的一项即使与美国没有明显联系但却适用于外国人的普遍权利。此种普遍权利不承认存在宪法拒绝保护的明确界限——一个人的公民身份是唯一的理由。反之,宪法保护是否实际上适用于美国以外的地方取决于务实地查询多种因素,这些因素当然包括申诉者与美国的联系程度。有时,正当程序要求宪法保障适用海外——因此就有了 Reid 一案中军人的配偶和其陪审团审理的权利或者关塔那摩的被监禁者及其人身保护权。然而,有时正当程序并不要求适用海外。例如,《美国联邦宪法》第四修正案之搜查许可证要求并不适用于应美国官员之请求在墨西哥进行的对墨西哥公民住宅的搜查。

V Interaction

Discuss with your tutor(s) or the People's judges in your locality about the implications of due process clause. Then based on the discussion, you are supposed to write a composition about the implications of due process on China's legal proceedings. Remember that you are required to express your ideas clearly.

VI A Appreciation of the Judge's Opinions

(1) Case Name(案件名称): *Lochner v. New York*

Lochner v. New York

Supreme Court of the United States

Argued February 23—24, 1905	
Decided April 17, 1905	
Full case name	Joseph Lochner, Plaintiff in Error v. People of the State of New York
Citations	198 U.S. 45 (more)
	25 S. Ct. 539; 49 L. Ed. 937; 1905 U.S. LEXIS 1153
Prior history	Defendant convicted, Oneida County Court, New York, February 12, 1902; affirmed, 76 N.Y.S. 396 (N.Y. App. Div. 1902); affirmed, 69 N.E. 373 (N.Y. 1904)
Subsequent history	None

Holding

New York's regulation of the working hours of bakers was not a justifiable restriction on the right to contract freely under the 14th Amendment's guarantee of liberty.

Court membership

Chief Justice
Melville Fuller
Associate Justices
John M. Harlan · David J. Brewer
Henry B. Brown · Edward D. White
Rufus W. Peckham · Joseph McKenna
Oliver W. Holmes, Jr. · William R. Day

Case opinions

Majority	Peckham, joined by Fuller, Brewer, Brown, McKenna
Dissent	Harlan, joined by White, Day
Dissent	Holmes

Laws applied

U.S. Const. amend. XIV; 1897 N.Y. Laws art. 8, ch. 415, §110

U.S. Supreme Court

LOCHNER v. PEOPLE OF STATE OF NEW YORK, 198 U.S. 45 (1905)

198 U.S. 45

JOSEPH LOCHNER, Plff. in Err.,

v.

PEOPLE OF THE STATE OF NEW YORK.

No. 292.

Argued February 23, 24, 1905.

Decided April 17, 1905.

(2) Case Summary(案情简介)

Lochner vs. New York(洛克纳诉纽约州政府), 198 U.S. 45 (1905), was a landmark United States Supreme Court case that held a "liberty of contract"(缔约自由) was implicit in the due process clause(正当程序条款) of the Fourteenth Amendment. The case involved a New York law that limited the number of hours that a baker

Lesson Fifteen Due Process and Targeted Killing of Terrorists

could work each day to ten, and limited the number of hours that a baker could work each week to 60. By a 5-4 vote, the Supreme Court rejected the argument that the law was necessary to protect the health of bakers, deciding it was a labor law attempting to regulate the terms of employment, and calling it an "unreasonable, unnecessary and arbitrary interference(蛮横干涉)with the right and liberty of the individual to contract."Justice Rufus Peckham wrote for the majority(代表多数法官撰写判决书), while Justices John Marshall Harlan and Oliver Wendell Holmes, Jr. filed dissents.

Lochner was one of the most controversial decisions in the Supreme Court's history, giving its name to what is known as the Lochner era. In the Lochner era, the Supreme Court issued several controversial decisions invalidating progressive federal and state statutes that sought to regulate working conditions during the Progressive Era(19世纪90年代至20世纪20年代美国政治改革和社会激进主义高速发展的时代) and the Great Depression(美国经济大萧条时期). Justice Harlan's dissent, joined by two other Justices, argued that the Court gave insufficient weight to the state's argument that the law was a valid health measure. Justice Holmes's famous lone dissent criticized the decision for discarding sound constitutional interpretation in favor of personal beliefs, writing: "the Fourteenth Amendment does not enact Mr. Herbert Spencer's Social Statics."This was a reference to a book in which Spencer advocated a strict laissez faire(放任自由的;自由主义的) philosophy.

During the quarter-century that followed *Lochner*, the Supreme Court generally upheld economic regulations, but also issued several rulings invalidating such regulations. The Court also began to use the Due Process Clause of the Fourteenth Amendment to protect personal (as opposed to purely property) rights, including freedom of speech and the right to send one's child to private school (which was the beginning of a line of cases interpreting privacy rights). The Lochner era is often considered to have ended with *West Coast Hotel Co. v. Parrish* (1937), in which the Supreme Court took a much broader view of the government's power to regulate economic activities.

Background of the case

In 1895, the New York Legislature unanimously enacted the Bakeshop Act (面包店法), which regulated sanitary conditions(卫生条件) in bakeries and also prohibited individuals from working in bakeries for more than ten hours per day or sixty hours per week. In 1899, Joseph Lochner, owner of Lochner's Home Bakery in Utica, was indicted(指控) on a charge that he violated the one hundred and tenth section of article 8, chapter 415, of the Laws of 1897, in that he wrongfully and unlawfully required and permitted an employee working for him to work more than sixty hours in one week and was fined $25. For a second offense in 1901, he drew a fine of $50 from the Oneida County Court.

Lochner chose to appeal his second conviction. However, the conviction was upheld by the Appellate Division of the New York Supreme Court(纽约高级法院,此处supreme不是纽约州的最高法院,而类似中国的高级法院) in a 3-2 vote. Lochner appealed again to the New York Court of Appeals(纽约州上诉法院,该州最高法院), where he lost by a 4-3 margin. After his defeat in the Court of Appeals (New York's highest court), Lochner took his case to the Supreme Court of the United States.

Lochner's appeal was based on the Fourteenth Amendment to the Constitution, which provides: "... nor shall any State deprive any person of life, liberty, or property, without due process of law."In a series of cases starting with *Dred Scott v. Sandford* (1857), the Supreme Court established that the due process clause (in both the 5th and 14th Amendments) is not merely a procedural guarantee(程序的保障), but also a "substantive"limitation (实体的限制)on the type of control the government may exercise over individuals. Although this interpretation of the due process clause is a controversial one, it had become firmly embedded in American jurisprudence(扎根于美国法学) by the end of the nineteenth century. Lochner argued that the "right to free contract"(缔约自由的权利)was one of the rights encompassed(包含,包括)by substantive due process.

The Supreme Court had accepted the argument that the due process clause protected the right to contract seven years earlier, in *Allgeyer v. Louisiana*(1897). However, the Court had acknowledged that the right was not absolute, but subject to the "police power" of the states(各州的行政权, police power 还可以表示"治安维护权,维持治安权,警察权"等). For example, *Holden v. Hardy* (1898), the Supreme Court upheld a Utah law setting an eight-hour work day for miners. In *Holden*, Justice Henry Brown wrote that while "the police power cannot be put forward as an excuse for oppressive and unjust legislation, it may be lawfully resorted to for the purpose of preserving the public health, safety, or morals." The issue facing the Supreme Court in *Lochner v. New York* was whether the Bakeshop Act represented a reasonable exercise of the state's police power.

Lochner's case was argued by Henry Weismann (who had been one of the foremost advocates of the Bakeshop Act when he was Secretary of the Journeymen Bakers' Union). In his brief(案情摘要), Weismann decried(谴责,厉声反对) the idea that "the treasured freedom of the individual... should be swept away under the guise of the police power of the State." He denied New York's argument that the Bakeshop Act was a necessary health measure, claiming that the "average bakery of the present day is well ventilated, comfortable both summer and winter, and always sweet smelling." Weismann's brief contained an appendix providing statistics showing that bakers' mortality rates(死亡率) were comparable to that of white collar professionals(白领专业人士).

The Supreme Court's decision

Justice Rufus Peckham delivered the opinion of the Court. The Supreme Court, by a vote of 5-4, ruled that the law limiting bakers' working hours did not constitute a legitimate exercise of police powers. The opinion of the Court was delivered by Justice Rufus Peckham. Peckham began by asserting that the Fourteenth Amendment protected an individual's "general right to make a contract in relation to his business." He acknowledged that the right was not absolute, referring disparagingly(以贬抑的口吻;以轻视的态度) to the "somewhat vaguely termed police powers" of the state. At the same time, Peckham argued that the police power was subject to certain limitations; otherwise, he claimed, the Fourteenth Amendment would be meaningless, and states would be able to pass any law using the police power as a pretext(借口). He asserted that it was the court's duty to determine whether legislation is "a fair, reasonable and appropriate exercise of the police power of the State, or... an unreasonable, unnecessary and arbitrary interference with the right of the individual... to enter into those contracts in relation to labor which may seem to him appropriate."

The Attorney General(州总检察长) of New York, Julius M. Mayer, had claimed in his brief that the government "has a right to safeguard a citizen against his own lack of knowledge." Peckham responded to this argument by writing that bakers "are in no sense wards(受监护人) of the State." He remarked that bakers "are... able to assert their rights and care for themselves without the protecting arm of the State, interfering with their independence of judgment and of action."

Next, Peckham proceeded to disclaim the idea that long working hours posed a threat to the health of bakers. He addressed the argument with the following words: "To the common understanding, the trade(行业,谋生手段) of a baker has never been regarded as an unhealthy one." He added that relevant statistics showed that baking was no more or less healthful, on average, than other common professions. Although conceding the "possible existence of some small amount of unhealthiness," Justice Peckham contended that it was insufficient to justify interference from the state.

Hence, Peckham and his fellow Justices reached the conclusion that the New York law was not related "in any real and substantial degree to the health of the employees." Consequently, they held that the New York law was not a valid exercise of the state's police powers. Lochner's conviction was accordingly vacated(判决、合同或指控等撤销;使无效).

Harlan's dissent

Justice John Marshall Harlan delivered a dissenting opinion, which was joined by Justices White and Day. Justice Harlan contended that the liberty to contract under the Due Process Clause of the Fourteenth Amendment is subject to regulation imposed by a State acting within the scope of its police powers. Justice Harlan offered the following rule for determining whether such statutes are unconstitutional:

The power of the courts to review legislative action in respect of a matter affecting the general welfare exists only "when that which the legislature has done comes within the rule that, if a statute purporting to have been enacted to protect the public health, the public morals or the public safety, has no real or substantial relation to those objects, or is, beyond all question(无可争辩), a plain, palpable invasion(公然侵犯) of rights secured by the fundamental law."

Justice Harlan asserted that the burden of proof should rest with the party seeking to have such a statute deemed unconstitutional.

Harlan contended that it was "plain that this statute was enacted to protect the physical well-being of those who work in bakery and confectionery establishments(面包店和糖果店里的工作人员)." Responding to the majority's assertion that the profession of a baker was not an unhealthy one, he quoted at length from academic studies describing the respiratory ailments(呼吸道疾病) and other risks that bakers faced. He argued that the Supreme Court should have deferred to the New York Legislature's judgment that long working hours threatened the health of bakery employees. According to Harlan, "If the end(目的,目标) which the legislature seeks to accomplish be one to which its power extends, and if the means(方法) employed to that end, although not the wisest or best, are yet not plainly and palpably unauthorized by law, then the court cannot interfere."

Holmes' dissent

Another dissenting opinion was penned by Justice Oliver Wendell Holmes, Jr..(霍姆斯大法官) Although only three paragraphs long, Holmes' dissent is well-remembered and often quoted. Holmes accused the majority of judicial activism(司法能动主义,中国之能动司法), pointedly claiming that the case was "decided upon an economic theory which a large part of the country does not entertain." He attacked the idea that the Fourteenth Amendment enshrined(使权利,传统,观念神圣不可侵犯,把……奉为神圣) the liberty of contract, citing laws against Sunday trading and usury(高利贷) as "ancient examples" to the contrary. He added, "Some of these laws embody convictions or prejudices which judges are likely to share. Some may not. But a constitution is not intended to embody a particular economic theory."

Subsequent developments

The Supreme Court's due process jurisprudence over the next three decades was inconsistent, but it took a narrow view of state police powers in several major labor cases after Lochner. For example, in *Coppage v. Kansas* (1915), the Court struck down statutes forbidding "Yellow Dog contracts"(以雇员不加入工会为条件的雇用契约). Similarly, in *Adkins v. Children's Hospital* (1923), the Supreme Court held that minimum wage laws violated the due process clause (although Chief Justice William Howard Taft strongly dissented, suggesting that the Court instead should have overruled Lochner). The doctrine of substantive due process was coupled with a narrow interpretation of congressional power under the commerce clause(贸易条款). Justices James McReynolds, George Sutherland, Willis Van Devanter, and Pierce Butler emerged during the 1920s and 30s as the foremost defenders of traditional limitations on government power on the Supreme Court; they were collectively dubbed by partisans of the New Deal(罗斯福新政) the "Four Horsemen of Reaction"(基督教《圣经》中的四骑士:指战争、饥馑、瘟疫、死亡四大害) as a result.

In 1934 the Supreme Court decided *Nebbia v. New York* stating that there is no constitutionally protected fundamental right to freedom of contract. In 1937, the Supreme Court decided *West Coast Hotel Co. v. Parrish*, which expressly overruled Adkins and implicitly signaled the end of the Lochner era. The decision repudiated(否定,批判,推翻建议;驳斥,驳倒;拒绝要求等) the idea that freedom of contract should be unrestricted.

The legislature has also recognized the fact, which the experience of legislators in many States has corroborated (证实,支持某种说法、信仰、理论等), that the proprietors(业主,所有者) of these establishments and their operatives(工人,职工) do not stand upon equality, and that their interests are, to a certain extent, conflicting. The former naturally desire to obtain as much labor as possible from their employees, while the latter are often induced by the fear of discharge(解雇,解聘) to conform to regulations which their judgment, fairly exercised, would pronounce to be detrimental to their health or strength. In other words, the proprietors lay down the rules and the laborers are practically constrained to obey them. In such cases, self-interest is often an unsafe guide, and the legislature may properly interpose(提出反对意见以便干涉) its authority.

Coming at a time of mounting political pressure over the judiciary's stance toward the New Deal, the Court's shift is sometimes called "The switch in time that saved nine."(源自 The stitch in time saved nine,小漏不补,大漏不断,此处的 stitch 改成 swtich,即改变,意思是"一变定天下").

Although the Supreme Court did not explicitly overrule Lochner, it did agree to give more deference to the decisions of state legislatures. The Court sounded the death knell(敲响了丧钟) for economic substantive due process several years later in *Williamson v. Lee Optical of Oklahoma* (1955). In that case, a unanimous Supreme Court declared: "The day is gone when this Court uses the Due Process Clause of the Fourteenth Amendment to strike down state laws, regulatory of business and industrial conditions, because they may be unwise, improvident, or out of harmony with a particular school of thought(与某一特定思想流派不符)."

In the post-Lochner era, the Supreme Court has applied a lower standard (rational basis test) in reviewing restrictions on economic liberty, but stricter standards in reviewing legislation impinging on personal liberties, especially privacy. A line of cases dating back to the 1923 opinion by Justice McReynolds in *Meyer v. Nebraska* has established a privacy right under substantive due process. More recently, in *Roe v. Wade* (1973), the Supreme Court held that a woman had a privacy right to determine whether or not to have an abortion. In 1992, *Planned Parenthood v. Casey* reaffirmed that right, though the Court no longer used the term "privacy" to describe it.

The Supreme Court's decision in *Lochner v. New York* has drawn the ire(怒火,愤怒) of some liberal and conservative legal scholars. For example, Robert Bork called the decision an "abomination"(厌恶,憎恨,可恶;令人憎恶的/讨厌的事物). Similarly, Attorney General Edwin Meese said that the Supreme Court "ignored the limitations of the Constitution and blatantly(公然地,露骨地) usurped legislative authority(立法权威)" However, the decision has attracted defenders, including the libertarian(思想或行动等的自由论者) Cato Institute, and scholars Richard Epstein and Randy Barnett who argue that Lochner was correct in its protection of individual economic liberty.

(3) **Excerpts of the Judgment**(法官判决词)

Mr. Justice Peckham delivered the opinion of the court:

The indictment, it will be seen, charges that the plaintiff in error(提请复审的当事人,取得复审令状的当事人,上诉人) violated the 110th section of article 8, chapter 415, of the Laws of 1897, known as the labor law of the state of New York(纽约州劳动法), in that he wrongfully and unlawfully required and permitted an employee working for him to work more than sixty hours in one week. There is nothing in any of the opinions delivered in this case, either in the supreme court or the court of appeals of the state, which construes the section(对该条款作出了解释), in using the word 'required,' as referring to any physical force being used to obtain the labor of an employee. It is assumed that the word means nothing more than the requirement arising from voluntary contract for such labor in excess of the number of hours specified in the statute. There is no pretense in any of the opinions that the statute was intended to meet a case of involuntary labor in any form. All the opinions assume that there is no real distinction, so far as this question is concerned, between the words 'required' and 'permitted.' The mandate(命令,训令;指令) of the statute, that 'no employee shall be required or permitted to work,' is the substantial equivalent of an enactment that 'no employee shall contract or agree to work,' more than ten hours per day; and, as there is no provision for special emergencies, the statute is mandatory(强迫性的,强制性的,义务性质的) in all cases. It is not an act merely fixing the number of hours which shall constitute a legal day's work, but an absolute prohibition upon the employer permitting, under any circumstances, more than ten hours' work to be done in his establishment. The employee may desire to earn the extra money which would arise from his working more than the prescribed time, but this statute forbids the employer from permitting the employee to earn it.

The statute necessarily interferes with the right of contract between the employer and employees, concerning the number of hours in which the latter may labor in the bakery of the employer. The general right to make a contract in relation to his business is part of the liberty of the individual protected by the 14th Amendment of the Federal Constitution. Under that provision no state can deprive any person of life, liberty, or property without due process of law(未经适当法律程序,任何州不得剥夺任何个人之人身、自由或财产). The right to purchase or to sell labor is part of the liberty protected by this amendment(修正条款,传统翻译为"修正案"), unless there are circumstances which exclude the right. There are, however, certain powers, existing in the sovereignty of each state in the Union, somewhat vaguely termed police powers, the exact description and limitation of which have not been attempted by the courts. Those powers, broadly stated, and without, at present, any attempt at a more specific limitation, relate to the safety, health, morals, and general welfare of the public. Both property and liberty are held on such reasonable conditions as may be imposed by the governing power of the state in the exercise of those powers, and with such conditions the 14th Amendment was not designed to interfere.

The state, therefore, has power to prevent the individual from making certain kinds of contracts, and in regard to them the Federal Constitution offers no protection. If the contract be one which the state, in the legitimate exercise of its police power, has the right to prohibit, it is not prevented from prohibiting it by the 14th Amendment. Contracts in violation of a statute, either of the Federal or state government, or a contract to let one's property for immoral purposes, or to do any other unlawful act, could obtain no protection from the Federal Constitution, as coming under the liberty of person or of free contract. Therefore, when the state, by its legislature, in the assumed exercise of its police powers, has passed an act which seriously limits the right to labor or the right of contract in regard to their means of livelihood(谋生方式,生计方式)between persons who are sui juris(有权处理自己的事务的,指已到法定年龄并精神健全者)(both employer and employee), it becomes of great importance to determine which shall prevail, the right of the individual to labor for such time as he may choose, or the right of the state to prevent the individual from laboring, or from entering into any contract to labor, beyond a certain time prescribed by the state.

This court has recognized the existence and upheld the exercise of the police powers of the states in many cases which might fairly be considered as border ones, and it has, in the course of its determination of questions regarding the asserted invalidity of such statutes, on the ground of their violation of the rights secured by the Federal Constitution, been guided by rules of a very liberal nature, the application of which has resulted, in numerous instances, in upholding the validity of state statutes thus assailed. Among the later cases where the state law has been upheld by this court is that of *Holden v. Hardy*. A provision in the act of the legislature of Utah was there under consideration, the act limiting the employment of workmen in all underground mines or workings, to eight hours per day, 'except in cases of emergency, where life or property is in imminent danger.' It also limited the hours of labor in smelting(熔炼、提炼、冶炼) and other institutions for the reduction or refining of ores or metals to eight hours per day, except in like cases of emergency. The act was held to be a valid exercise of the police powers of the state. A review of many of the cases on the subject, decided by this and other courts, is given in the opinion. It was held that the kind of employment, mining, smelting, etc., and the character of the employees in such kinds of labor, were such as to make it reasonable and proper for the state to interfere to prevent the employees from being constrained by the rules laid down by the proprietors in regard to labor. The following citation from the observations of the supreme court of Utah in that case was made by the judge writing the opinion of this court, and approved: 'The law in question is confined to the protection of that class of people engaged in labor in underground mines, and in smelters(冶炼厂) and other works wherein ores are reduced and refined. This law applies only to the classes subjected by their employment to the peculiar conditions and effects attending underground mining and work in smelters, and other works for the reduction and refining of ores. Therefore it is not necessary to discuss or decide whether the legislature can fix the hours of labor in other employments.'

It will be observed that, even with regard to that class of labor, the Utah statute provided for cases of emergency wherein the provisions of the statute would not apply. The statute now before this court has no emergency clause in it, and, if the statute is valid, there are no circumstances and no emergencies under which the slightest violation of the provisions of the act would be innocent. There is nothing in *Holden v. Hardy* which covers the case now before us. Nor does *Atkin v. Kansas* touch the case at bar(审理中的案件). The Atkin Case was decided upon the right of the state to control its municipal corporations, and to prescribe the conditions upon which it will permit work of a public character to be done for a municipality. *Knoxville Iron Co. v. Harbison* is equally far from an authority for this legislation. The employees in that case were held to be at a disadvantage with the employer in matters of wages, they being miners and coal workers, and the act simply provided for the cashing of coal orders when presented by the miner to the employer.

The latest case decided by this court, involving the police power, is that of *Jacobson v. Massachusetts*, decided at this term and reported in 197 U. S. 11. It related to compulsory vaccination(种痘;预防注射), and the law was held vaild as a proper exercise of the police powers with reference to the public health. It was stated in the opinion that it was a case 'of an adult who, for aught(任何事物, anything。如:He may starve for aught I care:他饿死也罢,我才不管呢;He may be rich for aught I know:他也许有钱,但我不大知道) that appears, was himself in perfect health and a fit subject of vaccination, and yet, while remaining in the community, refused to obey the statute and the regulation, adopted in execution of its provisions, for the protection of the public health and the public safety, confessedly endangered by the presence of a dangerous disease.' That case is also far from covering the one now before the court.

Petit v. Minnesota was upheld as a proper exercise of the police power relating to the observance of Sunday, and the case held that the legislature had the right to declare that, as matter of law, keeping barber shops open on Sunday was not a work of necessity or charity.

It must, of course, be conceded that there is a limit to the valid exercise of the police power by the state. There is no dispute concerning this general proposition. Otherwise the 14th Amendment would have no efficacy and the legislatures of the states would have unbounded power, and it would be enough to say that any piece of legislation was enacted to conserve the morals, the health, or the safety of the people; such legislation would be valid, no matter how absolutely without foundation the claim might be. The claim of the police power would be a mere pretext, become another and delusive name for the supreme sovereignty of the state to be exercised free from constitutional restraint. This is not contended for. In every case that comes before this court, therefore, where legislation of this character is concerned, and where the protection of the Federal Constitution is sought, the question necessarily arises: Is this a fair, reasonable, and appropriate exercise of the police power of the state, or is it an unreasonable, unnecessary, and arbitrary interference with the right of the individual to his personal liberty, or to enter into those contracts in relation to labor which may seem to him appropriate or necessary for the support of himself and his family? Of course the liberty of contract relating to labor includes both parties to it. The one has as much right to purchase as the other to sell labor.

This is not a question of substituting the judgment of the court for that of the legislature. If the act be within the power of the state it is valid, although the judgment of the court might be totally opposed to the enactment of such a law. But the question would still remain: Is it within the police power of the state? and that question must be answered by the court.

The question whether this act is valid as a labor law, pure and simple, may be dismissed in a few words. There is no reasonable ground for interfering with the liberty of person or the right of free contract, by determining the hours of labor, in the occupation of a baker. There is no contention that bakers as a class are not equal in intel-

Lesson Fifteen Due Process and Targeted Killing of Terrorists

ligence and capacity to men in other trades or manual occupations, or that they are not able to assert their rights and care for themselves without the protecting arm of the state, interfering with their independence of judgment and of action. They are in no sense wards of the state. Viewed in the light of a purely labor law, with no reference whatever to the question of health, we think that a law like the one before us involves neither the safety, the morals, nor the welfare, of the public, and that the interest of the public is not in the slightest degree affected by such an act. The law must be upheld, if at all, as a law pertaining to the health of the individual engaged in the occupation of a baker. It does not affect any other portion of the public than those who are engaged in that occupation. Clean and wholesome bread does not depend upon whether the baker works but ten hours per day or only sixty hours a week. The limitation of the hours of labor does not come within the police power on that ground.

It is a question of which of two powers or rights shall prevail,-the power of the state to legislate or the right of the individual to liberty of person and freedom of contract. The mere assertion that the subject relates, though but in a remote degree, to the public health, does not necessarily render the enactment valid. The act must have a more direct relation, as a means to an end, and the end itself must be appropriate and legitimate, before an act can be held to be valid which interferes with the general right of an individual to be free in his person and in his power to contract in relation to his own labor.

This case has caused much diversity of opinion in the state courts. In the supreme court two of the five judges composing the court(组成合议庭审理此案的五个法官) dissented from the judgment affirming the validity of the act. In the court of appeals three of the seven judges also dissented from the judgment upholding the statute. Although found in what is called a labor law of the state, the court of appeals has upheld the act as one relating to the public health, in other words, as a health law. One of the judges of the court of appeals, in upholding the law, stated that, in his opinion, the regulation in question could not be sustained unless they were able to say, from common knowledge, that working in a bakery and candy factory was an unhealthy employment. The judge held that, while the evidence was not uniform, it still led him to the conclusion that the occupation of a baker or confectioner was unhealthy and tended to result in diseases of the respiratory organs. Three of the judges dissented from that view, and they thought the occupation of a baker was not to such an extent unhealthy as to warrant the interference of the legislature with the liberty of the individual.

We think the limit of the police power has been reached and passed in this case. There is, in our judgment, no reasonable foundation for holding this to be necessary or appropriate as a health law to safeguard the public health, or the health of the individuals who are following the trade of a baker. If this statute be valid, and if, therefore, a proper case is made out in which to deny the right of an individual, sui juris, as employer or employee, to make contracts for the labor of the latter under the protection of the provisions of the Federal Constitution, there would seem to be no length to which legislation of this nature might not go. The case differs widely, as we have already stated, from the expressions of this court in regard to laws of this nature, as stated in *Holden v. Hardy*, and *Jacobson v. Massachusetts*. We think that there can be no fair doubt that the trade of a baker, in and of itself, is not an unhealthy one to that degree which would authorize the legislature to interfere with the right to labor, and with the right of free contract on the part of the individual, either as employer or employee. In looking through statistics regarding all trades and occupations, it may be true that the trade of a baker does not appear to be as healthy as some other trades, and is also vastly more healthy than still others. To the common understanding the trade of a baker has never been regarded as an unhealthy one. Very likely physicians would not recommend the exercise of that or of any other trade as a remedy for ill health. Some occupations are more healthy than others, but we think there are none which might not come under the power of the legislature to supervise and control the hours of working therein, if the mere fact that the occupation is not absolutely and perfectly healthy is to confer that right upon the legislative department of the government. It might be safely affirmed that almost all occupations more or less affect the health. There must be more than the mere fact of the possible existence of some small amount of unhealthiness to warrant legislative interference with liberty. It is unfortunately true that labor, even in any department, may possibly carry with it the seeds of unhealthiness. But are we all, on that account, at the mercy of legislative majorities? A printer, a tinsmith(白铁匠), a locksmith(锁匠), a carpenter, a cabinetmaker(家具师,桌椅匠), a dry goods (美国绸缎呢绒类货品;英国杂粮等) clerk, a bank's, a lawyer's, or a physician's clerk, or a clerk in almost any kind of business, would all come under the power of the legislature, on this assumption. No trade, no occupation, no mode of earning one's living, could escape this all-pervading power, and the acts of the legislature in limiting the hours of labor in all employments would be valid, although such limitation might seriously cripple the ability of the laborer to support himself and his family. In our large cities there are many buildings into which the sun penetrates for but a short time in each day, and these buildings are occupied by people carrying on the business of bankers, brokers, lawyers, real estate, and many other kinds of business, aided by many clerks, messengers, and other employees. Upon the assumption of the validity of this act under review, it is not possible to say that an act, prohibiting lawyers' or bank clerks, or others, from contracting to labor for their employers more than eight hours a day would be invalid. It might be said that it is unhealthy to work more than that number of hours in an apartment lighted by artificial light during the working hours of the day; that the occupation of the bank clerk, the lawyer's clerk, the real estate clerk, or the broker's clerk, in such offices is therefore unhealthy, and the legislature, in its paternal wisdom, must, therefore, have the right to legislate on the subject of, and to limit, the hours for such labor; and, if it exercises that power, and its validity be questioned, it is sufficient to say, it has reference to the public health; it has reference to the health of the employees condemned to labor day after day in buildings where the sun never shines; it is a health law, and therefore it is valid, and cannot be questioned by the courts.

It is also urged, pursuing the same line of argument, that it is to the interest of the state that its population should be strong and robust, and therefore any legislation which may be said to tend to make people healthy must be valid as health laws, enacted under the police power. If this be a valid argument and a justification for this kind of legislation, it follows that the protection of the Federal Constitution from undue interference with liberty of person and freedom of contract(保护个人自由与缔约自由不受不当干预) is visionary, wherever the law is sought to be justified as a valid exercise of the police power. Scarcely any law but might find shelter under such assumptions, and conduct, properly so called, as well as contract, would come under the restrictive sway of the legislature. Not only the hours of employees, but the hours of employers, could be regulated, and doctors, lawyers, scientists, all professional men, as well as athletes and artisans, could be forbidden to fatigue their brains and bodies by prolonged hours of exercise, lest the fighting strength(战斗力) of the state be impaired(受害,损害). We mention these extreme cases because the contention is extreme. We do not believe in the soundness of the views which uphold this law. On the contrary, we think that such a law as this, although passed in the assumed exercise of the police power, and as relating to the public health, or the health of the employees named, is not within that power, and is invalid. The act is not, within any fair meaning of the term, a health law, but is an illegal interference with the rights of individuals, both employers and employees, to make contracts regarding labor upon such terms as they may think best, or which they may agree upon with the other parties to such contracts. Statutes of the nature of that under review, limiting the hours in which grown and intelligent men may labor to earn their living, are mere meddlesome interferences with the rights of the individual, and they are not saved from condemnation by the claim that they are passed in the exercise of the police power and upon the subject of the health of the individual whose rights are interfered with, unless there be some fair ground, reasonable in and of itself, to say that there is material danger to the public health, or to the health of the employees, if the hours of labor are not curtailed. If this be not clearly the case, the individuals whose rights are thus made the subject of legislative interference are under the protection of the Federal Constitution regarding their liberty of contract as well as of person; and the legislature of the state has no power to limit their right as proposed in this statute. All that it could properly do has been done by it with regard to the conduct of bakeries, as provided for in the other sections of the act. These several sections pro-

Lesson Fifteen Due Process and Targeted Killing of Terrorists

vide for the inspection of the premises where the bakery is carried on, with regard to furnishing proper wash rooms and waterclosets, apart from the bake room, also with regard to providing proper drainage, plumbing, and painting; the sections, in addition, provide for the height of the ceiling, the cementing or tiling of floors, where necessary in the opinion of the factory inspector, and for other things of that nature; alterations are also provided for, and are to be made where necessary in the opinion of the inspector, in order to comply with the provisions of the statute. These various sections may be wise and valid regulations, and they certainly go to the full extent of(尽力) providing for the cleanliness and the healthiness, so far as possible, of the quarters in which bakeries are to be conducted. Adding to all these requirements a prohibition to enter into any contract of labor in a bakery for more than a certain number of hours a week is, in our judgment, so wholly beside the matter of a proper, reasonable, and fair provision as to run counter to that liberty of person and of free contract provided for in the Federal Constitution.

It was further urged on the argument that restricting the hours of labor in the case of bakers was valid because it tended to cleanliness on the part of the workers, as a man was more apt to be cleanly when not overworked, and if cleanly then his 'output' was also more likely to be so. What has already been said applies with equal force to this contention. We do not admit the reasoning to be sufficient to justify the claimed right of such interference. The state in that case would assume the position of a supervisor, or pater familias(男性家长、户主;一家之父,男性家长;家长权;不再受家长权束缚的成年市民) over every act of the individual, and its right of governmental interference with his hours of labor, his hours of exercise, the character thereof, and the extent to which it shall be carried would be recognized and upheld. In our judgment it is not possible in fact to discover the connection between the number of hours a baker may work in the bakery and the healthful quality of the bread made by the workman. The connection, if any exist, is too shadowy and thin to build any argument for the interference of the legislature. If the man works ten hours a day it is all right, but if ten and a half or eleven his health is in danger and his bread may be unhealthy, and, therefore, he shall not be permitted to do it. This, we think, is unreasonable and entirely arbitrary. When assertions such as we have adverted to become necessary in order to give, if possible, a plausible foundation for the contention that the law is a 'health law,' it gives rise to at least a suspicion that there was some other motive dominating the legislature than the purpose to subserve(对事业、目的等有利、促进、推动;有用,有利于;对……起作用;促进) the public health or welfare.

This interference on the part of the legislatures of the several states with the ordinary trades and occupations of the people seems to be on the increase. In the supreme court of New York, in the case of *People v. Beattie*, a statute regulating the trade of horseshoeing, and requiring the person practising such trade to be examined, and to obtain a certificate from a board of examiners and file the same with the clerk of the county wherein the person proposes to practise such trade, was held invalid, as an arbitrary interference with personal liberty and private property without due process of law. The attempt was made, unsuccessfully, to justify it as a health law.

The same kind of a statute was held invalid (*Re Aubry*) by the supreme court of Washington in December, 1904. The court held that the act deprived citizens of their liberty and property without due process of law, and denied to them the equal protection of the laws. It also held that the trade of a horseshoer is not a subject of regulation under the police power of the state, as a business concerning and directly affecting the health, welfare, or comfort of its inhabitants; and that, therefore, a law which provided for the examination and registration of horseshoers in certain cities was unconstitutional, as an illegitimate exercise of the police power.

The supreme court of Illinois, in *Bessette v. People*, also held that a law of the same nature, providing for the regulation and licensing of horseshoers, was unconstitutional as an illegal interference with the liberty of the individual in adopting and pursuing such calling as he may choose, subject only to the restraint necessary to secure the common welfare.

It is impossible for us to shut our eyes to the fact that many of the laws of this character, while passed under what is claimed to be the police power for the purpose of protecting the public health or welfare, are, in reality, passed from other motives. We are justified in saying so when, from the character of the law and the subject upon which it legislates, it is apparent that the public health or welfare bears but the most remote relation to the law(与法律的关联不甚紧密). The purpose of a statute must be determined from the natural and legal effect of the language employed; and whether it is or is not repugnant(冲突的,与……不一致的,不调和的) to the Constitution of the United States must be determined from the natural effect of such statutes when put into operation, and not from their proclaimed purpose. The court looks beyond the mere letter of the law in such cases.

It is manifest to us that the limitation of the hours of labor as provided for in this section of the statute under which the indictment was found, and the plaintiff in error convicted, has no such direct relation to, and no such substantial effect upon, the health of the employee, as to justify us in regarding the section as really a health law. It seems to us that the real object and purpose were simply to regulate the hours of labor between the master and his employees (all being men, Sui juris), in a private business, not dangerous in any degree to morals, or in any real and substantial degree to the health of the employees. Under such circumstances the freedom of master and employee to contract with each other in relation to their employment, and in defining the same, cannot be prohibited or interfered with, without violating the Federal Constitution.

The judgment of the Court of Appeals of New York, as well as that of the Supreme Court and of the County Court of Oneida County, must be reversed(推翻原判) and the case remanded(发回重审) to the County Court for further proceedings not inconsistent with this opinion.

REVERSED.

Lesson Sixteen

Sexual Predator Laws: A Two-Decade Retrospective

> **Learning objectives**
>
> After learning the text and having done the exercises in this lesson, you will be able to:
>
> —acquire relevant knowledge of legal characteristics and the nature of sexual predator laws in common-law countries;
>
> —familiarize yourself with the vocabulary, grammar, or syntax concerned in this text;
>
> —become aware of the information required to understand the sexual predator laws;
>
> —cultivate practical abilities to put to use the language in the specific context; and
>
> —translate relevant materials from Chinese to English and from English to Chinese.

 Text

Sexual Predator Laws: A Two-Decade Retrospective

Introduction

The year 2009 approaches the twentieth anniversary of the birth of sexual predator legislation, a family of laws aimed at controlling sexual violence through "regulatory" schemes of prevention—schemes that claim exemption from the constraints surrounding the normal "charge and conviction" paradigm① of the criminal justice system. This same two-decade time span has witnessed the most energetic, sweeping legislative agenda on sexual offenders in memory.

The underlying tenet of sexual predator legislation is the notion of exceptionalism: the assertion that sexual violence—at least in some forms—is different in kind from the common expressions of antisocial behavior that are the everyday object of the criminal justice system. Whether this no-

---

① paradigm: 范式, 范例, 示例。

tion of exceptionalism spawned the regulatory initiatives, or vice versa, is not entirely clear. What seems clear, however, is that the idea itself has been highly influential in driving multiple regulatory approaches to controlling sexual violence. Moreover, it has put pressure on (or created incentives for) developments in the behavioral sciences and it may provide a model for preventive detention[①]in other areas of the law, such as antiterrorism legislation[②]. The real danger is that the notion of exceptionalism is a pretext that will eventually be forgotten or discarded, and we will be left with a new and unbridled regulatory approach to criminal behavior ungoverned by any principled limitations.

Early litigation challenged the constitutionality of the major forms of regulatory laws. A common theme in these challenges was the argument that the laws were in reality punitive[③], and therefore they violated a variety of constitutional limitations on punishment. Uniformly, however, the courts have held that the states acted with a proper, nonpunitive motive, and rejected these challenges. Another challenge to the commitment[④]laws argued that they violated substantive due process rights[⑤]. Essentially, this is an argument, rejected by the Supreme Court, that sexually violent predator (SVP) laws fail to satisfy a key constitutional prerequisite of civil commitment, proof of "mental disorder." A related due process right, the provision of treatment for the presumptive mental disorder, was given short shrift[⑥]by the Supreme Court in Hendricks.

This Article traces some of the more significant developments arising from the introduction of this regulatory approach. First, we comment about the spread of civil commitment laws. Second, we describe some of the mutations that this legal approach has spawned. Third, we examine several ways in which SVP laws have had an impact on behavioral sciences (and vice versa), offering some observations about the potential import(意义,含义) of this interdependence. Fourth, we provide some brief and speculative comments about the future of the regulatory approach in dealing with sex offenders. Finally, we offer an observation, and a warning, about the potential spread of the approach beyond sexual violence and into other traditional areas of the criminal law.

I The Spread of Civil Commitment Laws

The use of civil approaches to dealing with sexual violence has had an up and down history. In its first incarnation, from the late 1930s through the 1970s, "sexual psychopath" laws were adopted by over half the states. In a brief period of time, between 1975 and 1981, half of those statutes were repealed[⑦]. By 1985, these statutes existed in only thirteen states, and were regular-

---

① preventive detention:预防监禁。
② antiterrorism legislation:反恐立法,反对恐怖主义的立法。
③ punitive:惩罚性的,如:punitive damages(民事法律中的惩罚性损害赔偿)。
④ commitment:拘禁令。civil commitment(民事关禁;民事拘禁令)。其英语解释为:post-sentence institutional detention of a sex offender with the intention of preventing a re-offense(为防止性犯罪者再犯,对性犯罪者宣判刑期后由某一机构对其进行拘禁)。
⑤ substantive due process rights:实体性正当程序。
⑥ be given short shrift:被冷待,不受重视。
⑦ repeal:(法令等的)废除,作废,取消,撤销;撤回;(英史)撤销合并运动;(美国)废除禁酒法。作动词使用时,表示"废除,作废,取消,撤销,撤回(法律、判决、决议等);召回"等的意思。

Lesson Sixteen Sexual Predator Laws: A Two-Decade Retrospective

ly enforced in only six states. The repeal of these statutes has been attributed to four factors: (1) the growing influence of the feminist movement①, which opposed the "medicalization"② of rape; (2) dissatisfaction among mental health professionals, primarily psychiatrists, as reflected in the 1977 report from the Committee on Forensic Psychiatry③ of the Group for the Advancement of Psychiatry④ (GAP), which dealt a mortal blow to the scientific legitimacy of these statutes, referring to them as "social experiments that have failed and that lack redeeming social value"; (3) the prevailing "due process revolution" raised procedural and substantive due process issues and recognized rights that eventuated in suits filed on behalf of mental patients; and (4) a wave of societal disapprobation⑤ with treatment of sexual offenders led to treatment-oriented interventions falling increasingly out of favor.

The second generation of these statutes, beginning in 1990, has, thus far, been unaffected by these four factors. By the eighteenth year of the new era, twenty states had adopted SVP laws, and the United States Congress had passed a civil commitment provision as part of the Adam Walsh Act⑥. In their earlier incarnation, the laws had a legitimate (if somewhat weak) theoretical grounding (coming from the progressive notion of the power of psychiatry and the redeemability of human beings), whereas the second manifestation was much more opportunistic, grabbing a handy tool to address a pressing political and social problem. No doubt, the biggest impediment to the spread of the laws in their second coming has been their cost. The average annual program cost has been estimated at $97,000 per person.

It is difficult, and likely premature, to predict whether the SVP meme has run its course⑦. As Dawkins and other meme theorists contend, some memes propagate poorly and become extinct, while other memes are heartier, spread, and mutate, much like the SVP meme. Curiously, some meme theorists have argued that memes most detrimental to their hosts are the ones most likely to thrive and spread.

Between 1990 and 1999, seventeen states passed SVP statutes. After a spate of adoptions, the spread slowed considerably, with no new SVP statute enacted for the next seven years. In 2006, Nebraska passed an SVP bill, followed by New York and New Hampshire in 2007. The federal version was added quietly to a bill whose main thrust⑧ was regularizing and nationalizing sex offender registration and notification laws and infrastructure⑨. Given the considerable struggle to pass the New York law, and the low visibility of the federal civil commitment law, it is likely that further spread of the civil commitment model will be sporadic.

---

① feminist movement:女权主义运动,并体现在法学研究中的"女性法学"(legal feminism, feminist legal studies)的兴起与发展。
② medicalization:用医学方法处理(非医学问题等)。
③ Forensic Psychiatry:法医心理分析学;司法精神医学。
④ psychiatry:精神病学,精神病治疗。
⑤ disapprobation:不认可,不答应,不赞成;指责,非难。
⑥ Adam Walsh Act:2006年的《亚当·沃尔什法》,是一部以被害儿童命名的法令,该法令规定所有各州必须尽快将性犯罪者的登记资料公开。
⑦ run its course:按常规发展。
⑧ thrust:要点,要旨;目标(the principal purpose or theme of a course of action or line of reasoning)。
⑨ infrastructure:本文指各州的"法律基础结构"。

II The Spawn of Other Mutations

The power of these frames is evidenced by their ability to generate new laws that contradict clear empirical findings about best practices. A key example is residential restrictions①, which continue to be enacted, despite a line up of studies, many conducted by law enforcement agencies, concluding that these restrictions are counterproductive. Similarly anti-empirical are the provisions specifically directed at juveniles② in the Sex Offender Registration and Notification Act (SORNA), part of the Adam Walsh legislation passed in 2006. Federal guidelines for the Adam Walsh Act prescribe an offense-based (no risk assessment) system of registration that will require everyone over the age of fourteen years who commits a sex offense to register. The Act will categorize all offenders into three "Tiers." Tier I requires registration and notification for fifteen years, Tier II for twenty-five years, and Tier III for life.

In practice, this requirement will fall especially heavily on juvenile sex offenders. The Act's requirements are especially onerous③ for offenders whose victims are under thirteen years old. Because juveniles are the largest group of offenders against other juveniles, experts argue, the provisions of the Adam Walsh Act will likely have a disproportionate impact on juveniles. The underlying premise of SORNA, like all registration and notification laws, is that the constraint on liberty entailed by registration and notification is offset and justified by the avoidance of future risk—indeed, the special and unique risk of sexual recidivism④. But much evidence suggests that juveniles who offend sexually are not at high risk of sexual recidivism, and, perhaps as importantly, not at higher risk than other juveniles who are delinquents.

Stepping back, we can make this comment on the spread of the regulatory paradigm beyond civil commitment. The regulatory paradigm correctly recognizes that all regulatory laws impose restrictions on liberty, and that such regulation must ordinarily be supported by some legislative assessment of harm or danger. The fundamental turn that the predator laws take is in asserting that the harm is manifested in risky persons (or the status of "dangerousness"), rather than risky behavior or risky things.

Most regulation prohibits risky behaviors (e.g., drunk driving, speeding, dumping pollutants), or controls risky or dangerous things (e.g., radioactive waste). The radical shift in the predator laws is that the risk of harm is conceived as being a condition of the person⑤, rather than simply a quality of the person's behavior. It is this radical shift that generates the need to establish the idea of exceptionality, that there are clear and principled limits on the legitimacy of regulating risky persons.

In the SVP commitment laws, the idea of exceptionality is made explicit, embodied in the mental disorder requirement. But, in the implementation of SVP laws, the mental disorder element

---

① restrictions:限定;法律;规章。
② juveniles:未成年人,青少年。
③ onerous:(law) involving heavy obligations (律)义务繁多的。
④ recidivism:再犯,累犯(行为或倾向)。
⑤ the risk of harm is conceived as being a condition of the person:伤害的风险/可能性被认为是惩诫该人的一个条件。

loses its pivotal role, and the notion of risk (harm) becomes ascendant as the real justification for the deprivation of liberty. This move from mental disorder to risk allows the regulatory paradigm to expand from civil commitment to public notification (akin to label warnings on dangerous products) and geographical separation (analogous to zoning restrictions on hazardous product disposal). The loss of the principled factor that makes predator laws exceptional (mental disorder) ominously opens the possibility of broad expansion of the paradigm.

III Interactions with the Behavioral Sciences

A key claim in the argument for the legitimacy of the sexual predator paradigm is its reliance on the putative expertise of the behavioral sciences. But the way in which science is presumed to legitimate predator laws has never been entirely clear, and this lack of clarity has led to confusion and ambivalence as courts seek to navigate the terrain of these laws①.

At the core of all of the sexual predator laws is the notion of risk—dangerousness—with a fundamental variation among the laws being whether risk is considered to be an adjudicated (individual) fact, or a legislative (group) fact. Many of the civil commitment laws, for example, contain legislative findings about the risk posed② by sex offenders as a group, but all require adjudication of individual risk. In contrast, many of the notification and residential restriction laws impose restrictions on liberty based on legislative categories, with no requirement (or opportunity) for individualized risk assessments③.

Perhaps by serendipity④, the rise of civil commitment laws corresponded with a growth in research aimed at developing and improving empirically based risk assessment methods⑤. This circumstance has confronted courts with an interesting set of predicaments. Had these risk assessment methods, including actuarial methods⑥, not been developed (as was the case in the adjudication of "sexual psychopathy⑦" under the old statutes), reliance on traditional clinical assessments of dangerousness would have been the only option. Despite the well-known weakness of clinical judgment in the prediction of dangerousness, SVP courts (following the lead of the Supreme Court in its death penalty jurisprudence⑧) refused to hold that prediction-based deprivation of liberty was unconstitutional. Of course, the courts always left open⑨ the possibility that the actual assessment in a particular case would not be sound enough to meet (constitutionally imposed) standards of proof, but these are weight-of-the-evidence assessments, and have been viewed uniformly as com-

---

① navigate the terrain of these laws：在法律领域中艰难前行，此处的 navigate 不是常见含义"导航"等，而是 make one's way with difficulty over (a route or terrain)(艰难地)走过，经过。
② pose：present or constitute (a problem, danger, or difficulty) (形成，构成(问题，危险，困难))。
③ individualized risk assessments：特别风险评估，individualize 在该处拟作"个别地加以考虑，个别化，个性化"的意思。
④ by serendipity：by chance, serendipity. 此处指的是 the occurrence and development of events by chance in a happy or beneficial way(意外发现珍奇的、令人喜悦的事物)。
⑤ empirically based risk assessment methods：基于经验法则的风险评估方法。
⑥ actuarial methods：精算方法，该处 actuarial 表示"保险精算师的、保险精算的"意思。
⑦ sexual psychopathy：性心理变态。
⑧ See *Barefoot v. Estelle*, 463, U.S. 880 (1983).
⑨ leave open：未解决；悬而未决。

prising only questions of fact. As such①, they generally escape appellate review, thus impeding the development of articulated legal standards of risk②.

The introduction of empirically developed and validated risk assessment scales cast the process in a new light. The long trail of empirical evidence finding that mechanistic methods are as good as (often better than) clinical predications pushed courts in the direction of allowing the use of these scales (an issue often framed as a question of admissibility under *Daubert or Frye*). The use of these mechanistic scales, however, has brought an unprecedented transparency to the risk assessment process, exposing clearly the nature and limitations of risk assessment. Suddenly, courts were confronted with a number of potentially embarrassing facts: the group-based nature of risk assessment, the tension of applying probabilistic estimates from life tables to defendants who departed significantly from the membership of the reference groups③ used to derive the estimates, the difficulty of evaluating and incorporating dynamic risk factors, and the problem of translating statutory language into scientifically meaningful terms all became quite clear. By quantifying key elements of the risk assessment process, actuarial risk assessment (ARA) has given courts the tools to answer some difficult questions: How much risk is required? What is the time horizon④ for risk assessment? How is error to be assessed? Should it be expressed using group-based confidence intervals⑤? What level of error is permissible? How is maturation (aging) to be adjusted for? How does treatment impact risk status? The science of empirical risk assessment, in short, gives courts a realistic opportunity to make clear decisions, set clear legal thresholds, and thus translate risk assessment into questions of law—legal standards—rather than unreviewable decisions of credibility or weight. To date, however, it is not at all apparent that this salutary effect of empirical risk assessment is materializing.

On the scientific side, there has been vigorous activity aimed at influencing the contours of the mental-disorder element⑥. As is known to all, the courts seem to assume that, though the mental disorder criterion is a legal creation, it must be grounded on a mental disorder that has some medical legitimacy. The clearest and most obvious source for "medical legitimacy," the DSM⑦, was never intended as a system for classifying criminal behavior, and consequently does not provide meaningful diagnoses for most of the individuals who are candidates for SVP commitments. The task of providing a legitimate diagnosis for SVP proceedings is further complicated by the fact that Antisocial Personality Disorder⑧, a DSM disorder that legitimately applies to many sex offenders, is often assumed to be a constitutionally inadequate predicate⑨ for commitment.

---

① as such:依其身份、资格或名义等;本身。
② articulated legal standards of risk:更为精准的有关风险的法律标准。
③ reference groups:参照组;参考群体。
④ time horizon:时间范围,时间跨度。
⑤ confidence intervals:(统计)置信区间;可靠区间。
⑥ the contours of the mental-disorder element:有关精神错乱/障碍因素的各种情形,此处的 contour 不是"轮廓、外形、围线、等高线、恒值线"的意思。
⑦ DSM:本文指 American Psychiatric Association's Diagnostic and Statistical Manual of Mental Disorders(美国精神病协会精神障碍)诊断数据手册。
⑧ Antisocial Personality Disorder:反社会性人格障碍。
⑨ predicate:(逻辑)谓项;本质;属性。

Lesson Sixteen　Sexual Predator Laws: A Two-Decade Retrospective

　　This confluence of factors has led to three scientifically unfortunate consequences, all of which are aimed at providing taxonomic① coverage for sex offenders who are subject to SVP petitions②. The first is a vigorous effort on the part of a few psychologists to develop and promote a new diagnosis, specifically for rapists, who otherwise would have no taxonomic home in the DSM. Second is the overuse of the DSM diagnosis pedophilia③, applying it indiscriminately to individuals who offend against children (anyone under the age of consent), whether or not they meet the rather specific diagnostic criteria. Third is a use of the term hebephilia④ to provide coverage for offenders whose victims are pubescent, but not yet adults (i.e., adolescents).

　　Pedophilia, a medical diagnosis defined by the DSM, is a distinct subgroup of individuals who sexually molest children. Indiscriminately diagnosing petitioned child molesters into this diagnostic category renders the diagnosis meaningless, undercutting⑤ the essential scientific purpose of classification—reduction of taxonomic heterogeneity⑥ by assigning cases to maximally homogeneous groups⑦. Lost is the diagnostic clarity that flows from⑧ assigning the offender to a differentiated⑨ subgroup of child molesters that might inform our judgment about that particular individual based on known subgroup characteristics.

　　Recognizing that pedophilia applies only to those whose victims are prepubescent, some examiners apply the label hebephilia to individuals who offend against adolescents. Specifically rejected by the American Psychiatric Association for inclusion in the DSM, the diagnosis refers to an arousal that, according to the testimony cited by one court, characterizes "a significant portion of adult men."

　　The diagnostic conundrum⑩ is perhaps even more serious for rapists, for whom the DSM provides no ready category. The result is a newly created "diagnosis of convenience": Paraphilia⑪: NOS-Nonconsent⑫. This diagnosis is not in the DSM. It is the creation of a psychologist who recognized the need to provide all rapists with a "home" in the DSM, just as child molesters have. As explained by one examiner in a New Jersey SVP case, "Rape or coercive sex is not listed as a paraphilia. So we generally use this diagnosis, paraphilia, NOS in order to code for rape or coercive or nonconsent sex."

　　Although this new diagnosis, which requires evidence of preferential arousal to nonconsenting partners, is plausible, it would be very rare. It must be determined that the mere "nonconsent" of the victim is the preferred source of sexual arousal. Discerning who, among all rapists, are con-

---

① taxonomic;(生物)分类学,分类系统。
② petition: an application to a court for a writ, judicial action in a suit, etc..(律)申请书,诉状。
③ pedophilia:恋童癖:对儿童有性欲异常的性变态。
④ hebephilia:恋青年癖:性犯罪受害者已进入青春期但尚未成年,应该与严格意义的恋童癖区分开来。
⑤ undercut: (figurative) weaken; undermine (喻)削弱;暗中破坏。
⑥ heterogeneity:异质性;不均匀性;不纯一性。
⑦ homogeneous groups:同类组。
⑧ flow from: 起因于,产生于。
⑨ differentiated:分化型。
⑩ conundrum:谜;猜不透的难题;难答的问题。
⑪ Paraphilia:性反常行为;性欲倒错。
⑫ NOS-Nonconsent:疾病分类学上"未经同意"之类;Nos- 意为 Nosology:疾病分类学,疾病分类。

sistently and intensely aroused by the knowledge that the victim does not consent, is extraordinarily difficult. After several thousand evaluations, one of us (Prentky) has identified one rapist who would qualify for this diagnosis. In our experience, however, this new diagnosis has become the ubiquitous classification in some jurisdictions for rapists, especially when Antisocial Personality Disorder does not apply. In our judgment, this diagnosis most often reflects bad science and faulty clinical judgment. It has no empirical support, no established criteria for classification, and highly questionable reliability. In contrast, there is a considerable body of science that has identified factors associated with sexual aggression against women, including misogynistic[①]anger, negative or hostile masculinity, rape-related cognitive distortions (rape myths[②]) and entitlement, and impersonal sex. But the imperatives of the SVP cases have pushed to the forefront a diagnosis that ignores these factors in favor of a weak new diagnosis that formalistically satisfies the SVP case law.

IV Future of the Regulatory Approach to Sexual Violence: Invalidity as Applied

What can we say about the future of the regulatory approach to the prevention of sexual violence? Is there any stopping point in politics or law? Or, will legislatures, unconstrained by political opposition, continue their imaginative quest for safety, enacting Halloween[③]quarantines[④]and chartreuse[⑤]license plate laws of increasing absurdity? Will SVP commitment laws continue to grow without short-term limit?

We see a future limited by four possible constraints.

A. Fiscal Constraint

States may simply run out of money to continue, or begin, expensive sex offender commitment regimes. Given the massive strains on the economy at the present time, this may be the most realistic outcome. However, most of the noncommitment regulatory approaches have the benefit of little or no upfront[⑥]costs. Registration, notification, and residential restrictions appear, in legislative analysis, to be low-cost, and are often enacted without forethought as to the real costs of enforcement.

B. Remedial Litigation

Most of the litigation about regulatory predator laws has focused on the facial validity of the laws, rather than on their implementation. In theory, an aggrieved individual could challenge improper implementation, forcing states to conform to the law (and the Constitution). But this kind of remedial litigation is problematic. The commitment and discharge[⑦]of individuals are matters of

---

① misogynistic:厌恶女人的。misogynist:厌恶女人的人。misogyny:the hatred of women by men,厌女症,仇视妇女。
② rape-related cognitive distortions (rape myths):强奸有关的认知扭曲(强奸谬论),myths 在此处非"神话"之意,而是 a widely held but false belief or idea:(普遍持有的)错误见解或想法。
③ Halloween:万圣节前夕,诸圣日前夕(10 月 31 日,诸圣日的前夜,起源于基督教创立以前,与凯尔特人的桑巴因节有关,该节日被认为是幽灵鬼怪四处出没的日子,后来被基督教作为节日,现已逐渐变为非宗教节日,庆祝方式包括化装和戴面具等)。
④ quarantines:(人或动物生病之后被隔离的)检疫期。
⑤ chartreuse:(法)查特酒(法国查特修道院僧侣酿制的黄绿色甜酒),黄绿色。
⑥ upfront:(of a payment) made in advance (报酬)预付的,先期的。
⑦ discharge:release (someone) from the custody or restraint of the law 解除对(某人)法律上的监管(或监禁)。

case-by-case litigation in state trial courts. Those individual litigations uniformly frame important boundary issues as questions of fact, thus giving appellate courts a ready excuse not to elaborate, and hence control, questions of legal compliance. For this reason, such enforcement lawsuits have been few and laborious. Nonetheless, it is probably the case, based on anecdotal comments, that the possibility of constitutional litigation is in the minds of many state program administrators①, and that this possibility serves as a modest curb on flagrantly unconstitutional implementation.

C. Invalidity as Applied

An alternative litigation approach would assert that SVP laws are "invalid as applied." The aim would be to invalidate a particular state SVP law, putting an end to the programs operated under that law. The legal claim seeks to show that the law has an improper (punitive) purpose based on systemic and persistent patterns of improper implementation. The early challenges to SVP laws were facial challenges, asserting that their legislative histories and statutory provisions made plain a punitive purpose. Though these initial facial challenges were uniformly unsuccessful, the initial facial evaluations of statutory purpose might have been mistaken, for two reasons. First, the explicit provisions of the SVP law might have masked a hidden legislative purpose that was improper. Second, despite a proper legislative purpose, the executive implementation of the statutory scheme might reveal an improper state purpose. This litigation approach is explored in more detail elsewhere.

D. Political Leadership to Change Frames

We have suggested that the regulatory approaches to sexual violence appear to be useful and attractive because they are viewed through a set of conceptual frames, in particular, the exceptionality of the "sexual predator," the concept of risk, and the idea of the degraded other. As we have written elsewhere, a key to changing the public policy and associated legal structures is the development and adoption of a new set of frames. Among other things, the new frames ought to insist on seeing sex offender policy comprehensively, through a public health approach, and on developing a greater sense of community ownership② of the problem of sexual violence.

V Spread beyond Sexual Violence

As we have suggested, the fundamental problem underlying the use of a regulatory approach to sexual violence is in establishing boundaries or limits. Advocates for SVP laws have consistently argued for the notion of exceptionality—that the expansion of civil commitment to sex offenders is sui generis③, not the first step on a slippery slope④ to the preventive state. Yet now, the existence and validity of SVP laws is being cited as justification⑤ for extending preventive detention into another area: preventive detention of suspected terrorists.

---

① program administrators:项目的行政管理者。
② sense of community ownership:社会主人翁精神。
③ sui generis:(Latin) literally of its own kind 独特的,唯一的。如:the sui generis nature of animals(动物的独特天性)。
④ slippery slope:灾难性的急剧下滑。
⑤ justification:正当的理由;辩解的理由。

Wittes and Gitenstein, for example, argue that preventive detention runs counter to core values, but that nonetheless it can be expanded to suspected terrorists because it has been used for a number of purposes such as the dangerously mentally ill or sexually deviant. In arguing for the extension, they do not focus on the grounds used to justify SVP laws—the supposed distinguishing characteristics of the mental status. Rather, they rely on the argument from necessity, the fact that we have no alternative, because evidence is inadmissible or no crimes have been committed, thereby undermining the utility of the criminal justice system. Goldsmith and Katyal also argue from this analogy.

But at present, even that much reliability would be absent in the anti-terrorism context, where (at least to our knowledge) no peer-reviewed, empirically developed actuarial risk assessment tools exist. But if the SVP context is predictive, a new market for detention based on prediction of danger will lead to the creation of new empirical tools for assessment of risk. We know, for example, that the government already uses a secret algorithm① to assess risk for all passengers arriving in the United States on international flights. The Los Angeles Police have undertaken a project to "map" and "Muslim enclaves②." The purpose is to "identify communities within the large Muslim community, which may be susceptible to violent, ideologically based extremism."

Profiling designed to identify "dangerous people" has a dishonorable legacy in this country, emerging, in only one example, in the days of the Cold War, and ultimately destroying the lives of many innocent Americans before Senator Joseph McCarthy③ was silenced. We have visited this shame on our citizens many times in history. Do we wish to go there again?

Conclusion

This Article identifies the broad arc of the developments of SVP laws, tracing key legal issues, as well as the ways in which the existence of this new legal approach has shaped both other areas of the law and the behavioral sciences.

The principal articulated impetus for sexual predator legislation was the belief that sexual violence was rampant, posed a more insidious threat to the welfare of society than other criminal behaviors, and, as such, needed to be addressed not simply in the criminal law but by using a variety of interventions that were civil or "regulatory" in nature. The central ideas are that the state commonly restricts liberty in the name of regulation, the key prerequisites derive from a nonpunitive purpose (perhaps benevolently parens patriae④ in spirit), and the risk of harm or danger is sufficient to balance the liberty-deprivation.

---

① algorithm:运算法则。
② enclave:飞地,指在一国境内的外国领土。
③ Joseph McCarthy: Joseph (Raymond) (1909—1957), American Republican politician. Between 1950 and 1954 he was the instigator of widespread investigations into alleged communist infiltration in US public life. 麦卡锡,约瑟夫·雷蒙德(1909—1957),美国共和党政客,1950 至 1954 年间,他是煽动对所谓共产党对美国公共生活的渗透进行广泛调查的始作俑者。
④ parens patriae:政府监护;政府监护权,政府监护权说,原意是"国家亲权"(parens patriae),来自于拉丁语,其字面上的含义即"国家家长"(parent of the country)。

Lesson Sixteen Sexual Predator Laws: A Two-Decade Retrospective

 Legal Terminology

1. aggrieved party、injured person 和 victim

乍看上去，上述单词或词组似乎均有"受害人"的含义，但究其内涵差异却极大。首先是 aggrieved party，因单词 aggrieve 在表示"伤害"或"不公正对待"时，只适用于法律场合情况下的伤害，故在法律英语中，aggrieved party（也称为 party aggrieved 或 person aggrieved）专指在司法或准司法程序中其合法权益受到伤害或不公正对待者，即受到认为不公正的判决、命令或惩处者，按规定，此种人具有上诉或申诉之权利地位（standing as an appellant or a petitioner or a complaint）。为与其他"受害人"相区别，最好将其译为"受屈人"或"权益受侵害人"或不服判决、命令等的"上诉人"或"申诉人"。因此，the aggrieved party in a case 便应为"案件受屈人"，指在案件中的受到不公正待遇者，或"案件申（上）诉人"，指案件中的 plaintiff 或 petitioner，而不应是有些词典中的"案件中受害的一方"或"被害人"。injured person 和 victim 则是指其权利、财产或人身等受到其他当事人伤害者，injured party 指法律诉讼中的曾受到另一方当事人行为伤害的"受害人"，即原告。victim 尤指犯罪、侵权或其他过错行为之受害人。

2. Due process

Due process，正当程序，也称为"正当法律程序"（亦称 due process of law）。源自于英美国家，核心内容是政府必须尊重任何依据国内法赋予人民的法律权利。正当法律程序起始于英国《大宪章》，后移植到美国，在美国宪法修正条款中具体呈现。美国宪法第五及第十四修正条款规定了除经过正当法定程序外，不得剥夺任何人之生命、自由或财产。第五修正条款规定:"... No person shall be ... deprived of life, liberty, or property, without due process of law ...."（未经正当法律程序，不得剥夺任何人的生命、自由或财产），主要适用于联邦。第十四修正条款规定:"nor shall any State deprive any person of life, liberty, or property, without due process of law ..."（亦不得未经正当法律程序剥夺任何人的生命、自由或财产），主要对各州具有约束力。

3. civil court、civil custody、civil prison 和 civil prisoner

在翻译以上术语时人们经常会犯错误，故务必要小心才行。首先应注意的是 civil court，该词组除在英、美等国指"民事法院"外，在其他地区，如在加拿大，它可用作指具有一般管辖权（包括具有简易审判程序）的刑事法院，其与民事无任何关系，civil 在此等同 ordinary，故应译为"普通刑事法院"。同样，civil custody 也是指警方或其他相关民政当局"对一般罪犯所作的拘留或关押"（普通监狱"civil prison"或教养所"penitentiary"的关押均包括在内）。civil prison 则可指任何关押由普通刑事法院（civil court）经简易审判程序（summary procedure）审判的罪行较轻刑期在 2 年以下罪犯之监狱（包括 jail 和其他场所），故为"普通监狱"。由此可知，civil prisoner 则是指由 civil court 所判处的被 civil prison 关押的刑期为 2 年以下的"普通服刑犯"。对于 civil prisoner 而言，《英汉法律词典》的新版本更正了其第一版将该术语译为"民事犯"之谬误，将其译为了"普通犯"，然而该词典援引的《法窗译话》之解释，即"普通犯"是"与政治犯、国事犯、军事犯、战犯等对称时用"的解释却仍然应为一谬误，这里的"普通"两字，实则应为"罪行较轻"的含义。

4. court of appeals 和 supreme court

在美国,court of appeals(在有些州也称为 court of appeal)可指联邦中级或州高级法院。如在加州和路易斯安那州,其是指中级法院,这些州的高级法院称为 supreme court;而在哥伦比亚特区、马里兰和纽约州,court of appeal 是指州高级,即州最高法院,这些州的 supreme court 反而成了州的中级法院。在英格兰,court of appeal 是最高司法法院"Supreme Court of Judicature"的一个分院,译为"上诉法院"。

5. mental disease 和 mental illness

两术语很容易被人混淆。总体说来,它们应基本算作同义,但两者在用法上有一定的差异。mental disease(也称为 emotional distress;emotional harm;mental anguish;mental suffering)(精神病)多限于法律事务中,现已发展成为专指刑法上导致反复的刑事犯罪或反社会行为的一种非正常精神病状。而 mental illness(精神疾患)则更多指医学界所认知的"精神上的疾病或病症",其也被称为 mental disorder。

Exercises

I Verbal abilities

Part One

Directions: *For each of these questions, read each item carefully to get the sense of it. Then, in the proper space, complete each statement by supplying the missing word or phrase.*

1. If a disaster manager can identify the unfolding scenarios, monitoring will ultimately be more important than _____.

   A. judgment   B. performance   C. occurrence
   D. assessment   E. concurrence

2. The social networks point out that they already have agreements that _____ the rights and responsibilities of application developers, and take action against those that misuse personal information.

   A. govern   B. manage   C. handle
   D. command   E. control

3. Be alert in your observations. Look for similarities, differences, as well as unique and _____ features in situations and problems.

   A. distributive   B. indifferent   C. destructive
   D. constructive   E. distinguishing

4. President Barack Obama signed orders earlier today to close the Guantanamo Bay _____ center.

   A. detainee   B. detention   C. detained
   D. detective   E. imprisoning

5. For those crimes he faces _____ discharge(开除军籍), forfeiture of pay, and up to 32 years in prison.

Lesson Sixteen Sexual Predator Laws: A Two-Decade Retrospective

A. dishonest   B. immoral   C. dishonorable
D. unethical   E. honorable

6. So if you are in a situation that isn't predictable you can't use a _____ methodology.

A. predictable   B. preventive   C. prophetical
D. purposeful   E. predictive

7. The one-China principle, resolutely adhered to by the Chinese Government, is also universally-recognized by the international _____.

A. countries   B. community   C. communist
D. society   E. profession

8. If certain provisions of a labor contract are invalid and such _____ does not affect the validity of the remaining provisions, the remaining provisions shall still remain valid.

A. validate   B. validity   C. invalidity
D. valid   E. invalidation

9. To encourage more institutional investors, an _____ system assessing fund companies' transactions should be established.

A. efficient   B. effective   C. effectuation
D. evaluation   E. efficiency

10. It is high time to introduce the _____ compensation system into Chinese public security area.

A. punitive   B. punishment   C. correctional
D. rehabilitative   E. revengeful

Part Two

Directions: *Choose the word or phase that best keeps the meaning of the original sentence if it substitutes for the underlined part.*

1. The existence of liability insurance <u>engenders</u> some impact on the punitive function and restrain injurious act function of tort law, but this influence is not absolute.

A. results from   B. generates   C. leads forward
D. actualizes   E. spawns

2. Foreign currency allowances for travelers are being cut, and more importers are finding that they have to <u>resort to</u> the parallel exchange market to obtain their dollars

A. be independent of   B. rely upon   C. give rise to
D. turn to   E. bring about

3. Two real options of theirs are simply capital controls and currency <u>appreciation</u>.

A. discernment   B. depreciation   C. upvaluation
D. inflation   E. deflation

4. Foreign direct investment (FDI) is less <u>volatile</u> than speculative capital inflows.

A. unstable   B. explosive   C. inchangeable
D. vaporific   E. vaporizable

5. The exchange rate is the price of foreign currency in terms of <u>domestic</u> currency, and it

varies from time to time.

  A. family   B. home   C. household

  D. internal   E. interior

  6. Indeed, even investment "demand" is <u>mitigated</u> by price as one need only buy a fourth as much of it as a decade ago to keep actual physical purchases constant.

  A. alleviated   B. aggravated   C. undermined

  D. deteriorated   E. strengthened

  7. Indeed there is every reason to think that policy independence would <u>benefit</u> systemic risk regulation as well.

  A. be detrimental to   B. allowance   C. do harm to

  D. advantage   E. welfare

  8. A Chinese will arrive on time or sometimes several minutes ahead of schedule when meeting an important person or keeping an important <u>appointment</u> to show respect to the other party.

  A. assignment   B. designation   C. engagement

  D. meeting   E. dating

  9. He spent six years in jail, mostly in solitary confinement, until his conviction was <u>overturned</u>.

  A. vacated   B. revoked   C. subverted

  D. reversed   E. overruled

  10. Huge reductions in phone call costs and new <u>access</u> to productivity-enhancing applications will revolutionize the business.

  A. accessory   B. admittance   C. retreat

  D. accession   E. retirement

II Cloze

  Directions: *For each blank in the following passage, choose the best answer from the choices given.*

  The implications of these two aspects of constitutional mental disorder have been instructive. Given the key constitutional ___(1)___ played by the notion of control dysfunction, it is shocking to see the consistently subversive way in ___(2)___ the courts have deprived the control dysfunction standard of any clear meaning. One of us wrote about this ___(3)___ in the mid-1990s, well before the Supreme Court in Crane confirmed the continuing constitutional centrality of the ___(4)___. His conclusion then was that in fifty-five years of implementing the first generation of sex psychopath (精神变态者,精神病患者) ___(5)___ in Minnesota, over 300 people had been ___(6)___ committed, and in none of the cases was the control-dysfunction element mentioned in appellate review. The vigorous ___(7)___ about the second-generation SVP laws focused intensely ___(8)___ the constitutional status, and meaning, of "inability to control." Janus ___(9)___ the first twenty-five appellate cases that discussed ___(10)___ dysfunction in the 1990s. His conclusion: "nowhere in the corpus of these cases can one find a straightforward declarative sentence ___(11)___ how one distinguishes incapacity to control (a mental disorder) from a failure to control (criminal behavior)." In a forthcoming publication, Prentky, Coward, and Gabriel call the control dysfunction element "an 800 pound diagnostic gorilla, an essential defining characteristic of an ___(12)___ statutory element that the weight of scholarly opinion regards in the same vein as divination." The essential problem is that courts have ___(13)___ almost any effort to define what control dysfunction might mean. Most courts simply hide the determination inside nested findings of fact. In several states, juries are not even ___(14)___ a specific jury instruction that uses the "difficulty controlling" terminology. A review of the appellate cases does not reveal any serious effort by courts to articulate standards governing the control dysfunction criterion. The closest any courts have come to attempting a definition of the term is a series of California cases, holding that the only evidence that could ___(15)___ difficulty controlling behavior was evidence that the individual had tried, but failed, to cease engaging in illegal behavior. This definition has clear failings.

(1) A. office   B. role   C. capacity
    D. function   E. character

(2) A. that   B. where   C. what
    D. how   E. which

(3) A. phenomenon   B. phenomena   C. element
    D. elementary   E. problem

(4) A. thought   B. idea   C. concept
    D. construction E. explanation

(5) A. ordinances   B. laws   C. regulations
    D. rules   E. decrees

(6) A. civil   B. criminal   C. civilly
    D. criminally   E. military

(7) A. procedure   B. proceeding   C. substantive
    D. litigation   E. mitigation

(8) A. in   B. on   C. through
    D. for   E. within

(9) A. reviewed   B. received   C. accepted
    D. refused   E. overturned

(10) A. monitor   B. supervise   C. complete
     D. control   E. confront

(11) A. explain   B. explaining   C. account for
     D. accounting   E. construct

(12) A. separable   B. dispensable   C. indispensable
     D. dispersive   E. dependant

(13) A. accepted   B. honored   C. made
     D. eschewed   E. put

(14) A. ordered   B. instructed   C. commanded
     D. placed   E. given

(15) A. present　　　B. demonstrate　　　C. establish
　　　D. clarify　　　E. certify

III Reading Comprehension

Part One

Directions: *In this section there a passage followed by questions or unfinished statements, each with suggested answers. Choose the one you think is the best answer.*

Sex Offender Registration

Australia

The Australian National Child Offender Register (ANCOR) is a web-based system used in all jurisdictions. Authorized police use ANCOR to monitor persons convicted of child sex offences and other specified offences once they have served their sentence. On 1 March 2011, there were 12,596 registered offenders across Australia.

Canada

Canada's National Sex Offender Registry (NSOR) came into force on December 15, 2004, with the passing of the Sex Offender Information Registration Act (SOIR Act)(性犯罪者信息登记法). The public does not have access to the registry.

Since 2001, the Province of Ontario operates its own sex offender registry concurrently with the federal registry.

United Kingdom

In the United Kingdom, the Violent and Sex Offender Register (ViSOR) is a database of records of those required to register with the Police under the Sexual Offences Act 2003, those jailed for more than 12 months for violent offences, and unconvicted(未经定罪的)people thought to be at risk of offending. The Register can be accessed by the Police, National Probation Service and HM Prison Service personnel. It is managed by the National Policing Improvement Agency of the Home Office(英国内政部).

United States

Sign at the limits of Wapello, Iowa; sex offender-free districts appeared as a result of Megan's Law. The Supreme Court of the United States has upheld sex offender registration laws twice, in two respects. Two challenges to state laws (in Hawaii and Missouri) have succeeded, however.

In 1947, California became the first state in the United States to have a sex offender registration program. Community notification of the release of sex offenders from incarceration(监禁;禁闭)did not occur until almost 50 years later. In 1994, a federal statute called the Jacob Wetterling Act required all states to pass legislation requiring sex offenders to register with state sex offender registries. Then again in 1996, based on a set of New Jersey laws called "Megan's Laws," the federal government required states to pass legislation mandating public notification of personal information for certain sex offenders. In Connecticut Dept. of Public Safety v. Doe (2002) the Supreme Court of the United States affirmed this public disclosure(向公众披露信息).

The Adam Walsh Child Protection and Safety Act became law in 2007. This law implements new uniform requirements for sex offender registration across the states (however, these laws can differ in each state). Highlights of the law are a new national sex offender registry, standardized registration requirements for the states, and new and enhanced criminal offenses related to sex offenders. Since its enactment, the Adam Walsh Act (AWA) has come under intense grassroots scrutiny for its far-reaching scope and breadth. Even before any state adopted AWA, several sex offenders were prosecuted under its regulations. This has resulted in one life sentence(无期徒刑) for failure to register, due to the offender being homeless and unable to register a physical address (实际地址).

Because of the act, all 50 states have now passed laws requiring sex offenders (especially child sex offenders) to register with police. Accordingly, the law requires offenders to report where they take up residence upon leaving prison or being convicted of any crime.

In 2006, California voters passed Proposition 83, which will enforce "lifetime monitoring of convicted sexual predators and the creation of predator free zones." This proposition was challenged the next day in federal court on grounds relating to ex post facto. The U.S. District Court for the Central District of California, Sacramento, found that Proposition 83 did not apply retroactively(具有追溯力的).

Patty Wetterling, the mother of Jacob Wetterling and a major proponent of the Jacob Wetterling Act, has openly criticized the evolution of sex offender registration and management laws in the United States since the Jacob Wetterling Act was passed, saying that the laws are often applied to too many offenses and that the severity of the laws often makes it difficult to rehabilitate(改造罪犯等,使恢复正常生活,使改过自新) offenders.

Constitutionality

U. S. Supreme Court Rulings

In two cases docketed for argument on November 13, 2003, the sex offender registries of two states, Alaska and Connecticut, would face legal challenge. This was the first instance that the Supreme Court had to examine the implementation of sex offender registries in throughout the U.S. The ruling would let the states know how far they could go in informing citizens of perpetrators of sex crimes. The constitutionality of the registries was challenged in two ways:

Ex post facto(有追溯力的) challenge. In *Smith v. Doe*, 538 U. S. 84 (2003), the Supreme Court upheld Alaska's sex-offender registration statute. Reasoning that sex offender registration deals with civil laws, not punishment, the Court ruled 6-3 that it is not an unconstitutional ex post facto law. Justices John Paul Stevens, Ruth Bader Ginsburg, and Stephen Breyer dissented.

Due process challenge. In *Connecticut Dept. of Public Safety v. Doe*, 538 U. S. 1 (2003), the Court ruled that Connecticut's sex-offender registration statute did not violate the procedural due process of those to whom it applied, although the Court "expresses no opinion as to whether the State's law violates substantive due process principles."

State Court Rulings

Hawaii. In State v. Bani, 36 P. 3d 1255 (Haw. 2001), the Hawaii State Supreme Court held that Hawaii's sex offender registration statute violated the due process clause of the Constitution of Hawaii, ruling that it deprived potential registrants of "of a protected liberty interest without due process of law." The Court reasoned that the sex offender law authorized "public notification of (the potential registrant's) status as a convicted sex offender without notice, an opportunity to be heard, or any preliminary determination of whether and to what extent he actually represents a danger to society."

Missouri. Many successful challenges to sex offender registration laws in the United States have been in Missouri because of a unique provision in the Missouri Constitution (Article I, Section 13) prohibiting laws "retrospective in their operation."

Pennsylvania. HARRISBURG①-May 27, 2011—The Pennsylvania Supreme Court says an Allegheny County ordinance barring sex offenders from living in certain areas is invalid.

In a strongly worded, 23-page decision released Thursday (5/26/2011), Chief Justice Ronald Castille said the ordinance is pre-empted by state laws that balance public safety and the goal of rehabilitation for sex offenders.

The prohibition against registered offenders living within 2,500 feet of schools, child-care facilities, community centers, public parks or recreational facilities would isolate many in what would amount to "localized penal colonies" distant from families and old neighborhoods, Castille wrote in the unanimous opinion.

In addition to Allegheny County, which includes the city of Pittsburgh, the decision affects many of the roughly 150 municipalities around the state that have similar ordinances, though lawyers involved in the Allegheny County case had different opinions about the decision's impact.

Buckingham solicitor Craig Smith said, "It is apparent from the decision that any effort by the municipality to restrict where paroled sex offenders(获得假释的性侵犯者)may live is in conflict with state law and therefore invalid."

Allegheny County passed its ordinance in 2007. A federal judge struck it down in 2009 and the county appealed. In a twist that lawyers described as unusual, a panel of the 3rd U. S. Circuit Court of Appeals(美国联邦第三巡回上诉法院)in Philadelphia sought the state court's input on whether state law pre-empted the county ordinance.

Nearly 11,000 sex offenders are registered with the state police under Pennsylvania Megan's Law.

People convicted of certain offenses—including kidnapping, indecent assault(强暴猥亵罪), and sexual abuse of children(对儿童的性侵犯)—must register for 10 years following their release on probation or parole(一旦缓刑或假释释放出来之后).

People convicted of multiple offenses or of any more serious offenses, including rape and involuntary deviate sexual intercourse, and offenders designated as "sexually violent predators" must register for life.

1. As to the sex offender registration in Australia, Which of the following is not true?

   A. It is a web-based system and all can have access to its information.

   B. People use the system to monitor those convicted of child sex offences.

   C. Only certain police with authorization have access to the web-based system.

---

① Harrisburg:哈里斯堡(美国宾夕法尼亚州的首府)。

D. The number that gets registered in the name of sex offences is really amazing.

2. According to the passage, all of the following countries have their sex offender registration systems except _____.

A. the United States   B. the United Kingdom   C. Canada   D. Mexico

3. Of all the countries mentioned in this passage, which of the following is the fundamental similarity as to the sex offender registration system?

A. They all have web-based system for such a registration.

B. Only those who are authorized can have access to the system.

C. All of the countries concerned have similar offender registration Acts.

D. All of the countries register the sex offenders throughout their own countries.

4. As to the U.S. sex offender registration program, which of the following is **NOT** true?

A. Community notification of the release of sex offenders from incarceration occurred in 1997.

B. In 1994, a federal Act required all states to pass legislation that would require states to register sex offenders.

C. "Megan's Laws" is a set of New Jersey laws and the said laws required states to pass legislation mandating public notification of personal information for certain sex offenders.

D. California was the first state in the Unites States that had a sex offender registration.

5. Which of the following is true of AWA?

A. AWA provided new uniform requirements for sex offender registration across the states.

B. AWA became law in 2007 and each state carried it out uniformly.

C. AWA highlighted its registration standards and it was new for sex offenders.

D. Adam Walsh Act came under intense grassroots scrutiny due to its new requirements.

6. According to AWA, a potential sex offender should do all of the following except _____.

A. register with police

B. register a physical address with police

C. monitor other convicted sexual predators and create a zone for predators

D. report where they take up residence upon leaving prison or being convicted of any crime

7. According to the passage, why was the constitutionality of the registries challenged?

A. Because sex offender registration deals with civil laws, not punishment.

B. Because the Court ruled 6-3 that it is not an unconstitutional ex post facto law.

C. Because the Court ruled that Connecticut's sex-offender registration statute did not violate the procedural due process.

D. Because the Court expresses no opinion as to whether the State's law violates substantive due process principles.

8. Why are there many successful challenges to sex offender registration laws in Missouri?

A. Because the sex offender law authorized public notification of the potential registrant's status as a convicted sex offender without notice.

B. Because there exists a unique provision in Missouri Constitution that prohibits laws "retrospective in their operation".

C. Because the registrant is given no opportunity to be heard in Missouri.

D. Because there is no preliminary determination of whether and to what extent the potential registrant actually represents a danger to society.

9. What kind of people convicted of offences must register for life?

A. those who are convicted of indecent assault and kidnapping

B. those convicted of multiple offences including rape or other serious offenses

C. those who are released on probation or on parol

D. those suspected to be would-be sexually violent predators

Part Two   True or False Questions

Direction: *In this part of the exercise, there is a passage with ten true or false questions. Read the passage carefully and mark T if it is true and F if it is false.*

The Diagnostic and Statistical Manual of Mental Disorders (DSM) is published by the American Psychiatric Association and provides a common language and standard criteria for the classification of mental disorders. It is used in the United States and in varying degrees around the world, by clinicians(临床医生;临床教师), researchers, psychiatric drug regulation agencies(精神病用药物管理机关), health insurance companies, pharmaceutical companies(制药公司), and policy makers. The DSM has attracted controversy and criticism as well as praise. There have been five revisions since it was first published in 1952, gradually including more mental disorders, although some have been removed and are no longer considered to be mental disorders, most notably homosexuality.

The manual evolved from systems for collecting census and psychiatric hospital(精神病院) statistics, and from a manual developed by the US Army, and was dramatically revised in 1980. The last major revision was the fourth edition ("DSM-IV"), published in 1994, although a "text revision"(文本修订) was produced in 2000. The fifth edition ("DSM-5") is currently in consultation(处于征求意见阶段), planning and preparation, due for publication in May 2013. ICD-10 Chapter V: Mental and behavioral disorders, part of the International Classification of Diseases produced by the World Health Organization (WHO)(世界卫生组织), is another commonly used guide, more so in Europe and other parts of the world. The coding system(代码系统) used in the DSM-IV is designed to correspond with the codes used in the ICD (International Classification of Diseases:联合国国际疾病分类法), although not all codes may match at all times because the two publications are not revised synchronously.

Many mental health professionals use the manual to determine and help communicate a patient's diagnosis after an evaluation; hospitals, clinics, and insurance companies in the US also generally require a 'five axis' DSM diagnosis of all the patients treated. The DSM can be used clinically in this way, and also to categorize patients using diagnostic criteria for research purposes. Studies done on specific disorders often recruit patients whose symptoms match the criteria listed in the DSM for that disorder. An international survey of psychiatrists in 66 countries comparing use of the ICD-10 and DSM-IV found the former was more often used for clinical diagnosis(临床诊断) while the latter was more valued for research.

History

The initial impetus for developing a classification of mental disorders in the United States was the need to collect statistical information. The first official attempt was the 1840 census which used a single category, "idiocy(白痴状态;极度愚蠢)/insanity(精神失常,神智迷乱)". In 1917, a "Committee on Statistics" from what is now known as the American Psychiatric Association (APA) (美国精神病协会,注意该协会与 American Psychological Association 美国心理学协会的缩写形式一样,注意区分), together with the National Commission on Mental Hygiene(心理卫生学全国委员会), developed a new guide for mental hospitals called the "Statistical Manual for the Use of Institutions for the Insane", which included 22 diagnoses. This was subsequently revised several times by APA over the years. APA, along with the New York Academy of Medicine, also provided the psychiatric nomenclature subsection of the US medical guide, the "Standard Classified Nomenclature of Disease(疾病标准分类名称)", referred to as the "Standard".

DSM-I (1952)

World War II saw the large-scale involvement of US psychiatrists in the selection, processing, assessment and treatment of soldiers. This moved the focus away from mental institutions and traditional clinical perspectives. A committee that was headed by psychiatrist Brigadier General(准将) William C. Menninger developed a new classification scheme called Medical 203 that was issued in 1943 as a "War Department Technical Bulletin"(存在于1789—1947年的美国陆军部技术通报) under the auspices of the Office of the Surgeon General(美国军医署). The foreword to the DSM-I states the US Navy had itself made some minor revisions but "the Army established a much more sweeping revision, abandoning the basic outline of the Standard and attempting to express present day concepts of mental disturbance(精神障碍). This nomenclature eventually was adopted by all Armed Forces, and "assorted modifications of the Armed Forces nomenclature were introduced into many clinics and hospitals by psychiatrists returning from military duty". The Veterans Administration(美国退伍军人管理局) also adopted a slightly modified version of Medical 203.

In 1949, the World Health Organization published the sixth revision of the International Statistical Classification of Diseases (ICD) which included a section on mental disorders for the first time. The foreword to DSM-1 states this "categorized mental disorders in rubrics similar to those of the Armed Forces nomenclature." An APA Committee on Nomenclature and Statistics was empowered to develop a version specifically for use in the United States, to standardize the diverse and confused usage of different documents. In 1950 the APA committee undertook a review and consultation. It circulated an adaptation of Medical 203, the VA(Veterans' Administration:美国退伍军人管理局) system and the Standard's Nomenclature, to approximately 10% of APA members. 46% replied, of which 93% approved, and after some further revisions (resulting in it being called DSM-I), the Diagnostic and Statistical Manual of Mental Disorders was approved in 1951 and published in 1952. The structure and conceptual framework were the same as in Medical 203, and many passages of text identical. The manual was 130 pages long and listed 106 mental disorders.

1. Homosexuality is not deemed as mental disorder in the Diagnostic and Statistical Manual of

Mental Disorders by the American Psychiatric Association. (   )

2. Classification of mental disorders is described in a commonly-used language in the Diagnostic and Statistical Manual of Mental Disorders. (   )

3. The coding system used in the DSM-IV will correspond with the codes used in the ICD and most codes will match each other. (   )

4. DSM is used by most mental health professionals to determine and help communicate a patient's diagnosis in the US. (   )

5. The DSM can be used clinically to categorize patients using diagnostic criteria for research purposes. (   )

6. APA's job in 1917 was to develop a new guide for mental hospitals, which was subsequently adopted by APA over the years. (   )

7. The new classification scheme called Medical 203 developed by psychiatrist Brigadier General William C. Menninger was later universally adopted in the U.S. Armed Forces. (   )

8. To standardize the diverse and confused usage of different documents, an APA Committee on Nomenclature and Statistics was empowered to develop a version specifically for use in the United States. (   )

IV Translation abilities

法律语言特征分析与法律翻译技能培养之十六：
同义与近义法律术语的翻译

法律语言中有不少同义和近义术语,使用和翻译时须特别留意。鉴于法律语言的严谨和准确,不少时候它们不能随便相互替换。如 sentence 专指刑事案件的"判刑"而非一般人心目中的"判决",故绝不能随便与 judgement 互换使用。又如 discovery 和 disclosure,它们都是诉讼法中常用的词汇,前者为"证据开示",后者为"证据披露"。区别在于前者多为非强制性,其较多体现一种"当事人主义"思想,即证据须经当事人申请则予以"开示"。其缺点在于有的当事人可扩大证据开示的范畴,借此以拖延诉讼,为此,目前国外所进行的民事诉讼改革中的一大举措便是用 disclosure 取代 discovery。disclosure 基本上属于强制性,体现出一种"职权主义"的味道,其由法官决定证据披露的范畴,目的主要在于解决长期困扰法院的诉讼"delay"问题。由此可知,这两个术语决不能混为一谈。

再以诉状为例,pleading, complaint, petition, clause, application, indictment, information, presentment, bill, statement of claim, particulars of claim 和 libel 等均有诉状的含义。其中,pleading 是指诉辩程序中,当事双方呈送法庭的各种诉辩文书,除指诉状(complaint)外,还指答辩状(answer),原告对被告抗辩的再答辩状(reply)等。complaint 多指向普通法法院所提交的民事诉状或刑事自诉状。petition 是指向大法官法院或衡平法法院以及在家事法院的离婚、子女抚养等案件中和遗嘱检验法院有关遗嘱检验的案件中所提交的诉状。clause 是指向宗教法院提交的诉状。application 多是指向国际法庭提交的要求得到法院某项专门命令的一种诉状。indictment, information 和 presentment 三个单词都是指刑事诉状,indictment 多指对重罪犯提起公诉时提交的诉状(在英格兰是以国王的名义,在苏格兰是以检察总长的名义,在美国是由大陪审团确认后向法院提交);在美国,information 与 indictment 的主要区别在于前者是以检察官个人名义,而不是经大陪审团确认后以大陪审团的名义所提交;在英国,如以 information 形式提起诉讼,检举人(informer)则可望得到一笔奖金,其有时也可用于民事诉讼的特权告发程序;在加拿大,information 可由警官直接向治安法官提出,如果治安法官认定其事实充足,便可签发传票或逮捕令(如果被传人不到庭);presentment 是指大陪审团(或其他团体)直接提交的控诉书。bill 源于法文的通知(libelle),多用于英格兰,为一般性用语,指对犯罪行为的书面告发(经大陪审团认定,告发书即成为诉状),还指向国王、大法官或议院提交的申诉状。statement of claim 和 particulars of claim 为英国或加拿大用于民事诉讼的文书,前者指向高等法院提交的诉状,后者指向郡法院提交的诉状,其作用有些等同美国的 complaint。libel 所指的诉状多用在海事和离婚案件(used especially in admiralty and divorce cases)中。

在法律翻译中,我们随时都可碰到上述十分棘手的同义或近义术语的问题。

Translation Exercises:

Part One *Put the following into Chinese*

The precise constitutional line between the two approaches has not been articulated, but it has been assumed that the deprivation of physical liberty (as in civil commitment) requires individual adjudication of risk, residential restrictions do not. Although the Supreme Court has never explicitly made this distinction, its treatment of the registration/notification cases suggests this outcome.

Equally as central as "risk" to the legitimacy of civil commitment laws is the notion of "mental disorder." Key decisions of the Supreme Court have given some content and potential distinguishing clarity to this legal concept. Nonetheless, strong forces prevail to insure that the mental disorder element does not limit the reach of regulatory control.

In the political and legal fights involving SVP laws, two important arguments have pointed to the central role for "mental disorder." Both of these arguments are designed to address the concern that surrounds the deprivation of liberty outside of the criminal "charge and conviction" paradigm. The first is a simple argument by analogy. Beginning with the established legitimacy of "standard" civil commitment, courts have asserted that SVP laws are "just like" traditional uses of civil commitment, because both require proof of some form of "mental disorder" proximately connected to risk.

Part Two *Put the following into English*

此种简单的论证证明是不够充分的,因为批评家争论道(在较早的是否合宪的诉讼中并未以严肃的方式提出):构成反暴力性犯罪法基础的这种精神障碍不同于传统上构成民事关禁的精神病,因而也就丧失了其权力的类比性。这就迫使法院清楚地表达了充分合宪的关于精神障碍的两个额外特征。首先,(美国联邦)最高法院突出了合宪性之法律方面,其裁定认为精神障碍要素构成了反暴力性犯罪法之民事关禁的例外性。为了宪法上理据充分,精神障碍必须不同于普通的、经常与刑事司法制度所处理的行为相联系的那种精神障碍。法院并未超越历史先例作过多的解释,而是为行使其职责选定了"控制机能障碍"这一概念。其次,(美国联邦)最高法院突出了科学性,其多次表明了医学上的合法性(依据的是美国精神病协会精神障碍诊断数据手册的认可)可作为支持反暴力性犯罪之民事关禁之合法性的要素。虽然高等法院从未真正解释过在什么意义上医学上的合法性运作使得此类方案合宪,但该概念似乎至少默示了其在很大程度上成为州法院之法理基础。

V Interaction

Discuss with your tutor(s) or the People's judges in your locality about whether there should be SVP laws in China and then based on the discussion, you are supposed to write a composition about the implications of such laws. Remember that you are required to express your ideas clearly.

VI Appreciation of Judge's Opinions

(1) Case Name(案件名):*Kansas v. Hendricks*

Kansas v. Hendricks

Supreme Court of the United States

Argued December 10, 1996
Decided June 23, 1997

Full case name	Kansas v. Leroy Hendricks
Citations	521 U.S. 346 (more)
Prior history	Certiorari to the Kansas State Supreme Court

Holding

Reverses Kansas State Supreme Court and agrees with the state's procedures for the indefinite civil commitment procedures for sex offenders meeting the definition of a "mental abnormality" upon release from prison

Court membership

Chief Justice
William Rehnquist
Associate Justices
John P. Stevens · Sandra Day O'Connor
Antonin Scalia · Anthony Kennedy
David Souter · Clarence Thomas
Ruth Bader Ginsburg · Stephen Breyer

Case opinions

Majority	Thomas, joined by Rehnquist, Scalia, O'Connor, Kennedy,
Dissent	Breyer, joined by Stevens, Souter, Ginsburg,

Lesson Sixteen Sexual Predator Laws: A Two-Decade Retrospective

Laws applied

Due Process, Miscellaneous; Criminal Procedure, Ex Post Facto

(2) **Case Summary**(案情简介)

Kansas v. Hendricks 521 U. S. 346 (1997) is a case in which U. S. Supreme Court set forth procedures for the indefinite civil commitment of prisoners convicted of a sex offense whom the state deems dangerous due to a mental abnormality(精神异常).

Fact of case

Under Kansas's Sexually Violent Predator Act, any person who, due to "mental abnormality"(精神异常) or "personality disorder(人格病态)", is likely to engage in "predatory acts of sexual violence" can be indefinitely confined. Leroy Hendricks and Tim Quinn had an extensive history of sexually molesting children(长期以来性侵害儿童). When they were due to be released from prison, Kansas filed a petition under the Act in state court to involuntarily commit Hendricks and Quinn. Hendricks and Quinn challenged the constitutionality of the Act and requested a trial by jury which the court granted. Hendricks and Quinn testified during the trial that they agreed with the diagnosis by the state psychiatrist that Hendricks and Quinn suffer from pedophilia and admitted that they continued to experience uncontrollable sexual desires for children when under extreme stress. The jury decided that they qualified as sexually violent predators. Since pedophilia is defined as a mental abnormality under the Act, the court ordered that Hendricks be civilly committed.

Hendricks appealed the validity of his commitment as well as claiming that the state was unconstitutional using ex post facto(事后的(adj.),在事后(adv.);追溯既往的/地,有追溯效力的/地,溯及既往) and double jeopardy(禁止对同一罪行重复起诉,禁止因同一罪名而受两次审理,一罪不二罚) law, to the State Supreme Court. The court ruled that the Act was invalid on the grounds that the condition of "mental abnormality" did not satisfy the "substantive" due process requirement that involuntary civil commitment must be based on the finding of the presence of a "mental illness". It did not address the claims of ex post facto and double jeopardy.

The Supreme Court granted Kansas certiorari.

Decision

The Supreme Court ruled against Hendricks in a 5-4 decision. It agreed with the Act's procedures and the definition of a "mental abnormality" as a "congenital or acquired condition(先天或后天的条件) affecting the emotional or volitional capacity(意志力) which predisposes(使预先有倾向,使预先有意向) the person to commit sexually violent offenses to the degree that such person is a menace(威胁) to the health and safety of others." It agreed with Kansas that the Act limits persons eligible for confinement to persons who are not able to control their dangerousness.

Further, the court decided the Act does not violate the Constitution's double jeopardy prohibition or the ban on ex post facto law because the Act does not establish criminal proceedings and therefore involuntary confinement under it is not punishment. Because the Act is civil, Hendricks' confinement under the Act is not a second prosecution nor is it double jeopardy. And finally, the court said the Act is not considered punitive if it fails to offer treatment for an untreatable condition.

(3) **Excerpts of the Judgment**(法官判决词)

JUSTICE THOMAS delivered the opinion of the Court.

In 1994, Kansas enacted the Sexually Violent Predator Act, which establishes procedures for the civil commitment of persons who, due to a "mental abnormality" or a "personality disorder," are likely to engage in "predatory acts of sexual violence." The State invoked the Act for the first time to commit Leroy Hendricks, an inmate(囚犯) who had a long history of sexually molesting children(性侵害儿童), and who was scheduled for release from prison shortly after the Act became law. Hendricks challenged his commitment on, inter alia(拉丁语,首先), "substantive"due process(正当法律程序), double jeopardy(一罪不二罚), and ex post facto grounds(溯及既往). The Kansas Supreme Court invalidated the Act, holding that its precommitment condition of a "mental abnormality" did not satisfy what the court perceived to be the "substantive"due process requirement that involuntary civil commitment must be predicated on a finding of "mental illness."The State of Kansas petitioned for certiorari(上级法院向下级法院发出的调卷令状). Hendricks subsequently filed a cross-petition(反控,反诉) in which he reasserted his federal double jeopardy and ex post facto claims. We granted certiorari on both the petition and the cross-petition, and now reverse the judgment below.

I A

The Kansas Legislature enacted the Sexually Violent Predator Act (Act) in 1994 to grapple with the problem of managing repeat sexual offenders(性侵害累犯). Although Kansas already had a statute addressing the involuntary commitment of those defined as "mentally ill,"the legislature determined that existing civil commitment procedures were inadequate to confront the risks presented by "sexually violent predators."In the Act's preamble, the legislature explained:

"A small but extremely dangerous group of sexually violent predators exist who do not have a mental disease or defect that renders them appropriate for involuntary treatment pursuant to the general involuntary civil commitment statute... In contrast to persons appropriate for civil commitment under the general involuntary civil commitment statute, sexually violent predators generally have anti-social personality features(具有反社会人格的特征) which are unamenable to existing mental illness treatment modalities and those features render them likely to engage in sexually violent behavior. The legislature further finds that sexually violent predators' likelihood of engaging in repeat acts of predatory sexual violence is high. The existing involuntary commitment procedure... is inadequate to address the risk these sexually violent predators pose to society. The legislature further finds that the prognosis(预测,预后,判病结局) for rehabilitating sexually violent predators in a prison setting is poor, the treatment needs of this population are very long term and the treatment modalities for this population are very different than the traditional treatment modalities for people appropriate for commitment under the general involuntary civil commitment statute."

As a result, the legislature found it necessary to establish "a civil commitment procedure for the long-term care and treatment of the sexually violent predator."The Act defined a "sexually violent predator"as:

"any person who has been convicted of or charged with a sexually violent offense and who suffers from a mental abnormality or personality disorder which makes the person likely to engage in the predatory acts of sexual violence."

A "mental abnormality"was defined, in turn, as a "congenital or acquired condition(先天或后天的条件) affecting the emotional or volitional capacity which predisposes the person to commit sexually violent offenses in a degree constituting such person a menace to the health and safety of others."

As originally structured, the Act's civil commitment procedures pertained to: (1) a presently confined person who, like Hendricks, "has been convicted of a sexually violent offense"and is scheduled for release(有待获释); (2) a person who has been "charged with a sexually violent offense"but has been found incompetent to stand trial; (3) a person who has been found "not guilty by reason of insanity of a sexually violent offense"; and (4) a person found "not guilty"of a sexually violent offense because of a mental disease or defect(精神疾病或缺陷).

The initial version of the Act, as applied to a currently confined person such as Hendricks, was designed to initiate a specific series of procedures. The custodial agency(监管机关) was required to notify the local prosecutor 60 days before the anticipated release of a person who might have met the Act's criteria. The prosecutor was then obligated, within 45 days, to decide whether to file a petition in state court seeking the person's involuntary commitment. If such a petition were filed, the court was to determine whether "probable cause"(正当理由) existed to support a finding that the person was a "sexually violent predator"and thus eligible for civil commitment. Upon

Lesson Sixteen Sexual Predator Laws: A Two-Decade Retrospective

such a determination, transfer of the individual to a secure facility for professional evaluation would occur. After that evaluation, a trial would be held to determine beyond a reasonable doubt whether the individual was a sexually violent predator. If that determination were made, the person would then be transferred to the custody of the Secretary of Social and Rehabilitation Services (Secretary)(社会服务与康复服务局) for "control, care and treatment until such time as the person's mental abnormality or personality disorder has so changed that the person is safe to be at large."

In addition to placing the burden of proof(举证证明责任) upon the State, the Act afforded the individual a number of other procedural safeguards. In the case of an indigent person(经济拮据者), the State was required to provide, at public expense, the assistance of counsel and an examination by mental health care professionals. The individual also received the right to present and cross-examine witnesses, and the opportunity to review documentary evidence(书证) presented by the State.

Once an individual was confined, the Act required that "the involuntary detention or commitment... shall conform to constitutional requirements for care and treatment." Confined persons were afforded three different avenues of review: First, the committing court was obligated to conduct an annual review to determine whether continued detention was warranted. Second, the Secretary was permitted, at any time, to decide that the confined individual's condition had so changed that release was appropriate, and could then authorize the person to petition for release. Finally, even without the Secretary's permission, the confined person could at any time file a release petition. If the court found that the State could no longer satisfy its burden under the initial commitment standard, the individual would be freed from confinement.

B

In 1984, Hendricks was convicted of taking "indecent liberties"(随意与……保持猥琐的关系) with two 13-year-old boys. After serving nearly 10 years of his sentence, he was slated for release to a halfway house. Shortly before his scheduled release, however, the State filed a petition in state court seeking Hendricks' civil confinement as a sexually violent predator. On August 19, 1994, Hendricks appeared before the court with counsel and moved to dismiss the petition on the grounds that the Act violated various federal constitutional provisions. Although the court reserved ruling on the Act's constitutionality, it concluded that there was probable cause to support a finding that Hendricks was a sexually violent predator, and therefore ordered that he be evaluated at the Larned State Security Hospital.

Hendricks subsequently requested a jury trial to determine whether he qualified as a sexually violent predator. During that trial, Hendricks' own testimony revealed a chilling history of repeated child sexual molestation and abuse, beginning in 1955 when he exposed his genitals to two young girls. At that time, he pleaded guilty to indecent exposure. Then, in 1957, he was convicted of lewdness(好色的,淫猥) involving a young girl and received a brief jail sentence. In 1960, he molested two young boys while he worked for a carnival(嘉年华会,狂欢节,节日表演节目). After serving two years in prison for that offense, he was paroled, only to be rearrested for molesting a 7-year-old girl. Attempts were made to treat him for his sexual deviance(性异常), and in 1965 he was considered "safe to be at large," and was discharged from a state psychiatric hospital.

Shortly thereafter, however, Hendricks sexually assaulted another young boy and girl-he performed oral sex on the 8-year-old girl and fondled the ll-year-old boy. He was again imprisoned in 1967, but refused to participate in a sex offender treatment program, and thus remained incarcerated(禁闭,监禁) until his parole in 1972. Diagnosed as a pedophile(恋童癖者), Hendricks entered into, but then abandoned, a treatment program. He testified that despite having received professional help for his pedophilia, he continued to harbor sexual desires for children. Indeed, soon after his 1972 parole, Hendricks began to abuse his own stepdaughter and stepson. He forced the children to engage in sexual activity with him over a period of approximately four years. Then, as noted above, Hendricks was convicted of "taking indecent liberties" with two adolescent boys after he attempted to fondle them. As a result of that conviction, he was once again imprisoned, and was serving that sentence when he reached his conditional release date in September 1994.

Hendricks admitted that he had repeatedly abused children whenever he was not confined. He explained that when he "gets stressed out," he "can't control the urge" to molest children. Although Hendricks recognized that his behavior harms children, and he hoped he would not sexually molest children again, he stated that the only sure way he could keep from sexually abusing children in the future was "to die.". Hendricks readily agreed with the state physician's diagnosis that he suffers from pedophilia and that he is not cured of the condition; indeed, he told the physician that "treatment is bull—."

The jury unanimously found beyond a reasonable doubt that Hendricks was a sexually violent predator. The trial court(一审法院)subsequently determined, as a matter of state law, that pedophilia qualifies as a "mental abnormality" as defined by the Act, and thus ordered Hendricks committed to the Secretary's custody.

Hendricks appealed, claiming, among other things, that application of the Act to him violated the Federal Constitution's Due Process, Double Jeopardy, and Ex Post Facto Clauses. The Kansas Supreme Court accepted Hendricks' due process claim. The court declared that in order to commit a person involuntarily in a civil proceeding, a State is required by "substantive" due process to prove by clear and convincing evidence that the person is both (1) mentally ill, and (2) a danger to himself or to others. The court then determined that the Act's definition of "mental abnormality" did not satisfy what it perceived to be this Court's "mental illness" requirement in the civil commitment context. As a result, the court held that "the Act violates Hendricks' substantive due process rights."

The majority did not address Hendricks' ex post facto or double jeopardy claims. The dissent, however, considered each of Hendricks' constitutional arguments and rejected them.

II A

Kansas argues that the Act's definition of "mental abnormality" satisfies "substantive" due process requirements. We agree. Although freedom from physical restraint "has always been at the core of the liberty protected by the Due Process Clause from arbitrary governmental action," Foucha v. Louisiana, 504 U. S. 71, 80 (1992), that liberty interest is not absolute. The Court has recognized that an individual's constitutionally protected interest in avoiding physical restraint may be overridden even in the civil context:

"The liberty secured by the Constitution of the United States to every person within its jurisdiction does not import an absolute right in each person to be, at all times and in all circumstances, wholly free from restraint(完全不受限制). There are manifold restraints to which every person is necessarily subject for the common good. On any other basis organized society could not exist with safety to its members."

Accordingly, States have in certain narrow circumstances provided for the forcible civil detainment of people who are unable to control their behavior and who thereby pose a danger to the public health and safety(对公共健康和安全造成了威胁).

The challenged Act unambiguously requires a finding of dangerousness either to one's self or to others as a prerequisite to involuntary confinement. Commitment proceedings can be initiated only when a person "has been convicted of or charged with a sexually violent offense," and "suffers from a mental abnormality or personality disorder which makes the person likely to engage in the predatory acts of sexual violence." The statute thus requires proof of more than a mere predisposition to violence(而非仅仅是具有暴力的倾向); rather, it requires evidence of past sexually violent behavior and a present mental condition that creates a likelihood of such conduct in the future if the person is not incapacitated. As we have recognized, "previous instances of violent behavior are an important indicator of future violent tendencies."

A finding of dangerousness, standing alone, is ordinarily not a sufficient ground upon which to justify indefinite involuntary commitment. We have sustained civil commitment statutes when they have coupled proof of dangerousness with the proof of some additional factor, such as a "mental illness" or "mental abnormality." These added statutory requirements serve to limit involuntary civil confinement to those who suffer from a volitional impairment (意志力受损) rendering them dangerous beyond their control. The Kansas Act is plainly of a kind with these other civil commitment statutes: It requires a finding of future dangerousness, and then links that finding to the existence of a "mental abnormality" or "personality disorder" that makes it difficult, if not impossible, for the person to control his dangerous behavior. The precommitment requirement of a "mental abnormality" or "personality disorder" is consistent with the requirements of these other statutes that we have upheld in that it narrows the class of persons eligible for confinement to those who are unable to control their dangerousness.

Hendricks nonetheless argues that our earlier cases dictate a finding of "mental illness" as a prerequisite for civil commitment. He then asserts that a "mental abnormality" is not equivalent to a "mental illness" because it is a term coined by the Kansas Legislature, rather than by the psychiatric community. Contrary to Hendricks' assertion, the term "mental illness" is devoid of any talismanic (法宝) significance. Not only do "psychiatrists disagree widely and frequently on what constitutes mental illness," but the Court itself has used a variety of expressions to describe the mental condition of those properly subject to civil confinement.

Indeed, we have never required state legislatures to adopt any particular nomenclature (分类法) in drafting civil commitment statutes. Rather, we have traditionally left to legislators the task of defining terms of a medical nature that have legal significance. As a consequence, the States have, over the years, developed numerous specialized terms to define mental health concepts. Often, those definitions do not fit precisely with the definitions employed by the medical community (医疗界). The legal definitions of "insanity" and "competency," for example, vary substantially from their psychiatric counterparts.

To the extent that the civil commitment statutes we have considered set forth criteria relating to an individual's inability to control his dangerousness, the Kansas Act sets forth comparable criteria and Hendricks' condition doubtlessly satisfies those criteria. The mental health professionals who evaluated Hendricks diagnosed him as suffering from pedophilia, a condition the psychiatric profession itself classifies as a serious mental disorder. Hendricks even conceded that, when he becomes "stressed out," he cannot "control the urge" to molest children. This admitted lack of volitional control, coupled with a prediction of future dangerousness, adequately distinguishes Hendricks from other dangerous persons who are perhaps more properly dealt with exclusively through criminal proceedings. Hendricks' diagnosis as a pedophile, which qualifies as a "mental abnormality" under the Act, thus plainly suffices for due process purposes.

B

We granted Hendricks' cross-petition to determine whether the Act violates the Constitution's double jeopardy prohibition or its ban on ex post facto lawmaking. The thrust of Hendricks' argument is that the Act establishes criminal proceedings; hence confinement under it necessarily constitutes punishment. He contends that where, as here, newly enacted "punishment" is predicated upon past conduct for which he has already been convicted and forced to serve a prison sentence, the Constitution's Double Jeopardy and Ex Post Facto Clauses are violated. We are unpersuaded by Hendricks' argument that Kansas has established criminal proceedings.

The categorization of a particular proceeding as civil or criminal (将某一特定程序界定为民事或刑事的范畴化) "is first of all a question of statutory construction.". We must initially ascertain whether the legislature meant the statute to establish "civil" proceedings. If so, we ordinarily defer to the legislature's stated intent. Here, Kansas' objective to create a civil proceeding is evidenced by its placement of the Act within the Kansas probate code. Nothing on the face of the statute suggests that the legislature sought to create anything other than a civil commitment scheme designed to protect the public from harm.

Although we recognize that a "civil label is not always dispositive," we will reject the legislature's manifest intent only where a party challenging the statute provides "the clearest proof" that "the statutory scheme is so punitive either in purpose or effect as to negate the State's intention" to deem it "civil," In those limited circumstances, we will consider the statute to have established criminal proceedings for constitutional purposes. Hendricks, however, has failed to satisfy this heavy burden.

As a threshold matter, commitment under the Act does not implicate either of the two primary objectives of criminal punishment: retribution(报应) or deterrence(威慑). The Act's purpose is not retributive because it does not affix culpability for prior criminal conduct. Instead, such conduct is used solely for evidentiary purposes, either to demonstrate that a "mental abnormality" exists or to support a finding of future dangerousness. We have previously concluded that an Illinois statute was nonpunitive even though it was triggered by the commission of a sexual assault, explaining that evidence of the prior criminal conduct was "received not to punish past misdeeds, but primarily to show the accused's mental condition and to predict future behavior." In addition, the Kansas Act does not make a criminal conviction a prerequisite for commitment-persons absolved of criminal responsibility may nonetheless be subject to confinement under the Act. An absence of the necessary criminal responsibility suggests that the State is not seeking retribution for a past misdeed. Thus, the fact that the Act may be "tied to criminal activity" is "insufficient to render the statute punitive."

Moreover, unlike a criminal statute, no finding of scienter is required to commit an individual who is found to be a sexually violent predator; instead, the commitment determination is made based on a "mental abnormality" or "personality disorder" rather than on one's criminal intent. The existence of a scienter requirement is customarily an important element in distinguishing criminal from civil statutes. The absence of such a requirement here is evidence that confinement under the statute is not intended to be retributive.

Nor can it be said that the legislature intended the Act to function as a deterrent. Those persons committed under the Act are, by definition, suffering from a "mental abnormality" or a "personality disorder" that prevents them from exercising adequate control over their behavior. Such persons are therefore unlikely to be deterred by the threat of confinement. And the conditions surrounding that confinement do not suggest a punitive purpose on the State's part. The State has represented that an individual confined under the Act is not subject to the more restrictive conditions placed on state prisoners, but instead experiences essentially the same conditions as any involuntarily committed patient in the state mental institution. Because none of the parties argues that people institutionalized under the Kansas general civil commitment statute are subject to punitive conditions, even though they may be involuntarily confined, it is difficult to conclude that persons confined under this Act are being "punished."

Although the civil commitment scheme at issue here does involve an affirmative restraint, "the mere fact that a person is detained does not inexorably lead to the conclusion that the government has imposed punishment." The State may take measures to restrict the freedom of the dangerously mentally ill. This is a legitimate nonpunitive governmental objective and has been historically so regarded. The Court has, in fact, cited the confinement of "mentally unstable individuals who present a danger to the public" as one classic example of nonpunitive detention. If detention for the purpose of protecting the community from harm necessarily constituted punishment, then all involuntary civil commitments would have to be considered punishment. But we have never so held.

Hendricks focuses on his confinement's potentially indefinite duration as evidence of the State's punitive intent. That focus, however, is misplaced. Far from any punitive objective, the confinement's duration is instead linked to the stated purposes of the commitment, namely, to hold the person until his mental abnormality no longer causes him to be a threat to others. If, at any time, the confined person is adjudged "safe to be at large," he is statutorily entitled to immediate release.

Furthermore, commitment under the Act is only potentially indefinite. The maximum amount of time an individual can be incapacitated pursuant to a single judicial proceeding is one year. If Kansas seeks to continue the detention beyond that year, a court must once again determine beyond a reasonable doubt that the detainee(被拘留者) satisfies the same standards as required for the initial confinement. This requirement again demonstrates that Kansas does not intend an individual committed pursuant to the Act to remain confined any longer than he suffers

Lesson Sixteen　Sexual Predator Laws: A Two-Decade Retrospective

from a mental abnormality rendering him unable to control his dangerousness.

Hendricks next contends that the State's use of procedural safeguards traditionally found in criminal trials makes the proceedings here criminal rather than civil. In Allen, we confronted a similar argument. There, the petitioner "placed great reliance on the fact that proceedings under the Act are accompanied by procedural safeguards usually found in criminal trials" to argue that the proceedings were civil in name only. We rejected that argument, however, explaining that the State's decision "to provide some of the safeguards applicable in criminal trials cannot itself turn these proceedings into criminal prosecutions." The numerous procedural and evidentiary protections afforded here demonstrate that the Kansas Legislature has taken great care to confine only a narrow class of particularly dangerous individuals, and then only after meeting the strictest procedural standards. That Kansas chose to afford such procedural protections does not transform a civil commitment proceeding into a criminal prosecution.

Finally, Hendricks argues that the Act is necessarily punitive (刑罚的,惩罚的) because it fails to offer any legitimate "treatment." Without such treatment, Hendricks asserts, confinement under the Act amounts to little more than disguised punishment. Hendricks' argument assumes that treatment for his condition is available, but that the State has failed (or refused) to provide it. The Kansas Supreme Court, however, apparently rejected this assumption, explaining:

"It is clear that the overriding concern of the legislature(立法机关首要关注的问题) is to continue the segregation of sexually violent offenders from the public. Treatment with the goal of reintegrating them into society(治疗并使其回归社会) is incidental, at best. The record reflects that treatment for sexually violent predators is all but nonexistent. The legislature concedes that sexually violent predators are not amenable(应服从的,顺从的) to treatment under the existing Kansas involuntary commitment statute. If there is nothing to treat under that statute, then there is no mental illness. In that light, the provisions of the Act for treatment appear somewhat disingenuous (不真诚的,无诚意的,虚伪的,奸诈的,阴险的)."

It is possible to read this passage as a determination that Hendricks' condition was untreatable under the existing Kansas civil commitment statute, and thus the Act's sole purpose was incapacitation. Absent a treatable mental illness, the Kansas court concluded, Hendricks could not be detained against his will.

Accepting the Kansas court's apparent determination that treatment is not possible for this category of individuals does not obligate us to adopt its legal conclusions. We have already observed that, under the appropriate circumstances and when accompanied by proper procedures, incapacitation may be a legitimate end of the civil law. Accordingly, the Kansas court's determination that the Act's "overriding concern" was the continued "segregation of sexually violent offenders" is consistent with our conclusion that the Act establishes civil proceedings, especially when that concern is coupled with the State's ancillary goal of providing treatment to those offenders, if such is possible. While we have upheld state civil commitment statutes that aim both to incapacitate and to treat, we have never held that the Constitution prevents a State from civilly detaining those for whom no treatment is available, but who nevertheless pose a danger to others. A State could hardly be seen as furthering a "punitive" purpose by involuntarily confining persons afflicted with an untreatable, highly contagious disease. Similarly, it would be of little value to require treatment as a precondition for civil confinement of the dangerously insane when no acceptable treatment existed. To conclude otherwise would obligate a State to release certain confined individuals who were both mentally ill and dangerous simply because they could not be successfully treated for their afflictions.

Alternatively, the Kansas Supreme Court's opinion can be read to conclude that Hendricks' condition is treatable, but that treatment was not the State's "overriding concern," and that no treatment was being provided (at least at the time Hendricks was committed). Even if we accept this determination that the provision of treatment was not the Kansas Legislature's "overriding" or "primary" purpose in passing the Act, this does not rule out the possibility that an ancillary purpose of the Act was to provide treatment, and it does not require us to conclude that the Act is punitive. Indeed, critical language in the Act itself demonstrates that the Secretary, under whose custody sexually violent predators are committed, has an obligation to provide treatment to individuals like Hendricks.

Although the treatment program initially offered Hendricks may have seemed somewhat meager, it must be remembered that he was the first person committed under the Act. That the State did not have all of its treatment procedures in place is thus not surprising. What is significant, however, is that Hendricks was placed under the supervision of the Kansas Department of Health and Social and Rehabilitative Services, housed in a unit segregated from the general prison population and operated not by employees of the Department of Corrections, but by other trained individuals. 4 And, before this Court, Kansas declared "absolutely" that persons committed under the Act are now receiving in the neighborhood of "31—'l2 hours of treatment per week."

Where the State has "disavowed(否认,推翻) any punitive intent"; limited confinement to a small segment of particularly dangerous individuals; provided strict procedural safeguards; directed that confined persons be segregated from the general prison population and afforded the same status as others who have been civilly committed; recommended treatment if such is possible; and permitted immediate release upon a showing that the individual is no longer dangerous or mentally impaired, we cannot say that it acted with punitive intent. We therefore hold that the Act does not establish criminal proceedings and that involuntary confinement pursuant to the Act is not punitive. Our conclusion that the Act is nonpunitive thus removes an essential prerequisite for both Hendricks' double jeopardy and ex post facto claims.

1

The Double Jeopardy Clause provides: "Nor shall any person be subject for the same offence to be twice put in jeopardy of life or limb." Although generally understood to preclude a second prosecution for the same offense, the Court has also interpreted this prohibition to prevent the State from "punishing twice, or attempting a second time to punish criminally, for the same offense." Hendricks argues that, as applied to him, the Act violates double jeopardy principles because his confinement under the Act, imposed after a conviction and a term of incarceration, amounted to both a second prosecution and a second punishment for the same offense. We disagree.

Because we have determined that the Kansas Act is civil in nature, initiation of its commitment proceedings does not constitute a second prosecution. Moreover, as commitment under the Act is not tantamount to "punishment," Hendricks' involuntary detention does not violate the Double Jeopardy Clause, even though that confinement may follow a prison term. Indeed, in *Baxstrom v. Herold* (1966), we expressly recognized that civil commitment could follow the expiration of a prison term without offending double jeopardy principles. We reasoned that "there is no conceivable basis for distinguishing the commitment of a person who is nearing the end of a penal term from all other civil commitments." If an individual otherwise meets the requirements for involuntary civil commitment, the State is under no obligation to release that individual simply because the detention would follow a period of incarceration.

Hendricks also argues that even if the Act survives the "multiple punishments" test, it nevertheless fails the "same elements" test of *Blockburger v. United States* (1932). Under Blockburger, "where the same act or transaction constitutes a violation of two distinct statutory provisions, the test to be applied to determine whether there are two offenses or only one, is whether each provision requires proof of a fact which the other does not." The Blockburger test, however, simply does not apply outside of the successive prosecution context. A proceeding under the Act does not define an "offense," the elements of which can be compared to the elements of an offense for which the person may previously have been convicted. Nor does the Act make the commission of a specified "offense" the basis for invoking the commitment proceedings. Instead, it uses a prior conviction (or previously charged conduct) for evidentiary purposes to determine whether a person suffers from a "mental abnormality" or "personality disorder" and also poses a threat to the public. Accordingly, we are unpersuaded by Hendricks' novel application of the Blockburger test and conclude that the Act does not violate the Double Jeopardy Clause.

2

Hendricks' ex post facto claim is similarly flawed. The Ex Post Facto Clause, which "forbids the application of any new punitive measure to a crime already consummated", has been interpreted to pertain exclusively to penal statutes. As we have previously determined, the Act does not impose punishment; thus, its application does not raise ex post facto concerns. Moreover, the Act clearly does not have retroactive effect(不具有溯及既往的效力). Rather, the Act permits involuntary confinement based upon a determination that the person currently both suffers from a "mental abnormality" or "personality disorder" and is likely to pose a future danger to the public. To the extent that past behavior is taken into account, it is used, as noted above, solely for evidentiary purposes. Because the Act does not criminalize conduct legal before its enactment, nor deprive Hendricks of any defense that was available to him at the time of his crimes, the Act does not violate the Ex Post Facto Clause.

III

We hold that the Kansas Sexually Violent Predator Act comports with(与……一致,相称,相适应) due process requirements and neither runs afoul of(和……碰撞/冲突、纠缠) double jeopardy principles nor constitutes an exercise in impermissible ex post facto lawmaking. Accordingly, the judgment of the Kansas Supreme Court is reversed(推翻).

It is so ordered.

Lesson Seventeen

Introduction to International Law

Learning objectives

After learning the text and having done the exercises in this lesson, you will:

—familiarize with knowledge of the legal characteristics and the nature of international law

—acquire an appreciation of the vocabulary and grammar or syntax relevant to the international law

—become aware of the information required in order to understand the international law;

—cultivate the practical abilities to put to use the language in the specific context;

—be able to do some translation from Chinese to English and from English to Chinese.

 Text

Introduction to International Law

Public international law has traditionally been regarded as a system of principles and rules designed to govern relations between sovereign states. As a point of departure for a study of international law, this description has the merit of emphasizing the central and still dominant position of states in international affairs. However, in recent times the scope of international law has been steadily expanding so that, in the words of Wilfred Jenks, "it represents the common law of mankind in an early state of development, of which the law governing the relations between states is one, but only one, major division". Perhaps the most significant development is the status newly accorded to individuals in the international legal process. In the field of human rights, for example, the individual now possesses international legal rights independently of, and even against, his national state.

While states remain the dominant actors in the international legal order, modern international law also reflects the new realities of international life, such as the interdependence of states, the

Lesson Seventeen　Introduction to International Law

growth of global organizations, the scientific and technological revolutions, the influence of giant multinational corporations, and the massive transnational movements of individuals and ideas. As this volume will demonstrate, international law is a dynamic system of norms which is capable of evolving to meet the regulatory needs of a rapidly changing international society.

　　The beginnings of international law as it is known today are usually traced to the sixteenth and seventeenth centuries, and coincide with the rise of the nation state. Hugo Grotius①, a Dutch jurist and diplomat, is widely regarded as the father of international law on account of his classic treatise *De Jure Belli Ac Pacis* written in 1625. The *treaties* of Westphalia②, which in 1648 ended the Thirty Years' War③, are often credited with the establishment of the system of sovereign states at the core of international law. History records also the existence of ancient systems of rules which governed relations between Greek states and between Roman citizens and foreigners, but these were not carried forward as a body of law during medieval times. Their influence has been felt mainly as an inspiration for the political philosophers of later centuries who sought to impose some rational order in inter-state relations following the break up of the Holy Roman Empire④ into many independent, warring political units.

　　Since international law originated in Europe, it has been infused with European social and political cultures and values. Politically speaking, international law was nourished by then new ideas about the sovereignty of independent states. It met the limited needs for diplomatic relations in the conduct of war and peace. Philosophically, international law was rooted in the law of nature as expounded by the classical text-writers. Some of these authors, reflecting a Christian heritage, based their theses on the Divine Order while others, in the rationalist tradition, derived their ideas from universal reason. In the face of a confused mass of local customs and bilateral treaties, natural law provided the text-writers with the basis for ordering the conduct of foreign affairs into a system of rules and for subjecting states and their leaders to the authority of the law. Later, the rise of positivism⑤ in political and legal philosophy exerted a powerful influence on international law. Positivist thought enhanced the concept of the sovereignty of states and imbued international law with the notion that legal obligations are based on consent.

　　In the course of colonial expansion, the ideas and values embodied in international law were carried by the European powers to other parts of the world. While the process of colonization and subjugation of foreign lands was not governed by international law, when some of the conquered territories, notably in North and South America, acquired independence the European practice of international law was extended to them. Only in the latter part of the nineteenth century were non-Christian countries, like Turkey, China and Japan, admitted as subjects of the international legal

---

　　① Hugo Grotius:雨果·格劳秀斯(1583—1645),荷兰法学家和诗人,曾任荷兰省检察长(1607年),出使英王詹姆斯一世宫廷(1613年),著有《战争与和平法》(De Jure Belli Ac Pacis),确立了国际法标准,还著有《诗集》、《圣诗》等。
　　② The Treaties of Westphalia:《斯特伐利亚条约》,Westphalia(斯特伐利亚),即 Westfalen(威斯特伐伦),德国西北部的一个地区。
　　③ Thirty Year's War:三十年战争,指1618年到1648年之间在欧洲以德意志为主要战场的国际性战争。
　　④ Holy Roman Empire:神圣罗马帝国(962—1806)。
　　⑤ Positivism:实证主义,由法国哲学家 Auguste Comte 创始的一种哲学。

system. Not until the adoption of the Covenant of the League of Nations①, following World War I, was international law formally applied to all states without discrimination. Even so, only through the process of de-colonization② after World War II, under the auspices of the United Nations, did the reach of international law become truly global.

Entry into the international legal system during this century, and particularly since 1945, of many new states with varied political, cultural, social and legal backgrounds has had, and is still having, a profound and lasting effect on international law. The original "Concert of Europe"③ has now been expanded to more than one hundred and sixty states on six continents. The number and diversity of the actors in the world arena have increased exponentially the difficulties of administering the <u>decentralized</u> system of nation states. More importantly, the new participants entered the community of states with very different perspectives and soon began to challenge the enduring validity of some of the Euro-centric concepts and principles of international law.④

The first major challenge to the simple belief in the universal acceptance of classical international law was posed after the Russian Revolution by the emergence of Soviet views on the role of the state, the sources of the law and the contents of many of its principles. More recently, the developing countries of Latin America, Africa and Asia have been urging a reformulation of international law, especially those parts governing foreign investment, development and other incidents of their former colonial circumstances. As a result, some of the traditional principles of international law have been either altogether abandoned (e. g., principles governing the acquisition of territory by force), or materially altered (e. g., rules relating to the amount of compensation payable upon the <u>expropriation</u> of foreign property), or, in other instances, wholly new concepts have been introduced (e. g., the right of self-determination of peoples, and the principle of a state's permanent sovereignty over its natural resources).

Phenomenal advances in science and technology have also profoundly affected international law. Thus the advent of nuclear energy, mass air travel, space flight, seabed mining and satellite telecommunications, to mention only a few major new activities, have prompted the creation of wholly new branches of international law, such as space law and environmental law, and great expansion of some traditional ones, most notably the law of the sea. In addition, the revolution in transportation and communications has enormously increased the movement and interaction of people all over the world, resulting in the need for international law to harmonize and accommodate many diverse and competing human interests. One conspicuous consequence has been the emergence of a great number of international organizations covering a wide variety of human activities. These organizations have become associated since 1945 with the United Nations, which has filled

---

① League of Nations:国际联盟,第一次世界大战后根据《凡尔赛和约》于1920年建立的国际组织,其目的在于促进国际和平和维护世界和平,总部设在日内瓦,于1946年解散,其某些职能由联合国取代。
② the process of de-colonization:去殖民化进程。
③ "Concert of Europe":"(欧洲)四国同盟",指1815年维也纳会议后奥地利、俄国、普鲁士和英国缔结的同盟。
④ some of the Euro-centric concepts and principles of international law:以欧洲为中心的一些理念和国际法原则。句中的 Euro-centric 意思是"以欧洲为中心的"。注意 Euro-可以和许多其他词构成新词,类似词语还有:Eurobond(欧洲债券);Eurocrat(欧洲经济共同体市场的官员);Euro-currency(欧洲货币);Euro-dollar(欧元);Euro-mart(= European Common Market,欧洲共同市场);Euro-centrism(欧洲中心主义);Eurosis(欧洲危机)等。

the role of a global coordinating organ, and they have been supported by the growth of a whole new body of law regarding international institutions. Second, the unprecedented growth of world trade, fueled by the huge energy of the modern multinational enterprise, has given rise to a growing corpus of international economic law to govern transnational commercial transactions.① Third, much greater awareness of the plight of millions of human beings, who suffer from poverty, hunger, disease, illiteracy and the effects of tyranny and war, has brought about organized efforts to improve human well-being everywhere and, particularly, to promote economic and social advancement in the less developed countries. These concerns have found their legal expression in such new developments as humanitarian laws, the protection of human rights and international development law. In sum, international law in the United Nations era has had to adapt to a much transformed, multinational and increasingly interdependent world.

In addition to this brief outline of the development of the international legal system, it is also necessary to examine the nature of the law itself. In one way or another, the questions raised in such an examination invariably focus on the basis of obligation and the means of enforcement in international law. Many writers have addressed these problems, including Professor Brierly who has provided the following lucid commentary.

Traditionally there are two rival doctrines that attempt to answer the question why states should be bound to observe the rules of international law.

The doctrine of "fundamental rights" is a corollary of the doctrine of "state of nature", in which men are supposed to have lived before they formed themselves into political communities, or states, for states, not having formed themselves into a super-state, are still supposed by the adherents of this doctrine to be living in such a condition. It teaches that the principles of international law, or the primary principles upon which the others rest, can be deduced from the essential nature of the state. Every state, by the very fact that it is a state, is endowed with certain fundamental, or inherent, or natural, rights. Writers differ in enumerating what these rights are, but generally five rights are claimed, namely self-preservation, independence, equality, respect, and intercourse. It is obvious that the doctrine of fundamental rights is merely the old doctrine of the natural rights of man transferred to states. That doctrine has played a great part in history; Locke② justified the English Revolution by it and from Locke it passed to the leaders of the American Revolution and became the philosophical basis of the Declaration of Independence. But hardly any political scientist today would regard it as a true philosophy of political relations and all the objections to it

---

① The unprecedented growth of world trade, fueled by the huge energy of the modern multinational enterprise, has given rise to a growing corpus of international economic law to govern transnational commercial transactions. "在现代跨国企业巨大的动力推动下,世界贸易得到史无前例的增长,导致了一整套不断发展的以调整国际商务交易为目的的国际经济法的出现。"句中的"fueled by the huge energy of"乃隐喻(metaphor),fuel 作为动词是"给……加燃料,给……加油"的意思;"现代跨国企业"在句中被作者比喻为"巨大的能源"。句中的"corpus"一词指"躯体、身体;法典等的全集或集成"等意思,但在法律英语中多用以表达"大全"等意思,如:Corpus Juris Civilis(《民法大全》或《国法大全》,也即《查士丁尼法典》、《学说汇纂》、《法学阶梯》、《新律》的总称);corpus delicti(犯罪事实之物证)等。句中 give rise to 为一个短语,意思是"导致,引起"等,如:Disarmament talk often gives rise to a great deal of conflict. (裁军谈判常常引起诸多争议。)

② Locke:全名是 John Locke(约翰·洛克)(1632—1704),英国唯物主义哲学家,反对"天赋观念"论,论证人类知识起源于感性世界的经验论学说,主张君主立宪政体,著有《政府论》、《人类理解论》等。

apply with even greater force when it is applied to the relations of states. It implies that men or states, as the case may be①, bring with them into society certain primordial rights②not derived from their membership of society, but inherent in their personality as individuals and that out of these rights a legal system is formed, whereas the truth is that a legal right is a meaningless phrase unless we first assume the existence of a legal system from which it gets its validity. Further, the doctrine implies that the social bond between man and man, or between state and state, is somehow less natural, or less a part of the whole personality, than is the individuality of the man or the state and that is not true; the only individuals we know are individuals-in-society. It is especially misleading to apply this atomistic view of the nature of the social bond to states. In its application to individual men, it has a certain plausibility because it seems to give a philosophical justification to the common feeling that human personality has certain claims on society; and in that way it has played its part in the development of human liberty. But in the society of states the need is not for greater liberty for the individual states, but for a strengthening of the social bond between them, not for the claimant assertion of their rights, but for a more insistent reminder of their obligations towards one another. Finally, the doctrine is really a denial of the possibility of development in international relations; when it asserts that such qualities as independence and equality are inherent in the very nature of states, it overlooks the fact that their attribution to states is merely a stage in an historical process; we know that until modern times states were not regarded either as independent or equal and we have no right to assume that the process of development has stopped. On the contrary it is not improbable and it is certainly desirable, that there should be a movement towards the closer interdependence of states and therefore away from the state of things which this doctrine would stabilize as though it were part of the fixed order of nature.

The doctrine of positivism, on the other hand, teaches that international law is the sum of the rules by which states have *consented* to be bound, and that nothing can be law to which they have not consented. This consent may be given expressly as in a treaty or it may he implied by a state acquiescing in a customary rule. But the assumption that international law consists of nothing save what states have consented to is an inadequate account of the system as it can be seen in actual operation and even if it were a complete account of the contents of the law, it would fail to explain why the law is binding. ③It is in the first place quite impossible to fit the facts into a consistently consensual theory of the nature of international law. Implied consent is not a philosophically sound explanation of customary law, international or domestic; a customary rule is observed, not because

---

① as the case may be:视情形而定,根据具体情况;类似结构还有:as the case stands(照现在的情况,事实上);as is often the case(此乃常有的事);such / that being the case(情况既然如此,因此);There are cases where...(……有时候)等。

② primordial rights:原初权利,自原始时代即有的权利。

③ But the assumption that international law consists of nothing save what states have consented to is an inadequate account of the system as it can be seen in actual operation and even if it were a complete account of the contents of the law, it would fail to explain why the law is binding. "但国际法除各国承诺之外不得为法的推定是对该制度的一种不恰当说明,这一点可以从实际运作得以证明;且即使它完全阐明了该法的内容,它也无法解释该法具有约束力的缘由。"句中的 save 可以作为介词,表示"除……之外"。如 Nothing was required of him on this ship save to entertain his guests.(在这条船上,除了招待客人以外,没有什么事需要他去做);save 还可以作为连词,表示"只要,要不是(that)"或者"用于从句主语之前,表'除了'"的意思,如:No one knows about it save she(这事除她外谁也不知道)。此外,save 在古语中还相当于 unless,表示"除……以外"的意思。Save 还可以与 for 连用,构成短语 save for,表示"除……之外,除去;撇开"的意思。

it has been consented to, but because it is believed to be binding and whatever may be the explanation or the justification for that belief, its binding force does not depend, and is not felt by those who follow it to depend, on the approval of the individual or the state to which it is addressed. Further, in the practical administration of international law, states are continually treated as bound by principles which they cannot, except by the most strained construction of the facts[①], be said to have consented to and it is unreasonable, when we are seeking the true nature of international rules, to force the facts into a preconceived theory instead of finding a theory which will explain the facts as we have them. For example, a state which has newly come into existence does not in any intelligible sense consent to accept international law; it does not regard itself and it is not regarded by others, as having any option in the matter. The truth is that states do not regard their international legal relations as resulting from consent, except when the consent is express, and that the theory of implied consent is a fiction invented by the theorist; only a certain plausibility is given to a consensual explanation of the nature of their obligations by the fact, important indeed to any consideration of the methods by which the system develops, that, in the absence of any international machinery for legislation by *majority vote*, a new rule of law cannot be imposed upon states merely by the will of other states.

But in the second place, even if the theory did not involve a distortion of the facts, it would fail as an explanation. For consent cannot of itself create an obligation; it can do so only within a system of law which declares that consent duly given, as in a treaty or a *contract*, shall be binding on the party consenting. To say that the rule *pacta servanda sunt*[②] is itself founded on consent is to argue in a circle. A consistently consensual theory again would have to admit that if consent is withdrawn, the obligation created by it comes to an end. Most positivist writers would not admit this, but to deny it is in effect to fall back on an unacknowledged source of obligation, which, whatever it may be, is not the consent of the state, for that has ceased to exist. Some modern German writers, however, do not shrink from facing the full consequences of the theory of a purely consensual basis for the law; they have inherited from Hegel[③] a doctrine known as the auto-limitation of sovereignty[④], which teaches that states are sovereign persons, possessed of wills which reject all external limitation and that if we find, as we appear to do in international law, something which limits their wills, this limiting something can only proceed from themselves. Most of these writers admit that a self-imposed limitation is no limitation at all; they conclude, therefore, that so-called international law is nothing, but "external public law", binding the state only because and only so long as, it consents to be bound. There is no flaw in this argument; the flaw lies in the premises, because these are not derived, as all positivist theory professes to be, from an observation of international facts. The real contribution of positivist theory to international law has been its insistence that the rules of the system be to be ascertained from observation of the practice of

---

① most strained construction of the facts: 严重歪曲事实,对事实作最为扭曲的解释。
② pacta servanda sunt: (Latin) Agreements must be kept, 有约必守。
③ Hegel: 全名是 George Wilhelm Friedrich Hegel(1770—1831),德国古典唯心主义哲学家,在客观唯心主义基础上提出了系统的辩证法理论,其哲学成为马克思主义哲学的理论来源之一,主要著作有:《哲学全书》、《逻辑学》等。
④ the auto-limitation of sovereignty: 主权的自我限制。

states and not from *a priori*①deductions, but positivist writers have not always been true to their own teaching; and they have been too ready to treat a method of legal reasoning as though it were an explanation of the nature of the law.

There need be no mystery about the source of the obligation to obey international law. The same problem arises in any system of law and it can never be solved by a merely juridical explanation. The answer must be sought outside the law and it is for legal philosophy to provide it. The notion that the validity of international law raises some peculiar problem arises from the confusion which the doctrine of sovereignty has introduced into international legal theory. Even when we do not believe in the absoluteness of state sovereignty, we have allowed ourselves to be persuaded that the fact of their sovereignty makes it necessary to look for some specific quality, not to be found in other kinds of law, in the law to which states are subject. We have accepted a false idea of the state as a personality with a life and a will of its own, still living in a "state of nature", and we contrast this with the "political" state in which individual men have come to live. But this assumed condition of states is the very negation of law and no ingenuity can explain how the two can exist together. It is a notion as false analytically as it admittedly is historically. The truth is that states are not persons, however convenient it may often be to personify them; they are merely *institutions*, that is to say, organizations which men establish among themselves for securing certain objects, of which the most fundamental is a system of order within which the activities of their common life can be carried on. They have no wills except the wills of the individual human kings who direct their affairs; and they exist not in a political vacuum, but in continuous political relations with one another. Their subjection to law is as yet imperfect, though it is real as far as it goes; the problem of extending it is one of great practical difficulty, but it is not one of intrinsic impossibility. There are important differences between international law and the law under which individuals live in a state, but those differences do not lie in metaphysics or in any mystical qualities of the entity called state sovereignty.

The international lawyer then is under no special obligation to explain why the law with which he is concerned should be binding upon its subjects. If it were true that the essence of all law is a command and that what makes the law of the state binding is that for some reason, for which no satisfactory explanation can ever be given, the will of the person issuing a command is superior to that of the person receiving it, then indeed it would be necessary to look for some special explanation of the binding force of international law. But that view of the nature of law has been long discredited. If we are to explain why any kind of law is binding, we cannot avoid some such assumption as that which the Middle Ages made and which Greece and Rome had made before them, when they spoke of natural law. The ultimate explanation of the binding tree of all law is that man, whether he is a single individual or whether he is associated with other men in a state, is constrained, in so far as he is a reasonable being, to believe that order and not chaos is the governing principle of the world in which he has to live.

---

① a priori:拉丁语,由原因推及结果的;演绎的;先验的;推测的（opp. a posteriori）。如:an a priori judgment 臆测的判断。

It has often been said that international law ought to be classified as a branch of ethics rather than of law. The question is partly one of words, because its solution will clearly depend on the definition of law which we choose to adopt; in any case it does not affect the value of the subject one way or the other, though those who deny the legal character of international law often speak as though "ethical" were a depreciatory epithet, but in fact it is both practically inconvenient and also contrary to the best juristic thought to deny its legal character. It is inconvenient because if international law is nothing but international morality, it is certainly not the whole of international morality, and it is difficult to see how we are to distinguish it from those other admittedly moral standards which we apply in forming our judgments on the conduct of states. Ordinary usage certainly uses two tests in judging the "rightness" of a state's act, a moral test and one which is somehow felt to be independent of morality. Every state habitually commits acts of selfishness which are often gravely injurious to other states, and yet are not contrary to international law; but we do not on that account necessarily judge them to have been "right". It is confusing and pedantic to say that both these tests are moral. Moreover, it is the pendantry of the theorist and not of the practical man; for questions of international law are invariably treated as legal questions by the foreign offices which conduct our international business, and in the courts, national or international, before which they are brought; legal forms and methods are used in diplomatic controversies and in judicial and arbitral proceedings, and authorities and precedents are cited in argument as a matter of course. It is significant too that when a breach of international law is alleged by one party to a controversy, the act impugned is practically never defended by claiming the right of private judgment, which would be the natural defense if the issue concerned the morality of the act, but always by attempting to prove that no rule has been violated.

But if international law is not the same thing as international morality, and if in some important respects at least it certainly resembles law, why should we hesitate to accept its definitely legal character? The objection comes in the main from the followers of writers such as Hobbes and Austin[①], who regard nothing as law which is not the will of a political superior. But this is a misleading and inadequate analysis even of the law of a modern state; it cannot, for instance, unless we distort the facts so as to fit them into the definition, account for the existence of the English Common Law.

Legal Terminology

1. treaty 与 executive agreement

Treaty 与 executive agreement 二者均是指美国政府和其他政府之间缔结的协定。executive agreement 为"行政协议",指由总统就其职权范围的事项与外国政府签订的,毋需经国会

---

① Hobbes and Austin:Hobbes 指 Thomas Hobbes(托马斯·霍布斯)(1588—1679),英国政治学家,机械唯物主义者,认为哲学对象是物体,排除神学,从运动解释物质现象,拥护君主立宪,提出社会契约说,主要著作有《利维坦》、《论物体》等。Austin 指 John Austin(约翰·奥斯汀)(1790—1859 年),英国法学家,分析法学派创始人,主要著作有《法理学范围》、《法理学讲义》等。

批准的协定。treaty 为"条约",指由正式授权的代表与两个或更多的主权国家等签署的书面协定,通常由国家立法机关批准。executive agreement 的权力通常不如 treaty,且其只能取代州法而非联邦立法,但 treaty 则能取代联邦立法。

2. decentralize

权力下放;将(权力、权限等)自中央政府转到地方政府。decentralization 与 devolution 二者均有中央政府将权力下放地方政府的含义,区别在于前者所下放的权力要少于后者。在实行 devolution 的国家,地方当局几乎等于是自治区政府,而在实行 decentralization 的国家则不然。如翻译"联邦政府将警察权下放各州"时便应使用 devolution 而非 decentralization。

3. expropriation, eminent domain 与 condemnation

三者均与财产的征用相关。eminent domain 为"国家征用权",在美国,多指州、市政府或经授权行使公职的个人或法人拥有的征用私人财产,尤指对土地的权力,征用之财产应用于公共目的,对征用财产应作合理补偿。condemnation 和 expropriation 都为"征用",是指对 eminent domain 这种权利的实施程序,但在路易斯安那州,expropriation 的含义则等同 eminent domain。

4. majority vote

(1) majority 与 plurality 二者均有多数的含义,但从严格的法律意义上讲,它们仍有很大的差异。关键在于 plurality 只是指"相对多数",而非构成过半数的多数,即:a large number or quantity that does not constitute a majority。相比之下,majority 则指"过半数多数",即 a number that is more than half of a total。

(2) poll, vote 和 ballot 三者均有投票表决的含义。相比之下,vote 为通用词,含义最广,包括表决的各种形式,如投票表决、举手表决、鼓掌表决等,因表决常用投票进行,故 vote 有时也就被人译为"投票",但其精确含义应为"表决",尤其是与 poll 用在一起时。而 poll 则多指表决的一种形式,即"投票表决"。ballot 则又属于投票表决中的一种形式,即不记名投票表决。

5. contract 与 agreement

两者均指表达两个或以上之当事人合意(mutual consent)之文件。在英美法中,agreement(协议)经常被作为 contract 的同义词,但其内涵比 contract(合同)要广(agreement is in some respects a broader term than contract),它还常用作指不具备合同要素或要件,即无对价(consideration)的某些协议。而合同总是含有对价的。总体说来,所有合同均是一种协议,而协议却未必一定是合同。要使协议成为合同,其必须符合合同的要件规定(only if it meets the requirements of a Contract),有时还需当事人在交易过程中通过语言或经交易过程或商业惯例等的默示予以补偿条件。

Lesson Seventeen Introduction to International Law

Exercises

I Verbal Abilities

Part One

Directions: *For each of these completing questions, read each item carefully to get the sense of it. Then, in the proper space, complete each statement by supplying the missing word or phrase.*

1. The fist _____ features of the international law is that it aims at regulating the behavior of States, not that of individuals.

   A. saintly   B. salient   C. salable
   D. salutary   E. sanatory

2. Within States individuals are the principal legal subject, and legal entities (corporations, associations) are merely secondary subjects whose possible suppression would not result in the demise of the whole legal system, in the international community the _____ holds true.

   A. opposite   B. contradictory   C. contrary
   D. diametric   E. reverse

3. H. Kelsen's 'monistic' theory postulates the existence of a _____ legal system, embracing all various legal orders existing at various levels, and the superiority of international law, which is at the top of the pyramid and validates or invalidates all the legal acts of any other legal system.

   A. solely   B. innumerable   C. unitary
   D. unreckonable   E. uni-axial

4. "The common heritage of mankind" _____ expresses, with all its merits and limitations, the new world model of world community which has gradually emerged since 1945.

   A. succinctly   B. shortly   C. epigrammatically
   D. sufficiently   E. reducibly

5. After forcefully contending that "the plows of the rich nation can do as much harm as their swords", Ivan Illiich points out that "rich nations now benevolently impose a straitjacket of traffic jams, hospital confinements and classrooms on the poor nations, and by international agreement call this 'development'".

   A. bicamerally   B. bifurcatedly   C. believably
   D. benevolently   E. beneficially

6. One of the principal reasons why developing countries endure increasingly worse conditions is because they do not actually control their own natural resources which are in fact in the hands of the foreign corporations, usually in the form of multinational _____.

   A. disquietude   B. concerns   C. watchfulness
   D. conciliation   E. concordance

7. All countries _____ themselves to pursue internal and external economic policies designed to accelerate economic growth throughout the world.

A. pleaded B. premeditate C. plotted
D. maneuvered E. pledged

8. Since 1945 international efforts for the promotion of development have made great _____ forward and undergone various changes.

A. rejoinder B. strides C. likeness
D. detour E. commotion

9. The IMF (International Monetary Fund) is the most important instrument of State monopoly in the field of international monetary policy, which the _____ States have established after the Second World War under the domination of the U. S.

A. imperishable B. shaky C. imperative
D. imperialistic E. implausible

10. The socialist countries consistently refer to sovereignty as the key concept in international relations and the principal legal means of _____ their freedom of action from external interference.

A. shielding B. shirking C. severing
D. screening E. signifying

Part Two

Directions: *Choose the one word or phase that best keep the meaning of the original sentence if it were substituted for the underlined part.*

1. Ethiopia strongly opposes any introduction or maintenance of troops by one country within the territory of another country under the pretext of protection of national interest, protection of lives of citizens or any other excuse.

A. pretermission B. presupposition C. excuse
D. sham E. substantiality

2. Socialist countries are now motivated in international relations by their political interests, which largely amount to the aims of strengthening the socialist camps, averting the intrusion of the Western States into their own domestic affairs.

A. deter B. promote C. aviate
D. avenge E. avail

3. Civil strife raged in North America between 1774 and 1783 and the fight between American settlers and the British colonial power lasted a long time and wrought havoc.

A. happenstance B. harbinger C. hazard
D. catastrophe E. hawkshaw

4. Pollock found an ingenious solution to the problem by saying that whatever a man chooses to do bargain for must be conclusively taken to be of some value to him.

A. ingenuous B. ingratiating C. informative
D. infuriating E. coony

5. Easements, covenants and equitable servitudes are restrictions imposed on the use of a landowner's property that are intended bind future owners of the same property.

A. ephemeral B. corruptible C. bigoted
D. disinterested E. uninterested

6. Wherever the international commercial dispute is resolved, time will be consumed and expenses <u>incurred</u>, and difficulties may arise in obtaining the necessary persons or documents required by the procedural rules of the appropriate forums.

A. inculcate B. indemnify C. undertake
D. discharge E. shun

7. The Securities Act of 1933 governs offerings of new securities in the United States and contains <u>material</u> misstatements in a registration statement or for an omission of a required fact.

A. earthly B. momentous C. materialistic
D. substantive E. mastodonic

8. There are rules in the study of international law that countries will <u>habitually</u> ignore because the official state position may not have kept pace with changes in the world.

A. chronically B. habitable C. sporadically
D. occasionally E. unwonted

9. The aggregate authority cited by the parties simply establishes that a trial court faced with a suit in which diplomatic recognition of a plaintiff has been withdrawn is to exercise its sound discretion in deciding whether to <u>suspend</u> or dismiss the suit.

A. temporize B. swat C. sustain
D. check E. dangle

10. The multinational enterprise <u>contemplating</u> an indirect selling arrangement in the EEC to determine what will happen legally on termination, what can or cannot be done during the term of the arrangement, and to what extent territorial protection and exclusivity can be guaranteed.

A. contemning B. construing C. excogitating
D. gazing E. contaminate

II Cloze

Directions: *For each blank in the following passage, choose the best answer from the choices given.*

A customary system of law can never be adequate to the needs of any but a primitive society, and the __(1)__ of the international society is that, whilst on the material side it is far from primitive, and therefore needs a strong and fairly elaborate system of law for the regulation of the __(2)__ to which the material interdependence of different states is constantly __(3)__, its spiritual cohesion is weak, and as long as that is so the weakness will inevitably be reflected in a weak and primitive system of law.

Whether we ought to conclude that international law is a failure depends upon what we assume to be its aim. It has not failed to serve the purposes for which states have chosen to use it; in fact it serves these purposes reasonably well. The __(4)__ hears little of international law as a working system, for most of its practice goes on within the walls of foreign offices, which __(5)__ are secretive; and even if the foreign offices were inclined to be more communicative the layman would not find what they could tell him very interesting, any more than he would normally be interested in the working of a solicitor's office. For in fact the practice of international law proceeds on much the same lines __(6)__ any other kind of law, with the foreign offices taking the place of the private __(7)__ and exchanging arguments about the facts and the law and later, more often than is sometimes supposed, with a hearing before some form of __(8)__. The volume of this work is __(9)__, but most of it is not sensational, and it only occasionally relates to matters of high political interest. That does not mean that the matters to which it does relate are unimportant in themselves; often they are very important to particular interests or individuals. But it means that international law is performing a useful and indeed a necessary function in international life in enabling states to __(10)__ their day-today intercourse along orderly and predictable lines. That is the role for which states have chosen to use it and for that it has proved a serviceable __(11)__.

Brierly's well-recognized book does not express the only acceptable view on these matters. It is best to form one's own opinion—not in __(12)__ but on the basis of the evidence to be found amongst the materials of international law collected in the rest of this volume. Chapters 2, 3 and 4 provide the basis for an assessment of the international legal system. These three chapters present the __(13)__ evidence of the legal organization of international society and the means to create and to apply international law. Successive chapters deal with the __(14)__ rights and obligations assumed by states as the principal subjects of international law. Chapter 5 canvasses one of the most longstanding aspects of international law, namely the rules governing the conduct of __(15)__. Chapters 6 to 9 discuss the existence of international controls on the __(16)__ of state power and authority under the legal rubrics of __(17)__ and responsibility. Chapters 10 and 11 add evidence of the growing __(18)__ of international law through the recent development of two particular subject areas, the protection of human rights and the law of the sea. In the context of some other new fields of international __(19)__, the final Chapter 12 invites concluding reflections on the scope, the force and the __(20)__ of international law.

(1) A. paradox   B. parachronism   C. parable
     D. panhandler   E. panacea

(2) A. crashes   B. clusters   C. clashes
     D. crutches   E. crotches

(3) A. giving way   B. giving rise   C. giving weight
     D. giving offence   E. giving origin

(4) A. professional   B. specialist   C. civilian
     D. layman   E. amateur

(5) A. in principle   B. in effect   C. in practice
     D. in gear   E. on principle

(6) A. than that   B. as that of   C. as that
     D. than   E. than that of

(7) A. legal adviser   B. consultant   C. advocate
     D. lawyer   E. practitioner

(8) A. bureau   B. department   C. international tribunal
    D. tributary   E. retributive
(9) A. considerate   B. consistent   C. constituent
    D. consonant   E. considerable
(10) A. carry out   B. carry forward   C. carry away
     D. carry on   E. carry off
(11) A. Instrument   B. note   C. draft
     D. deed   E. paper
(12) A. ahead   B. advance   C. preparation
     D. superiority E. priority
(13) A. sustainable B.   B. attainable C. present
     D. existing   E. available
(14) A. substantiate B. adjective   C. substantive
     D. substantial E. procedural
(15) A. diplomatic relations B. personal relations   C. interpersonal relationship
     D. diplomatic relationships   E. diplomatic sovereignty
(16) A. command   B. commandeer   C. exercise
     D. control   E. regulate
(17) A. discreetness B. discretion   C. justification
     D. adjudication E. jurisdiction
(18) A. domain   B. region   C. area
     D. limitation   E. restraint
(19) A. reflection   B. concern   C. consideration
     D. provocation E. worry
(20) A. nature   B. consternation   C. consolidation
     D. character   E. characteristics

III Reading Comprehension

Part One

Directions: *In this section there are passages followed by questions or unfinished statements, each with suggested answers. Choose the one you think is the best answer.*

Passage One

A major ethical (and) legal problem in international business dealings has to do with the legitimacy of certain side payments to government officials. In the United States, the majority of contracts are formed within the private sector. In many foreign countries, however, decisions on most major construction and manufacturing contracts are executed and made by government officials because of extensive government regulation and control over trade and industry. Side payments to government officials in exchange for more favorable business contracts are not unusual in such countries, nor are they considered to be unethical in some areas. In the past, the United States corporations doing business in developing countries largely followed the maxim, "When in Rome, do as the Romans do".

In the 1970's, however, the United States—and government officials as we—uncovered a number of business scandals involving large side payments by American corporations, such as Lockheed Aircraft, to foreign representatives for the purpose of securing advantageous international contracts. In 1977 to prohibit American firms from this unethical conduct, Congress passed the Foreign Corrupt Practices Act (FCPA), which prohibits American businesspersons from bribing foreign officials to secure advantageous contracts. The act has made it difficult for American companies to compete as effectively as they otherwise might in the global marketplace.

1. What might be the title of this passage?
   A. The Bribery of Foreign Officials   B. When in Rome, Do as the Romans Do.
   C. FCPA's Intention   D. Ill Effects of FCPA.
2. Why do the U. S. firms become less competitive in the world marketplace after the passage of FCPA?
   A. The U. S. FCPA prohibits the American businesspersons from bribing the foreign officials.
   B. Bribery and Corruption in some countries are not curbed.
   C. The U. S. firms hope to gain advantageous business contracts.
   D. Though American firms are inhibited from bribing foreign officials, the bribery and corruption in some countries are not altogether checked.

Passage Two

The Foreign Corrupt Practices Act (FCPA) of 1977 is divided into two major parts. The first part applies to all U. S. companies and their directors, officers, shareholders, employees and agents. This part of FCPA prohibits the bribery of most officials of foreign governments if the purpose of the payment is to get the official to act in his or her official capacity to provide business opportunity.

The FCPA does not prohibit payment of substantial sums of minor officials whose duties are ministerial. These payments are often referred to as "grease" payments. They are meant to ensure that administrative personnel "do what they are supposed to do" and that government services that might otherwise be performed at a slow pace are sped up. Thus, is a firm makes a payment to a minor official to speed up an import-licensing process, the firm has not violated the FCPA. Generally, the act, amended, permits payments to foreign officials if such payments are lawful within the foreign country. Furthermore, the act does not prohibit payments to provide foreign companies or other third parties unless the American firm knows that the payment will be passed on to a foreign government in violation of the FCPA.

The second part of the FCPA is directed toward accountants, because in the past bribes were often concealed in corporate financial records. All companies must keep detailed records that "accurately and fairly" reflect the company's financial activities. In addition, all companies must have an accounting system that provides "reasonable assurance" that all transactions entered into by the company are accounted for and legal. These requirements further prohibits any person from making false statements to accountants or false entries in any record or account.

Business firms that violate an act may be fined up to $2 million. Individual officers or directors who violate the FCPA may be fined up to $100,000 (the fine cannot be paid by the company) and may be imprisoned for up to five years.

FCPA is the only law of its kind in the world. No other country imposes penalties on businesspersons for bribing foreign officials. Increasingly, however, multinational initiatives are being undertaken to stem corruption and bribery in business dealings in the international arena.

Consider, for example, developments that occurred in 1996. The organization for Economic Cooperation and Development, to which twenty-six of the worlds' leading industrialized countries belong, called on its member nations to both criminalize the bribery of foreign officials and eliminate the tax deductibility of bribes. The International Chamber of Commerce also announced that it had updated its "Rules of Conduct to Combat Extortion and Bribery" which were first adopted in 1977. These rules prohibit the payment and receipt of bribes by business firms. In addition, the General Assembly of the United Nations adopted the "Declaration against Corruption and Bribery in International Commercial Transactions". This declaration grew out of efforts begun in 1975 to encourage countries to attack corruption. The 1996 declaration, however, was more forceful than earlier efforts in that it went beyond mere encouragement and committed member nations to act.

Part of the incentive behind these and other multinational initiatives has to do with the opening up of new markets in Asia and in the Eastern European countries that formerly wee part of the Soviet Union. The media attention given to these new markets have led to concerns over real or imagined corruption and bribery. If the momentum of joint international actions to curb such practices continues, eventually U.S. and world businesspersons may face a more level playing field with respect to international business transactions.

1. Which of the following is true according to the passage?

A. FCPA facilitates the American firms to bribe the foreign officials.

B. Agents of the American firms in the foreign countries can offer grease money to foreign government officials to obtain advantageous business contracts.

C. An accounting system must provide assurance that all transactions entered into the American firms are accounted for and legitimate.

D. The directors or the managers have to pay heavy fines on behalf of the company if the company violates the FCPA.

2. The word "grease" in the passage may probably mean _____.

A. slippery
B. lubrication
C. facilitating payments
D. payments for the purpose of corruption

3. The conclusion we can draw from the passage is that _____.

A. More implicit measures will be taken by the businesspersons to bribe the foreign officials.

B. World corruption can be, in the long run, discouraged and eliminated.

C. Joint international actions against corruption and bribery will be discontinued.

D. The measures taken by the United Nations were less stricter than those taken by the U.S.A.

Passage Three

The first UN Conference on Trade and Development was held in 1964 under the auspices of the UN, and was attended by practically all members of the world community (120 states). After three months of hard and protracted labors, it adopted a set of resolutions which laid down the basic principles on which the institution was to work in future. The General Assembly then decided to establish the Conference as one of its institutions, to be convened at intervals of no more than three years, and also set up a permanent executive body, the "Trade and Development Board" (consisting of fifty-five members elected by the Conference, to meet twice yearly), as well as a Secretariat, headed by a Secretary-General (appointed by the UN Secretary—General and confirmed by the General Assembly). Among the general principles laid down by the Conference the following stand out:

(1) 'Economic development and social progress should be the common concern of the whole international community'. Accordingly, all countries pledged themselves to pursue internal and external policies designed to accelerate economic growth throughout the world, and in particular to help promote in developing countries a rate of growth consistent with the need to bring about substantial and steady increase in average income in order to narrow the gap between the standards of living in developing countries and that in developed countries.

Thus, a general political philosophy propounded was whereby the development of less advanced countries was of concern to everybody, in particular to industrialized nations. While until that time backward countries had merely requested to be assisted as a concession on the part of advanced States, now they proclaimed that they were entitled to international help.

(2) A new idea was launched, that of an international division of labor.

(3) Existing trade barriers hampering the access of primary products of developing countries were to be eliminated by developed countries.

(4) A further important measure was to be the stabilization of the price of primary commodities so as to avoid their fluctuation and decline to the detriment of producers.

(5) Finally, developed countries were requested to grant commercial concessions to developing countries, in particular the most-favored-nation treatment, without, however, requiring any concession in return from developing countries. In other terms, the most-favored-nation clause ought not to be reciprocal when applied to less advanced nations. Furthermore, technologically advanced States were invited to make preferential concessions, both tariff and non-tariff, to developing countries, and the latter were to be allowed not to extend to the former preferential treatment inn operation amongst them.

In short, the liberal, free-market approach was to be dropped as far as developing countries were concerned, and they had to enjoy a 'discriminatory treatment', that is treatment different and more advantageous than that existing between developed countries. This was, indeed, a conspicuous departure from the basic principles which had governed international relations until that time.

It is apparent from the foregoing that UNCTAD does not constitute a 'traditional' international organizations, nor has it brought about a set of standards legally binding on all the participating

States. UNCTAD is, rather, a felicitous combination of a body of general guidelines destined to serve as a blueprint for action, and a political forum where developed and developing countries meet on an equal footing, exchange views, and gradually try to implement these guidelines. The establishment of UNCTAD marks the real divide in international action for development, for it was in 1964 that developing countries became aware that aid was no longer sufficient and that it was necessary to come to grips with the basic causes of international disequilibrium. Subsequently, it was within UNCTAD that backward States gradually evolved their new philosophy of development and, as we shall see, came to formulate a global strategy, which was expounded in 1974, thus changing from a specific sector (that of international trade) to an overall approach to economic relations between North and South.

More specifically, UNCTAD is important in the following three respects. First, as emphasized by Abi Saab, its real significance "is reflected... in the forces which brought it into being but which were given more shape and self-awareness through it. Thus for the first time a vast grouping of all the underdeveloped countries was formed and is learning to co-operate and to act as one bloc in defense of their common interests. The importance of this factor is not reduced by the occasional awkwardness and deviation which are part and parcel of any process of learning".

A second merit of UNCTAD lies in 'educating world public opinion, especially in developed countries' as to the conditions and causes of underdevelopment in the Third World, so as to persuade industrialized States to take action at least to reduce the most glaring international economic injustices.

The third, and perhaps most important, merit of UNCTAD is its piecemeal construction of a set of international standards designed to expand and apply the general guidelines set forth in 1964.

One of the areas where the effects of pressure UNCTAD are most visible is that of commodity agreements, that is, those multilateral treaties calculated to impinge upon the free play of international market forces controlling the sale of primary commodities raw materials by developing countries. "Precisely because developing nations are mostly geared to monocultures, that is, to the exploitation of one basic natural resource, for many years a crucial issue has been the stabilization of the international price of such commodities. Since the early 1960s the terms of trade of raw materials have deteriorated, for a number of reasons: (1) the influence of natural causes (weather, vegetal diseases, etc.) on the production of such resources; (2) the inherent instability of the international market, which moves in unpredictable cycles"; (3) the tendency of industrialized countries to replace natural products such as rubber and fibres with synthetic products; (4) the tendency of developed countries to draw on goods they themselves produce. UNCTAD has strongly pressed for the conclusion of agreements designed to eliminate or attenuate short-term market instability by preventing or moderating pronounced fluctuations in the price of those commodities. Urged on by UNCTAD, States felt impelled to undertake commodity agreements (no novelty in 1964 since an agreement on wheat had been conclude as early as 1949) because this was the best way to guarantee sovereignty over natural resources and stable earnings from them.

1. Before the meeting of UNCTAD, the principles that governed the international relations

was that _____.

A. developed countries enjoy more preferential treatment than those less developed countries.

B. developing countries encounter more tariff and nontariff barriers.

C. the price of primary products in the developing nations was higher because of the pressure from the developed countries.

D. economic development and social progress is not what the developed countries want to expect from.

2. Which of the following statements is true according to the passage?

A. UNCTAD constitutes a routine institution to tackle the world problems of development.

B. UNCTAD sets back a blueprint for the development of the world States.

C. Developing countries can still not feel they are on the equal footing with the developed countries.

D. Economic relations between North and South for the first time become globally concerned.

3. Which of the following is not the reasons why the terms of world trade of raw materials become worsened?

A. Fluctuation in the world marketplace.

B. Self-sufficiency of developed countries in providing the raw materials.

C. Replacement of natural products with synthetic products by the developing countries.

D. Typhoon, hurricane and other natural catastrophe.

4. The merit of UNCTAD can be seen from which of the following statements?

A. Developing nations now join hands to defend their common interests.

B. The public in the developed countries can now fully understand the plight in the underdeveloped countries.

C. General guidelines for the international standards need be formulated once and for all.

D. All of the above.

5. The conclusion we can draw from the passage is that _____.

A. UNCTAD contributes a great deal to development of the world States, developed or developing, but it may still be affected by great many factors.

B. UNCTAD will affect world market forces to the utmost extent.

C. UNCTAD will continue to play a major role in the harmonization of world States.

D. UNCTAD seems far from what the world, especially the developing countries, expects.

Part Two Short Answer Questions

Direction: *In this part, you are required to read the case carefully and answer the questions briefly.*

Case Study

Frummer v. Hilton Hotels International, Inc.

227 N. E. 2d 851 (1967)

Fuld, Chief Justice

The plaintiff alleges that in 1963, when he was on a visit to England, he fell and was injured

Lesson Seventeen Introduction to International Law

in his room at the London Hilton Hotel while attempting to take a shower in an ovular, modern bathtub. He seeks $150,000 in damages not only from the defendant Hilton (U. K.), but also from the defendants Hilton Hotels Corporation and Hilton Hotels International, both of which are Delaware corporations doing business in New York. The defendant Hilton (U. K.) which is the lessee and operator of the London Hilton Hotel, has moved for an order dismissing the complaint against it on grounds that the court lacks jurisdiction of the defendant's person.

Both parties argue that "the applicable statute" is CPLR 302 (sbd. [a], par. I) which authorizes our courts to exercise personal jurisdiction over a foreign corporation if it "transacts any business within the state" and the cause of action asserted against it is one "arising from" the transaction of such business.

Jurisdiction was, however, properly acquired over Hilton (U. K.) because the record discloses that it was "doing business" here in the traditional sense.

As we have frequently observed, a foreign corporation is amenable to suit in our courts if it is "engaged in such a continuous and systematic course of 'doing business' here as to warrant a finding of its 'presence' in this jurisdiction". Although "mere solicitation" of business for an out-of-state concern is not enough to constitute doing business, due process requirements are satisfied if the defendant foreign corporation has "certain minimum contacts with [the State] such that the maintenance of the suit does not offend 'traditional notions of fair play and substantial justice'".

In the case before us, services are provided for the defendant Hilton (U. K.) by the Hilton Reservation Service which has a New York office, as well as a New York bank account and telephone number. The Service advertises that it was "established to provide the closest possible liasion with Travel Agents across the country", that lodging "rates for certified wholesalers and/or tour operators [could] be obtained [from the Service] on request" and that it could "confirm availabilities immediately... and without charge" at any Hilton hotel including the London Hilton. Thus it does "public relations and publicity work" for the defendant Hilton (U. K.), including "maintaining contacts with... Travel agents" and tour directors; and it most certainly "helps to generate business" here for the London Hilton—which, indeed, was the very purpose for which it was established.

The "presence" of Hilton (U. K.) in New York, for purposes of jurisdiction, is established by the activities conducted here on its behalf by its agent, the Hilton Reservation Service, and the fact that the two are commonly owned its significant only because it gives rise to a valid inference as to the broad scope of the agency in the absence of an express agency agreement.

We are not unmindful that litigation in a foreign jurisdiction is a burdensome inconvenience for any company. However, it is part of the price that may properly be demanded of those who extensively engage in international trade. When their activities abroad, either directly or through an agent, become as widespread and energetic as the activities in New York conducted by Hilton (U. K.), they receive considerable benefits from such foreign business and may not be heard to complain about the burdens.

Since, then, Hilton (U. K.) was "doing business" in New York in the traditional sense and was validly served with process in London, as provided by statute (CPLR 313), our courts acquired "person jurisdiction over the corporation for any cause of action asserted against it, no matter where the events occurred which gave rise to the cause of action."

1. What is doing business?
2. What are the reasons for the appeal?
3. What is the jurisdiction argument raised in the Hilton?

IV   Translation Abilities

法律语言特征分析与法律翻译技能培养之十七：

法人法语

　　法律翻译过程中，有时表达似乎更难于理解，原因主要在于法律翻译必须做到"法人法语"(Talking like a lawyer or writing like a lawyer)。法律语言是一种"专门技术语言"，包括了许多法律专门技术术语和特殊法律概念，其中的技巧和奥秘绝非一般人可以轻易掌握或破解，只有谙晓外语和母语两种法律知识的"法律人"才可真正做到法人法语。但法律部门繁杂，分工细致，不少知识具有极强的专业性，即便在"法律内部"(intra-law)不同部门的人士也时有隔行如隔山的感觉。精通不同法律体系中各种部门法的"通才"在实践中实在难求，致使不少人哀叹"普通法"不可译(香港普通法翻译纲要编辑组，1997年)，或至少无法做到Groot所说的"确保将一种法律语言翻译成另一种法律语言"，而不是"将一种法律语言翻译成另一种语言"。由于不熟悉法律知识以及法律文化背景，非法律人在翻译法律时经常出现语用层面上的表达"失格"。"尤其是法律概念，译文中纰漏之多，令人吃惊"(张龙，2002年)，致使译文读者有时根本无法解读或无法完全理解译文的真正含义，如：

原文	非法律人之译文	适格法律翻译主体之译文
access right	通行权	（父母对子女的）探视权
apparent agency	明确的代理	表见代理
case of first impression	未发生过的案件	无先例案件
construction of law	法律构建	法律解释
contributory negligence	被害人本身的过失	混合过失，与有过失
derivative acquisition	派生获得	（所有权的）继受取得
discharge	结束合同	终止合同
dominant owner	主要所有人	需役地所有人
indeterminate sentence	不特定刑罚	不定期刑
law reports	法律报告	（普通法）判例汇编
mortgagee	承受抵押者	按揭权人
overlapping of laws	法律的重叠	法规竞合
prize law	奖惩法则	捕获法
procurement	做淫媒罪、拉皮条罪	介绍卖淫罪
proper law of contract	管合同的合适法律	合同准据法
res judicata	已判决的事件	既判力
security measures	保安措施	（诉讼）保全措施
separation of powers	权力的分开	权力的分立
servient owner	从属所有人	供役地所有人

Lesson Seventeen   Introduction to International Law

英译汉过程中要做到"法人法语"之困难尚且如此,汉译英的难度更可想而知,如:

原文	适格法律翻译主体之译文
法教义学	legal dogmatic
法学自治	autonomy of jurisprudence
法制	nomocracy; government in accordance with a system of law
信赖赔偿责任	liability of reliance damages
物权请求权	claim of real right
行政紧急权力	administrative emergency power
意思自治	self-governance; party autonomy
越权立法	ultra vires legislation
治外法权	extraterritoriality
主观恶性	subjective malice
罪责刑相适应原则	*nullum crimen sine lege*

Translation Exercises:
Part One   *Put the Following into Chinese*

If, as Sir Frederick Pollock (*First Book of Jurisprudence*, at 28) writes, and as probably most competent jurists would today agree, the only essential conditions for the existence of law are the existence of a political community, and the recognition by its members of settled rules binding upon them in that capacity, international law seems on the whole to satisfy these conditions.

But it is more important to understand the nature of the system than to argue whether it ought to be called law or something else. The best view is that international law is in fact just a system of customary law, upon which has been erected, almost entirely within the last two generations, a superstructure of "conventional" or treaty-made law, and some of its chief defects are precisely those that the history of law teaches us to expect in a customary system. It is a common mistake to suppose that of these the most conspicuous is the frequency of its violation. Violations of law are rare in all customary systems, and they are so in international law. The explanation of that fact is simple, and so too is the explanation of the common belief to the contrary. For the law is normally observed because, as we shall see, the demands that it makes on states are generally not exacting, and on the whole states find it convenient to observe it; but this fact receives little notice because the interest of most people in international law is not in the ordinary routine of international legal business, but in the occasions, rare but generally sensational, on which it is flagrantly broken. Such breaches generally occur either when some great political issue has arisen between states, or in that part of the system which professes to regulate the conduct of war. But our diagnosis of what is wrong with the system will be mistaken if we fail to realize that the laws of peace and the great majority of treaties are on the whole regularly observed in the daily intercourse of states. And this is no small service to international life, however far it may fall short of the ideal by which we rightly judge the achievements of the system. If we fail to understand this, we are likely to assume, as many people do, that all would be well with international law if we could devise a better system for enforcing it; but the weakness of international law lies deeper than any mere question of sanctions. It is not the existence of a police force that makes a system of law strong and respected, but the strength of the law that makes it possible for a police force to be effectively organized. The imperative character of law is felt so strongly and obedience to it has become so much a matter of habit within a highly civilized state that national law has developed a machinery of enforcement which generally works smoothly, though never so smoothly as to make breaches impossible. If the imperative character of international law were equally strongly felt, the institution of definite international sanctions would easily follow.

Part Two *Put the Following into English*

尽管协商和起草国际协议时已尽一切可能去预测或避免产生争议,但在履行协议的过程中,分歧仍然会产生或的确存在。国际大背景中,存在着两种基本形式的争议:一种是有关同权利和义务的争议,另一种乃政府试图通过变革运作规则而更改合同所产生的争议。

国家商务环境中争议的解决主要有如下各种方式,即在内国法院提起商事诉讼的传统方式以及国际诉讼。有些问题,如内国法律的域外适用、法律选择以及国家主权豁免权等,有时大大限制了诉讼的作用,使其不大具有用武之地。为此,仲裁在人们心中就成了诉讼的一种任择方式。当然,这不是说该方式乃一种允许外国企业能够避免诸如美国式的法律环境的方式,因为,诸如美国等国的诉讼程序制度于他们而言是陌生的。同样,对于诸如美国等国的企业而言,他们对外国法律制度的了解一样是微乎其微的。

V Interaction

1. Write about the nature of the international public law.

2. Discuss with your tutor/s or your friends specializing in the international public law and offer your opinion as to the doctrine of "fundamental rights" and the positivistic doctrine.

VI Appreciation of the Judge's Opinions

(1) Case Name(案件名):*Medellín v. Texas*

Medellín v. Texas	

Supreme Court of the United States	
Argued October 10, 2007 Decided March 25, 2008	
Full case name	José Ernesto Medellín v. Texas
Docket nos.	06-984
Citations	U.S. [1] (more) 552 U.S. 491; 128 S. Ct. 1346; 170 L. Ed. 2d 190; 2008 U.S. LEXIS 2912; 76

Lesson Seventeen Introduction to International Law

	U. S. L. W. 4143; 2008-1 U. S. Tax Cas. (CCH) P50,242; 21 Fla. L. Weekly Fed. S 126
Prior history	Medellín v. State, No. 71,997 (Tex. Crim. App., May 16, 1997); petition denied, S. D. Tex.; certificate of appealability denied, 371 F. 3d 270 (5th Cir. 2004); cert. granted, 543 U. S. 1032 (2005); cert. dismissed, 544 U. S. 660 (2005) (per curiam) (Medellín I); Ex parte Medellín, 223 S. W. 3d 315 (Tex. Crim. App. 2006); cert. granted Ex parte Medellín, 550 U. S. _____ (2007)
Subsequent history	Stay and petition denied, 554 U. S. _____ (2008) (Medellín III)
Argument	Oral argument

Holding

Neither Case Concerning Avena and Other Mexican Nationals (Mex. v. U. S.), 2004 I. C. J. 12 (Judgment of Mar. 31) nor the President's Memorandum to the Attorney General (Feb. 28, 2005) constitutes enforceable federal law that pre-empts state limitations on the filing of habeas corpus petitions.

Court membership

Chief Justice
John G. Roberts
Associate Justices
John P. Stevens · Antonin Scalia
Anthony Kennedy · David Souter
Clarence Thomas · Ruth Bader Ginsburg
Stephen Breyer · Samuel Alito

Case opinions

Majority	Roberts, joined by Scalia, Kennedy, Thomas, Alito
Concurrence	Stevens
Dissent	Breyer, joined by Souter, Ginsburg

Laws applied

Optional Protocol Concerning the Compulsory Settlement of Disputes to the Vienna Convention, April 24, 1963, (1970) 21 U. S. T. 325, T. I. A. S. No. 6820; Article 36(1)(b) of the Vienna Convention on Consular Relations; Article 94 of the United Nations Charter; U. S. Const., Art. II, §3

(2) **Case Summary**(案件简介)

This is the second time this matter has reached the Supreme Court. Medellín, a citizen of Mexico, was convicted of capital murder(因罪杀人) in Texas state court and sentenced to death. Medellín filed a petition for a writ of habeas corpus(人身保护令) arguing that the state violated his rights as a foreign national to consular access under the Vienna Convention(《维也纳公约》). His petition was denied in the lower courts, despite a ruling by the International Court of Justice(国际法院) that Medellín and others were entitled to review of their convictions based on violations of the Vienna Convention. While Medellín's case was pending (当……的时候,在……中;审理中的,未定的,未决的) in the United States Supreme Court, the Bush administration filed a brief urging the Court to rule that Medellín had no private right to seek enforcement of the Convention, but also announced that the U. S. Government would comply with(遵循) the World Court decision and directed state courts to reexamine the claims of Medellín and other Mexican nationals. Accordingly, Medellín filed a new state habeas petition and asked the Supreme Court to stay its consideration of the case pending state review. The Supreme Court in a 5-4 decision dismissed Medellin's petition and allow the state habeas case to go forward.

The Texas Court of Criminal Appeals(德克萨斯刑事上诉法院) denied Medellin's habeas petition because Medellin had not raised the issue at his trial, as required by Texas law. It held that the International Court of Justice decision was not binding federal law and, thus, did not preempt(美国为取得先买权预先占据公地,以先买权取得;先占,先取) the state procedural rule requiring petitioners to raise issues at trial, and furthermore, that under the separation of powers doctrine, President Bush had no authority to order the state to reconsider Medellin's conviction.

Question Presented:

In the *Case Concerning Avena and Other Mexican Nationals* (*Mex. v. U. S.*), I. C. J. No. 128 (judgment of Mar. 31, 2004), the International Court of Justice determined that 51 named Mexican nationals, including petitioner, were entitled to receive review and reconsideration of their convictions and sentences through the judicial process in the United States. On February 28, 2005, President George W. Bush determined that the United States would comply with its international obligation to give effect to the judgment by giving those 51 individuals review and reconsideration in the state courts. However, the Texas Court of Criminal Appeals held that the President's determination exceeded his powers(超越权限), and it refused to give effect to the *Avena* judgment or the President's determination.

This case presents the following questions:

1. Did the President of the United States act within his constitutional and statutory foreign affairs authority when he determined that the states must comply with the United States' treaty obligation to give effect to the *Avena* judgment in the cases of the 51 Mexican nationals named in the judgment?

2. Are state courts bound by the Constitution to honor the undisputed international obligation of the United States, under treaties duly ratified by the President with the advice and consent of the Senate, to give effect to the *Avena* judgment in the cases that the judgment addressed?

(3) Excerpts of the Judgment(法官判决词)

CHIEF JUSTICE(首席大法官) ROBERTS delivered the opinion of the Court.

The International Court of Justice (ICJ)(国际法院), located in the Hague, is a tribunal established pursuant to the United Nations Charter to adjudicate(进行裁判) disputes between member states(各成员). In *the Case Concerning Avena and Other Mexican Nationals* (*Mex. v. U. S.*), 2004 I. C. J. 12 (Judgment of Mar. 31) (*Avena*), that tribunal considered a claim brought by Mexico against the United States. The ICJ held that, based on violations of the Vienna Convention(违反《维也纳公约》) 51 named Mexican nationals(国民) were entitled to review and reconsideration of their state-court convictions and sentences in the United States. This was so regardless of any forfeiture of the right to raise Vienna Convention claims because of a failure to comply with generally applicable state rules governing challenges to criminal convictions.

In *Sanchez-Llamas v. Oregon* (2006)—issued after Avena but involving individuals who were not named in the Avena judgment—we held that, contrary to the ICJ's determination, the Vienna Convention did not preclude the application of state default rules. After the Avena decision, President George W. Bush determined, through a Memorandum to the Attorney General (Feb. 28, 2005), that the United States would "discharge its international obligations"(履行国际义务) under Avena "by having State courts give effect to the decision."

Petitioner José Ernesto Medellín, who had been convicted and sentenced in Texas state court for murder, is one of the 51 Mexican nationals named in the Avena decision. Relying on the ICJ's decision and the President's Memorandum, Medellín filed an application for a writ of habeas corpus(人身保护令状) in state court. The Texas Court of Criminal Appeals dismissed Medellín's application as an abuse of the writ under state law, given Medellín's failure to raise his Vienna Convention claim in a timely manner under state law. We granted certiorari to decide two questions. First, is the ICJ's judgment in Avena directly enforceable as domestic law in a state court in the United States? Second, does the President's Memorandum independently require the States to provide review and reconsideration of the claims of the 51 Mexican nationals named in Avena without regard to state procedural default rules? We conclude that neither Avena nor the President's Memorandum constitutes directly enforceable federal law that pre-empts state limitations on the filing of successive habeas petitions. We therefore affirm(维持原判)the decision below.

I

A

In 1969, the United States, upon the advice and consent of the Senate, ratified the Vienna Convention on Consular Relations (Vienna Convention or Convention)(《维也纳领事关系公约》), and the Optional Protocol Concerning the Compulsory Settlement of Disputes to the Vienna Convention Optional Protocol or Protocol(《维也纳领事关系公约关于强制解决争端之任择议定书》). The preamble(序言) to the Convention provides that its purpose is to "contribute to the development of friendly relations among nations." Toward that end(目的), Article 36 of the Convention was drafted to "facilitate the exercise of consular functions." It provides that if a person detained(扣留,拘留) by a foreign country "so requests, the competent authorities of the receiving State(接受国) shall, without delay, inform the consular post of the sending State(派出国)" of such detention, and "inform the detainee(被拘留者,多指政治犯等) of his right" to request assistance from the consul of his own state.

The Optional Protocol provides a venue(犯罪地点;现场;审判管辖区,审判地点;起诉书上对审判地点的指示,此处可以理解为"路径或渠道") for the resolution of disputes arising out of the interpretation or application of the Vienna Convention. Under the Protocol, such disputes "shall lie within the compulsory jurisdiction of the International Court of Justice" and "may accordingly be brought before the ICJ... by any party to the dispute being a Party to the present Protocol".

The ICJ is "the principal judicial organ of the United Nations." It was established in 1945 pursuant to the United Nations Charter(《联合国宪章》). The ICJ Statute(《国际法院规约》)—annexed to the U.N. Charter—provides the organizational framework and governing procedures for cases brought before the ICJ.

Under Article 94(1) of the U.N. Charter, "each Member of the United Nations undertakes to comply with the decision of the ICJ in any case to which it is a party." The ICJ's jurisdiction in any particular case, however, is dependent upon the consent of the parties(基于各成员国的同意). The ICJ Statute delineates (叙述,描写) two ways in which a nation may consent to ICJ jurisdiction: It may consent generally to jurisdiction on any question arising under a treaty or general international law, or it may consent specifically to jurisdiction over a particular category of cases or disputes pursuant to a separate treaty. The United States originally consented to the general jurisdiction of the ICJ when it filed a declaration recognizing compulsory jurisdiction under Art. 36(2) in 1946. The United States withdrew from general ICJ jurisdiction in 1985. By ratifying(批准,许可) the Optional Protocol to the Vienna Convention, the United States consented to the specific jurisdiction of the ICJ with respect to claims arising out of the ICJ's judgment in *Avena*, the United State gave notice of withdrawal from the Optional Protocol to the Vienna Convention.

B

Petitioner José Ernesto Medellín, a Mexican national, has lived in the United States since preschool. A member of the "Black and Whites" gang, Medellín was convicted of capital murder and sentenced to death in Texas for the gang rape(轮奸,几个袭击者对同一受害者进行连续强奸) and brutal murders of two Houston teenagers.

On June 24, 1993, 14-year-old Jennifer Ertman and 16year-old Elizabeth Pena were walking home when they encountered Medellín and several fellow gang members. Medellín attempted to engage Elizabeth in conversation. When she tried to run, petitioner threw her to the ground. Jennifer was grabbed by other gang members when she, in response to her friend's cries, ran back to help. The gang members raped both girls for over an hour. Then, to prevent their victims from identifying them, Medellín and his fellow gang members murdered the girls and discarded their bodies in a wooded area(抛尸丛林). Medellín was personally responsible for strangling(扼死,勒死,绞死) at least one of the girls with her own shoelace.

Medellín was arrested at approximately 4 a.m. on June 29, 1993. A few hours later, between 5:54 and 7:23 a.m., Medellín was given Miranda warnings; he then signed a written waiver(放弃,弃权;弃权声明书) and gave a detailed written confession(供述). Local law enforcement officers did not, however, inform Medellín of his Vienna Convention right to notify the Mexican consulate of his detention. Medellín was convicted of capital murder and sentenced to death; his conviction and sentence were affirmed on appeal.

Medellín first raised his Vienna Convention claim in his first application for state post conviction relief. The state trial court(一审法院) held that the claim was procedurally defaulted (欠缺,缺乏) because Medellín had failed to raise it at trial or on direct review. The trial court also rejected the Vienna Convention claim on the merits (案件的实质内容), finding that Medellín had "failed to show that any non-notification of the Mexican authorities impacted on the validity of his conviction or punishment."

Medellín then filed a habeas petition in Federal District Court. The District Court denied relief, holding that Medellín's Vienna Convention claim was procedurally defaulted and that Medellín had failed to show prejudice arising from the Vienna Convention violation.

While Medellín's application for a certificate of appealability was pending in the Fifth Circuit, the ICJ issued its decision in *Avena*. The ICJ held that the United States had violated Article 36(1)(b) of the Vienna Convention by failing to inform the 51 named Mexican nationals, including Medellín, of their Vienna Convention rights. In the ICJ's determination, the United States was obligated "to provide, by means of its own choosing, review and reconsideration of the convictions and sentences of the affected Mexican nationals." The ICJ indicated that such review was required without regard to state procedural default rules.

The Fifth Circuit denied a certificate of appealability. The court concluded that the Vienna Convention did not confer individually enforceable rights. The court further ruled that it was in any event bound by this Court's decision in *Breard v. Greene* (1998) (per curiam), which held that Vienna Convention claims are subject to procedural default rules, rather than by the ICJ's contrary decision in *Avena*.

This Court granted certiorari. Before we heard oral argument, however, President George W. Bush issued his Memorandum to the United States Attorney General(致美国总检察长的备忘录), providing:

I have determined, pursuant to the authority vested in me as President by the Constitution and the laws of the United States of America, that the United States will discharge its international obligations under the decision of the International Court of Justice in *Avena*, by having State courts give effect to the decision in accordance with general principles of comity(国际礼让原则) in cases filed by the 51 Mexican nationals addressed in that decision.

Medellín, relying on the President's Memorandum and the ICJ's decision in *Avena*, filed a second application for habeas relief in state court. Because the state-court proceedings might have provided Medellín with the review and reconsideration he requested, and because his claim for federal relief might otherwise have been barred, we dismissed his petition for certiorari as improvidently granted.

The Texas Court of Criminal Appeals subsequently dismissed Medellín's second state habeas application as an abuse of the writ. In the court's view, neither the Avena decision nor the President's Memorandum was "binding federal law" that could displace the State's limitations on the filing of successive habeas applications. We again granted certiorari.

II

Medellín first contends that the ICJ's judgment in Avena constitutes a "binding" obligation on the state and federal courts of the United States. He argues that "by virtue of the Supremacy Clause, the treaties requiring compliance with the Avena judgment are already the 'Law of the Land' by which all state and federal courts in this country are 'bound.'" Accordingly, Medellín argues, Avena is a binding federal rule of decision that pre-empts contrary state limitations on successive habeas petitions.

No one disputes that the Avena decision—a decision that flows from the treaties through which the United States submitted to ICJ jurisdiction with respect to Vienna Convention disputes—constitutes an international law obligation on the part of the United States. But not all international law obligations automatically constitute binding federal law enforceable in United States courts. The question we confront here is whether the Avena judgment has automatic domestic legal effect such that the judgment of its own force applies in state and federal courts.

This Court has long recognized the distinction between treaties that automatically have effect as domestic law, and those that—while they constitute international law commitments—do not by themselves function as binding federal law. The distinction was well explained by Chief Justice Marshall's opinion in Foster v. Neilson (1829), overruled on other grounds, United States v. Percheman (1833), which held that a treaty is "equivalent to an act of the legislature," and hence self-executing, when it "operates of itself without the aid of any legislative provision." When, in contrast, "treaty stipulations are not self-executing they can only be enforced pursuant to legislation to carry them into effect." In sum, while treaties "may comprise international commitments... they are not domestic law unless Congress has either enacted implementing statutes or the treaty itself conveys an intention that it be 'self-executing' and is ratified on these terms."

A treaty is, of course, "primarily a compact between independent nations." It ordinarily "depends for the enforcement of its provisions on the interest and the honor of the governments which are parties to it." "If these interests fail, its infraction becomes the subject of international negotiations and reclamations... It is obvious that with all this the judicial courts have nothing to do and can give no redress." Only "if the treaty contains stipulations which are self-executing, that is, require no legislation to make them operative, will they have the force and effect of a legislative enactment."

Medellín and his amici(法庭之友) nonetheless contend that the Optional Protocol, United Nations Charter, and ICJ Statute supply the "relevant obligation" to give the Avena judgment binding effect in the domestic courts of the United States. Because none of these treaty sources creates binding federal law in the absence of implementing legislation, and because it is uncontested that no such legislation exists, we conclude that the Avena judgment is not automatically binding domestic law.

A

The interpretation of a treaty(条约的解释), like the interpretation of a statute, begins with its text. Because a treaty ratified by the United States is "an agreement among sovereign powers," we have also considered as "aids to its interpretation" the negotiation and drafting history of the treaty as well as "the postratification understanding" of signatory nations(签署国,签字国).

As a signatory to the Optional Protocol, the United States agreed to submit disputes arising out of the Vienna Convention to the ICJ. The Protocol provides: "Disputes arising out of the interpretation or application of the Vienna Convention shall lie within the compulsory jurisdiction of the International Court of Justice." Of course, submitting to jurisdiction(提交国际法院管辖) and agreeing to be bound(受国际法院判决约束) are two different things. A party could, for example, agree to compulsory nonbinding arbitration. Such an agreement would require the party to appear before the arbitral tribunal without obligating the party to treat the tribunal's decision as binding.

The most natural reading of the Optional Protocol is as a bare grant of jurisdiction. It provides only that "disputes arising out of the interpretation or application of the Vienna Convention shall lie within the compulsory jurisdiction of the International Court of Justice" and "may accordingly be brought before the ICJ... by any party to the dispute being a Party to the present Protocol." The Protocol says nothing about the effect of an ICJ decision and does not itself commit signatories to comply with an ICJ judgment. The Protocol is similarly silent as to any enforcement mechanism(履行/执行机制).

The obligation on the part of signatory nations to comply with ICJ judgments derives not from the Optional Protocol, but rather from Article 94 of the United Nations Charter—the provision that specifically addresses the effect of ICJ decisions. Article 94(1) provides that "each Member of the United Nations undertakes(承诺)to comply with the decision of the ICJ in any case to which it is a party." The Executive Branch contends that the phrase "undertakes to comply" is not "an acknowledgement that an ICJ decision will have immediate legal effect in the courts of U. N. members," but rather "a commitment on the part of U. N. Members to take future action through their political branches to comply with an ICJ decision."

We agree with this construction of Article 94. The Article is not a directive to domestic courts. It does not provide that the United States "shall" or "must" comply with an ICJ decision, nor indicate that the Senate that ratified the U. N. Charter intended to vest ICJ decisions with immediate legal effect in domestic courts. Instead, "the words of Article 94…call upon governments to take certain action." In other words, the U. N. Charter reads like "a compact between independent nations" that "depends for the enforcement of its provisions on the interest and the honor of the governments which are parties to it."

The remainder of Article 94 confirms that the U. N. Charter does not contemplate(期待,预期;企图,打算) the automatic enforceability(自动履行) of ICJ decisions in domestic courts. Article 94(2)—the enforcement provision—provides the sole remedy for noncompliance: referral to the United Nations Security Council by an aggrieved state.

The U. N. Charter's provision of an express diplomatic—that is, non judicial—remedy is itself evidence that ICJ judgments were not meant to be enforceable in domestic courts. And even this "quintessentially international remedy," is not absolute. First, the Security Council(安理会) must "deem necessary" the issuance of a recommendation or measure to effectuate the judgment. Second, as the President and Senate were undoubtedly aware in subscribing to the U. N. Charter and Optional Protocol, the United States retained the unqualified right to exercise its veto of any Security Council resolution.

This was the understanding of the Executive Branch(行政机关) when the President agreed to the U. N. Charter and the declaration accepting general compulsory ICJ jurisdiction.

If ICJ judgments were instead regarded as automatically enforceable domestic law, they would be immediately and directly binding on state and federal courts pursuant to the Supremacy Clause. Mexico or the ICJ would have no need to proceed to the Security Council to enforce the judgment in this case. Noncompliance with an ICJ judgment through exercise of the Security Council veto—always regarded as an option by the Executive and ratifying Senate during and after consideration of the U. N. Charter, Optional Protocol, and ICJ Statute—would no longer be a viable alternative. There would be nothing to veto. In light of the U. N. Charter's remedial scheme, there is no reason to believe that the President and Senate signed up for such a result.

In sum, Medellín's view that ICJ decisions are automatically enforceable as domestic law is fatally undermined by the enforcement structure established by Article 94. His construction would eliminate the option of noncompliance contemplated by Article 94(2), undermining the ability of the political branches to determine whether and how to comply with an ICJ judgment. Those sensitive foreign policy decisions would instead be transferred to state and federal courts charged with applying an ICJ judgment directly as domestic law. And those courts would not be empowered to decide whether to comply with the judgment—again, always regarded as an option by the political branches—any more than courts may consider whether to comply with any other species of domestic law. This result would be particularly anomalous in light of the principle that "the conduct of the foreign relations of our Government is committed by the Constitution to the Executive and Legislative—'the political'—Departments."

The ICJ Statute, incorporated into the U. N. Charter, provides further evidence that the ICJ's judgment in Avena does not automatically constitute federal law judicially enforceable in United States courts. To begin with, the ICJ's "principal purpose" is said to be to "arbitrate particular disputes between national governments." More important, Article 59 of the statute provides that "the decision of the ICJ has no binding force except between the parties and in respect of that particular case." The dissent does not explain how Medellín, an individual, can be a party to the ICJ proceeding.

Medellín argues that because the Avena case involves him, it is clear that he—and the 50 other Mexican nationals named in the Avena decision—should be regarded as parties to the Avena judgment. But cases before the ICJ are often precipitated(拼命催促,促成,促使危机等早现；使突然发生) by disputes involving particular persons or entities, disputes that a nation elects to take up as its own.

It is, moreover, well settled that the United States' interpretation of a treaty "is entitled to great weight." The Executive Branch has unfailingly adhered to its view that the relevant treaties do not create domestically enforceable federal law.

The pertinent international agreements, therefore, do not provide for implementation of ICJ judgments through direct enforcement in domestic courts, and "where a treaty does not provide a particular remedy, either expressly or implicitly, it is not for the federal courts to impose one on the States through lawmaking of their own."

B

The dissent faults our analysis because it "looks for the wrong thing (explicit textual expression about self-execution) (明确的有关自动履行的文本表达) using the wrong standard (clarity) in the wrong place (the treaty language)." Given our obligation to interpret treaty provisions to determine whether they are self-executing, we have to confess that we do think it rather important to look to the treaty language to see what it has to say about the issue. That is after all what the Senate looks to in deciding whether to approve the treaty.

The interpretive approach employed by the Court today—resorting to the text—is hardly novel. In two early cases involving an 1819 land-grant treaty between Spain and the United States, Chief Justice Marshall found the language of the treaty dispositive. In Foster, after distinguishing between self-executing treaties (those "equivalent to an act of the legislature") and non-self-executing treaties (those "the legislature must execute"), Chief Justice Marshall held that the 1819 treaty was non-self-executing. Four years later, the Supreme Court considered another claim under the same treaty, but concluded that the treaty was self-executing. The reason was not because the treaty was sometimes self-executing and sometimes not, but because "the language of" the Spanish translation (brought to the Court's attention for the first time) indicated the parties' intent to ratify and confirm the land-grant "by force of the instrument itself."

As against this time-honored textual approach, the dissent proposes a multifactor, judgment-by-judgment analysis that would "jettison(抛弃,放弃)relative predictability for the open-ended rough-and-tumble(混战，混乱，战斗,漫无计划的生活；adj. 乱七八糟的,混乱的,杂乱的,莽撞的) of factors." The dissent's novel approach to deciding which (or, more accurately, when) treaties give rise to directly enforceable federal law is arrestingly indeterminate. Treaty language is barely probative(证明的，作证据用的). ("The absence or presence of language in a treaty about a provision's self-execution proves nothing at all"). Determining whether treaties themselves create federal law is sometimes committed to the political branches(委托给政府机关完成) and sometimes to the judiciary. Of those committed to the judiciary, the courts pick and choose which shall be binding United States law—trumping(胜过；捏造)not only state but other federal law as well—and which shall not. They do this on the basis of a multifactor, "context-specific" inquiry. Even then, the same treaty sometimes gives rise to United States law and sometimes does not, again depending on an ad hoc judicial assessment.

Our Framers(制宪者)established a careful set of procedures that must be followed before federal law can be created under the Constitution—vesting that decision in the political branches, subject to checks and balances(制衡,制约与平衡). They also recognized that treaties could create federal law, but again through the political branches, with the President making the treaty and the Senate approving it. The dissent's understanding of the treaty route, depending on an ad hoc judgment of the judiciary without looking to the treaty language—the very language negotiated by the President and approved by the Senate—cannot readily be ascribed to those same Framers.

The dissent's approach risks the United States' involvement in international agreements. It is hard to believe that the United States would enter into treaties(缔结条约)that are sometimes enforceable and sometimes not. Such a treaty would be the equivalent of writing a blank check to the judiciary(给司法机关开空白支票). Senators could never be quite sure what the treaties on which they were voting meant. Only a judge could say for sure and only at some future date. This uncertainty could hobble the United States' efforts to negotiate and sign international agreements.

In this case, the dissent—for a grab bag of no less than seven reasons—would tell us that this particular ICJ judgment is federal law. That is no sort of guidance. Nor is it any answer to say that the federal courts will diligently police international agreements and enforce the decisions of international tribunals only when they should be enforced. The point of a non-self executing treaty is that it "addresses itself to the political, not the judicial department; and the legislature must execute the contract before it can become a rule for the Court." The dissent's contrary approach would assign to the courts—not the political branches—the primary role in deciding when and how international agreements will be enforced. To read a treaty so that it sometimes has the effect of domestic law and sometimes does not is tantamount to vesting with the judiciary the power not only to interpret but also to create the law.

C

Our conclusion that Avena does not by itself constitute binding federal law is confirmed by the "postratification understanding" of signatory nations. There are currently 47 nations that are parties to the Optional Protocol and 171 nations that are parties to the Vienna Convention. Yet neither Medellín nor his amici have identified a single nation that treats ICJ judgments as binding in domestic courts. In determining that the Vienna Convention did not require certain relief in United States courts in *Sanchez-Llamas*, we found it pertinent that the requested relief would not be available under the treaty in any other signatory country. So too here the lack of any basis for supposing that any other country would treat ICJ judgments as directly enforceable as a matter of its domestic law strongly suggests that the treaty should not be so viewed in our courts.

Our conclusion is further supported by general principles of interpretation(法律解释的一般规则). To begin with, we reiterated in *Sanchez-Llamas* what we held in *Breard*, that "'absent a clear and express statement to the contrary, the procedural rules of the forum State govern the implementation of the treaty in that State.'" Given that ICJ judgments may interfere with state procedural rules, one would expect the ratifying parties to the relevant treaties to have clearly stated their intent to give those judgments domestic effect, if they had so intended. Here there is no statement in the Optional Protocol, the U.N. Charter, or the ICJ Statute that supports the notion that ICJ judgments displace state procedural rules.

Moreover, the consequences of Medellín's argument give pause. An ICJ judgment, the argument goes, is not only binding domestic law but is also unassailable(无懈可击,没有争论/批评余地). As a result, neither Texas nor this Court may look behind a judgment and quarrel with its reasoning or result. (We already know, from *Sanchez-Llamas*, that this Court disagrees with both the reasoning and result in Avena.) Medellín's interpretation would allow ICJ judgments to override(蔑视,藐视法规;制服,压倒;废弃;推翻决议)otherwise binding state law; there is nothing in his logic that would exempt contrary federal law from the same fate. And there is nothing to prevent the ICJ from ordering state courts to annul criminal convictions and sentences, for any reason deemed sufficient by the ICJ. Indeed, that is precisely the relief Mexico requested.

Even the dissent flinches at(退缩,畏缩)reading the relevant treaties to give rise to self-executing ICJ judgments in all cases. It admits that "Congress is unlikely to authorize automatic judicial enforceability of all ICJ judgments, for that could include some politically sensitive judgments and others better suited for enforcement by other branches." Our point precisely. But the lesson to draw from that insight is hardly that the judiciary should decide which judgments are politically sensitive and which are not.

In short, and as we observed in *Sanchez-Llamas*, "nothing in the structure or purpose of the ICJ suggests that its interpretations were intended to be conclusive on our courts." Given that holding, it is difficult to see how that same structure and purpose can establish, as Medellín argues, that judgments of the ICJ nonetheless were intended to be conclusive on our courts. A judgment is binding only if there is a rule of law that makes it so. And the question whether ICJ judgments can bind domestic courts depends upon the same analysis undertaken in *Sanchez-Llamas* and set forth above.

Our prior decisions identified by the dissent as holding a number of treaties to be self-executing, stand only for the unremarkable proposition that some international agreements are self-executing and others are not. It is well settled that the "interpretation of a treaty... must, of course, begin with the language of the Treaty itself." As a result, we have held treaties to be self-executing when the textual provisions indicate that the President and Senate intended for the agreement to have domestic effect.

Medellín and the dissent cite *Comegys v. Vasse* (1828), for the proposition that the judgments of international tribunals are automatically binding on domestic courts. That case, of course, involved a different treaty than the ones at issue here; it stands only for the modest principle that the terms of a treaty control the outcome of a case. We do not suggest that treaties can never afford binding domestic effect to international tribunal judgments—only that the U. N. Charter, the Optional Protocol, and the ICJ Statute do not do so. And whether the treaties underlying a judgment are self-executing so that the judgment is directly enforceable as domestic law in our courts is, of course, a matter for this Court to decide.

D

Our holding does not call into question the ordinary enforcement of foreign judgments or international arbitral agreements. Indeed, we agree with Medellín that, as a general matter, "an agreement to abide by the result" of an international adjudication—or what he really means, an agreement to give the result of such adjudication domestic legal effect—can be a treaty obligation like any other, so long as the agreement is consistent with the Constitution. The point is that the particular treaty obligations on which Medellín relies do not of their own force create domestic law.

The dissent worries that our decision casts doubt on some 70-odd treaties under which the United States has agreed to submit disputes to the ICJ according to "roughly similar" provisions. Again, under our established precedent, some treaties are self-executing and some are not, depending on the treaty. That the judgment of an international tribunal might not automatically become domestic law hardly means the underlying treaty is "useless." Such judgments would still constitute international obligations, the proper subject of political and diplomatic negotiations. And Congress could elect to give them wholesale effect (rather than the judgment-by-judgment approach hypothesized by the dissent) through implementing legislation, as it regularly has.

Further, that an ICJ judgment may not be automatically enforceable in domestic courts does not mean the particular underlying treaty is not. Indeed, we have held that a number of the "Friendship, Commerce, and Navigation" Treaties(友好通商条约) cited by the dissent, are self-executing—based on "the language of these Treaties." In *Kolovrat v. Oregon* (1961), for example, the Court found that Yugoslavian claimants denied inheritance under Oregon law were entitled to inherit personal property pursuant to an 1881 Treaty of Friendship, Navigation, and Commerce between the United States and Serbia.

Contrary to the dissent's suggestion, neither our approach nor our cases require that a treaty provide for self-execution in so many talismanic words; that is a caricature(false impression) of the Court's opinion. Our cases simply require courts to decide whether a treaty's terms reflect a determination by the President who negotiated it and the Senate that confirmed it that the treaty has domestic effect.

In addition, Congress is up to the task of implementing non-self-executing treaties, even those involving complex commercial disputes. The judgments of a number of international tribunals enjoy a different status because of implementing legislation enacted by Congress.

Further, Medellín frames his argument as though giving the Avena judgment binding effect in domestic courts simply conforms to the proposition that domestic courts generally give effect to foreign judgments. But Medellín does not ask us to enforce a foreign-court judgment settling a typical commercial or property dispute. Rather, Medellín argues that the Avena judgment has the effect of enjoining(命令，吩咐；告诫；责成) the operation of state law. What is more, on Medellín's view, the judgment would force the State to take action to "review and reconsider" his case. The general rule, however, is that judgments of foreign courts awarding injunctive relief, even as to private parties, let alone sovereign States, "are not generally entitled to enforcement."

In sum, while the ICJ's judgment in Avena creates an international law obligation on the part of the United States, it does not of its own force constitute binding federal law that pre-empts state restrictions on the filing of successive habeas petitions. As we noted in *Sanchez-Llamas*, a contrary conclusion would be extraordinary, given that basic rights guaranteed by our own Constitution do not have the effect of displacing state procedural rules. Nothing in the text, background, negotiating and drafting history, or practice among signatory nations suggests that the President or Senate intended the improbable result of giving the judgments of an international tribunal a higher status than that enjoyed by "many of our most fundamental constitutional protections."

Ⅲ

Medellín next argues that the ICJ's judgment in Avena is binding on state courts by virtue of the President's February 28, 2005 Memorandum. The United States contends that while the Avena judgment does not of its own force require domestic courts to set aside ordinary rules of procedural default, that judgment became the law of the land with precisely that effect pursuant to the President's Memorandum and his power "to establish binding rules of decision that preempt contrary state law." Accordingly, we must decide whether the President's declaration alters our conclusion that the Avena judgment is not a rule of domestic law binding in state and federal courts.

A

The United States maintains that the President's constitutional role "uniquely qualifies" him to resolve the sensitive foreign policy decisions that bear on compliance with an ICJ decision and "to do so expeditiously." We do not question these propositions. In this case, the President seeks to vindicate United States interests in ensuring the reciprocal observance of the Vienna Convention, protecting relations with foreign governments, and demonstrating commitment to the role of international law. These interests are plainly compelling.

Such considerations, however, do not allow us to set aside first principles. The President's authority to act, as with the exercise of any governmental power, "must stem either from an act of Congress or from the Constitution itself."

Justice Jackson's familiar tripartite scheme provides the accepted framework for evaluating executive action in this area. First, "when the President acts pursuant to an express or implied authorization of Congress, his authority is at its maximum, for it includes all that he possesses in his own right plus all that Congress can delegate." Second, "when the President acts in absence of either a congressional grant or denial of authority, he can only rely upon his own independent powers, but there is a zone of twilight in which he and Congress may have concurrent authority, or in which its distribution is uncertain." In this circumstance, Presidential authority can derive support from "congressional inertia(不活动,不活泼,迟钝,惰性), indifference or quiescence(默许)." Finally, "when the President takes measures incompatible with the expressed or implied will of Congress, his power is at its lowest ebb," and the Court can sustain his actions "only by disabling the Congress from acting upon the subject."

B

The United States marshals(引,领,带,引导)two principal arguments in favor of the President's authority "to establish binding rules of decision that preempt contrary state law." The Solicitor General first argues that the relevant treaties give the President the authority to implement the Avena judgment and that Congress has acquiesced in the exercise of such authority. The United States also relies upon an "independent" international dispute-resolution power wholly apart from the asserted authority based on the pertinent treaties. Medellín adds the additional argument that the President's Memorandum is a valid exercise of his power to take care that the laws be faithfully executed.

1

The United States maintains that the President's Memorandum is authorized by the Optional Protocol and the U. N. Charter. That is, because the relevant treaties "create an obligation to comply with Avena," they "implicitly give the President authority to implement that treaty-based obligation." As a result, the President's Memorandum is well grounded in the first category of the Youngstown framework.

We disagree. The President has an array of political and diplomatic means available to enforce international obligations, but unilaterally(单方面地) converting a non-self executing treaty into a self-executing one is not among them. The responsibility for transforming an international obligation arising from a non-self-executing treaty into domestic law falls to Congress. As this Court has explained, when treaty stipulations are "not self-executing they can only be enforced pursuant to legislation to carry them into effect." Moreover, "until such act shall be passed, the Court is not at liberty to disregard the existing laws on the subject."

The requirement that Congress, rather than the President, implement a non-self-executing treaty derives from the text of the Constitution, which divides the treaty-making power between the President and the Senate. The Constitution vests the President with the authority to "make" a treaty. If the Executive determines that a treaty should have domestic effect of its own force, that determination may be implemented "in making" the treaty, by ensuring that it contains language plainly providing for domestic enforceability. If the treaty is to be self-executing in this respect, the Senate must consent to the treaty by the requisite two-thirds vote, consistent with all other constitutional restraints.

Once a treaty is ratified without provisions clearly according it domestic effect, however, whether the treaty will ever have such effect is governed by the fundamental constitutional principle that "'the power to make the necessary laws is in Congress; the power to execute in the President.'" As already noted, the terms of a non-self-executing treaty can become domestic law only in the same way as any other law—through passage of legislation by both Houses of Congress, combined with either the President's signature or a congressional override of a Presidential veto. Indeed, "the President's power to see that the laws are faithfully executed refutes the idea that he is to be a lawmaker."

A non-self-executing treaty, by definition, is one that was ratified with the understanding that it is not to have domestic effect of its own force. That understanding precludes the assertion that Congress has implicitly authorized the President—acting on his own—to achieve precisely the same result. We therefore conclude, given the absence of congressional legislation, that the non-self executing treaties at issue here did not "expressly or impliedly" vest the President with the unilateral authority to make them self-executing. Accordingly, the President's Memorandum does not fall within the first category of the Youngstown framework.

Indeed, the preceding discussion should make clear that the non-self-executing character of the relevant treaties not only refutes the notion that the ratifying parties vested the President with the authority to unilaterally make treaty obligations binding on domestic courts, but also implicitly prohibits him from doing so. When the President asserts the power to "enforce" a non-self executing treaty by unilaterally creating domestic law, he acts in conflict with the implicit understanding of the ratifying Senate. His assertion of authority, insofar as it is based on the pertinent non-self-executing treaties, is therefore within Justice Jackson's third category, not the first or even the second.

Each of the two means described above for giving domestic effect to an international treaty obligation under the

Constitution—for making law—requires joint action by the Executive and Legislative Branches: The Senate can ratify a self-executing treaty "made" by the Executive, or, if the ratified treaty is not self-executing, Congress can enact implementing legislation approved by the President. It should not be surprising that our Constitution does not contemplate vesting such power in the Executive alone. As Madison explained in The Federalist No. 47, under our constitutional system of checks and balances, "the magistrate(君主,元首,治安法院法官) in whom the whole executive power resides cannot of himself make a law." That would, however, seem an apt description of the asserted executive authority unilaterally to give the effect of domestic law to obligations under a non-self executing treaty.

The United States nonetheless maintains that the President's Memorandum should be given effect as domestic law because "this case involves a valid Presidential action in the context of Congressional 'acquiescence'." Under the Youngstown tripartite framework, congressional acquiescence is pertinent when the President's action falls within the second category—that is, when he "acts in absence of either a congressional grant or denial of authority." Here, however, as we have explained, the President's effort to accord domestic effect to the Avena judgment does not meet that prerequisite.

In any event, even if we were persuaded that congressional acquiescence could support the President's asserted authority to create domestic law pursuant to a non-self executing treaty, such acquiescence does not exist here. The United States first locates congressional acquiescence in Congress's failure to act following the President's resolution of prior ICJ controversies. A review of the Executive's actions in those prior cases, however, cannot support the claim that Congress acquiesced in this particular exercise of Presidential authority, for none of them remotely involved transforming an international obligation into domestic law and thereby displacing state law.

The United States also directs us to the President's "related" statutory responsibilities and to his "established role" in litigating foreign policy concerns as support for the President's asserted authority to give the ICJ's decision in Avena the force of domestic law. Congress has indeed authorized the President to represent the United States before the United Nations, the ICJ, and the Security Council, but the authority of the President to represent the United States before such bodies speaks to the President's international responsibilities, not any unilateral authority to create domestic law. The authority expressly conferred by Congress in the international realm cannot be said to "invite" the Presidential action at issue here. At bottom, none of the sources of authority identified by the United States supports the President's claim that Congress has acquiesced in his asserted power to establish on his own federal law or to override state law.

None of this is to say, however, that the combination of a non-self-executing treaty and the lack of implementing legislation precludes the President from acting to comply with an international treaty obligation. It is only to say that the Executive cannot unilaterally execute a non-self executing treaty by giving it domestic effect. That is, the non-self-executing character of a treaty constrains the President's ability to comply with treaty commitments by unilaterally making the treaty binding on domestic courts. The President may comply with the treaty's obligations by some other means, so long as they are consistent with the Constitution. But he may not rely upon a non-self executing treaty to "establish binding rules of decision that preempt contrary state law."

2

We thus turn to the United States' claim that—independent of the United States' treaty obligations—the Memorandum is a valid exercise of the President's foreign affairs authority to resolve claims disputes with foreign nations. The United States relies on a series of cases in which this Court has upheld the authority of the President to settle foreign claims pursuant to an executive agreement. In these cases this Court has explained that, if pervasive enough, a history of congressional acquiescence can be treated as a "gloss(解释)on 'Executive Power' vested in the President by §1 of Art. II."

This argument is of a different nature than the one rejected above. Rather than relying on the United States' treaty obligations, the President relies on an independent source of authority in ordering Texas to put aside its procedural bar to successive habeas petitions. Nevertheless, we find that our claims-settlement cases do not support the authority that the President asserts in this case.

The claims-settlement cases involve a narrow set of circumstances: the making of executive agreements to settle civil claims between American citizens and foreign governments or foreign nationals. They are based on the view that "a systematic, unbroken, executive practice, long pursued to the knowledge of the Congress and never before questioned," can "raise a presumption that the action had been taken in pursuance of its consent." As this Court explained in *Garamendi*,

"Making executive agreements to settle claims of American nationals against foreign governments is a particularly longstanding practice... Given the fact that the practice goes back over 200 years, and has received congressional acquiescence throughout its history, the conclusion that the President's control of foreign relations includes the settlement of claims is indisputable."

Even still, the limitations on this source of executive power are clearly set forth and the Court has been careful to note that "past practice does not, by itself, create power."

The President's Memorandum is not supported by a "particularly longstanding practice" of congressional acquiescence, but rather is what the United States itself has described as "unprecedented action". Indeed, the Government has not identified a single instance in which the President has attempted (or Congress has acquiesced in) a Presidential directive issued to state courts, much less one that reaches deep into the heart of the State's police powers and compels state courts to reopen final criminal judgments and set aside neutrally applicable state laws. The Executive's narrow and strictly limited authority to settle international claims disputes pursuant to an executive agreement cannot stretch so far as to support the current Presidential Memorandum.

3

Medellín argues that the President's Memorandum is a valid exercise of his "Take Care" power. The United States, however, does not rely upon the President's responsibility to "take Care that the Laws be faithfully executed." We think this a wise concession(让步, 迁就; 让与; 政府的核准, 许可, 特许; 特许权; 特许使用的场地). This authority allows the President to execute the laws, not make them. For the reasons we have stated, the Avena judgment is not domestic law; accordingly, the President cannot rely on his Take Care powers here.

The judgment of the Texas Court of Criminal Appeals is affirmed.

It is so ordered.

Lesson Eighteen

Recent Developments in International Intellectual Property Litigation

> **Learning objectives**
>
> After learning the text and having done the exercises in this lesson, you will:
>
> —familiarize with knowledge of the nature and the development of International Intellectual Property Litigation;
>
> —acquire an appreciation of the vocabulary and grammar or syntax relevant to International Intellectual Property Litigation;
>
> —become aware of the information required in order to understand International Intellectual Property Litigation;
>
> —cultivate the practical abilities to put to use the language in the specific context;
>
> —be able to do some translation from Chinese to English and from English to Chinese.

Text

Recent Developments in International Intellectual Property Litigation

Introduction

Increased global exploitation of copyrighted works and trademarked products has forced courts and scholars to reconsider the apparent simplicity of choice of law① issues in intellectual proper-

---

① choice of law: 法律选择，在冲突法中，决定适用何种法律的问题。法院在决定应适用的准据法（applicable law）时，可依据不同的法律选择原则，例如：区分实体法和程序法原则、重力中心说原则、反致、适用法院地法原则、连结点聚集原则以及最密切联系原则等。

ty①cases. Notions of conceptually defined places of conduct governing an infringement action②become problematic when works are distributed, and allegedly infringing trademarks are used, on the internet. Where does "publication"③of a work occur when it is made available online? Everywhere? If a work can be accessed from the United States, has publication occurred in the United States? If a person uses an allegedly infringing mark④without authorization on a web site in France, but that site is accessible from the United States, where has the mark been used? These are vexing questions. The shift in the attitude of intellectual property law to conflicts questions is perhaps best captured by the title of a recent review of U.S. case law published in a European journal: in conflicts matters, intellectual property law has gone "from dodging the bullet to biting it." In this Part, I will outline some recent developments in international intellectual property irrigation, first in copyright law⑤, and second in trademark law⑥, that reflect this sentiment.

A. International Copyright Litigation

In 1998, in *Itar-Tass Russian News Agency v. Russian Kurier, Inc.*, the Court of Appeals for the Second Circuit offered one of the most detailed choice of law analyses seen in modern copyright cases. The court commented that "choice of law issues in international copyright cases have been largely ignored in the reported decisions and dealt with rather cursorily by most commentators," and noted (with some irony) that this dearth of treatment could be attributed to a perception among scholars that conflicts issues were "rarely troublesome" in copyright law. The Second Circuit thought otherwise and sought to develop a federal rule on choice of law in copyright cases.

The court rejected the conventional wisdom that public international law (and in particular, the national treatment principle) compelled any particular choice of law rule. After reviewing various options, the court applied a variation on the approach of the Second Restatement of Conflicts⑦, but gave primary weight in infringement matters to the lex loci delicti⑧. I have serious doubts about the cogency of the Second Circuit's approach, especially when pushed to the limits by digital uses, and have elsewhere advocated an approach using the development of substantive rules applicable to international copyright cases. Where a work is made available online, and courts

---

① intellectual property: (1) 知识产权,无体财产权的一种,它保护人的智慧创造的具有商业价值的产品。它主要包括商标权、版权和专利权,也包括商业秘密权、公开权、精神权利以及反不正当竞争权。简作(IP)。有时为了与下一含义相区别,亦写作(intellectual property rights)。(2) 知识产品,该术语亦指上述权利的保护对象,即人的智慧创造的、具有商业价值的产品。例如可以版权保护的作品、可以受到保护的商标、可以被授予专利的发明、商业秘密等。

② infringement action: 侵犯版权诉讼。

③ Publication: 出版,在版权法中,出版指向公众发行作品的复制件。同时,由于专利保护的发明创造须具有新颖性,所以已在出版物上公开的技术方案,一般不能再获得专利保护。在美国的普通法中,作品是否出版决定其版权是受州还是联邦的保护,但1976年《版权法》(Copyright Act)已取代了绝大部分普通法版权,所以出版在这方面的意义也被降低。

④ infringing mark: 侵权商标。

⑤ copyright law: 著作权法,copyright,版权,是就独创的文学、戏剧、音乐或美术作品而授予其作者的一组权利,包括对作品进行复制、表演与其他使用行为的专有权。

⑥ trademark law: 商标法,trademark,指产品的制造商或销售商用以表示产品来源、将其与他人的产品相区别的文字或图形标志。此为狭义的、亦是最常用的商标含义。在广义上,该词还可以泛指表示商品或服务来源的任何形式,包括产品商标、服务商标(service marks)、集体商标(collective marks)、证明商标(certification marks)、商号(trade names)和商品外观装潢(trade dress)。有时即以"mark"一词表示其广义。

⑦ The Second Restatement of Conflicts: 第二次冲突法重述。

⑧ lex loci delicti: 侵权行为地法。

treat accessibility in their country as publication, the *lex loci delicti* rule localizes the unitary act of uploading in too many disparate *loci delicti*. But, putting aside for present purposes the debate concerning the best copyright choice of law rule, the sudden recognition by courts that choice of law analysis in copyright litigation might require more substantial development than heretofore is noteworthy.

Before addressing the significance of increased attention to choice of law in copyright cases, however, a second development in recent international copyright litigation merits brief mention. As noted above, until recently, U. S. courts were extremely reluctant to adjudicate claims of infringement arising under foreign intellectual property laws. If U. S. law did not apply, the complaint was dismissed[①]. Many other countries adopted a similar approach to the (non-)application of foreign law.

This approach—using the binary switch of justiciability—precludes the development of a nuanced methodology designed to reconcile the competing claims of different national laws. Such a rule of self-abnegation[②] also forces intellectual property owners to pursue infringers serially in a large number of countries. Digital use of marks and copyrighted works has highlighted this inefficiency. It is not surprising therefore that in the past two years several courts, with the encouragement of the Second Circuit, have permitted actions alleging claims under several foreign copyright laws to proceed, although none of these cases has gone to trial. British courts have also reversed their historical reluctance and indicated a similar willingness.

At its most uncontroversial, the mere fact that national courts are now engaging in serious copyright choice of law analysis and that they are contemplating the application of foreign law requires us to know foreign law more intimately and thus enhances the need for comparative work. This is a relatively low-intensity kind of comparative work that arises from the mere willingness to accept the possibility of applying some law other than the lex fori[③]. It thus seems remarkably untaxing. Indeed, the task is not inherently comparative; it involves the mere supply of information to the courts. But translating information into knowledge, and thence into understanding, such that the information is properly understood and applied, is facilitated by exposure to comparative scholarship. Understanding foreign substantive law often requires a more generalized appreciation of foreign systems and methods that does not neatly correlate to the specialized division of substantive law[④].

To be sure, the routine application of foreign law itself arguably does not require such comparativist immersion (although the quality of the process by which lawyers supply, and courts apply, foreign law, would surely benefit). From a conflicts perspective, courts and scholars will now have to develop choice of law rules for copyright as they have done in the past for all sorts of torts. And those who think that the internet merely requires the further application of traditional tech-

---

① dismissed:驳回(起诉);(未经开庭审理而)终结诉讼。
② self-abnegation:为信仰或为他人而自欺欺人,克制,自我牺牲,克己。
③ lex fori:拉丁语,法院地法;诉讼地法;审判地法。在冲突法中,对于诉讼程序、证据规则和所采用的法律救济作出规定的诉讼所在地的法律。
④ substantive law:实体法。

Lesson Eighteen　Recent Developments in International Intellectual Property Litigation

niques devised for domestic problems can find ready analogies to the problem of digital publication, for example, in the single publication rule of defamation law①.

In fact, however, the possible analogy to multistate defamation merely highlights the difference between conflicts in the domestic multistate and transnational context, a difference that the internet brings into sharp focus and to which we need to attend. While state defamation law in the United States has substantial commonality, and has been given a unifying federal overlay by virtue of the constitutionalization of some aspects of the tort, there is a gulf between the defamation laws of such apparently similar societies as the United Kingdom and the United States. (Or at least U.S. courts who refuse to enforce U.K. libel②judgments appear to think so.) And any unifying overlay could only be international in nature, where no supreme adjudicative body exists. The ongoing tribulations of Yahoo before the French courts confirms that countries of similar economic development, but quite different historical circumstance, might reach fundamentally different conclusions on the appropriate balance between free speech rights and ensuring a climate of equality for its citizens. Transnational answers may more often require a much harder analytical tussle, and the reconciliation of competing values may need to be pursued in a quite different way.

These divides exist throughout the field of copyright, and not simply through the free speech concerns that are often implicated. There are fundamental philosophical differences on central matters of copyright protection throughout the world. Reconciling instrumentalist economic philosophies with personality-based notions of rights, for example, requires a real grasp of these different philosophies. Such reconciliations are not impossible, however, especially when attempted in the setting of concrete litigated disputes. And there are also some legislative arenas (a classical locus for the use of comparative scholarship) in which these efforts at compromise have borne fruit, including, most notably, in the EU (which includes countries with laws reflecting each of these different philosophies).

Although U.S. courts are largely resorting to existing choice of law methodologies to resolve international copyright conflicts, by either refining traditional connecting factors or suggesting variations on the Second Restatement, scholars have been more inventive. In addition to my own efforts to advocate substantive rules generated from an amalgam of national sources and international standards, Jane Ginsburg has argued for a more traditional waterfall of connecting factors, but all undergirded by the substantive standards found in international treaties. And cyber-enthusiasts have floated the notion of autonomous standards governing internet conduct.

---

① defamation law:诽谤法。Defamation,诬蔑;诽谤;中伤;损害(他人)名誉,故意以口头或书面方式散布不实之词以败坏他人声誉,或使公众对该人萌生有损其声誉的情绪或看法。

② libel:诽谤;书面诽谤;诽谤罪:恶意地以虚假的、内容不实的书面(文字、图画、符号等)形式公开诋毁和损害他人名声、人格、信誉的行为,其后果是使被侵害者遭受他人或公众愤恨、鄙视、嘲笑,并使其工作、社交和社会地位受损。符合上述任何情况的行为均属诽谤,一般可以侵权行为起诉,在普通法上,情节严重的可构成妨害社会治安的诽谤罪,以轻罪〔misdemeanor〕论处。但在现代美国,基于对言论自由的宪法性保护,诽谤已不再受到刑事追诉。一般地说,诽谤的构成条件有三:(1) 公开散布内容虚伪不实的信息,意在诋毁他人名誉;(2) 采用书面,包括文字、图画、摄影、电影、广播等持久性形式散布,从而扩大对受害者名誉的损害程度;(3) 主观上具有恶意,即明知内容不实而故意散布,或明知有内容不实的可能而不予详察即公开散布;如果内容虚伪且具有诋毁性质,即应理解为恶意,至于行为人动机如何并不重要。需注意的是,在英美法中,凡采用口头形式诽谤他人的称 slander,口头诽谤传播范围较小,只能以侵权行为起诉,尚不构成轻罪。

What each of these proposals has in common is a commitment to comparative analysis as part of the solution to (certain) copyright conflicts. The substantive law method that I have advocated in international copyright cases would require courts to consider international agreements and practices, national and regional laws, the norms of developing post-national groupings, and systemic conflicts values in fashioning an applicable substantive rule. Professor Ginsburg would require courts to determine whether the potentially applicable national copyright law is consistent with the norms found in the Berne Convention, the TRIPS Agreement and the WIPO Copyright Treaty.

At first blush, the notion of universal autonomous standards would in contrast appear to conclude, rather than re-energize, the comparativist task. This appearance is deceptive. The initial development of such rules should, of course, ideally proceed from detailed comparative analysis. But, even after the unified rules are formulated, the practical reality of current international relations is that certain matters will be reserved to, or dependent upon, national laws or rights. The supranational Community Trade Mark system operating within the EU, as well as the ICANN domain name dispute resolution policy discussed below, confirm this suspicion. Mediating between the unified non-national rules and the relevant remaining national rules—vertical choice of law analysis—will benefit greatly from comparativist insight.

These recent developments in international copyright litigation thus suggest the need for greater comparative thought. The adoption of proposals for reform currently pending would bolster this need. The similar willingness to adjudicate foreign copyright claims in Europe is partly a result of the provisions of the Brussels Convention on Jurisdiction and Enforcement of Judgments in Civil and Commercial Matters. The Brussels Convention is similar (but not identical) to the proposed Hague Convention on Jurisdiction and Judgments that is being considered by the Hague Conference on Private International Law. Some copyright owners would like to see the Brussels system extended more broadly in the belief that this would streamline international enforcement of national copyrights. It has thus attracted the attention of international intellectual property policymakers. The provisions addressing intellectual property have, however, proved controversial and some delegates to the Hague Conference would like to exclude intellectual property from the scope of the new convention.

Copyright claims appear likely to be governed by any Hague (or Hague-like) regime that ensues. The greatest opposition to the inclusion of intellectual property claims within the Hague system has arisen with respect to registered rights such as accorded under patent and trademark laws; many countries remain unwilling to permit foreign courts to review the administrative determinations made by their patent and trademark officials. Moreover, even if all intellectual property rights (including copyright) are excluded from the Hague Convention as it emerges from the negotiations, or no such treaty is concluded, scholars and international intellectual property organizations have been considering the possibility of a standalone treaty on jurisdiction and recognition of judgments in intellectual property cases.

This last proposal, a standalone treaty authored by Professors Rochelle Dreyfuss and Jane Ginsburg, was first discussed at a two-day forum organized by the World Intellectual Property Organization in Geneva in January 2001, immediately preceding a meeting of the delegates to the

Hague Conference. The draft of the Dreyfuss/Ginsburg proposal debated in Geneva would arguably implicate comparative work (and, in particular, comparative analysis of conflicts) even more extensively than the current draft of the Hague Convention. The negotiation process itself (and the process of preparing for possible implementation) forces participants to engage in comparative analysis of the content and merits of different approaches to jurisdiction and recognition and enforcement. But the draft of the Dreyfuss/Ginsburg proposal would include a ground for non-recognition of judgments not found in the Hague proposal, namely, the application by the rendering court of a law that is arbitrary or unreasonable. Of itself, this provision would require courts to engage in comparative assessment of the conflicts analysis of foreign courts. And this salutary effect is heightened by the inclusion of a standard for that assessment that includes the choice of law rule suggested by Professor Ginsburg (which may require reference to international treaties).

Indeed, either treaty will increase the need for comparative expertise in conflicts. Although, unlike the Brussels Convention, the Hague and Dreyfuss/Ginsburg systems would operate without any court with supreme jurisdiction over questions raised by the Convention, both seek to achieve uniformity by requiring national courts to interpret the Convention in light of its international character, the need for uniformity, and the case law of other contracting states. This appeal to what might be called "interpretive comity" establishes a bare set of "conflicts-influencing" considerations that, situated within a conflicts treaty, constitute a direct invitation to comparative analysis of conflicts methodology. The Hague Convention, or the Dreyfuss/Ginsburg proposal, would thus increase the already-developing need for comparative analysis of copyright law, of conflicts, and of legal systems generally, that recent developments in international copyright litigation have generated.

B. International Trademark Litigation

In the trademark context, the internet has caused immense problems of private international law. Because trademark rights are territorial in nature, different producers may own rights in the same mark for the same class of goods in different countries. Producer X may use the mark APPLE for a particular good in State A, and that mark may be separately used (and owned and registered) by Producer Y for the same goods in State B. Both parties may have legitimate, discrete national trademark rights that conflict only when one or both seek to operate in the international marketplace. Which of the different owners of legitimate national trademark rights in the word APPLE is entitled to ownership of the domain name registration apple.com (of which there can, under the current configuration of the internet, only be one registration)? And what remedies might either of these mark owners have against a third person, with no trademark rights in the mark APPLE, who in bad faith secures the domain name registration apple.com as a result of the first-come first-served philosophy underlying current domain name registration processes?

These problems have thus far been addressed largely through existing devices of trademark law and conflict of laws. An alternative solution has been developed to address a particular problem, namely the question of cybersquatting, which is loosely defined as the bad faith registration and use of a domain name consisting of or including a trademark of another in which the domain name registrant has no rights. When ICANN① approved registrars to allocate domain names in the leading generic top level domain names (such as. com, or. net), it imposed certain conditions. One was that the registrar require domain name registrants to agree in their registration application to resolve any complaints brought by a trademark owner before an ICANN approved dispute settlement provider. These complaints are resolved according to the Uniform Domain Name Dispute Resolution Policy (UDRP) promulgated by ICANN. The UDRP articulates the elements that a trademark owner must show in order to make out a claim. If the claim is sustained, the dispute settlement panelist may order that the domain name registration be transferred to the trademark owner.

Trademark owners, well pleased with this non-national form of resolving the conflict between their national rights and domain name registrants whose rights are not nationally rooted, would like to see the system expanded. And suggestions that the UDRP system might be adopted for other internet-based disputes can be found both in congressional hearings and in aspirational recitals in a recent EU Directive. The potential, and perhaps appropriate limits on the use, of UDRP-like systems as a means of resolving conflicts issues on the internet is worth sustained analysis. For present purposes, however, I focus only on the approach of the UDRP to applicable law. The Rules promulgated by ICANN to accompany the UDRP instruct dispute resolution panels to "decide a complaint on the basis of the statements and documents submitted and in accordance with the Policy, these Rules and any rules and principles of law that it deems applicable." The Policy and the Rules are skeletal. To where should panels look when additional guidance is required? This choice of law rule invites comparative analysis in at least three important respects.

The first opportunity for comparative analysis is presented by the need to develop or select an appropriate substantive rule. Some scholars have argued that the UDRP choice of law provision should not be regarded as an instruction to develop lex-mercatoria-like, substantive rules applicable to certain international disputes. And, to be sure, language in the travaux préparatoires to the UDRP suggests that in certain cases where a particular national interest predominates, national sources may be the appropriate basis for finding interpretive guidance. But nothing appears to preclude the development and application of autonomous standards drawn from any number of sources, national, international or any other, in appropriate circumstances. Indeed, the entire UDRP project is premised upon the development of substantive non-national rules so as to obviate the problems of disparate national laws and national rights operating in the context of a ubiquitous online environment.

A second role for comparative thought in the UDRP system is more closely linked to comparative conflicts scholarship. In an era when international or non-national rules assume greater importance, determining when to develop or apply a substantive international rule, and when to insist instead on the predominant claim of one prescriptive national source, will become crucial. This is a vertical choice of law, and is an analysis that will be greatly aided by comparative and historical

---

① ICANN:互联网名称与数字地址分配机构的简称,是总部设在美国加利福尼亚州的一个非营利性国际组织,在美国商务部的提议下于1998年10月成立的,负责互联网协议(IP)地址的空间分配、协议标识符的指派、通用顶级域名(GTLD)以及国家和地区顶级域名(CCTLD)系统的管理以及根服务器系统的管理。之所以由它管理全球顶级域名,是因为互联网的雏形源于美国国防部的一个项目,后来才被转为民用。

analysis. Guidance on the question of balancing centralized order and local autonomous rights can be found in numerous federal systems, including the increasingly developed jurisprudence of the European Court of Justice, and parallels the tension found in every international intellectual property agreement.

Comparison must always be informed, of course. Structurally, one might regard the contest between national and international norms and institutions as the natural successor to the contest between state and federal authority that occurred in federal systems when regional activity became more national in nature. But the current competition between national and international norms deviates from the most obvious examples of this parallel in one important way. How to resolve these new "local-federal" disputes will be determined without any federal political or legal structure, whether established by constitutional document or by treaty. The extent to which the applicable norms will derive from the broader community and institutions and the scope of their application will be determined in large part by the local institutions and local rules.

Finally, comparative awareness of other systems in which the substantive law method has been applied will also assist in the UDRP context. Should a panelist apply the best substantive rule? Are there still systemic or conflicts concerns that might over-ride preferred substantive results? But, here again, our inclination to compare must be informed. For example, the modern lex mercatoria found in international commercial arbitration may be only of limited use in the UDRP setting because it operates in a quite different context. In particular, it exists within a system where there is genuine party consent to the panels' terms of reference, and there is only a limited publication of opinions. In this regard, the UDRP is closer to a judicial system; involvement is not optional on the part of domain name registrants, and every decision is published, creating a systemic value of precedent and expectation that might not be present in other contexts.

Legal Terminology

1. property

该词可指财产或物(thing or things capable of ownership),也可指产权,即 ownership of a thing。总体说来,property 可分为 real property(不动产)和 personal property(动产)两大类。其中,personal property 又可分为 chattels real(土地附属动产)和 chattels personal(属人动产)。chattels real(土地附属动产,也称为 real chattels)指从土地或房屋等派生出的非永赁或自由保有土地权益(a real property interest that is less than freehold or fee),如土地租赁权或租借土地保有权等。chattels personal(属人动产,也称为 person chattels)则指有形动产和无形权利,如 patent 等,其又可分为 choses in possession(占有上的物)和 choses in action(诉讼上的物)两类。choses in action(诉讼上的物)指可以通过法律程序请求或强制实施的属人财产权利,如尚未征收的关税即可为诉讼上的物。

2. copyright

版权是就独创的文学、戏剧、音乐或美术作品而授予其作者的一组权利,包括对作品进行复制、表演与其他使用行为的专有权。根据(思想—表现)二分法(idea-expression dichotomy),版权并不保护抽象的思想(idea),而只是保护对思想的特定、具体的表现(expression)。而且,构成一个有效的有版权作品(copyrighted work),除了该表现必须具备独创性(originality)外,还应达到最低创作程度。在英美法上,版权是文艺复兴运动与印刷技术发展的产物。1556年,英国的书籍出版业公会(Stationers Company)根据特许权而享有书籍出版的垄断权,所有书籍均须经其登记官的同意与注册方得出版。1709年,英国一制定法承认作者享有印刷其作品的专有权利,已印刷作品的保护期为21年,未印刷作品之保护期为14年。这被认为是世界上第一部版权法,即《安娜女王法》(Statute of Anne)。英国版权法随时代发展而历经修改,逐步增加了受版权保护的作品范围与作者权限及保护期限。当前的英国版权法是1988年《版权、外观设计和专利法》(Copyright, Designs and Patents Act)。该法规定受版权保护的作品除文学、戏剧、音乐、美术作品外,还包括录音作品(sound recordings)、电影、广播、有线节目以及已出版版本的印刷排版设计(typographical arrangement)。版权的保护期一般为作者有生之年加死后50年。版权的内容包括对作品进行复制、发行、表演、公开展览、广播、改编等权利,而且,在该法中第一次增加规定了精神权利(moral rights)。在美国,国会于1790年仿照英国1709年版权法制定了第一部联邦的版权法。该法亦历经多次修订。最近的一次版权立法是在1976年10月,即《1976年版权法》(Copyright Act of 1976),该法于1978年1月1日生效。在此之前,美国存在着普通法保护与制定法保护两套版权保护体系,通常,普通法版权(common law copyright)保护出版前的作品,而出版后的作品则产生制定法上的版权(statutory copyright),受联邦版权法的保护。《1976年版权法》意在取消普通法版权而创设一套统一的版权保护体系。该法保护已被固定在有体载体上的所有表现(expression),故只要某一作品已被某种确定的方式记载下来,其作者的权利即受版权法保护。《1976年版权法》对版权的保护期限也为作者有生之年加死后50年。此外,为使其国内法符合加入《伯尔尼公约》(Berne Convention)的条件,美国又专门制定了《伯尔尼公约执行法》(Berne Convention Implementation Act)。在该法生效(1989年3月1日)之前,如果没有在发行的版本上适当标注版权标记,则该作品的版权可能被没收,但在该法生效之后,进行版权登记或标注版权标记不再是取得版权的前提条件。这是美国版权法在形式要件上的重大变更。

3. litigation, action, suit, proceedings 与 procedure

上述单词均有诉讼的含义。action, litigation 和 proceedings 都为一般术语,可指各种诉讼案件。Action 现在多指民事诉讼,如果要表示刑事诉讼则在此之前加 criminal 予以区别。litigation 尤指在普通法院,即"court of law"争辩的案件,是为实现法定权利或维持某种法律救济而实施的一种民事法律行为,为普通法上的诉讼,即 legal action。同时,litigation 还有诉讼程序的含义。传统英国法上,action 和 suit 之间的差异主要在于,action 指普通法法院的诉讼,其程序到法院判决(judgment)即终止;而 suit 则为衡平法法院的用语,其程序包括判决和执行(judgment and execution)。在美国则不存在此差别。Procedure 主要是指诉讼程序。

4. court of appeals 与 supreme court

在美国,court of appeals(在有些州也称为 court of appeal)可指联邦中级法院或州中级法院。如在加州和路易斯安那州,其指中级法院,这些州的高级法院称为 supreme court;而在哥伦比亚特区、马里兰和纽约州,court of appeal 是指州高级,即州最高法院,这些州的 supreme court 反而成了州的中级法院。在英国,court of appeal 是最高司法法院"Supreme Court of Judicature"的一个分院,译为"上诉法院"。

5. conflict of laws 与 private international law

均为国际法中的术语,指不同国家私法之间的冲突。前者多为普通法系国家采用,尤其是美国,除可以指国家见的法律冲突外,还可以用语指美国各州之间的法律冲突;后者最初主要用于大陆法系国家,后逐渐为普通法系国家普遍接受。

6. brand, trademark 与 trade name

均用作指商业、商品或服务的名称,但它们并非同义。差异在于 brand(品牌)主要指已经树立的,经常是著名的且用于广告的商品名称,其不是正式的法律用语,一般不具备法律上的排他权。Trademark(商标)为典型的法律术语,表示经登记注册之商标,具有排他权,其可以是词语或符号。Trade name(商号)是指用于区分业务或职业的名字或标记,有时也可当作商标使用,与 trademark 一样,其也受法律保护,多用于表示经营某种业务的公司、企业、团体等实体的名称的区分。

Exercises

I Verbal Abilities

Part One

Directions: *For each of these completing questions, read each item carefully to get the sense of it. Then, in the proper space, complete each statement by supplying the missing word or phrase.*

1. The Agreement on Trade Related Aspects of Intellectual Property Rights (TRIPS) is an international agreement _____ by the World Trade Organization (WTO) that sets down minimum standards for many forms of intellectual property (IP) regulation as applied to nationals of other WTO Members and was negotiated at the end of the Uruguay Round of the General Agreement on Tariffs and Trade (GATT) in 1994.

  A. effectuated   B. administered   C. regulated   D. oversaw

2. The TRIPS agreement introduced intellectual property law into the international trading system for the first time and remains the most comprehensive international agreement on intellectual property _____.

  A. to all appearances   B. to the end   C. to date   D. to the letter

3. In 2001, developing countries, concerned that developed countries were insisting on an overly narrow reading of TRIPS, *initiated* a round of talks that resulted in the Doha Declaration.

  A. initiated   B. conceived   C. originated   D. pre-instructed

4. The Doha declaration is a WTO statement that clarifies the scope of TRIPS, stating for example that TRIPS can and should be interpreted _____ the goal "to promote access to medicines for all."

  A. in dispute   B. in entirety   C. in the aggregate   D. in light of

5. TRIPS _____ requirements that nations' laws must meet for copyright rights, including the rights of performers, producers of sound recordings and broadcasting organizations; geographical indications, including appellations of origin; industrial designs; integrated circuit layout de-

signs; patents; monopolies for the developers of new plant varieties; trademarks, trade dress; and undisclosed or confidential information.

 A. contains   B. subsists in   C. encircles   D. encroaches

 6. TRIPS also specifies enforcement procedures, remedies, and dispute _____ procedures.

 A. determination   B. deliverance   C. resolution   D. pronoouncement

 7. Protection and enforcement of all intellectual property rights shall meet the objectives to contribute to the promotion of technological innovation and to the transfer and dissemination of technology, to the mutual advantage of producers and users of technological knowledge and in a manner _____ social and economic welfare, and to a balance of rights and obligations.

 A. conducive to   B. encourageable to   C. cooperative with   D. perceptive to

 8. The United States strategy of linking trade policy to intellectual property standards can be traced back to the entrepreneurship of senior management at Pfizer in the early 1980s, who *mobilized* corporations in the United States and made maximizing intellectual property privileges the number one priority of trade policy in the United States.

 A. intensified   B. intimidated   C. instigated   D. mobilized

 9. Because ratification of TRIPS is a compulsory requirement of World Trade Organization membership, any country seeking to obtain easy _____ to the numerous international markets opened by the World Trade Organization must enact the strict intellectual property laws mandated by TRIPS.

 A. entry   B. opportunity   C. access   D. means

 10. It has therefore been argued that the TRIPS standard of requiring all countries to create strict intellectual property systems will be _____ poorer countries' development.

 A. detrimental to   B. dilapidated to

 C. disadvantageous over   D. decadent to

Part Two

Directions: *Choose the one word or phase that best keep the meaning of the original sentence if it were substituted for the underlined part.*

 1. Should the states disappear, present international society would either <u>fall apart</u> or change radically.

 A. diverge   B. retrograde   C. split

 D. retrocede   E. fall flat

 2. If we desire sincerely and passionately the safety, the welfare and the free development of the talents of all men, we should not be <u>in want of</u> the means to approach such a state.

 A. deficient   B. by lack of   C. in default

 D. needy   E. sufficient

 3. If the issues <u>brought up</u> by Judge Edwards do become the subject of debate in the United Kingdom, what do you think of it?

 A. incriminated   B. impeached   C. renewed

 D. posed   E. inflicted

4. Judge Edward's plea for a return to doctrinal legal analysis has <u>provoked</u> relatively little comment in the United Kingdom.

A. aggravated
B. enraged
C. occasioned
D. irritated
E. denounced

5. Russia claimed to have <u>implemented</u> pricing policies in 1992 similar to those by Poland in 1990.

A. enforced
B. carried on
C. employed
D. allocated
E. cited

6. <u>Pursuant to</u> the WTO agreement, the US has an obligation to make an injury determination before imposing a countervailing duty on the goods.

A. According to
B. Agreeable to
C. Compatible to
D. Consonant with
E. In harmonious with

7. <u>A multitude of</u> people gathered there to hear the president's speech

A. large heard
B. gigantic fleet
C. big pack
D. huge crowd
E. clever ear

8. Personal interest is not always <u>consistent</u> with public interest.

A. agreeable
B. compatible
C. suitable
D. adaptable
E. comfortable

9. If their statutes permit it, international organizations or agencies may resort to <u>expulsion</u> of an offending member.

A. bombardment
B. getting rid of
C. wiping out
D. retaliation
E. expelling

10. In its deceptive simplicity this very definition betrays the <u>ambivalence</u> that pervades out subject.

A. dissimulation
B. culmination
C. disquisition
D. lampoon
E. Uncertainty

II Blank-Filling

Directions: *Fill in the blanks in the following sentences with the words or phrases from the text.*

1. The United States is a large and _____ country comprising many autonomous political sub-units that enjoy _____ and prescriptive authority. As commerce, culture, and communication became more national in nature, conflicts between different states within the United States were sufficiently plentiful to provide _____ for the mills of both courts and conflicts scholars.

2. Patent protection is _____ federal; the 1976 Copyright Revision Act federalized the entire corpus of copyright law, bringing unpublished works as well as published works within its reach; and _____ over trademarks, which may nominally be protected, under both state and federal law, are typically _____ under federal law such that state standards have converged around the federal.

3. Indeed, the Court of _____ for the Ninth Circuit has in recent years used the frenetic public international _____ by the U. S. government to explain the court's reluctance to become involved in international intellectual property _____.

4. Numerous intellectual property concepts reflect underlying _____ of the appropriate balance between ensuring competition and stimulating innovation; but different competitive climates may subsist in different national markets, _____ a different balance and thus divergent _____ of the (supposedly harmonized) concept in question.

5. The principle of _____ led naturally, at least in the crucial matter of determining _____, to the proposition that the lex loci delicti was the applicable law, meaning in copyright cases that the _____ of a defendant's conduct in copying a work would be determined by where the allegedly unauthorized copying or publication occurred.

6. But, putting aside for present purposes the debate _____ the best copyright choice of law rule, the sudden _____ by courts that choice of law analysis in copyright litigation might require more _____ development than heretofore is noteworthy.

7. And there are also some _____ arenas (a classical locus for the use of comparative scholarship) in which these efforts at _____ have borne fruit, including, most notably, in the EU (which includes countries with laws reflecting each of these different _____).

8. Although, unlike the Brussels _____, the Hague and Dreyfuss/Ginsburg systems would operate without any court with supreme _____ over questions raised by the Convention, both seek to achieve uniformity by requiring national courts to interpret the Convention in light of its international character, the need for _____, and the case law of other contracting states.

9. In an era when _____ or non-national rules assume greater importance, determining when to develop or _____ a substantive international rule, and when to insist instead on the predominant claim of one _____ national source, will become crucial.

10. The _____ of international intellectual property litigation, stemming from the need to reconcile territorialist legal _____ with inherently non-territorial activity, may serve as a vehicle for the pursuit of that task. Comparative thought will be central to _____ that goal with any degree of success.

III Reading Comprehension

Part One

Directions: *In this section there is a passage followed by questions or unfinished statements, each with suggested answers. Choose the one you think is the best answer.*

Recent developments in international intellectual property litigation demand an intensified commitment to comparative work. This takes many forms. The recent recognition that conflicts in intellectual property law are not straightforward, but require a more sophisticated approach, has finally engaged conflicts and intellectual property scholars.

Many of the approaches being considered by scholars, if not yet by courts, would elevate the role of comparative analysis, whether in developing substantive private international copyright law

Lesson Eighteen Recent Developments in International Intellectual Property Litigation

or interpreting the provisions of international treaties as baseline elements of choice of law analysis.

Moreover, the acceptance that courts might apply foreign copyright law introduces the potential for comparative analysis to play its most practical role of supplying information about foreign law. Although this role is often seen as purely informational (and arguably non-comparative) the informed application of foreign law requires broader comparative exposure, especially if that foreign law in any way references or incorporates international treaty standards.

The growing liberal attitude toward the procedural structure of international intellectual property litigation has vastly multiplied the number of cases pursued in ways that challenge the traditional model of serial national litigation. This development of itself generates a number of issues that require comparative analysis, including not only application of foreign law, but consideration of foreign law as part of *forum non conveniens*(不方便法院) analysis and in assessing requests for antisuit injunctions.

The proposed Hague Convention, which some of the intellectual property community view as a vehicle for the more effective enforcement of rights on an international basis, would establish a multinational judicial network requiring constant comparative analysis of conflicts thought. The Dreyfuss/Ginsburg proposal would heighten this need by its choice of lawbased ground for non-recognition of judgments, although even the grounds for non-recognition in the current Hague proposal (e.g., lack of jurisdiction in the rendering court) would require comparative analysis that is sufficiently informed to understand the different conceptual approach to jurisdiction outside the United States.

Developments in international trademark law, and the ICANN UDRP in particular, also illustrate the ways in which a re-orientation of choice of law analysis might occur in a more globalized world. Choice of law analysis is about the allocation of prescriptive power, and that contest is increasingly waged between national and international (or non-national) institutions rather than merely national ones. It will involve not only the horizontal choice between laws of competing nation-states, but also the question of whether national prescriptive authority should accede to international or non-national standards. Which aspects of society should be treated in law according to national norms rather than regional or international or non-national norms?

Upon which issues can universal solutions be developed at the expense of local values? As noted above, the first question suggests a re-orientation toward vertical choice of law issues. The second presents a more fundamental political debate about the competing (and perhaps complementary) values of universality and diversity.

Professor Fauvarque-Cosson characterizes this second question as the battle between comparatavism (or internationalism)(比较学派,国际主义学派) and conflictualism(冲突论派). But one can strive for greater uniformity on certain matters without wholly undermining the local values that conflictual methodology sustains.

Comparative knowledge and comparative method will contribute to a better understanding of when, and how, each of these sometimes competing values should be given greater weight. The project of comparativists therefore is not to reveal universal truths, nor merely destructively to declare that the individuality of perspective renders the discipline an irrelevance and common values a fraud. Instead, the goal of contemporary comparative work has to be to facilitate a dialogue about when and in what ways these values are at work. It is to build a bridge between unity and diversity, between internationalism and conflictualism. The complexities of international intellectual property litigation, stemming from the need to reconcile territorialist legal structures with inherently non-territorial activity, may serve as a vehicle for the pursuit of that task. Comparative thought will be central to achieving that goal with any degree of success.

Finally, the developments achieved will require lawyers and judges to cross borders in a number of different ways that comparative analysis can assist. These include not only the provision of information about other vertical allocations of authority and how to understand international laws that are (ideally) the amalgamated product of comparative analysis. But also, involving more conceptual borders, this will encompass how to apply public international laws in the private international context; and, correlatively, whether and how to extend privately generated bodies of law, such as the modern lex mercatoria(国际商法), in settings that are substantively less private in nature (such as ICANN panels). A comparativist perspective will always aid appreciation of laws. But the increasingly multidimensional nature of international intellectual property litigation may mean that only a comparativist can fully appreciate these dimensions and accord them the proper weight.

1. The conflicts and intellectual property scholars are engaged in _____.

   A. the procedural structure of international intellectual property litigation

   B. the recognition of the difficulty of handling the intellectual property cases

   C. the interpreting the provisions of international treaties

   D. the intensified commitment to comparative work

2. To what extent might the domestic courts apply foreign copyright law?

   A. The introduction of foreign law can enable the domestic judges to be well informed of the foreign practices.

   B. The informed application of foreign law requires broader comparative exposure.

   C. The substantive private international property rights law or interpreting the provisions of international treaties can help divert the focus.

   D. The substantive private international property law or interpreting the provisions of international treaties has served as the baseline elements of choice of law analysis.

3. What has greatly multiplied the number of cases pursued in ways that challenge the traditional model of serial national litigation?

   A. consideration of foreign law as part of forum non conveniens analysis

   B. application of public international laws in the private international context

   C. the growing liberal attitude toward the procedural structure of international intellectual property litigation

   D. the enforcement of the Hague Convention

4. Which of the following statements is not True according to the text?

   A. Choice of law analysis will involve not only the horizontal choice between laws of competing nation-states, but also the question of whether national prescriptive authority should accede to international or non-national standards.

B. A re-orientation of choice of law analysis occurring in a more globalized world cannot benefit the solution of the intellectual property cases in the United States.

C. Comparative knowledge and comparative method will be beneficial to a better understanding of when, and how, each of these sometimes competing values should be given greater weight.

D. A comparative analysis can sufficiently be undertaken to understand the different conceptual approach to jurisdiction outside the United States in the intellectual property right litigation.

5. Which of the following can be considered the title of the passage?

A. The multidimensional nature of international intellectual property litigation

B. Modern lex mercatoria and international intellectual property rights litigation

C. The international intellectual property litigation and comparativist thought

D. The internationalism and conflictualism in international intellectual property rights litigation

Part Two   True or False Questions

Direction: *In this part of the exercise, there is a passage with several true or false questions. Read the passage carefully and mark T if it is true and F if it is false.*

Marketing agreements

There are various types of marketing agreements including:

Agency agreement

A traditional sales agency agreement is an agreement whereby a company (known as the principal) authorizes another company or individual (known as the agent) to sell the principal's goods on its behalf. The agent thus sells the goods on behalf of the principal (rather than purchase the goods itself). When a customer purchases from the agent the contractual relationship (known as 'privity of contract') will thereby legally exist directly between the principal and the purchaser (the agent receiving commission on such sales).

Distribution agreement

This is an agreement whereby a company (termed the supplier) actually sells its goods to another company (the distributor). When the distributor then sells the goods on to its own customer there is no contract created between the supplier and the final customer (the contract being between the distributor and its customer). The distributor therefore receives no commission from the supplier, instead earning profit from the 'mark-up' between the price it paid the supplier and the price it sold the goods on for. (Distribution agreements must be drafted very carefully since many agreements which restrict competition and therefore consumer choice are now illegal under European Community law.)

Franchise agreement

A company (the franchisor) can expand its business nationally and internationally by entering into franchise agreements with other parties (known as franchisees). This is known as franchising a business. Franchising is appropriate to businesses with an established brand. A franchise agreement imposes requirements on the franchisee to operate the business in accordance with a uniform business model (for instance by stipulating the colour scheme and interior layout of the franchisee's premises). The franchisee benefits however by being associated with a well recognized brand-name. Many well-known high street brands are franchises, such as fast-food restaurants.

Joint venture agreement

This is an arrangement in which two or more businesses agree to co-operate or in other words 'join forces' on a particular business venture or project. This enables companies to undertake initiatives which they may not have the resources to undertake individually, sharing risks while also combining their financial and skills resources. Care is again required in drafting joint venture agreements in order to avoid contravening European Community law competition rules and/or US competition law (known as 'anti-trust' law).

1. An agent purchases goods directly from a principal. (　)
2. Under an agency agreement a contract exists between the principal and ultimate customer. (　)
3. Under a distribution agreement the distributor purchases goods directly from a supplier. (　)
4. An entirely unknown company would usually be a suitable business to franchise. (　)
5. Franchisor with an established brand can imposes requirements on the franchisee to operate the business in accordance with a uniform business model. (　)
6. Joint venture agreement means an arrangement in which two or more businesses agree to join forces on a particular business venture or project so as to avoid the taxation. (　)

IV Translation Abilities

法律语言特征分析与法律翻译技能培养之十八：

法律文化与翻译策略的选择

译者的文化态度不仅与其所处的时代背景和文化因素相关，而且与译者对原语文化和目标文化在其心中的地位的看法紧密相连。

译者所处的时代背景及当时的文化取向影响其对文本的选择。我们总结19世纪以前中国与西方的接触中法律文化的交流史，可以发现这样一些特点：第一，在交流中起主要媒介作用的是东来的欧洲传教士，即中西间的文化交往从一开始就是在西方主动而中国被动的情况下发生的。第二，从交流的内容看，东来之西学以西方古典的自然知识为主，鲜有西方社会政治法律风俗的内容；而传教士寄往欧洲的众多书简、札记和游记里却关注了中国的政教风俗。比如在意大利商人马可波罗那部举世闻名的游记中就零星记录了元朝的一些法律制度，特别是刑事司法，例如刑法和刑事诉讼法方面的内容。这主要是由于当时中国经济文化等方面的相对繁荣对外界的吸引所致。而此后，由于政府采取的闭关锁国政策使得中国与外界的联系甚少，在西方列强（包括日本）的向外扩张过程中，我们对敌人知之甚少，从而处于更加被动的局面。在此情况下，我们被迫关注"西学"，尤其是政治法律制度方面，诸如接受马礼逊、丁韪良、傅兰雅等对西方政法知识的介绍和改良主张。当然，西方法学知识的输入也是依附于对世界一般地理历史知识的介绍后出现的，诸如《海国图志》、《海国四说》以及《瀛寰志略》等著作都是以介绍世界地理知识为核心的综合性书籍。到了19世纪60年代以后,由于西方国际法著作的大量翻译,近代西方法学的输入才获得了相对独立的意义。而且,由于传教士国籍的性质决定了输入中国的政法知识以英美国家的内容为主。

同时,译者自身的文化因素,如文化取向也会影响译者对文本的选择。对此,我们可以当前中国的法学著作翻译为例。自1978年中国改革开放以来,法学著作的翻译构成了中国法学发展的一个重要组成部分。由于中国理论法学的落后以及各个部门法的修改,法学界的诸多活跃学者都在各自学科领域精心选题,如高鸿钧、贺卫方、梁治平、刘星、米健、沈宗灵、王晨光、舒国滢、夏勇、信春鹰、许章润、张文显、张志铭、郑成良、郑永流等在广义的理论法学界作过不少翻译。而在方流芳、梁慧星、孙宪忠、王利明、王卫国、徐国栋等民商法领域学者的著作中,我们都可以强烈感受到德国、日本、英美、罗马法的影响。从储槐植、张明楷等人在刑法领域的著作中也可以看到英美和日本的影响。

此外,原语文化和目标文化的地位也影响译者对翻译策略的选择。我们认为,"文化地位之所以能影响译者的翻译策略的选择,正是因为它通过潜移默化的方式让翻译活动的执行者意识到了原语文化和目标文化之间的差距,从而赋予了他特定的文化态度"。因此,译者的文化态度对翻译策略的制约作用是不容忽视的。"五四"运动时期,中国译界出现了归化式与异化式两种不同的翻译策略共处的现象,两种翻译策略实际上代表了两种不同的文化势力。这说明译者对原语文化和目标文化的文化地位的认同,在翻译策略的选择上起着至关重要的作用。近现代中国法制模式是在清末民初学习借鉴西方法制,按照大陆法系法制模式建立起来的,尤其是中国在大力进行法制建设的过程中,法律翻译直接影响和促进着现代中国法制的发展进步。故而译者往往对国外的法律采取一种吸收的态度,引进了不少汉语中原本没有的法律术语,比如:不可抗力、一事不再理、共同海损、引渡,等等。同时,由于法律文化的差异,翻译者也创制了法律术语,最典型的是将法律英语中律师之 barrister 和 solicitor 分别译为"巴律师(出庭律师)"和"沙律师(不出庭律师)"。

Translation Exercises:

Part One *Put the Following into Chinese*

1. Interestingly, many of the leading international copyright and trademark disputes also involve Canada or Mexico. And, although globalization has expanded the range of recent disputes beyond North America, a steady flow of Canadian and Mexican intellectual property conflicts continues to generate U. S. litigation. Yet, courts addressing conflicts in the leading intellectual property cases have not treated the Canadian or Mexican disputes as akin to domestic conflicts.

2. To be sure, the routine application of foreign law itself arguably does not require such comparativist immersion (although the quality of the process by which lawyers supply, and courts apply, foreign law, would surely benefit). From a conflicts perspective, courts and scholars will now have to develop choice of law rules for copyright as they have done in the past for all sorts of torts.

3. Copyright claims appear likely to be governed by any Hague (or Hague-like) regime that ensues. The greatest opposition to the inclusion of intellectual property claims within the Hague system has arisen with respect to registered rights such as accorded under patent and trademark laws; many countries remain unwilling to permit foreign courts to review the administrative determinations made by their patent and trademark officials.

Part Two *Put the Following into English*

美国的著作权保护以登记为主要原则。负责登记的部分是美国版权办公室。经过登记的作品,一旦遭到别人侵权就可以即使主张自己的权利了。侵权最常见的形式是抄袭。但是,法律对默写情况下的使用(法律上称为"合理使用"(fair use))别人作品还是会有所支持。

如果确定某一情况是否为"合理使用",必须考虑以下几种因素:(1)使用的目的和性质,即该使用是否属于商业性质或非盈利的教育目的;(2)已获得版权作品的性质;(3)与整体已获得版权作品相关的使用数量及实际使用程度;(4)已获得版权作品之价值或其潜在的市场利用的价值。举个例子,在编写教科书以及非营利目的的作用时,如果在复制他人作品的问题上产生争议,法庭会充分考虑以上四个因素,维护社会的公平正义。

著作权侵害的救济包括禁令、损害赔偿金、诉讼费用以及扣留或销毁侵权资料。

V Interaction

Discuss with your tutor(s) or the People's judges in your locality about the trends in the intellectual property litigation. Then based on the discussion, you are supposed to write a composition about the intellectual property litigation (overview, types of handled cases, suggestions for future work, and difficulties encountered). Remember that you are required to express your ideas clearly.

VI Appreciation of Judge's Opinions

(1) 案件名(Case Name):*Dastar Corp. v. Twentieth Century Fox Film Corp.*

Dastar Corp. v. Twentieth Century Fox Film Corp.

Supreme Court of the United States

Argued April 2, 2003
Decided June 2, 2003

Full case name	Dastar Corporation, Petitioner v. Twentieth Century Fox Film Corporation, et al.
Citations	539 U.S. 23 (more)
	123 S. Ct. 2041; 156 L. Ed. 2d 18; 2003 U.S. LEXIS 4276; 71 U.S.L.W. 4415; 66 U.S.P.Q.2D (BNA) 1641; Copy. L. Rep. (CCH) P28,622; 194 A.L.R. Fed. 731; 2003 Cal. Daily Op. Service 4554; 2003 Daily Journal DAR 5799; 16 Fla. L. Weekly Fed. S 330
Prior history	Judgment for plaintiffs, 2000 U.S. Dist. LEXIS 22064 (C.D. Cal. Nov. 27, 2000);

Lesson Eighteen Recent Developments in International Intellectual Property Litigation 557

	affirmed in part, sub nom. Twentieth Century Fox Film Corp. v. Entertainment Distributing, 34 Fed. Appx. 312 (9th Cir. 2002); cert. granted, sub nom. Dastar Corp. v. Twentieth Century Fox Film Corp., 537 U.S. 1099 (2003)
Subsequent history	Judgment for plaintiffs, 2003 U.S. Dist. LEXIS 21194 (C.D. Cal. Oct. 14, 2003); affirmed, sub nom. Twentieth Century Fox Film Corp. v. Entertainment Distributing, 429 F.3d 869 (9th Cir. 2005)

Holding

A former copyright holder could not bring a Lanham Act claim for false designation of origin against a subsequent distributor who labelled itself the "producer" rather than the work's original author, because "origin" under the Lanham Act refers only to the origin of the physical goods rather than the intangible ideas contained therein. Ninth Circuit Court of Appeals reversed and remanded.

Court membership

Chief Justice
William Rehnquist
Associate Justices
John P. Stevens · Sandra Day O'Connor
Antonin Scalia · Anthony Kennedy
David Souter · Clarence Thomas
Ruth Bader Ginsburg · Stephen Breyer

Case opinions

Majority   Scalia, joined by Rehnquist, Stevens, O'Connor, Souter, Thomas, Kennedy, Ginsburg

Breyer took no part in the consideration or decision of the case.

Laws applied

15 U.S.C. §1125(a) (Lanham Act §43(a))

DASTAR CORPORATION, PETITIONER v.
TWENTIETH CENTURY FOX FILM CORPORATION et al.
on writ of certiorari to the united states court of
appeals for the ninth circuit
[June 2, 2003]

(2) Case Summary(案情简介)
Facts of the Case

Doubleday published the WWII book, *Crusade in Europe*, registered the work's copyright, and granted exclusive television rights to Twentieth Century Fox Film Corporation(20世纪福克斯电影公司). In 1975, Doubleday renewed the book's copyright(书的著作权), but Fox never renewed the copyright on the television series(电影连续剧), leaving the series in the public domain(公共/公知领域). In 1988, Fox reacquired the television rights. In 1995, Dastar Corporation released a video set, *World War II Campaigns in Europe*(欧洲战线上的第二次世界大战), which it made from tapes of the original version of the Crusade television series. Fox filed suit, alleged that Dastar's sale of Campaigns without proper credit to the Crusade television series constituted "reverse passing off" (反向假冒) in violation of the Lanham Act. The District Court granted Fox summary judgment. In affirming, the

Court of Appeals held that, because Dastar copied substantially the Crusade series, labeled it with a different name, and marketed it without attribution to Fox, Dastar had committed a "bodily appropriation" of Fox's series, which was sufficient to establish reverse passing off.

Question:

Does the Lanham Act prevent the unaccredited copying of a work? If so, may a court double a profit award under the Act in order to deter future infringing conduct?

Conclusion:

Decision: 8 votes for Dastar Corp. , 0 vote(s) against

Legal provision(法律规定): 15 U.S.C. 1125

No; the Court did not answer the question. In an 8-0 opinion delivered by Justice Antonin Scalia, the Court held that section 43(a) of the Lanham Act does not prevent the unaccredited copying of an uncopyrighted work(非著作权作品). Under the Lanham Act, the Court reasoned that no false designation of origin was shown since the phrase "origin of goods," as used in the Act, did not connote the person or entity that originated the ideas contained in the video, but instead referred only to the producer's tangible video product(制片商的有形视频产品). Thus, Dastar was the "origin" of the products it sold as its own, without acknowledging the series, because it marketed a video that copied a public domain television series. Justice Stephen G. Breyer took no part in the consideration or decision of this case.

(3) Excerpts of the Judgment(法官判决词)

Justice Scalia delivered the opinion of the Court.

In this case, we are asked to decide whether §43(a) of the Lanham Act, 15 U.S.C. §1125(a), prevents the unaccredited copying of a work, and if so, whether a court may double a profit award under §1117(a), in order to deter future infringing conduct.

I

In 1948, three and a half years after the German surrender at Reims, General Dwight D. Eisenhower completed *Crusade in Europe*, his written account of the allied campaign(盟军的战斗) in Europe during World War II. Doubleday published the book, registered it with the Copyright Office in 1948, and granted exclusive television rights(独家电视权利)to an affiliate(附属公司) of respondent Twentieth Century Fox Film Corporation (Fox). Fox, in turn, arranged for Time, Inc., to produce a television series, also called *Crusade in Europe*, based on the book, and Time assigned its copyright in the series to Fox. The television series, consisting of 26 episodes, was first broadcast in 1949. It combined a soundtrack (音带)based on a narration of the book with film footage from the United States Army, Navy, and Coast Guard(海岸警备队), the British Ministry of Information and War Office, the National Film Board of Canada, and unidentified "Newsreel Pool Cameramen." In 1975, Doubleday renewed the copyright on the book as the "'proprietor of copyright in a work made for hire.'" Fox, however, did not renew the copyright on the Crusade television series, which expired in 1977, leaving the television series in the public domain.

In 1988, Fox reacquired the television rights in General Eisenhower's book, including the exclusive right to distribute the Crusade television series on video and to sub-license others to do so. Respondents SFM Entertainment and New Line Home Video, Inc., in turn, acquired from Fox the exclusive rights to distribute Crusade on video. SFM obtained the negatives(底片) of the original television series, restored them, and repackaged the series on videotape; New Line distributed the videotapes.

Enter petitioner(原告/诉人)Dastar. In 1995, Dastar decided to expand its product line from music compact discs to videos. Anticipating renewed interest in World War II on the 50th anniversary of the war's end, Dastar released a video set entitled World War II Campaigns in Europe. To make Campaigns, Dastar purchased eight beta cam tapes of the original version of the Crusade television series, which is in the public domain, copied them, and

Lesson Eighteen Recent Developments in International Intellectual Property Litigation

then edited the series. Dastar's Campaigns series is slightly more than half as long as the original Crusade television series. Dastar substituted a new opening sequence, credit page, and final closing for those of the Crusade television series; inserted new chapter-title sequences and narrated chapter introductions; moved the "recap" in the Crusade television series to the beginning and retitled it as a "preview"; and removed references to and images of the book. Dastar created new packaging for its Campaigns series and (as already noted) a new title.

Dastar manufactured and sold the Campaigns video set as its own product. The advertising states: "Produced and Distributed by: Entertainment Distributing" (which is owned by Dastar), and makes no reference to the Crusade television series. Similarly, the screen credits state "DASTAR CORP presents" and "an ENTERTAINMENT DISTRIBUTING Production," and list as executive producer, producer, and associate producer, employees of Dastar. The Campaigns videos themselves also make no reference to the Crusade television series, New Line's Crusade videotapes, or the book. Dastar sells its Campaigns videos to Sam's Club, Costco, Best Buy, and other retailers and mail-order companies(邮售商行/公司) for $25 per set, substantially less than New Line's video set.

In 1998, respondents(被告/被上诉人)Fox, SFM, and New Line brought this action alleging that Dastar's sale of its Campaigns video set infringes Doubleday's copyright in General Eisenhower's book and, thus, their exclusive television rights in the book. Respondents later amended their complaint to add claims that Dastar's sale of Campaigns "without proper credit" to the Crusade television series constitutes "reverse passing off" in violation of §43(a) of the Lanham Act, 15 U. S. C. §1125(a), and in violation of state unfair-competition law(反不正当竞争法). On cross-motions for summary judgment, the District Court found for respondents(作出有利于被告的判决) on all three counts, treating its resolution of the Lanham Act claim as controlling on the state-law unfair-competition claim because "the ultimate test under both is whether the public is likely to be deceived or confused". The court awarded Dastar's profits to respondents and doubled them pursuant to §35 of the Lanham Act, 15 U.S.C. §1117(a), to deter future infringing conduct by petitioner.

The Court of Appeals for the Ninth Circuit affirmed the judgment for respondents on the Lanham Act claim, but reversed as to the copyright claim and remanded. With respect to the Lanham Act claim, the Court of Appeals reasoned that "Dastar copied substantially the entire Crusade in Europe series created by Twentieth Century Fox, labeled the resulting product with a different name and marketed it without attribution to Fox, and therefore committed a 'bodily appropriation(挪用,擅用)' of Fox's series." It concluded that "Dastar's 'bodily appropriation' of Fox's original television series is sufficient to establish the reverse passing off." The court also affirmed the District Court's award under the Lanham Act of twice Dastar's profits. We granted certiorari.

II

The Lanham Act was intended to make "actionable the deceptive and misleading use of marks," and "to protect persons engaged in... commerce against unfair competition." While much of the Lanham Act addresses the registration, use, and infringement of trademarks and related marks, §43(a), 15 U. S. C. §1125(a) is one of the few provisions that goes beyond trademark protection. As originally enacted, §43(a) created a federal remedy against a person who used in commerce either "a false designation of origin, or any false description or representation" in connection with "any goods or services." As the Second Circuit accurately observed with regard to the original enactment, however—and as remains true after the 1988 revision—

§43(a) "does not have boundless application as a remedy for unfair trade practices", "Because of its inherently limited wording, §43(a) can never be a federal 'codification' of the overall law of 'unfair competition'", but can apply only to certain unfair trade practices prohibited by its text.

Although a case can be made that a proper reading of §43(a), as originally enacted, would treat the word "origin" as referring only "to the geographic location in which the goods originated." Moreover, every Circuit to consider the issue found §43(a) broad enough to encompass reverse passing off. The Trademark Law Revision Act of 1988 made clear that §43(a) covers origin of production as well as geographic origin. Its language is amply inclusive, moreover, of reverse passing off—if indeed it does not implicitly adopt the unanimous court-of-appeals jurisprudence on that subject.

Thus, as it comes to us, the gravamen(控诉理由,控诉的要点) of respondents' claim is that, in marketing and selling Campaigns as its own product without acknowledging its nearly wholesale reliance on the Crusade television series, Dastar has made a "false designation of origin, false or misleading description of fact, or false or misleading representation of fact, which... is likely to cause confusion... as to the origin... of his or her goods." That claim would undoubtedly be sustained if Dastar had bought some of New Line's Crusade videotapes and merely repackaged them as its own. Dastar's alleged wrongdoing, however, is vastly different: it took a creative work in the public domain—the Crusade television series—copied it, made modifications (arguably minor), and produced its very own series of videotapes. If "origin" refers only to the manufacturer or producer of the physical "goods" that are made available to the public (in this case the videotapes), Dastar was the origin. If, however, "origin" includes the creator of the underlying work that Dastar copied, then someone else (perhaps Fox) was the origin of Dastar's product. At bottom, we must decide what §43(a)(1)(A) of the Lanham Act means by the "origin" of "goods."

III

The dictionary definition of "origin" is "the fact or process of coming into being from a source," and "that from which anything primarily proceeds; source." *Webster's New International Dictionary* 1720—1721 (2d ed. 1949). And the dictionary definition of "goods" (as relevant here) is "wares; merchandise." We think the most natural understanding of the "origin" of "goods"—the source of wares—is the producer of the tangible product sold in the marketplace, in this case the physical Campaigns videotape sold by Dastar. The concept might be stretched (as it was under the original version of §43(a)) to include not only the actual producer, but also the trademark owner who commissioned or assumed responsibility for ("stood behind") production of the physical product. But as used in the Lanham Act, the phrase "origin of goods" is in our view incapable of connoting the person or entity that originated the ideas or communications that "goods" embody or contain. Such an extension would not only stretch the text, but it would be out of accord(与……不协调/不一致) with the history and purpose of the Lanham Act and inconsistent with precedent(先例).

Section 43(a) of the Lanham Act prohibits actions like trademark infringement that deceive consumers and impair a producer's goodwill(商誉). It forbids, for example, the Coca-Cola Company's passing off its product as Pepsi-Cola or reverse passing off Pepsi-Cola as its product. But the brand-loyal(信守某一品牌的) consumer who prefers the drink that the Coca-Cola Company or PepsiCo sells, while he believes that that company produced (or at least stands behind the production of) that product, surely does not necessarily believe that that company was the "origin" of the drink in the sense that it was the very first to devise the formula(配方). The consumer who buys a branded product does not automatically assume that the brand-name company is the same entity that came up with the idea for the product, or designed the product—and typically does not care whether it is. The words of the Lanham Act should not be stretched to cover matters that are typically of no consequence to purchasers.

It could be argued, perhaps, that the reality of purchaser concern is different for what might be called a communicative product—one that is valued not primarily for its physical qualities, such as a hammer, but for the intellectual content that it conveys, such as a book or, as here, a video. The purchaser of a novel is interested not merely, if at all, in the identity of the producer of the physical tome(书的一卷,一册;大书,大部头的书,一本巨著)(the publisher), but also, and indeed primarily, in the identity of the creator of the story it conveys (the author). And the author, of course, has at least as much interest in avoiding passing-off (or reverse passing-off) of his creation as does the publisher. For such a communicative product (the argument goes) "origin of goods" in §43(a) must be deemed to include not merely the producer of the physical item (the publishing house Farrar, Straus and Giroux, or the video producer Dastar) but also the creator of the content that the physical item conveys

Lesson Eighteen　Recent Developments in International Intellectual Property Litigation　　561

(the author Tom Wolfe, or—assertedly—respondents).

　　The problem with this argument according special treatment to communicative products is that it causes the Lanham Act to conflict with the law of copyright, which addresses that subject specifically. The right to copy, and to copy without attribution, once a copyright has expired, like "the right to make an article whose patent has expired—including the right to make it in precisely the shape it carried when patented—passes to the public." "In general, unless an intellectual property right such as a patent or copyright protects an item, it will be subject to copying." The rights of a patentee or copyright holder are part of a "carefully crafted bargain," *Bonito Boats, Inc. v. Thunder Craft Boats, Inc.* (1989), under which, once the patent or copyright monopoly has expired, the public may use the invention or work at will and without attribution. Thus, in construing the Lanham Act, we have been "careful to caution against misuse or over-extension" of trademark and related protections into areas traditionally occupied by patent or copyright. "The Lanham Act," we have said, "does not exist to reward manufacturers for their innovation in creating a particular device; that is the purpose of the patent law and its period of exclusivity." Federal trademark law "has no necessary relation to invention or discovery," but rather, by preventing competitors from copying "a source-identifying mark," "reduces the customer's costs of shopping and making purchasing decisions," and "helps assure a producer that it (and not an imitating competitor) will reap the financial, reputation-related rewards associated with a desirable product". Assuming for the sake of argument that Dastar's representation of itself as the "Producer" of its videos amounted to a representation that it originated the creative work conveyed by the videos, allowing a cause of action under §43(a) for that representation would create a species of mutant(变异的,变异所引起的,与突变有关的) copyright law that limits the public's "federal right to 'copy and to use'" expired copyrights.

　　When Congress has wished to create such an addition to the law of copyright, it has done so with much more specificity than the Lanham Act's ambiguous use of "origin." The Visual Artists Rights Act of 1990(《视觉艺术家权利法》), §603(a), provides that the author of an artistic work(艺术作品的作者) "shall have the right... to claim authorship of that work." That express right of attribution(作品权属的明确性) is carefully limited and focused: It attaches only to specified "works of visual art," is personal to the artist, and endures only for "the life of the author." Recognizing in §43(a) a cause of action for misrepresentation of authorship of noncopyrighted works (visual or otherwise) would render these limitations superfluous. A statutory interpretation that renders another statute superfluous is of course to be avoided.

　　Reading "origin" in §43(a) to require attribution of uncopyrighted materials would pose serious practical problems. Without a copyrighted work as the basepoint, the word "origin" has no discernable limits. A video of the MGM film Carmen Jones, after its copyright has expired, would presumably require attribution not just to MGM, but to Oscar Hammerstein II (who wrote the musical on which the film was based), to Georges Bizet (who wrote the opera on which the musical was based), and to Prosper Mérimée (who wrote the novel on which the opera was based). In many cases, figuring out who is in the line of "origin" would be no simple task. Indeed, in the present case it is far from clear that respondents have that status. Neither SFM nor New Line had anything to do with the production of the Crusade television series—they merely were licensed to distribute the video version. While Fox might have a claim to being in the line of origin, its involvement with the creation of the television series was limited at best. Time, Inc., was the principal if not the exclusive creator, albeit under arrangement with Fox. And of course it was neither Fox nor Time, Inc., that shot the film used in the Crusade television series. Rather, that footage came from the United States Army, Navy, and Coast Guard, the British Ministry of Information and War Office, the National Film Board of Canada, and unidentified "Newsreel Pool Cameramen." If anyone has a claim to being the original creator of the material used in both the Crusade television series and the Campaigns videotapes, it would be those groups, rather than Fox. We do not think the Lanham Act requires this search for the source of the Nile and all its tributaries.

Another practical difficulty of adopting a special definition of "origin" for communicative products is that it places the manufacturers of those products in a difficult position. On the one hand, they would face Lanham Act liability for failing to credit the creator of a work on which their lawful copies are based; and on the other hand they could face Lanham Act liability for crediting the creator if that should be regarded as implying the creator's "sponsorship or approval" of the copy. In this case, for example, if Dastar had simply "copied the television series as Crusade in Europe and sold it as Crusade in Europe," without changing the title or packaging (including the original credits to Fox), it is hard to have confidence in respondents' assurance that they "would not be here on a Lanham Act cause of action."

Finally, reading §43(a) of the Lanham Act as creating a cause of action for, in effect, plagiarism—the use of otherwise unprotected works and inventions without attribution—would be hard to reconcile with our previous decisions. For example, in *Wal-Mart Stores, Inc. v. Samara Brothers, Inc.*, we considered whether product-design trade dress(商业外观,商业包装,商品外观,商品形象) can ever be inherently distinctive. Wal-Mart produced "knockoffs" of children's clothes designed and manufactured by Samara Brothers, containing only "minor modifications" of the original designs. We concluded that the designs could not be protected under §43(a) without a showing that they had acquired "secondary meaning," so that they "identify the source of the product rather than the product itself." This carefully considered limitation would be entirely pointless if the "original" producer could turn around and pursue a reverse-passing-off claim under exactly the same provision of the Lanham Act. Samara would merely have had to argue that it was the "origin" of the designs that Wal-Mart was selling as its own line. It was not, because "origin of goods" in the Lanham Act referred to the producer of the clothes, and not the producer of the (potentially) copyrightable or patentable designs that the clothes embodied.

Similarly under respondents' theory, the "origin of goods" provision of §43(a) would have supported the suit that we rejected in Bonito Boats, where the defendants had used molds to duplicate the plaintiff's unpatented boat hulls (apparently without crediting the plaintiff). And it would have supported the suit we rejected in TrafFix: The plaintiff, whose patents on flexible road signs had expired, and who could not prevail on a trade-dress claim under §43(a) because the features of the signs were functional, would have had a reverse-passing-off claim for unattributed copying of his design.

In sum, reading the phrase "origin of goods" in the Lanham Act in accordance with the Act's common-law foundations (which were not designed to protect originality or creativity), and in light of the copyright and patent laws (which were), we conclude that the phrase refers to the producer of the tangible goods that are offered for sale, and not to the author of any idea, concept, or communication embodied in those goods. To hold otherwise would be akin to finding that §43(a) created a species of perpetual patent and copyright, which Congress may not do.

The creative talent of the sort that lay behind the Campaigns videos is not left without protection. The original film footage used in the Crusade television series could have been copyrighted, as was copyrighted (as a compilation) the Crusade television series, even though it included material from the public domain. Had Fox renewed the copyright in the Crusade television series, it would have had an easy claim of copyright infringement. And respondents' contention that Campaigns infringes Doubleday's copyright in General Eisenhower's book is still a live question on remand. If, moreover, the producer of a video that substantially copied the Crusade series were, in advertising or promotion, to give purchasers the impression that the video was quite different from that series, then one or more of the respondents might have a cause of action—not for reverse passing off under the "confusion... as to the origin" provision of §43(a)(1)(A), but for misrepresentation under the "misrepresents the nature, characteristics or qualities" provision of §43(a)(1)(B). For merely saying it is the producer of the video, however, no Lanham Act liability attaches to Dastar.

* * *

Because we conclude that Dastar was the "origin" of the products it sold as its own, respondents cannot prevail on their Lanham Act claim. We thus have no occasion to consider whether the Lanham Act permitted an award of double petitioner's profits. The judgment of the Court of Appeals for the Ninth Circuit is reversed, and the case is remanded for further proceedings consistent with this opinion.

It is so ordered.

Justice Breyer took no part in the consideration or decision of this case.